Frisian Land Law

Medieval Law and Its Practice

Edited by

John Hudson (*University of St Andrews*)

VOLUME 33

The titles published in this series are listed at *brill.com/mlip*

Frisian Land Law

A Critical Edition and Translation of the Freeska Landriucht

Edited by

Han Nijdam
Jan Hallebeek
Hylkje de Jong

BRILL

LEIDEN | BOSTON

Cover illustration: Freeska Landriucht (c. 1484–1486), first page of the main text with large initial. With kind permission of Tresoar, Leeuwarden.

This book is made open access with funding support from:
Fryske Akademy
Fryske Akademy Fûns
Koninklijk Fries Genootschap voor Geschiedenis en Cultuur
Old Burger Weeshuis
Ottema-Kingma Stichting
St. Anthony Gasthuis Fonds

FRYSKE AKADEMY

FAF OKS Ottema-Kingma Stichting ST. ANTHONY GASTHUIS

The Library of Congress Cataloging-in-Publication Data is available online at https://catalog.loc.gov
LC record available at https://lccn.loc.gov/2022054028

Typeface for the Latin, Greek, and Cyrillic scripts: "Brill". See and download: brill.com/brill-typeface.

ISSN 1873-8176
ISBN 978-90-04-51471-3 (hardback)
ISBN 978-90-04-52641-9 (e-book)

Contents

Maps

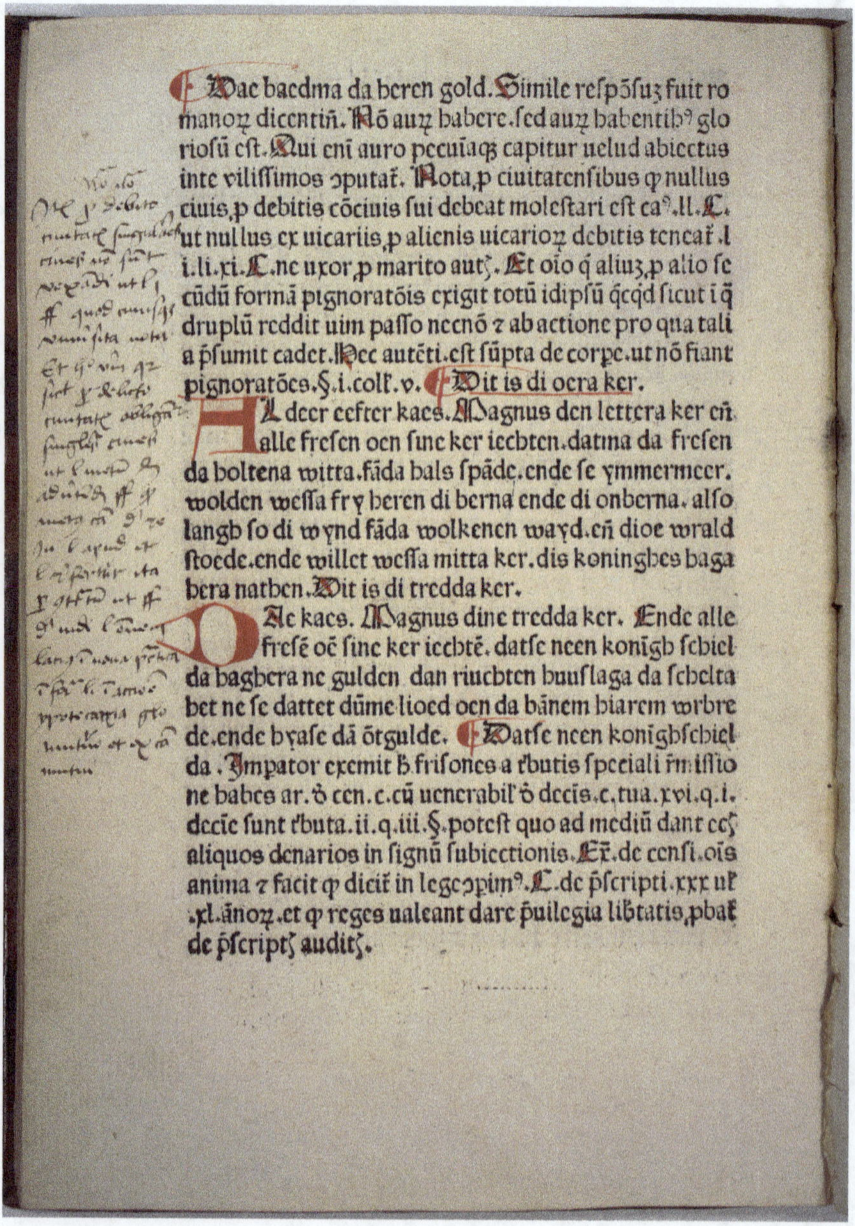

Freeska Landriucht (c. 1484–1486), p. 50 (see pp. 174–176 of this edition), showing a part of text v, The Statutes of Magnus, with a marginal handwritten gloss by the first owner, Hemma Oddazin (see p. 36–37 of the Introduction). With kind permission of Tresoar, Leeuwarden.

Introduction

Preface to the Edition and Translation of the Old Frisian Main Text

Han Nijdam

At the end of the 15th century—between 1484 and 1487—the core collection of medieval Frisian law texts was reproduced in the new technology of book printing that was spreading rapidly over Europe. It is unclear how many copies of this book were printed but today nine have survived.

Printing this archaic collection of law texts was remarkable in itself, since many of these law texts had become more and more outdated since the beginning of the 15th century. Whatever its practical use, however, it did showcase the classical legal tradition of the Frisians which was so intrinsically connected to the famous Frisian Freedom, the autonomy which the Frisian lands had enjoyed since the 11th century. The book became generally known as *Freeska Landriucht* or 'Frisian land law'. In Old Frisian studies it is generally referred to as Druk ('printed book'), since this is the only printed work among the Old Frisian law manuscripts.

In this introduction I will first provide some context by sketching medieval Frisia and its society. A short overview f classical Old Frisian law follows, in which I also try to describe some of the peculiarities of legal procedure. This is intended as an aid to better understand the texts presented in this edition. Needless to say, this introduction to medieval Frisia and Frisian law can by its very nature be no more than concise.

Next I will focus on the book itself; first its history and what is known about the project of printing this collection of Old Frisian law texts and then a brief introduction to the various texts in *Freeska Landriucht*. Finally, I will explain the editorial principles for rendering the Old Frisian text. The Latin Gloss is introduced separately.

1 Medieval Frisia

During the Roman period a people who called themselves Frisians lived along the coastal shores of the North Sea. Their material culture and the little linguistic material they left behind indicate they were a Germano-Celtic people.[1]

1 Seebold, 'Die Friesen'; Schrijver, 'Frisian between the Roman and Early-Medieval Periods'.

 | DOI:10.1163/9789004526419_002

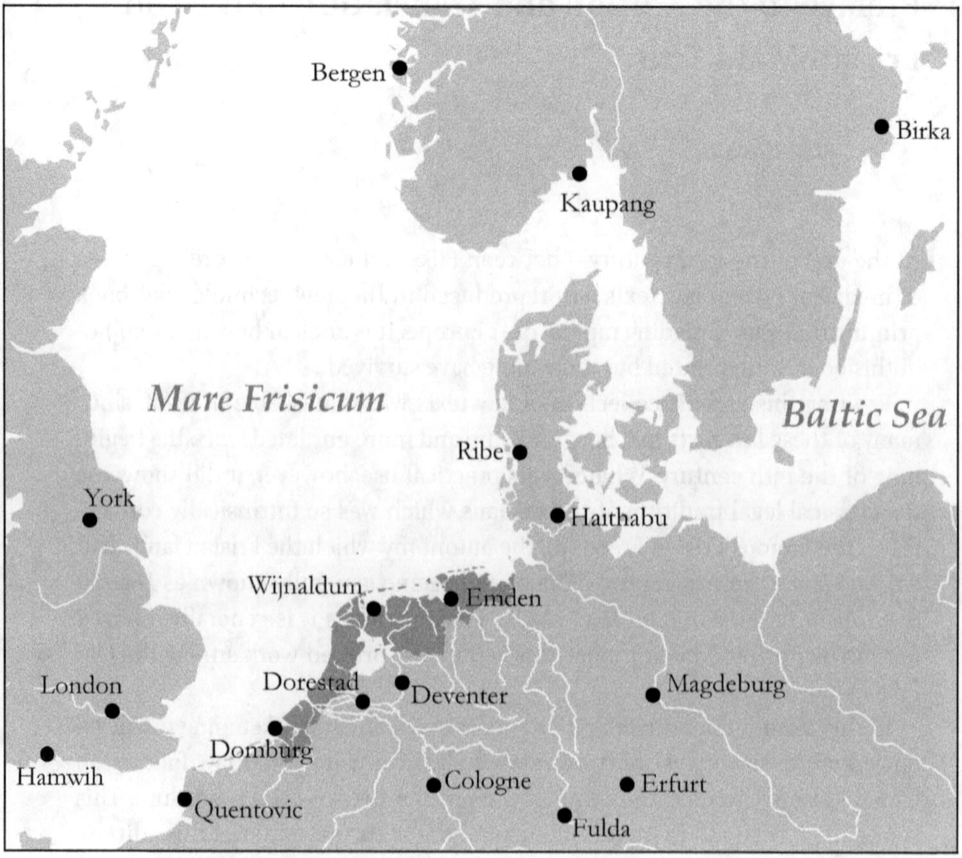

MAP 1 Early medieval Frisia and the surrounding North Sea area
VERSLOOT-KARTOGRAFY

During the Migration Period (4th century) the Frisian settlements were largely depopulated. Shortly after 400 AD, new inhabitants coming from the Saxon region of the Elbe–Weser triangle settled there. These soon called themselves Frisians too.[2]

The new Frisians were a Germanic people and their language and culture were related to those of the Scandinavians and the Anglo-Saxons in England around the same time. Frisia was thus very much a member of the cultures and communities around the North Sea. They were famous for their wealth and trade (see Map 1).[3]

2 Hines and IJssennagger-van der Pluijm (eds.), *Frisians of the Early Middle Ages*.
3 Lebecq, *Marchands et navigateurs frisons*; Nicolay, *The Splendour of Power*.

In the course of the 8th century the Frisians were defeated by the Franks. After the demise of the powerful Frisian king Radbod (Frisian: Redbad) in 719, the Frisian territories were conquered from West to East, the East being subdued in 785.

At the end of that century the *Lex Frisionum* was composed by order of the Frankish rulers. This 'Law of the Frisians' is a remarkable and valuable source of the indigenous law of the period. Since the surviving text is a draft, it contains information that would otherwise surely have been edited out.[4]

The *Lex Frisionum* is also the first historical source to describe the three Frisian core regions:

1. West Frisia: between the rivers Sincfal (Zwin) and Vlie (i.e. the present-day provinces of Zealand, South- and North-Holland in the Netherlands).
2. Central Frisia: between the rivers Lauwers and Vlie (i.e. the present-day province of Fryslân / Friesland in the Netherlands);
3. East Frisia: between the rivers Lauwers and Weser (i.e. the present-day provinces of Groningen in the Netherlands and the region Ost-Friesland in Germany).

The Central Frisian area, coinciding with the current province of Friesland (Dutch) or Fryslân (Frisian), is the point of departure or default of the law text: the *Lex Frisionum* gives the provisions for this area and notes divergences that apply in the other areas. This is done by adding marginal notes and two sets of *additiones* from legal experts coming from West and East Frisia (more on these below), called Wlemar and Saxmund.

These three regions were conglomerations of the real core territories of the Frisians: the various *pagi* (Dutch *gouw*, German *Gau*) or shires. These have now also been firmly reconstructed, as is shown in Map 2.[5] Each pagus must have had a *thing* or assembly where the inhabitants of the *pagus* met a few times a year to hold council and to hold court (on which more below).

The Carolingian dominion over the Frisians had a few consequences. First, they had to swear loyalty to the king and pay a tax or tribute in recognition of the Carolingian rule. This tax is called *huslotha* or *huslaga* in the Old Frisian sources.[6] Also, a count was appointed by the king to safeguard the internal and external affairs of the Frisians. These matters were standard procedure for all peoples that were subdued by the Franks.

---

4 Siems, *Studien zur Lex Frisionum*; Nijdam, 'The Body Legal in Frisian Law'.

5 De Langen and Mol, 'Vikingen en de Kerk in de Friese landen', De Langen and Mol, 'Koning Redbad'.

6 Henstra, *Friese graafschappen*, 20–22.

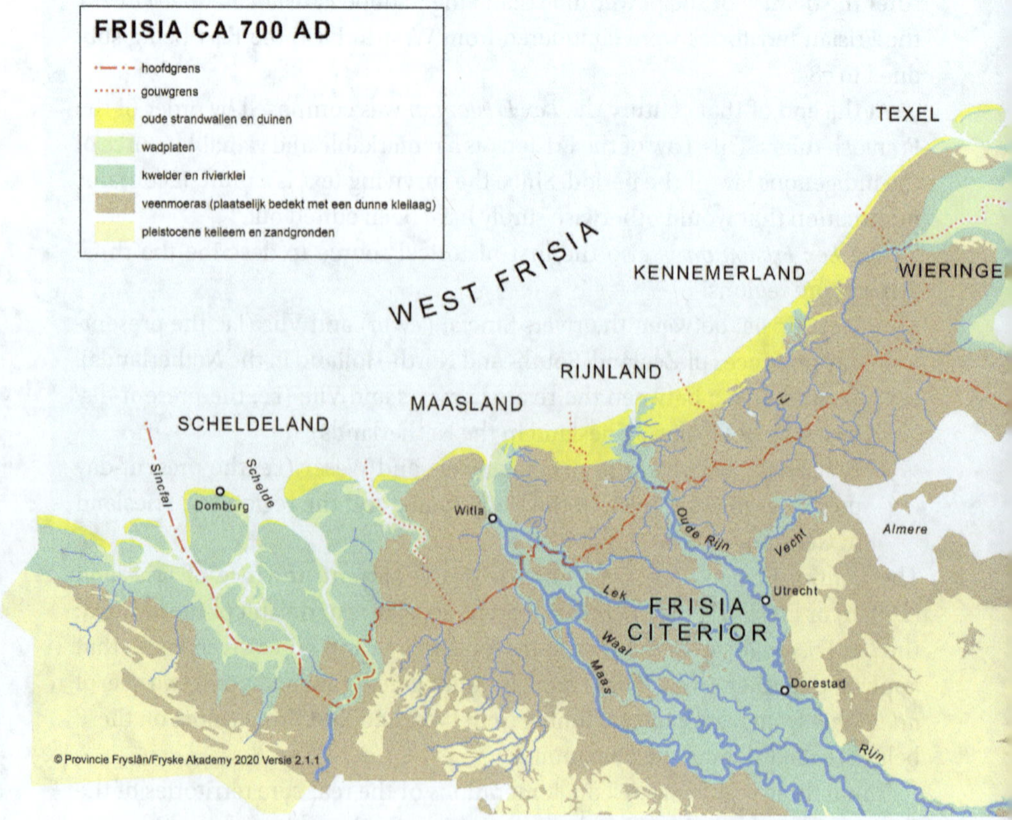

MAP 2 Early medieval Frisia
DE LANGEN AND MOL (2020)

Shortly after the Frankish or Carolingian rule had been established in Frisia, the Viking Age started. The Viking raids on the European mainland, starting at the end of the 8th century, were a reaction to Charlemagne's ongoing conquests of large parts of Europe, eventually pushing northward towards the Danish border. Also, he implemented a monetary reform that did not go well with the Scandinavians, nor did the fact that Carolingisation meant Christianisation.

It has now been established that the Viking Age affected the Frisians in various ways. First, the Frisians continued to trade with the Scandinavians. The Frisians also went on a Viking expedition with them every now and then. Lastly, the Frisian coasts were raided by the Vikings.[7] For Frisia, the most intense

7 IJssennagger, 'Between Frankish and Viking'.

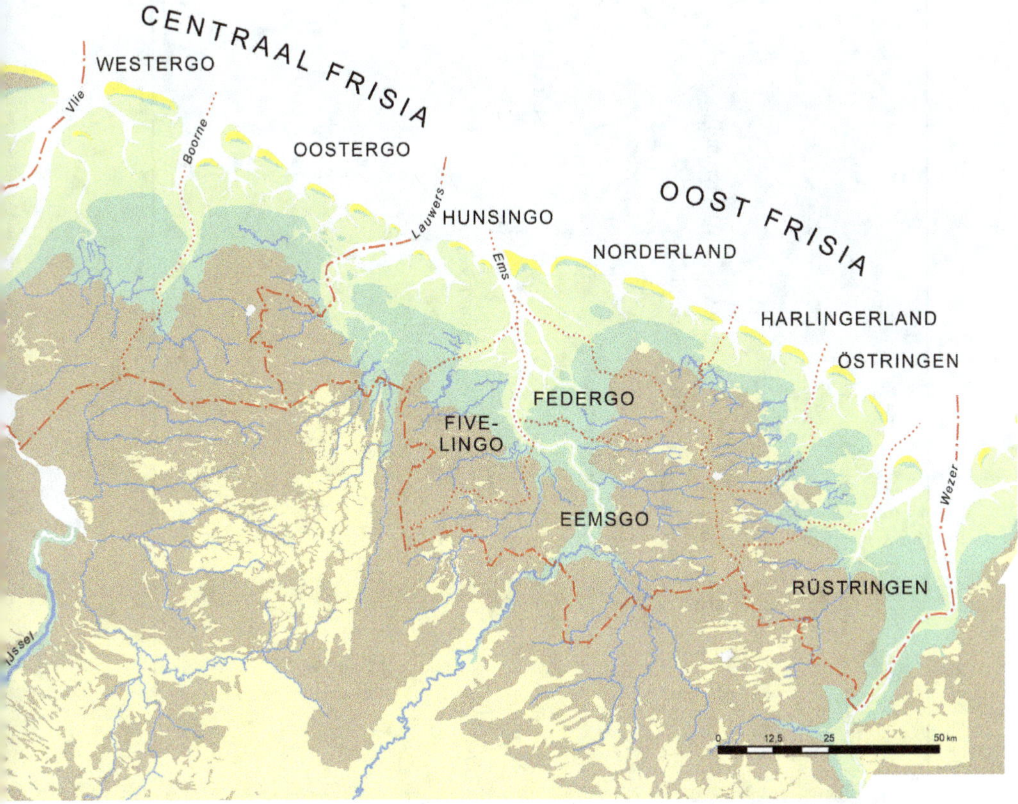

period in this respect was between c. 850–950. It caused the Carolingians to lose their grip on this newly conquered part of their realm. Louis the Pious even gave a few Frisian regions in fief to Viking rulers.

In the second half of the 10th century the Viking threat had abated and the bishops of both Utrecht and Münster (the two bishoprics under which the Frisian lands fell) started a restoration campaign which resulted in establishing a finely knit grid of parishes and main churches in the Frisian lands.[8] In order to get these churches built and funded, the bishops had to negotiate with the local Frisian elite to finance them by means of dotations of land. During this same

8 De Langen and Mol, 'Church Foundation and Parish Formation'.

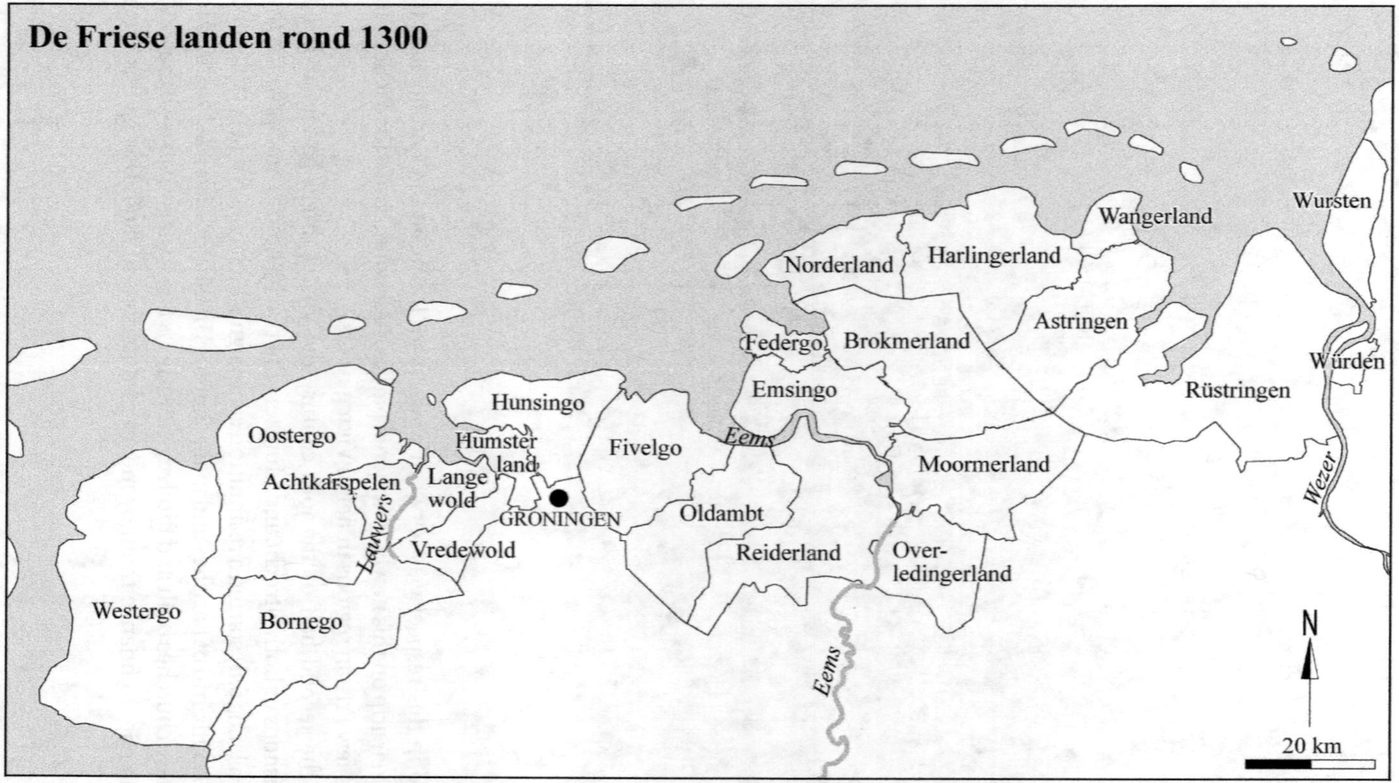

MAP 3 The Frisian regions that were part of the Frisian Freedom
VERSLOOT-KARTOGRAFY

period Carolingian counts were established again in Frisia but never resided in the region itself, ruling from a distance.[9]

This mix of events and circumstances must have been the reason the so-called Frisian Freedom or Frisian autonomy developed. Officially the Frisians were part of the Carolingian realm, but basically they ruled themselves, using their age old infrastructure of local and supralocal assemblies or *thing* meetings to build a grass roots government structure. All freeholders and nobles were eligible for the office of judge-administrator, which rotated every year. During the later Middle Ages, this autonomy was formalised by charters from a number of emperors of the Holy Roman Empire.[10]

The exception was West Frisia. Here the counts of Holland succeeded in bringing the territory under their authority. The region of the Frisian Freedom thus comprised of Central and East Frisia (see Map 3).

The end of the Frisian Freedom is said not to have come about by threats from the outside, but as a consequence of internal strife. For centuries, the Frisian elite had been divided in two large factions, the *Schieringers* and the *Vetkopers*. They had held each other in balance for a long time, but after 1480, due to military innovations and the recruitment of ever larger armies of hired soldiers, the whole fabric of society started to tear. In a last effort to come out on top, the *Schieringers* requested Duke Albert (Albrecht) III of Saxony (1443–1500) to become *gubernator* of Frisia. This was granted by Emperor Maximilian I (1459–1519), who had borrowed huge sums of money from Albert.[11] The year 1498 thus marked the end of the Frisian Freedom.

2 A Chronological Overview of the Classical Old Frisian Law Texts

The political developments described above had an important effect on Old Frisian law: it was allowed to grow on its own accord, organically. The legal tradition evolved without interruption, caused by legislative interventions by a king or count aimed at modifying existing law. This is an important observation because this is what has always been the charm of Old Frisian law since legal historians in the 19th century started looking at the various Germanic law traditions.[12] Recent research confirms this: classical Old Frisian law is very archaic,

9 Henstra, *Friese graafschappen*.
10 Vries, 'Frisonica libertas'.
11 Mol, 'Hoofdelingen en huurlingen'.
12 Nijdam, 'Indigenous Or Universal?'; Schwartz, 'Comparative Legal Reconstruction'.

and a continuity of legal tradition and practice can be observed from the *Lex Frisionum* to the later Old Frisian sources. At the same time the tradition grew and evolved organically.

The oldest Frisian law texts are undoubtedly the compensation tariffs or injury lists.[13] In many societies across the world, the institution of blood money or *wergild* (literally 'man compensation') was invented in order to stop or prevent an ongoing chain of revenge between factions and families after a homicide had taken place. This meant that the killer would pay a fixed amount of money and valuables to the heirs of his victim in order to buy off revenge.[14] This was often accompanied by a ritual of swearing peace between the families involved.

The *wergild* was then seen as the worth of a man. In early medieval Europe, a specific *wergild* was attributed to the various estates: half free men (*liti*), free men (*liberi*) and noblemen (*nobiles*). The default always was that for a free man, a nobleman usually having a *wergild* that was twice that of a free man.

In many societies that had invented the institution of *wergild*, the concept was used to also put a price on not losing a life, but losing a limb. What is the value of a hand that has been cut off, or an eye that has been poked out or is blinded for the rest of the victim's life?[15] Out of this secondary system, tariff lists grew, which indicated what a perpetrator had to pay a victim if he had injured him in some way. These lists must be seen as the starting point of the negotiations between the two parties, or of the claim that would be presented in court if the matter could not be resolved without legal procedures.

In Frisia, the practice of paying *wergild* and compensating injuries with money and other valuables was present until the end of the Middle Ages. The oldest attestation of this practice is recorded in the *Lex Frisionum*, dating to the end of the 8th century. But the tradition was already old by the time it was recorded. Not only do the provisions show a cultural affinity with the law of king Aethelberht of Kent (c. 600), but the *wergild* in the *Lex Frisionum* of 53 1/3 gold *solidi* seems to have originally been based on the Byzantine gold *solidus*, which had been replaced by the slightly lighter Roman *solidus* after 575. This would mean that the original *wergild* had been a round figure of 50 Byzantine *solidi*.[16] So in all, it seems safe to say that the Frisians brought the *wergild* sys-

13 Nijdam, *Lichaam, eer en recht*; Nijdam, 'Belichaamde eer, wraak en vete'; Nijdam, 'Compensating Body and Honor'; Nijdam, 'Indigenous Or Universal?'.

14 Boehm, 'The Natural History of Blood Revenge'.

15 Miller, *Eye for an Eye*; Oliver, *The Body Legal*.

16 Nijdam, 'A Comparison'; Henstra, *The Evolution of the Money Standard*, 289–290.

tem and a more primitive version of the compensation tariffs with them when they settled on the Frisian shores in the 5th century.

Obviously, this compensation tariff tradition was transmitted orally for a long time. Even between the *Lex Frisionum* and the later Old Frisian tradition there is no written continuity.[17] The continuity of the orally transmitted legal tradition indirectly attests to the fact that the whole legal infrastructure that was necessary to uphold it stayed in place during the centuries between the 8th century and the later Middle Ages, when the Old Frisian corpus of law texts emerged.

This brings us to the question when the first Old Frisian law texts were composed and written down. This question has been heavily debated, since although the oldest texts have traditionally been dated to the 11th century on the basis of their contents, the oldest Old Frisian manuscripts that have survived date to the end of the 13th century.[18]

Carolingian monasteries had been founded in Frisia in the 8th century, introducing written culture to the Frisian lands on a permanent basis, albeit on a small scale.[19] More importantly, a broad infrastructure necessary to kickstart a culture of writing can be argued to have come into existence with the parochial infrastructure that was built in the second half of the 10th century, as shown by De Langen and Mol.[20] This consisted of a network of main churches and parishes. Some of the churches in the larger towns, such as Leeuwarden, are known to have had schools attached to them, were pupils could learn to read and write Latin.[21]

In this respect, it should be kept in mind that the Reformation in the Frisian lands, which took place around 1580 and the dissolution of the monasteries had a decimating effect on the medieval archives and books that were present there.[22] Only a small percentage of the books and manuscripts that had been around survived. But every now and then discoveries are made. In 2015 two tiny fragments of parchment came to light which contained interlineair psalm glosses in Old Frisian, dated 1100–1125 on palaeographic grounds.[23]

17 Nijdam, 'Law and Political Organisation', 143. Siems, *Studien zur Lex Frisionum*.

18 Bremmer, *Hir is eskriven*; Bremmer, 'The Orality of Old Frisian Law Texts'.

19 Dirk Jan Henstra suggests *The Seventeen Statutes* might have been written down with the assistance of the monastery of Reepsholt: see Henstra, *Fon Jelde*, 109. For the monastery of Staveren: see Mol and Van Vliet, 'De oudste oorkonden'.

20 De Langen and Mol, 'Church Foundation and Parish Formation'.

21 Bremmer, *Hir is eskriven*, 30.

22 Nijdam and Savelkouls, 'The Manuscript Collection'; Bremmer, *Hir is eskriven*: 11–17.

23 Langbroek, 'So viel geschrieben, so wenig geblieben'.

Until then the oldest piece of Old Frisian had been a fragment with interverbal psalm glosses dated c. 1200.[24]

It therefore seems most likely to assume that the first Old Frisian legal texts were composed and written down in the 11th century and grew considerably in the 12th and 13th centuries (and that the language of the texts was updated to the Old Frisian of that period). The dating of three different texts point to the first half of the 11th century.

First, the text widely seen as the oldest Old Frisian law text, *The Seventeen Statutes*, was traditionally dated to the 11th century because the Vikings are still mentioned, while the Viking threat in Frisia disappeared after that century, and because the town of Münster is still called by its archaic name Mimigerdaford, a tradition which fell out of use after the 11th century.[25] More recently, Henstra has argued that the *wergild* mentioned in the 15th statute can be dated to the first half of the 11th century. He moreover argues that the text was originally drafted in East Frisia, after which it was received in Central Frisia, and the *wergild* was expressed in the pounds and ounces that were used in that region.[26] (Other scholars think *The Seventeen Statutes* originated in Central Frisia).[27]

As already discussed earlier, *The Seventeen Statutes* probably contain even older material, going back to the Carolingian age. In this respect it is interesting to note that the first ten statutes deal with the relationship between the king and the Frisians, making them almost a political pamphlet rather than a law text (see the introduction to text VI below). For now it is important to note that even though the text may contain even older material, the first half of the 11th century seems to be the period it has been written down.

The second Old Frisian law text that has traditionally been dated to the 11th century is *The Synodical Law of Central Frisia*. This has recently been confirmed by Jan Hallebeek (see the introduction to text XI below for more detail). Again, this text both seems to contain older material, as it is said to have been partially based on a handbook from the beginning of the 10th century, and younger material, since the text shows various signs of later development.

The third text that deserves attention in this context concerns a small text, called *Fon Jelde* ('concerning *wergild*'), which describes how the *wergild* was updated in various stages. It is explicitly linked to the 16th statute, which says

---

24 Langbroek, 'Condensa atque Tenebrosa'.

25 Algra, *Zeventien Keuren en Vierentwintig Landrechten*, 252–255; Bremmer, 'Het boek is af', 80, arguing in favour of a dating after 1200, points to a last mention of *Mimigerdaford* in a charter from 1202.

26 Henstra, *Fon Jelde*, 99–126.

27 Algra, *Zeventien Keuren en Vierentwintig landrechten*, 210–213.

that all free Frisians (i.e. the freeholders and nobles) have the right to compensate their deeds by means of paying money rather than having to undergo corporal punishment (text VI,16). The beginning of *Fon Jelde* reads:

> Concerning *wergild*
> 1. In order to be able to compensate crimes with money, the people chose the first *wergild* to be set at 12 marks. After that, the kin received 6 marks on top of that, to distribute among themselves.[28]

In all, the text describes nine stages, which Henstra analysed and dated. He dated the first stage at the beginning of the 11th century.[29]

A secondary question that comes into view is whether the first versions of these texts were written in Frisian, i.e. the vernacular, or in Latin.[30] This question—Latin first or Frisian first—also has been debated for a long time in Old Frisian studies, for a number of Latin versions of various Old Frisian law texts are indeed extant. Only, these existing texts have all evidently been translated from Old Frisian into Latin. If the oldest Frisian law texts would have started off in Latin, these versions would then have been translated into Frisian in the 12th century at the latest (because the Old Frisian of the most archaic texts goes back to at least the 12th century and is possibly even older: this is currently under discussion), after which these Latin prototexts would have disappeared without a trace. Subsequently, some of the texts would then again have been translated into Latin in the 13th century.[31] This is not a likely scenario.

The last complicating factors to be mentioned are firstly that the law texts continued to develop for a long time, making them fluid and hard to pinpoint, i.e. they do not stem from one moment in time, but paragraphs were added, the language of the text was updated, etc. Secondly, the legal practice out of which these texts grew and in which context they were used, continued to have a strongly oral character for a long time, at least until the beginning of the 15th century. This orality is also reflected in the law texts.[32]

---

28 Buma and Ebel (eds.), *Das Fivelgoer Recht*, 170–171. See text XII,1 in the edition below for a detailed description of the distribution of the kin's share of the *wergild*.

29 Henstra, *The Evolution of the Money Standard*, 299–302; 304–313.

30 Bremmer, *Hir is eskriven*, 81–86.

31 Popkema, 'Old Frisian'; Reinders, 'Die Sprache'. The only exception might be the Latin part of the *The Synodical Law of Central Frisia*, which is only present in *Freeska Landriucht*, but which needs further analysis. See Van Buijtenen, *De grondslag van de Friese Vrijheid*, 153; Nijdam, 'Het Westerlauwers Seendrecht', 316.

32 Bremmer, 'The Orality of Old Frisian Law Texts'; Nijdam, *Lichaam, eer en recht*; Nijdam, 'A Comparison'; Nijdam, 'The Body Legal'.

To conclude this discussion on the origins and earliest development of the Old Frisian laws in the 11th–13th centuries, it may be clear that there are still many issues to be addressed. However, the hypothesis seems justifiable that the oldest texts were written down in the 11th century. More texts arose in the course of the following centuries.

With a focus on the texts presented in this edition, I will now give a short overview of the chronology of the Old Frisian text corpus. The classical tradition comes to an end around 1400 in Central Frisia, when it is replaced by a younger tradition, on which more below.

2.1 *The Manuscripts*

First I will briefly discuss the manuscript traditions of East and Central Frisia.[33] From the East Frisian region the most archaic manuscripts have survived. At the same time, the tradition comes to a halt earlier than the Central Frisian tradition. The oldest manuscripts stem from the easternmost parts of East Frisia: Rüstringen and Brokmerland. Both regions have produced two complete manuscripts with compilations of Old Frisian law texts stemming from the end of the 13th century. Hunsingo has yielded two almost identical manuscripts with Old Frisian law, stemming from the period around 1350. Three manuscripts from the Emsingo region have survived, the oldest of which stems from c. 1400 (but which is very archaic), the other two from c. 1450. Fivelgo, finally, has given us one manuscript, dating from c. 1430. In all, this amounts to ten manuscripts containing compilations of Old Frisian law texts, beside which a number of fragments have come to light, testifying to what has been lost to us.

The manuscript tradition from Central Frisia starts later and is more diffuse. I will focus on the manuscripts which contain compilations of classical Old Frisian law that are comparable to *Freeska Landriucht*. There are only two of such manuscripts left today. The voluminous manuscript *Jus Municipale Frisonum* (Jus or J for short) is a copy from c. 1530 of several older Old Frisian manuscripts.[34] It goes back to at least four older Old Frisian text compilations. These original compilations dated from the end of the fifteenth century.[35]

The second manuscript is called *Codex Unia* (Unia or U for short).[36] It was copied from one or several older manuscripts by the nobleman Syds Unia in 1475.[37] In the 17th century, it was in the possession of state historian Simon

33 For a more detailed overview: see Johnston, 'The Old Frisian Law Manuscripts'.
34 Buma, Ebel and Tragter-Schubert (eds.), *Westerlauwerssches Recht I*.
35 Nijdam. *Lichaam, eer en recht*, 486.
36 Sytsema, 'Codex Unia: Edition and Reconstruction'.
37 Siebs, *Westfriesische Studien*.

Abbes Gabbema (1628–1688) but disappeared after his death.[38] Fortunately, his acquaintance Franciscus Junius (1591–1677) copied it, probably shortly before or in 1674.[39] He made the copy partly in the margins of his copy of *Freeska Landriucht* (see below, copy J109), partly in a blanc notebook. Even though we are looking at *Codex Unia* through at least two filters, namely the copying by Syds Unia and Franciscus Junius, this is the most archaic manuscript from Central Frisia we have at our disposal. The language of the oldest, most archaic texts could perhaps date back to the (early) 13th century.[40]

2.2 *The Texts*

Focusing on the texts that are in *Freeska Landriucht* yields the following chronological overview of classical Old Frisian law texts from c. 1000 to c. 1400.[41]

2.2.1 From the 11th and 12th Centuries

1. *The Seventeen Statutes* (text VI)
2. *The Twenty-Four Land Laws* (text VIII)
3. *Exceptions to the 17th Statute* (text X)

These three texts are so-called Pan Frisian texts, which means that they can be found in manuscripts both from Central and East Frisia.

4. *The Synodical Law of Central Frisia* (text XI)
5. *The Older Skelta Law* (text III)
6. *The Younger Skelta Law* (text XII)
7. *The Eight Provisions* (text IX)

These seven are the oldest law texts from Central Frisia. Especially the older and the younger *Skelta Law* show a considerable degree of development and growth.

2.2.2 From the 13th Century

8. *What Is Law?* (text II)
9. *Of the Two Kings Charles and Radbod* (text IV)
10. *The Statutes of Magnus* (text V)

---

38 The function of state historian or 'landshistorieschrijver' was created in 1590 by the States of Friesland. Nijdam and Savelkouls, 'The Manuscript Collection', 308; Eekhoff, 'Lijst'.

39 Nijdam and Savelkouls, 'The Manuscript Collection', 323–324.

40 Versloot, *Mechanisms of Language Change*, 70–75. More recently, Versloot has expressed the uncertainty that exists for reconstructing Old Frisian back to the 11th century. In other words, by absence of actual written sources it is hard to reconstuct how Old Frisian exactly looked like in the 11th century. Personal communication Arjen Versloot (Amsterdam University).

41 For a description of the contents of these texts, see section 8 of this introduction.

11. *Prologue to the Seventeen Statutes and Twenty-Four Land Laws* (text VII)

These four texts were added to the oldest core, i.e. the texts which were written down in the 11th and 12th centuries. The 13th century was a prosperous and productive period in the history of Frisia. It also gave rise to a new ideological embellishment of Frisian law, leading to such texts as *Of the Two Kings Charles and Radbod* and *The Statutes of Magnus*, all relating how the Frisian Freedom and Law go back to a privilege granted by Charlemagne. The list of all Old Frisian texts which were created during this period is long and will not be treated here.[42] Together, these 11 texts form the core canon of classical Old Frisian law texts from Central Frisia.

12. *The Statutes of the Five Districts* (text XIII)
13. *The Calculated Tariffs* (text XIV)
14. *Currency Conversion and Wergilds* (text XV)
15. *The Book of Emperor Rudolf* (text XVI)
16. *Market Law* (text XVII)
17. *On Forceful Robberies* (text XIX)

These additional texts, including nos. 18 and 19 below appear very frequently in the Old Frisian manuscripts. The only text that looks slightly out of place is *The Statutes of the Five Districts*, which seems to be confined to the area around the town of Franeker. Its alternative title, however, is 'the old statutes of Opstalsbam'. This might be the reason that this is the only text that pertains to only a part of and not the entire Central Frisian area.

2.2.3 From 14th and early 15th Centuries

18. *Unmendable Crimes* (text XVIII)
19. *The Statutes of Opstalsbam* (text XX)
20. *A Treatise on the Seven Sealands* (text XXI)

These are the youngest texts to have been added to the *Freeska Landriucht* compilation. *The Statutes of Opstalsbam* date from 1323 as is stated in the text itself. The *Treatise on the Seven Sealands* might go back to an older tradition, but this version was probably created in 1417, making this the last but also the absolute youngest text in *Freeska Landriucht*.

2.3 *Jurisprudentia Frisica*

After 1400, a new legal tradition came to fruition in Central Frisia.[43] It was based on a selection of the paragraphs and provisions from the classical corpus, com-

42 For an overview of Frisian law texts: Gerbenzon, *Apparaat voor de studie van Oudfries recht*. For the dynamics of the 13th century: Bremmer, *Hir is eskriven*, 91–118.

43 Gerbenzon, *Excerpta Legum*; Gerbenzon, 'Aantekeningen over de *Jurisprudentia Frisica*'.

bined with new material in Frisian, which leaned heavily on Roman and Canon law. The entire text was built up more systematically. It was subdivided into titles, each with its own subject, after the model of the titles in the different parts of the *Corpus iuris civilis* and the *Liber Extra*.[44] It was also heavily glossed with Latin glosses. The Frisian and Latin texts show a high degree of mutual dependence.

This tradition was called *Excerpta Legum* or *Jurisprudentia Frisica*, after the names of the texts in the two major Old Frisian manuscripts which have been handed down: *Codex Aysma* and *Codex Roorda*.[45] Both manuscripts stem from the end of the 15th century, but *Codex Aysma* contains a version of this tradition that can be dated to the beginning of the 15th century, whereas *Codex Roorda* contains the youngest redaction, dating from the end of the 15th century.

Although Frisian charters from the 15th century show that this tradition was used in day to day legal practice, it was not meant to last, since the Frisian Freedom came to a halt in 1498, when Albert III, Duke of Saxony (1443–1500) was appointed as *gubernator* of Frisia by the Holy Roman Emperor. In 1504 the so-called *Saxon Ordinance* was issued by this new government, instituting Roman law as the official legal system in Frisia. Since the influence of Roman and Canon law had already been vast in the 15th century, this was not an enormous break with the past.

3 Family and Inheritance

As in many societies throughout the world and ages, family was of key importance to the medieval Frisians. They relied on their family and relatives on more than one occasion. These relationships are reflected in a number of ways in Frisian law.

The closest relatives (father, mother, brother, sister, son, daughter) were called 'the six hands', the body metaphor attesting to the closeness that was felt to these primary relatives. The Frisians had a system of bilateral descent: the father's side (called *swirdsida* 'sword side') and the mother's side (called *spindelsida* 'spindle side') were both equally important, although at the end of the medieval period, the father's side gained importance.[46]

44 On the *Corpus iuris civilis* and the *Liber Extra* see below, 'Preface to the Edition and Translation of the Gloss'.

45 Buma, Gerbenzon and Tragter-Schubert (eds.), *Codex Aysma*.

46 Noomen, 'Consolidatie van familiebezit'.

Inheritances ideally fell within the six hands. Sons were entitled to a double share of the inheritance of their parents whereas daughters received a single share. If none of the 'six hands' were present to inherit, this was very much lamented in Frisian law: it was called an *unwene lawa* 'unhoped-for inheritance' (text VIII,16).

The six hands were also entitled to the *wergild* of their slain relative. Conversely, they had the responsibility to help raise a *wergild* if one of their relatives had killed somebody. Another half wergild was raised by and given to the next of kin of both families involved in a homicide. This was called the *meitele* or 'kin's share'. So the ratio of a simple *wergild* to the kin's share was 2:1. Put in another way, one third of a full *wergild* consisted of the kin's share. In the sources it is sometimes difficult to discern which *wergild* is referred to: the simple or the full *wergild*.[47] In the first paragraph of *The Younger Skelta Law* an detailed account is given of which kin receives which share of the *wergild*, including the *meitele* (text VI,1).

Children came of age at 12 years. From that time onwards they had legal capacity and could act as a litigating party. For women, this meant being able to choose a husband and marry. The classic description of a Frisian marriage ritual is given in *The Synodical Law of Central Frisia* (text XI,62).

At the wedding, a woman received a dowry from her father. This was kept separate from her husband's goods. In addition, the wife was entitled to half of the mutually built increase in capital that took place during the marriage (Old Frisian *be*), but not to her husband's original inheritance. She could claim her dowry and the *be* in the event of her husband's death. However, another legal construction was possible, namely that the wife went into an agreement with her husband, whereby the possessions that the woman had brought into the marriage were declared common property. In return, the man made his wife an heir, so she would inherit together with their children. In the event of his death, she would then inherit a third of the assets.[48]

Lawful marriage was very important for the status of the children: a free Frisian was born from a free Frisian man and and a free Frisian woman who were lawfully married (text IX,8). And these legitimate children were in turn entitled to the inheritances of their parents.

---

47 Henstra, *The Evolution of the Money Standard*, 265–266.

48 Algra, *Oudfries Recht*, 353–355.

4 The Farm or Estate

Just as the family was the core unity of Frisian medieval society from a social point of view, so was the farm or the estate from a socio-economic point of view. In Frisia, the fertile lands had been wrought from the sea by building terps or artificial mounds on which houses were built. Later, from the 12th century onwards, the Frisians succeeded in building dikes and thus keeping larger stretches of land dry. This also meant that the total area of land in Frisia grew, as more and more land was reclaimed from either the sea but especially from marshes and peat lands that were surrounded by dikes and thus became arable.

The Frisian farm was an agricultural unit that consisted of a farmstead (the house) and farmland, which could be a combination of arable fields, pasture lands and meadows. Some parts of the wild lands or the communal lands (Old Frisian *hemrik*) could also be used. The farms could be managed by either noblemen, freeholders or tenants. On the farms, cattle was raised, yielding milk, butter and cheese. Also grain and vegetables were grown. The produce was sold at local and regional markets.

Farms varied in size. There is a tax list from 1479, which gives a nice overview of the categories reckoned with by then. These can be used retrospectively.[49] The largest farms counted 100 pondemaat or acres.[50] The aristocracy usually owned several of these farms. The freeholders roughly owned one farm, and these could vary between 30 acres up to 50 or even 100 acres. The quality of the soil also varied. Along the coast line of the North Sea lay the most fertile clay soil. Further inland, the land became more peaty or sandy, yielding less produce per acre. According to the tax list from 1479, the number of cows on a farm varied between four and twenty.

The aristocracy would often have erected a simple motte-and-bailey castle (Old Frisian stins 'stone house') next to the farm where their residency was. These could be used to defend themselves in a war or a feud. Over the course of the middle ages, some of these grew into real castles where the nobility would take up permanent dwelling.[51]

The ownership of a farm was an important way to measure someone's social and legal status. Having a farm made one eligible to the function of *gretman* or judge-administrator for a period of a year. Also, the size of one's farm(s) was

---

49 De Langen en Mol, 'The Distribution and Subdivision of Farmland', 6.

50 The pondemaat was a unity of acreage. Measured with the 'royal rod' it amounted to .375 hectare and was thus roughly comparable to the English acre (.405 hectare).

51 Noomen, *De stinzen in middeleeuws Friesland.*

used to determine which weapons one should bring with him on a military expedition to defend the land (text III,22). The unity of measurement is the worth of the land. It yields this list:

1. thirty pounds worth of land = a horse and weapon
2. twenty pounds worth of land = a forged weapon
3. twelve pounds worth of land = spear and shield
4. less than twelve pounds worth of land = bow and arrow

Obviously, the highest category must have been reserved for the nobility. The other three categories probably referred to three types of freeholders, attesting to the variation of farm land (in size and quality) they could own.

On ownership, an important remark should be made. In classic Old Frisian law, absolute ownership did not seem to exist. The person who most was considered the owner of a farm was the one who had the most rights of the *were* 'guardianship' or 'authority'. He would possess the *einlike were* 'own authority' of a farm.[52] So although Old Frisian *ein* does mean 'own', ownership seems to have been considered relative and not absolute. This can be inferred from a number of court procedures discussed in the *Older Skelta Law*, as well as from the institution of the *ferdban* 'peace ban', which meant that the *gretman* would pronounce peace over the one who held the *neste were* over a farm.[53] This would ensure the owner of the title to sit on his farm undisturbed. The right of *niār* 'pre-emption' or 'taking over a sale' (on which more below) also points to the fact that absolute property did not exist.

5 The Church

The Church had been present since the first missionaries came to convert the Frisians in the course of the 7th century. After the Carolingians conquered the Frisians, a few principal churches and a monastery were founded in Frisia. However, as mentioned at the beginning of this introduction, the Viking Age caused a period of turmoil during which the church was practically absent from Frisia. This changed during the second half of the 10th century.

Between c. 920 and 1024 the Ottonian or Saxon dynasty ruled over the Holy Roman Empire. In Central Frisia members of the house of Billung were appointed as count for a few generations.[54] During this period the counts of Frisia were members of the highest Saxon nobility. Because they were thus actively

---

52 Agra, *Ein*, 74 vv.
53 Vries, 'Also dat wy habbet ferdban kloppet'.
54 Henstra, *Friese graafschappen*, 84–92.

involved in the highest politics of the realm, they partly allowed Frisia to take care of its own affairs. This would then also explain the development of the function of the *frana* (< Proto-Germanic *frawan- 'belonging to the lord'), the substitute of the count in Frisia in his absence.[55] The count himself would only visit Frisia once a year, and then visit the various local courts to preside over them. The Salian dynasty started when Conrad II or the Elder (c. 990–1039) became king in 1024. This dynasty ended with Henry V (1081/1086–1125).

It is within this political context that the bishops of Utrecht started their restoration activities in Central Frisia in the 10th century, after the Viking raids had abated. Bishop Balderic of Utrecht (897–975) was a very influential and successful political actor, who succeeded in bringing the episcopal residence back to the city of Utrecht in 922, after the Utrecht bishops had been forced into exile in the previous decades. He was well connected to the Ottonian kings.

Under Balderic's initiative, a planned infrastructure was created in Frisia, resulting in a closed network of parishes and churches. This meant that each Frisian now belonged to a parish and a church, where funerals and baptisms were held, and where he had to pay tithes.

This infrastructure also included the creation of a synod in Frisia. Frisia was divided into three deaneries, presided over by an archdeacon. The synod also meant the implementation of an ecclesiastical court system in Frisia. Once every four years, the bishop of Utrecht visited Frisia (called the *circatus*) and then presided over the synodical court. For the remaining three years, the bishop transferred his *ban* (his authority) to the dean. The bishop's synod was his visitation of the lay people in his diocese to monitor the progress of the Christianization process and the well-being of the clerics and churches. Parallel to this, an ecclesiastical court was organised.

During the court session of the synod, matters concerning the church were settled. This could concern a number of categories. Firstly, everything connected with the church, the faith and clerics (such as the position of the clerics and acts of violence against them, the observance of Sundays and holidays, sacrilege and violation of the immunity of the church building, altar theft and corpse theft, but also superstitions and sorcery). Secondly, matters pertaining to marriage and morality (such as abortion, prostitution, adultery, paternity of a child, marriage). Lastly, there were matters that touched on secular law, such as perjury and oath-breaking.

A striking feature of the organization of the synod was that it relied heavily on lay people, who had pledged themselves to the courts and had the duty

55 Boutkan and Siebinga, *Old Frisian Etymological Dictionary*, s.v. frana.

to bring cases which concerned the synod before the court.[56] These sworn witnesses 'must be free, Frisian, born out of a lawful marriage, sufficiently wealthy to be able to pay a possible fine for perjury and not have forfeited their rights'.[57]

These local elites from which these sworn witnesses were recruited, had also played an important role in fundraising a number of the original churches out of which the parish infrastructure had been built. These relationships with the local elite are described by De Langen and Mol:

> How the fundraising under the local elite was organized is still unclear, though one can form an idea based on what is known about the *circatus*, the four-year visitation and inspection cycle of the bishop. On this repeated and systematic round through his diocese, the bishop not only had to hold court, but it was also his task to administer confirmations, ordain priests, and consecrate churches and altars, which also implied that he and his staff had to carry a treasure of relics with them. In the churches that served as synodal 'chairs' he was of course welcomed by the dean and the local priests. He was, however, also hailed and hosted by the most prominent local laymen, who, in their function as synodal witnesses, were responsible for the proper settlement of the ecclesiastical court cases. In this way, the bishop came into direct contact with the local elite on a regular basis. This offered him ample opportunity to put initiatives for new foundations on the agenda, to be realized within the next visitation cycle.[58]

It is thus clear that from the 10th century onwards, the Church, together with ecclesiastical law through the synod, had become an intrinsic part of Frisian society.

6 Legal Procedure in Classical Old Frisian Law

At certain times during the year the free Frisians gathered at *thing* or assembly meetings.[59] The Germanic term *thing* has been translated in a number of ways:

---

56 De Langen and Mol, 'Church Foundation and Parish Formation', 17.
57 Hallebeek, *Layci erant coiudices*, 16.
58 De Langen and Mol, 'Church Foundation and Parish Formation', 51.
59 Green, *Language and History*, 35–39; Iversen, '*Concilium* and *Pagus*'.

MAP 4 The districts in late medieval Central Frisia
MOL (2017)

'court' (our general choice in the text edition), 'court meeting', 'assembly'.[60] The etymology of the word can be retraced to 'time appointed for a particular purpose'.[61] The *thing* fulfilled several purposes. It was a meeting which was held at specific times during a year, where all kinds of matters (legal, military, polit-

60 Vogt and Nijdam, 'Translating a Medieval Legal System', 38–53; Green, *Language and History*, 36.

61 Green, *Language and History*, 35.

ical and religious) concerning the people in a certain district or region (Latin *pagus*, OFris. *gā*)[62] were discussed.

Free Frisians had the right, but also the duty, to attend the *thing* meetings (text III). The legal system was primarily accusatorial: cases could be brought before court by the men who attended the *thing* meetings. There was no government yet which actively pursued crimes.

Apart from the three regular *thing* meetings a free Frisian could also be summoned to attend a special meeting. Three types are mentioned in *Freeska Landriucht*. The first two are related: the *bodthing* 'commanded *thing* / court session' was ordered by the bishop or the count and took place once every four years. It consisted of two parts, of which the second was called *fimelthing* (text III,24–25).[63] The third, the *bōdelthing*, was a court meeting concerning a claim to an estate, held at that particular estate (text III,69).

The *thing* was the assembly of the inhabitants of a certain region. For Frisia the oldest *pagi* or districts are now firmly established (see Map 2). In Central Frisia, they were called Eastergoa (Dutch Oostergo) and Westergoa (Dutch Westergo), by their very names showing that Central Frisia was an old unity. In the course of the Middle Ages sub-districts came into being. In the 13th century, Westergoa was divided into three sub-districts: Franekeradeel, Wonseradeel and Wymbritseradeel. In Eastergoa, matters are more complicated. The southern part became the district of Bornego, but it is unclear how the northern part was divided in the 13th century. Later, even more subdistricts arose, yielding a situation where there were some 28 districts by the end of the 15th century (see Map 4). These newer districts always followed the borders of the church parishes. Also military obligations continued to be organised according to the districts.[64] In short, the districts were an important factor in the lives of medieval Frisians.

During the *thing* meetings peace was to be observed by all present.[65] Old Frisian *frethe, ferd* 'peace' had a temporal as well as a spatial aspect: a peace was ordained both for a specific time and for a specific place. In time, more specific kinds of peace were ordered, such as peace during a market. In *Freeska Landriucht*, a general peace can be seen to be in place. If someone committed a crime, often a penalty was also exacted for breaking this general peace.

---

62 I will only indicate vowel lengths in Old Frisian words in this introduction the first time the term is mentioned.

63 Alrga, 'Rechtshistorische aspecten', 121–125.

64 Mol, *De Friese volkslegers*.

65 Lambert and Rollason (eds.), *Peace and Protection*.

A peace was ordered and warranted by an authority. In Old Frisian this was called a *ban*. The *ban* too was a Germanic phenomenon. The meaning of the Proto-Germanic verb *banna- is 'to speak' (OFris. *banna*), so the original meaning must have been 'to order, to command'.[66] The authority to issue a *ban* rested in final instance with the king who could delegate it to his officials who were active in Frisia (see below). If the *ban* or order had been disobeyed, the authority of the one who had ordered the *ban* had been infringed upon, and a fine was exacted from the perpetrator. By extension, *ban* came to mean more than simply 'command': it could also mean 'jurisdiction' and 'district'. This was because similar to the concept of peace, *ban* also had a spatial aspect.

The officials involved at a *thing* or court meeting were first of all the count (OFris. *greva*) or his representative, the *frana*. We encountered these officials earlier. The count visited Frisia once a year and held court throughout the territory. The lower, day to day jurisdiction was overseen by the *skelta*, a term which is derived from *skeldhata* 'the one who calls out the guilt' (cf. German *Schultheiß*, Dutch *schout*). Thus, the function of the *skelta* originally was to admonish the congregation of free men to perform the duties they had towards the count, such as paying taxes.[67] In Frisia, the *skelta* thus was an important administrator and also presided over the court. From the end of the 13th century he was called *gretman*, (OFris. *grētmon*: literally 'the man who pronounces the accusations'), to signal that the Frisians had started appointing this official themselves.[68] In the translation, I have decided not to translate the terms *frana* and *skelta* because of the inadequacy of terms such as 'magistrate' or 'judge' or any other solution.

Another prominent figure in litigation was the legal expert who was called the *āsega*, a compound of *ā* 'law' and *sega* 'to speak'.[69] There has been some debate on what exactly the function of the *asega* was: whether he would actively recite the entire corpus of law once every year just as the Icelandic *lögsögumaðr* did, or whether he knew the appropriate rules for specific cases and would deliver them when asked to do so.

In the Old Frisian law texts, the *asega*—the term is also left untranslated in this edition—can be seen doing a number of things. He tells the *skelta* what happens next during a procedure: which party should take which oath at a certain phase of the procedure, dictating the oath formulas to the parties, and

66 Boutkan and Siebinga, *Old Frisian Etymological Dictionary*, s.v. Bon1. Note that Modern English has only retained the negative aspect of these semantics: *to ban* means 'to forbid'.

67 Algra, 'Rechtshistorische aspecten', 103, 107; Erler and Neidert, 'Schultheiß, Schulze'.

68 Noomen, *De stinzen in middeleeuws Friesland*, 84.

69 Algra, *Oudfries Recht*, 99–100; Gerbenzon, 'Der altfriesische *asega*'.

giving 'expert legal judgment', which is the translation I chose for OFris. *dōm dela*. The first word of this pair is a cognate of English *doom*, which however, just as with *ban*, has retained only the negative aspect of the semantics of this term in modern times. It originally meant 'judgment, verdict, decree'.[70] The verb *dela* means 'to deal out, to give'.

Several scholars have argued that the legal experts mentioned in the *Lex Frisionum*, Wlemar and Saxmund, probably were *asegas* as well, and that the *asega* was a pre-Carolingian official. They are called *sapientes* 'wise men' in a caption, but this was probably an addition by the 16th-century editor Johannes Herold.[71] But even though the *sapientes* are not called *iudex* explicitly, they do 'dictate' a 'decree': *Haec iudicia Saxmundus dictavit* 'Saxmund dictated these sentences'.[72] In other words, the *sapientes* and the *iudex* in *Lex Frisionum* as well as the *asega* were all legal experts who knew the rules of the law and of legal procedure: which oaths to take, which formulas to utter, etc.

The glosses to *Freeska Landriucht* provide some information as well: two glosses to text III,3 (*The Older Skelta Law*) read: 23. *Scelta id est iudex ex parte comitis* 'Scelta i.e. the judge on behalf of the Count'; 24. *Aesgha id est iudex terre ex parte potestatis* 'Aesgha i.e. the judge of the territory on behalf of the authorities'. Thus, in the medieval glosses, the *skelta* and the *asega* are both called *iudex* 'judge' or 'magistrate'. I have nevertheless chosen to retain the original Old Frisian terms in the translation in order to keep the distinction between and the special meanings of the terms visible.

The most archaic legal procedure encountered in the Old Frisian law texts (and already in the *Lex Frisionum*) is also known from other Germanic peoples. A claimant (OFris. *klagere, onsprekere, onthingere*) brought a case before court (OFris. *thing*), and the defendant (OFris. *haldere, sittere*) had the right to deny the charges and to swear innocence (OFris. *undswera*). If more oaths were required because of the severity of a case, the defendant had to find compurgators to take an oath in his favour. They would swear under oath that the defendant was a man of honour who always spoke the truth. Their function was thus that of a character witness rather than to bear witness of what had actually happened concerning the case at hand.

This again underlines how important honour was in this society. A man of honour did everything out in the open and not secretly, and could be held

70 On this, also see the individual introduction to tekst IX, *The Eight Provisions*, in paragraph 5 below.

71 Gerbenzon, 'Der altfriesische *asega*', 88–90.

72 *Lex Frisionum, Additio Sapientum* Tit. III,59: Eckhardt and Eckhardt (eds.), *Lex Frisionum*, 94.

responsible for his deeds. By extension, the difference between homicide (OFris. *daddel, dadslachta, dath, monslachta*) and murder (OFris. *morth*) was whether the killing was performed in the open and openly admitted or whether it was done secretly.[73] The same applied to taking something openly (OFris. *rāf*) or secretly, which was theft (OFris. *thiūvethe*).[74] In honour societies such as medieval Frisia a man of honour could thus deny charges simply by swearing on his honour that he had not done the matter brought against him.

The most common oath form was probably that on the holy relics (OFris. *wīthēth*) and which had probably replaced an older pre-Christian custom (plausibly by swearing on an oath ring).[75] A second type of oath is that on clothing which meant the person took his own garment in his hands and pledged upon those clothes.[76] A third type is the *fiāēth*, which meant one swore on his own possessions.

Because of the rich corpus of Old Frisian law, we are able to fill in some more details of the classical Frisian legal procedure. In order to start a procedure, the claimant would pronounce a complaint before court (OFris. *onsprēke*) and take an oath in which he formally declared and pronounced his claim against the defendant.

The next step would be that a summons (OFris. *lathinge*) would be formally announced to the defendant at his home by the *bannere*, a term which could be translated by bailiff: the *bannere* assisted the court officials and proclaimed the *ban* that had been decreed by the officials. If the defendant would refuse to appear before court after he had been summoned up to five times, the community would go to his house and destroy it.[77] Appearing before court was a privilege, but also a duty.

If the defendant appeared before court, the *skelta* or the legal representative of the claimant (OFris. *forspreka*) would formally put forward the claim. The defendant then was granted a term (OFris. *ferst*) during which he could decide to either confess (OFris. *jā, jechta*) or deny (OFris. *biseka*). If he denied, the claimant would address the defendant personally in court. This was called 'to accuse higher / more severely' (OFris. *hagra grēta*). At this point, the defendant might choose to say he was not obligated to answer. If that happened, the

73 Nijdam, *Lichaam, eer en recht*, 166; Miller, *Bloodtaking and Peacemaking*, 26–34.

74 Nijdam, *Lichaam, eer en recht*, 71; 124; Miller, *Bloodtaking and Peacemaking*, 93–101, 206.

75 On oaths in Old Frisian: Popkema, 'Die altfriesischen Eidesbezeichnungen'. On oath rings: Beck, 'Eidring'.

76 Nijdam, *Lichaam, eer en recht*, 179.

77 A custom known in large parts of medieval Europe (German *Wüstung*, French *arsin et abattis de maison*).

asega, after having been asked by the *skelta*, would declare that the defendant was obligated to either deny or confess and that if he wished to deny, he had to swear innocence (OFris. *undriuchta*) with so many compurgators (depending on the severity of the case). The only option that the claimant then had was to refuse to listen to these oaths, thus breaking off the procedure.

If a matter could not be resolved by the legal procedure described here, a solution could be found in a so-called ordeal, in which God would decide a case. A number of ordeals are described in Old Frisian law (texts III and XI). Most frequently used were first the ordeal by water, where the defendant would take an object out of a kettle filled with boiling water. After a certain term had elapsed, officials would assess how well the hand had healed. If it had healed sufficiently, the defendant had won the case. For more serious cases, an ordeal by combat or judicial duel could be held. This meant that the claimant and the defendant, or—as seemed to have become standard practice in medieval Frisia—hired champions would fight each other. After the Fourth Council of the Lateran, held in 1215, forbade the practice of putting God to the test in this way, ordeals slowly died out.[78]

At the end of the procedure, a verdict was reached. The *asega* would propose a verdict to the free Frisians present at the court or *thing* meeting and these would let their assent with the proposed verdict know by some means. This is not described in the Old Frisian sources but is known from other Germanic people.[79] After this, the *skelta* would find in favour (OFris. *forth finda*) of one party and against (OFris. *urbek finda*) the other. The Old Frisian terms literally mean: find in front of one and find behind one, indicating that the *skelta* would stand between the two parties and face the party that had won. This party was then in front of him while the other party was behind him.

Once the verdict had been pronounced in favour of the claimant by the *skelta*, the claimant had to execute the verdict himself, since medieval Frisia had no strong public authorities, capable of enforcing the judgment.[80] Only the community could be adhorted to act as a collective and go to the house of someone not willing to abide by the law, as we saw earlier. In the *Younger Skelta Law* it is explicitly stated thus (text XII,29):

> This is the law, if a thief has been caught and brought before the *skelta*, and if he is sentenced to death, then the *skelta* is not obligated to either hang the thief or blind him. Then the *bannere* has to bind him and lead

78 Buma, *Het Godsoordeel*; Neumann, *Der gerichtliche Zweikampf*.
79 Algra, 'Rechtshistorische aspecten', 165–166.
80 Nijdam, *Lichaam, eer en recht*, 172–173.

> him to the gallows. Then the claimant has the choice between hanging him himself or paying someone to do it for him.

It also becomes apparent from this clause that the *bannere* was the closest to an executioner or bailiff with a public law authority, since he was assisting in the execution of the verdict, but only to a certain extent.

The last subject that deserves attention in relation to the verdict and the end of the legal procedure is the concept of compensation. The privilege to compensate all crimes by paying a certain amount of money to the other party was so important, that it forms one of the paragraphs of *The Seventeen Statutes*. Here it is stated that 'all Frisians have the right to compensate their wrongdoings with valuables. Because of this, all Frisians will not have to be subjected to punishment by stick or pillory, hot scissors, flagellation or any other corporal punishment' (text VI,16).

The Old Frisian term for 'compensation' is *bōte*, from which a verb *bēta* 'to compensate' was derived. The etymology of the term is 'to make better again, repair'.[81] The compensation was thus meant to repair what had been damaged. In this edition, I have chosen to use the term 'compensation' rather than composition, settlement, or the like. It should be clear, however, that the term 'compensation' used here encompassed not only what was needed to repair or make good what had been caused by the act of injuring the victim, but also some penal elements: everything that was necessary to make the victim and his relatives feel that justice had been done and the victim's honour and position had been restored and at the same time a proper penalty for the crime committed. Needless to say this was a delicate process.[82]

In some languages the cognates of the Frisian word *bote* (Modern Dutch, Modern Frisian *boete*, Modern German *Buße*) have acquired the meaning 'fine': a sum of money to be paid by the wrongdoer as a punishment, which after criminal prosecution was monopolised by the state commonly has to be paid to the public authorities. It is interesting to see that a precursor of this secondary meaning of the term *bote* already occurs in the Old Frisian texts. Sometimes, *bote* refers to a compensation (with some penal elements) to be paid horizontally, from the wrongdoer to the victim, but sometimes, it refers to a fine that is to be paid to the community or the count (or his officials, the *skelta* and the *frana*). This is expressed in the translation by using the terms 'compensation' (in the broad sense as indicated) and 'fine' respectively.

---

81 Boutkan and Siebinga, *Old Frisian Etymological Dictionary*, s.v. beta, bote; Nijdam, *Lichaam, eer en recht*, 60–62.

82 Miller, *Eye for an Eye*.

Over time—probably in the 12th century—legal procedure started to change. Proof became more important. If things were publicly known (OFris. *būrkūth*) or if people had seen the defendant doing what he later denied in court, swearing innocence was no longer allowed. This element was already present at an early stage, as the *Exceptions to the Seventeenth Statute* (text X) which has been dated to the 11th century shows. This text enumerates six cases in which something is done in public, so that it cannot be denied afterwards in court.

Alongside this development towards truth finding, a new group of officials was introduced into the higher and lower courts: the OFris. *tolva* or *konings orkenen* 'king's witnesses'. The Old Frisian term *tolva* literally means 'twelve': this was a bench of twelve men from a certain district who had sworn an oath to serve the truth. They were respectable men, a delegation of the bystanders at the *thing* meeting one could say, who knew what was going on in the district, and who also started to actively find the truth concerning cases brought before court. The consent of a majority, or seven of the twelve, was necessary to win a dispute.

Finally, in the context of this evolution of the way proof was dealt with in court, two technical terms deserve some attention: OFris. *onbring* / *onbrinze* and OFris. *niār*.[83] If a claim or a crime was *burkuth* 'publicly known', then the defendant could no longer exonerate himself by swearing an oath. In those cases where the defendant had lost this right, the claimant had the right of *onbring* (noun) or the case was called *onbrinze* (adjective). The term literally means 'to bring forth, to present'. This meant the claimant had the right to affirm his claim by swearing an oath. This in turn annulled the right of the defendant to swear innocence.

A term that is related to this is OFris. *niār* which literally means 'closer'. It meant that one of the parties had 'more right' to either pursue the claim or deny it. A fine example of the game of moves and countermoves these legal rules led to can be found in paragraph 3 of *The Younger Skelta Law* (text XII,3). A few illustrative sentences from this section:

> Nu aegh dy grewa dyne aesgha toe bannen dat hi riucht deeroen deel. Nu deelt dy aesgha dat hy nyaer se mitta oenbring him schieldich toe winnane dan hy se mitta edem deer hy byoeth oenschieldich toe wirdane.

> Now the count has to order the *asega* to come to a lawful judgment concerning this matter. Now the *asega* declares that the claimant has more

83 Nijdam, *Lichaam, eer en recht*, 166–167.

right to accuse the defendant under oath and thus get him convicted than the defendant is allowed to produce oaths of innocence and thus be found innocent.

The right of *niar* could also apply if a plot of land was sold. Either relatives or neighbours owning land adjacent to the plot being put up for sale could claim the right to buy that land.[84]

Overall, it has hopefully become clear that classical Frisian law was built on ancient Germanic foundations, and that the right to exonerate oneself remained firmly in place throughout this classical period, but that regulations and the importance of truth finding grew over time, creating an intricate chess-like legal game with moves and countermoves.

7 The Book

The book *Freeska Landriucht* consists of 11 quires plus one bifolium on which the prologue and the table of contents are printed (text I in the edition). The quires are numbered A to I and L to M. This means that a quire K seems to be missing exactly at the point where the text reads *Hyr eyndighet dat Landriucht der Fresena ende alhyrnei folged Keiser Rodulphus boeck* 'Here ends the land law of the Frisians and after this begins the book of Emperor Rudolf' (text XV in the edition).[85] Also, half a page is left empty at this point.

This observation leads to two conclusions. In the first place it makes it highly likely that texts II to XV were seen as the core canon of Central Frisian law: *Freeska Landriucht* in the narrow sense of the word. Secondly, the missing quire K might give some clues about the printing process, although it is very hard to see what this actually reveals. It is unlikely that two separate Old Frisian manuscripts had been presented to the printer, since all other Old Frisian law manuscripts that have survived show a collection of texts similar to the entire *Freeska Landriucht*. Furthermore, the texts in quires L and M also contain Latin glosses (unlike any other extant Old Frisian manuscript), so there is no clear break in that respect either.

It is still a mystery who printed *Freeska Landriucht*. For centuries, authors have speculated about this. As we will see below, already around 1567 the Frisian nobleman Botte van Holdinga wrote that it had been printed by the

84 Algra, *Ein*, 76–79; Vries, 'Nijaer is sijd ende pliga'.

85 Popkema, 'Aspekten fan it Freeska Landriucht', 173.

priest Hidde van Camminga (the Van Camminga's were a very prominent noble family). This information can also be found on two younger handwritten title pages in the copies BL (nr. 2) and RA (nr. 8), described below.

Later authors, the first of whom was the historian Ubbo Emmius (1547–1625), thought that the book had been printed in Cologne. The discussion has continued in the centuries since.[86]

The jury is still out on the question who printed this work. It has become clear by now, however, that this print shop printed five more—Latin—works in the fields of theology and law.[87] On the basis of the watermarks in the paper that was used to print *Freeska Landriucht*, the date has been pinpointed to 1484–1487.[88]

None of the nine copies of *Freeska Landriucht* that exist today are identical, as is not uncommon for early printed books. Corrections were made during the printing process, as a result of which all copies show some mutual dissimilarities.[89] Despite these mistakes, however, printing *Freeska Landriucht* was a carefully planned project. This becomes clear when we first look at the Old Frisian text and then compare it to the Latin glosses. This will yield some interesting insights.

First, the detailed table of contents was created with the help of the complete Old Frisian text. The captions that were in the main text were used to create it. Since many of the paragraphs of the *Old Skelta Law* have captions, this text is overrepresented. Mistakes that were made in these captions are repeated in the table of contents, testifying to the close link between the two. An example of this is text III,16, where the caption reads: *Nen Fresa thoer schelta ban tielda* 'No Frisian has to observe the authority of the *skelta*', where *schelta* should read *grewa* 'count', as becomes clear from the actual text of this paragraph. The mistake was repeated in the table of contents (text I). Another example is the caption to text III,52, which erroneously reads *Van enis ovirlandis guedes mannes daed* 'Concerning the death of a good foreigner', which can again be found in the same form in the table of contents, but which should read *Van enis overlandis daedes mannes gued* 'Concerning the goods of a dead foreigner'.

A second observation is that the entire Old Frisian text as a whole has been modernised and edited, in various respects. The language of all texts has been updated to the late 15th century. One example of this is the preponderance

86 Schouten, 'Hypothese op hypothese stapelen'.

87 Kruitwagen, 'De Freeska Landriucht-drukkerij'; Van Thienen, 'A Date for the Freeska Landriucht Press', 141–142; Schouten, 'Hypothese op hypothese stapelen', 168.

88 Van Thienen, 'A Date for the Freeska Landriucht Press'.

89 Popkema, 'Aspekten fan it Freeska Landriucht'.

of the spelling *mit* for OFris. *mith* 'with'.[90] Another example can be found in the *Younger Skelta Law*, where the archaic word OFris. *uta* was clarified by adding the interjection *dat is biwiis* 'that means proof' (text XII,3 in the edition). This addition is not present in any of the other redactions of this text. On the whole then, the archaic Old Frisian law texts have been carefully dusted off and presented in such a way that they were readable and understandable to a late 15th-century audience.

The Latin glosses, on the other hand, seem to have eluded this update. They date, as Jan Hallebeek and Hylkje de Jong show below in their 'Preface to the Edition and Translation of the Gloss', from the period between c. 1250 and 1400.[91] The fact that the glosses themselves have not been updated is not surprising, since the *Freeska Landriucht* tradition had become out of fashion after 1400, becoming more or less replaced by the *Excerpta Legum / Jurisprudentia Frisica* tradition. But that is not all. A closer inspection of the Old Frisian lemmata with which a number of the glosses start, show that these in several cases point to a variant redaction of the main text in *Freeska Landriucht*. In total, 139 glosses begin with one or a few words of Old Frisian (a lemma from the Old Frisian main text). Out of these, 18 references in the glosses point to a variant redaction of the Old Frisian text that is alluded to; there is, in other words, a mismatch between the reference in the Gloss and the main text.

One example can be found in gloss 68, which comments the second of the *Seventeen Statutes*. The reference in the gloss reads *alle godes mannen*. The main text, however, reads (text VI,2): *Dio oder kest is: alle godeshusem, alle godesliodem ferd bi LXXII pondem* 'The second statute is: peace to all churches and all clerics, on penalty of 72 pounds'. So whereas the main text has *godesliodem*, the reference in the Gloss reads *godesmannen*. The redaction in Jus, however, does read *godesmannum* at this point.[92]

In four instances, the Old Frisian lemmata in the glosses are missing altogether in the main text. One instance is a very special case. In the middle of gloss 182, the following short sentence in Old Frisian can be found: *inda scheltena riucht: Iefma ane man biiclaghet itta how and hiine wtoer ferd to liidsene* 'In the *Skelta Law*: If a case against someone is brought before the court of the count in order to have him outlawed'. The paragraph to which this refers can indeed be found in the *Older Skelta Law*, in III,56–57. But this exact short sentence is sought for in vain: not only are these exact wordings not found in the *Freeska Landriucht* redaction, they cannot even be found in any of the extant

90 Nijdam and Versloot, 'Kodeks Siccama', 141–144.

91 See also: Hallebeek, 'The Gloss to the *Saunteen Kesta*'.

92 Buma and Ebel, *Westerlauwerssches Recht I*, 136 (J VI,2).

redactions. We might even be dealing with a translation of a Latin sentence or an addition, which for some reason was not phrased in Latin, but then this would be the only instance in the entire Gloss. The language of this short sentence has been dated to the beginning of the 15th century.[93]

In short then, a close analysis of *Freeska Landriucht* yields a number of insights. The Old Frisian archaic law texts were carefully edited so that they could easily be read and understood by a late 15th century audience. The Latin Gloss however, was not updated, thus giving testimony to the fact that this tradition had come to an end by around 1400. The Gloss thus show that there must have existed several manuscripts with glossed compilations of Old Frisian law texts. None of these have survived today, save the first two texts of *Codex Roorda*, which seems to be the beginning of a *Freeska Landriucht* like compilation.[94] But this compilation breaks off after a few pages. The only other glosses that survived are the handwritten glosses in the copy FG of the *Freeska Landriucht* (i.e. the copy that was taken as the basis of this edition).

7.1 *Early Attestations until the End of the 17th Century*

Attestations of copies from past centuries come not only from Central Frisia, but also from East Frisia, both from the Ommelanden (province of Groningen) and Ostfriesland in Germany.

In the Ommelanden, the 14th century saw the decline of Frisian as a written language. Its replacement by Low German (Low Saxon) is often contributed to the influence of the city of Groningen but is more likely the consequence of the strong position of Low German as *lingua franca* in the North Sea and Baltic Sea regions. In the course of the 15th and 16th centuries a corpus of translations of Old Frisian law texts into Low Saxon grew, which today consists of some 150 manuscripts. In this corpus, there is a marked influence of *Freeska Landriucht*, which means that one or (probably) more copies circulated there.[95]

Around 1567, the Frisian nobleman Botte van Holdinga (c. 1500–1577) wrote a history of the Frisians, titled *De origine, antiquitate et situ totius Phrysiae libri decem*.[96] Holdinga was the first to mention *Freeska Landriucht*. He said it was printed a century earlier:

93 Personal communication Arjen Versloot (Amsterdam University).

94 Gerbenzon, 'Aantekeningen over de *Jurisprudentia Frisica*'.

95 Gerbenzon, *Excerpta Legum*, 42–43; Meijering and Nijdam, *Wat is recht?*, 28–29; 589; Sytsema, *De 17 Keuren en de 24 Landrechten*.

96 Tresoar Leeuwarden, 9056 Hs B.

> Caeterum Dns. Hiddo a Camminga, vir nobilis, olim apud Doccumates et postea apud Angumaeos parochus, sub idem fere tempus eundem libellum, ex quo hanc Phrysiae divisionem mutuati sumus, suis praelis in excusum in lucem edidit, licet nomen suum ut typographi ille non addiderit, cujusmodi passim adhuc apud non paucos nostratium extant.[97]
>
> Around that time, Sir Hiddo of Camminga, first priest in Dokkum and later in Anjum, printed the book on which our division of Frisia is based on his own press, without adding his name or that of the printer, of which many copies are still around today.

In 1599 Bernardus Furmerius, the second state historian of Friesland, borrowed three books from the library of the city hall of Leeuwarden. One of these can be identified as *Freeska Landriucht*, since the municipal administrative source in which this event was documented accurately gives the incipit and explicit.[98] It is unclear whether he ever returned the books.

Also at the end of the 16th century a strange book was printed which would have a profound influence on Frisian historiography in the centuries to come. It concerns a fictional history of the Frisians, entitled *Croniicke ende waarachtige Beschrijvinge van Vrieslant*.[99] It was written by a certain Andreas Cornelius, who claimed to have used as sources the works of otherwise unkown authors Ocko Scharlensis (purportedly 10th century) and Johannes Vlietarp (purportedly 14th century). The book also recites the story of Magnus, the leader of the Frisian war band, who conquered Rome on behalf of Charlemagne, thus obtaining the Frisian freedom as a reward for this feat. Here Cornelius cites a paragraph from *Freeska Landriucht* which describes pope Leo giving the Frisians a charter to confirm their privileges (see text V,7 in the edition, and see section 5 below for a more detailed description of this text).[100]

In 1617 the Frisian scholar Sibrandus Siccama (1571–1622) published an annotated edition of the *Lex Frisionum*. To demonstrate the continuity from this ancient law of the Frisians to the Middle Ages, he adduced a number of shorter or larger text fragments from Old Frisian law manuscripts. These quotations show that he had access to a distinct Old Frisian manuscript, similar but not

---

97 Tresoar Leeuwarden, 9056 Hs B, fol. 49^{v}–50^{r}.

98 Historisch Centrum Leeuwarden, Recesboek F4, fol. 361^{v}; on this source see: http://www.mpaginae.nl/ResolRaad/StedBibl1599vv.htm.

99 Bolhuis van Zeeburgh, *Kritiek der Friesche geschiedschrijving*; Noomen, 'Suffridus Petrus'.

100 Cornelius, *Croniicke ende waarachtige Beschrijvinge*, fol 21^{v} (2nd edition 74/75).

identical to any of the few that have survived today (Unia and Jus). But they also show he had *Freeska Landriucht* at his disposal.[101]

Franciscus Junius (1591–1677) was one of the first scholars to study the various Germanic languages, such as Gothic, Old English and Old Frisian. The fact that he was a cosmopolite who travelled between England and the Netherlands gave him access to both Old English source material and to sources of the continental Germanic languages. During his stay in the Netherlands he went to great lengths to learn Frisian and to acquire Old Frisian manuscripts. For this, he built a cultural network in Frisia. One of his contacts was the Frisian nobleman Doeke Hemmema (1603–1698), who probably helped him to acquire a copy of *Freeska Landriucht* (see below, copy J109), but who also reported on his own and other copies he had seen in a letter to Junius dating from 1657.[102]

In 1664 Christianus Schotanus published his *Beschryvinge van de Heerlyckheydt van Friesland tusschen 't Flie end de Lauwers met nieuwe Caerten*. On pages 36–106, he rendered *Freeska Landriucht* integrally, including the Latin glosses. We do not know whether he used one of the still existing copies or a copy that is now lost.

More could be said about attestations of *Freeska Landriucht* after 1700, but these attestations partly overlap with information on the provenances of the nine existing copies.

7.2 *FG = Leeuwarden, Tresoar Fries Genootschap A III 31 / B 38831 Kluis*

This copy is the source text of our edition. All initials have been filled in in red ink, the initial to the prologue (text I in the edition) with a large capital letter in blue ink and the initial of the first text, *What Is Law?* (text II in the edition), rather elaborately in blue ink with red decorative penwork. FG is bound in a brown leather binding. A quire of five leaves has been added at the front in the 18th century, on which earlier owners left some marks. Among them are notes by Petrus Wierdsma (1729–1811) in which he refers to earlier works which mention *Freeska Landriucht*.

The copy was well used by contemporaneous users. It has been established that one of the two hands that can be discerned in this copy can be identified as that of Hemma Oddazin, scribe to the city of Leeuwarden from 1486–1493 and 1501–1508. On two pages Hemma Oddazin wrote down three currency conversion tables.[103] He also added handwritten glosses to the Gloss, which might be a testimony of part of a larger Gloss tradition to *Freeska Landriucht* which is now

---

101 Nijdam and Versloot, 'Kodeks Siccama'.

102 Nijdam and Savelkouls, 'The Manuscript Collection', 321–322.

103 Henstra, *Fon Jelde*, 253–273.

lost to us.[104] Because of the strong link to the municipality of Leeuwarden, this might even be the copy the state historian Bernardus Furmerius had borrowed from the city library of Leeuwarden in 1599 (see earlier).

In later times, the copy belonged to Petrus Wierdsma, who probably had it bound and who left notes in the extra quire at the front.[105] In 1858 it was bought by J.G. Ottema (1804–1879) when Wierdsma's collection was auctioned. Ottema then donated this copy to the Fries Genootschap, of which he was a member.[106] This copy filled the gap that had been left in the collection of the Fries Genootschap after they had donated their only copy to the Royal Library in The Hague in 1855 (see copy KB, nr. 5 below).

7.3 *BL = London, British Library A I 48951*

This copy has remained quite blank. There are almost no marginal notes left by previous owners and the initials have not been filled in. It does however contain one very important handwritten note in Dutch at the very end of the book, which reads: *In 't jaer ons Heren dusent vier hondert ende acht ende tachtig geschreven op den dach doet screven woert* [*maria amor*] 'In the year of our Lord 1488 on the day it was written [maria amor]'.[107] This gives an important hard *datum ante quem* for *Freeska Landriucht* and fits well with the date that was deduced from an analysis of the paper and its watermarks: 1484–1487.

The copy is bound in a 20th-century brown leather cover.[108] On the verso side of the blank leaf that was bound in front of *Freeska Landriucht*, a handwritten note can be found in Dutch, which relates that this copy originally contained a loose leaf with a handwritten title page. Because this leaf had been so tattered, it had been left out of the new binding. The note does, however, give the text of the title on that discarded leaf:

> It Rjuechtboeck fen alre fryja Freezena Freeska Landrjuecht, ien aade tieden Beschrioewen, so az dat Baad di Keizer Kaarl Magnus to Room, om it 800e jeer nei Christus, der nei Rodolf de Keizer, om it 1273e jeer. Droekt ien't kleaster by Jr Hidde fen Camminga, Parochijaan eerst to Dokkum, da to Aanjum.

---

104 See 'Preface to the Edition and Translation of the Gloss'.

105 De Vries, 'Midsiuwske Fryske rjochtshânskriften'.

106 *Een en dertigste verslag der handelingen*, 30.

107 It is unclear what *maria amor* means. At the moment, this entry is difficult to read. It should be reexamined.

108 Personal communication Anne Tjerk Popkema and Herre de Vries, who inspected this copy in 2018.

> The lawbook of all free Frisians *Freeska Landriucht*, written in old times, as commanded by Emperor Charlemagne around the year 800 AD, and afterwards by Emperor Rudolf around the year 1273. Printed in the monastery by Hidde van Camminga Esq., priest, first in Dokkum, later in Anjum.

This title is identical to that of the copy RA (nr. 8 below).

This copy had been in the book collection of Gerardus Meerman (1722–1771) and his son Johannes Meerman (1753–1815) since at least 1767. One of them thus probably wrote the note just mentioned, and Gerardus or Johannes probably had the copy bound after they had purchased it for their collection.

The Meerman collection was auctioned in 1824, at which point the copy was sold. It ended up in the collection of Richard Heber (1773–1833) a well-known bibliophile who amassed a huge collection during his life. It probably came to the British Museum after the auction of Heber's collection in 1835.[109] At the end of the 20th century the book was moved to the British Library but maintained its shelf mark.

7.4 *BN = Paris, Bibliothèque Nationale Ms. Néerl. 45*

This copy lacks the bifolium with the prologue and table of contents (text I in the edition). It has no marginal notes, but all initials are filled in, some even rather elaborately. The copy is part of a convolute manuscript consisting of four different parts which were bound together between c. 1570 and c. 1590, probably in Groningen.[110] The earliest possessor of the convolute is an otherwise unknown Geerd Klaasz schipper. The first two parts of this convolute are manuscripts with Low Saxon translations of Old Frisian law. The first part stems from the middle of the 16th century, but the second part—dubbed Paris II—stems from the end of the 15th century and is important to the study of the Low Saxon corpus.[111] The third part contains 15th century law texts from the province of Drenthe. The convolute came into the Bibliothèque Nationale—then called Bibliothèque du Roi—between 1682 and 1730. This is based on the fact that the copy BN is mentioned in the handwritten catalogue of the library that was created in 1730.

Through an analysis of the handwritten addendum of eight texts to this copy of *Freeska Landriucht*, which has become known as Codex Parisiensis in Old Frisian studies, Gerbenzon has been able to show that this copy has been in

109 Pollard et al., *Catalogue of books*, 110.

110 Gerbenzon, *Codex Parisiensis*, 1–26; Gerbenzon, 'Canon and Roman Law'; Popkema, 'On the Provenance'.

111 Meijering and Nijdam, *Wat is recht?*, 35–36, *passim*.

use in the South East of Central Frisia (Sânwâlden and Stellingwerf regions) in the late 15th and early 16th centuries. It thus gives a unique insight in the daily legal practice in this period.[112]

7.5 *J109 = Oxford, Bodleian Library MS Junius 109*

This copy is bound in a parchment binding. At the front and at the back, leaves have been inserted. A few initials have been filled in. Otherwise, this copy shows no traces of any previous owners other than those of its only known owner, Franciscus Junius (1591–1677). Junius acquired his copy of *Freeska Landriucht* around 1657.[113] In 1659 he lent it to his friend Jan van Vliet (Janus Vlitius), who returned it a year later and eventually succeeded in acquiring a copy for himself (see below, copy M60, nr. 6). After Junius's death, his collection of manuscripts, including this copy of *Freeska Landriucht*, was transferred to the Bodleian Library.

7.6 *KB = The Hague, Royal Library 150 C 36*

This copy is bound in parchment and interleaved.[114] Most of the interleaved pages have been left blank. On the first pages, however, someone has translated the Frisian text into Dutch. This seems to be a 16th-century hand. On the last page of this copy one of the earliest owners left a trace: *Dit boeck hoert toe Sybout Aysma* 'This book belongs to Sybout Aysma'.[115] Sybout Aysma (ca 1534–1604) also owned a manuscript with Old Frisian law texts, belonging to the younger tradition of the *Jurisprudentia Frisica*, which was named after him: Codex Aysma.[116]

A second trace was left by state historian Simon Abbes Gabbema (1628–1688), in the form of a marginal note in his handwriting.[117] After Gabbema, the copy came into the hands of Nicolaas Tholen (1725–1770), assistant editor of the *Groot Placaat en Charterboek van Vriesland*. This Gabbema-Tholen connection makes it highly likely that this copy too (see below, copy RA, nr. 8) had been part of the library of the state historians of Friesland, which was placed in the Gabbema Gasthuis after the death of Simon Abbes Gabbema in 1688. This library was rediscovered by Georg thoe Schwartzenberg en Hohenlansberg (1733–1783)

---

112 Gerbenzon, 'Canon and Roman Law'.

113 Nijdam and Savelkouls, 'The Manuscript Collection', 324.

114 It can be consulted online here: https://archive.org/details/ned-kbn-all-00001690-001.

115 Nijdam and Savelkouls, 'The Manuscript Collection', 313.

116 Gerbenzon, *Excerpta Legum*, 21–24; Buma, Gerbenzon and Tragter-Schubert (eds.), *Codex Aysma*.

117 Nijdam and Savelkouls, 'The Manuscript Collection', 313.

when he was preparing his monumental edition of Frisian sources, the *Groot Placaat en Charterboek van Vriesland* around 1765.[118] Although the details are unknown, KB was later acquired by J.M. van Beyma thoe Kingma (1781–1847) and finally bought by the Fries Genootschap at the auction of Van Beyma thoe Kingma's library after his demise.

As a consequence of the rediscovery of the Gabbema collection by the Schwartzenberg team, several manuscripts of this immensely important library, which contained many unique medieval Frisian manuscripts, ended up in the possession of J.F.M. Herbell (1752–1819), who became assistant to Schwartzenberg after the untimely death of Tholen. This separated a number of important manuscripts from the original Gabbema collection, which had remained relatively intact until then. After Herbell's death in 1819, his collection of books and manuscripts was put to auction. A sizable part of this collection was then bought by the Royal Library ('Koninklijke Bibliotheek') in The Hague. The purchase of the Royal Library remained in the care of H. Amersfoordt (1796–1842)—one of the three founding fathers of the Fries Genootschap (founded 1827)—until 1832, when it was transferred to The Hague.

In 1855 an agreement was reached between the Fries Genootschap and the Minister of the Interior, which entailed that the important collection of manuscripts which had been bought by the Royal Library at the auction of the collection of Herbell in 1819 (and which mostly had come from the Gabbema collection) would return to Frisia and be placed under the care of the Fries Genootschap.

In return for this gesture, the Royal Library received the copy KB from the Fries Genootschap. For the occasion of the exchange, the Leeuwarden municipal archivist, historian and member of the Fries Genootschap, Wopke Eekhoff (1809–1880), who had managed the practicalities of the deal with the Royal Library on behalf of the Fries Genootschap, included a handwritten introduction to this *Freeska Landriucht* copy.[119]

7.7 *M60 = Oxford, Bodleian Library MS Mareschalli 60*

This copy is bound in a parchment binding. All initials have been soberly filled in. The book is interleaved. This copy was acquired by Jan van Vliet (1622–

118 Nijdam and Savelkouls, 'The Manuscript Collection'. Much remains unclear about the Gabbema collection and its fate: it has recently become apparent that part of it was transferred to his successor in office and after that followed a different route, also to end up eventually with Schwartzenberg. See: Popkema, 'On the Provenance', (Fs).

119 Nijdam and Savelkouls, 'The Manuscript Collection', 313. This text, also handwritten by Eekhoff, can also be found in Leeuwarden, Tresoar Hs 1327.

1666), a colleague of Franciscus Junius who worked on an edition of *Freeska Landriucht* between 1659 and 1665.[120] He originally borrowed the copy owned by Junius (J109) but in 1660 he received this copy (M60) as a gift from his friend Thomas Browne (1604–1673).[121] After Van Vliet's demise, his copy came into the possession of Junius, who in turn gave it to his long time friend and former pupil Thomas Marshall (1621–1685). This copy then became part of the collection of manuscripts of Marshall that was transferred to the Bodleian Library after his death.[122]

7.8 PB = *Leeuwarden, Tresoar Hs 1074 R*

This copy is bound in a brown leather binding. It contains two bifoliums with the prologue and table of contents (text I of the edition), of which one is a misprint, bound after each other.[123] The copy shows marginal notes in various hands, the oldest of which seems to be from the early 16th century.

This copy formed part of the library of Oldersum Castle situated in East Frisia in the 16th century and is the only surviving book of that library today.[124] After the death of the nobleman Hero II of Oldersum in 1589, an inventory of the library was made in the context of the legal affairs that had to be seen to, since Hero had left no heir. In the aftermath of these legal affairs, the copy came into the hands of Henricus Reiningius of Coevorden, a public notary. A year later, on 15 October 1590, he in turn gifted the book to Rembartus Ackema, a *legum doctor*, who at the time was prefect of nearby Leerort but originated from Groningen. A handwritten note by mr. Jacob Warmolt Keiser (1737–1821), dated 1792, relates that he acquired this copy from Samuel Wolther Tjassens (1739–1814) in exchange for a number of manuscripts. At this point, it is unknown how the copy ended up in the Provincial Library in Leeuwarden (now Tresoar).

7.9 RA = *Leeuwarden, Tresoar, Toegang 326 (Familie thoe Schwartzenberg en Hohenlansberg) No. 3945a*

This copy is bound in parchment and interleaved. The first bifolium containing the prologue and the table of contents (text I in the edition) is missing. All initials are filled in blue and red ink. Other than this, the copy shows no traces of contemporary use.

---

120 Dekker, *The Origins of Old Germanic Studies*, 115–122.

121 Dekker, 'The Old Frisian Studies', 118.

122 Hunt et al., *A Summary Catalogue*, 992, 999.

123 De Vries, 'Misprintinge leit skiednis bleat'; Popkema, 'The *Freeska Landriucht* (1074R)'.

124 Popkema, 'The *Freeska Landriucht* (1074R)'.

The interleaving was heavily used by the first known owner, Simon Abbes Gabbema (on whom and on what follows see earlier, copy KB, nr. 5). On these leaves he noted variant forms of the texts in *Freeska Landriucht*, which he copied from the various Old Frisian and Low German law manuscripts he either owned himself, or which he had borrowed from acquaintances in his network.[125]

By a 'great coincidence' as he himself describes it, this copy was bought by the same man who had rediscovered the Gabbema collection around 1765: Georg thoe Schwartzenberg en Hohenlansberg.[126] It still forms part of the family archive of the Schwartzenberg family, which is now housed at Tresoar, Leeuwarden.

A quire of two leaves was later added to this copy, by means of which a title page was created. The text of this title page is the same as in copy BL (nr. 2, earlier). Moreover, to this was added: *doorsteeken met schoon papier, en vergeleeken met verscheidene hantschriften door Simon Abbes Gabbema, gelastigde geschiedschrijver van Friesland* 'interleaved with blank paper and compared with various manuscripts by Simon Abbes Gabbema, state historian of Frisia'. This text seems to date to the 18th century: further research is required, also on the relation between this copy and the BL copy.

7.10 *UB = Utrecht, University Library J Oct 1112*

This copy also is part of a convolute.[127] It was bound together with one of the five other books that are known to have been produced by the workshop of the '*Freeska Landriucht* printer': the *Statuta provincialia et synodalia Trajectensia*.[128] The works are bound together in a greenish brown leather binding with some decorative gold tooling on the covers dated to the second half of the 18th century.[129]

This copy has some of the initials filled in with a green ink, which has now faded considerably. It shows a fair number of old marginal notes, dating to the late 15th / early 16th centuries. It has, in other words, been used.

---

125 Nijdam and Savelkouls, 'The Manuscript Collection', 319–320.

126 Schwartzenberg, *Groot Placcaat en Charterboek* II (1773), lxix; Popkema, 'On the Provenance', (Fs).

127 It can be consulted online here: http://objects.library.uu.nl/reader/index.php?obj=1874-301851&lan=en#page//70/98/59/70985995877195695080521019824924727705.jpg/mode/1up.

128 Incunabula Short Title Catalogue (*Statuta Traiectensia* (*Utrecht*): *Provincialia et synodalia*): https://data.cerl.org/istc/is00754300.

129 Janssen, '"Freeska Landriucht"'.

The copy was once—in the early 16th century judging from the writing—in the possession of Fecke Sipkes, as can be read on f. 87r: *fecke sipk zoon possidet me*. We do not know who Fecke was or what happened to this copy in the centuries to follow. It was finally bought by the University Library of Utrecht in 1899 at the auction of the library of mr. Willem Jan Royaards van den Ham (1829–1897), who had been an avid collector of rare books and manuscripts during his life.[130] The library's main reason for buying this copy probably was the second book of this binding, *The Provincial and Synodical Statutes of Utrecht*.

8 A Short Introduction to the Individual Texts

8.1 *Text I. Prologue*

The compilation starts with a prologue and a table of contents. This text falls into three parts. It begins with a dedication to St. Mary and a commemoration of Frisian law, which Charlemagne granted the Frisians because they had fought valiantly for him in Rome (a reference to the story told in text V).[131] After that a concise overview of the contents is given, consisting of seventeen parts. This cannot be coincidental, for *The Seventeen Statutes* (text VI) is the oldest and most important Old Frisian law text; in other words, the number seventeen had a special meaning.[132] Thirdly, a more detailed table of contents is given. This overview gives all the captions that are present in the compilation. The effect of this is that *The Older Skelta Law* (text III) is overrepresented, taking up almost two thirds of this table.

8.2 *Text II. What Is Law?*

This text can be best be viewed as a general preface or introduction to Old Frisian law. That is why it always appears as the first text in the law manuscripts from Central Frisia. It tells where law originally came from, tracing its origin back to Mosaic law and then through the ancient empires on to the Holy Roman Emperors and finally to Old Frisian law. In terms of its content, the text shows similarities with the *Book of Emperor Rudolf* (text XVI) and with the *Prologue to the Seventeen Statutes and Twenty-Four Land Laws* (text VII).

---

130 Janssen, '"Freeska Landriucht"'.

131 Johnston, 'Old Frisian Law and the Frisian Freedom Ideology', 194–195. On the Frisians and their relationship with Saint Mary see: Van Lengen, 'Karl der Große, Jungfrau Maria und andere Heilsbringer'.

132 Stein, 'Seventeen'; Bremmer, 'More than Language', 105–109.

The form of the text is that of a catechism: the paragraphs begin with a question which is then answered. Pieter Gerbenzon has demonstrated that its main source is the *Summa Coloniensis* (the *Summa Elegantius in iure divino*), an anonymous commentary on the first and second part of Gratian's *Decretum*, dating from 1169. He also manages to shed more light on the canonistic source of the extensive pseudohistorical continuation: the *Decretum Gratiani* (c.1140), in which for this section elements from the *Etymologiae* of Isidore of Seville (560–636) have been adopted. On the basis of this, and because the *Summa Coloniensis* fell into disuse after 1220, Gerbenzon dates *What Is Law?* to the early 13th century. However, as Gerbenzon indicates himself, once the text had reached Frisia, it might have been used until the late 13th century.[133]

8.3 *Text III. The Older Skelta Law*

After the introduction to Old Frisian law provided by the previous text, *The Older Skelta Law* forms the start of the core of archaic law texts from Central Frisia. It ends with its counterpart, namely the *Younger Skelta Law* (text XII). As their names suggest, these two texts are related. They both contain comparable material. *The Older Skelta Law* shows a long history of development over the centuries: this collection of jurisprudence is thought to have originated in the 11th century, but material was added until the 13th century.[134]

The text starts with regulating how the count, who visited the land once a year, should hold court, which as we saw earlier seems to be a preamble that was added to the text at a later stage. It then continues with a great amount of information on procedural law, one of the reasons for the fame of this text in scholarship. The text is long: the version in *Freeska Landriucht* comprises 83 paragraphs. Earlier I explained the function of the *skelta*, who appears so often in the text that it was named after him. Apart from procedural law, it contains information concerning a.o. which weapons a free Frisian should own and use in defence of the land. A lot of attention is also given to the various types of ordeals. The procedure for the ordeal by combat is described in detail.

The title given to this text has changed somewhat over the last decades. Karl von Richthofen (1811–1888), who might be called the founding father of Old Frisian studies, used the title 'Das Schulzenrecht' in his 1840 edition of Old Frisian law texts.[135] He in turn refers to the introduction of Matthias von Wicht's

---

133 Gerbenzon, 'Bijdrage tot het bronnenonderzoek', 18. This is also suggested by Jan Hallebeek (personal communication).

134 See: Steller, *Das altwestfriesische Schulzenrecht*; Fairbanks, *The Old West Frisian Skeltana Riucht*; Algra, 'De datearring fan it Skeltarjocht'.

135 Von Richthofen, *Friesische Rechtsquellen*, 387–400.

(1694–1778) edition of the *East Frisian Land Law*. Von Wicht was the first to give the title 'Schulzenrecht' (*Skelta Law*) to the text, referring to a Latin gloss to *Freeska Landriucht*, which provides a confirmation that the title *Skelta Law* was also used in medieval Frisia.[136] This is gloss 182, which I discussed earlier. The short Old Frisian sentence that can be found in this gloss begins with a reference to the *Older Skelta Law*, as it reads: *in da scheltena riucht* 'in the *Skelta Law*'.

Interestingly, the copy FG of *Freeska Landriucht* that was chosen as the basis for this edition yields another name for the text that seems to have been overlooked until now. At the bottom of p. 84, a marginal gloss can be found to a paragraph in *The Eight Provisions* (text IX) made by the late medieval possessor of this copy, Hemma Oddazin. It connects a paragraph in this text with one in the *Older Skelta Law*. The gloss reads: *Vide autem int grewe riucht de eodem* 'However see about this also in "the Count's Law"'. This also is a logical way to refer to the *Older Skelta Law*, since it indeed starts with describing the authority and jurisdiction of the count when he arrives in Frisia to hold court.

Some redactions of the *Older Skelta Law*, such as the one in Jus and the Middle Dutch translation *Landrecht der Vriesne*, start with '(this is) land law of the Frisians'. Especially after de Middle Dutch translation had been edited in 1996, it was thought by scholars that this must have been the title after all.[137] However, since the whole compilation is also called *Freeska Landriucht* 'Frisian land law', Nico Algra opted for the title *Landrecht van Westergo* ('Land Law of Westergoa'). Eventually, Old Frisian scholars went back to using the traditional name, since this caused the least confusion and had been the custom for so long.

8.4 *Text IV. Of the Two Kings Charles and Radbod*

This is the first of a number of mythological texts in this collection, which at first glance seems like a foreign body in a collection of legal texts.[138] It tells the story of how 'king Radbod' and 'king Charles' both came to Frisia and claimed dominion over the land. The battle which followed was fought out in the form of what is known as the ordeal by cross, performed by both kings. This ordeal consists of each party standing on either side of a cross and stretching out their hands horizontally; whoever lowers his arms first loses. The story tells how the kings 'stood still' for 24 hours, after which king Charles won the duel through

136 Von Wicht, *Das Ostfriesische Land-Recht*, Vorbericht, 97.

137 Breuker (ed.), *Landrecht der Vriesne*.

138 Buma and Ebel, *Westerlauwerssches Recht I*, 126–131 (J IV); An edition of all three redactions can be found in: Steller, *Abriß der altfriesischen Grammatik*, 121–125.

a ruse. He dropped his glove, which Radbod then graciously picked up from the ground and returned to Charles. Upon this, Charles exclaimed: "Now you have become my vassal!". The story ends with Radbod retreating from Frisia and returning to Denmark.

In the second episode of the story, Charles ordered the Frisians to choose a law for themselves. In order to accomplish this, he called twelve delegates of the Frisians before him. Several times, they asked for a delay and in the end they were still unable to choose law. Enraged, Charles condemned them to be put in a ramshackle boat which would withstand only a small amount of strong weather. Once at sea, they prayed to God. Suddenly, a thirteenth man appeared who steered the ship to shore and taught them law there. This, in other words, is a story about the divine origin of Frisian law.

King Radbod was the greatest Frisian king from the early Middle Ages, who died 719.[139] In this text he is presented as a Danish king. King Charles must refer to Charlemagne (747–814), who according to the ideology granted the Frisians their freedom, as is also narrated in the next text, *The Statutes of Magnus*. Historically then, this clash of kings is problematic since they were never contemporaries. One might be inclined to think that in that case Charlemagnes grandfather Charles Martel (688–741) might be meant by 'king Charles', but this is highly unlikely, for the outcome of the text is that 'king Charles' gives the Frisians their freedom. Hence Charlemagne must certainly be meant.

Obviously then this text does not date from the early Middle Ages, but correctly dating it is difficult. It is probably safest to say it dates from the flowering period of Old Frisian law, the 13th century. The seal of the West Frisian city of Medemblik from 1294 shows a boat with 13 persons on board. It is generally thought that this image refers to the story of the thirteenh man and the divine origin of Frisian law.[140]

Some elements, such as the ordeal by cross and the dropping of the glove hint at a familiarity with the *chansons de geste* and chivalric romances. At the same time, a link has been suggested to a few 14th-century monasteries in the first episode of the story,[141] whereas the second episode has been interpreted as reflecting a Germanic myth of the origin of law.[142] In conclusion then this story still presents us with a number of unsolved puzzles. The main reason for its inclusion in this compilation must have been to show the divine origin of Frisian law.

---

139 Nijdam and Knottnerus, 'Redbad, the Once and Future King'.

140 Bremmer, *Hir is eskriven*, 125–126.

141 Noomen, 'Hachens en Wachens'.

142 Birkhan, 'Eine altfriesische Tradition'.

8.5 *Text V. The Statutes of Magnus*

This text first relates how the Frisians won their freedom from Charlemagne by conquering the city of Rome for him. The second part however, the actual seven statutes, can be seen as a legal text. These statutes for the most part echo the older *Seventeen Statutes* (text VI).

The story in this text, also called the *Saga of Magnus* tells how pope Leo was taken prisoner by the Romans and blinded. Charlemagne, who is said to be Leo's brother in this story proclaimed a call to arms across the nations who fell under his control. The Frisians, led by Magnus, travelled to Rome to come to Charlemagne's aid. They are portrayed as naked and slaves to the Vikings, in other words, the lowest of the lowest. They were sent ahead to do the dirty work, but miraculously succeeded in taking Rome. Once inside, they would only let Charlemagne enter the city if he promised them freedom. This left Charlemagne with no other option than proclaiming the Frisians to be a free people. They then received a charter signed and sealed by both Charlemagne and Leo as proof. Back home, they stored the precious charter in the church of Almenum (now part of the town of Harlingen).

Magnus is not a typical Frisian name. Presumably, a few traditions have come together here. Firstly, the name can refer to Saint Magnus of Trani who lived in the third century. His relics ended up in the church of the Frisians in Rome, which dated to the 8th century and in later times was devoted to both Saint Michael and Saint Magnus. Magnus could also be interpreted as a reference to Carolus Magnus—Charlemagne. In 846 the Frisians, Franks and Saxons assisted emperor Lothar in fighting of an attack of the Saracens on Rome. This might be the kernel of historical truth behind this story.[143]

The fictional story of Magnus is thought to date to the 12th century. It was then retold until the end of the Middle Ages. The seal of the land Westergoa, dating 1270 shows Magnus standing upright, holding the Frisian banner he planted on the highest tower in Rome. According to the story, this banner was brought home and later revered as one of the holy Frisian regalia. The seal bears the inscription *Sanctus Magnus Dux Frisonum*.

8.6 *Text VI. The Seventeen Statutes*

This text represents the absolute core of classical Old Frisian law. Together with its standard companion *The Twenty-Four Land Laws* it can be found in all Old Frisian law manuscripts, both from Central and East Frisia, as well as in numerous Low German translations. This in itself is proof of regular contacts between

143 Salomon, *Friesische Geschichtsbilder*, 78–121.

the Frisian lands and the notion of a shared Frisian identity. *The Seventeen Statutes* are slightly older than *The Twenty-Four Land Laws* and date from the 11th century.

The title does not really convey what this text contains: the 'Frisian Declaration of Independence' or 'Frisian Magna Charta' would have been more apt. The text enumerates the privileges the Frisians enjoy in relation to the Holy Roman Emperor. They are free to be left undisturbed on their own estate, have to pay only a small amount of taxes to the emperor and to the church, do not have to go on a military expedition for too long and too far, etc.

Because of their prominence in Old Frisian law, *The Seventeen Statutes* and *The Twenty-Four Land Laws* are the most studied texts.[144] Yet not all puzzles are solved. There is for instance the peculiar fact that it has been observed that linguistically the text originated in East Frisia, whereas the content points to Central Frisia.[145]

Another enigma is the age of the text. Nico Algra came to the conclusion that in the course of time the text grew out of a core of the first ten paragraphs. He assumed that this core was based on a capitulary Louis the Pious issued in 814, in which he gave the Frisians and the Saxons back their ancestral lands. These lands had been confiscated by Charlemagne to punish them for their rebellion around 785.[146]

8.7 *Text VII. Prologue to the Seventeen Statutes and Twenty-Four Land Laws*

This prologue provides historical and divine legitimacy for Old Frisian law. It traces back the history of law to Moses and the Jewish people. Since Moses received the stone tablets from God, law has a divine origin. The text then traces the law from the Roman emperors to the German emperors. Since the last emperor mentioned is Emperor Frederick II (1220–1250), it is assumed that the prologue was written in the first half of the thirteenth century. This historical legitimation of Old Frisian law is also addressed in text II *What Is Law?* Both texts thus show intertextuality. This material can also be found in *The Book of Emperor Rudolf* (text XVI).

---

144 See a.o.: Algra, *Zeventien Keuren en Vierentwintig landrechten*; Algra, 'The Relation between Frisia and the Empire'; Hallebeek, 'The Gloss to the *Saunteen Kesta*'; Henstra, 'De eerste optekening'; Schmidt, 'Friesische Freiheitsüberlieferungen'; Hoekstra, *Die gemeinfriesischen Siebzehn Küren*; Vries, *Asega is het Dingtijd?*, 51–53.

145 Munske, *Der Germanische Rechtswortschatz*, 202–205; Algra, 'The Relation between Frisia and the Empire'.

146 Algra, 'The Relation between Frisia and the Empire', 7–14.

Brian Murdoch not only shows that these kinds of prologues to law texts are a near universal phenomenon, already starting with the laws of the Mesopotamian king Hammurabi (c. 1810–c. 1750 BC), but also analyses the medieval European background of this text tradition.[147] In that sense, this short prologue is a small window to the way in which medieval Frisia took part in the learned tradition of medieval Europe.

8.8 *Text VIII. The Twenty-Four Land Laws*

This text is the standard companion of *The Seventeen Statutes* (text VI). It is thought to be slightly younger, which would mean that it dates from the late 11th or 12th century. It continued to evolve until the 13th, perhaps even the 14th century.[148] *The Twenty-Four Land Laws* can be characterised as a collection of jurisprudence from Frisian courts. Hence, its focus is far more on internal legal affairs than *The Seventeen Statutes*.

Just as the number seventeen bore a special symbolic meaning, so did twenty-four.[149] Therefore it is interesting to see that the number of twenty-four provisions was contained at all costs. In the East Frisian tradition it can be observed that in some older redactions the number of twenty-four paragraphs was exceeded, so that one version even has 26 paragraphs.[150] Also, there is variation between the various redactions, more so than in *The Seventeen Statutes*.

The final result is a collection of jurisprudence plus some reiterations of *The Seventeen Statutes*. The text was clearly intended for internal use: there is no mention of any king or count, and the matters that are addressed concern sale of land, matrimonial assets, inheritances, protection of widows and orphans, rape, and arson by night, to name but a few.

8.9 *Text IX. The Eight Provisions*

The Old Frisian title of this text, *Da Acht Doemen*, literally translates as 'The Eight Dooms'. Old Frisian *dōm*, just as all occurrences in the other Old Germanic languages of the same etymon, means 'judgment, verdict, decree'. The original meaning in Proto-Germanic seems to have been 'to have an opinion', as is still reflected in the English verb 'to deem'.[151] I decided on a more neutral translation for the title of this text, and thus arrived at 'provisions'.

147 Murdoch, 'Authority and Authenticity'.

148 Algra, *Zeventien Keuren en Vierentwintig Landrechten*, 349–371.

149 Bremmer, 'More than Language', 107–108.

150 Algra, *Zeventien Keuren en Vierentwintig Landrechten*, 349–350.

151 Green, *Language and History*, 44–49.

It is almost impossible to discern a common thread throughout the paragraphs in this text. They deal with matters such as at which age a girl is allowed to marry (§1), the payment a son has to give his mother for having kept him safe from harm when he marries (§2), rent (§3), and inheritances (§§4–8).[152] As far as the content is concerned, there are some links to *The Older Skelta Law*. Partly because of this, this apparently archaic text is usually dated to the 12th century.

8.10 *Text X. Exceptions to the Seventeenth Statute*

This short text describes six cases in which a free Frisian is not allowed to swear innocent or deny the accusations brought against him. It concerns acts or circumstances in which the defendant has either made public statements or commitments himself, or has been caught red-handed, such as the second exception, where a moneyer is apprehended with counterfeit coins.

The text is directly linked to *The Seventeen Statutes* (text VI), because these cases are exceptions to the 17th statute in that text, which states that a free Frisian is always allowed to swear innocent in court. Since these two texts are related and also describe the same archaic phase of law, this text too is thought to have originated in the 11th century.[153]

8.11 *Text XI. The Synodical Law of Central Frisia*

The infrastructure of parishes and churches that was established in the Frisian lands in the second half of the 10th century also brought the synod to these regions. With this, Central Frisia was divided into three deaneries (Eastergoa, Westergoa and Sudergoa). The synod court session was a by-product of the bishop's synod, the original goal of which was a visitation to monitor the progress of Christianization, whether the lay people were behaving virtuously as well as the well-being of the clerics and the churches. The bishop of Utrecht visited Frisia once every four years and then presided over the synodical court. For the remaining three years, the bishop transferred his *ban* (his authority) to the rural deans.

During the synodical court sessions, matters were discussed and tried that concerned the church. First, everything related to the church, religion and clerics (such as the position of clerics and acts of violence against them, the observance of Sundays and holidays, sacrilege and violating the immunity of the church building, altar robbery and corpse robbery, but also superstition

152 Vries, *Asega, is het dingtijd?*, 65.

153 Algra, *Zeventien Keuren en Vierentwintig Landrechten*, 273–278.

and sorcery). Second, matters related to marriage and morality (such as abortion, prostitution, adultery, paternity of a child, marriage). Lastly, matters that touched on secular law, such as perjury and oath breaking.

This text bears testimony of the antiquity of the synod in Frisia. The oldest core of the text was traditionally dated to the 11th century.[154] This has recently been confirmed by Jan Hallebeek. Because the text testifies of the undivided jurisdiction of the diocesan bishop and the fact that no mention is yet made of the Utrecht archdeacons who came into function around the year 1000, he dates the oldest phase of this text to the period before 1050.[155] Note that again, just as was the case with the dating of *The Seventeen Statutes*, the dating is pinpointed to the first half of the 11th century. Finally, Mari van Buijtenen was the first to observe that this text was inspired by the *Libri duo de synodalibus causis et disciplinis ecclesiasticis* by Regino of Prüm (840–915), dating from the beginning of the 10th century.[156]

The Old Frisian text that has reached us is however a version that grew considerably in time. A recent philological analysis shows that at least three sections can be discerned.[157] Only the *Freeska Landriucht* version includes the first of these three sections, which is partly written in Frisian, but for the most part in Latin. This section is missing in all other redactions. Van Buijtenen suspected that this is a younger part because mention is made of *postsynodalia* (a session that was held after the official meeting ended, to settle and conclude certain matters) and of a tax called *cathedraticum*, which is supposed not to have existed in the bishopric of Utrecht before 1300.[158] The Latin installation form and oath form for a new parish-priest, which are only printed in *Freeska Landriucht* at the very end of the text also seem to be part of this text layer.

Structure of the text	
Section I	paragraphs 1–17
Section II	paragraphs 18–38
Section III	paragraphs 39–63

154 Van Buijtenen, *De grondslag van de Friese Vrijheid*.
155 Hallebeek, *Layci erant coiudices*, 8–9.
156 Van Buijtenen, *De grondslag van de Friese Vrijheid*, 154, 168–182.
157 Nijdam, 'Het Westerlauwers Seendrecht'.
158 Van Buijtenen, *De grondslag van de Friese Vrijheid*, 153.

The transition between section II and III is marked by a paragraph that resembles a prologue, which tells how Pope Leo gave the Frisians the synodical law. This puts us in familiar ideological territory, for this is a reference to *The Statutes of Magnus* (text V).

At the beginning of section III of the text in the versions in Jus and Unia, a block of paragraphs that could already be found at the beginning of section II is repeated: it is as if the text starts again.[159] A few other paragraphs are repeated as well in these two sections: on grave robbery (§§25 and 46), abortion (§§24 and 60), adultery (§§31 and 61), and proof of marriage (§§36 and 62). Sections II and III thus must be seen as parallel versions of the text, which at a later stage were merged together.

Finally, the relationship with the *Older Skelta Law* deserves some attention. Both texts originated in the 11th century, and both continued to grow and evolve until the 13th century. One text dealt with secular matters, the other with ecclesiastical matters. Just as these two domains touched every now and then, so do these two texts.

The most striking parallel is the fact that only in these two texts the same provision can be found about the state the four roads leading to a church must be in, and how things must be arranged if the church borders on water or on a main road. Although these two provisions are not literally the same, the wording is such that they seem to go back to a common original text.[160] Lastly, only in these two texts do we find a large amount of paragraphs on ordeals. The ordeals quickly disappeared, certainly in an ecclesiastical context, after the Fourth Council of the Lateran of 1215: another clear sign that the evolution of these texts came to a halt in the 13th century.

8.12 *Text XII. The Younger Skelta Law*

This is the last text of the old core of archaic law texts from Central Frisia, that started with *What Is Law?* (text II) and the pendant of this *Younger Skelta Law* namely *The Older Skelta Law* (text III). These two *Skelta Laws* are strongly linked. They probably once formed one big collection of jurisprudence and formulas, that was split up in the course of time.

One of the signs that the two texts are strongly linked is that the first two paragraphs of the text in the *Freeska Landriucht* and Unia redactions form the last paragraphs of the *Older Skelta Law* in the Jus redaction.[161] Interestingly,

159 J IX,25–28 / U 26–30.

160 *Old Skelta Law*: text III,14; *Synodical Law*: text XII,43.

161 Algra, 'Een datering van het "jong" Schoutenrecht', 90.

these two paragraphs are used in the prologue in *Freeska Landriucht* to describe the entire text: 'The ninth part contains the compensations for homicide'.[162]

This intertextuality does however not mean that they are not two distinguishable texts. Nico Algra shows that ordeals are no longer mentioned in *The Younger Skelta Law*, while they are very prominent in *The Older Skelta Law*. On the other hand, *The Younger Skelta Law* describes in detail how dikes and sluices should be maintained. Algra connects this with the regular flooding which took place in the years 1248 and 1249.[163] In all, Algra suspects this text came into existence around 1160 and grew until c. 1270.[164]

Just as *The Older Skelta Law*, this text provides an enormous amount of procedural law. It is famous for containing a large number of formulas which should be spoken by claimant or defendant at certain stages during the procedure.

8.13 *Text XIII. The Statutes of the Five Districts*

This is the most understudied text in the compilation. It is dated to the late 13th or early 14th century. The five districts (OFris. *dēl* 'part, district') referred to in the title are situated in the north of Westergoa in Central Frisia (Barradeel, Menaldumadeel, Franekeradeel, Baarderadeel, Hennaarderadeel). Franeker was one of the very old administrative centres in Central Frisia.

Apart from *Freeska Landriucht*, the statutes can be found in the manuscripts Jus and Unia. The version in Jus carries an enigmatic title: 'The Old Statutes of Opstalsbam'. This would then imply a relation to the actual *Statutes of Opstalsbam* (text XX below), dated 1323. Almost no one has tried to find an explanation for this, thinking it must have been a mistake. Nico Algra, however, points to parallels between these statutes and the *Statutes of Opstalsbam* and suggests this text might have been drawn up by the same type of organisation as the actual *Statutes of Opstalsbam*.[165]

It is clear that more study is needed. What can be observed for now is that the text varies considerably from one version to the next. The size varies between 35 and 41 paragraphs (the *Freeska Landriucht* redaction consists of 38 paragraphs). On top of that, the various versions have quite a number of unique paragraphs, not shared by the other versions.[166]

---

162 See text II.
163 Algra, 'Een datering van het "jong" Schoutenrecht', 64.
164 Algra, 'Een datering van het "jong" Schoutenrecht', 78.
165 Algra, 'Rechtshistorische aspecten', 160.
166 Nijdam, 'Old West Frisian *bī thā sida*', 20–21.

MAP 5 Districts in 13th century Central Frisia
VERSLOOT-KARTOGRAFY

8.14 *Text XIV. The Calculated Tariffs*

As stated earlier, the compensation tariffs form the oldest layer of Old Frisian law, going back to the early Middle Ages. In East Frisia, one single tariff, the *General East Frisian Compensation Tariff*, was in use, probably dating back to the 11th century (as a written text), until it was gradually replaced in the course of the 13th and 14th centuries by regional tariffs.

In Central Frisia, all surviving manuscripts stem from the 15th century or are direct copies from 15th-century exemplars. They contain a large number of regional compensation tariffs. Most of these tariffs are rather concise: c. 130 provisions on average. It has become clear that these younger tariffs can be traced back to tariff groups (A to D), which can be ascribed to the 13th century districts of which Central Frisia then consisted (Map 5).

Group A: (Northern) Eastergoa
Group B: Wymbritseradeel (Westergoa)
Group C: Franekeradeel (Westergoa)
Group D: Wonseradeel (Westergoa)

Only the texts in Group C, represented by two redactions—one in Jus, one in *Freeska Landriucht*—grew in size. And it seems that the text present in *Freeska Landriucht*, entitled *The Calculated Tariffs*, developed into a general Central Frisian tariff, reaching a size of 262 paragraphs (i.e. twice that of the tariffs in the other groups). The fact that this tariff is the only one present in *Freeska Landriucht* supports this assumption.

8.15 *Text XV. Conversion Directive for Wergilds*

It is quite understandable that a text like this one follows the previous compensation tariff, for here the *wergilds* in the various districts in Central Frisia are listed and conversions are provided. At the same time, this is not a common text in the Old Frisian compilations. It only also appears in Jus.[167] For a long time, this text had not been studied. That changed with the studies Dirk Jan Henstra made of the money systems in medieval Frisia, on which he published several works. Henstra dates the text to (the beginning of) the 15th century.[168]

Even though much has now become more clear concerning this text, some problems remain. Henstra found a few inconsistencies in the conversions which are hard to explain. In his first analysis of this text, he suggested that the term *grata* 'groat' might refer to a groat which Emperor Sigismund (1368–1437) allowed the Frisians to mint in Leeuwarden, but which seems to have never been struck in reality. If this is true, then this text is directly connected to the negotiations of the Frisians with the Emperor in order to have their ancient freedom formally acknowledged by him. Text XXI below almost certainly was written shortly before 1417 as part of the lobby to obtain the charter from Sigismund.

In his second analysis of this text, Henstra was more hesitant to link the inconsistencies to the Sigismund groat. Instead, he considered the possibility that during ca. 1275 and 1375 the compensations of the tariffs were doubled as a result of the so-called Truce of God or *Treuga Dei* movement of the 12th century, which tried to curb violence and feuding.[169] The inconsistencies in the conversion text might then be an attempt to solve this problem and convert

167 Buma and Ebel, *Westerlauwerssches Recht I*, 424–429.
168 Henstra, *The Evolution of the Money Standard*, 337–349. Henstra, *Fon Jelde*, 253–274.
169 Henstra, *Fon Jelde*, 270.

the compensations to the then current situation, which meant dividing the old compensations by two.

Finally, this text forms the end of an entire section, for at the end this sentence is inserted: 'Here ends the land law of the Frisians and after this begins the book of Emperor Rudolf.' Apparently, these first fifteen texts were seen as *Freeska Landriucht per se* as mentioned earlier.

8.16 *Text XVI. The Book of Emperor Rudolf*

This is a long and enigmatic text. It is a mixture of historical fiction and law. Moreover, it is partly written in rhyme. As observed earlier, as far as its historical fiction is concerned, it is related to the texts *What Is Law?* (text II) and the *Prologue to the Seventeen Statutes and Twenty-Four Land Laws* (text VII).

The structure of the text is roughly as follows. It tells how the Frisians had a meeting with Emperor Rudolf, who had summoned them before him at a place called *Bordeus*. After an introduction (§§1–3), Rudolf addresses the Frisians directly and gives them four 'exceptions' (§§4–8), six 'key provisions' (§§9–21), then he gives an historical overview of the origin of law (§§22–23), four things 'because of which I commanded you to come' (§24), five peace orders (§25), after which the main text comes to a conclusion and the Frisians are said to return home (§§26–27). But although this seems to mark the end of the text, it still continues with a number of regulations (§§28–30).

On the whole, many of the provisions that are given in this text are not new, but can be found in the various previous law texts in this compilation. So what was the purpose of this text and at what moment in time was it drawn up?

In this respect, one of the main questions is of course who is Emperor Rudolf? One candidate is Rudolf of Swabia, also known as Rudolf of Rheinfelden (1025–1080). He was an important figure in the 11th century, as he revolted against his brother-in-law, Emperor Henry IV (1050–1106), and was elected as anti-king in 1077 at the onset of the Investiture Controversy, which had begun as a conflict between Henry IV and Pope Gregory VII (1015–1085) an ended in 1122. This would fit one solution for the date given in the text, which would yield 24 June 1080.

This solution also fits the mentioning of Alemania 'Germany'. This would then mean that the place were Rudolf and the Frisians meet, Bordeus, is not to be interpreted as Bordeaux in France, but as Bardowick in Saxony (between Hamburg and Lüneburg), which used to be called *Bordeus vicus*. If *Bordeus* indeed refers to Bardowick, then it must also be assumed that, for whatever reason, the element *vicus* was dropped in the Old Frisian text.[170]

170 Bos-van der Heide, *Het Rudolfsboek*, 17–19.

The other candidate is king Rudolf I of Germany (1218–1291). The whole text does indeed point to a later date: it has all the characteristics of a younger text. Also, the text contains an attestation of the concept of 'the Frisian Freedom' (text XVI,1), which is another argument for a later date.[171]

As for the date, the text is dated to the 13th century. This is then almost two centuries after the meeting of Rudolf of Swabia with the Frisians would have taken place, if this ever happened at all. It has even been suggested that both Rudolf and Bordeus are perhaps better viewed as fictional names, created in order to deliver the message that was intended by the text.[172] Even though this argument seems to fit the character of the text, it must be said that the Frisians have sought to have their freedom and privileged status confirmed by the Holy Roman Emperor throughout their history (see earlier and see below, text XXI).

8.17 *Text XVII. Market Law*

This text regulates the competence of the *skelta* concerning a market with respect to the normal situation of the land law. A market was an event that usually took place once a year and often during special holidays. For that reason it is specifically mentioned that these holidays should not be an impediment for the *skelta* to hold court. The text is dated to the 13th century[173]

8.18 *Text XVIII. Unmendable Crimes*

This text enumerates five crimes for which only the Pope can grant absolution; so-called *casus papales*. In Old Frisian the term *swarta swengen* is used, which is odd: the term literally means 'black pourings' and occurs in the compensation tariffs (see text XIV). It concerned an insulting act, in which the perpetrator poured unclean liquid (urine, but also beer) over the victim with the aim of insulting him. The text must have originated in a clerical environment and is thought to date from the 14th century. The text is always accompanied by the following text.

8.19 *Text XIX. On Forceful Robberies*

In every Old Frisian manuscript in which this text occurs, it is accompanied by the previous text. It is then also dated to the 14th century. The three extant versions (Unia, Jus[174] and *Freeska Landriucht*) all have the first seven paragraphs in common. The first three paragraphs deal with instances of robbery.

171 Vries, 'Frisonica libertas', 7.

172 Bremmer, 'More than Language', 123–124.

173 Van Buijtenen, *Frieslands middeleeuwse marktrechten*.

174 Buma and Ebel, *Westerlauwerssches Recht I*, 246–250.

The last four however describe instances where a person should enjoy peace, for instance when he visits the secular and synodical courts. Jus and *Freeska Landriucht* then each have a separate eighth paragraph. These thus must have been added later.[175]

8.20 *Text XX. The Statutes of Opstalsbam*

The Opstalsbam was a court assembly located near Aurich in East Frisia. The first attestations of a League of the Opstalsbam stem from the early 13th century (c. 1220). The league was an alliance of all Frisian lands. Representatives from the various Frisian regions convened once a year at the Opstalsbam to hold an assembly where international legal and political matters were discussed. Also, its members would assist each other if they were threatened by foreign attacks. In what era this League first originated is unknown.[176]

Because of its location, it is thought that the League of the Opstalsbam was created in East Frisia, and that Central Frisia joined later. *The Statutes of Opstalsbam*, however, were drawn up in Central Frisia on 18 September 1323. This was a time when the Frisians from this region were more and more threatened by the claims the Count of Holland made to this part of Frisia. The text then is interpreted as an attempt to revive the old League of the Opstalsbam which had slowly gone into hibernation.

The Statutes of Opstalsbam is generally acknowledged as the first Old Frisian law text in which a demonstrable influence of Canon law can be observed.[177] Furthermore, there is talk of Frisian sealands: an ideological way to refer to the Frisian lands. In one of the myths of origin of the Frisians, the Frisian lands were founded by one of three brothers, Friso, Saxo and Bruno, who travelled from India to these regions. Friso begot seven sons to each of whom he gave one of the seven Frisian sealands.

A few other peculiarities of the text are first that there are two Old Frisian versions, a short one consisting of 24 paragraphs (this version can be found in *Freeska Landriucht*) and long one consisting of 36 paragraphs, as well as a Latin version, also consisting of 24 paragraphs. According to Henk Meijering the Latin version was the original text. The Frisian short versions were translations of this original Latin version. The longer versions, both the Latin and the Frisian are seen as secondary developments.

Finally, a striking detail of the text is that paragraphs 22 and 23 are left blank in the version encountered in *Freeska Landriucht* (i.e. the short Frisian version).

---

175 Meijering and Nijdam, *Wat is recht?*, 402.
176 Meijering, *De Willekeuren van de Opstalsboom*, 288–297.
177 Meijering, *De Willekeuren van de Opstalsboom*, 279–280.

Paragraph 22 was designed to determine which mendicant order was allowed to ask for alms in the various lands.[178] Paragraph 23 deals with currency: the long version describes which currency was allowed in the Frisian lands and gives the conversion tables for the various coins.[179] It is thought that the short versions have retained the original reading of the text. According to this view, each land would fill in these paragraphs according to their specific situation.

8.21 *Text XXI. A Treatise on the Seven Sealands*

The final text of the compilation is a short description of the free Frisian lands, symbolically designated as 'seven sealands'. The description starts in the west, with Westfriesland and ends at the Weser area in Germany. Surprisingly enough, it also mentions the regions to the south of the Frisian lands in the Netherlands, Drenthe and part of Overijssel, which traditionally were Saxon territories. Apparently, they were seen as potentially becoming part of the political union of the Free Frisian lands.

Because the text describes the political situation of the time, this redaction can be dated rather precisely around 1417. It is thought, however, that it made use of an already existing text on the topic. The hypothesis is that the treatise formed a part of the file of manuscripts that were used during the negotiations the Frisians had with Emperor Sigismund in 1416–1417, which eventually led to the famous privilege Sigismund granted the Frisians.[180] This sealed charter acknowledged and confirmed the ancient freedom of the Frisians.[181] The Frisians had first started petitioning for obtaining such a charter from the Roman Emperor in the 13th century.[182]

9 Principles Underlying the Edition and Translation

In order to make *Freeska Landriucht* as accessible as possible to a wider audience, I have chosen for a critical edition of the text. This means I have added punctuation and created complete sentences which start with capitals. I have also added text numbers and paragraph numbers. These make it possible to compare the texts with the other surviving text versions. Numerals have been

178 Meijering, *De Willekeuren van de Opstalsboom*, 57; 150–152.
179 Meijering, *De Willekeuren van de Opstalsboom*, 59; 152–162.
180 Vries, 'Frisonica libertas', 4.
181 Vries, *Asega, is het dingtijd?*, 71–72. Edition and Dutch plus Frisian translation of this text according to the *Freeska Landriucht* version: Vries, *Asega, is het dingtijd?*, 496–499.
182 Meijering, 'De zeven zeelanden'.

written as words if the Old Frisian text does so and given as Arabic numerals if the Old Frisian text renders them as Roman numerals. These Roman numerals have always been rendered in capitals in the edition. The page numbers of the original are given in the left margin.

The spelling of the Old Frisian is made as transparent as possible and has been as much as possible conformed to the standard spelling used in the most recent dictionary of Old Frisian, the *Altfriesisches Handwörterbuch*.[183] This mainly effected the spellings of ⟨i⟩ and ⟨j⟩ on the one hand and of ⟨u⟩, ⟨v⟩ and ⟨w⟩ on the other. A few examples: ⟨houe⟩ is rendered as *hove*, ⟨wrherich⟩ as *urherich* in the edition.

This choice also effected compounds, which were written together according to the *Altfriesisches Handwörterbuch*. Conversely, certain words that were written together in the source text were separated, for instance ⟨schilma⟩ became *schil ma* 'shall one'. But because we are dealing with a word pair that was highly frequent, we encounter a contracted form ⟨schima⟩ twice. These were left as they were. The same applies to a contracted form ⟨endma⟩ < *ende ma* 'and one'. Another contraction is ⟨schilmet⟩ which should be read as *schil ma hit* which I decided to render as *schil met*.

For this edition, the copy Fries Genootschap (FG) was chosen as the source text.[184] Only the printed text of this copy is rendered, not the marginal handwritten notes made by the medieval owner, Hemma Oddazin.[185] Since the nine surviving copies of *Freeska Landriucht* show some variation, as we described earlier, the following approach for the main text, i.e. the Old Frisian text, was chosen. If the text in FG is corrupt and one of the other copies has a correct reading, this correct form is given in the footnote to the emendation with a reference to the copy which has this correct reading.[186]

Acknowledgments

In the spring of 2014, Chris Lutgendorff made the preliminary edition and preliminary translation of three texts (IV, XIII and XXI) as part of a traineeship he did at the Fryske Akademy. Second, a big thank you to Jorieke Savelkouls, who checked the English of the translation on several occasions. Third, I would

---

183 Hofmann and Popkema, *Altfriesisches Handwörterbuch*.

184 Leeuwarden, Tresoar Fries Genootschap A III 31 / B 38831 kluis.

185 Henstra, *Fon Jelde*, 253–273, also see earlier.

186 For the principles underlying the transcription of the glosses and emendations of this transcription see below, 'Preface to the Edition and Translation of the Gloss'.

like to thank the Pastei research group (Wytze Fopma, Riemer Janssen, Anne Popkema and Herre de Vries) for their feedback on this introduction, which especially involved the history of *Freeska Landriucht* as a book project and the provenance of the extant copies. Finally, I would like to thank my co-editors Jan Hallebeek and Hylkje de Jong. Without their expertise in the field of legal history and especially on Canon and Roman law, this edition would never have come about.

Preface to the Edition and Translation of the Gloss

Jan Hallebeek and Hylkje de Jong

1 Introduction: Glosses

Various parts of the *Freeska Landriucht* (Frisian Land Law), edited in the incunable *Druk*,[1] are provided with glosses. Glosses are notes to certain words and phrases of another text, reflecting an explanation or commentary. Usually a gloss starts with quoting one or more words, derived from the main text, to which the gloss specifically relates. These words are called the *lemma* (plural *lemmata*). The glosses on a certain text in their entirety are indicated as 'the Gloss'. In case there is a kind of coherence between the single glosses, one also speaks about an apparatus of glosses. In the Middle Ages, many authoritative texts were provided with a Gloss: the Vulgate Bible, Law books as the *Corpus iuris civilis*, the *Ars commentata* of Galenus, etc. Not infrequently, these glosses came into being in a scholarly environment as a result of academic teaching and were elaborated by some generations of scholars before they settled as the Standard Gloss or *Glossa Ordinaria* to a certain text.

The glosses to *Freeska Landriucht* are written in Latin. For the most part they deal with learned law, i.e. not the indigenous law of Frisia, but law as it was taught in the law schools and universities, i.e. Canon law and Roman law. This law is also called the *ius commune*, since it became the foundation of the common legal culture of continental Europe until the time that law was codified in national Codes. The glosses show that its authors must have been familiar with medieval legal scholarship, its sources and its literature, even to such an extent that it is inconceivable they were not academically trained at some university.

2 Learned Law: Canon Law and Roman Law

Canon law was the law of the Catholic Church. In the twelfth century it developed into a discipline of its own, independent from theology. The teaching started in Bologna, but soon it spread to other places in Southern Europe. The main authoritative texts of Canon law were the following.

1 *Dat aelde freeska landriucht* [s.l.] [c. 1486–1487].

DOI:10.1163/9789004526419_003

1. The *Decretum Gratiani* (1135/1140)—a compilation of old papal letters, canons of Councils (both local and oecumenical) and quotations from Church Fathers, in three parts
2. The *Liber Extra* or Decretals of Gregory IX (1234)—a compilation of papal decretals in five books, subdivided into titles
3. Some later additions, such as the *Liber Sextus* of Boniface VIII (1298)

In later times these texts were termed *Corpus iuris canonici.*

The study of Roman law started at the beginning of the twelfth century, after some important Roman law texts from antiquity were rediscovered. Initially, the study of Roman law was a purely academic occupation, since Roman law was the law of an ancient society. Unlike Canon law, it lacked force of law. However, from the beginning it had some authority. Subsequently, the Church adopted it as an additional source of law, and it started to influence legal thinking. By so doing it could affect the interpretation of indigenous law, which eventually led—especially from the time judges in the European supreme courts were professionally educated—to a reception of Roman law, starting in the South of Europe and spreading gradually from there to the North. The main authoritative texts of Roman law were the following.

1. *Digestum Vetus*—the Digest of Justinian, books I–XXIV.2
2. *Infortiatum*—the Digest of Justinian, books XXIV.3-XXXVIII
3. *Digestum Novum*—the Digest of Justinian, books XXXIX–L
4. *Codex Justinianus*—the Justinian Code, books I–IX
5. *Volumen parvum*—*Authenticum*, *Tres Libri* (*Codex* books X–XII), *Libri Feudorum* and Institutes

The Digest of Justinian is a compilation of replies of jurists from the classical period of Roman law (0–300 AD), elaborated in postclassical times, selected, compiled and interpolated in the sixth century. The *Codex Justinianus* is a compilation of imperial constitutions, dating from the second to the sixth century AD. Three books (X–XII) are enshrined in the *Volumen parvum.* The *Authenticum* is a collection of constitutions which Justinian issued after the *Codex* was completed, the so-called Novels. The *Libri Feudorum* contain Lombard feudal law and the Institutes is a textbook of Roman law, promulgated by Justinian with force of law. In later times these texts were termed *Corpus iuris civilis.*

3 The Gloss to the Frisian Land Law

Despite the fact that the Frisian Land Law was not taught anywhere in an academic setting, these texts were provided with glosses, albeit that some parts

had little or even no glosses. This was not unusual for late medieval compilations of customary, indigenous law. The *Usatges* (Usages) of Barcelona (12th century) were provided with a Standard Gloss (1251/1257) and also the *Sachsenspiegel* (Mirror of the Saxons) had a Gloss, composed *inter alia* by Johann von Buch (c. 1285/90-after 1356) and Nikolaus Wurm († after 1401).[2] These Glosses referred copiously to the sources of Roman and Canon law.

The edition of the Gloss to the Frisian Land Law in *Druk* must have been preceded by a manuscript tradition. This explains why some glosses show mutual similarities, as if the one is a shortened version or an earlier draft of the other, or both go back to a common source. This is the case with the gloss *intellige de puero doli capace* (n. 171) to text XIV (*The Calculated Tariffs*) and the gloss *intellige de puero doli capace* (n. 126) to text VIII (*Twenty-Four Land Laws*). Moreover, some glosses can be traced back in manuscripts which are just slightly younger than the edition of *Druk*. Some glosses to text II (*What Is Law?*) and text III (*Older Skelta Law*) can also be found at the beginning of the *Codex Roorda*, dating from about 1500, which starts with *Haet is riucht?*, followed by a part of the *Older Skelta Law* before turning to the *Jurisprudentia Frisica*.[3] Moreover, two glosses to text XIV (*The Calculated Tariffs*), viz. the gloss *supradicta emenda fiunt* (n. 170) and the gloss *intellige de puero doli capace* (n. 171), mentioned above, can be found in the manuscript *Jus Municipale Frisonum*, a copy from around 1530 of several fifteenth century manuscripts. They were adopted there as additions to the *Injury Tariff of Wonseradeel and the Vijf Delen*.[4] Other glosses can be found in the manuscript *Codex Aysma*, also a collection of Frisian legal texts from around 1500.[5]

It should be noted here, that the copy of *Druk* used as source text for our edition, i.e. *Leeuwarden, Tresoar Fries Genootschap A III 31/B 38831 kluis* (FG), also contains some handwritten glosses. These were added by the jurist and Municipal Secretary of Leeuwarden Hemma Odda zin (c. 1455–1525), who was prob-

2 Kaufmann (ed.), *Glossen zum Sachsenspiegel-Landrecht* and Kaufmann (ed.), *Glossen zum Sachsenspiegel-Lehnrecht*. As early as the fourteenth century a Dutch version of the *Sachsenspiegel* was available, provided with a Gloss, based on the Gloss of Johann von Buch to the Land Law. This Gloss was only partly edited. See De Geer van Jutphaas (ed.), *De Saksenspiegel in Nederland*.

3 *Codex Roorda* (Leeuwarden, Tresoar, ms. Richthofen 6), pp. 1–7. The Gloss in the *Codex Roorda* to *Haet is riucht?* and the *Landrecht der Friezen* is for the major part more extensive than the one printed in *Druk*, to texts II and III.

4 *Jus Municipale Frisonum* (Leeuwarden, Tresoar, ms. Richthofen 5); they can be found in the edition of this manuscript, see Buma et al. (eds.), *Westerlauwersches Recht I*, 526 (n. 272) and 528 (n. 277). See about these glosses: Nijdam, *Lichaam, eer en recht*, 99.

5 The *Codex Aysma* (Oxford, Bodleian Library, MS Junius 78) was edited and translated into German. See Buma et al. (eds.), *Codex Aysma*.

ably the first owner of this copy of the incunable.[6] It is by no means excluded that these glosses also go back to a medieval manuscript tradition and were added by hand, since they were not incorporated in the edition (*Druk*).

After its first edition in *Druk*, the Gloss was re-edited in the seventeenth century by the Franeker professor Christianus Schotanus (1603–1671), together with the main text. He wrote out in full many of the abbreviated words and corrected some obvious spelling errors in the running text of the glosses.[7] Only some parts of the Gloss were re-edited in the twentieth century. The Gloss to text XI (*Synodical Law of Central Frisia*) was edited by J.G.C. Joosting (1866–1944), who for some time was archivist of the Province of Drenthe and later of the Province of Groningen.[8] The Gloss to text XVI (*Book of Emperor Rudolf*) was edited by the Groningen professor Pieter Gerbenzon (1920–2009).[9] The handwritten glosses in FG to text XI (*Synodical Law of Central Frisia*) were also edited by Joosting.[10]

In the present volume only the Gloss as printed in *Druk* is edited, not the handwritten glosses. Glosses in manuscripts are usually positioned between the lines of the main text (interlinear glosses) or in the margin of the main text (marginal glosses). In *Druk* the glosses are reproduced within the text area itself, i.e. integrated within the Frisian main text to which the glosses refer. This format is not uncommon; the same layout can be seen in late medieval manuscripts, for example of the *Usatges*[11] and in some early editions of the *Sachsenspiegel*.[12]

4 Allegations

The 188 Latin glosses contain i.a. references to provisions of Canon law and Roman law, so-called allegations. In sum there are 545 allegations, i.e. 340 allegations from the *Corpus iuris civilis* and 205 from the *Corpus iuris canonici*. *Alle-*

6 See Vries, 'Hemma Odda zin', 218 and 220.

7 Schotanus, *Beschryvinge van de Heerlyckheydt*, 36–98.

8 Joosting and Muller (eds.), *Bronnen voor de geschiedenis, Vol 5*, 354–367.

9 Gerbenzon, *Rudolfsboekmateriael*, 58–62.

10 Joosting, *Bronnen voor de geschiedenis, Vol 5*. For some of these glosses see also Hallebeek, *Layci erant coiudices*.

11 Some manuscripts of the *Usatges* of Barcelona display two *apparatus* of glosses in this way, while still leaving the margins blank, for example the manuscript Escorial lat. Z-1-3. See Iglesia Ferreirós, *Cataluña Medieval*. This pattern was also followed by the sixteenth century *Antiquiores*-edition of the *Usatges* (*Antiquiores Barchinonensium leges*).

12 Such as the *Sassenspegel mit velen nyen Addicien*.

gatio literally means that what is adduced, brought up. These allegations quote the sources of learned law in the way this was practiced in the Middle Ages and the Early Modern Period. The Digest, *Codex*, Institutes, Decretals and *Liber Sextus* are composed of books which are subdivided in titles. Specific provisions from these sources are quoted by an abbreviation for the source (ff. is Digest, C. is *Codex*, X is *Liber Extra*, etc.), followed by the initial words of the title and the initial words of the specific provision. Texts from the first part of the *Decretum Gratiani* are quoted by the number of the *distinctio*, followed by the initial words of the canon, texts from the second part by the number of the *causa*, followed by the number of the question and the initial words of the canon. In the edition by Schotanus, mentioned above, the allegations are still reproduced in this way.

Since the Friedberg edition of the *Corpus iuris canonici* (1879–1881) and the *editio stereotypa* of the *Corpus iuris civilis* (1872–1895) became the most commonly used editions, generally available in libraries all over the world, the old way of reference was replaced by an internationally standardised method of quotation. In the present edition we have identified all allegations by their usual present-day reference in brackets. The numbering corresponds with the editions just mentioned, also if it deviates from the old editions, e.g. the Vulgate edition of the Digest.[13] For some parts of the Frisian Land Law, the allegations had been identified previously. Joosting did so for text XI (*Synodical Law of Central Frisia*) and Gerbenzon for text XVI (*Book of Emperor Rudolf*).[14]

For the reader not so familiar with the sources of *ius commune* and the way of reference to specific provisions within these sources, the following overview of abbreviations and references may be helpful.

	Corpus iuris civilis
Dig.	the books of the Digest, adopted in the *Digestum Vetus*, *Infortiatum* and *Digestum Novum*; the numbers that follow indicate the book, the title and the specific provision (sometimes also the paragraph)
Cod.	the *Codex Justinianus*, adopted in the *Codex* (books 1–9) and the *Tres Libri* (books 10–12), part of the *Volumen*; the numbers that follow indicate the book, the title and the specific provision
Inst.	the Institutes, part of the *Volumen*; the numbers that follow indicate the book, the title and the paragraph

13 See *Traditio* 11 (1955) 438–439.

14 Not without flaws. The text from *De regulis iuris*, referred to in the gloss *de hoc vide* (n. 176), is *Dig.* 50.17.122 and not *Dig.* 50.17.106.

LF the *Libri Feudorum*, part of the *Volumen*; the numbers that follow indicate the book, the title and the paragraph

Auth. the *Authenticum*, part of the *Volumen*; the numbers that follow indicate the volume (*collatio*), title, and chapter (*caput*); in the *editio stereotypa* of the *Corpus iuris* not the *Authenticum*, but another compilation of Novels is adopted; the corresponding site in this edition is always given in parentheses (*Nov.* …)

post *Cod.* an *authentica*, adopted in the *Codex Justinianus*; after *Cod.* follows the site in the *Codex* the *authentica* is connected to; the *authenticae* are short summaries, derived from the *Authenticum*; their origin in the Novels (*editio stereotypa*) is given in parentheses (ex *Nov.* …)

Corpus iuris canonici

D.c. each letter followed by numbers, which indicate the *distinctio* and *capitulum* (or *canon*) in the first part of the *Decretum Gratiani*

C.q.c. each letter followed by numbers, which indicate the *causa*, *quaestio* and *capitulum* (or *canon*) in the second part of the *Decretum Gratiani*

De con. (*De consecratione*) D.c. each letter followed by numbers, which indicate the *distinctio* and *capitulum* (or *canon*) in the third part of the *Decretum Gratiani*

DG *Dictum Gratiani*, i.e. an introductory or connecting text by Gratian in the *Decretum* following or preceding a specific provision

X *Liber Extra*; the numbers that follow indicate the book, the title and the *capitulum*

VI *Liber Sextus*; the numbers that follow indicate the book, the title and the *capitulum*

The Gloss also contains references to fragments in the Frisian main text. The exact locations of these texts are reproduced in the footnotes. The Roman numerals refer to the various parts of the Frisian Land Law, the Arabic numerals to the specific fragment (paragraph) within that text.

5 References to Scholarly Literature

The Gloss also contains references to scholarly writings, such as the Standard Glosses to the *Corpora iuris* as well as to other works of learned jurists. We refer to these works in the footnotes and not in a separate *apparatus fontium*. When identifying these quotations or references, we consistently recorded the specific site in the work (Book, Title, Part, Chapter, Paragraph, etc.),

where the relevant fragment can be found, i.e. in the commonly available editions. We have refrained from referring to specific pages or folios in specific editions, since for the greater part these works had not yet appeared in print at the time the incunable was edited. Moreover, the page numbers will vary in the subsequent reprints.[15] We did not identify, for obvious reasons, the specific fragments of two authors, whose works referred to are not available in print or easily accessible through digitalised manuscripts, i.e. those of Vincentius Hispanus and Petrus de Sampsone. Moreover, we were unable to identify the unknown brother Otto, mentioned in the gloss *palmerum romerum* (n. 83) to text VI (*The Seventeen Statutes*). He may be the same scholar as the Otto mentioned in the *Codex Roorda* and the *Codex Aysma*. According to the Gloss of the Frisian Land Law, Otto would have enshrined circulating materials (of which some fragments are quoted) in his additions to X 5.39.[16] According to the *Codex Roorda* and the *Codex Aysma*,[17] Otto is the author of additions to a *Summa Confessorum*.[18] In 1292 it was decided that Frisian students in Bologna were assigned to the *natio Germanica*. In the Acta of the year 1297 a 'dominus Otto de Frisia' is mentioned who bequeathed three solidi.[19]

Standard Glosses (*Glossae Ordinariae*) and referred works of learned law are the following (the Roman numerals refer to the various texts of the Frisian Land Law, the Arabic numerals to the specific gloss or glosses within that text).

1. Azo, *Summa Codicis* | VI (85), VIII (140), IX (152, 154), XI (157)

Azo († c. 1230) belonged to the glossators of Roman law; he taught at the law school of Bologna. His *Summa Codicis* (1208–1210) remained influential throughout the Middle Ages, also after the Standard Gloss to the *Corpus iuris civilis* was compiled in the middle of the thirteenth century.

---

15 We do not deny the importance of distinguishing between the various editions of legal works in early modern times and the connection between these incunables (and early prints) and the preceding medieval manuscript tradition, but for our purpose we decided to limit ourselves to indicating the site of the quotations or reference in an available copy of the work.

16 The gloss *palmerum romerum* (n. 83) to text VI (*The Seventeen Statutes*).

17 Both manuscripts belong to the so-called *excerpta legum*-tradition, which started to develop from the beginning of the fifteenth century.

18 The gloss *Jtem een gued reedlick pli* to JF 30:26 in *Codex Roorda*, p. 140. For the *Codex Aysma* see the edition by Buma et al. (eds.), *Codex Aysma*, 388.

19 See Friedländer and Malagola (eds.), *Acta Nationis Germanicae*, 47.

2. Tancredus, *Ordo iudiciarius* | VIII (98)
Tancredus (c. 1185–c. 1236) taught Canon law at Bologna from 1210 onwards. His *Ordo iudiciarius* (1216) is a work on procedural law. It was widely spread during the Middle Ages.

3. Raymundus de Pennaforte, *Summa de poenitentia* | VIII (123)
Raymundus de Pennaforte (c. 1175–1275) was General of the Dominican Order. He compiled on request of Innocent IX the *Liber Extra*. His *Summa de poenitentia et matrimonio* (1234) is a manual for confessors.

4. The *Glossa Ordinaria* to the *Corpus iuris civilis* | II (14), III (31, 33, 38, 47, 52, 60bis), VIII (96, 124, 127), XII (170), XVI (183, 184)
The Standard Gloss to the *Corpus iuris civilis* was composed by Accursius (c. 1182–1260/63), who taught Roman law at Bologna. It was probably completed not long after 1235. The Standard Gloss replaced almost all previous scholarly literature.

5. Vincentius Hispanus, Apparatus to the *Liber Extra* | VIII (98)
Vincentius Hispanus (†1248) taught Canon law in Bologna. He was one of the first who wrote an *apparatus* to the *Liber Extra* (1234–1243). It is preserved in manuscripts and has never been printed.

6. The *Glossa Ordinaria* to the *Decretum Gratiani* | II (11), III (18)
The Ordinary Gloss to the *Decretum* was composed by Johannes Teutonicus (c. 1170–1245), who at the beginning of the thirteenth century taught Canon law at Bologna. Around 1240 it was revised and supplemented by Bartolomaeus de Brixiensis, a student of Tancredus, who in the middle of the thirteenth century also taught at Bologna.

7. Goffredus de Trano, *Summa in titulos decretalium* | II (6), VIII (98)
Goffredus de Trano (†1245) was a student of Azo. He taught Roman law in Naples and was from 1240 attached to the papal Curia. During that period he wrote his *Summa in titulos decretalium*, which is a textbook on the *Liber Extra*.

8. Innocentius IV, *Commentaria* | VI (82bis), VIII (98, 123, 135)
Sinibaldo de Fieschi (†1254) worked for the papal Curia until 1243 after which he was elected pope (Innocent IV). He completed his commentary on the Decretals, later edited as *Commentaria super libros quinque decretalium*, around 1245.

9. Guilelmus Redonensis, Gloss to the *Summa de poenitentia* of Raymundus de Pennaforte | III (32)
Guillaume de Rennes or Guilelmus Redonensis was a Dominican theologian from Brittany. Around 1250 he wrote his glosses to the manual for confessors of Raymundus.

10. Petrus de Sampsone, *Lectura* on the decretals | VI (82)
Petrus de Sampsone, a French canonist, taught canon law in Bologna. His *Lectura* on the *Liber Extra* dates from about 1250 and was never printed.

11. Hostiensis (Henricus de Segusio), *Summa aurea* and *Lectura* | VI (82), VIII (96, 140), IX (154bis)
Henricus de Segusio († 1271) was from 1262 bishop of Ostia (hence Hostiensis). His *Summa aurea*, a commentary on the decretals, dates from around 1253. He worked on the *Lectura*, a more extensive commentary, from his early years in Paris until the end of his life.

12. The *Glossa Ordinaria* to the *Liber Extra* | II (13), III (42), VI (68bis, 82), VIII (111, 124, 130, 147), IX (149), XVI (174, 177)
The Standard Gloss to the *Liber Extra* was compiled around 1263 by Bernardus Parmensis († 1266), a student of Tancredus and Vincentius Hispanus, who taught at Bologna.

13. Guillaume Durand, *Speculum iudiciale* | VIII (95, 96, 97, 100, 111, 126), IX (154), XI (156)
Guillaume Durand (c. 1239–1296) taught in Modena and worked for the papal Curia. His *Speculum iudiciale* (1271) was the most important and influential work on procedural law during the Middle Ages.

14. Johannes de Friburgo, *Summa confessorum* | III (32), VIII (123)
Johannes de Friburgo or Johannes von Freiburg († 1314) lectured theology in Freiburg. His *Summa confessorum* (before 1290) is a compilation and elaboration of the *Summa de poenitentia* of Raymundus de Pennaforte.

15. The *Glossa Ordinaria* to the *Liber Sextus* | XII (170)
The Standard Gloss to the *Liber Sextus* was compiled in 1301 by Johannes Andreae (c. 1270–1348), a student of Guido de Baysio (c. 1250–1313), who lectured on the Decretals in Bologna and Padua.

16. Archidiaconus (Guido de Baysio), *Lectura super* VI *decretalium* | VIII (147)
Guido de Baysio was Archdeacon of Bologna (hence Archidiaconus) and worked for the papal Curia. He compiled his apparatus on the *Liber Sextus* around 1306.

17. Cinus de Pistoia, *Commentaria in Codicem* | III (33)
Cinus de Pistoia (Guittoncino dei Sinibaldi, 1270–1336/37) taught Roman law at several Italian universities. He wrote his commentary on the *Codex Justinianus* around 1313.

18. Johannes Andreae, *Novella Commentaria* | VIII (111, 123)
Johannes Andreae (c. 1270–1348) from 1300 onwards lectured on the Decretals in Bologna. His *Novella Commentaria* were composed and elaborated over a long period of time (1311–1338). The title is said to refer to his youngest daughter Novella who would have replaced her father as lecturer (from behind a screen), when he was ill.

19. Henricus Boich, *Commentaria* | VI (82), VIII (135)
Henricus Bohich or Boich (1310-after 1370) lectured on the Decretals at the University of Paris and practiced law. His Commentary to the Decretals was finalized in 1349.

20. Panormitanus (Nicolaus de Tudeschis), *Commentaria* | II (8bis)
Nicolaus de Tudeschis (1386–1445) taught Canon law in Bologna and in 1435 became archbishop of Palermo (hence Panormitanus). He wrote his extensive and authoritative commentary to the Decretals over a long period (1411–1433).

6 Relation of the Gloss to the Main Text of the Frisian Land Law

In which way the Gloss relates to the main text of the various parts of the Frisian Land Law should be revealed by analysing and comparing the content of both. Their mutual coherence may clarify what purpose the author(s) of the Gloss may have had in mind. Until now only the Gloss to the Text VI (*Seventeen Statutes*) was cautiously investigated in search of an answer.[20] Although the findings may not be generalized, we can establish, also on the basis of the

20 Hallebeek, 'The Gloss to the *Saunteen Kesta*'.

process of transcribing, editing and translating the glosses, that their nature is divergent. They relate to the main text heterogeneously. It also appeared that a relevant statement sometimes seems to be absent in the text referred to, but that it does appear in the Gloss to that text. Referring to a certain provision in one of the *Corpora iuris* apparently includes referring to the Gloss to that text.

Some glosses merely make mention of provisions of Canon law and/or Roman law, without any commentary. Apparently these provisions are considered to be relevant for the main text or comparable as regards their content. Sometimes glosses have a mere comparative nature and explain in which way learned law is deviating from the Frisian Land Law. There are also glosses which adduce texts from learned law in order to endorse the indigenous Frisian rule. These glosses are more complicated. The reference sometimes seems to be far-fetched and one wonders what objective there could have been to adopt such an allegation. Is it meant to suggest a kind of accordance? Is it meant to provide the indigenous rule with some kind of universal, ideological foundation by tracing it back to compilations of legal texts, resting upon the authority of the Pope or the Emperor? When we do discover some kind of support in the *ius commune*, the Latin concepts used there and the scholarly context they are derived from are never identical. Moreover, the statements of learned law are sometimes slightly different as regards content or they encompass (much) more than the rule of indigenous law. Hence, juxtaposition of indigenous rules and rules of learned law, may be 'misleading'. Through a dialectical process, it may lead to reciprocity and increasingly affect the perspective from which the rules and concepts of indigenous law are read and interpreted.

Just identifying a notion of indigenous law as its Roman equivalent may be a first step towards adopting rules of Roman law into indigenous law. Once a Frisian, indigenous concept is labelled as its Roman law equivalent, and presented in a scholarly, Latin disguise, Roman rules, derived from the *Corpus iuris*, may suddenly be present. We see this, for example, in the gloss to § 14 (n. 85) of text VI (*The Seventeen Statutes*). The Frisian right to regain one's property without judicial decree when returning from captivity is qualified as the Roman law *ius postliminii*. That Roman provisions, related to the *ius postliminii*, suddenly appear seems almost obvious now: provisions concerning *restitutio in integrum* (D. 4.6.1 and C. 8.50.2) and the return after being ransomed (D. 49.15.20.2).[21] This mechanism reflects what happened in West-

21 Cf. Hallebeek, 'The Gloss to the *Saunteen Kesta*', 61.

ern Europe on a larger scale, legitimised by the doctrines of the learned jurists such as Bartolus de Saxoferrato (1313–1357): to use *ius commune* when applying *ius proprium*.[22]

Some glosses even appear to pronounce upon the question to what extent the main text, recording indigenous law, can be considered operative: glosses which say that ordeals, mentioned in the main text, are no longer put into practice (glosses 35 and 160) and glosses which describe ecclesiastical competence, whereas the main text only talks about secular law and secular courts dealing with the issue (gloss 82). Ordeals were for the greater part prohibited by papal decrees at the time of the Fourth Lateran Council (1215). Ecclesiastical jurisdiction in case of widows and other *personae miserabiles* and in case of possessory remedies developed in the twelfth and thirteenth centuries and curtailed the competences of secular courts. We may not exclude the possibility that the purpose of such glosses was also to bring the main text up to date. The idea that recordings of law can only be updated by alterations in the texts themselves is based on the nineteenth century ideal that law can be found in the Codes and nowhere else. Substantial law cannot change without revision of the Code. Justinian, however, did not replace any constitution in his *Codex*, but merely promulgated new ones. *Lex posterior derogat legi priori*. Even nowadays Canon Law is developed and altered by adding Novels to the *Codex iuris canonici* (1983), not by revising it.

Although it is difficult to assess the exact significance of the Gloss in its entirety, it may be clear that its relation to the main text has to be determined by a meticulous analysis of the texts, main text and Gloss, in their mutual relationship. It may also be clear that the indigenous Frisian law of the Late Middle Ages cannot be properly understood and pronounced upon without observing the Gloss.

7 Author and Date of the Gloss

The author of the Gloss to the Frisian Land Law is unknown, but it is not unlikely there was more than one author. The texts which constitute the Frisian Land Law do not have the same origin and date, so neither is it to be expected that the glosses do. The glosses may have gradually developed and may have been elaborated several times before they found their way into the incunable. In any event, their coming into existence and their further development pre-

22 Bellomo, *The common legal past*, 184–195.

supposes the presence of Frisian jurists who were academically educated in Canon law, Roman law or both. It is known that many clerics from Friesland were involved in litigation and were often academically trained in both Canon and Roman law. In the Netherlands, studying law became possible only in 1425 with the foundation of the University of Louvain, but it is known that Frisian jurists were educated elsewhere in Europe. The most famous example is that of the early decretalist Emo van Huizinge (†1237), who had studied Canon law at Paris, Orleans and Oxford before becoming abbot of the Norbertine Abbey of Bloemhof near Wittewierum.[23] That the knowledge of Roman law was extant in Friesland during the fifteenth century is beyond doubt, since this appears from the *Jurisprudentia Frisica* and from various charters.[24]

Somehow, students must have brought the knowledge of Canon and Roman law to Frisia, by taking home handwritten lecture notes and manuscripts of scholarly works. It is hardly conceivable that the Gloss was composed without the presence of such kind of literature. Some of the works the Gloss referred to, belonged to the common literature every academic jurist would have known, such as the Standard Glosses, the *Speculum iudiciale* and the *Summa Codicis* of Azo.

The less common works referred to in the Gloss may reveal something more about the transplant of legal scholarship to the North, although it is difficult to pronounce upon these things with certainty. We just bring up some intriguing examples. In the gloss *nen tingh keth* (n. 98) to text VIII (*Twenty-Four Land Laws*), there is a reference to Vincentius Hispanus (†1248), probably to his Apparatus to the *Liber Extra*, dating from 1234–1243. Not one copy of this work (and neither copies of Vincentius' Apparatus to the *compilationes antiquae*) is

23 Various publications by Van Apeldoorn and Gerbenzon have pointed out that long before the Frisian Land Law was compiled and edited, there was professional knowledge of Canon Law and Roman Law in Frisia. Van Apeldoorn, *Het Romeinsche recht in Friesland*, 26–28; Gerbenzon, *Emo van Huizinge*; Gerbenzon, 'Bijdrage tot het bronnenonderzoek'; Gerbenzon, 'Aantekeningen over de *Jurisprudentia Frisica*'.

24 Sipma (ed.), *Oudfriesche oorkonden Vol. II*, 31 (p. 40) and 43 (p. 59). The former charter, dating from c. 1450, refers to *Cod.* 4.1.3 and the *casus* in the Accursian Gloss to *Cod.* 4.1.3. The second one (from 1458) refers to four maxims, all derived from learned law, i.e. *Jura vigilantibus subveniunt, et non dormientibus* (*Dig.* 42.8.24, which is also quoted in gloss 51 of the Frisian Land Law), *Qui tacet, consentire videtur* (VI *de regulis iuris, regula* 43), *Notoritas non indiget probatione* (the gloss *quia manifestum fuit* ad *Dig.* 19.1.11.12) and *Quod semel placuit, amplius non displicet* (VI *de regulis iuris, regula* 21). Volume IV of the *Oudfriese oorkonden* contains a statement of claim, dating from around 1500, which has many references to the *Corpora iuris*, the Gloss and learned jurists as Henricus de Piro (1403–1473) and Cinus de Pistoia. See Vries (ed.), *Oudfriese Oorkonden Vol. IV*, 112 (pp. 123–129). The latter document had previously been edited in Gerbenzon, *Excerpta* legum, 451–457.

preserved nowadays somewhere in the Netherlands, despite the fact that these works were never printed. Is it possible that some Frisian student brought one of these works to Frisia? Similarly, the *Lectura decretalium* (c. 1250) of Petrus de Sampsone is referred to in the gloss to § 11 (n. 82) of text VI (*The Seventeen Statutes*). Sixteen manuscripts of this work have been preserved, but none of these in the Netherlands, and again this work never appeared in print.[25] Is it possible that the reference to Petrus de Sampsone was added by a Frisian jurist who studied in Bologna, where around 1270 the *Lectura decretalium* of Sampsone was edited or at some other university in the South of Europe? Thirdly, there is the work *In quinque libros decretalium commentaria* (1349) of Henricus Boich. An extensive quotation from this work can be found in the gloss, just mentioned, to § 11 (n. 82) of text VI (*The Seventeen Statutes*). Could this have been achieved by a Frisian student who in the middle of the fourteenth century had studied under this Parisian Professor? As regards this work, Boich's commentary on the Decretals, we know that the Chapter of Saint Martin in Utrecht had a copy of the first book, the very part quoted in the Gloss.[26] As a matter of fact, the questions must remain unanswered. However, pre-reformation Frisia must have had connections with the academic centres of learned law and there must have existed some kind of common Frisian tradition of legal scholarship and monasteries with libraries, where the legal heritage of learned law was cherished. It is striking that the three canonists just mentioned, Vincentius Hispanus, Petrus de Sampson and Henricus Boich, reappear in the *Jurisprudentia Frisica*.[27]

As regards the date of the Gloss, we should realize that a number of *lemmata* cannot be found back in the principal text. The reason for this is, that the main text contains an updated redaction, whereas the *lemmata* of the glosses refer to an earlier text redaction. Obviously, the editor(s) of the Frisian Land Law adapted the main text to the common parlance of their own days, but did not adapt the *lemmata* of the glosses. The *lemmata* correspond with an older version of the main text, and this may indicate that they came into being quite some time before the end of the fifteenth century. Our hypothesis would be therefore that, now that we know that the main text was not further elaborated after the end

25 Soetermeer, 'Petrus de Sampsone'.

26 De Groot and Coppens, *Manuscripta canonistica latina*, 405 (n. 1466).

27 Vicentius Hispanus is referred to in the glosses *dat riucht seyt beda paus* ad JF 37:13, *dij aerste pont is fan* ad JF 64:17 and *joff een man wrda noes* ad JF 76:6; see *Codex Roorda*, pp. 159, 251 and 275. Petrus de Sampsone is referred to in JF 59:19–20; see *Codex Roorda*, pp. 236–237. Henrichus Boich is quoted in the glosses *dat keysers riucht seyt aldus* ad JF 10:1 and *dat riucht seyt beda paus* ad JF 37:13; see *Codex Roorda*, pp. 45, 159.

of the fourteenth century, the same holds good for the glosses. This is more or less confirmed by the fact that hardly any works from the fifteenth century are mentioned, the youngest author being Nicolaus de Tudeschis (Panormitanus, 1386–1445), who is only mentioned once in text II (*What Is Law?*) and influential authors such as Bartolus de Saxoferrato (1313–1357), Baldus de Ubaldis (1327–1400) and Paulus de Castro (†1441) are entirely absent.

8 Principles Underlying the Edition and Translation

For the edition of the Gloss we used the same copy of the incunable (FG) as used for editing the main text. We could consult an earlier transcription of FG, an ostensibly unfinished draft, which was made in the early Sixties by Prof. Hans (J.A.) Ankum (1930–2019) and Prof. Klaas Fokkema (1898–1967). They did not only transcribe the text, but also identified the allegations and references. Occasionally the abbreviated text appeared to be misinterpreted, which sometimes put us on the wrong track. Moreover, some allegations were identified incorrectly. All in all, however, this preliminary work was a tremendous support and we realize very well that identifying allegations has become much easier than in the old days thanks to the availability of digitalized sources.

Not infrequently, the text of the Gloss to the Frisian Land Law appeared to be corrupt: the Latin was grammatically incorrect and quotations lacked certain words or contained homoioteleutons. Compared to their origin in the Vulgate text of e.g. the Digest—as available for example through the late fifteenth century editions of the Venetian printer Baptista de Tortis—quotations from the *Corpus iuris civilis* appeared to contain an extensive number of flaws. This may be due to errors by the printer or to a corrupt manuscript which served as a model for the edition. The texts may have been repeatedly copied by scribes who did not master law and had a poor knowledge of Latin.

For reproducing the text of the Gloss we followed the international transcription rules for medieval writings of Canon law and *ius commune*.[28] Conjectural emendations and homoioteleutons are indicated in the footnotes, which serve *inter alia* as *apparatus criticus*. Orthographic variants of minor importance in other remaining copies of the incunable are not recorded. The medieval spelling is retained. For editorial reasons we did not adopt line numbers and did not produce a separate *apparatus fontium*.

---

28 As standardized by Stephan Kuttner (1907–1996). See Kuttner, 'Note on the presentation', and Kuttner, 'Note on the presentation. Addition'.

The English translation follows the Latin original as closely as possible. The result may sometimes look cryptic, but the Latin glosses are equally cryptic for those who do understand the Latin, but are not familiar with Roman and Canon law and the medieval way of glossing legal texts. Reading the glosses in coherence with the Frisian main text and consulting the allegations can be helpful.

For various reasons it was no easy task to translate the Gloss into English. Apart from the fact, that 'proper' English terminology for describing continental learned law does not exist, there was the serious methodological problem that Latin terms derived from the sources of learned law (*Corpus iuris civilis* and *Corpus iuris canonici*) are used for commenting upon indigenous, Frisian law. Consequently, the issue became which denotations and connotations of the words should prevail for translating: those originating from Canon and Roman law or those originating from Frisian law? Ultimately, we opted for the learned law to be decisive. The Gloss is strongly imbued with Canon and Roman law reasoning. The *ius commune* seems to be its author's paradigm. Only where a gloss appeared to have a mere exegetical nature, i.e. just explaining certain words from the Frisian main text, did it become obvious that the Latin words were meant as pure equivalents of the Frisian terms. In such cases we opted for English words which come as close as possible to the Frisian terms. It should be clear that translating the Gloss required a continuous and thorough consultation with the translator of the main text, Dr. Han Nijdam. We owe him a debt of gratitude as well as Frances M. Gilligan LL.M, who was willing to linguistically correct our translations which again, due to the complexity of the material, was only possible through close consultation.

Bibliography

Source Editions

Buma, W.J., and W. Ebel (eds.), *Das Fivelgoer Recht* (Göttingen 1971).

Buma, W.J., W. Ebel, and M. Tragter-Schubert (eds.), *Westerlauwerssches Recht I. Jus Municipale Frisonum*. (Göttingen 1977).

Buma, W.J., P. Gerbenzon and M. Tragter-Schubert (eds.), *Codex Aysma: die altfriesischen Texte* (Assen/Maastricht 1993).

Eckhardt, K.A., and A. Eckhardt (eds.), *Lex Frisionum*. Monumenta Germaniae Historica. Fontes iuris Germanici antiqui in usum scholarum separatim editi XII (Hannover 1982).

Friedländer, E., and C. Malagola (eds.), *Acta Nationis Germanicae Universitatis Bononiensis* (Berlin 1887).

Geer van Jutphaas, B.J.L. de (ed.), *De Saksenspiegel in Nederland, Tweede stuk, Vermeerderde tekst met de glosse* (The Hague 1888).

Gerbenzon, P., *Codex Parisiensis* (The Hague 1954).

Joosting, J.G.C., and S. Muller (eds.), *Bronnen voor de geschiedenis der kerkelijke rechtspraak in het bisdom Utrecht in de Middeleeuwen. Vol 5: 4e afdeling: Provinciale en synodale statuten; 5e Afdeling: Seendrechten, door J.G.C. Joosting* (The Hague 1914).

Kaufmann, F.M. (ed.), *Glossen zum Sachsenspiegel-Landrecht. Buch'sche Glosse, 3 vols*. MGH Fontes iuris Germanici antiqui, N.S. 7 (Hannover 2002).

Kaufmann, F.M. (ed.), *Glossen zum Sachsenspiegel-Lehnrecht. Die längere Glosse, 3 vols*. MGH Fontes iuris Germanici antiqui, N.S. 9 (Hannover 2013).

Richthofen, K. von (ed.), *Friesische Rechtsquellen* (Göttingen 1840).

Sassenspegel mit velen nyen Addicien fan dem Leenrechte unde Richtstige (Augsburg 1516).

Sipma, P. (ed.), *Oudfriesche oorkonden Vol. II*. Oudfriese taal- en rechtsbronnen 2 (The Hague 1933).

Vries, O. (ed.), *Oudfriese oorkonden Vol. IV*. Oudfriese taal- en rechtsbronnen 14 (The Hague 1977).

Vries, O., *Asega, is het dingtijd? De hoogtepunten van de Oudfriese tekstoverlevering* (Leeuwarden and Utrecht 2007).

Literature

Algra, N.E., *Ein. Enkele rechtshistorische aspecten van de grondeigendom in westerlauwers Friesland* (Groningen 1966).

Algra, N.E., *Zeventien Keuren en Vierentwintig Landrechten* (Doorn 1992).

Algra, N.E., 'De datearring fan it Skeltarjocht', *It Beaken* 53 (1991) 1–33.

Algra, N.E., 'Een datering van het "jong" Schoutenrecht', *It Beaken* 59 (1997) 57–91.

Algra, N.E., 'Rechtshistorische aspecten van het *Landrecht der Vriesne*', in: Ph.H. Breuker (ed.), *Landrecht der Vriesne: tekstuitgave en commentaar* (Leeuwarden 1996) 91–223.

Algra, N.E., 'The Relation between Frisia and the Empire from 800–1500 in the Light of the Eighth of the Seventeen Statutes', in: R.H. Bremmer, T.S.B. Johnston and O. Vries (eds.), *Approaches to Old Frisian Philology*. Amsterdamer Beiträge zur älteren Germanistik 49 / Estrikken 72 (Amsterdam, Atlanta/GA and Groningen 1998) 1–76.

Algra, N.E., *Oudfries Recht 800–1256* (Leeuwarden 2000).

Antiquiores Barchinonensium leges, quas vulgus usaticos appellat, cum comentariis supremorum Iurisconsultorum Iacobi a Monte Iudaico, Iacobi et Guielermi a Vallesicca et Iacobi Calicii, cum Indice copiosissimo non antea excussae (Barcelona 1544).

Apeldoorn, L.J. van, *Het Romeinsche recht in Friesland*. Mededeelingen der Nederlandsche Akademie van Wetenschappen, Afdeling Letterkunde, Nieuwe Reeks, Deel III, No. 10 (Amsterdam 1940).

Beck, H., 'Eidring. Literarisches', in: H. Beck et al. (eds.), *Reallexikon der Germanischen Altertumskunde* 6 (Berlin and New York 1986) 549.

Bellomo, M., *The common legal past of Europe 1000–1800* (Washington 1995).

Birkhan, H., 'Eine altfriesische Tradition zur Konstituierung von Recht und Freiheit', *Rostocker Beiträge zur Sprachwissenschaft* 7 (1999) 63–85.

Boehm, C., 'The Natural History of Blood Revenge'. In: J. Büchert Netterström and B. Poulsen (eds.), *Feud in Medieval and Early Modern Europe* (Aarhus 2007) 189–203.

Bolhuis van Zeeburgh, J., *Kritiek der Friesche geschiedschrijving* (The Hague 1873).

Bos-van der Heide, H.S.E., *Het Rudolfsboek* (Assen 1937).

Boutkan, D., and S.M. Siebinga, *Old Frisian Etymological Dictionary*. Leiden Indo-European Etymological Dictionaries 1 (Leiden 2005).

Bremmer, R.H., *Hir is eskriven. Lezen en schrijven in de Friese landen rond 1300* (Hilversum 2004).

Bremmer, R.H., 'Het boek is af, maar mag de schrijver spelen? Reacties op mijn *Hir is eskriven*', *Us Wurk* 56 (2007) 63–87.

Bremmer, R.H., 'The Orality of Old Frisian Law Texts'. In: R.H. Bremmer Jr., S. Laker and O. Vries (eds.), *Directions for Old Frisian Philology*. Amsterdamer Beiträge zur älteren Germanistik 73 / Estrikken 96 (Amsterdam / New York 2014) 1–48.

Bremmer, R.H., '"Thi Wilde Witsing": Vikings and Otherness in the Old Frisian Laws', *The Journal of English and Germanic Philology* 119/1 (2020) 1–26.

Bremmer, R.H., 'More than Language. Law and Textual Communities in Medieval Frisia', in: T. Gobbit (ed.), *Law, Book, Culture in the Middle Ages* (Leiden and Boston 2021) 98–125.

Breuker, Ph.H., (ed.), *Landrecht der Vriesne: tekstuitgave en commentaar* (Leeuwarden 1996).

Buijtenen. M.P. van, *De grondslag van de Friese Vrijheid* (Assen 1953).

Buijtenen, M.P. van, *Frieslands middeleeuwse marktrechten* (Leeuwarden 1965).

Buma, W.J., *Het Godsoordeel in de Oud-Friese literatuur. Rede uitgesproken bij de aanvaarding van het ambt van bijzonder hoogleraar in de Friese taal- en letterkunde aan de Rijksuniversiteit te Utrecht* (Groningen/Batavia 1949).

Cornelius, A., *Croniicke ende waarachtige Beschrijvinge van Vrieslant* (Leeuwarden 1597, 2d edition 1742).

Dekker, K., 'The Old Frisian Studies of Jan van Vliet (1622–1666) and Thomas Marshall (1621–1685)', in: R.H. Bremmer Jr, T.S.B. Johnston and O. Vries (eds.), *Approaches to Old Frisian Philology* (Amsterdam 1998) 113–138.

Dekker, K., *The Origins of Old Germanic Studies in the Low Countries*. Brill's Studies in Intellectual History 92 (Leiden 1999).

Eekhoff, W., 'Lijst van de opvolgende Lands Historieschrijvers van Friesland', *De Vrije Fries* 11 (1868) 339–342.

Een en dertigste verslag der handelingen van het Friesch Genootschap van geschied-, oudheid- en taalkunde, over het jaar 1858/9, uitgebragt in de vergadering van den 4 augustus 1859 (Leeuwarden 1859).

Erler, A., and M. Neidert, 'Schultheiß, Schulze', in: A. Erler et al. (eds.), *Handwörterbuch zur deutschen Rechtsgeschichte* (Berlin 1971) 1519–1521.

Fairbanks, F., *The Old West Frisian Skeltana Riucht* (Cambridge, Ma. 1939).

Folz, R., *Le souvenir et la légende de Charlemagne dans l'Empire germanique médiéval* (Paris 1950).

Gerbenzon, P., *Excerpta Legum. Onderzoekingen betreffende enkele Friese rechtsboeken uit de vijftiende eeuw* (Groningen/Djakarta 1956).

Gerbenzon, P., *Rudolfsboekmateriael. Gearfandele en biarbeide fan in stúdzjerounte oan de Ryksuniversiteit to Utert*. Estrikken 32 (Groningen 1962).

Gerbenzon, P., *Emo van Huizinge, een vroege decretalist. Rede uitgesproken bij de aanvaarding van het ambt van gewoon hoogleraar aan de Rijksuniversiteit te Groningen op 8 juni 1965* (Groningen 1965).

Gerbenzon, P., 'Bijdrage tot het bronnenonderzoek van *Haet is riocht*', *Us Wurk* 20 (1971) 1–18.

Gerbenzon, P., 'Der altfriesische *asega*, der altsächsische *eosago* und der althochdeutsche *esago*', *Tijdschrift voor Rechtsgeschiedenis* 41 (1973) 75–91.

Gerbenzon, P., *Apparaat voor de studie van Oudfries recht*. 2 vols. (Groningen 1981).

Gerbenzon, P., 'Aantekeningen over de *Jurisprudentia Frisica*. Een laat-vijftiende-eeuwse Westerlauwers-Friese bewerking van de *Excerpta legum*', *Tijdschrift voor Rechtsgeschiedenis* 57 (1989) 21–67; 339–374.

Gerbenzon, P., 'Canon and Roman Law in the So-Called Codex Parisiensis', in: R.H. Bremmer et al. (eds.), *Aspects of Old Frisian Philology*. Amsterdamer Beiträge zur älteren Germanistik 31–32 (Amsterdam 1990) 125–145.

Gosses, G., 'By it Rudolfsboek', *It Beaken* 4 (1942) 113–117.

Green, D.H., *Language and History in the Early Germanic World* (Cambridge 1998).

Groot, A.J. de, and E.C.C. Coppens, *Manuscripta canonistica latina. Elenchus codicum necnon diplomatum iuris canonici ante a. 1600 in bibliothecis et archivis neerlandicis* (Nijmegen 1989).

Hallebeek, J., 'The Gloss to the *Saunteen Kesta* (Seventeen Statutes) of the Frisian Land Law', *Tijdschrift voor Rechtsgeschiedenis* 87 (2019) 30–64.

Hallebeek, J., *Layci erant coiudices. Over de rol van leken in de Westerlauwerse seendprocedure. Rede in verkorte vorm uitgesproken bij het afscheid als hoogleraar Europese rechtsgeschiedenis aan de Vrije Universiteit te Amsterdam op 26 april 2019* (Amsterdam 2019).

Henstra, D.J., *The Evolution of the Money Standard in Medieval Frisia. A Treatise on the History of the Systems of Money of Account in the Former Frisia* (c. 600–c. 1500), (Groningen 2000).

Henstra, D.J., 'De eerste optekening van de algemeen-Friese Keuren', *It Beaken* 64 (2002) 99–128.

Henstra, D.J., *Fon Jelde. Opstellen van D.J. Henstra over middeleeuws Frisia* (Groningen 2010).

Henstra, D.J., *Friese graafschappen tussen Zwin en Wezer. Een overzicht van de grafelijkheid in middeleeuws Frisia* (ca. 700–1200) (Assen 2012).

Hines, J., and N. IJssennagger-van der Pluijm (eds.), *Frisians of the Early Middle Ages* (Woodbridge 2021).

Hoekstra, J., *Die gemeinfriesischen Siebzehn Küren* (Assen 1940).

Hunt, R., et al., *A Summary Catalogue of Western manuscripts in the Bodleian Library at Oxford Which Have Not Hitherto Been Catalogued in the Quarto Series* (Oxford 1953).

Iglesia Ferreirós, A., *Cataluña Medieval, I Estudio, II Edición del ms. lat. Z-I-3 del Real Monasterio de El Escorial* [Colección Efímera n.º 4.1–2]. Associació Catalana d'Història del Dret "Jaume de Montjuïc" (Barcelona 2008).

IJssennagger, N.L., 'Between Frankish and Viking: Frisia and Frisians in the Viking Age', *Viking and Medieval Scandinavia* 9 (2013) 69–98.

IJssennagger, N.L., *Central because Liminal. Frisia in a Viking Age North Sea World* (Groningen 2017).

Iversen, F., '*Concilium* and *Pagus*—Revisiting the Early Germanic *Thing* System of Northern Europe', *Journal of the North Atlantic, Special Volume* 5 (2013) 5–17.

Janssen, R., '"Freeska Landriucht". Het oudste Friese boek en diens onbekende drukker'. Internet publication. https://www.uu.nl/bijzondere-collecties-universiteitsbibliotheek-utrecht/collecties/oude-en-bijzondere-drukken/freeska-landriucht

Johnston, T.S.B., 'Old Frisian Law and the Frisian Freedom Ideology: Text and Manuscript Composition as a Marketing Device', in: R.H. Bremmer, T.S.B. Johnston and O. Vries (eds.), *Approaches to Old Frisian Philology* (Amsterdam, Atlanta/GA and Groningen 1998), 179–214.

Johnston, T.S.B., 'The Old Frisian Law Manuscripts and Law Texts', in: H.H. Munske et al. (eds.), *Handbuch des Friesischen. Handbook of Frisian Studies* (Tübingen 2001), 571–586.

Kruitwagen, F.J.B., 'De Freeska Landriucht-drukkerij. [Friesland?, omstreeks 1485–1490]', *Het boek* 29 (1947/48) 213–237.

Kuttner, S., 'Note on the presentation of text and apparatus in editing works of the decretists and decretalists', *Traditio* 15 (1959) 452–464.

Kuttner, S., 'Note on the presentation of text and apparatus in editing works of the decretists and decretalists. Addition', *Traditio* 26 (1970) 432.

Lambert, T.B., and D. Rollason (eds.), *Peace and Protection in the Middle Ages*. Durham Medieval and Renaissance Monographs and Essays 1 (Durham and Toronto 2009).

Langbroek, E., 'Condensa atque Tenebrosa; die altfriesischen Psalmen: Neulesung und Rekonstruktion (UB Groningen Hs 404)', in: R.H. Bremmer, G. van der Meer and O. Vries (eds.), *Aspects of Old Frisian Philology*. Amsterdamer Beiträge zur älteren Germanistik 31–32 (Amsterdam and Groningen 1990), 255–284.

Langbroek, E., 'So viel geschrieben, so wenig geblieben. Eine neue Entdeckung: unbekannte altfriesische Psalmglossen', *Amsterdamer Beiträge zur älteren Germanistik* 74 (2015) 135–146.

Langen, G.J. de, and J.A. Mol, 'Church Foundation and Parish Formation in Frisia in the Tenth and Eleventh Centuries: A Planned Development?', *The Medieval Low Countries* 4 (2017) 1–55.

Langen, G.J. de, and J.A. Mol, 'Vikingen en de Kerk in de Friese landen', in: M. Stoter and D. Spiekhout (eds.), *Wij Vikingen. Friezen en Vikingen in het kustgebied van de Lage Landen* (Zwolle 2019) 22–41.

Langen, G.J. de, and J.A. Mol, 'Koning Redbad en zijn bewegingsruimte', *De Vrije Fries* 100 (2020) 28–41.

Langen, G.J. de, and J.A. Mol, 'The Distribution and Subdivision of Farmland on the Medieval and Prehistoric Salt Marshes of the Northern Netherlands. A Retrogressive Model of the (pre-)Frisian farm, Based on Historical Sources from the Early Modern Period', in print (2021).

Lebecq, S., *Marchands et navigateurs frisons du haut moyen âge*. 2 Vols. (Lille 1983).

Lengen, H. van, 'Karl der Große, Jungfrau Maria und andere Heilsbringer als Garanten und Patrone Friesischer Freiheit. Zu den Siegeln der Landesgemeinden Frieslands im Mittelalter', in: H. van Lengen (ed.), *Die Friesische Freiheit des Mittelalters—Leben und Legende* (Ostfriesische Landschaftliche Verlags- und Vertriebsgesellschaft mbH: Aurich 2003), 90–133.

Meijering, H.D., 'De zeven zeelanden—het traktaat en de traditie', in: *Studia Frisica in memoriam Prof Dr. K. Fokkema 1898–1967 scripta* (Grins/ Groningen 1969) 100–111.

Meijering, H.D., *De Willekeuren van de Opstalsboom (1323). Een filologisch-historische monografie* (Groningen 1974).

Meijering, H.D., and H. Nijdam (ed. and transl.), *'Wat is Recht?'. De receptie van Oudfries recht in de Groninger Ommelanden in de 15e en 16e eeuw. Een editie met vertaling* (Bornmeer 2018).

Miller, W.I., *Bloodtaking and Peacemaking. Feud, Law, and Society in Saga Iceland* (Chicago and Londen 1990).

Miller, W.I., *Eye for an Eye* (Cambridge 2006).

Mol, J.A., and K. van Vliet, 'De oudste oorkonden van het Sint-Odulfusklooster van Staveren', *Jaarboek voor Middeleeuwse Geschiedenis* 1 (1998) 73–134.

Mol, J.A., 'Hoofdelingen en huurlingen. Militaire innovatie en de aanloop tot 1498', in: J. Frieswijk et al. (eds.), *Fryslân, staat en macht 1450–1650. Bijdragen aan het historisch congres te Leeuwarden van 3 tot 5 juni 1998* (Hilversum and Leeuwarden 1999) 65–84.

Mol, J.A., *De Friese volkslegers tussen 1480 en 1560* (Hilversum/Leeuwarden 2017).

Murdoch, B., 'Authority and Authenticity: Comments on the Prologues to the Old Frisian Laws', in: R.H. Bremmer Jr, T.S.B. Johnston and O. Vries (ed.), *Approaches to Old Frisian Philology* (Amsterdam/Atlanta, GA 1998) 215–244.

Neumann, S., *Der gerichtliche Zweikampf: Gottesurteil–Wettstreit–Ehrensache* (Ostfildern 2010).

Nicolay, J.A.W., *The splendour of power. Early medieval kingship and the use of gold and silver in the southern North Sea area (5th to 7th century AD)*. Groningen Archaeological Studies 28 (Groningen 2014).

Nijdam, H., 'Old West Frisian *bī thā sida* 'according to the custom': A Case of Intertextuality', *Us Wurk* 50 (2001), 14–26.

Nijdam, H., *Lichaam, eer en recht in middeleeuws Friesland. Een studie naar de Oudfriese boeteregisters* (Hilversum 2008).

Nijdam, H., 'Klinkende munten en klinkende botsplinters in de Oudfriese rechtsteksten: continuïteit, discontinuïteit, intertekstualiteit', *De Vrije Fries* 89 (2009), 45–66.

Nijdam, H., 'Belichaamde eer, wraak en vete. Een historisch- en cognitief-antropologische benadering', *Tijdschrift voor Geschiedenis* 123 (2010), 192–207.

Nijdam, H., 'Compensating Body and Honor: The Old Frisian Compensation Tariffs', in: W.J. Turner and S.M. Butler (eds.), *Medicine and Law in the Middle Ages*. Medieval Law and its Practice 17 (Leiden and Boston 2014), 25–57.

Nijdam, H., 'Indigenous Or Universal? A Comparative Perspective On Medieval (Frisian) Compensation Law', in: P. Andersen, K. Salonen, H. Sigh, H. Vogt (eds.), *How Nordic are the Nordic Laws? Ten years after. Proceedings of the Tenth Carlsberg Conference on Medieval Legal History 2013* (Kopenhagen 2014), 161–181.

Nijdam, H., 'A Comparison of the Injury Tariffs in the Early Kentish and the Frisian Law Codes', in: J. Hines and N. IJssennagger (eds.), *Frisians and their North Sea Neighbours. From the Fifth Century to the Viking Age* (Woodbridge 2017) 223–242.

Nijdam, H., 'The Body Legal in Frisian Law. Bridging the Gap Between the *Lex Frisionum*

and the Old Frisian Compensation tariffs'. In: A. Rabin and S. Jurasinski (eds.), *Languages of the Law in Early Medieval England. Essays in Memory of Lisi Oliver* (Leuven / Paris / Bristol 2019) 101–125.

Nijdam, H, 'Het Westerlauwers Seendrecht: een filologische analyse', in H. van Engen, H. Nijdam en K. van Vliet (eds.), *Macht, bezit en ruimte. Opstellen over de noordelijke Nederlanden in de middeleeuwen, aangeboden aan Hans Mol bij zijn afscheid als bijzonder hoogleraar Geschiedenis van de Friese landen in de Middeleeuwen aan de Universiteit Leiden* (Hilversum 2021) 305–321.

Nijdam, J.A., 'Law and Political Organisation of the Early Medieval Frisians (c. AD 600–800)', in: J. Hines and N. IJssennagger-van der Pluijm (eds.), *Frisians of the Early Middle Ages* (Woodbridge 2021) 137–170.

Nijdam, H., and O.S. Knottnerus, 'Redbad, the Once and Future King of the Frisians'. In: S. Halink (ed.), *Northern Myths, Modern Identities. The Nationalisation of Northern Mythologies Since 1800* (Leiden–Boston 2019) 87–114.

Nijdam, H., and J. Savelkouls, 'The Manuscript Collection of the Frisian State Historian Simon Abbes Gabbema (1628–1688) from an Old Frisian Perspective.', in: M. de Vaan and S. Laker (eds.), *Frisian Through the Ages. Festschrift for Rolf H. Bremmer Jr.* Amsterdamer Beiträge zur älteren Germanistik 77 (Leiden 2017) 303–332.

Nijdam, H., and A.P. Versloot, 'Kodeks Siccama. Spoaren fan in ferdwûn Aldwestfrysk rjochtshânskrift', *Us Wurk* 61 (2012) 1–56.

Noomen, P.N., 'Suffridus Petrus en de Friese identiteit', *It Beaken* 56/2–3 (Leeuwarden 1994) 146–187.

Noomen, P.N., 'Consolidatie van familiebezit en status in middeleeuws Friesland', in: J.A. Mol (ed.), *Zorgen voor zekerheid. Studies over Friese testamenten in de vijftiende en zestiende eeuw* (Leeuwarden 1994) 73–174.

Noomen, P.N., 'Hachens en Wachens: Feit en fiksje yn midsieusk Fryslân', in: R.H. Bremmer et al. (eds.), *Speculum Frisicum. Stúdzjes oanbean oan Philippus H. Breuker* (Leeuwarden and Leiden 2001) 3–22.

Noomen, P.N., *De stinzen in middeleeuws Friesland en hun bewoners* (Hilversum 2009).

Oliver, L., *The Body Legal in Barbarian Law* (Toronto etc. 2011).

Pollard, A.W., et al., *Catalogue of books, printed in the xvth century now in the British Museum*, part IX (London 1962).

Popkema, A.T., 'Die altfriesischen Eidesbezeichnungen', in: Rolf H. Bremmer et al. (eds.), *Advances in Old Frisian Philology*. Amsterdamer Beiträge zur älteren Germanistik 64 / Estrikken 80 (Amsterdam and New York 2007) 325–356.

Popkema, A.T., 'On the Origin of All Evil: The Old Frisian Collocation *grimme herne* and its Modern Use', in: J. Hoekstra (ed.), *Twenty-Nine Smiles for Alastair. Freundesgabe für Dr. Alastair G.H. Walker* (Kiel 2013) 195–207.

Popkema, A.T., 'The *Freeska Landriucht* (1074R): A Book from Oldersum Castle Library Retrieved', in: M. de Vaan and S. Laker (eds.), *Frisian Through the Ages. Festschrift for*

Rolf H. Bremmer Jr. Amsterdamer Beiträge zur älteren Germanistik 77 (Leiden 2017) 333–347.

Popkema, A.T., 'Old Frisian: a Legal Language in Principle', in: R.H. Bremmer et al. (eds.), *Directions for Old Frisian Philology* (Amsterdam/New York 2014) 369–395.

Popkema, A.T., 'On the Provenance of the Old Frisian Law Manuscripts' (in preparation 2022).

Reinders, A., 'Die Sprache der erstmaligen Verschriftlichung der 17 Küren und der 24 Landrechte—Altfriesisch oder Latein?', *Us Wurk* 68 (2019), 99–118.

Salomon, A., *Friesische Geschichtsbilder. Historische Ereignisse und kollektives Gedächtnis im Mittelalterlichen Friesland* (Aurich 2000).

Schmidt, H., 'Friesische Freiheitsüberlieferungen im hohen Mittelalter', in: *Festschrift für Hermann Heimpel zum 70. Geburtstag am 19. September 1971*. Bd. III (Göttingen 1971) 518–545.

Schotanus, C., *Beschryvinge van de Heerlyckheydt van Friesland tusschen 't Flie end de Lauwers met nieuwe Caerten* (Franeker 1664).

Schouten, D., 'Hypothese op hypothese stapelen. Theorieën over de *Freeska Landriucht*-drukkerij: een overzicht', *De Boekenwereld* 17 (2000/2001) 167–194.

Schrijver, P., 'Frisian between the Roman and Early-Medieval Periods. Language contact, Celts and Romans', in: J. Hines and N. IJssennagger (eds.), *Frisians and their North Sea Neighbours. From the Fifth Century to the Viking Age* (Woodbridge 2017) 43–52.

Schwartz, S.P., 'Comparative Legal Reconstruction in Germanic', in: J. Puhvel (ed.), *Myth and Law among the Indo-Europeans. Studies in Indo-European Comparative Mythology* (Berkeley 1970) 39–53.

Schwartzenberg en Hohenlansberg, G.F. thoe, *Groot Placaat en Charterboek van Vriesland*. 5 vols. (Leeuwarden 1768–1793).

Seebold, E., 'Die Friesen im Zeugnis antiker und spätantiker Autoren', in: H.H. Munske et al. (eds.), *Handbuch des Friesischen. Handbook of Frisian Studies* (Tübingen 2001) 479–487.

Siebs, T., *Westfriesische Studien*. Anhang zu den Abhandlungen der königlichen preussischen Akademie der Wissenschaften (Berlijn 1895).

Siems, H., *Studien zur Lex Frisionum* (Ebelsbach 1980).

Soetermeer, F., 'Petrus de Sampsone', in: *Biographisch-Bibliographisch Kirchenlexikon* 23 (Nordhausen 2004) 1097–1101.

Stein, R., 'Seventeen: The Multiplicity of a Unity in the Low Countries', in: J. Boulton and J. Veenstra (eds.), *The Ideology of Burgundy. The Promotion of National Consciousness, 1364–1565* (Leiden 2006)

Steller, W., *Das altwestfriesische Schulzenrecht* (Breslau 1926).

Sytsema, J., *De 17 Keuren en de 24 Landrechten in de Ommelander Rechtshandschriften* (Amsterdam 1998).

Sytsema, J., 'Codex Unia: Edition and Reconstruction of a Lost Old Frisian Manuscript', in: R.H. Bremmer Jr., S. Laker and O. Vries (eds.), *Directions for Old Frisian Philology*. Amsterdamer Beiträge zur älteren Germanistik 73 / Estrikken 96 (Amsterdam / New York 2014) 497–526.

Thienen, G. van, 'A Date for the Freeska Landriucht Press (1481–1487) from Paper Evidence. With a note on Codex Roorda', in: M. Davies (ed.), *Incunabula. Studies in Fifteenth-Century Printed Books presented to Lotte Hellinga* (London 1999) 141–167.

Versloot, A.P., *Mechanisms of Language Change. Vowel Reduction in 15th century West Frisian* (Doctoral Dissertation 2008).

Vogt, H., and H. Nijdam, 'Translating a Medieval Legal System into Modern English', in: *Translation and Medieval Documents. Voices of Law: Language, Text and Practice* (Digital Online publication Voices of Law 2018) 38–53.

Vries, O., 'Hemma Odda zin, stedsskriuwer fan Ljouwert om 1500 hinne', *It Beaken* 43 (1981) 217–239.

Vries, O., *Het Heilige Roomse Rijk en de Friese Vrijheid* (Leeuwarden 1986).

Vries, O., '*Her Bendix is wrbeck fonden*. Die altfriesische Terminologie im Bereich des Zivilprozeßrechtes', in: R.H. Bremmer, S. Laker and O. Vries (eds.), *Advances in Old Frisian Philology* (Amsterdam 2007) 325–355.

Vries, O., 'Nijaer is sijd ende pliga allijnna in Freesland. Die Terminologie bei der Ausübung des Näherrechts im altfriesischen', in: O. Vries, *De taal van recht en vrijheid* (Gorredijk 2012) 262–283.

Vries, O., 'Also dat wy habbet ferdban kloppet. Die Terminologie des Friedebannes bei der Eigentumsübergabe von Immobilien in der altfriesischen Urkundensprache', in: O. Vries, *De taal van recht en vrijheid* (Gorredijk 2012) 243–261.

Vries, O., '*Frisonica Libertas*. Frisian Freedom as an Instance of Medieval Liberty', *Journal of Medieval History* 1 (2015) 1–20.

Vries, H. de, 'Misprintinge leit skiednis bleat', *Letterhoeke* 11/1 (2016) 20–21.

Vries, H. de, 'Midsiuwske Fryske rjochtshânskriften', *Letterhoeke* 16/3 (2020) 16–17.

Waterbolk, E.H., *Twee eeuwen Friese geschiedschrijving. Opkomst, bloei en verval van de Friese historiografie in de zestiende en zeventiende eeuw* (Groningen 1952).

Wicht, M. von, *Das Ostfriesische Land-Recht, nebst dem Deich und Syhlrechte* (Aurich 1746).

Wumkes, G.A., 'De frijheitsmythe fen it Rudolfsboek', *It Beaken* 1 (1938) 4–11.

Text and Translation

I. Prologue

1 Ther era Godes, synre liaver moder Maria, alle des himelsche heerschipes ende alre fria Fresena fridom. Ende in een sonderlinge memorie des Freeska landriuchtis deer us haeth joun di koningh Kaerl, keyser to Roem, dae dae Fresen da burich to Roem ursteerden. Want hya alderaerst ayn weren ende da holtena witta droghen ende deernei des koninghes heernaten worden. Hwelka riuchten di koningh Kaerl dae Fresen bifael ende di paeus Leo dat hiaet hilden als hia dine Cristena naema.

Om disse riuchten thi bet to finden ende to onthalden ende deer ma naet onthalda mey weer to sekane, soe folged hyrnei een taefla of een register deer joe ut wisa schil huoe y mogen fynda dae punten deer dit boeck fan rorende is. Ende wirt deeld in XVII delen.

Dat arste bighint aldus: 'Haet is riucht? List ende konst'.
Dat oder deel: fan da Saun Kerren.
Dat tredde is fan da Kesten.
Dat fiarde is fan da XXIIII Landriuchta.
Dat fyfte is fan da Acht Domen.
Dat sexte is fan da Sex Wenden.
Dat saunde is fan dat Sind riucht int generael.
Dat achtende is fan dat Sind riucht int speciael.
Dat niogende is fan da jelden enis daedslachtis.
Dat tiende is fan dae Wilkerren fan da Fyf Delen.
Dat alfte is fan dae Birecknada Boeta.
Dat toelfte is dat Boeck des keysers Rodulphi.
Dat trettiende is fan da Merkedriucht.
Dat fiarteende is fan da Swerte Swenghen.
Dat fyftiende is fan da Schaeckraeff.
Dat sexteende is fan da Wilkeren fan Opstallisbaem.
Dat sauntiende is fan da Saun Zelanden.

Hyr bighinnet dae capitulen fan disse delen forscrioun

2 Haet is riucht? List I
Hwa fand ende sette[1] riucht III
Hwa band den arsta ferdban
Hwa scriou riucht arst IIII

[1] FG: set.

© KONINKLIJKE BRILL NV, LEIDEN, THE NETHERLANDS, 2023 | DOI:10.1163/9789004526419_005

1. Prologue

In honour of God, his dear mother Mary, all of the heavenly hosts and the Frisian Freedom. And in special memory of the Frisian land law, which was given to us by King Charlemagne, the Roman emperor, when the Frisians conquered the citadel in Rome. For they had first been slaves wearing wooden neck bands and after that had become the king's vassals. Charlemagne and Pope Leo ordered the Frisians to honour these laws in the same way they should obey the Christian faith.

In order to better find and remember these laws, or to look them up again if one is unable to remember them, a table or register follows after this, which will allow you to find the subject matter contained in this book. It is divided into seventeen parts.

Here Begin the Captions of the Parts Just Mentioned

Hwa da wilkerren aerst sette[1]
Hoe sinte Willibrord da Fresen bikeerde[2] V
Hwana caem riucht aerst
Van da tien wird
Van dis grewa incomst VI
Van friheed der Freesna
Elck Fresa aeg syn selvis deda to witan beth dan ma op hem brengha mey
Fan grete des dikes ende weys
Fan helgane gued naet toe litikiane
Fan leengued to bihalden VII
Dat di fader sine dochter naet onwillens ne gewe
Fan mondscipes lawa an der wedua
Fant mondschet der famna
Fan der pine des mondschets deert lasta nelle
Fant laen des mondschipes des moers fant kynd
Hweerom dat kind ne toer dat laen naet jaen
Fant laen des jongera broders diin jeldera als hi siin breid hala
Fan tzierckwegum ende fan hiara brede VIII
Van dio brede des weis om dat tzierckhou
Nen Fresa thoer grewa[3] ban tielda
Nen fresa thoer grewa ban tielda buta scelta wroginge
Fan dike to hodane bi sinte Benedictus.
Van sile to haldene tiaende bi sinte Benedictus.
Van Freesna wepen to halden
Van des grewa riucht
Van schelta ladinga IX
Efter sonnaschyn ne doer ma an stride staen
Dat da schelta bodting eer ond biginne
Van needmond ende hyara betteringha X
Van helgene ende hofguede toe delane XI
Van tinge om eerve to delane
Van eerfschip toe delane
Van forkapa land da frionden dat nier toe bisitten
3 Van graetheid dis forkapa | guedis XII
Hweer ma ketelfang duaen schil[4]
Hu ma ontingia schil fan dae kampa
Fan da stryd ende fan ayder igghe XIII

---

[1] FG: set. [2] FG: bikedrde. [3] FG: schelta. [4] FG: *schil* is missing.

Fan dio strydede XIIII
Fan landhera nier to witane
Fan riucht des fruchtbare vrouwes deer di man bygraven is XV
Fan enis overlandis daedes mannes gued[1]
Di fria Fresa is niaer toe witane off hy aefte tingh halden habbe
Fan schada ende urhlest
Fan mene tinghriucht to houwe.
Hu ma een man ferdloes deth XVI
Jef ma bi sonnaschiin naet ladet
Fan urhericheit dis hoves
Fan tinge ferst to da howe
Fan da lettera fersta
Hu ma da tiughe[2] al moge forwysa XVII
Fan dada tiughe[3] ut to riuchtane
Fan tinghe binna oers epenbere slaet
Fan tiufftigha gued toe sekan XVIII
Fan tiuftiga gued toe sekane
Fan bodeltingha toe dae huse
Fan bodel to bitinghien binna dae jeer XIX
Fan boedel riucht dine sibsta in dat huis to wisane
Fan lawede bodel XX
Dit is di bodeleed
Fan fordele in dae cladem onder aefta sidem eeffter des oderis dade
Fan bodel toe delane
Fan di deer[4] onwillich is toe delen XXI
Di schelta schil biaede him self to riuchta[5] anderde
Fan sonderinga fordela ende dis aesgha riuchtes
Fan da tweer koninghen Kaerl ende Radbod XXII
Hyr biginnet dae kerren deer Magnus kaes toe Roem XXIII
4 Hyr biginnet dae saunteen kesta |
Fan frede alle godeshusem XXV
Hyr bighinnet da fyouwer ende XX landriuchta XXXII
Als dio moder her kindes eerfschip forkaped XXXIII
Hyr bighinnet dae acht doemen XLI
Hyr bighinnet dae sex[6] wenden XLIII
Hyr bigint dat sindriucht[7] int ghemeen XLV

[1] FG: guedes mannes daed. [2] FG: tinghe. [3] FG: tinghe. [4] FG: dees. [5] FG: rtuchta. [6] FG: acht.
[7] FG: si*n*driuch|te.

Hyr bighinnet dae sindriuchta XLVII
Hyr biginnet da wilkerren dis landis mitta V delem LXI
Hyr[1] bighinnet da birecknada bota LXIIII
Hyr bighint keyser Rodulphus boeck LXXIII
Hyr bighinnet dae merkedriucht LXXXIIII
Hyr bighinnet dae swarta swenghen
Hyr bighinnet da scaeckraeff LXXXV
Hyr biginnet da wilkerren fan Opstallisbame LXXXVI
Hyr bighinnet da saun zelanden LXXXVIII

[1] FG: Hy.

Here begin the synodical laws—**fol. 47** (XI,39)
Here begin the statutes of the land with the five districts—**fol. 61** (XIII)
Here begin the calculated tariffs—**fol. 64** (XIV)
Here begins the book of Emperor Rudolf—**fol. 73** (XVI)
Here begins the market law—**fol. 84** (XVII)
Here begin the unmendable crimes (XVIII)
Here begins 'on forceful robberies'—**fol. 85** (XIX)
Here begin the statutes of Opstalsbam—**fol. 86** (XX)
Here begins (a treatise on) the seven sealands—**fol. 88** (XXI)

II. What Is Law?

5 **1.** Haet is riucht? List ende konst riuchtes ende goedes. Haet meent dat, riuchtes ende goedes? Riuchtes, dat meent riuchtlikera ende eerlikera tinga, alsoe bitiothet hit us di paeus. Haet bitiothet wird goedes? Netlikera ende eerlikera tinga, alsoe spreckt di keyser. Hoe manich riucht ister? Twa: een godlic ende een menslic. Dat aerste is di oenbern ende dat oeder scheltu lera. Dat een is natuerlic ende dat oeder is taulic.

2. Haet is Godlic riucht? Oenwerp Godis gastis deer dat gued luvet ende dat eerge leth by mannes wytem. Jeta beth sey mi haet Godes riucht se. Ewa, deer des mannes sin leert hym selff to biriuchten ende dat oenriucht to urfiuchten, dae onschield to helpane ende da onmyldicheed fordriwa.

3. Haet is menschelic riucht? Koninges setma ende lyoda pliga, deer netlic is ende eerlic. Koninges setma haet ma scrioun riucht ende alset riucht scrioun is, so haet met een ewa. Wer da ewa mei nen wilker dae ewa brecka. Taulic pliga fan langher wennicheed is alsoe gued so scrioun riucht, jeft se naet ne swiwet.

GLOSSA 1. *Sprect di keyser etc.* Concordat i. di. Humanum genus (DG ante D.1 c.1), ff. de iusti. et iu. l. i. in fi. (*Dig.* 1.1.1.4) cum lege sequenti.

GLOSSA 2. *Haet is mensclic riucht etc.* Insti. de iu. natu. gen. et ci. in prin. et § Scriptum et § Ex non scripto (*Inst.* 1.2. in pr., 3 and 9). Item lex est constitutio populi qua maiores natu aliquid cum plebe sanxerunt.[a] Constitutio uel edictum est quod tantum rex uel imperator constituit.[b] Ius commune siue constitutionem cessare facit necessitas, lxxxi di. Cum omnibus (D.81 c.27) et de re. iu. Quod non est licitum (X 5.41.4). Ius naturale quod in lege
6 moysaica uel in euangelio continetur ut iniusticiam nemini | inferre d.i. c.i. (DG ante D.1 c.1).

4. Hweerom is dat riucht seth? Dat ma fruchta da wreeck, binda den duriga fan da lust der sonda, bischyrme da onschield ende scheppe da wreecke.

GLOSSA 3. *Hweer um is dat riucht set.* Diuerse pene in canonibus sunt statute ad malitiam hominum peruersorum reprimendam, extra de of. iud. or. Ad reprimendam (X 1.31.8). Nam per leges nemo benefacere cogitur sed malefacere prohibetur, xxiii q.v Ad fidem (C.23 q.5 c.33).

---

a Cf. *Inst.* 1.2.4 and Isidore of Sevile († 636), Etymologies 5.11 and D.2 c.1.

b Cf. *Inst.* 1.2.8 and Isidore of Sevile, Etymologies 5.14 and D.2 c.4.

 | DOI:10.1163/9789004526419_006

II. What Is Law?

1. What is law? The craft and the knowledge of that which is fair and good. What does 'that which is fair and good' mean? 'That which is fair' means fair and honourable things, as the pope explains to us. What does the word 'good' mean? Useful and honourable things, the emperor tells us. How many types of law are there? Two: one is divine and the other is human. The former is innate and the latter has to be learnt. The former is natural and the latter is man-made.

2. What is divine law? An inspiration of the divine spirit in human minds, which loves good things and refrains from bad things. Tell me more about divine law. It is the law which helps the human mind to judge oneself and to defeat injustice, to aid the innocent and to drive out mercilessness.

3. What is human law? The rule of the king and the customs of the people, which are useful and honourable. The king's rule is called written law and if law is written down, it is called *ewa*. No chosen statute can go against *ewa*. Useful customs which have been upheld for a long time are as good as written law, as long as they do not contradict each other.

GLOSS 1. *Sprect di keyser etc.* (*the emperor tells etc.*). This is in conformity with DG ante D.1 c.1 and *Dig.* 1.1.1.4–5.

GLOSS 2. *Haet is mensclic riucht etc.* (*What is human law? etc.*) See *Inst.* 1.2. in pr., 3 and 9. A statute is an enactment of the people whereby those by nobler birth have established something together with the common people. An enactment or edict is that which only the king or the emperor decrees. The *ius commune* or an enactment is rendered inoperative by necessity, see D.81 c.27 and X 5.41.4. Natural law is what Mosaic Law or the Gospel teaches, i.e. that no injustice should be done to anyone, see DG ante D.1 c.1.

4. Why was the law established? So that people will fear its wrath, restrain villains from the desire to commit a sin, protect the innocent and create an instrument for vengeance.

GLOSS 3. *Hweer um is dat riucht set* (*Why was the law established?*). In the canons, various penalties are laid down in order to suppress the malice of villains, see X 1.31.8. After all, legal provisions do not compel anyone to do good, but prohibit doing wrong, see C.23 q.5 c.33.

5. Haet is der ewa riucht? Erlykera tinga reda, treftlykera tingh bieda, urbieda dat onriucht, hinzia moetlykera ting ende aec behwilen oenmoetlikera tingh truch fruchta des erra.[1] Hor so dat riucht is naturalis jefta taulic[2] ende ayder mit scrift jefta mit ewa schel met sceda. Soe haet ma dat een setma ende dat oer wenheed.

GLOSSA 4. *Haet is ewa etc.* Lex siue constitutio, ut patet in memoria supra allegata. Constitutio est ius humanum quod duplex est, aliud in scriptis redactum, quod proprie dicitur constitutio, aliud solo usu utentium approbatum, quod proprie consuetudo dicitur, idest, i.d. ca. Ius naturale (D.1 c.7). Quis potest constituere? Resp. Papa in spiritualibus, ut decretales etc., in secularibus Imperator unde et leges statuit. Ciuitas enim potest legem municipalem constituere. Causa constituendi leges est ut precepta iuris seruentur, ut honeste uiuere, alterum non ledere, ius suum unicuique tribuere, d.i c.i. (DG ante D.1 c.1), Inst. de iust. et iur. § iii (*Inst.* 1.1.3). Modus instituendi legem est ut lex talis sit quod contineat in se honestatem, quia lex debet esse honesta, iusta, possibilis secundam naturam et consuetudinem patrie, tempori et loco conueniens, necessaria, utilis et manifesta, ne aliquid propter obscuritatem contigat, ut potest colligi d.i. c. Consuetudo (D.1 c.5) et ff. de const. prin. l. In his rebus (*Dig.* 1.4.2) cum suis concordantibus.

GLOSSA 5. *Wrbieda dat onriucht* ff. de iust. et iu. l. Iustitia § i (*Dig.* 1.1.10.1) et melius ff. de leg. l. Leg. uirtus (*Dig.* 1.3.7).

6. Haet is wenheed? Een Godlic pliga deer ma to riucht haut. Als di setma brect
7 ende deer en ny sek uphliaept der naet fan scrioun is, so moet | ma dyn pliga
to riucht[3] halda. Fan disse wenheed jefta pliga habbet alleer koninghen mislic deeld. Di aerste spreckt aldus: dattet riucht schel altyd dyne pliga opnyma. Di ora sprect: ald pliga fan netliker wenheed is een kerstenlic maesterscyp. Di tredda sprect: aldeer dat riucht redelic is deer wyckt dy plyga, want thet riucht[4] deer en naemlic onriucht[5] urbioet dat schel nen pliga wyka. Di fiarda sprect: mislic is pliga; netlic pliga is kerstenlic maesterscyp, onredelic pliga wyecht dat riucht.[6] Di fyfte sprect: truch landis reed ende teerwa wyecht onder tydem dat riucht[7] dan pliga. Di sexta sprect: dat[8] riucht is al riucht, dy pliga is kerstenlic, deer era leert ende onera ursteert. Dat riucht is Godlic riucht[9] deer da sonda urdilighied mit heyliga boedem. Dat is riucht[10] wraudesc riucht, deer da eedlingen set habbet mitta elmeente, to halden truch landes reed. Di saunda sprecht:

[1] FG: era. [2] FG: taulic?. [3] FG: riuccht. [4] FG: riuct. [5] FG: onriuct. [6] FG: riuct. [7] FG: riuct. [8] FG: dat Dat. [9] FG: riuct. [10] FG: riucdt.

5. What is *ewa*? To advise honourable things, to order useful things, to forbid injustice, permit appropriate things and also sometimes inappropriate things out of fear for worse. A distinction should be made whether law is natural or man-made and whether it is written law or *ewa*. One is called codified law and the other customary law.

GLOSS 4. *Haet is ewa etc.* (*What is ewa? etc.*). This is a statute or enactment, as appears in the statement adduced above. An enactment is human law, which is twofold, i.e. sometimes set down in writing, which is termed enactment in the proper sense, and sometimes approved by the mere practice of those who use it, which is termed custom in the proper sense, see D.1 c.7. Who is competent to promulgate enactments? This is the answer: The pope in spiritual affairs, such as decretals, etc.: the emperor in secular affairs; and hence the latter has also enacted statutes. For, the citizens can enact municipal statutes. The reason for enacting statutes is so that legal precepts be observed, such as to live honestly, not to cause damage to another and to give everyone his due, see DG ante D.1 c.1 and *Inst.* 1.1.3. A statute should be enacted in such a way that the statute is intrinsically honourable because a statute should be honest, just, possible to perform, in accordance with nature and indigenous customs, appropriate in time and place, necessary, useful and clear so that it does not corrupt something by lack of clarity, as one can derive from D.1 c.5, *Dig.* 1.4.2 and similar provisions.

GLOSS 5. *Wrbieda dat onriucht* (*to forbid injustice*). See *Dig.* 1.1.10.1 and even better *Dig.* 1.3.7.

6. What is customary law? A custom which is in accordance with the divine law and which is considered law. If a statute is found wanting and a new case presents itself on which nothing has been written, then that which is customary should be regarded as law. In olden times, various kings have evaluated customary law in divergent ways. The first said that the law should always adopt custom. The second king said: an old custom which is useful can be considered on a par with Christian authority. The third said: if the law is fair then the custom should give way because a law which forbids blatant injustice should not give way to a custom. The fourth said: custom is diverse; a useful custom can be considered on a par with Christian authority, an unreasonable custom should give way to the law. The fifth said: because of the protection and requirements of the land, sometimes the law has to give way to custom. The sixth said: that law is just and that custom is Christian which teaches honour and destroys disgrace. Divine law is law which eradicates sins by means of holy commandments. Virtuous secular law is law which the nobles have decreed together with

dat riucht is alle riucht deer mey mena reed jefta bode wysera lioedena is set to twang dera sondan deer by willa ende by dumheed ophliaept, ty meena[1] frede ende to mena fere. Dat riucht[2] urwint alle pligan ende alle kerran. Dit riucht is alle riucht, deer toejenst da wird naet ne fiucht ende netlic is ende eerlick. Dat is falsc riucht,[3] deer da wird mit tyogem oenfiucht:[4] dat mei blynda[5] syande aegen.

GLOSSA 6. *Hat is wenheed iefte pliga*. Consuetudo. De hac uide extra de consuetu. per totum (X 1.4) et ff. de leg. l. Diuturna consuetudo (*Dig*. 1.3.33) et Inst. de iure natu. gen. et ci. § Ex non scripto[a] (*Inst*. 1.2.9). Etiam consuetudo dicitur optima legum interpres, extra de consue. cap. Cum dilectus (X 1.4.8). Sed ubi consuetudo repugnat iuri, non dicitur consuetudo sed quaedam corruptela uel abusio, extra e. c. ult. (X 1.4.11) de sy. c. Tua
8 (X 5.3.34). | Nota secundum Goffredum quod consuetudo inducitur, cum expresse populo placet aliquid obseruari in futurum pro consuetudine.[b] Vnde non eo ipso quod aliquid fit, ius consuetudinarium inducitur, arg. ff. de iti. actuque[c] priuato l. fi. (*Dig*. 43.19.7). Inducit enim unus actus consuetudinem, xxv q.ii Ita nos (C.25 q.2 c.25).

GLOSSA 7. *Als die setma breckt etc*. In his in quibus nil certi statuit, ecclesia uel diuina scriptura, mos populi Dei et instituta maiorum pro lege sunt tenenda, xi. d. In his rebus (D.11 c.7) et ca. Consuetudinis (D.11 c.4), xii d. ca. Diuturni (D.12 c.6). Item tria sunt necessaria ad hoc, ut consuetudo pro iure habeatur, scilicet diurnitas temporis et sanioris uel maioris partis autoritas, ac illius tamen ecclesie approbatio, in qua aboleuit xi. d. Catholica (D.11 c.8) et tunc alios non constringit.

GLOSSA 8. *Nen pligaa wyka etc*. Consuetudo habet enim proprietates tres. Imitatur enim legem, interpretatur legem et derogat legi. De hac materia uide Panormitanum in c. Clerici de iudi. extra. (X 2.1.8).[d] Quando uero canones cedunt legibus et econuerso, uide plenius Panormitanum in c.i. extra de no. op. nuncia. (X 5.32.1).[e] Et uide in x d. c.ii (D.10 c.2), quod leges imperiales debent cedere canonibus generaliter, econuerso uero quando canon precipit, ut ecclesia soluat tributum, xi. q.i. Si tributum (C.11 q.1 c.27), sed imperator dat legem, ut ecclesia libera sit a tributo.

---

[1] FG: meeua. [2] FG: riuckt. [3] FG: riuct. [4] FG: oe*n*fiuct. [5] FG: blynd.

---

a scripto *scripsimus cum Institutionibus*: scrcripto FG.
b Goffredus de Trano, Summa in titulos decretalium, X 1.4, n. 3.
c actuque *scripsimus cum Digesto Novo et J109*: actusque FG.
d Panormitanus (Nicolaus de Tudeschis), Commentaria, X 2.1.8, n. 4.
e Panormitanus (Nicolaus de Tudeschis), Commentaria, X 5.32.1, n. 7.

the community, to be upheld for the protection of the territory. The seventh said: law is fully just if it has been decreed with the consent of the community or ordered by wise men to stop sins which arise intentionally or out of stupidity in order to promote common peace and common benefit. Such law prevails over all customs and local statutes. Such law is fully just which does not fight against the truth and which is useful and honourable. Unjust law is law which violates the truth with the help of witnesses: such law can blind seeing eyes.

GLOSS 6. *Hat is wenheed iefte pliga* (*What is custom or usage?*). Custom. See on this the entire title X 1.4, *Dig.* 1.3.33 and *Inst.* 1.2.9. Custom is also said to be the best interpreter of legal provisions, see X 1.4.8. However, where custom is in contradiction with the law, it is not called custom, but some kind of corruption or abuse, see X 1.4.11 and X 5.3.34. Please note, that according to Goffredus a custom is established, when it clearly suits the people to observe something in the future as a custom. Therefore, a customary right is not established by the mere fact that something occurs. An argument can be found in *Dig.* 43.19.7, since one act may establish custom, see C.25 q.2 c.25.

GLOSS 7. *Als die setma breckt etc.* (*If a statute is found wanting, etc.*). In matters where nothing specific is laid down the Church or the divine scripture, the custom of God's people and the institutions of the ancestors, should be considered as the law, see D.11 c.7, D.11 c.4 and D.12 c.6. Three things are required for regarding custom as the law, namely a long duration, the authority of the sounder and greater part and, moreover, approval by the Church, if the custom nullifies something, see D.11 c.8. Otherwise it does not bind others.

GLOSS 8. *Nen pligaa wyka etc.* (*should not give way to a custom etc.*). For, custom has three qualities. Since it imitates the law, it interprets the law and it derogates from the law. See Panormitanus about this matter in his commentary on X 2.1.8. However, for cases where canon law provisions give way to Roman law provisions and conversely, see Panormitanus in his copious commentary on X 5.32.1. And see in D.10 c.2, that generally, imperial provisions have to give way to canon law provisions. It is the opposite, however, when canon law prescribes that the Church pays tax, see C.11 q.1 c.27, but the Emperor issues a statute, exempting the Church from tax.

GLOSSA 9. *Dy saunda mey mena reed etc.* Priuilegium paucorum non facit legem communem, xxv q.i. c. Ideo § ult. (C.25 q.1 c.16).

Hwae fand ende seth dat riucht alleraerst

7. Hwae fand ende sette riucht alleraerst? Foroneus in Kreka land, Mercurius in Egiptera land, Solon in Athenera land, Ligurius in Lacedemera land. Disse Ligurius nomet op bi enis afgoedis wirden bi Appollonius fiindenisse. Ende dae Kreken noment op fan Moyses fiif boekem deer hya scryoun heden fan da Joedem. Dy koninck heet Numa Pompilius deer da riucht sette alleraerst toe Roem, ende di fand aeck alleraerst dae taele oen der Latynscha tonga *unus, duo etcetera* hwant da Latynscha leyden eer stenen deer dyo tale mey biwared
9 was: hwite stenen to liaeflika | seckem ende swarte stenen toe leedlika seckem. Di Numa was di aersta koningh[1] efter Romulo deer aerst da burich toe Roem timmerade ende naemde. Deerom heet hi Numa, want hy waes di forma deer dyn penningh montya heet mit keyserlika forma. Deereefter worden alsoe manich riucht so deer riken weren. Hwant da koninghen settent to riucht deer him alderbest tuchte. So worden da riucht wandeled als dy koningh waes daed ont Romeran dat bycronghen, dat se da wrald to mena frede bytwongen. Doch ne muchtent da Romera heren ho wys ende ho wieldich dat se weren, sceppa dae riucht alsoe steed ende also fest, dat se dae koninghen naet wandelia dorsten, eer dat da koninghen[2] cristen worden ende dae riucht ney Goedes jefta schoepen.

GLOSSA 10. *Hwa fand ende set.* De hoc habetur vii. di. Moyses (D.7 c.1). Cum enim leges propter discordias plebeorum a nobilibus fere per xxx annos in dissuetudinem abissent, creati sunt x. uiri qui de grecis ciuitatibus leges collectas transtulerunt in latinum et eas in tabulas eburneas scriptas detulerunt, qui decemuiri sequenti anno, accepta potestate corrigendi et interpretandi leges, uidentes multa deesse tabulis, duas tabulas addiderunt et appellata sunt leges xii tabularum ff. de origine iuris l. ii per totum (*Dig.* 1.1.2). Quis primo constituit[a] ius, vii di. Moyses et c. sequenti. (D.7 c.1–2).

GLOSSA 11. *Foronius in kreka land etc.* Immo Romulus primo ⟨tradidit⟩[b] sed paucas et Foronius postea multas, vii di. c.ii super uerbo primus.[c] Nota. Ius consuetudinis statim cepit post legem naturalem ex quo homines

---

[1] FG: koniugh. [2] FG: koningden.

---

a constituit *scripsimus*: constitnit FG.

b Emendavimus ex Decreto Gratiani.

c The gloss *primus* ad D.7 c.1.; primus *scripsimus cum Decreto Gratiani*: primo FG.

GLOSS 9. *Dy saunda mey mena reed etc.* (*the seventh said ... with the consent of the community etc.*). The privilege of a few does not result in a general provision, see C.25 q.1 c.16.

Who Found and Laid Down Law for the First Time

7. Who found and laid down law for the first time? Phoroneus in Greece, Mercurius in Egypt, Solon in Athens, Ligurius in Lacedaemon. Ligurius obtained it through the words of an idol on the authority of Apollo. The Greeks obtained it from the Five Books of Moses, which they had copied from the Jewish people. The king who first decreed law in Rome was called Numa Pompilius and he also invented the first numbers in Latin: *unus, duo, et cetera*, because before that the Latin people piled up stones as a way of counting: white stones to count positive things and black stones to count negative things. Numa was the first king after Romulus who built the citadel in Rome and who gave it its name. He is called Numa because he was the first to have coins struck showing the Emperor's bust. After that as many laws arose as there were empires. For the kings decreed law as they deemed best. In this way, laws changed after the demise of a king until the Romans imposed a common peace on the whole world. No matter how wise and powerful the Roman rulers were, however, they were unable to create law which was so constant and strong that the kings did not dare to change it. This only happened after the kings had become Christian and created law in line with God's gift.

GLOSS 10. *Hwa fand ende set.* (*Who found and laid down?*). This subject is discussed in D.7 c.1. After approximately thirty years the statutes had become obsolete due to the discord between plebeians and nobles. Ten men were appointed to translate into Latin, statutes collected from Greek cities and presented these, written on ivory tables. The next year the same *decemviri* (ten men), after having obtained the authority to correct and interpret the statutes, added two tables, when they saw that many things were lacking in the tables. And they were called the statutes of the Twelve Tables; see the entire text of *Dig.* 1.1.2. For the one who for the first time established law see D.7 c.1–2.

GLOSS 11. *Foronius in kreka land etc.* (*Phoroneus in Greece etc.*). Indeed Romulus issued statutes for the first time, but not many. Later Phoroneus issued many, see the gloss *primus* to D.7 c.1. Note. Customary law emerged right after men started to live together on the basis of the natural law. Statutory

ceperunt simul habitare. Ius uero constitutionis cepit a Moyse qui primus omnium diuinas leges sacris litteris explicauit, uidelicet Foronius grecis ut
10 in textu continetur. |

Hwa bande den aersta ferdban

8. Hwa bande dine aersta ferdban oen da wrald? Octavianus di keyser. Da Romera heren al da wrald fan aesta to westa, fan noerda to suda ende alle da eylanden bi heves muda mit heerschielde bitwonghen heden ende Octavianus dine lesta ferdban fan Pardland brochte, da hy mit goldena waynen to Roem in foer ende by da waynem trowaden koninghen, spand mit goldena keden. Da heet hy to handes Janes porta sluta. Dat was tredda stond fan saunhundert ende XXII jeren soer dat Roem bigonde to biclywen. Dis bagaden dae van Roem dat deer dis deys mitta koninghe[1] mara kostelicheit ende syrheed coem dan se eer aller havena heden. Da scopen se da koninghe enen nyen nama. Eer heet hy Octavianus, dae heten se him Augustus. Dis deys schyden twa wonder grate teyken to Roem. Hya saeghen oen da hymel fan da moern alont middey tria sonna schinen. Deerom ghingh een reynboga also lyacht als di logha, ende garen se toe lesta. Aeck ontsprungh dis deys to Roem een burna fan olya ut een hoerna huus ende flaet ut in dine Tiber mit fulla straeme, een etmal alomme. Dae dat folck toe stede coem, da spreeck di koningh mit hleste: "Nu is al dyo wrald truch Romes drede wiges bilowid ende toe mena freda commen. Nu wille ick dyne ferd mit duegheden sterkia ende fan treftelika tinghen twa nye riucht[2] setta, deer da durige were ende dine eerma bischirma, ho dattet land mit riuchte stande ende den freed nimmen oenfiuchte. Dit is dat aersta deer ick biede: dat alle dyo tiade deer hyoda aen ellende se, to hyara ayn land weder kere, fri
11 fan alla mannem ende jow tins dae Roemera heran, boeghia mit hyara | frionden ende wise hiara ayn eerwe ende fee op hiara ayn. Dat oer is dat ick banne wiwem ende mannem frede an lyf, frede an gued, dat mannick mitta sinem bisitte soe langhe so hyt onfoerwrocht ne habbe." Dat was di aerste ferdban deer disse wrald enich wan. Fan oenbighin ont hyoda so ne schyd hit na dat onder een[3] man alle dyo wrald coeme to mena ferdbanne. Hit timade aeck wel dat di eerdscha koningh dine ferd bande, dae di himelscha koningh was commen to mannem. Hwant hit was di selva dey deer Cristus in der cribba lay: dat was een scheen dey toe Roem, alsoe scheen was dyoe nacht in Jherusalemra land, dae[4] di enghel coem toe dae herderem ende kette frede alla gueda willigha lyoedem: *Gloria in excelsis Deo*.

[1]FG: kon*in*gde. [2]FG: riueht. [3]FG: eeu. [4]FG: dat.

law emerged, however, with Moses who was the first of all to promulgate the divine laws in the sacred Scriptures, and for example Phoroneus for the Greek, as is stated in the text.

Who Ordered the First Peace

8. Who ordered the first peace in the world? Emperor Octavian. When the Roman rulers had conquered the entire world from east to west and from north to south and all islands along the coasts with their armies and Octavian brought home his last victory from Parthia, he rode into Rome on golden chariots whilst kings walked to the sides of those chariots, fettered in golden chains. He then ordered the gate of Janus to be closed immediately. This was the third time in seven hundred and twenty-two years since Rome had begun to rise. The Romans prided themselves on the fact that on this day, together with their king, more valuables and jewellery entered Rome than they had ever possessed together before. They gave their king a new name then. Before, he was called Octavian, but after that they called him Augustus. That day two great omens happened in Rome. Three suns could be seen in the sky from morning till noon. Around them was a rainbow as bright as a burning fire and in the end they merged into one. Also on this same day in Rome, a fountain of oil welled up from a brothel and flowed into the river Tiber with a strong current for a day and a night. When the people came to that place, they all listened while the king spoke: 'Now the whole world has been freed from war out of fear for Rome and a common peace has been attained. Now I want to make this peace stronger by solidifying certain virtues and create two new laws from useful things, which will punish inconsiderate people and protect the poor, so that the land will be held upright by law and no-one will compromise the peace. This is my first order: that everyone who is abroad today shall return to their native country completely free from any bonds and pay tithes to Rome, live together with their relatives and point out their own homes and cattle on their own estates. My second order is peace to all men and women, both to their bodies and to their properties, so that each has possession of his own property as long as he has not forfeited it.' This was the first peace that anyone had ever proclaimed in this world. Since the beginning of time up until that day, it had never occurred that the whole world was brought under the peace of one man. It was fitting that a worldly king proclaimed peace to the world at the same time that the heavenly king had come to mankind. For that very same day Christ lay in his crib: just as beautiful as the day was in Rome, so was the night in Jerusalem when the angel came to the shepherds and proclaimed peace to all people of good will: *Gloria in excelsis Deo*.

Hwa scryou riucht alleraerst

9. Hwa screef dae riucht alleraerst? Pomponius di grewa, di bygonde se toe scryuwen. Dae woex him soe graet nyd dat hyt leet bliuwa. Julius ende Octavianus heden se bigonnen, dae worden hya mitta gaelika daed byronnen. Deerney dae dyoe cristenheed oenstoed, dae worden dae riucht steed ende gued, dae God syn folck dae nede joe. Theodosius heet di hera deer se alleraerst screef ende dae herde wel folbrochte, deer na wralda neen keyser mochte fan[1] alle dae deer bifarra him weren fan M ende C ende XXXIII jera soer Numa ende Romulus storen, deer da riucht mit Romerem alleraerst ophoven. Deerefter ward een wys keyser to Roem. Justinianus was syn nama, deer dae riucht alleraerst enigad aldeer se entwa spreken.

GLOSSA 12. *Justinianus was*. C. de no. co. com. (Constitutio *Haec*) in prin. et
12 per totum et de emen. Iustiniani co. (Constitutio *Cordi*) in prin. |

Ende kirte se aldeer se[2] toe manichfald weren. Deerom sit hi jeta to Roem, melad op een goldena troen, een boec aen synre hand deer dae riucht oen standet. Op dat paellaes meled, deer mey met jeta schoya aldus: "Da se Justinianum toe keyser setten dat was al dyoe wrald nette, want hi al onse riucht gette ende myt grata frewelheed[3] kirte."

Hwae dae wilkeren alderaerst sette

10. Hwae sette dae wilkeren alleraerst? Justinianus di keyser. Disse Justinianus saegh oen manychfalda landa mislika derwa. Dae joe hi oerlef dat aller landick truch syn sonderinga bihoef wilkerren kerre ende toe riucht hilde ende dat se se naet toejenst den lawa ne sette ner tojenst Goedes hulde. Dat selve fynt ma in syne boeke aldus: 'Landes deerwa deer eerlyck sint ende myt meene frede prowet, dae bied ick to halden alse dat riucht.'[4] Disse Justinianus waes dy tria ende fiiftichsta keyser fan Octavianus deer dae wrald mitta aersta ferdban gette. Een tusent ende twa hundert ende LXXVII jera fan Numa deer dae riucht aerst sette. Fiif hundert ende LXXVII jera eefter Cristus berthe. Hy was hundert ende XXXVII jera eefter Theodosius deer dae riucht aerst screef. Twa hundert ende XXVII eer Kaerl, deer da Fresen den fridoem joe. Manich man deer wys haet weent, dat Kaerl da riucht habbe seth. Fresen haet hy se bihulpen dat se riuchtes pligia moeten deer eer sonder era weren onder alla manna foetem.

---

[1] FG: *fan* is missing. [2] FG: aldeers. [3] FG: frewelhheed. [4] FG: riudht.

Who Wrote the First Laws

9. Who wrote the first laws? Count Pomponius began to put them to paper. But then he became so angry that he let the matter rest. Julius and Octavian had begun to write them but they were struck by untimely deaths. When the Christian faith blossomed and God gave mercy to his people, the laws became strong and good. Theodosius was the name of the emperor who first put them to paper and he did this very well: no emperor in the world before him would have been able to do this during the 1133 years that had passed since the demises of Romulus and Numa, who had begun to lay down law for the Romans. After Theodosius, a wise emperor sat on the throne in Rome. He was called Justinian and for the first time, he unified the laws when they contradicted each other.

GLOSS 12. *Justinianus was* (*was … Justinian*). See the constitution *Haec* at the beginning and in its entirety and the constitution *Cordi* at the beginning.

And he shortened them whenever they were redundant. For this he can still be found in Rome, painted on a golden throne, holding a book in his hand in which the law is written. This can still be seen today, painted on the palace: 'When the people chose Justinian as their emperor, this was beneficent to the entire world because he unified all of our law and shortened them with great energy.'

Who Enacted the First Statutes

10. Who enacted the first statutes? Emperor Justinian. Justinian saw a variety of needs in the various countries of the empire. He then gave permission to all countries to come up with statutes which would meet their particular needs and to take them on as law, provided these statutes would not go against the faith or against God's worship. This can also be found in his books: 'The needs of a country which are honourable and in concordance with the common peace I command to be accepted as law.' Justinian was the fifty-third emperor since Octavian, who had enriched the world with the first peace. One thousand, two hundred and 77 years since Numa who first decreed law. Five hundred and 77 years since the birth of Christ. He lived one hundred and 37 years after Theodosius who wrote down the first laws. Two hundred and 27 years before Charlemagne, who gave the Frisians their freedom. Many a man who is thought to be wise thinks that Charlemagne laid down the laws. He helped the Frisians—who previously were without honour and beneath the feet of all men—to uphold their law.

GLOSSA 13. *Manich man deer wys haet et cetera* Qualiter Frisones uenerunt
ad libertatem de isto magno Karulo et patre eius in translatione regni
Grecorum in Germanos siue Allemanos, nota extra electione c. Venera-
13 bilem (X 1.6.34), ubi notatur in glosa super uerbo transtulit:[a] | "Et legi-
tur in cronicis, quod cum romana ecclesia opprimeretur ab Astulfo rege
Lombardorum petiit auxilium a Constantino et Leone simul eius impe-
ratoribus[b] Constantinopolis et cum nollent patrocinari romane ecclesie,
que petebat eorum auxilium, Stephanus papa secundus natione romanus
transtulit imperium ad Karolum, qui fuit filius Pippini, quem Zacharias
predecessor eius substituerat Lodowico regi Francorum, quem deposue-
rat, de quo legitur xv q. vi Alius (C.15 q.6 c.3). Et translatio illa facta est
anno Domini septingentesimo[c] lxxvi. Qui Karolus coronatus est a Leone
papa tercio, elapsis post hoc xv annis."

Hoe sinte Willibrord dae Fresen bikeerde

11. Dae sinte Wiilbrord dat land bikeerde,
Fresen hy dat leerde,
dat se capeden myt guede
dat se dy koningh Kaerl noem in synre huede,
hoe se da Nordman ontcoeme.
Deerom flegen hia to da herem fan Roeme.
Deereefter deer se dae heerferd byswoeren
ende mit him toe Roem foren
ende dae burich tostoerden,
dae weren hya des koninghes heranaeten worden.
Da se da burich wonnen, dae weren se burchheren toe Roem.
Dae camen se mit riuchta ordel toe fridome.
Want hit een ald riucht was
dat dy man fri was in alle landem deer to Roem burgher was.
Dat en man onder da galga stoed
ende coemet[1] him to moede
dat hi op da Roemscha burgherschip teghe
ende hyt aller wirdic leghe,
hi moste wessa ontbonden

[1] FG: coemct.

a The gloss *transtulit* ad X 1.6.34.

b imperatoribus *scripsimus cum Glossa Ordinaria*: imperatoribns FG.

c septingentesimo *scripsimus cum Glossa Ordinaria*: septengesio FG.

GLOSS 13. *Manich man deer wys haet et cetera* (*Many a man who is thought to be wise et cetera*). For how the Frisians were liberated from this Charlemagne and his father, when the kingdom of the Greek was transferred to the Germanics or Germans, see X 1.6.34, where the gloss *transtulit* states: "And one reads in the chronicles that when the Roman Church was oppressed by Astulfus, king of the Lombards, he asked Constantine and Leo, concurrently Byzantine emperors, for help. And because they did not want to protect the Roman Church, which was asking for their help, Pope Stephen II, a Roman by birth, transferred the empire to Charles, who was a son of Pepin, whom his predecessor Zachary had put in the place of Louis, king of the Franks, whom he had deposed, about which you can read in C.15 q.6 c.3. And this transfer took place in the year of our Lord 776. When 25 years had subsequently elapsed, the same Charles was crowned by Pope Leo III".

How Saint Willibrord Converted the Frisians

11. When Saint Willibrord converted the land he taught the Frisians to buy the protection of Charlemagne with valuables in order to escape from the Northmen. Therefore, they fled to the Roman rulers. After that, when they had sworn to take up their weapons for him and had travelled with him to Rome and had destroyed the citadel for him, they had become the king's vassals. When they had taken the citadel, they became lords of the citadel in Rome. According to a just judgment, they then were pronounced free. For it was an old rule of law that if a man was a Roman citizen, he was considered a freeman in all countries. When a man stood underneath the gallows and he suddenly remembered that he could invoke Roman citizenship, even though he lied, he should be set free until the truth of the matter had been ascertained in Rome. By God's will,

alont hit toe Roem worde onderfonden.
Aeck joe hy him dat truch God
dat hya mosten halda Justinianus[1] bod
ende hetet eer se van him schate, dat se al hiara landis therwa bytochte ende hyt himmen habba lethe ende se dat ymmermeer toe riuchte hilde.[2] Ende
14 hi sine ban deeroen leide ho se deereefter neen koningh ofnete. |

GLOSSA 14. *Fri was deer to roem* Inst. de nup. in prin. (*Inst.* 1.10.pr), Inst. de liberti. in fi., ibi in ciuitate romana decorauimus glossa,[a] id est libertate, supra eodem titulo § Libertinorum (*Inst.* 1.5.3); ad idem de sen. ex. c. Si iudex laycus li. vi. (VI 5.11.12), id est si in iudicio esset sententialiter iudicatum an esset liber uel seruus, quia aliter iudicabitur liber secundum leges et aliter seruus; et innocens dimittitur et reus nocens furto condempnatus, uinculatur et suspenditur, ff. de pe. l. Capitalium § Famosos et § Grassatores[b] (*Dig.* 48.19.28.15 et 10) et in constitutione Fridrici imperatoris de pace tenenda c. Si duo homines § Si quis quinque solidos id est aureos (*LF* 2.27.18). Non caret scrupulo societatis occulte, qui manifesto facinori desinit obuiare, lxxxiii d.c. Error (D.83 c.3), extra de homi. c. Sicut dignum (X 5.12.6) cum suis concordantibus.

Hwana caem riucht alleraerst

12. Nu haestu my seid, hwa riucht aerst sette to Rome.
Ende ic wil wita hwana dattet riucht alleraerst coem.
Dat was VIII hundert jeer
ende aeck fiif jeer meer
eer Romulus ende Numa oen da wrald comen,
deer da burich timmeraden ende riucht setten to roem,
da God Moyses twa tafela jo
derer tyen wird mey syn fingher oen screef.
Ende dae wirden spreeck hi aec also hluud
dattet heerden al dae Israhelscha lyoed
ende dae hwile deer hi se spreeck,
dat weet ick dat di himel ontbreeck
mit tonghere ende mit blixen
ende mit[3] so freeslika bere datter neen sonna schynd

---

[1] FG: iusti*n*anus. [2] FG: hildde. [3] FG: mlt.

---

a The gloss *ciuitate romana* ad *Inst.* 1.5.3.
b Grassatores *scripsimus cum Digesto Novo*: Crassatores FG.

Charlemagne also granted them to uphold Justinian's rule and before they took their leave he ordered them to record all the special needs of their land and he allowed them to indefinitely observe these as their law. And he issued a prohibition that no king after him should deprive them of these rights.

GLOSS 14. *Fri was deer to roem* (*free was who in Rome*). See *Inst.* 1.10.pr and *Inst.* 1.5.3, particularly the gloss *ciuitate romana* to *Inst.* 1.5.3 "we have honoured with citizenship", that is, with liberty, see *Inst.* 1.5.3; VI 5.11.12 deals with the same issue, that is to say when in a verdict it is decided as final sentence whether someone is free or slave, because sometimes one is deemed free according to the provisions of Roman law and sometimes slave; and the innocent is dismissed and the defendant, guilty of theft and sentenced, is chained and hanged, see *Dig.* 48.19.28.15, *Dig.* 48.19.28.10 and *LF* 2.27.18. Whosoever abstains from preventing a manifest crime, does not escape suspicion of partaking in a clandestine conspiracy, see D.83 c.3, X 5.12.6 and similar provisions.

Whence the Law First Came

12. Now that you have told me who first laid down law in Rome, I would like to know whence law first came. It was 800 years and five more before Romulus and Numa who built the citadel and laid down law in Rome came to this world, that God gave Moses two tables on which he wrote Ten Commandments with his finger. He also spoke these words so loud that the whole people of Israel could hear them and I know that while he said them the heavens burst open with thunder and lightning and with such terrifying noise that no sunlight could be seen for the fire that blazed down from the sky. They also heard

oers dan dat fyoer deer fan da himel ran.
Ende aeck heerden se also hera hoerna hluud.
Ende dat folc was eer truch da eewa teyn ut.
Da worden se so seer foerfeerd fan da gryslika bere
datter nimmen libba dorste eer
Moyses van da birgh caem aef
ende tfolck traest ghaef.
Di birgh deer moyses op stoed,
di barnde aen liachter gloed
dat dy logha oen den himel rachte
alle da XL nachte
deer God mit Moyse uppa bogade
ende hem alle riuchte leerde ende wegade. |

Van da tiaen wird

13. Dit sint dae tyaen wird.

Israhel, dyn God is een weer God. Him scheltu tienia ende syn era mit nene fraemde godem menzia.
Israhel, dyn God scheltu neen byld makia fan alle da creatura deer bi da himel fliucht jefta op der eerde swerft ende in da wettere swomt, want ick mine ontanck wreck al ti da fyarda ende myne tanck laenie al toe da tyenda.
Israhel, dyn Godes naema scheltu naet forswerra ner to nen ydelnisse optyaen sonder need.
Israhel, dis sonnendeis fira scheltu naet foerjetta.

Disse fyower boeden weren in eenre taefla ende disse sex deer[1] hyrney folgiet weren in een ander taefla.

Israhel, era dyn fader ende dyn moder hoe du lange libbe op der eerda.
Hoed di van hoerdom.
Hoed di van manslachta.
Hoed di fan tyefta.
Hoed di fan falsch tiuch.
Hoed di van onnetter bijeringe alle der tingena deer dyn[2] nesta aegh mit mara riucht dan du.

---

[1] FG: *deer* is missing. [2] FG: dyu.

war horns sounding. Because of this covenant the people had gathered outdoors. But then they grew so anxious from the terrible pandemonium that no-one dared breathe until Moses came down the mountain and comforted the people. During the 40 nights that God stayed there with Moses and taught him all laws and aided him, the mountain on which Moses stood burnt so bright that the flames reached the sky.

On the Ten Commandments

13. These are the Ten Commandments.

Israel, your God is a true God. Him you shall serve and you shall not mingle your devotion to him with that for other gods.
Israel, you shall not make an image of your God out of any of the creatures who fly in the sky or wander on the earth or swim in the water, for I take revenge for my wrath until the fourth generation and reward my gratitude until the tenth generation.
Israel, you shall not commit perjury in the name of your God nor use his name idly without there being a necessity.
Israel, you shall not forget to hallow the Sunday.

These four commandments were written on one table and the six which come after this were on another table.

Israel, honour your father and your mother so that you may live long on this earth.
Refrain from adultery.
Refrain from homicide.
Refrain from theft.
Do not commit a false testimony.
Refrain from unrightfully desiring the things your neighbour has with more rights than you.

Bi disse x wirdem schoep Moyses Goedes riucht ende menslick riucht ende syn fyf boeka ende deereefter alle da propheten ende apostolen ende al hiara buecka. Ende al haet so dyo wrald scriftes haet ende riuchtes deer netlic ende eerlic is, dat bighint ende eyndiget in disse tien wirdem.

14. Hwa sette aller[1] aerst godlyck riucht ende menslyck riucht? *Deus*, God, da hi screef ayder riucht an syner tafela, da jo hi se Moisi bede. Derom schil di prester wessa een fogid der wird to tiuge ende to ede.

[1] FG: allet.

With these ten words Moses created divine law and human law and his five books. After him came all the prophets and apostles and all their books. And all writings and laws existing in the world which are useful and honourable begin and end with these ten words.

14. Who first laid down divine law and human law? *Deus*, God, when he wrote each law on his tables and gave them both to Moses. Because of this, the priest shall be a guardian of the truth at testimonies and at oath-takings.

III. The Older Skelta Law

Van dis grewa incomst

1. Dit is landriucht der Freesna. Di grewa deer an Freslande grewa wessa schel, dy schel wessa fulre bertha boren ende syn riucht onforloren. Hi schil to Sudermuda incomma ende comma to Franeker in dat Del mit wirder were, | mit des
16 koninghes jefta ende myt breve ende myt insigel. Deer agen him da Fresen to ontfaen ende to riucht to staen. Deer aegh him di aesga een ferd to delen ende hi him self to bannen, dat him nimmen aet onriuchtes dwe. Soe aghen dae lyoed dyne ferd toe sterkiane. Deer aegh dy grewa aller manlikum syn leen toe gewane als hiit oen synre wer hede, sonder fya.

GLOSSA 15. *Ende siin riucht onforloren etc.* Item iudex non debet esse excommunicatus, nec hereticus, de hereticis per totum (X 5.7); nec proscriptus id est *ferdloos*, etc.

GLOSSA 16. *Mit des koninghes iefta* Nota comitem esse iudicem delegatum. Et si dicis eum ordinarium, requirit tamen regalem confirmationem. Nec ante suam confirmacionem potest alios confirmare.

GLOSSA 17. *Deer aegh hi di aesga.* Minor iudex dat pacem superiori, id est permittit eum uti sua iurisdictione per partes Frisie, uisis litteris regalibus et sic inferior examinat et sic est suus superior.

GLOSSA 18. *Fia* id est pecunia, quia pecunia dicitur a pecude, i q. iii Totum (C.1 q.3 c.6) in glossa;[a] et ibi distinctionem glossa notat.

Van friheed der Freesna

2. Dit is riucht, dat dy frya Fresa oen nen heerferd thoer fora fara, dan mitta ebba ut ende mitta floed op, truch dae need dat hy dyne owera biwarria schil alle daghen tojenst diin salta se ende toejenst dyn wylda Wysingh mit vyf wepen: myt spada ende mit furka, myt schield ende myt swird ende myt etkeris oerd, by eenre lyoedwirden, jeftit hem keth wirt mit boeda jefta bakene jefta sexasum onzwara dattet hym naet keth were hor myt boda ner myt bakene.

a The gloss *pecunia* ad C.1 q.3 c.6.

III. The Older Skelta Law

Concerning the Entry of the Count

1. This is the land law of the Frisians. The count who is to hold office in Frisia must be of legitimate birth and not have forfeited his rights. He shall land at Sudermuda and then travel to Franeker at the location called the Del, fully authorised by the King's appointment and by a sealed charter. There, the Frisians shall welcome him and allow him to hold court. There also, the *asega* has to proclaim a peace and the count has to proclaim a peace over himself, so that no man does anything unlawful to him. Then the people have to confirm this peace. There also, the count shall grant every man his fief, just as they already possessed it, without having to pay a fee for this.

GLOSS 15. *Ende siin riucht onforloren etc.* (*and not have forfeited his right etc.*). Similarly, a judge may not have been excommunicated, nor be a heretic, see the entire title X 5.7; nor outlawed, that is, *ferdloos*, etc.

GLOSS 16. *Mit des koninghes iefta* (*by the King's appointment*). Note that the Count is a delegated judge. And were you to state he is an ordinary judge, he still needs Royal confirmation. And before his confirmation, he cannot confirm others.

GLOSS 17. *Deer aegh hi di aesga* (*there also the asega has to*). The inferior judge 'grants peace' to the superior one, that is, he allows him to exercise his jurisdiction in the regions of Frisia after having inspected his Royal credentials. And in this way the inferior judge is the one who performs the examination and in this way he is his superior.

GLOSS 18. *Fia* (*a fee*). that is money, because the word *pecunia* (money) derives from *pecus* (cattle), see the gloss *pecunia* to C.1 q.3 c.6; and there, this gloss notes a distinction.

Concerning the Freedom of the Frisians

2. This is the law, that a free Frisian is not obliged to take part in a military expedition which would take longer than leaving at low tide and returning at high tide because of the necessity for a Frisian to guard the coast, day in, day out, against the salt sea and against the wild Vikings, with five weapons: with spade and with fork, with shield and with sword and with spear. This he shall do on pain of a small wergild, whenever notice was given by a messenger or by means of a beacon, or he may exonerate himself with five compurgators that no notice was given, either by means of a messenger or a beacon.

GLOSSA 19. *Heerferd thoer et cetera* Causa huius priuilegii eciam recitatur infra *inda fiifta ker* et infra *inda tyaenda kest*.

17 GLOSSA 20. *Lyoedwirden et cetera* | Hoc est secundum penam limitatam et taxatam a Frisonibus, et est summa octo librarum seu talentatum.

Elck Fresa aegh syn selvis deda toe wytan bet dan ma[1] op hem brengha mey

3. Dit is riucht, dat di fria Fresa syn selvis deda aegh to wytan op dae helgum myt mara riucht dan him ymmen aegh toe urtyoghane, hit ne se dat hi soe fiir bitinget se mit scelta banne ende mit aesegha doeme dat dae nyoghen tyoegh synes aynes eed binyme.

GLOSSA 21. *Seluis deda etc.* Quia nemini factum proprium licet ignorare. C. de rei uendi. l. Si quis (*Cod.* 3.32.11 in pr.).

GLOSSA 22. *Op da helghum etc.* Iurant homines per maiorem suum, ad hebreos vi,[a] extra de iureiur. Et si Cristus (X 2.24.26).

GLOSSA 23. *Scelta* id est iudex ex parte comitis.

GLOSSA 24. *Aesgha* id est iudex terre ex parte potestatis.

Fan grete des dikes ende weys

4. Dit is riucht dat di fria Fresa wyta moet mit hwelker meta dikes ende weyes hy lida moeghe myt mara riucht dan him di grewa deer toe banne dat hy dat wirtse[2] deer hy naet moege.

GLOSSA 25. *Hwelker meta etc.* Nota. Credendum est cuilibet in oneribus predialibus que iura dicuntur quantum ualeat supportare, ff. de cen. l. Forma (*Dig.* 50.15.4.pr), ne dicat "me grauat ille labor sub cuius pondere labor id est cado", quia impossibilium nulla est obligatio, de reg. iur. li. vi. Nemo ad impossibile (VI *de regulis iuris, regula* 6).

---

[1] FG: denma. [2] FG: witse.

---

a Ad Hebraeos 6.16.

GLOSS 19. *Heerferd thoer et cetera* (*obliged military expedition, etc.*) The reason for this privilege is also mentioned below under *inda fiifta ker*[1] and *inda tyaenda kest.*[2]

GLOSS 20. *Lyoedwirden et cetera* (*a small wergild, etc.*). This is in conformity with the fine as fixed and assessed by the Frisians and it is the sum of eight pounds or talents.

Every Frisian Has More Right to Testify to His Own Acts Than Any Man's Testimony Against Him

3. This is the law, that a free Frisian has more right in establishing the facts of his own acts by means of an oath on the holy relics against any man's testimony, unless he has been prosecuted, by order of the *skelta* and decree of the *asega*, to such an extent that the ninefold testimony invalidates his own oath.

GLOSS 21. *Seluis deda etc.* (*his own acts etc.*). Since no-one is allowed to ignore his own act, see *Cod.* 3.32.11 in pr.

GLOSS 22. *Op da helghum etc.* (*on the holy relics etc.*). People swear allegiance to a higher authority, see the Epistle to the Hebrews chapter 6 and X 2.24.26.

GLOSS 23. *Scelta* (*skelta*). i.e. the judge on behalf of the Count.

GLOSS 24. *Aesgha* (*asega*). i.e. the judge of the territory on behalf of the authorities.

Concerning the Dimensions of Dykes and Roads

4. This is the law, that a free Frisian has more right to declare under oath for the maintenance of which part of the dyke and road he is responsible than the count is entitled to command him to perform more than he is able to.

GLOSS 25. *Hwelker meta etc.* (*which part etc.*). Note that regarding predial obligations, termed as '*iura*', we should have trust in anyone's statement as to what extent he can contribute, see *Dig.* 50.15.4, so that he cannot say "I cannot sustain this burden, under which weight I succumb, i.e. I collapse", since an obligation to perform something impossible is null and void, see VI *de regulis iuris, regula* 6.

1 See text V,5.

2 See text VI,10.

Fan helgene guede naet toe litickiane

5. Dit is riucht, dat dy fria Fresa dat wyta moet oen da hemmerick deer hy oen eerwed is ende ayn aen synre wer haet, hweer se dis santis ende dis koninges eerwe, dat hy dat wise ende naet ne litikie.

GLOSSA 26. *Dis santis* Id est episcopi uel ecclesie. Vbi enim predia publica et priuata simul sunt sita et contigua, tunc priuatorum est demonstrare, quia circa illa magis sunt solliciti.

Fan leengued toe bihaldene

18 6. Dit is riucht: hweer soe dy frya Fresa een onderhava lawiget wirdet dat hy dat winna[1] scil enen pennige, aldeer hyt mit kape wint by[2] tween penningen. Jeft him dy foget deerum sanna wil, dat hy oen onwonna land sitta, so is hy nyer mit syne saun orkenen to jechtane dine foget ende da allerlyc scellet sidza mit sonderlinga ede. Jeft him[3] dis brect, di foget due deermede syne willa.

GLOSSA 27. *Onder haua* id est bona feudalia.

GLOSSA 28. *Foget* id est procurator regis uel domini feudi.

Dat di faeder syne dochter[4] naet onwillens ne gewe

7. Dit is riucht dat di fader aech syn dochter nen man to jaen ur hern willa um dat hyo naet waldes aech oers dan her ledena. Ende jeft hy se jout ur her willa ende her on da oenwilla misscy, so aech hyt to betane dyne ferd als jeft hy se mit synre hand[5] urslayn hede.

GLOSSA 29. *Ur herne willa* De potentia patris et matris in filia. Item matrimonia debent esse libera, extra de sponsa. et matrimo. capi. Requisiuit et ca. Cum locum (X 4.1.17 et 14), quia inuite nuptie difficiles exitus solent habere, ut dicto capitulo Requisiuit (X 4.1.17); et uide glosam in capitulo primo de spon. inpube. (X 4.2.1)[a] et doctores ibidem.

Fan mondscypes lawa ander wedua

8. Dit is riucht, datter nimmen aech dyne mondscet oen der wedue dan her soen, so fyr als hi jerich se, jefta dy selva deer dan da aeftingha aech. Lywet ny dy soen, soe aegh hy dan des mondes[6] fyower penninghen min dan twa merck.

[1] FG: winua. [2] FG: hy. [3] FG: hi. [4] FG: docher. [5] FG: haud. [6] FG: monnadeys.

a The gloss *consentit* ad X 4.2.1.

On Not Diminishing the Goods of the Church

5. This is the law, that in the village district in which he inherited property and possesses property, a free Frisian has the obligation to declare by an oath on the holy relics where the land of the church and the land of the king are located: he must point it out and not declare it to be smaller than it actually is.

GLOSS 26. *Dis santis* (*of the Church*). i.e. of the Bishop or the Church, because where public and private tenements are adjacent and contiguous, the private tenements should be clearly identified, since people are more concerned about such.

On Retaining a Fief

6. This is the law: whenever a fief is bequeathed to a free Frisian, he has the right to obtain it at half the rate that would be owed if it were bought. If the representative of the count wants to accuse him that he is occupying land not rightly obtained, he can defend himself with his seven witnesses, and each of these shall testify with a separate oath. If he is unable to procure these testimonies, let the representative of the count do with the fief what he wants.

GLOSS 27. *Onder haua* (*fief*). i.e. feudal goods.

GLOSS 28. *Foget* (*representative of the count*). i.e. the Procurator of the King or of the Feudal Lord.

That the Father Shall Not Give away His Daughter against Her Will

7. This is the law, that a father is not allowed to give away his daughter to any man against her will because the only authority she has is that over her own body. And if he does give her away against her will and she is harmed because she resisted it, he shall compensate for it as if he had hit her with his own hand.

GLOSS 29. *Ur herne willa* (*against her will*). This concerns parental authority over the daughter. Likewise, marriages should be voluntary, see X 4.1.17 and X 4.1.14, because marriages under coercion usually produce an unfortunate outcome, as in X 4.1.17 aforementioned; and see the Gloss to X 4.2.1 and the commentary of the scholars on that provision.

On Passing on the Guardianship of a Widow

8. This is the law, that no man shall have guardianship of a widow but her son, provided he is of age, or the man she remarries. If there is no son alive anymore, the new husband shall receive four pennies less than two marks for the guardianship.

Fant mondschet der famna

9. Deer famna riucht is: dyjen deer se aeftighet tweer schillinghen[1] des mondes.[2]

Fan der pyne des monschets deert lasta nelle

19 **10.** Dit is riucht:[3] jeft hy dyne mondschet naet lasta en wille ende hi dat wyf toe aefta onfucht, soe schel hy dis monnadeis ende aec foerd al da fyf daghen alont des saterdys ban tielda ende alle da daghen des halsfanges twyrasum onswerre, jefta dyne mondschet laesta des saterdeys twifald, jefta oen stride staen, jefta—tredda kest—half boedel jaen binnia dae balkem.

Fant[4] laen des mondschypes des moers vant kynd[5]

11. Dit is riucht luterslaen, dat dy soen aegh syne[6] moeder toleff jera aller jeerkis toe laen toe jaen fyff schillinghen, als hy synre breid halled, so fyr dat hi onwemed see fan warlasheed fan fyf seckum: fan swynes tusch, fan honna eetsle, fan hundes bythe, fan hynxstes hoeff ende[7] fan reederis hoerne.

Hweerum dat kynd ne thoer dat laen naet jaen

12. Dit is riucht: jeft hi weemd se ende hit syn moeder naet bycanna wil, so aech hyt mit syn ede oen her toe winnen ende deermey byhalda dat laen synre moeder.

Fant laen des jonghera broders dyn jeldera als hy syn breid halla

13. Dit is riucht: als di jonghera broder een wyf halle, so schel syn wyf syn jeldera broeder jaen fyff schillinghen ende dat deerum dat hy dat bed reme syn jonghera broeder ende syne wive. Dat is takeris jefta.

Fan tzierkweghum ende fan hiara brede

14. Dit is riucht,[8] dat to der haedstoe scellet ghaen fyower weghen.[9] Da schillet allerlyc wessa fiower[10] mollesfoten breed um da fiower halva sida, hit ne stande aen stedis overe. Jef dat disse fiower een an dine heerwei[11] coem, so mei
20 di heerwei wessa bede herwei ende kercwei, al bi eenre meta. |

[1] FG: schillingden. [2] FG: monnadeys. [3] FG: rincht. [4] FG: Faut. [5] FG: kyud. [6] FG: synre. [7] FG: eude. [8] FG: riuct. [9] FG: waeghen. [10] FG: friower. [11] FG: heernei.

On the Guardianship of a Maiden

9. This is the law concerning a maiden: he who marries her has to pay two shillings for the guardianship.

On the Fine for Not Wanting to Pay for the Guardianship

10. This is the law: if a man does not want to pay for the guardianship and he denies to be married to the woman, he shall come to court on Monday and all subsequent five days until Saturday and each day he shall exonerate himself of (the claim of) cohabitation, with the help of one compurgator, and on Saturday he shall either pay a twofold fee for the guardianship, undergo a trial by ordeal, or—as a third option—give half of his household goods.

On the Payment for the Mother's Guardianship of the Child

11. This is the lawful 'swaddling-payment', that the son has to pay his mother five shillings for each of the twelve years (he was underage) when he brings his bride home, when he has remained uninjured as a consequence of neglect by these five things: the tusk of a swine, the spur of a cock, the bite of a dog, the hoof of a horse and the horn of cattle.

In Which Cases the Child Does Not Have to Give the Payment

12. This is the law: if he has been injured and his mother does not want to acknowledge this, then he must take an oath to convince her and so retain the payment to his mother.

On the Payment of the Younger Brother to the Older Brother When He Brings His Bride Home

13. This is the law: if a younger brother takes a wife, then his wife shall give the older brother five shillings because he yields the bed to his younger brother and his wife. This is called the gift to the brother-in-law.

Concerning Church Roads and Their Measurements

14. This is the law, that four roads shall lead to the head-church. These shall all be four standard feet wide, on the four sides of the church, unless it stands on the shore of open water. If one of these four roads leads to a main road, the latter may constitute both, main road and church road at the same time, included in the same measurement.

Van dioe brede des weyes om dat tzerckhou

15. Dit is riucht, dat om dat tzerckhou, buta des wideles werp, scel een wey ghaen deer XXI mollesfoeta breed se ende diin aegh[1] di schelta mit ban toe haldene. Deer aghen ferd oen alle daejen deer dat goedeshuus seket. Of him deer ymmen oen bischadighet, soe schel hyt twybeet beta.

Nen Fresa thoer grewa[2] ban tielda

16. Dit is riucht, dat di fria Fresa ne thoer dis grewa ban tyelda twisscha sumerisnacht ende lettera ewennacht.[3] Deer en twisscha ne thoer hi neen ban tyelda, ner bod, oers dan tree dagen. Comt hi onbiclaghet fan dana, soe ne thoer hi nen koninges ban tyelda eer dat jeer omcomt.

Nen Fresa thoer grewa ban tielda buta scelta wroegingha

17. Dit is riucht, dat di fria Fresa ne thoer bi des grewa ban an stride toejenst him staen, hit ne se datter him syn schelta urherich urtioga.[4]

Van dike to hodane bi sinte Benedictus

18. Dit is riucht, dat di fria Fresa[5] schel dine ovir deer hi bi banne wareth tojenst dyne salta see toe sinte Benedictus missa wrocht habba, jefta mit twaem schillingen aldus urnacht beta tojenst dine scelta, alsoe langh als hit oen wanwirke is, ont sumerisnacht. Ende eefter sumerisnacht, jef dat grundjeth dat saute wetter inleth ende lyoedem schaede deth oen hyara noth, aldus urnacht ont lettera evennacht mit twaem pondem beta.

Van sile to haldene tyaende bi sinte Benedictus

19. Dit is riucht, dat di fria Fresa dyne syl deer hi bi banne wareth toe sinte Benedictus missa schel tyaende ende temande habba, jefta mit twaem schillingen aldus urnacht tojens diin scelta beta.

21 20. Dit is riucht: jeff di scelta deer ur diin siil dae ban | lath to wanwirke schowat dyn syl mit des koninges orkenen ende mitta aesgha, jef da lyoed bisecka willet, soe is di schelta nyer mitta tiuge da lyoede to jechtane so da lyoed to onswarene.

---

[1] FG: aecgh. [2] FG: schelta. [3] FG: ewa nacht. [4] FG: schelta urtioga. [5] FG: di fresa.

Concerning the Measurements of the Road Around the Churchyard

15. This is the law, that around the churchyard, outside the cemetery, there shall be a road which is to be twenty-one standard feet broad and which is to be maintained under the authority of the *skelta*. On that road, everyone who goes to the church should be left in peace. If someone is injured there by someone else, he is to be compensated twofold.

No Frisian Has to Observe the Authority of the Count

16. This is the law, that a free Frisian is only obligated to attend the count's court between midsummer night and between the autumn equinox. And during that period, he is only obligated to attend the court, whether under proclamation or summons, for three days. If he comes from this court without having been formally accused, he does not have to obey any royal summons before the end of the year.

No Frisian Has to Observe the Authority of the Count without Order of the Skelta

17. This is the law, that a free Frisian is not obligated to appear before the count in his court, unless his *skelta* has convicted him of disobedience.

On the Maintenance of Dykes before Saint Benedict's Day

18. This is the law, that a free Frisian shall see to it that the dykes he has been ordered to maintain as a protection against the salt sea are in good order by Saint Benedict's Day, or pay a fine of two shillings a day up to Midsummer Night for as long as it remains unrepaired. And after Midsummer Night, if a hole in the dyke lets through salt water and harms the people in their harvests, he shall have to pay a fine of two pounds a day until the autumn equinox.

On the Maintenance of Sluices before Saint Benedict's Day

19. This is the law, that a free Frisian shall see to it that the sluice he has been ordered to maintain is letting water in and out by Saint Benedict's Day, or pay a fine of two shillings a day to the *skelta*.

20. This is the law: if the *skelta* who has jurisdiction over the sluice inspects it and finds it in a poor state of maintenance, together with the king's witnesses and the *asega*, and if the people want to contest this, then the *skelta* can refute the people's testimony with the help of the testimony of the king's witnesses and the *asega*, against their oath of innocence.

21. Dit is riucht, dat to der sylroda by da syle dat dat meenwirck schel wessa ur tria ende sexstich fota.

Van Freesna wepen to halden

22. Dit is riucht:[1] aldeer di fria Fresa XXX pond wird eerwis haet oen synre wer dat hi hoers ende wepen halda schil to der landwer. Jef him dis breckt, so schil hi tojenst dine frana mit twam pondem beta. Hwa so haet XX ponda wird eerwis oen synre wer, di schel habba truchslayn wepen jefta mit twam pondem beta. Hwa so haet XII ponda wird eerwis, di schil habba speer ende schield toe der landwer jefta mit twam pondem beta. Di deer haet lessa, di schel habba koeker ende bogha to der landwer, jefta mit twam pondem beta.

Van des grewa riucht

23. Dit is riucht: di grewa deer hyr da ban lath, dat hi des fyarda jeris bodtingh halda moet, also fyr so hi wil. Dat is riucht, als hi se halda wil, dat ma se keda schil ith aller kerkane liick, di prester efter Cristes morne eer jerisdey, dat se di grewa halda wil efter sumerisnacht eer lettera ewennacht. Ende als di grewa bodtingh halda wil, dat hi schil da ban opja saun wiken da schelten eer ma se halde ende neen doem to delen, bihalva om needsecken, hit ne se datter een hera oen dit land coemme[2] jefta dat ma een wyf an nede nym, jefta dat ma een man in sine huse slee, so moet hi deer rida ende ban leda.

Van schelta ladingha

22 **24.**Dit is riucht dat da schelten keda schellet allerlyck binna sine banne des monnendeys toe aller doerna lyck sex wiken eer ma se halde ende aldus keda: 'Bodtingh kede ick joe ur sex wikem aen dis selva dei, dis monendeys to haldene ende dis tysdeys, dis wernsdeys, dis tonerdeys, dis fredis, dis saterdeys ende dis monendeys.' Alle dagen aegen hya se toe bannen bi des koninges banne ende also to haldene ende to lastan. Soe hwa soe naet ne seeckt, di schel toejenst dyn schelta mit twam pondem beta.

GLOSSA 30. *Bodtingh kede ick* Citatio est fundamentum ordinis iudiciarii de const. c. Ecclesie sancte Marie (X 1.2.10). Nota. Citatus ad duo tenetur, scilicet ut ad iudicem ueniat et ad diem sibi prefixam accedat. Et si non potest ad diem sibi assignatam uenire, nihilominus tenetur postea se iudici presentare, quia cum mandatur alicui ut alii ad certum diem rem certam

[1] FG: riuct. [2] FG: ceomme.

21. This is the law, that along the canal leading to the sluice the revetment is to be more than sixty-three feet and to be constructed and maintained by the entire community.

Which Weapons Frisians Are Obligated to Own

22. This is the law: when a free Frisian possesses land worth thirty pounds as his property, he shall have a horse and weapon for the defence of the land. If he is unable to procure this, he shall pay a fine of two pounds to the *frana*. He who possesses land worth twenty pounds as his property shall have a forged weapon or pay the fine of two pounds. He who possesses land worth twelve pounds as his property shall have spear and shield for the defence of the land or pay the fine of two pounds. If someone possesses less than this he shall have bow and arrow for the defence of the land or pay the fine of two pounds.

Concerning the Court of the Count

23. This is the law: the count who has jurisdiction here may hold a *bodthing* every four years if he wishes. This is the law, that if he wishes to hold it, between Christmas and New Year's Day the priest shall announce at every church that the count will be holding it between Midsummer Night and the autumn equinox. And if the count wants to hold a *bodthing*, he shall confer his jurisdiction to the *skeltas* seven weeks before it is held, and he shall give no judgment unless in cases of emergency, if a foreign army invades the land, or if a woman is raped, or if a man is killed inside his own house; in those cases he must ride there and exercise his authority.

Concerning the Summons by the Skelta

24. This is the law, that on Monday six weeks before it is held, the *skeltas* shall give notice to everyone within their jurisdiction at every door, saying: 'I give you notice of a *bodthing* which will be held on this same day six weeks from now, to be held on Monday, Tuesday, Wednesday, Thursday, Friday, Saturday and Monday'. They shall give notice of it every week, saying that it is to be performed and held by the authority of the king. If someone does not attend he shall pay a fine of two pounds to the *skelta*.

GLOSS 30. *Bodtingh kede ick* (*I give notice of a bodthing*). The summons constitutes the basis for the proceedings, see X 1.2.10. Note that the defendant is obligated to do two things; namely, to appear before the judge and to turn up on the day assigned to him. If the defendant is incapable of appearing on the day assigned to him, he nevertheless must present himself at a later date to the judge. For, when someone is ordered to perform a certain thing for another within a fixed term, he will not be discharged

exsoluat, non ideo erit a mandato solutus, si soluere nequiuerit die assignata. Ymmo ad solutionem elapso etiam die solutioni prefixo tenetur. Extra de dol. et contu. c. Cum dilecti (X 2.14.6). Citatus ad causam a suo iudice, licet interea incipiat esse alterius iurisdictionis, propter hoc tamen non potest declinare iudicium prioris iudicis quo ad illam causam siue sit ordinarius siue delegatus, extra de fo. compe. c. Proposuisti (X 2.2.19), quia ubi inceptum est iudicium, ibi debet habere finem, ff. de iuris. omni. iu. l. Cum quedam (*Dig.* 2.1.19.pr).

Efter sonnaschyn ne doer ma an stride staen

25. Dit is riucht, dat da schelten des monendeys deer komma ende dis tysdeys ende dis koninges ban opja da grewa aldeer hyaet ontfinghen.

26. Dit is riucht, dat di grewa dine tysdei ende den wernsdey ende den tonghersdey da tre dagen also riuchta schil da lyoden als ma oen dae bannena[1] bodtingh
23 deed, deer ma deer naet to eynd riuchta mocht. So hetet da tre daghen | fimeltingh.

Dat dae schelta bodtingh eer ond biginne

27. Dit is riucht, dat dae schelten deer bodtingh haldet toe middey eer unden bannes bigonnen habba schillet om dat stryd deer ma aldeer greta schil bi sonnaopgongh.

28. Dit is riucht: als dyoe sonne sighende is ende dyoe kuu da klewendene deth, so ne thoer di fria Fresa efterdam dis deys an stride withstaen om dat hy eer gret ne was.

29. Dit is riucht, dat di fria Fresa ne thoer dis grewa ner dis schelta ban tyelda efter sonnasedel.

GLOSSA 31. Nota. Exceptio peremptoria est actionis exclusio de of. dele. c. Consuluit (X 1.29.24). Nota. Tribus modis dicitur aliquis contumax: primo quando peremptorie citatus non comparuit, secundo quando comparet et non uult respondere, tertio quando comparet et praeter consensum iudicis recedit. Hec omnia uide in c. ii de do. et con. (X 2.14.2), sed plenius in l. Contumacia ff. de re iudi. (*Dig.* 42.1.53.pr) in glosa.[a] Item nota. Si

[1] FG: bannenda.

a The gloss *contumacia* ad *Dig.* 42.1.53.pr.

from such mandate for the reason that he could not perform on the assigned day. Similarly, one remains compelled to perform an obligation, after the lapse of the term, fixed for the performance. See X 2.14.6. Anyone who has been summoned to a case by a competent judge, even though in the meantime he has begun submitting to another's jurisdiction, may not escape the sentence of the first judge for this reason, no matter whether the judge is an ordinary judge or a delegated one, see X 2.2.19, since where proceedings are initiated, there they should be brought to an end, see *Dig.* 2.1.19.pr.

One Is Not Obligated to Appear before Court after Sunset

25. This is the law, that the *skeltas* shall come there (i.e. the *bodthing*) on Monday and Tuesday and return the king's authority to the count, from whom they received it.

26. This is the law, that on Tuesday, Wednesday, and Thursday, on these three days the count shall judge the people as was done at the *bodthing*, with respect to any matters that could not be decided there. Those three days are called the *fimelthing*.

That the Bodthing *of the* Skelta *Should Begin in the Morning*

27. This is the law, that the *skeltas* who are holding the *bodthing* shall open court before noon because a lawsuit is to be initiated while the sun is climbing.

28. This is the law: when the sun is setting and the cow lays down her hoofs, a free Frisian is not obligated to stand suit on that day, since he was not charged before.

29. This is the law, that a free Frisian is not obligated to attend the court of the count or the *skelta* after sunset.

GLOSS 31. Note that a peremptory exception implies an exclusion of the claim, see X 1.29.24. Note that someone can be said to make default in three ways. First, when peremptorily summoned, he does not appear. Secondly, when he appears and does not wish to respond. In the third place when he appears and leaves without permission of the judge. All these things you will find in X 2.14.2, but more fully in the Gloss to *Dig.* 42.1.53.pr.

aliquis citari debet et non inueniatur, sufficit ut citationis edictum apud ecclesiam uel domum suam publice proponat, extra de do. et contu. c. Venerabilis (X 2.14.10).

30. Dit is riucht, dat da lyoed deer dae bodtingh ende dae fimelthingh halden habbet, dae ne thoeren[1] efterdam dis koninges ban tyelda in dat jeer.

Van needmund ende herre betteringa

31. Dit is riucht: hweer so ma een wif an nede nimpt endma dat claget da frana, soe schel ma her folgia mitta aesga ti da fordel deer hio binna is. Ende di frana schel heer fregia, ho se deer komme, hor willens so onwillens. Hockera hio dan spreckt, so schel hio in des frana wald wessa tria nachta truch da need, deer ma
24 aldeer claghet. | Dis tredda deys aeghse di frana oen den werf to bringhen ende tweer steven to setten,[2] her willa to barien. Bi da ena steve stande her meghen ende bi da ora her man. Jef hyo ti da man geet, so brucke se dis mannes mit willa om dat hyo her ledena wald aegh. Jef hyo to da megen geet, so schil hi se twede jelda ende brand ende breeck tielda ende tachtich pond herem ende lyodem jaen. Ende dera allerlyck, deer aldeer in bitinged wirdet, brand ende breck tielda ende mit hiara haedlesene beta. So hwam so ma dis jelkirs bitiget, dat hi deermede an folliste were, so schil hi mit twam pondem beta jefta sexasum ontswara.

GLOSSA 32. Nota de raptu mulierum, qui committitur, cum puella uiolenter rapitur, xxxvi q.i. c. de raptoribus § Ex hac (DG post C.36 q.1 c.3). Et tunc demum committitur, cum ipse raptor non desponsauerat primo puellam, xxxvi q.i. Lex illa (C.36 q.1 c.2) et q.ii. De puel. Si quis uirginem (C.36 q.2 c.4 and 5), extra c. Cum causam (X 5.17.6). Idem, si uiduam uel sanctimonialem, xxxvi q.ii Raptores c. Si quis uiduam (C.36 q.2 c.2 and 5), secundum canones excomunicatur, ut xxxv q.ii. Si quis uirginem[a] (C.36 q.2 c.5), secundum leges decapitatur.[b] Eciam raptorem ad ecclesiam fugientem secundum legem non defendit, ut in Aut. coll. iii. de mandatis principum § Neque enim homicidiis[c] (*Auth.* 3.4.7 [*Nov.* 17.7]). Nec etiam potest esse matrimonium raptoris et rapte, eciam si illa consentiat, C. de raptu uirginum l.i § i (*Cod.* 9.13.1.pr). Et in ueteri lege qui sponsam uel uxorem alterius ui oppresserit, lapidabatur, xxxiiii q.iii. Non

---

[1] FG: dae thoeren. [2] FG: setteu.

---

a uirginem *scripsimus cum Decreto Gratiani*: uirginam BL BN FG RA.

b decapitatur *scripsimus*: dcapitatnr BL BN FG KB J109 PB RA UB: deapitatnr *male praem.* M60.

c homicidiis *scripsimus*: hdmicidas *male praem.* FG.

Note also the following. When someone ought to be summoned, but is not to be found anywhere, it is sufficient to publicly display the writ of summons at the church or at his house, see X 2.14.10.

30. This is the law, that people who have attended the *bodthing* and the *fimelthing* after that are not obligated to attend the court of the count or the *skelta* in that same year.

Concerning Raping a Woman and Compensating Her

31. This is the law, whenever a woman is raped, and complaint is made to the *frana*, she shall be visited, in the company of the *asega*, at the dwelling she is in. And the *frana* has to ask her how she came there, willingly or unwillingly. Whatever she says, she shall remain in the custody of the *frana* for three nights because of the case of violence. On the third day, the *frana* shall bring her to the court and set up two staves with which she can show her desire. Her kinsmen shall stand at one stave, and her abductor at the other. If she goes to the abductor, let her have him in peace for she has the right to dispose of her own body. If she goes to the kinsmen, the abductor shall pay a double wergild and his house shall be burnt down and laid to waste and he shall pay eighty pounds to the lords and to the people. And all who are convicted of complicity shall suffer that their house to be burnt down and laid to waste and shall pay their own wergild to avert a death penalty. And if someone is accused of assisting this, he shall pay a fine of two pounds or exonerate himself with five compurgators.

GLOSS 32. See regarding rape of women, which is committed when a girl is raped by force, DG post C.36 q.1 c.3. This is only committed in case the rapist himself had not previously betrothed himself to the girl, see C.36 q.1 c.2, C.36 q.2 c.4–5 and X 5.17.6. Moreover, anyone who rapes a widow or a nun, as in C.36 q.2 c.2 and 5, according to canon law is excommunicated, see C.36 q.2 c.5; according to Roman law he shall be decapitated. According to a Roman rule, no protection is even afforded to a rapist who takes sanctuary in a church, see *Auth.* 3.4.7 (*Nov.* 17.7). Neither can matrimony take place between the rapist and the woman raped, even should she consent, see *Cod.* 9.13.1.pr. According to the law of the Old Testament, the one who had seized by force another's fiancée or wife, was lapidated,

satis (C.34 q.1–2 c.3). Hoc uerum est de iure ueteri. Hodie secus est, si prior discensus transeat in consensum, extra de rapto. c. fi. (X 5.17.7). Sed qui uirginem solutam oppresserit, soluebat patri quinquaginta dragmas argenti, eam uxorem habebat, e. q.ii. Denique (C.36 q.2 c.9), uel pater eam eadem pecunia dotatam alii in matrimonium dabat, e. q.ii. Tria. (C.36 q.2 c.8). Sed qui deflorauit eam uoluntariam, non tenetur ducere nec maritare; hoc notat Ioannes in summa confessorum li. ii., | ti.v de rapto q.vi.[a] Nota ideo in summa in loco allegato, quid de eo qui deflorat uirginem solutam. Nunquid tenetur eam ducere uel maritare, secundum quod uidetur dicere decretalis, extra de adult. c. ult. (X 5.16.7)? Resp. secundum Guilelmum hoc, super verbo 'contrahere',[b] potest. Si deflorat ipsam uoluntariam, non tenetur eam ducere uel maritare. Si autem inuitam uel per dolum inductam ad consensum, in foro penitentiali iniungenda est ei, quod satisfaciat uel componat cum ea. Ad penam autem predicte decretalis non tenetur,[c] nisi in foro causarum. Et glosatores exponant eam de raptore qui seducit eam a domo patris et detrahit uirginem per uiolentiam.

Van helghene ende hofguede to delane

32. Dit is riucht, dat oen da himrick deer dis santis ende dis koninges ende des huismannes land oenlenth ende leyt, dat hyt dis fiarda jeris dela moet alsoe fyr dat di clagere deer se deer dat oppe dae helgem bringe dat dyo jeertale omcommen se ende hiit mit mara riucht dela schil dan hit langera aldus oendeeld staen schil. Soe schil hi to da tinge efter toelfta dey tinghes biginna ende syn land meta mit riuchta wirde mit sine tinghmanne.[1] Jef se sine eed nellet ontfaen, dat hi da tinge alle fiower tingia schil. To da fiifta tinge soe is hy nyer dine eed to swarane ende syn deel to nimane ende toe winnane soe hiit bilia schil. Jof hit so comt dat hi da fiif tinge eer dae festa naet tingia moge, so moet hi in der festa aefte ban leda om een hemrickdeel alont hit fol bitinget is.

[1] FG: tiuchmanne.

a Johannes de Friburgo, Summa confessorum, Lib. II, tit. 5, q. 6.
b The gloss *contrahere potest* of Guilelmus Redonensis ad Raymundus de Pennaforte, Summa de poenitentia, Lib. II, tit. 5, § 3.
c tenetur *scripsimus*: tenentur FG.

see C.34 q.1–2 c.3. For the Old Testament this is correct. Nowadays it is different when initial disagreement turns into consent, see X 5.17.7. Anyone who had seized a young single woman, paid the father 50 drachms and married her, see C.36 q.2 c.9, or the father gave her, provided with a dowry of this amount of money, in marriage to another, see C.36 q.2 c.8. The person who deflowered her with her consent, is not compelled to marry her or provide her with a dowry; Johannes notices this in the second book of his *Summa confessorum*, title V on abduction, question VI. Thus, see in this *Summa loco citato* what happens to the person who deflowers an unbetrothed virgin. Is he compelled to marry her or provide her with a dowry, in conformity with what decretal X 5.16.7 seems to maintain? The answer, in accordance with the gloss of Guilelmus to the word *contrahere*, is that this is possible. If he deflowers her with her consent, he is not compelled to marry her or provide her with a dowry. However, if he does the same while she is not willing or by deceit seduced to consent, in the court of penance it should be imposed upon him to grant her satisfaction or composition. However, he is not held to the penalty of the decretal mentioned above, unless in a trial because of interrelated matters. And the glossators deal with this penalty in connection with the abductor who takes a girl away from her parental home and carries away a virgin by force.

Concerning the Partitioning of Church Land and King's Land

32. This is the law regarding the common pasture which neighbours and borders on the lands of the church, the king and the freeman, that it shall come up for distribution every fourth year, provided that the claimant is present and pronounces on the holy relics that the term of years has expired and he then is more entitled to partition it, rather than it will remain undistributed any longer. He shall then begin the proceeding in the court meeting held after Twelfth Day (Epiphany) with his solicitor and describe the dimensions of his land in a proper complaint. If they will not accept his oath, then he must bring the case before the usual four successive court meetings. At the fifth court meeting he has a stronger right to swear the oath and obtain his share rather than to do without it. If it so happens that he does not succeed to complete his proceedings at the fifth session before Lent, then the *skelta* must hold court during Lent in the matter of the distribution of the common pasture until the proceedings are completed.

Van helgena ende hofguede to delane

33. Dit is riucht om eenre hemrickdeel deer ma bigint itta afta[1] tinge efter tolefta dei, dat di schelta moet omme saun nacht aefte ban leda al ti da fiifta tinge,
26 alont dy mensingeed swerren is. Soe ist riucht | dat di aesgha aegh toe delane dat hya schillet itta haud bighinna. Bi evennacht bi sinte Benedictus buppa der clesie schellet hya alle deeld habba, truch dat dyo kuu oen den field schil. Dat aegh di schelta toe bannen dat set alsoe laste. Soe ist riucht dat di schelta dat fregia schil, her hya so deen habbe als him di aesga deelde.[2] Jef se also naet deen habbe, so aegh hi aller husekem tweer schellingen ur to delen. So aegh di schelta dae biwysda bota toe monien: fyouwer tingh om saun nachta ende dat fiifte thingh to hiara fordele ende deer to tingiane da ban. Soe ist riucht jef ma da acht schillingen naet utachtia moet, dat di aesgha schel twa pond dae grewa toedela ende dae schelta x schellingen. Soe ist riucht, dat hi da boete it aller manlikum mit sonderinga eed winna schil.

34. Dit is riucht: jof di hemrick oendeeld is ont sumerisnacht, so is dera allerlyck, deer des weygeret, da grewa twa pond schieldich.

Van tinge om eerwe toe delane

35. Dit is riucht: jef dae lyoed enich onwillich se, dat hi dela nelle, so schil di schelta dis onwilliga deel waria ende mitta williga an field fara ende da hemrick deermede dela.

Van eerfscip toe delane

36. Dit is riucht: aldeer di fria Fresa op een eerwe tinghia wil dat hi an bannena tingh comma schil mit sine tinghmanne ende schil greta mit aefte greetwird ende bitigia him des dat hi een eerwe an synre wer habbe onriucht, deer hi mit riuchta rema schil. So aegh him di ora to anderien ende fregia him hweer dat eerwe lidse. Soe aegh him di aesga toe delen dat hi dat eerwe wise mit steve ende mit tiuge. Dat tiuch schil wessa[3] dis selva deys ur saun nachten op dat
27 eerwe. |

Van forkapa land da fryonden dat nyer to bisitten

37. Dit is riucht dat hi him dis selva deys bi midda moern, bi sonnaopgongh, mit twam scheltem ende mit saun synre buren ende mitta aesga ende mit dis

[1] FG: fiifta. [2] FG: deeld. [3] FG: wes.

Concerning the Partitioning of Church Land and King's Land

33. This is the law regarding distribution of the common pasture which should begin in the court held after Twelfth Day; that the *skelta* must hold court for seven days until the fifth proceeding, when the oath of distribution is sworn. Then it is the law that the *asega* shall declare that they shall begin at the farthest end of the common pasture. By the equinox, at Saint Benedict's Day, they shall have everything distributed up to the hedges, because of the cattle that have to go to the pasture. The *skelta* has to order them to do it exactly like this. Then the *skelta* shall ask if they have done as the *asega* declared. If they have not done so, the *asega* shall decree a fine of two shillings for every house. And the *skelta* shall demand the prescribed penalty from them on four weekly court days, and hold the fifth proceeding at their estate, and there exact the fine. Then it is the law, if they are unwilling to pay the eight shillings, that the *asega* shall decree a fine of two pounds to the count and ten shillings to the *skelta*. And then it is the law that the *skelta* shall obtain the fine from each man by swearing a separate oath for each.

34. This is the law: if the common pasture remains undistributed by Midsummer Day, each one of those who refused to distribute it has to pay a fine of two pounds to the count.

Concerning the Procedure for Partitioning Land

35. This is the law: if any of the people is unwilling to accept his share, the *skelta* shall confiscate the unwilling one's share and go into the field with those who are willing, and distribute the common pasture among them.

On Assigning a Piece of Land

36. This is the law: if a free Frisian wishes to go to court over a piece of land, he shall come to the proclaimed court session with his solicitor, and challenge the defendant with the proper formula, and charge him with unlawfully having a piece of land in his possession, which he must by law surrender to him. Then the defendant must answer him and ask him where the land lies. Then the *asega* must decree that the claimant point out the land both by swearing an oath and with the help of a testimony. The testimony shall be performed on the land itself, a week from the same day.

Concerning the Right of Kinsmen to Sold Land

37. This is the law, that on the same day of the week, in the middle of the morning, while the sun is climbing, he shall summon the defendant, accompanied

andera bura saun mitta aefta tiuge[1] ladia schil to der landwer to sine fordele. Ende di aesga aegh him to delane dat hi in den field fare jef hyt wara wil. Jof hi naet comma wil to der landwer, so is dat riucht, dat ma efta tinghia schil, dat een tingh, dat oer, dat tredde ende dat fyarde. Itta fyfta tinghe dine ferd deeroen winna als ma mit riuchta landriuchte schil.

Van graetheit des forkapa guedis

38. Dit is riucht, dat neen man syn eerwe foercapia moet, hit ne se bi syn[2] eerfnama moede, him ne dere hongher jefta heer need, jef dat hy also sondich se dat hi dat land rema wil ende syn sonda bettria: soe aech hyt syn erfnama toe bieden dae fyaerda penningh lichtera dan hit wird se. Jef hit aeck ymmen capet buta dis eerfnama mode, als di odera man sterft deer dat eerwe seld haet, so aech di eerfnama een ferd oen da gued ende eerwe ende di odera nene fyafellingha.

GLOSSA 33. Hoc ius habet textum pro se Leuitici xxv., ubi dicitur 'Si attenuatus fuerit, uendiderit possessionem, potest redimere propinquus'.[a] Sed lex contradicit C. de contrahen. emp. l. Dudum proximis consortibus concessum erat ut extraneos ab emptione remouerint (*Cod.* 4.38.14). Primum tenetur in Frisia et utentium moribus approbatur iiii di. Leges dicunt, sic secundum Cinum super Codice,[b] quod quilibet potest emptorem querere et uendere. Sed lex non prohibit, quando proximiores et uiciniores possunt emptores expellere et redimere, ad hoc ff. de contrahen. emp. l. Qui offi. (*Dig.* 18.1.62), ff. de mino. xxv an. l. Si ⟨in⟩ emptione (*Dig.* 4.4.35). Pro
28 uicinioribus facit | ff. de lega. ii, Si cui fundus (*Dig.* 31.1.54)[c] et in constitutione Fredrici imperatoris de feudis Per quos fiat inuestitura post principium (*LF* 2.3) et ibi in glossa.[d]

GLOSSA 34. *Ende di odera nene fia follinga* id est pecuniam uel solutionem. Quia pecunia a pecude, i q.iii Totum quod (C.1 q.3 c.6), item de reg. iuris ea que contra ius fiunt li. vi. (VI *de regulis iuris, regula* 64), C. de legi. l. Non dubium (*Cod.* 1.14.5), C. de pactis l. Pacta que contra leges (*Cod.* 2.3.6).

---

[1] FG: tinge. [2] FG: se syn.

---

a Leviticus 25.25.
b Cinus de Pistoia, Commentaria in Codicem, *Cod.* 4.38.14, n. 1–2.
c Si cui fundus *scripsimus*: l. Si emp. *male praem.* FG.
d The gloss *proximiori* ad *LF* 2.3 in pr.

by the two *skeltas* and seven of the neighbours and the *asega* and seven of the defendant's neighbours, at his house in order to defend his possession of the land. And the *asega* must decree that he shall go into the field if he wishes to defend it. If he will not come to the defence, the law is that the claimant shall again hold proceedings, a second time, a third, and a fourth. At the fifth proceeding he shall be entitled to undisturbed possession, according to the true law of the land.

Concerning the Dimensions of Sold Land

38. This is the law, that no man may sell his inheritance, save by consent of his heir, unless he is constrained by hunger or military necessity, or if he is so sinful that he wishes to give up the land in order to make atonement for his sins: he must then offer it to his heir for the fourth penny less than it is worth. If anyone buys it without the consent of the heir, then, when the man who sold it dies, the heir shall have a right to undisturbed possession of the goods and the land, and the other will not be compensated.

GLOSS 33. This provision is supported by Leviticus 25, where it is said "when someone became impoverished and sold his possession, his relative may redeem it". However, Roman law contradicts this in *Cod.* 4.38.14. The former is observed in Frisia and customs of those who observe these are approved of in the fourth distinction. The Roman law provisions say, at least according to Cinus in his commentary on the Codex, that anyone can look for a buyer and sell. But Roman law does not prevent that close relatives and next-door neighbours can expel the buyers and redeem what was sold. See for this *Dig.* 18.1.62 and *Dig.* 4.4.35. An argument for the neighbours can be found in *Dig.* 31.1.54 and in the constitution *LF* 2.3 of Emperor Frederick and the Gloss to the latter.

GLOSS 34. *Ende di odera nene fia follinga* (*and the other will not be compensated*). i.e. money or payment, because the word 'money' (*pecunia*) is derived from the word 'cattle' (*pecus*), see C.1 q.3 c.6, and also VI *de regulis iuris, regula* 64, *Cod.* 1.14.5 and *Cod.* 2.3.6.

Hweer ma ketelfange dwaen schil

39. Dit is riucht: di deer to dae striid tingia wil, dat met lessa bigreta ne mei toe dae ketelfangh dan fyower eynsa ende fioertiensta trimene[1] penningh. Jef syn kempa oen da ordel bifalt, soe schel hi dat twibeet beta ende dae grewa twa pond dis raefferda ende twa pond dis strydferda.

40. Dit is riucht: als ma to lessa stryd tinghia wil, dat di oentingere neen kempa winna thoer men di haldere schillen winna ende deer schellet se bede oen jechta.

41. Dat is riucht, dat di aesgha deer dat stryd mede bitinget is, dela schil dat dat ordel oen da kerkewalle schil wessa to des haudstoed deer dy deeckma to geed, hit ne se mit dis haudpresters oerlef dattet se itter capella, deer di schelta da ban urlath deer dat stryd mede bitinghet is.

Hu ma ontingia schel fan da kampa

42. Dit is riucht, dat di ketel oen dae kerckwalle hingia schil buta dis widelis werp on da walle ende di prester op da hofwal staen ende dat ordel wya with ane schillingh penninga. Soe aegh di kempa buta hofwal toe staen ende al stede in to faen, als di strydeed swerren is. So aegh di schelta ende di aesga ende di prester ende fyower dis koninges orkenen, hya saun, dis tredda deis da hand to schoyen binna dae kerka; dae tre mitta prester ende di ena mitta schelta
29 ende mitta aesga. Jof | se aet sanet, soe is di prester nyer ende dae tree mit him dae hand toe helane, so dae tre to urbaernene. Wirt hi schowet to heelre hand, so schil di ora den meeneed festia ende da grewa twa pond jaen. Ende wirth hy baernd, soe schil hi ja da grewa twa pond dis strydferda ende twa pond dis raefferda ende syn decken ja heer ende heed, jefta mit sine fia laesta[2] ende den meneed festia.

GLOSSA 35. Nota. Hec est ratio quare ⟨usus⟩ aque bulientis uel frigide sit prohibitum scilicet ne sors cadit super innocentem, ii q.v Consuluisti (C.2 q.5 c.20), de purgatione uulgari per totum (X 5.35). Item nota. Vulgaris purgatio dicitur quia sibi uulgus inuenit scilicet per duellum, aquam et ignem, ut extra de purgatione uulgari per totum (X 5.35). Triplex est ratio quare huiusmodi purgatio prohibetur: prima quia facta fuit inuidia fabri-

[1] FG: trimone. [2] FG: lesti.

Where the Ordeal by Water Shall Be Held

39. This is the law: if someone wishes to continue the proceedings until an ordeal must be held, that the claim in case of the ordeal by water may not involve less than four ounces and thirteen and a third pennies. If the defendant's champion fails the ordeal, he shall pay double the amount claimed and two pounds to the *frana* as a penalty for violently robbing someone's goods and another two pounds as a penalty for breaking the peace by failing an ordeal.

40. This is the law: if the minor ordeal is to be held, the claimant does not have to hire himself a champion but the defendant does, and both shall be bound by the outcome of the ordeal.

41. This is the law, that the *asega* before whom the case is tried shall decree that the ordeal shall be held at the church wall of the main church to which the tithes are paid, unless, with the permission of the parish priest, it may be held at the chapel where the *skelta* before whom the case is tried holds court.

How One is to Proceed Concerning the Champion

42. This is the law, that the kettle shall hang on the church wall outside the holy ground on the outside of the wall and the priest shall stand on the churchyard wall and consecrate the ordeal and receive one shilling for this. The champion has to stand outside the churchyard and reach into the kettle right after the ordeal oath has been sworn. On the third day the *skelta* and the *asega* and the priest and four of the king's witnesses, seven in total, shall inspect the hand inside the church; three of the king's witnesses shall form a group together with the priest, and the remaining one with the *skelta* and the *asega*. If they disagree to any extent, then the priest and the three king's witnesses have more rights to declare the hand to be healed than the other three to declare it to be burnt. And if his hand is declared healed, then the claimant shall compensate for his false oath by means of a fast and pay two pounds to the *frana*. And if his hand is declared burnt, the defendant shall pay the *frana* two pounds for breaking the peace by holding an ordeal and another two pounds for robbing someone's goods and he shall offer his hair and hide to his dean or pay for it with his goods and fast as compensation for the false oath.

GLOSS 35. Note that this is the reason why the use of boiling or cold water is prohibited, viz. to avoid fate indicating someone innocent, see C.2 q.5 c.20 and the entire title X 5.35. Also, note that the ordeal is called a 'public purge', because the public becomes aware of it through duel, water and fire, as in the entire title X 5.35. There is a threefold reason why such a purge is prohibited. In the first place because performing it arouses dis-

cante, ut in c. Mennam ii q.v. (C.2 q.5 c.7) et c. Consuluisti (C.2 q.5 c.20), secunda quia Deus in ea temptari uidetur, ut e. ti. c. ult. (X 5.35.3), tertia quia plurimus innocens condempnatur, ut e. ti. Significantibus (X 5.35.2) et officium etiam atletarum hodie reprobatur, et secundum leges ut C. de gladiatis l.i lib. xi[a] (*Cod.* 11.44.1).

43. Dit is riucht: jef di fria Fresa toe stride bitinget wirth ende hi queth dat hi aynlikes guedes soe fula oen synre wer naet habbe dat hi wepen ende wrichten winna moge ende beta jof hit op him falt, soe aegh hit di aesga to delen dat dit saun synre buren sidsa schillet bi da ede deer se da koninge to hulde sworen ende bi hyara selvis siele, hor hi also graet gued an synre wer hede dis deis da ma him mit stride bigrette. Sidset hia him so graet gued da hi mit stride bigret ward soe schel hi dat mara striid oenghaen. Sidset hia so graet syn guet naet, so schil hi lessa stryd oenghaen.

Van da stryd ende van ayder igghe

44. Dit is riucht, jef hi toe ene swirdkempa tinghia wil, dat hi naet lessa bigreta mey dan tria pond | ende acht eynsa: dat is di strydwirdiga schat. Soe schil di fria Fresa da odera totingia een thingh, ende dat oder, dat tredde, ende dat fiaerde an bannena tinghe ende toe da fiarda tinge schil ma dat stryd weddia. So ist riucht dat hi een burga habba schil. Ende di burga schil alsoe graet gued habba dat hi dine strydwerdigha schat lasta mey. Also schil hi oen der burghschip[1] staen alont di strydeed swerren is.

45. Dat is riucht, dat hi to dae fyfta tingh dine strydeed[2] swara schil ende dine wedereed[3] hera. Soe ist riucht dat hy syn hand op da helligha lidsa schil ende di aesga schil hem dine eed stowia, dat hem God alsoe help ende dae helligha. Soe aegh di aesgha dyn oentingere toe monien dat hi oplidse jef hi riucht habbe. So schil hi oplidsa ende di aesga schil him dine eed stowia dat him God also help ende da helliga. So schil hi swigia ende di ora swara. Nu schil ma him stowia, soe hi dine eed riucht swerre ende onmeens. Nu schil hi swigia ende di ora swara ende di aesgha schil him dine eed stowia, dat hi him na bira-

[1] FG: buurschip. [2] FG: tingh dat hi dine stryd eed. [3] FG: wedereede.

a l.i lib. xi *scripsimus*: li. l. xi FG.

gust, see C.2 q.5 c.7 and C.2 q.5 c.20, secondly because it seems to put God to the test, see X 5.35.3, and in the third place because many an innocent is condemned, see X 5.35.2, and even the profession of athletes is nowadays disapproved of, also according to Roman law, as in *Cod.* 11.44.1.

43. This is the law: if a free Frisian is challenged to an ordeal and he declares that he does not possess sufficient goods of his own to be able to buy a sword and armour, and on top of that pay the amount claimed if he loses, then the *asega* has to decree that seven of his neighbours shall declare on their souls and by the oath they swore to the king, whether or not he had so many goods on the day he was challenged to the ordeal. If they say he did have that many goods on the day he was challenged to the ordeal, then he shall have to undergo the major ordeal (of the duel). If they say he did not have so many goods, then he is allowed to undergo the minor ordeal (of the kettle proof).

Concerning the Ordeal and How Each Party Shall Act

44. This is the law, if one wants to continue the proceedings until an ordeal by combat must be held, the claim should not involve less than three pounds and eight ounces: that is the duel-worthy sum. Then the free Frisian shall bring proceedings against the other man at one court meeting, a second, a third, and a fourth, all decreed court meetings, and at the fourth court meeting, a financial security shall be provided for the duel. And it is the law that the defendant shall have a surety. And the surety shall have enough goods to be able to pay the duel-worthy sum. Thus the defendant shall be under surety until the duel oath is sworn.

45. This is the law, that at the fifth court meeting he (the claimant) shall swear the duel oath and hear the counter oath. It is law, that he shall lay his hand on the holy relics and the *asega* shall administer the oath to him and pray that God and the saints may help him. Then the *asega* shall request the claimant to lay his hand on the holy relics if he is in the right. Then he shall lay his hand on the holy relics and the *asega* shall administer the oath to him and pray that God and the saints may help him. Now he shall be silent and the other one shall swear.[3] Now the oath shall be administered to him, so that he shall swear lawfully and not falsely. Now he shall be silent and the defendant shall swear and the *asega* shall administer the oath to him, that he has never robbed the

3 *Freeska Landriucht* has condensed this text somewhat in comparison to the other redactions, found in *Codex Unia* and *Jus Municipale Frisonum*. Because of this, the taking of roles turns defective: *hi* suddenly means the defendant where one would expect it to be the claimant.

wede oen hae ner oen stree, aen gued ner oen eetber[1] fya. Nu schil hi swigia
ende di ora swara, dat hi him birawet habbe oen ha ende oen stree ende oen
gueda eetber fya. Nu schil hi swigia ende di ora swara dat hi him so gued naet
birawet hab so tria pond ende acht eynsa. Nu schil hi swigia ende di ora swara
dat hi him so gued birawet hab so tria pond ende acht eynsa, hit were bettera
jof hit scholde. Nu schil hi swigia ende di ora swara, so hy ne juwe onnette ful-
liste sonder riuchte frana wald. Nu schil hi swigia ende di ora swara: "So ic mit[2]
31 riuchta dat raef tojeens him naet | beta thoer". Nu schil hi swigia ende di ora
swara: "So y nu mit riuchte tojens mi beta schillet".

Van dyoe striidede

46. Nu di strydeed swerren is, nu ist riucht dat hi habba schil een burga, jef
him[3] di naet burghia wil, deer him eer burged haet. Soe schil hi him burgia XXI
nachta. Di burga schel alsoe ryck wessa dat hi dine strydwirdiga schat al lasta
moge deer onder gretwird aldeer lat was. Soe schil hi dae burghschip[4] hoda
alont da etkeren biwixled sint. Jef hi dine kempa naet winna mey, soe aegh hyt
op da helligem toe bringen dattet him need ofnaem, so aegh hi efta XXI nachta.
Jef him des efta breckt, dat hi dine kempa winna ne mey, so aegh hi eft XXI
nachta. Als da LXIII nachta omcommen sint, so schil ma dat stryd bifiuchta
binna dae ban deer hit binna biswerren is. So aegh di schelta dine ker hweer hi
dat tingh keda leth. Nu agen hya da kempen deer to bringen deer dat stryd ledat
ende di aesga aegh him dine kampstal to wisen. Di kampstal schil wessa LXIII
mollesfota breed allerweikes. Deer agen da kempen binna to wessen ende da
greetwirderen ende di schelta ende di aesga. Hwa so deer jelkirs ingeet di is dae
grewa schieldich twa pond. Efter dam deer di schelta bannis bigint, so aegh him
di aesga to delen dat se binna dae trim degem dat stryd bifiuchta schillet mit sex
wepen. Nu schillet dae swird even lang wessa. Di schelta ende di aesga schillet
da wepen schoia jondis ende morns. Soe schillet dae wepen oen da kampstal
bidia alder se da kempen bringet. Hia schillet aider twa swird habbe, jeft een
brect, dat hi ti da odera fe jef hi moge. Dioe leste hetene deer da kempen dis
tredda deys fiuchtet, dyo haet dyo luckhetene. Dan schel ma naet fiuchta ors
32 dan om een needmond ende om een moerdbrand ende om een nomelsmoerd. |

[1] FG: eeth. [2] FG: iemit. [3] FG: hi. [4] FG: buurschip.

claimant in hay nor straw, in goods nor cattle. Now the defendant shall be silent and the claimant shall swear that he did rob him in hay and straw, in goods and good cattle. Now he shall be silent and the defendant shall swear that he did not rob him of so much as three pounds and eight ounces. Now he shall be silent and the claimant shall swear that he did rob him of so much as three pounds and eight ounces, or more if it came down to it. Now he shall be silent and the other shall swear that he did not give illegal help without the consent of the *skelta*. Now he shall be silent and the other shall swear: "That I am lawfully not obligated to compensate the robbery performed on him". Now he shall be silent and the other shall swear: "That you shall now lawfully compensate me".

Concerning the Duel Oath

46. Now that the duel oath has been sworn, it is law that the defendant shall procure a surety, if the man who has stood surety from him until now does not want to continue to do so. The surety shall stand surety for him for 21 days. The surety shall be rich enough to be able to pay the duel-worthy sum completely for the person who has been summoned in court. And he shall continue his suretyship until the spears have been crossed. If the defendant is unable to hire a champion, he has to swear on the holy relics that necessity prevented him and he shall have twenty-one more days. If he is again unsuccessful in finding a champion, let him again have twenty-one days. When sixty-three days have passed, the duel has to take place within the jurisdiction where the indictment was made. And the *skelta* shall decide where the meeting is to be held. Now the champions who will fight the duel are to be brought there, and the *asega* has to point out the ring to them. The ring shall be sixty-three standard feet wide all around. Inside the ring shall be present the champions, the umpires, the *skelta* and the *asega*. Anyone else who enters it has to pay two pounds to the count. After the *skelta* has opened the proceedings, the *asega* must decree that they shall fight the duel within three days, using six weapons. Now the swords shall be of the same length. The *skelta* and the *asega* shall examine the swords in the evening and in the morning. The weapons shall remain in the ring where the champions put them. Each champion shall have two swords, so that he may try to reach the other one if the first one breaks. The last round which the champions fight on the third day is called the closing round. This round shall only be fought in cases concerning rape, arson or murder.

47. Dit is riucht: hweer so di fria Fresa op een oderne een stryd tinghia wil, dat hi comma schil een thingh ende dat oer ende dat tredde ende binna da trim tinghem schil sine steden alle naemna, jef hi se habba wil. Itta fiaerda tinghe aegh hy nene ferd jefta dat strid biwedia, jefta dat fyfte schil ith sine fordele wessa om dat tinghlase.

48. Dat is riucht: als ma dyn fria Fresa toe stride tingia wil ende di oera da uta habba wil, dat hi binna trim degem comma schil jef hi dae uta habbe wil. Jef ma him deer mitta striid bigret, so schil hi sprecka ende sidsa hi ne thoer bi dis schelta ban hor jechtwird ner seckwird dwaen ner neen tinger ontfaen om dat hi deer huis ner hof haet.

49. Dat is riucht, dat hi sine schelta naemne schil deer hi to tiucht ende sine nesta buren. Soe aegh him syn aesga deer to delane, dat hyt op dae helgum wita moet, hweer syn huis ende syn hof se, hit ne se dat him di schelta mitta tiuge inhalia wil. Jof di schelta him bilyout, so aech hyt op da helgem to swaren ende di aesga aegh him dyn eed toe stowien, hweer syn huis ende syn hof se. Nu schil hi sine bura tweer habba deer hine burgie ende dat se alsoe ryck se, dat hya dine strydwirdiga schet al lasta moghe, jef him di schelta hana leth dat hi aldeer anderda schil.

Van landhera nyer toe witane

50. Dit is riucht: jef di landsata queth dat hi dat land toe aheer ontfensen habbe, dat di hera nyer is toe witane op da hellighem hoe langhe dae forwerda se, soe di landsata.

Van riucht des fruchtbare vrouwes deer di man bigraven is

33 **51.** Dit is riucht. Aldeer een man oflyvich wirth[1] ende her dat wyf al urmeth, dat hyo ur dat gref quaen schil dat hyoe een berthe oen her habbe, deer hy oen her bytylet habbe ende hyoes her alle[2] biweent. Nu schel di eerfnama her dat gued ende dyn sitma bifella to her riuchta deytingh. So is di riuchte deytingh tyen monaden. Nu schil hyoe binna dat jeer ende binna dae dey dae berthe byrecknia. Nu schil ma her dat gued bisetta oen da hand mitta schelta ende mitta aesga ende mit des koninges orkenen ende mitta aefta tiuge.[3] Ende brin-

---

[1] FG: wirht. [2] FG: hyose alle. [3] FG: tinge.

47. This is the law, whenever a free Frisian wants to continue the proceedings until an ordeal must be held; that the defendant shall attend the first court meeting, the second and the third and in the course of these three sessions he has to bring his defences if he wishes to raise them. At the fourth session he has no remedy at his disposal but provide surety for the ordeal, or the fifth court session shall be held at his house because of his absence from court.

48. This is the law: if a free Frisian is challenged to the ordeal and the defendant wishes to plead lack of jurisdiction, he shall come within three days if he wants to establish the plea. If he is required to litigate there, he shall say that he is not obligated to confess nor deny at the order of that *skelta*, nor stand trial in any way, because he does not own a house and enclosure there.

49. This is the law, that he then shall name his own *skelta*, under whose jurisdiction he falls, and his closest neighbours. Then his *asega* shall decree that he may establish by an oath on the holy relics where his house and enclosure are, unless the *skelta* will overrule this with a testimony. If the *skelta* believes him, he has to swear on the holy relics and the *asega* has to administer the oath to him where his house and enclosure lie. Now he shall have two neighbours who will stand surety for him and who are so rich that they can pay the duel-worthy sum for him, when the *skelta* lets him go from there to defend himself at the other court.

Concerning the Rights of the Landlord

50. This is the law: if a tenant says that he holds the land on eternal lease, the landlord has a stronger right to confirm that the period of lease has lapsed by swearing an oath on the holy relics than the tenant (has to deny this).

Concerning the Right of a Pregnant Woman Whose Husband Lies Buried

51. This is the law. If a man dies and his wife is certain that she is pregnant, then she shall declare at the funeral that she is with child, begotten by her late husband, and that she is quite certain of it. Now the heir shall hand over to her the goods and property for the lawful term allotted to her. This term is ten months. Now she shall compute when the child-birth is due within the next period of a year and a day. Now the possession of the property is to be transferred to her with the help of the *skelta* and the *asega* and with the king's witnesses and legal

ckt hyo dyo berthe naet, so schel hyo dat gued also gued opanderda, so hyoet ontfengh. Nu aghen her[1] twa wyf toe biwarien, van aydera konne een, dat hyo naet eerges ne dwe. Aeck schellet se waria tween maen, fan aydere kenne een, dat ma her naet onriuchtes dwe. Nu schellet hya fyf dat gued nettigia ont dyo bertte bireckened is, dat dyo berthe libben oen dyo wrald coem. Jef hya om da berthe sanet; jef dat wyf queth deer van des eerfnama hallem warade dat dat kind naet libbende oen da wrald coem, nu hya da berthe jechtet dat hyo deer were, nu sint dae twa nier op da helghem oen to bringhane dat dyo berthe libben oen da wrald coem. Soe aegh[2] dyoe frowe een ferdban oen dae guede, dat her nimmen naet rawie jefte aet onriuchtes dwe.

GLOSSA 36. De postumo. *Dit is riucht* Nota. In sex mensibus et uno die potest quis nasci et ad decimum mensem finitum, in auct. de resti. et de ea que parit in undecimo mense § Viuum siquidem coll. iiii (*Auth*. 4.6.2 [*Nov*. 39.1.2]).

GLOSSA 37. *Dat gued an seta bifella* ff. de uent. in poss. mitten. l. i. § Sed et si quis[a] uentrem (*Dig*. 37.9.1.9).

GLOSSA 38. *Tien monaden langh* Per decem menses et duos dies potest mulier portare filium in uentre suo et non plus, ut notat Accursius in dicto § Viuum siquidem super uerbo *perfecto*,[b] allegans ff. de suis et le. here. l. Intestato §. fi. (*Dig*. 38.16.3.12). Et ibi uide ab annunciatione dominica, ut uterus uirginalis fieret templum diuinitatis. Habitauit Cristus cc et lxxvi diebus et natus fuit ex ea altissimus. Psalmista ⟨dicit⟩: homo natus.[c]

GLOSSA 39. *Libbende oenda wrald coem* Nota. Etiam si nullam uocem emiserit uel in manibus obstetricis decesserit, ut in dicta l. iii. C. de postu. here. in fi. (*Cod*. 6.29.3). Secus si mulier peperit abortiuum, Inst. de exhere. li. § i (*Inst*. 2.13.1), ff. de uer. signi. l. Qui mortui (*Dig*. 50.16.129).

Van enis ovirlandis daedes mannes gued[3]

52. Dit is riucht: jefter een ovirlandich man sterft, so aech di frana dat gued to ontfaen jeer ende dey to haldene. Jof deer enich eftercomt[4] fan syn eerven binna jeer ende binna dei, dae eerfnamen toe jaen. Jef deer nimmen comt: di frana nym een deel ende di ora deel to Godes tyenst.

---

[1] FG: hyer. [2] FG: aecgh. [3] FG: Van enis ovirlandis guedes mannes daed. [4] FG: enich synre efter comt.

---

a quis *scripsimus cum Infortiato*: qnis FG.

b perfecto *scripsimus cum Authentico*: profecte FG. The gloss *perfecto* ad *Auth*. 4.6.2 (*Nov*. 39.1.2).

c Psalmi 86.5.

testimony. And if no child is born, she shall return the property in the same condition she received it. Now two women, one from each side of the family, are to watch over her, so that she does not do anything wrong. Also, two men, one from each side of the family, are to watch over her, to see that she is not harmed. These five people are entitled to use the property until the baby is due and the child is born alive. If there is a dispute about the birth; if the woman who kept watch on behalf of the heir states that the child came stillborn into the world, but concedes that a child was born, the other two have more right to swear upon the holy relics that the child was born alive. And the mother shall have a right to peaceful possession of the property, so that no-one may rob her or do her any wrong.

GLOSS 36. On offspring. *Dit is riucht* (*This is law*). Note that a person can be born in six months and one day and until the tenth month has elapsed, see *Auth.* 4.6.2 (*Nov.* 39.1.2).

GLOSS 37. *Dat gued an seta bifella* (*hand over the goods and the property*), see *Dig.* 37.9.1.9.

GLOSS 38. *Tien monaden langh* (*ten months*). A woman can carry a son in her womb for ten months and two days and not longer, as notices Accursius in the gloss *perfecto* to *Auth.* 4.6.2 (*Nov.* 39.1.2), referring to *Dig.* 38.16.3.12. And see there that from the Annunciation of the Lord, the virginal womb became the temple of divinity; Christ lived there 276 days and the Most High was born from her. The psalmist says: a man was born.

GLOSS 39. *Libbende oenda wrald come* (*born alive*). Note, even if it has emitted no sound or has died in the hands of the midwife, as in *Cod.* 6.29.3. It is different when a woman has lost it through a miscarriage, see *Inst.* 2.13.1 and *Dig.* 50.16.129.

Concerning the Goods of a Dead Foreigner

52. This is the law: if a foreigner dies, the *frana* shall take custody of his goods and keep them for a year and a day. If any of his heirs come for them within a year and a day, he shall give them to the heir. If no-one comes then the *frana* takes half and the other half goes to the church.

GLOSSA 40. De rebus peregrinorum uide C. communia de succes. auth. Omnes peregrini et aduene libere hospitentur ubi uoluerint etc. (post *Cod.* 6.59.10 [Constitutio Friderici II]), ut patet in textu.

GLOSSA 41. *Ende di ora deel to goedes tyenst* Item libere apud eos qui uolunt sponte suscipere liberam habeant testandi facultatem, dummodo legittime testentur, C. de ino.[a] testa. l. Si quando (*Cod.* 3.28.35) et nota de sacrosanctis et l. i. (*Cod.* 1.2.1).

Di fria Fresa is nyaer toe witanne of hi aefte tingh halden habbe

53. Dat is riucht: jef di fria Fresa trya aefte thingh habbe socht binna dae jeer, soe mey di frana naet nyer komma, soe hyt op dae helghum wyta moet hor hi dae socht habbe, soe hi da naet socht habbe.

54. Jef di schelta bitighet een man dat hy syn tingh naet socht habbe als hy mit riuchta schulde, soe | schil hy hem twirasum onswara op da helghum.

Van schaede ende urhlest

55. Jef ma een man deth ureer ende ovirscheer, overmeet ende ovirdelta, so schil met mit twam schillingen beta, also langh so hit naet oflat is. Wirt hit oflat, so schil hi dyn schada foerfulla twyschet ende da grewa twa pond to ferda.

GLOSSA 42. *Schillingh* De his solidis qualiter sunt intelligendi, uide extra de maledic. c. Statuimus in fi. (X 5.26.2), et de iniur. c. Olim super uerbo usualis monete.[b] Item infra hoc libro de iure sinodali in titu. de pena adulterantis et ibi glo. inferius,[c] etiam ad hoc ff. de lega. i. Si seruus § Si numerus (*Dig.* 30.50.3).

Van mene thinghriuchte toe howe

56. Jef ma een man ti da how opclaget, so schil di grewa da schelta bieda dat hine to how bodie. So schel di schelta da bannere bieda dat hyne to how bodie. So schel di schelta da bannere byeda dat hi dine man toe howe bodie tweer daghen aen syne bura andert. Jef hy dan naet komma wil, soe aegh him di schelta dis tredda deys selff toe bodyen oen synre bura andert. Jef hy dan jeta naet komma wil, soe aegh hy hym dis fyaerda deys thi dae houwe urherich toe thyoeghen. Soe aegh hym dy aesgha twae pond to urdelane om dae urherichnisse

---

a de ino. *scripsimus cum Codice*: de I n o I FG.

b The gloss *usualis* ad X 5.36.7.

c *Infra* gloss 161.

GLOSS 40. See for matters concerning foreigners auth. *Omnes peregrini* (post *Cod.* 6.59.10), as appears in the text.

GLOSS 41. *Ende di ora deel to goedes tyenst* (*and the other half goes to the church*). Likewise, it is at the discretion of those who wish to do this by their own free will, that they have the free competence to make a last will and testament, as long as they do so in a legitimate way, see *Cod.* 3.28.35 and notice *Cod.* 1.2.1.

A Free Frisian Has More Rights to Establish Whether He Has Attended the Compulsory Court Meetings

53. This is the law: if a free Frisian has attended three duly held court meetings during the year, then the *frana* does not have the right to make him testify with an oath on the holy relics whether he has attended them or not.

54. If the *skelta* accuses a free Frisian of not having attended the court meetings he is legally obligated to, he shall exonerate himself with an oath on the holy relics, with the assistance of one compurgator.

Concerning Damage and Nuisance

55. If any man unlawfully ploughs or reaps or digs or mows on another man's land, he shall compensate with two shillings, as long as nothing is carried away. If something is carried away, then the man shall compensate the damage twofold and pay two pounds to the count for breaking the peace.

GLOSS 42. *Schillingh* (*shillings*). For how these coins should be understood, see X 5.26.2 and the gloss *usualis* to X 5.36.7. See also below in this book on synodical law, in the title on the penalty for the adulterer, and there in the lower gloss, and on this matter also *Dig.* 30.50.3.

Concerning the Common Procedure at the Court of the Count

56. If a case against someone is brought before the court of the count, the count shall order the *skelta* to summon the defendant to court. Subsequently, the *skelta* shall order the *bannere* to summon the defendant to court. The *skelta* shall order the *bannere* to summon the defendant to court in the presence of his neighbours on two successive days. If he then refuses to come, the *skelta* himself has to summon him in the presence of his neighbours on the third day. If he still refuses to come, the *skelta* shall proclaim him disobedient at the court on the fourth day. Then the *asega* shall decree that the defendant has to pay a

thi dae how. Soe schel dy grewa dae schelta ende da[1] aesgha byeda dat se toe syne fordele faere ende deer twa pond ut toe achtiane oen synre bura andert, jeff hya moeten, ende thoe how thoe bringhaene. Jef hith ymmen werth, soe aegh hym di aesgha allerliick twae pond thoe urdelane deer hit werden.

Hu ma een man ferdloes deth

36 57. Nyogen werva aegh ma him to bodien ende tria di schelta[2] urherich to tioghen mit saun des koninges orkenen, eer ma him mit riuchta to brand ende to breck dela moge. Jef hi des alles urherich wirt, soe aech ma him to sekane mit here ende mit brand. Ende als hi barnd is soe aeg di grewa, of hi deer is, dine aesga to bannen dat hi riucht[3] dele. Jef di grewa deer naet is, soe aegh di schelta dine aesga to bannen dat hi riucht dele. So aegh di aesga him ferdloes to lidsen ende syn gued. So aegh di aesga to delen dat di schelta dat eerwa bifaen schil to heerna ende to lyodena hand alont hi tinghet heerna hulde ende lyoda mit sodeenre boete als hi urberd haet, hit ne se dat hi bet tingia moge. Jef hi naet tinget binna jeer ende binna dei heerren ende lyoda hulde, so aegen heran ende da lyoed mitta eerwe to dwaen deer hiara wille se.

GLOSSA 43. *Ferdloes* De hoc uide in libro Rodulphi imperatoris.

GLOSSA 44. *Dit is di odera* Et nota quod condempnato in actione personali scilicet super debitis pecuniariis debent primo capi mobilia bona per iudicem et tradi actori secundum debiti quantitatem. Quibus deficientibus fiet executio in immobilibus. Tercio peruenitur ad nomina scilicet suorum debitorum et ad iura reddituum et ad ea que sibi debentur ff. de re iud. l. A diuo Pio[a] § primo et § In uendicione (*Dig.* 42.1.15 in pr. et 2), extra ut li. non contest. c. Quoniam frequenter § fi. (X 2.6.5).

Jef ma bi sonnaschyn naet ladet

58. Aldeer di fria Fresa[4] truch claghe toe how bodet wirt ende hi to andert comt ende greetwird urnimpt ende hi dat wert also langh als dyoe sonne schynt, so thoer hi to da dey efter sonnasedel hor anderda ner ban tielda. Soe schel ma him nyes bodia als jef hy eer naet bodet were.

37 GLOSSA 45. Exceptio dilatorie. De hoc | uide de offici. deleg. c. Consuluit (X 1.29.24).

GLOSSA 46. *Ende spreckt hy dat dyo sonne al onder da eerda is* Excipiendo, sed si tacet in exceptionibus, ualet processus contra ipsum factus.

---

[1] FG: di. [2] FG: sdhelta. [3] FG: riuct. [4] FG: di fria fria Fresa.

---

a A diuo Pio *scripsimus cum Digesto Novo*; Adinopiam FG.

fine of two pounds for disobedience to the count's court. Then the count shall order the *skelta* and the *asega* to go to the house of the defendant and collect the two pounds in the presence of his neighbours, if they can, and bring them to court. If someone hinders them in doing this, the *asega* shall decree a fine of two pounds against each of those who hindered them.

How to Decree a Man Outlawed

57. Nine times shall he be summoned, and the *skelta* shall decree him disobedient three times with seven of the king's witnesses, before it may lawfully be decreed against him that his house and goods are to be burnt down and laid to waste. If he remains disobedient in spite of all this, then a militia is to besiege his house with fire. And if his house is burnt down, the count, if he is present, shall order the *asega* to proclaim the decree. If the count is not present, then the *skelta* shall order the *asega* to proclaim the decree. Then the *asega* shall declare him and his property outlawed. Then the *asega* shall decree that the *skelta* shall take possession of the property on behalf of the lords and the people until the defendant has won back the favour of the lords and the people by paying the fine he was decreed to, unless he can offer a better defence. If he starts no proceedings within a year and a day to win back the favour of the lords and the people, then the lords and the people may do with the property as they deem fit.

GLOSS 43. *Ferdloes* (*outlawed*). See on this Emperor Rudolph's Book.

GLOSS 44. *Dit is di odera* (*this is the other*). And note that when someone is sentenced in a personal claim, i.e. for money debts, the judge should first take the moveable things and transfer these to the claimant in conformity with the amount of debt. When these are inadequate, execution occurs on the immovable properties. In the third place, recourse is taken to claims, viz. against his debtors, and to his rights to claim restitution and to the things owed to him, see *Dig*. 42.1.15 at the beginning and 2, and X 2.6.5.

If a Man Is Not Tried before Sunset

58. When a free Frisian is summoned to (the count's) court to answer a claim, and he appears to defend himself, and hears the claim, and defends himself as long as the sun shines, then he need not respond nor remain at court after sunset that day. Then he shall be summoned again as if he had not been summoned before.

GLOSS 45. A dilatory exception. See about this X 1.29.24.

GLOSS 46. *Ende spreckt hy dat dyo sonne al onder da eerda is* (*and if he says that the sun has set*). By way of defence; but if he fails to bring proper defences, the legal proceedings brought against him are valid.

Van urhericheyt des howes

59. Jef di grewa een man bitighet dat hi urherich fan da how ging ende dat him di aesga twa pond urdeelde ende hy him nenis weddis bitiged, so is hy nyer twyrasum to onriuchtane dan enich ban to ontfaen. So ne thoer hy deer an nene riucht staen om dat hy deer onbodet coem.

Van thinge ferst toe da houwe

60. Jef ma een man to how bodet ende hi deer greetwird urnimpt ende nachtferst jaret so aegh him di grewa nachtferst toe jaen sonder aesga doem ende hi syn andert to jaen dat hy dys moerns comme ende an riuchte stande.

Van da lettera fersta

61. Hweer so ma een man to how bodeth[1] ende hi deer greetne urnimpt ende hi to hand to riuchte wil staen ende di grewa dan fersta wil ende haet him syn andert toe jaen[2] soe ne thoer hy neen wed jowa[3] ner neen urheergens beta, want hi deer an riuchte staen wil. Soe schil hy deer mit riuchta dana gaen sonder schada. Jef ma him fora opsprecka wil, so schil ma him nyes bodia.

62. Jef ma da bannere in da boedschip duustsleken jefta bloedresena deth, jefta dera enich, deer hy mit boetschipe utladeth, soe is syn boete twybeet ende dae grewa twae pond jefta sexasum ontswara.

Hu ma da tiuge[4] alle moge forwisa

63. Dit is riucht: aldeer een stryd mit schelta ban ende mit aesga doem seend is
38 ende di onspreker in een oderis schelta ban beth an den odera | spreckt ende hi him to stride ladet, so schil hi quaen hine moghe him naet to stride laya om dat hyt him eer tosochte bi des schelta ban deer eer dissem waes ende bi dis aesgha doem ende an da bura eheer, "Dat hi mi mit[5] XII edem kestigade ende di aesgha dat deytingh deelde ende ick dae alle to dae bewysda deytingh taech alsoe aeft ende alsoe riucht dat ick nu mit riuchta naet thoer toejeens di toe stride staen. Jeftu des bisecka wilt so weddia ick di alsodeen tiuch[6] als di aesga deelt." So deelt him di aesga dat aefte tiuch[7] of hi libben is. So schil hit sidsa di schelta deer ur him da ban lath ende di aesga deer da eden stowad, ist dat hia libbe. Jef hia naet ne libbet so schillet saun dis koninges orkenen deer binna da

---

[1] FG: bodeht. [2] FG: ioun. [3] FG: neen iowa. [4] FG: tinge. [5] FG: hi mit. [6] FG: tinch. [7] FG: tinch.

Concerning Disobedience to the Count's Court

59. If the count accuses a man of having disobediently left the court, and if the *asega* has fined him with two pounds but if the count did not accuse him of having not given any financial security to appear, then the man can exonerate himself with one compurgator without further legal proceedings. And he is not obligated to stand suit because he originally came without being summoned.

Concerning Lawful Delay at the Count's Court

60. If a man is summoned to (the count's) court and he hears the complaint and asks for a day's delay, then the count shall grant him this without the decree of the *asega* and the defendant has to declare that he will come again the next day and stand before court again.

Concerning the Subsequent Delay

61. If a man is summoned to court and he hears the complaint and wishes to answer the claim immediately and the count wishes to grant him delay and orders him to give a promise, he does not have to give a financial security nor will he be fined for disobedience because he is willing to stand suit. Then he may leave the court without any penalty. If the claimant want to proceed against him further, he must be summoned anew.

62. If the *bannere* is attacked while on duty, be it hard blows or bleeding wounds, or by any of those who are summoned by him (the *bannere*), he shall receive a double compensation and two pounds for the count or he must exonerate himself with five compurgators.

How One Should Repudiate a Claim

63. This is the law: where a lawsuit has been settled by judgment of the *skelta* and decree of the *asega*, and the claimant then again makes the same complaint against the defendant when a new *skelta* has come into office, then the defendant shall declare that he cannot challenge him because he brought suit against him previously, under the jurisdiction of the previous *skelta*, and with a decree of the *asega* and in the presence of the neighbours, "That he demanded twelve oaths of me and the *asega* decreed a trial day, and on the appointed trial day I did all that was required in such a lawful manner that I now do not have to go to trial with you. If you wish to deny this, I will provide financial security for whatever testimony the *asega* may decree." And if the *asega* is still alive, he shall decree the proper testimony. Then the *skelta* who formerly held office and the *asega* who administered the oaths will testify, if they are still alive. If they are not, then seven of the king's witnesses which have been appointed within

ban setten sent allerlyck swara een sonderinga eed, dat hyaet mit agenen sagen ende mit aren heerden, dat di aesga da eden stowade ende him da laden alle taegh bi des schelta ban ende bi des aesga doem. Ende soe schillet saun swara fan dis koninges orkenen ende foerfulla des aesga doem ende swara dat hiaet mit aegenem sagen ende mit aren heerden dat di aesga da eden alle stowade. So schillet hya saun sidsa, een afara ende sex folgia, dat hya deermey weren dat hyt him eer tosochte bi des schelta ban ende bi des aesga doem ende dat hy him tolef eden weddade ende da alle taegh also fyr soe hi se hera wolde ende nu mit mara riucht staen schil soe dan hi se slita schil.

Van dada tiuge[1] ut to riuchtane

64. Dit is riucht, dat ma mit des dada tiuch naet fora ne waria mey, bihalva om fiouwer deden. Dyoe ene om een stryd, hoer hit biseend si soe bifuchten. Dat oer om een eerwe, hoer aen hit bitinget se so naet. Dat tredde om een bodel-
39 deel, hor hit him eer tosocht were. Dat | fyaerde om een hofferd.

Van tinge binna enis oers epenbere slaet

65. Dit is riucht. Jof deer ymmen in oderis epena slaet sprecka wil ende oen syn eerwe,[2] so schil hi hem tocomma mit twira tele ende mit aesga dome. Jef hi deer inoer wil, so schil hy him kestigia mit XII eden jefta toe een swirdkempa. Dat schil ma bitingia mit aefta ban ende mit aefta[3] deytingh.

Van tiuftiga gued toe sekan[4]

66. Aldeer ma een man syn gued ofstelt ende hi mitta[5] frana comt to sines bures huis ende deerin seka wil, so schil hi oerlef bidde ende dat gued naemna der hi seka wil. Jef hit soedeen gued se dat met moege oen der hand biluka jefta onder dae schaet bihiella, soe schil di frana ingaen ende saun dis koninges orkenen mit hem, al gripende eermen ende ongert ende onbroket ende berfoet, dat hia[6] neen gued indraga moge deer hya mede schadigie da onschieldiga manne. Jef hia dat tiuftigade gued deerin fyndet, is hit wollen claed ende onfarwed, so moet hyt to sine oenwirke tiaen. Jef hit linnen is, so moet hyt to sine eckere tyaen, deer dat flax oen woex deer ma dat claed of makede. Soe schillet swara tweer synre buren dat hi alsodeen land heed deer dat flax oen woex jefta da scheep hede deer ma dae wolle of scheer. Jef hit wrocht gold is, so moet hyt to

[1] FG: tinge. [2] FG: sprecka wil oen syn eerwe. [3] FG: aesga. [4] FG: ne|kan. [5] FG: ende mitta. [6] FG: hi.

this jurisdiction, shall each swear with an oath that they saw with their own eyes and heard with their own ears, that the *asega* administered the oaths and accepted the purgatory oaths by order of the *skelta* and the decree of the *asega*. And seven of the king's witnesses will swear and obey the decree of the *asega* to swear that they saw with their own eyes and heard with their own ears, that the *asega* administered the oaths. Then they will all declare, one first, followed by the other six, that they were present when the claimant brought a case against this defendant previously under the former *skelta's* jurisdiction and the decree of the *asega* and that the defendant offered him twelve oaths and performed them all in so far as he would hear them, and that according to law the judgment must stand and not be invalidated.

How to Deal With the Testimony of a Dead Man

64. This is the law, that the testimony of a dead man cannot be used any further with the exception of four instances. First, about an ordeal, whether it was settled or fought out. Second, about a piece of land, as to whether it has been under litigation or not. Third, regarding a specific asset, as to whether it was claimed from him previously or not. Fourth, concerning a infringement on someone's enclosure.

Concerning a Case Concerning Someone's Public Ditch

65. This is the law. If a man wishes to claim another man's open ditch and his adjacent land, he shall make a lawsuit with claim and defence, followed by a decree from the *asega*. If he wants to pursue this further, the claimant must challenge the defendant to twelve oaths or to an ordeal by combat. And proceedings shall be brought under proper jurisdiction and according to proper legal periods which have passed.

How to Search for Stolen Goods

66. If a man's goods are stolen and he comes to his neighbour's house accompanied by the *frana* and wants to search it, he shall ask permission and name the goods he wishes to search for. If it is something that can be held in the hand or hidden under a coat, the *frana* and seven of the king's witnesses with him shall enter with open hands, ungirt, without breeches and barefoot, so that nothing can be carried in with which they might damage the innocent man. If they find the stolen goods inside, and if it is undyed woollen cloth, let him show that it is his own manufacture. If it is linen, let him show his farmland, on which the flax grew out of which the cloth was made. In that case two of his neighbours shall swear that he does own land on which flax grows or that he owns sheep of which the wool was shorn. If it is wrought gold, he must show that it is his

sine inwirke tyaen. Jef hit onwrocht is, so schil hyt toe sine warende tyaen jefta to da tolneda merked jefta to da fieldfarende manne.

67. Jef ma een gued binna enis mannes huse in synre camer bifaert ende deer een reeckhol in is ende hit soedeen gued se dat ma hit deerin werpa moge, so is hi nyer sexasum op da helligem to witen ende schaedloes dat gued wer to jaen dan hi tief aegh to wessen. | Jef hit binna sine huse bidulven se, jefta dat ma hit fynt binna sine tredda slette, soe schil hi schieldich wessa jefta een schieldigra[1] winna. Jef hy aeck neen schieldigra wint so schil hy dat gued eenschet ende dat oder wederjae ende da frana deer dat gued binna sine banne nimmen is dat wederjeld jaen ur al sine hinden deer jerich sint ende hi binna sine dorem haet. So is dat wederjeld IIII einsa ende fyoerteensta trimene penningh.

GLOSSA 47. *Twischet* Res furtiue in duplum sunt restituende, Insti. de oblig. que ex maleficio nascuntur § Pena (*Inst.* 4.1.5) et loquitur[a] de furto non manifesto, quia actio furti manifesti est quadrupli, ut in § predicto (*Inst.* 4.1.5). Quare punitur manifestum magis quam occultum, cum clam facta magis sunt punienda, ff. de amminist. tuto. l. Non estimo (*Dig.* 26.7.54)? Sed ymmo magis delinquit qui palam quam qui clam ammouet, ut Insti. de ui bono. rapto. in princi. (*Inst.* 4.2.pr.); unde magis punitur, ff. de offi. pret. l. Diuus (*Dig.* 1.18.14); concordat xiiii q.v Penale (C.14 q.5 c.13). Et hec que dicta sunt ad pene persecutionem pertinent, Insti. de oblig. que ex maleficio nascuntur § ult. (*Inst.* 4.1.19[21]). Quia qui furatur, tenetur in quadruplum, cum ipsa re, secundum Accursium ibi.[b] Fur de iure autenticorum pro furto non suspenditur, nec occiditur nec membrum ei absciditur, sed aliter castigatur in auct. ut nulli iudic. § Furto (*Auth.* 9.9.13.1 [*Nov.* 134.13.1]), sed antiquo iure ff. furca suspenditur ff. de pe. l. Capitalium § Famosos § Grassatores[c] (*Dig.* 48.19.28.15 et 10). Sed secundum constitutionem Fredrici imperatoris, si quis quinque solidos ualens uel amplius furatus fuerit laqueo suspendatur, si minus scopis et forpice excorietur et tondatur, ut in lege Fredrici de pace tenenda uel tuenda in c. Si duo homines § Si quinque solidos (*LF* 2.27.18), sed secundum leges furtum manifestum est quadrupliciter restituendum, ut est Inst. ut supra (*Inst.* 4.1.5). Item si propterea non facis furtum, quia timens ne uidearis, id est ne iudiceris, intus in corde fecisti reus furti. Teneris, quamuis inde nil tulisti.

---

[1] FG: schiedigra.

---

a loquitur *scripsimus*: loquitnr FG.

b The gloss *condicendo* ad *Inst.* 4.1.19(21).

c Grassatores *scripsimus cum Digesto Novo*: Crassatores FG.

own manufacture. If it is unwrought gold, he must show that it came from his supplier, or the toll-market, or a traveling merchant.

67. If a good is found in a man's room, and there is a chimney in it, and the good is so small it could have been thrown in, then the owner of the house has more rights to exonerate himself with five compurgators and return the good without having to compensate for it rather than be proclaimed a thief. If it is found buried in his house or locked behind three locks, then he shall be found guilty of theft or produce a guiltier person. If he is unable to do so, he shall return the good and give its value on top of that, and he will pay a wergild for all adult members of his household to the *frana* within whose jurisdiction the good was stolen. And the wergild is 4 ounces and thirteen and a third pence.

GLOSS 47. *Twischet* (*twofold*). Things stolen have to be restored in twofold, see *Inst.* 4.1.5. And this text speaks about non-manifest theft, because the *actio furti manifesti* is for fourfold, as in the same text. Why is manifest theft punished more severely than occult theft, since what is done secretly should be punished more severely? see *Dig.* 26.7.54. But on the other hand the one who takes something away openly, is misbehaving more seriously than the one who takes something away secretly, see *Inst.* 4.2.pr.; hence he is punished more severely, see *Dig.* 1.18.14; this is in conformity with C.14 q.5 c.13. And the things mentioned here refer to claiming the penalty, see *Inst.* 4.1.19(21). Because someone who steals something owes the fourfold value as well as the thing itself, according to Accursius to that text. According to the law of the Authenticum the thief is not hanged, neither killed or deprived of a limb, but chastised in a different way, see *Auth.* 9.9.13.1 (*Nov.* 134.13.1), but according to the ancient law of the Digest he is hanged on the gallows, see *Dig.* 48.19.28.15 and 10. But according to a constitution of Emperor Frederick, if someone has stolen something of a value of five *solidi* or more, he gets the rope, if not skinned and shaved with rods and tongs, as in *LF* 2.27.18, but according to Roman law something manifestly stolen has to be restored fourfold, as in *Inst.* 4.1.5. Likewise, if you do not commit theft, but solely out of fear to be detected, i.e. to be sentenced, inside in your heart you have committed theft. You will be held,

41 Teneris quo ad Deum, non quo ad hominem, cum rem non tractaueris, | ff. de acquiren. possess. (*Dig*. 41.2), quia solo animo furtum non committitur secundum leges ut ibi dicitur.[a]

Van tiuftiga gueden to sekane

68. Jef di frana mitta lyoden een tiuftigada guede folget ende hi to enis mannes huus comt, soe aech hyt to bariane haet hi deer in seka wil. Jef ma him deer wert mit wighe ende mit wepen ende hy dat binaemde gued deer naet in seka moet, jef hi bisecka wil dat hi da seecknisse na ne werde, so schil dat bitiughe di bannere ende saun synre gaelioed. Als hit di bannere tiughet haet, soe schil hi dat gued jefta alsoe graet gued weerjaen ende da grewa twa pond.

GLOSSA 48. Pena recusantis, qui negat inquisitionem rei furtiue. Ex presumptione iuris reus dicitur furti, Extra de presump. c. Nullus (X 2.23.4).

GLOSSA 49. *So schil dat bitiuge da bannere* Nota. Vnus solus, licet deputatus sit ad officium, non est testis sufficiens, Extra de proba. c. Quoniam contra falsam (X 2.19.11).

Van bodeltinga to da huse

69. Jef een man in een bodel tingia wil ende deer een sibbera binna is, so schil hy da fiower thingh alle tingia bi aefta deytinghen. To da fyfta tinghe so aegh hi dae inferd jof hy moet. Jof hy naet moet, soe aegh di schelta dine waegh in to brecken ende him deer in toe bringen jef hi moet. Alle da deer him wareth mit wych ende mit wepen, dera is allerlyck da grewa schieldich twa pond. Ende jef hy deerin moet so schil hi alle bifara flette tinga. Ende jef di ora haet da tawa, so haet hy deermey bihalden sin bodel ende sin gued. Jef him deer tawa brect, soe aegh di oentingere een ferd oen da gued dat him nimmen aet onriuchtes dwe ende di ora dat gued rema.

Van bodel toe bitingien binna dae jeer

70. Jef ymmen oen oderis bodel tingia wil ende hi sit jeer ende dei onbitinget,
42 so ne thoer di ora him | to nenis riuchtis staen om dat hi jeer ende dey werloes was.

GLOSSA 50. Nota annalem prescriptionem. Heres habet annum ad deliberandum an uelit adire hereditatem uel repudiare, C. de iure deliber. l. Cum antiquioribus (*Cod*. 6.30.19). Et hoc est uerum, cum non petit deliberationem. Si uero petit et hoc si ab imperatore habet annum. Si uero a iudice

a Cf. *Dig*. 41.2.3.18.

although you did not take anything. You will be held towards God, not towards men, because you did not touch a thing, see *Dig*. 41.2, because according to Roman law one cannot commit theft by the mere intention, as is maintained there.

How to Search for Stolen Goods

68. If the *frana* is tracing stolen goods with the people and he comes to a man's house, he shall declare what he wants to search for in that house. If he is resisted with force and weapons and he is unable to search for the goods, and if the party afterwards denies that they obstructed the search, the *bannere* and seven of his militia will testify to this. If the *bannere* has done so, the party who resisted will return the goods or an equal amount of money and pay two pounds to the count.

GLOSS 48. As punishment for the obstinate one who opposes the search for the stolen thing. By presumption he is regarded culpable of stealing it, see X 2.23.4.

GLOSS 49. *So schil dat bitiuge da bannere* (*the bannere will testify to this*). Note that just one person, although designated for the task, does not suffice as a witness, see X 2.19.11.

Concerning a Court Meeting Over an Estate Held at the House

69. If a man wishes to claim an estate and a nearer of kin than he is in possession, he shall bring four proceedings at the proper intervals. At the fifth proceeding he has the right to enter the house if he can. If he cannot, the *skelta* has to break in the wall and conduct him in if he can. All those who then resist with force and weapons each are liable to the count for two pounds. If he can get in, he shall litigate the whole question in the front part of the house. And if the defendant establishes his case, he thereby retains his estate and his property. If the defendant fails to deliver the proof, the claimant gets a right to peaceful possession of the property so that no man may wrong him, and the defendant shall leave the property.

A Lawsuit to Claim an Estate Must Start Within a Year

70. If a man wishes to claim an estate and the defendant has been in possession of the estate for a year and a day, he is no longer obligated to stand suit over this claim because no complaint has been brought before court for a year and a day.

GLOSS 50. Note that prescription is annual. The heir has one year to deliberate whether he wants to accept or reject the inheritance, see *Cod*. 6.30.19. And this holds good, when he did not enter a petition for deliberation.

habet nouem menses, ut C. e. l. fi §. Sed quia (*Cod.* 6.30.22.13a) et ff. e. l. i §. ult. (*Dig.* 28.8.1.2).

GLOSSA 51. *So ne doer* Inanis est actio, quia infra annum non egit. Ergo neglexit ipsum, quia infra tempus statutum a iure non egit. Et iura non subueniunt dormientibus sed uigilantibus.[a] Et quia tanto tempore dormiuit, non est actio sua audienda nec sibi per iudicem ecclesiasticum uel temporalem subueniendi.

Van bodel riucht dine sibsta in dat huis to wisane

71. Hweer so een bodel laweged is ende di sibsta mit tinge to da huis comt, soe aegh di aesga dine alre sibsta in to delen to da forma tinge. Als hi incommen is, so aegh hi een ferd oen da gued an fara flette alont hit bitinget is, huckera hiara di aeftera eerwa se. Ende huckera fan hiarem deer dat biradeth dat hi aeftera eerwa se, so aegh hi dine ferd oen da gued.

GLOSSA 52. *So aegh di aesga* id est iudex terre ex parte potestatis et iudex competens habens merum et mixtum imperium ut et iudex ordinarius loci, ubi res hereditarie sunt constitute, mittit in possessionem, C. ubi de heredi. agi opor. l.i. (*Cod.* 3.20.1), et notatur C. de edic. diu. adri. l.iii §. Sancimus (*Cod.* 6.33.3 in pr.) super uerbo competenti iudici.[b]

GLOSSA 53. *Den alre sibsta* Verum est ab intestato uenienti, secus in herede scripto qui primo mittendus est in possessionem omnium rerum testatoris que fuerunt ipsius tempore mortis testatoris, ut in dicta l. iii C. de edic. diui adri. toll. libro sexto Codicis (*Cod.* 6.33.3).

GLOSSA 54. *Hueckera hiara di aeftera* Id est missus in possessionem uel antea uel detinens uel contradicens.

GLOSSA 55. *Ende hueckera fan hiaren* id est potiora iura; ex legitimis proba-
43 tionibus ostenderit, ut dicta. l. ul. § Sin autem | C. de edic. diui adri. tol. (*Cod.* 6.33.3.1).

Van lawede bodele

72. Hweer so ma een bodel lawiget nevem ende niftem ende hia evenkne sint als hia to da fordel commet, soe agen hia in to farane ende des boedels to moniane mit aefta orkenschip fan dam deer kamer ende kayen der warade. So aech him di aesga to delane dat se agen to weddien elkerlyck orem riucht bodeldeel. Als hia dat riuchte boedeldeel biweddet habbet, soe schellet se[1] foerd draga

[1] FG: schelles.

a Cf. *Dig.* 42.8.24.

b The gloss *competenti iudici* ad *Cod.* 6.33.3 in pr.

However, if he did, and he did so to the Emperor, he has one year; to the judge, however, nine months, see *Cod.* 6.30.22.13a and *Dig.* 28.8.1.2.

GLOSS 51. *So ne doer* (*no longer obligated*). The claim is inane, since he has not sued within one year. He thus neglected this period, since he did not bring the claim within the time determined by law. Legal provisions do not support those who sleep, but those who are awake. And because he has been sleeping for such a long time, he has no admissible claim and neither should he be rescued by the ecclesiastical or secular judge.

Concerning Temporarily Allotting an Estate to the Next of Kin

71. Whenever an estate has been bequeathed and the relatives come to the house to litigate their claims, the *asega* must allot the right of entry to the next of kin on the first court session. When the next of kin has entered, he shall have a right to peaceful possession of the property in the front part of the house until the question has been litigated as to which of them is the more lawful heir. And which of them shows that he is the more lawful heir, let him have a right to peaceful possession of the property.

GLOSS 52. *So aegh di aesga* (*the asega must*). This is the judge of the territory on behalf of the authorities and the competent judge, having a 'pure' and 'mixed' power, so that he, also as ordinary judge of the place where the hereditary goods are situated, authorizes to take possession, see *Cod.* 3.20.1 and what is stated in the gloss *competenti iudici* to *Cod.* 6.33.3 in pr.

GLOSS 53. *Den alre sibsta* (*the next of kin*). This is true for the heir-at-law. It is different for the testamentary heir who first must be authorized to take possession of all the testator's things, which were his from the time of the testator's death, as in *Cod.* 6.33.3 mentioned above.

GLOSS 54. *Hueckera hiara di aeftera* (*which of them is the most lawful heir*). That is, the one authorized to take possession, either previously, or by retaining the estate or by contradicting (the other's right).

GLOSS 55. *Ende hueckera fan hiaren* (*and which of them*). That means stronger claims; this is shown by legitimate evidence, as in *Cod.* 6.33.3.1.

Concerning an Estate

72. When a man leaves an estate to nephews and nieces, and when those who come to the house are of the same degree of relationship to him, they must go in with the proper evidence and claim the estate from the keeper of the rooms and keys. Then the *asega* must decree that they shall pledge one another a fair share of the estate. When they have pledged one another a fair share, they shall carry

gold ende weed jof hit deer is, ku ende ey ende hiara quickfia ende inka ende anderke. So agen hia in den field to farane ende dat eerwe to delen, dat fyrste alleraerst ende dat neste allerlest. Dat schillet hia binna saun nachtem deen habba al to da huse, hit ne se dattet him need ofnime. Deer schil hia di schelta tobanna dat hiaet alsoe dwe: dat schil wessa dis winters als des summers, dat ne mei urfaen fira ner festa mer deer schil ma tingia om saun nacht om een bodeldeel.

Jef dis buirblicande guedis aet forloren is, deer hi eer aynlike oen siner wer hede da hi aller[1] nest oen sonda live was, oen schepena weed jefta oen wrochta golde jefta oen fyower fotada schettum, soe schil hi deer kamer ende kayen warade dat winna jefta foer fuldeel nima, hit ne se dattet him an needraef ofnimmen se.

Ende jef ma deer enich schielda aeschet, willet hia naet jechta,[2] so schil di swara, deer dat gued aeschet, dat hi dat oen dat meenbodel jo dam, deer da kamer ende kayen biwarade. Soe schil di ora swara dat hi[3] dat ontfingh ende in dat meenbodel biwarade. Nu mei fordera neen schielda jechta deer kamer ende kayen warade dan hy mit ku ende ey jelda mei ende binnia da balken mit bodel. Jef hi fordera jecht, so sint da erfnamen nyer dine ker to habben hor hia
44 onswerre[4] dan hia jelde. |

GLOSSA 56. *Ueddia schil riucht bodedeel* Primo mobilia de inde immobilia sunt diuidenda, ut C. quo. bono. per totum (*Cod.* 8.2), Institut. de interdic. § Adiscipendum (*Inst.* 4.15.3), ff. quo. bono. l. i. (*Dig.* 43.2.1).

GLOSSA 57. *Dat fyrsta alleraerst* Nota quod in iudicio sunt ignoti prius expediendi.

GLOSSA 58. *Aen schepna weed* Nota quod bona hereditaria tempore mortis derelicta integraliter sunt representanda.

GLOSSA 59. *Jefta foer fol deel nima* lib. v. C. de rerum amota[a] per totum (*Cod.* 5.21), C. de iure deliberan. l. Sanci. § Simili modo (*Cod.* 6.30.22.1b).

Dit is di boedeleed

73. Dit is di riuchta boedeleed deer dijeen swara schil deer kamer ende kayen warade. So aegh hy op to nymen mit siner winster hand sine winstera ghara[5] ende deer op toe lidsen tween fingeren mit sine fora hand ende swara dan. Ende di aesga schil him dine eed stowia aldus: "Dat y[6] nabbe oen da meenbodel helleth ner[7] hindereth oen ha ner oen coern, oen field ner oen terp, oen wepen ner

[1] FG: alier. [2] FG: willet hia jechta. [3] FG: hit. [4] FG: onswer. [5] FG: hara. [6] FG: hyo. [7] FG: hel|lenner.

a lib. v. C. de rerum amota. *scripsimus cum Codice*: lib. vi C. de rerum an moto. FG.

out gold and cloth, if there is any, cows and sheep and other cattle, and tools for fishing and farming. After that, they must go to the fields and divide the land, the farthest part first, and that which is nearest to the house last. They must have finished this up to the house within the week, unless necessity prevents them. The *skelta* shall order them to do so, whether it be winter or summer, nor shall a fast-day or a feast-day prevent it, but the distribution of the estate must be done within a week.

If anything is missing which was openly known to be in the possession of the deceased when he was last alive, whether it be woven cloth or wrought gold or cattle, then the keeper of the rooms and keys shall produce it or consider it as part of his share, unless it was taken from him by robbery.

And if any debts are claimed against the estate and the heirs are not willing to concede these, then the claimant shall swear that he delivered it to the main estate, handing it over to the keeper of the rooms and the keys. The latter shall swear that he received it and kept it as part of the general estate. The keeper of the rooms and keys cannot acknowledge more claims than he can pay out of cattle and sheep and goods within the household. If he concedes more, the next of kin have a stronger right to choose between taking an oath of non-liability or paying.

GLOSS 56. *Ueddia schil riucht bodedeel* (*must pledge a fair share of the estate*). First the moveables and subsequently the immoveables must be distributed, see the entire title *Cod.* 8.2, *Inst.* 4.15.3 and *Dig.* 43.2.1.

GLOSS 57. *Dat fyrsta alleraerst* (*the farthest part first*). Note that in the proceedings, the unknown heirs should first be traced.

GLOSS 58. *Aen schepna weed* (*woven cloth*). Note that the hereditary goods that were abandoned at the time of death must be produced in their entirety.

GLOSS 59. *Jefta foer fol deel nima* (*or consider it as part of his share*). See the entire title *Cod.* 5.21 and *Cod.* 6.30.22.1b.

This is the Estate Oath

73. This is the legal oath which the keeper of the rooms and the keys must swear. He must take up the left part of his coat with his left hand and place two fingers of his right hand on it and swear. And the *asega* shall administer the oath thus: "That you have not kept or withheld anything of the general estate, in hay nor in corn, in fallow land nor in ploughland, in weapons nor in cloth, in gold nor

oen weed, oen gold ner oen steente, oen selvir ner oen slayn penningen, oen heer ner oen heed, binnia der eerda ner buppa der eerda, also gued so fiower penningen. Also bruke y lives ende ledena ende alle der havena deer y nu habbe ende[1] foerd winne ende also mote joe tigia quick ende bern ende bodel ende al juwe hava dat joe God alsoe helpe ende syn helligha als y dine eed riucht swerre ende onmeens, hit ne se dat y jo bet bitensa moghe binna jeer ende binna dey ende riuchta den eed ende betterie den eed tojenst dyn deer y[2] oen urbritsen haet."

Van fordele in da cladem under aefte sidem efter des oderis dade

74. Dit is riucht: hueckera hyara sidena deer lingera lywet, so aegh hi tria da besta claen oen toe habben als ma dyn andera toe der molde bifalt. | Als hya dat bodel delet, so schil hi da nima tojenst dat beerweed ende deer ne schil oen wessa goud noch selvir ner paleftreda, ner weed ner worma.

Van bodel to delane

75. Dat is riucht: hweer so ma een boedel dela schil dat met also dela schil als met samanade. Jef hyara een quet dat him bodeldeel laweged se, so schil met utreda mitta koninges orkenen alset deer inkommen is oen scheppena weed jefta oen wrochta gold jefta oen fyowerfoeteda schet, dat hyt binna jeer ende binna dey in dat meenbodel coem.[3]

GLOSSA 60. *Mit des koninges orkenen* Id est tabellionum siue notariorum publicorum qui iurant suum officium fideliter exercere pro utraque parte de his qui audient et uidebunt, Extra de prescript. c. Ad audien. (X 2.26.13), de presumpt. Illud (X 2.23.11), in auct. de tabel. coll. iiii (*Auth.* 4.7 [*Nov.* 44]), C. de tabella. l. iii. libro decimo[a] (*Cod.* 10.71[69].3) et uide glossam super uerbo publicarum personarum C. de ammistr. tut. l. Tutor uel curator[b] et sufficit unus tabellarius uel iudex ordinarius ut ibi in glossa et C. ubi de hereditate agi oportet l. i (*Cod.* 3.20.1) et C. de edic. di. adri. l. iii § Sancimus (*Cod.* 6.33.3 in pr.) super uerbo competenti iudici.[c]

76. Dat is riucht ti da meenbodel. Jef di man queth dat hi sin eerwe seld habbe ende in dat meenbodel brocht, so schil met him forfulla jef hit mitter wirde

---

[1] FG: habbee.nde. [2] FG: hy. [3] This entire sentence was misplaced in the incunable: it was printed after the last sentence of § 74 (after *weed ner worma*) but belongs here.

---

a decimo *scribimus*: undecimo *male praem.* FG.
b The gloss *publicarum personarum* ad *Cod.* 5.37.24.
c The gloss *competenti iudici* ad *Cod.* 6.33.3.pr.

in gemstones, in silver nor in coined money, in hair nor in hide, beneath the earth nor above the earth, so much as four pennies. And so may you have the use of your life and limbs and all the goods you now have and will have, and so may you win cattle and children and property and all of your goods, that God so help you and all his saints, that you will swear this oath truly and not falsely, unless you reconsider this within a year and a day and set the oath right and compensate the false oath to him you have injured".

Concerning the Division of Clothes between Spouses When One of Them Has Died

74. This is the law: whichever spouse lives the longest, shall have the three best garments to wear when the other is being buried. When dividing the estate, they shall take these clothes to counterbalance the graveclothes and on these garments shall be neither gold nor silver or expensive silk, nor shall they be coloured blue or purple.

Concerning the Division of an Estate

75. This is the law: when an estate is distributed, it shall be distributed in the order in which it was accumulated. If someone maintains that part of the estate was bequeathed to him, it shall be proven with the king's witnesses that this part was added to the estate within the past year and a day, be it woven cloth or wrought gold or cattle.

GLOSS 60. *Mit des koninges orkenen* (*with the king's witnesses*). That means, of the notaries or public clerks who take an oath to practice their office faithfully for both parties as regards the things heard and seen, see X 2.26.13, X 2.23.11, *Auth.* 4.7 (*Nov.* 44), *Cod.* 10.71(69).3 and see the gloss *publicarum personarum* to *Cod.* 5.37.24; and one notary or ordinary judge is sufficient as in the gloss mentioned and *Cod.* 3.20.1 and the gloss *competenti iudici* to *Cod.* 6.33.3 at the beginning.

76. This is the law regarding the common estate: if the husband says that he sold his land and included the revenue into the common estate, he shall be compensated for it, if he can prove it by testimony of the inhabitants of the

biwisa mei oen da buirschip der hit seld is. Jef dyo frouwe queth dat hio dat her seld habbe, mei hioet awa an da buirschip deer hioet seld haet,[1] so schil met her forfulla. Jef dat bern dat queth, dat hit syn seld habbe, so agen dae bern dat selve riucht jef hia da helpe habbe oen der buirscip deer hit sield is als deerto heert.

Van di deer onwillich is to delen

77. Aldeer een bodel bitinget is ende hiara een onwillich is syn deel to nimen, soe aegh di frana des onwilliga deel to nimen oen torp ende oen fielda ont hit
46 to da | huis comme. So aegh hy to da huis dine deel to nimmen ende to warien ur al.

Di schelta schil biade him self to riuchta anderde

78. Dat is riucht: hweer soe di schelta een tingh halt, so schil hy riuchtes bieda aller manlikum. Jef him ymmen aet bitiget: lada ende bota. Jef him ymmen aet op to sprecken haet, soe schil di huuskeerl dae bannere bieda dat hy dine schelta aeschie. So schil di bannere quaen: "Her schelta, ick aeschie jo ende banne jo deertoe mit mines hera banne, dat y disse manne riucht andert jouwe." Jef hy naet wil, so aech him nimmen to jaen lada ner bota ner nimmen syn lada tielda.

79. Dit is riucht. An hwelka ban soe di aesga comt ende him ymmen aet op to sprecken[2] haet, soe schil hy an da selve banne aller manlikum jaen lada ende bota, jef hy moet neen doem dela.

Van sonderinga fordela ende dis aesga riuchtes

80. Dit is riucht. An hwelka banne so di aesga een man aeschet dat hi him aldeer schil ja lada ende boeta, hit ne se dat hyt bi willa fersta wil.

81. Als di grewa in dat land comt ende hi urherige lioed seka schil, so schil di syn fana fera deer dyn mena ferd dis landis feert ende biwareth.

82. Wideken heet di forma aesga deer dyn aersta doem deelde in Freescha merkum.[3]

83. Hwa so een hors to dada slacht, so is syn lives riucht dat met jelda schil mit trim eynsem ende mit twam schillingem dyn ferd beta, hit ne se dat di ora

[1] FG: hioet haet. [2] FG: op him to sprecken. [3] FG: merknm.

settlement where he sold it. If the wife says she sold hers, and she can prove it by testimony of the inhabitants of the settlement where she sold it, she shall be compensated for it. If the child says that he sold his, then the children are entitled to the same rights provided they can get the help of the inhabitants of the settlement where it was sold, as is required.

Concerning Someone Unwilling to Take Part in the Division

77. Where an estate is being distributed and one of the heirs is unwilling to accept his share, the *frana* shall take possession of the unwilling party's share, existing of meadow and ploughland until it comes to the house. Then he shall take his share of (goods in) the house and guard everything.

The Skelta *Shall Lawfully Defend Himself*

78. This is the law: whenever the *skelta* holds court, he shall offer legal satisfaction to all men alike. If any man accuses him of anything: (then he must exonerate himself with) oaths or (pay) compensation. If someone wishes to pursue the claim, let the freeman order the *bannere* to make a demand to the *skelta*. The *bannere* shall say: "Lord *skelta*, I ask of you and command you by the authority of my lord that you give this man a proper answer." If the *skelta* refuses to do so, no man needs to pay him for claims or compensations nor obey his orders.

79. This is the law. In whatever court the *asega* comes and someone makes a claim against him, he shall give answers or compensations to all men or he may make no decree.

Concerning Specific Privileges and the Rights of the Asega

80. This is the law. In whatever court the *asega* makes demand upon a man, that man shall defend himself or give compensation, unless he (the *asega*) is willing to grant him a delay.

81. When the count enters the land and has to prosecute disobedient people, the man in charge of keeping the general peace in the land shall carry his banner.

82. Wideken is the Name of the First *asega* who First Gave Judgment Within the Frisian Territory.

83. If someone's horse is killed, it is the law that it shall be compensated with three ounces and a fine of two shillings for breaking the peace, unless the owner

quaen wil, deer dat hors aegh, dat him deer mara schada oen schyn is ende him
47 deer omme kestigia wil. Dis hinxstes bote dis lives: | tredde[1] hael eynse. Dis oxa
bota dis lives: twae eynsa. Der ku bote dis lives: tritich penningen. Dis feringes
bote dis lives: acht penningen ende twa eynsa ende II schillinghen di ferd.

[1] FG: boe|de.

of the horse asserts that he suffered more damage than that and wants to sue for it. The compensation for a stallion is two and a half ounces. The compensation for an ox: two ounces. The compensation for a cow: thirty pennies. The compensation for a bull: eight pennies and two ounces and for all these a fine of 2 shillings for breaking the peace.

IV. Of the Two Kings Charles and Radbod

Van da tweer koningen Kaerl ende Radbod

Da di koningh Kaerl ende di koningh Radbod fan Deenmerkum in dat land comen, da bisette ellick syn oerd ende syn eynd in Franekeragae mit een heerschielde, ende elkerlyck seide dat land were syn. Da woldent wise lioed sena ende da heren woldent bifiuchta. Da wysdma da soen alsoe langh, dat met op dae tweer koningen gaf, huckera hiarem deer orem an stille stalle urstoed, dat hyt wonnen heed. Da brocht ma da heren togara. Da stoden se een etmel al omme, da leet him[1] di koningh Karl syn handschoech ontfalla. Da rachten him di koningh Radboed. Da spreeck di koningh Kaerl: "Ha, ha, dat land is myn!" ende hlackade. Aldeerom haet syn oerd Hachense. "Hweerom?" spreeck Radboed. Da spreeck Kaerl: "Y sint myn man worden!" Dae spreeck Radboed "O wach!" Deerom[2] haet syn oerd Wachense.

Da foer[3] di koningh Radboed uta lande, ende di koningh Kaerl wolde tingia. Da ne mostere, hwant deer lediges landis so fula naet was, deer hi op tingia mochte. Da seyntere boede[4] in da saun selanden ende hetet hiarem, dat hya him wonnen[5] een frie stoe, deer hi op tinghia mochte. Dae caepeden hya mit schat ende mit schillinge Deldemanes.

Deer tingadere op ende layde da[6] Fresen tofara him, ende heet dat hya riucht kerren,[7] als hya halde wolden. Da baden hia ferstis to hiara foerspreka. Da jo hy hiarem oerlef. Dis ora deis heet hi dat se tofara dat riucht coemen.[8] Da comen se, ende kerren foerspreken: XII fan da saun seelanden. Dae heet hy
48 dat se riucht kerren. Dae byjaraden se ferstis. | Dis tredda deis het hi se commen, da tagen se needschyn. Dis fyaerde deys also, dis fyfta also. Dit sint da twae ferst ende da tria needschyn deer di Fria Fresa mit riuchta habba mey. Dis sexta deis heet hi dat se riucht kerren. Da spreken se hya ne konden. Da spreeck di koningh: "Nu lidse ick jo toefara tree kerren, hor jemna lyawera se: dat ma jemna deye, dan y alle ayn werde, joff dat ma jemna een schip jow, also fest ende also sterck deer een ebba ende een floed mey urstaen ende dat sonder rema ende roer, ende sonder tow." Da kerren hya dat schip, ende folen ut mitta ebba also fyr dat se neen aland syaen mochten. Dae was hyarem leed toe moed. Dae spreeck di ena deer fan Wydeken slachte was, dis forma aesga: "Ick hab heerd dat us hera God, da hi op eertrike was, tolef jongheren hede, ende hi self di tretteensta were, ende coem to hyarem bi bislettena dorem ende traeste se ende leerde se. Hoe bidda wy naet dat Hi us een tretteensta seinde, deer us riucht lere ende toe lande wise?" Dae folen se alle op hyara kne ende

[1] FG: *him* is missing. [2] FG: deer. [3] FG: foeer. [4] FG: *boede* is missing. [5] FG: won. [6] FG: da da. [7] FG: ker. [8] FG: coem.

IV. Of the Two Kings Charles and Radbod

When King Charles and King Radbod of Denmark came into the land, each occupied his site and end in the district of Franeker with an armed muster and each claimed that the land was theirs. Then wise men wanted to come to reconciliation, but the lords wanted to battle out the dispute. Then they insisted on a truce for such a long time, that they convinced the two kings that the one who would outstrip the other in the ordeal of the cross, would have won. Then the lords were brought together. They had stood still for a full day and night, when King Charles let his glove fall from his hand. Then King Radbod picked it up for him, and King Charles spoke: "Ha, ha, this land is mine!" and laughed. For that reason his site is called *Hachense*. "Why?" Radbod said. Then Charles said "You have become my vassal!" Then Radbod said: "Woe is me!" which is why his site is called *Wachense*.

Then King Radbod left the land, and King Charles wished to hold court. Yet he could not, for there was no vacant plot of land where he could hold court. So he sent envoys throughout the Seven Sealands and bade them to acquire for him a free place where he could hold court. Then they bought *Deldamanes* for him with assets and money.

There he held court and summoned the Frisians before him, and ordered them to choose a law they would want to uphold for themselves. Then they requested a term to choose their delegates. This he granted them. The next day he summoned them before the court. Then they came, and chose their delegates: twelve from the Seven Sealands. Then he ordered them to choose law. Then they requested a term. The third day he ordered them to come, and then they appealed to legal impediment. The fourth day, too, as well as the fifth day. These are the two terms and the three impediments to which a free Frisian is legally entitled. The sixth day he ordered them to choose law. Then they stated that they could not. Then the king spoke: "Now I am going to give you three options which you can choose from, namely that you be put to death, that you all become serfs, or that you are given a ship, as strong and as firm as to withstand but one ebb and one flow tide, without a rudder and oars, and without rigging." Then they chose the ship, and set out on an ebb tide and went so far that they could no longer see land. Then they despaired. Then the one of them who was of Widekin's kin, the first *asega*, spoke: "I have heard that our lord God, when he was on Earth, had twelve disciples, and he himself was the thirteenth, and he came to them through closed doors and comforted them and taught them. Why should we not pray so that He may send us a thirteenth, who may teach us the law and guide us to land?" Then they fell to their knees and prayed fervently.

beden inlike. Da se da bedinge heden deen, da sagen se een tretteensta oen der stioerne sitten ende een axa op synre aexla deer hi mey toe lande stioerde tojenst straem ende wynd. Da se toe lande coemen, da worp hy mitter axa op dat land ende worp een tura op. Da ontsprongh deer een burna. Aldeerom haet dat to Axenthove ende to Eeswey comen se to land, ende seten om dae burna. Ende haet so him di tretteensta leerde, dat nomen se toe riucht, doch ne wistet nimmen haet di tretteensta were deer to hyarem commen was, alsoe lyck was hy hyarem elkerlyck. Dae hy hyaerem dat riucht wysd hede, dae weren deer mer
49 toelef. | Aldeerom schillet aldeer der in da land wessa tretteen aesgen, enda hyara domen schillet hya dela to Axenthove ende to Eeswey. Ende hweer so hia entwa sprecket, so agen da saun da sex in to halien. Aldus ist landriucht aller Fresena.

When they had prayed, they saw a thirteenth man sitting at the helm, with a golden axe on his shoulder, with which he steered them to land against the tides and the wind. And when they made landfall he threw the axe to the ground and upheaved a turf. Then a well sprung from that spot. For that reason that place is called *Axenhove* and they came to land at *Eswei*, and sat around the well. And whatsoever the thirteenth taught them, they adopted as law, yet no-one knew who the thirteenth was who came to them, to such an extent he resembled each of them. And after he had taught them the law, only twelve remained. For that reason there shall be thirteen *asegas* in the land, and they shall pronounce their judgments at *Axenhove* and at *Eswei*. And when there is no consensus, the seven shall have precedence over the six. Such is the land law of all Frisians.

v. The Statutes of Magnus

Hyr bighinnet dae kerren deer Magnus kaes thoe Roem

Will y harkya ende letet joe sidsa fan da aersta kerren deer da Fresen kerden da hya toe roem den fridoem bicronghen. Ende da dat stryd opheven ward twischa Romera heren ende den koningh Kaerl om des paeus Leo aeghen deer Romera heren blyndet heden, da brocht ma da nakena Fresen alla fara, ho se aerst foerslayn worden. Da binettent da Fresen mitta live ende efter bifuchten hyaet mitta handen manlike dat[1] hya Romera burich wonnen an dera tredda tyd dis deys, da da Romera heran ur hiara moes weren. Da brochte Magnus, deer di Freesna fanadreger was, syn fana op da alrehagista thoer deer waes binna Roem. Hoe leed dat koningh Kaerl was: eer weren se alle naken Fresen, da heet se di koning alle heren. Da baed ma da heren gold ende goedwob. Da baed ma da heren allerlikum syn breda schield mitta rada golde to bislaen. Da baed ma da heeren allerlikum to setten in een sonderinga rike ende dat ma deer of doch tyenade als ma een wieldigha koninghe schulde. Alle dae jeften deer di koningh baed dae urspreck Magnus ende kaes een oer hael bettera ende alle Fresen oen Magnus ker jechten.

1. Ende kaes, dat alle Fresen fryheren weren,[2] di berna ende di oenberna, alsoe langh soe di wynd fan da wolkenen wayd ende dyoe wrauld stoede ende willet
50 wessa mit kerre dis koninghes haga heranathen. |

GLOSSA 61. *Dae baedma da heren gold* Simile responsum fuit romanorum, dicentium "Non aurum habere, sed aurum habentibus ⟨imperare⟩[a] gloriosum est".[b] Qui enim auro pecuniaque capitur, uelud abiectus inter uilissimos computatur. Nota pro ciuitatensibus quod nullus ciuis pro debitis conciuis sui debeat molestari. Est casus duo, C. ut nullus ex uicariis pro alienis uicariorum debitis teneatur l. i libro undecimo (*Cod.* 11.57[56].1), C. ne uxor pro marito auth. (post *Cod.* 4.12.4 [ex *Nov.* 52.1]): "Set[c] omnino qui alium pro alio secundum formam pignorationis exigit totum id ipsum quicquid sit[d] in quadruplum reddit uim passo necnon et ab actione pro qua talia presumit cadet". Hec autentica est sumpta de corpore ut non fiant pignorationes § i. coll. v. (*Auth.* 5.5.1 [*Nov.* 52.1]).

---

[1] FG: da. [2] FG: weer.

---

a Emendavimus ex Servio.
b Maurus Servius Honoratius (4th century AD), Commentary on the Aeneid, 6.844.
c Set *scripsimus cum Codice*: Et FG.
d sit *scripsimus cum Codice*: sicut FG.

v. The Statutes of Magnus

Here Begin the Statutes Which Magnus Formulated in Rome

Listen and hear about the first statutes the Frisians formulated after they had won their freedom in Rome. When the war between the Roman nobility and King Charlemagne began because the Romans had gouged out Pope Leo's eyes, they brought all Frisians into the front line, so that they be slain first. Then the Frisians put their lives at risk and with their own hands fought so valiantly that they conquered the Roman stronghold on the third hour of the day, when the Romans were having their meals. Then Magnus, the standard-bearer of the Frisians, placed his standard on the highest tower in Rome. Charlemagne regretted this very much: before this they had been naked Frisians, but now the king had to consider them all lords. Then the lords were offered gold and precious textiles. Then the lords were offered to have their wide shields studded with red gold. Then the lords were each offered a separate territory in which they would be served as if they were mighty kings. All gifts the king offered were declined by Magnus and he chose a better one, and all Frisians agreed with Magnus's choice.

1. And he determined, that all Frisians were to be free, the born and the unborn, for as long as the wind will blow from the clouds and the world stands firm, and that the Frisians by statute would be high comrades-in-arms to the king.

GLOSS 61. *Dae baedma da heren gold* (*Then the lords were offered gold*). Similar to this was the response of the Romans who said 'It is honourable not to have gold, but to rule over those who have gold'. For, he who is obsessed by gold and money, being a despicable person, is rated amongst the lowest of the low. Note that for citizens, it holds that no citizen may be burdened by the debts of his fellow citizen. There are two cases: *Cod.* 11.57(56).1 and the authentica *Sed omnino* (post *Cod.* 4.12.4): "Surely the one who by way of pledge takes something from the wrong person, has to restore that all, whatever it is, in fourfold to the one afflicted by the infringement and he will also abandon the claim for which he assumed such behaviour". This authentica is taken from the core of *Auth.* 5.5.1 (*Nov.* 52.1).

Dit is di oera ker

2. Aldeerefter kaes Magnus den lettera ker ende alle Fresen oen sine ker jechten, dat ma da Fresen da holtena witta fan da hals spande ende se ymmermeer wolden wessa fryheren, di berna ende di onberna, also langh so di wynd fan da wolkenen wayd ende dioe wrald stoede ende willet wessa mitta ker dis koninghes haga heranathen.

Dit is di tredda ker

3. Dae kaes Magnus dine tredda ker ende alle Fresen oen sine ker jechten, dat se neen koninghschielda haghera ne gulden dan riuchten huuslaga da schelta, het ne se dattet dumme lioed oen da bannem hiarem urberde[1] ende hya se dan ontgulde.

GLOSSA 62. *Datse neen koninghschielda* Imperator exemit hic Frisones a tributis speciali remissione. Habes arg. de cen. c. Cum uenerabil. (X 3.39.21), de decimis c. Tua (X 3.30.25), xvi q. i. Decime sunt tributa (C.16 q.1 c.66), ii q. iii § Potest quoad medium (?).[a] Dant ecclesie aliquos denarios in signum subiectionis, extra de censi. Omnis anima (X 3.39.2); et facit quod dicitur in lege Comperit C. de prescripti. xxx uel xl. annorum (*Cod.* 7.39.6). Et quod reges ualeant dare priuilegia libertatis, probatur de prescriptio-
51 nibus Auditis (X 2.26.15). |

Dae fyaerde ker

4. Dae kaes Magnus dine fyaerde ker ende alle Fresen oen sine ker jechten ende kaes een bettera dan alle da jefta deer di koningh baed, dat se neen himelschielda haghera gulden[2] dan riuchten deeckma dae prester deere da haudstoed bisunch, hit ne se dattet dumme lioed oen da bannem hyara urberde ende hya se dan ontgulde.

Dit is di fyfta ker

5. Deerefter kaes Magnus dine fifte ker ende alle Fresen oen syn ker jechten, dat se neen heerferd fordera folgia wolden enich hera dan aester to da Wisere ende wester toe da Flee, ut mitta ebba ende op mitta floed, om dat se dine owirra wariet deis ende nachtis tojenst dyn noerdkoninck ende tojenst dyn wylda Wising mitta fyf wepen: mit swird ende schield, mit spada ende furka ende mit etkeris oerd.

[1] FG: urbrede. [2] FG: guld.

a Locus corruptus esse videtur.

This Is the Second Statute

2. After that, Magnus determined the second statute and all Frisians agreed with Magnus's choice, that the Frisians would be released of the wooden band they wore around their necks and that they would be forever free, the born and the unborn, for as long as the wind will blow from the clouds and the world stands firm, and that the Frisians by their own choice would be high comrades-in-arms to the king.

This Is the Third Statute

3. Then Magnus determined the third statute and all Frisians agreed with his choice, that the Frisians were not obligated to pay a higher tax to the king than the legal tax called *huslaga* they paid the *skelta*, unless someone was foolish enough to be fined for something, which they then had to pay.

GLOSS 62. *Datse neen koninghschielda* (*that they were not ... tax to the king*). Here the emperor exempted the Frisians from taxes by means of a special remission. You may find an argument for this in X 3.39.21, X 3.30.25, C.16 q.1 c.66 and C.1 q.3 c.4 (i.m.). The churches give some pennies as sign of subjection, see X 3.39.2; this is also the purport of what is written in *Cod.* 7.39.6. And that Kings are competent to grant privileges, is acknowledged in X 2.26.15.

The Fourth Statute

4. Then Magnus determined the fourth statute and all Frisians agreed with his choice, and he chose something better than all the gifts the king offered him, which was that the Frisians were not obligated to pay a higher tax to the church than the legal tithes which are to be paid to the priest who says masses at the main church, unless someone is foolish enough to be fined for something, which they then have to pay.

This Is the Fifth Statute

5. After that, Magnus determined the fifth statute and all Frisians agreed with his choice, that the Frisians would not have to answer a call for a military expedition which would lead them further to the east than the river Weser or further to the west than the river Vlie, leaving at low tide and returning at high tide because, day and night, they guard the coast against the northern king and against the wild Vikings with these five weapons: sword and shield, spade and fork, and spear.

Dit is di sexsta ker

6. Da kaes Magnus dine sexsta ker ende alle Fresen oen sine ker jechten, dat se hyra ayn riucht halda wolden binna hyaera ayn saun seelanden, bi des paus ende dis koninghes jeften, bi riuchta banne ende bi aesgha dome ende bi papena ordel, als hyae heden tween leken to folgerum.

GLOSSA 63. *Ayn saun selanden* Nota. Frisones non sunt citandi extra eorum terras. Ratio ⟨est⟩ quia ad bella publica auctoritate gerenda citari non possunt extra suos fines; ergo multo minus pro utilitate priuata; concordat in auc. ut omnes obedi. iudicibus § iv. coll. v.[a] (*Auth.* 5.20.4 [*Nov.* 69.4]).

GLOSSA 64. *Ende biriuchta papena ordel* Nota. Sacerdotes et clerici uocandi sunt ad arduas causas laicorum et eorum consilio tentari debent et expediri, Deut. xvii. c.,[b] et extra qui filii sunt legitimi c. Per uenerabilem ad finem (X 4.17.13), ubi dicitur "Si difficile et ambiguum apud te iudicium ⟨esse⟩[c] perspexeris inter sanguinem et sanguinem, causam et causam,
52 lepram et lepram et | iudicium inter portas tuas uideris uariari, surge et ascende ad locum, quem elegerit dominus Deus tuus, ueniesque[d] ad sacerdotes Leuitici generis et ad iudicem qui fuit illo tempore, queresque[e] ab eis qui iudicabunt tibi iudicii ueritatem et facies quecunque dixeriint tibi etc.", ut ibi.

Dit is di saunda ker

7. Dae kaes Magnus dine saunda ker ende alle Fresen oen sine ker jechten, dat him di paeus Leo ende di koningh Kaerl een breef wolden jaen ende een insighel, deer hya mosten oen scriwa Saun Kerren, Saunteen Kesta, Fyower ende XX Landriuchta ende XXXVI Sindriuchta.

Dat oerlef jo him di paeus Leo ende di koningh Kaerl mitta monde ende efter weddadent hya mitta handem. Een heylich biscop seet ende screeft mitta handen ende Magnus spreckt mitta monde uter taefla deer God self hede joun Moysi op da birghe to Synai. Dae dat breef reed was hoe froe dat manich Fresa was! Da ginghen se allegaer toe fara diin paeus ende dyn koningh staen. Dit breef joe him di paeus. Hoe hage hyt hyarem bifeel! Hi hetet dat dae Fresen dat also herde hilde als hya dine Cristena nama habba wolde ende dat se da suderna

---

a § iv. coll. v. *scripsimus*: § iii. coll. iiii. *male praem.* FG.

b Deuteronomium 17.8–10.

c Emendavimus ex Biblia et Decretalibus.

d ueniesque *scripsimus cum Decretalibus*: ueniensque FG.

e queresque *scripsimus cum Decretalibus*: quaerensque FG.

This Is the Sixth Statute

6. Then Magnus determined the sixth statute and all Frisians agreed with his choice, that they would uphold their own law within their own seven sealands, as a privilege bestowed by the pope and the king, through legal commands and judgments of the *asega* and according to the judgment of priests, as long as they had two laymen as fellow judges.

GLOSS 63. *Ayn saun selanden* (*own seven sealands*). Note that the Frisians are not to be summoned outside their territory. The reason is that, since they cannot be summoned beyond their borders to wage war, they can to an even lesser extent be summoned for some private matter. This is in conformity with *Auth.* 5.20.4 (*Nov.* 69.4).

GLOSS 64. *Ende bi riuchta papena ordel* (*and according to the legitimate judgment of priests*). Note that priests and clerics should be called in for difficult cases of laics and they should be questioned and appealed to for their counsel, see Deuteronomy 17.8, and X 4.17.13, which rules: 'If you notice that the sentence is difficult and unclear to you, in a case between blood and blood, cause and cause, leprosy and leprosy, and you notice that the sentence is disputed within your gates, stand up and go to the place which the Lord your God shall chose. And you shall go to the priests of the tribe of the Levites and to the judge who is in office that time, and request from them who judge that they shall explain the truth of the sentence to you and do whatever they tell you, etc.'.

This Is the Seventh Statute

7. Then Magnus determined the seventh statute and all Frisians agreed with his choice, that Pope Leo and King Charles would give him a sealed charter, on which they would write Seven Statutes, Seventeen Statutes, Twenty-Four Land Laws and Thirty-Six Synodical Laws. Pope Leo and King Charles first agreed to this with their mouths and subsequently they shook hands on it. A holy bishop sat and wrote it down with his hands, and Magnus spoke from his mouth, reading from the tablet which God himself had given to Moses on the mountain in Sinai. When the charter was finished, many a Frisian was overcome with joy! Then they all positioned themselves before the pope and the king. The pope gave Magnus the charter. How much he recommended it to them. He enjoined them to uphold their law just as much as they wanted to be called Christians

riucht ende hera herich were, want hya alle in dat noerdsche[1] koninghryck heerden ende alle heyden weren.

Alleraerst dae him dat bref in da hand coem, da hoef op Magnus een leysa ende sangh 'Cristus onse nade, kyrioleys!'. Da reemden se des koningh Kaerlis ende al Romera land. Aeck bond Magnus oen syn stef dis koninghes heerteken, hoed alle da folke trou were dat alle Fresen weren fryheren, di berna ende di
53 oenberna, also langh soe di wynd fan da wolkenen wayd | ende dyo wrald stode. Dat breef brochte Magnus binna Frescha merkum, dat lest ma, in Almenum in sinte Michelsdoem, deer to der tyd was ramed mit holt ende reyl. Deer was to der tyd binna Freesland jelkirs naet manich. Deer lest ma uta breve VII Kerren, XVII Kesta, XXIIII Landriucht ende XXXVI Sindriucht, alle Fresen to lof ende toe erem.

[1] FG: noetdsche.

and that they would from now on be loyal to the southern law and to the southern army because, up until then, they were all subjects to the northern kingdom and were all pagans. The moment the charter was placed in his hands, Magnus began a song of victory and sang: 'Christ is our salvation, Kyrie Eleison!'. Then they left King Charles's and all Roman lands. Magnus tied the king's banner to his staff as proof to all people that all Frisians were free, the born and the unborn, for as long as the wind will blow from the clouds and the world stands firm. Magnus brought the charter into the Frisian territory, as one can read, to the church of Saint Michael in Almenum, which in those days was made of wood and tarp. In those days, there were not many churches in Frisia. There, one can consult from the charter the Seven Statutes (of Magnus), the Seventeen Statutes, the Twenty-Four Land Laws and the Thirty-Six Synodical Laws, as a symbol of honour and fame to all Frisians.

VI.The Seventeen Statutes

Hyr biginnet da saunteen kesta

1. Dit is dyo forme kest: dat aller mannick syn selvis walde also langhe als hyt naet foerwrocht habbe.

GLOSSA 65. Nullus rebus suis sit spoliandus nisi legitime[a] coram iudice conuictus.[b] Fas est unicuique disponere de rebus suis qualitercunque sibi placet, ff. si a paren. quis man. fue. l. ii. (*Dig.* 37.12.2), C. de dona. Si quis argen. (*Cod.* 8.53.35.5), C. manda. In re[c] mandata (*Cod.* 4.35.21), C. de actio. et obliga. l. Sicut (*Cod.* 4.10.5). Quilibet est arbiter et moderator in re propria, ff. si quis a parente manu. fuerit l. ii. (*Dig.* 37.12.2), xiii. q. ii. c. Placuit (C.13 q.2 c.7), sed aliud de sepult. c. De his in fi. (X 3.28.4).

GLOSSA 66. *Also langh* De hoc ff. et. C. de bonis damp. per totum (*Dig.* 48.20 et *Cod.* 9.49), C. de here. l. Manichaeos[d] (*Cod.* 1.5.4), in auth. de nupt. § Ingratitudinem[e] (*Auth.* 4.1.46.4 [*Nov.* 22.46.4]).

Van frede alle goedeshuesem

2. Dio oder kest is: alle godeshusem, alle godesliodem ferd bi LXXII pondem. Ende dat pond schil wessa bi saun penningen Agripsera penningen, dat sint Colensche penningen, want Colen heet bi alda tiden Agrippina efter alle da wrald ney da koninge deer da burich stifte. Hy heet Agrippa to riuchta nama. Dae was dyoe monthe alto fyr ende di penningh alto sweer. Da kerren da lyoed een nyara montha ende een lichtera penningh leyden da lyoed. Toejenst dae twa ende sauntich ponda waest hare bilowad LXXII schillingen Reynades
54 slachta jefta Kanga slachta. Ende tria pond da frana dat is XXI | schillingen.[1] Hyr is also manich schillingh des koninges[2] ban.

GLOSSA 67. *alle godes husem* Hoc ius uidetur extractum C. de his qui fugiunt ad ecclesiam per totum (*Cod.* 1.12), extra de emuni. eccl. Inter alia (X 3.49.6), de for. conpet. Conquestus (X 2.2.16), xviii q. iiii ⟨Id⟩[f] constituimus (C.17 q.4 c.36).

GLOSSA 68. *alle godes mannem* exceptis publicis latronibus et populatoribus agrorum quos non defendit ecclesia, sed licite extrahuntur in auc.

[1] FG: pond. [2] FG: koniuges.

a legitime *scripsimus*: legittime FG.
b conuictus *scripsimus*: conuictns FG.
c In re *scripsimus*: Iure *male praem.* FG.
d Manichaeos *scripsimus cum Codice et J109 et M60*; Manitheos BL BN FG KB PB RA UB.
e Ingratitudinem *scripsimus cum Codice*: Ingratitudo FG.
f Emendavimus ex Codice.

VI. The Seventeen Statutes

Here Begin the Seventeen Statutes

1. This is the first statute: that each man has authority over his own property as long as he did not lose it as a consequence of having committed crimes.

GLOSS 65. Nobody should be deprived of his goods unless he is legitimately sentenced by the court. Everyone is allowed to make use of his goods as he pleases, see *Dig.* 37.12.2, *Cod.* 8.53.35.5, *Cod.* 4.35.21 and *Cod.* 4.10.5. Everyone manages and administrates his property, see *Dig.* 37.12.2 and C.13 q.2 c.7, but it is different in X 3.28.4.

GLOSS 66. *Also langh* (*as long as*). See the entire titles *Dig.* 48.20 and *Cod.* 9.49, *Cod.* 1.5.4 and *Auth.* 4.1.46.4 (*Nov.* 22.46.4).

Peace to All Churches

2. The second statute is: peace to all churches and all clerics, on penalty of 72 pounds. And the pound shall consist of seven pennies, Agrippinal pennies, that is, pennies of Cologne because Cologne was called Agrippina in the olden days throughout the entire world, after the king who founded the city. His given name was Agrippa. Then the Frisians considered the mint too far and the penny too heavy. Then the people chose a new mint and set a new standard penny. Against the seventy-two Cologne minted pounds, theirs was set at 72 shillings minted by Reynad or by Kanga. And three pounds (are to be added to the penalty) for the *frana*: that makes 21 shillings (in new coins). Here the same amount of shillings is to be paid as penalty for disobeying the king's authority.

GLOSS 67. *alle godes husem* (*all churches*). This provision seems to derive from the entire title *Cod.* 1.12, X 3.49.6, X 2.2.16 and C.17 q.4 c.36.

GLOSS 68. *alle godes mannen* (*all clerics*) except notorious robbers and plunderers of the fields, to whom the Church offers no protection and who may

de manda. prin. Quod si delinquentes[a] coll. iii. (*Auth*. 3.4.2 [*Nov*. 17.4.2]), extra de emuni. ecclesiarum c. Inter alia (X 3.49.6). Nota. Qui uiolat emunitatem ecclesiasticam duplici ratione punitur. Primo est excomunicatus illo facto, si bona rapiendo uel furando subtrahit ecclesie, xvii. q. iii. c. Nullus (C.17 q.4 c.19). Secunda pena relinquitur arbitrio iudicis et dabitur persone uel loco ubi delinquit[b] uel cui immunitas[c] est lesa, extra de sen. excommuni. c. Parochianis (X 5.39.9). Nota. Bona ecclesiarum et locorum religiosorum et persone earum eadem gaudent priuilegio; concordat infra penultimum ius sinodale[d] et xvi. q. i. Similiter[e] (C.16 q.1 c.58), extra de pigno. c. Ex litteris in glossa penultima,[f] et de censi. Quamquam in vi (VI 3.20.4) et xii q.ii c. Ecclesiarum[g] (C.12 q.2 c.69), et de priuilegiis c. Licet li. vi (VI 5.7.11). Nota. Vbicumque certa quantitas pecunie ponitur in lege ut est solidorum denariorum, semper intelligendum est de moneta usuali currente per terram, ff. de contrahen. empti. l. Imperatores (*Dig*. 18.1.71), extra de censi. ex parte et de maledic. c. Statuimus (X 5.26.2) et de iniur. et c. Olim super uerbo usualis,[h] quia lex debet esse loco et tempori et patrie conueniens, iiii.[i] d. c. Erit (D.4 c.2), ut patet eciam supra 'Quid sit lex?' in principio.[j]

3. Dio tredde kest is dat aller mannick oen da sinen bisitte onbirawet, hit ne se dat met hem ofwinne mit tale ende mit reden ende mit riuchta tinge. So dwere als him di aesga deelt ti riuchta doem ende ti lyoda landriucht jefta ney nedem.

Di aesga aegh nen doem, hit ne se dat him da lioed kerren habbe ende hy tofara dyn keyser to Roem swerren | habbe. So aegh hi dan to witen alle riuchtlika tingh, dat sint kesta ende landriuchta. So aegh hy to delen da fynden als da fryonden om dat hi swer tofara dyn keyser to Roem, alle wesem like ende sine tredkninge. Ende als di aesga aec nympt onriuchte mede ende urlowade penningen so ne aegh hi neen doem to delane om dat di aesga biteykenet di

a delinquentes *scripsimus cum Authentico*: delinquens FG.
b delinquit *scripsimus*: deliquit FG.
c immunitas *scripsimus*: emunita FG.
d See text XI,44.
e Similiter *scripsimus*: Si mulier *male praem*. FG.
f The gloss *obligata* ad X 3.21.5.
g Ecclesiarum *scripsimus cum Decreto Gratiani*: Ecclesia FG.
h The gloss *usualis* ad X 5.36.7.
i iiii *scripsimus*: vii *male praem*. FG.
j *Supra* gloss 4.

legitimately be expelled according to *Auth.* 3.4.2 (*Nov.* 17.4.2) and X 3.49.6. Note. Whoever violates ecclesiastical immunity is punished in two ways. In the first place, he is excommunicated by the fact that he, by robbing and stealing goods, has taken away something from the Church, see C.17 q.4 c.19. The second punishment is left to the good sense of the judge and this fine is granted to a person or to a place where the delict took place or whose immunity was violated, see X 5.39.9. Note. The goods of Churches and religious places and persons enjoy the same privilege; this is in conformity with the section below on synodical law in the penultimate provision and with C.16 q.1 c.58, the gloss *obligata* to X 3.21.5, VI 3.20.4, C.12 q.2 c.69 and VI 5.7.11. Note. Whenever a provision determines a certain quantity of money in coins or pennies, this should always be understood as referring to the currency commonly in circulation throughout the land, see *Dig.* 18.1.71, X 5.26.2 and the gloss *usualis* to X 5.36.7, because a provision has to be in accordance with the place, the time and the land, see D.4 c.2, as also appeared above at the beginning of the paragraph on the question 'what is law?'.

3. The third statute is that each man has the right to live on his own property undisturbed, unless he forfeits it as a consequence of legal proceeding brought against him. In that case he has to act according to the legal judgment which the *asega* gives, and according to the land law or according to the exceptions to the land laws.

The *asega* is not allowed to give judgment unless he was chosen in office by the people and swore an oath before the emperor in Rome. In order to be fit for office, he has to know all legal matters, that is statutes and land laws. He has the obligation to give judgment to both foes and friends because he swore before the emperor in Rome to treat all people, including orphans, as if they were his relatives in the third degree. And if an *asega* accepts illegal gifts or unauthorised pennies he loses the right to pass judgment because the function of the

prester want hya sint agen der cristenheed. Hya schillet helpa dam, ende dyn wei wisa, deer him self naet helpa ne mey.

GLOSSA 69. Item quod nemini facienda est iniuria in re propria uel possessione sua. Hoc ius scriptum est, Insti. de interdic. § Retinende (*Inst.* 4.15.4) cum § Commode⟨m⟩ aut possedendi (*Inst.* 4.15.4 in fine), C. de eden. l. Qui accusare (*Cod.* 2.1.4), C. de rei uindicati. l. fi. (*Cod.* 3.32.28), ff. si usuf. petatur l. Vtifrui (*Dig.* 7.6.5 in pr.), C. de peti. heredita. l. Cogi (*Cod.* 3.31.11), C. de probati. l. ii (*Cod.* 4.19.2).

GLOSSA 70. *Onbirawed* Extra de resti. spo. c. Olim (X 2.13.12). Vnde cuilibet[a] licitum est mouere bellum pro defensione sui et rerum suarum, nec hoc proprie dicitur bellum,[b] sed defensio. Eciam si eiciatur de possessione sua, licet ei in continenti pugnare, ut ibi et ff. de u. obli. l. Continuus (*Dig.* 45.1.137.pr.), c. unde ui l. i (*Cod.* 8.4.1), ff. de ui et ui ar. l. i. § Quod igitur (*Dig.* 43.16.1.15), et Innocentius, de resti. spolia. c.[c] Olim (X 2.13.12).[d] Simile ius inueniri potest in primo iure ciuili quod dicitur *landriucht*.

GLOSSA 71. *Datmet him mit tele* C. de probati. l. Possessiones[e] (*Cod.* 4.19.2).

GLOSSA 72. *Ende deer aegh nen aesga* Hoc sumptum est C. de iudi. l. Rem non nouam (*Cod.* 3.1.14 in pr.).

GLOSSA 73. *Doer dis edis wille* Nota quod presumitur pro iudice ratione iuramenti i. q. vii. c. Sancimus (C.1 q.7 c.26), de presump. c. Ad audienciam circa medium (X 2.26.13 i.m.).

GLOSSA 74. *Ende als di aesga nympt onriucht* Sentencia uenalis ipso facto est nulla, C. quando prouoca. ne. Venales (*Cod.* 7.64.7). Et iudex accusari potest pena legis Iulie repetunda,[f] C. ad leg. iu. repet. l. Iubemus (*Cod.* 9.27.4) et munera percepta in quadruplum restituat, C. e. ti. l. i (*Cod.* 9.27.1) et litem facit suam, ff. de iudi. l. Si filius fa. (*Dig.* 5.1.15 in pr.) et qui corrumpit causam amittit, C. de pen. iudi. l. i. et ii. (*Cod.* 7.49.1–2), sed nouo iure
56 quadruplum.[g] |

4. Dio fyaerde kest is dat hy tyen merka schieldich se—ende dera merka ellick bi fyouwer wedem[1] ende dera weda ellick bi XII penningen—deer oen oderis

[1] FG: merka bi fyouwer ellick wedem.

a cuilibet *scripsimus*: quilibet FG.
b bellum *scripsimus*: bellun FG.
c c. *scripsimus*: cum *male praem.* FG.
d Innocentius IV, Commentaria, X 2.13.12, n. 9.
e Possessiones *scripsimus cum Codice*: Possessionis FG.
f Repetunda *scripsimus*: repetenda FG.
g Cf. auth. *Nouo iure qui dicit* post *Cod.* 7.49.1 (ex *Nov.* 124.2).

asega is on a par with that of the priest because they are the eyes of Christianity. They should help and guide those who cannot help themselves.

GLOSS 69. Likewise, it can be said that no damage should be caused to anyone's property or possession. This is written law, see *Inst.* 4.15.4, with *Inst.* 4.15.4, *Cod.* 2.1.4, *Cod.* 3.32.28, *Dig.* 7.6.5.pr., *Cod.* 3.31.11 and *Cod.* 4.19.2.

GLOSS 70. *Onbirawed* (*undisturbed*). X 2.13.12. Hence, anyone may cause a 'war' to defend himself or his goods and this is actually not termed war, but defence. Even if one is ejected from his possession, he may immediately take up arms, as here (X 2.13.12) and in *Dig.* 45.1.137.pr., *Cod.* 8.4.1, *Dig.* 43.16.1.15, and Innocent in his commentary on X 2.13.12. A similar right can be found in the first civil provision which is termed *landriucht.*

GLOSS 71. *Datmet him mit tele* (*as a consequence of legal proceeding*). See *Cod.* 4.19.2.

GLOSS 72. *Ende deer aegh nen aesga* (*and the asega is not allowed*). This is derived from *Cod.* 3.1.14 in pr.

GLOSS 73. *Doer dis edis wille* (*because of his oath*). Note that this is presumed to apply to the judge in view of his oath, see C.1 q.7 c.26 and X 2.26.13.

GLOSS 74. *Ende als di aesga nympt onriucht* (*and if the asega accepts illegal gifts*). A venal sentence is ipso facto null, see *Cod.* 7.64.7. And the judge can be prosecuted for the punishment of the *lex Iulia repetundarum*, see *Cod.* 9.27.4, and he should reimburse the gifts received in quadruple, see *Cod.* 9.27.1, and he will be liable for 'making the litigation his own', see *Dig.* 5.1.15.pr. and the one who bribed the judge loses his claim, see *Cod.* 7.49.1 and 2, but according to the new law he forfeits the fourfold value.

4. The fourth statute is that a ten mark fine is to be paid by anyone—and each mark equals four *wedmarks* and each *wedmark* equals 12 pennies—who

wald in syn wara faert onbitingades tinghes, buta des aesga ledene ende lyoda orlef.

5. Dio fiifte kest is dat ma tredknies[1] lawa ende alderis lawa mit dededen bihalde sonder striid mit tolef manna edem.

6. Dio sexta kest is dat ma caepland ende godeshuses land deer to da helligem joun is jefta boked is jefta caped halda moet mit saun manna wyteden. Ende deer ne schil neen wessa meenedich ner manslachtich ner mit hoerdome biwollit ner oen neen sonda, dat hy Karina schieldich se. Ende dae schillet alle kona hiara *pater noster* ende *credo in deum* ende da scrifta, dat se papen ende wise leken deer naet oen sanne.

GLOSSA 75. *Jefta caped* De hoc in l. Iubemus C. de sac. sanc. eccl. (*Cod.* 1.2.14).

GLOSSA 76. *Uessa menedich* Extra de testi. c. Testimonium (X 2.20.54), quia enormibus criminibus heretici testificari non possunt. Nota. Quatuor modis corrupitur iudicium, scilicet amore, timore, odio et munere, xi. q. iii Quatuor (C.11 q.3 c.78), de sen.[a] et re iudi. Cum eterni li. vi (VI 2.14.1).

GLOSSA 77. *Karina schieldich* De karena uide extra de sponsa duorum c. Accepisti (X 4.4.2).

7. Dio saunde kest is dat alle Fresen oen fria stoele bisitte—also fyr so se friboren se—ende fri spreke habbe. Dat jo him koningh Kaerl om dat hya cristen worden ende hensich ende herich da suderne koningh ende klipschielda foertege ende huuslaga golde bi aesga dome ende bi lyoda landriucht. Ende capeden[2] deermey edeldoem ende hiara fria hals, want alle Fresen in dat noerd-
57 koninghryck eer heerden oen da grimma herna. |

8. Dio VIII kest is dat neen huusman toejenst syn hera to swide ne winne. Ende haet soe dis were deer ma fan des koninges hallem urseyde and enich man of hit him mit riuchte urcoem dat hi sines haudis[3] schieldich were dat hyt ontgulde. Jef hyt biseke dat hi hem sikerade mit XII manna[4] wiitedem. So ne thoer

[1] FG: tredkines. [2] FG: caped. [3] FG: handis. [4] FG: mana.

a de sen. *Scripsimus cum Libro Sexto*: de sina *male praem.* FG.

intrudes upon someone else's property without an injunction, without the judgment[4] of the *asega*, and without the consent of the people.

5. The fifth statute is that one has the right to retain an inheritance of a relative in the third degree or of grandparents by swearing an oath, with the help of eleven compurgators, without having to undergo an ordeal.

6. The sixth statute is that the church has the right to ascertain her claim to land bought by the church or traditionally belonging to the church with the oaths of seven men, whether the land was given to, bequeathed to, or bought by the church. And these men shall not have committed perjury or murder or adultery, nor be indicted for any sin which has obligated them to do a forty days penance (*carena*). And they must all know the Lord's Prayer and *credo*, and the Scripture, so that no priest or educated layman can disqualify them.

GLOSS 75. *Jefta caped* (*or bought*). See on this *Cod.* 1.2.14.

GLOSS 76. *Uessa menedich* (*committed perjury*). See X 2.20.54, since heretics cannot testify due to their hideous crimes. Note. In four ways a sentence can be corrupted, namely by love, fear, hate and donation, see C.11 q.3 c.78 and VI 2.14.1.

GLOSS 77. *Karina schieldich* (*obligated ... forty days penance*). See on *carena* (40 days fasting) X 4.4.2.

7. The seventh statute is that all Frisians have a right to a free seat (in court)—if they are freeborn—and have the right to bring a case to court. This privilege was given to them by King Charlemagne because they converted to Christianity and became loyal to the southern king and abandoned the tax called *klipskelde* and started paying the *huslaga* in conformity with the judgment of the *asega* and the people's land law. And with that, they bought their nobility and their free necks because, before that time, all Frisians belonged to the northern kingdom, to the grim region.

8. The eighth statute is that no freeman should prosecute a lawsuit against his lord too vehemently. Moreover, whatever it is that is laid against any man on behalf of the king, and if he is sentenced to pay his own wergild to avert a death penalty, let him pay. If he denies, let him confirm this with twelve com-

4 The Old Frisian text (in almost all redactions) has *ledene* 'leading the host', which must be wrong because this was not one of the duties of the *asega*. Hence we have chosen for the implicit correction to OFris. *dom* 'judgment'. See Algra, *Zeventien Keuren*, 298.

di huiskeerl tojenst dyn koningh neen kamp leda want di koningh ryck is ende haet aller kempana anoegh bi dam dat alle kempen fyuchtet binna dis koninges banne. So schil di huusman anderda ende aerst swara. Jof hit landriucht is, so schillet deerefter swara fyouwer edele man ende deerney fyower friheren ende fiower leethslachta[1] maen. Aldus schil ma da koningh riuchta.

GLOSSA 78. *Huisman* Hoc potest intelligi de iure emphiteotico C. de iure emphi. l. ii. (*Cod.* 4.66.2) uel monopoliis C. eodem libro (*Cod.* 4.59) ut dicitur C. ut nemo priuatus l. ii. (*Cod.* 2.15[16].2). Quilibet tenetur dominum suum reuereri nec ipsum exasperare consilio Salomonis ne exasperaueris animum potentis.

GLOSSA 79. *Sikarade mit xii.* Nam rusticitati et simplicitati parcendum est, C. de testamentis[a] l. ult. (*Cod.* 6.23.21). Et potest hec lex anullari ad multa hic posita *inda landriucht*.

9. Dio nyogende kest is dat ma ferdpenninghen jelde ende huuslaga bi des koninghes ban by twam penninghen Reynaldis slachta. Ende di penningh schil alsoe wichtich wessa dat men moghe hera clinnen in een lewyn ur nyogen fecke huses. Hwae so dat riucht ursitte soe bete hi des keysers ban da frana mit XXI schillingen.[2] Om de riuchta tins soe agen alle Fresen saun streta ruum ende rennende suder to farane, fyower oen da wettere ende tria oen da lande.

58 GLOSSA 80. *Ferd peuningen* Nota. Causa pacifice ambu |

GLOSSA 81. *Ferd penninghen* Nota. Causa pacifice ambulationis in stratis marinis et terrenis quilibet tenetur soluere regi nummum et non alii,[b] nisi seruauerit pacem, ut xxiii. q. viii Tributum (C.23 q.8 c.22).

Dio aerste strete oen da wettere is dio Elve, dio oder is dio Wesere, dio tredde dioe Eemse, dioe fiaerde is dat Ryn. Dio forme strete oen da lande: op to Hamersten ende ut to Jewere. Dio oder: op[3] to Irmegardafoerda ende ut to Eemda. Dio tredde: op to Coforda ende ut to Starem.

Hwa soe us dera saun streta enich binaert so breckt hy deeroen tien lyoedmerck ende dis frana allerhagista ban, dat is XXI schillingen. Jof dae Fresen jefta[4] hira caeplioed dera saun streta enich birawed wirt ende hit comme fan des koninges hallem so aegh met to nimen of da huislaga ende lioda fia ende deerof hiara schada to follane ende deer tojens to wariane.

---

[1] FG: leeckslachta. [2] FG: .xxi. schillingen deer mede to capien. [3] FG: wt. [4] FG: *jefta* is missing.

---

a De testamentis *scripsimus*: de testibus *male praem.* FG.

b alii *scripsimus*: alius FG.

purgators. The freeman cannot be compelled to fight a duel against the king because the king is powerful and has more than enough champions to choose from because all champions fight under the authority of the king. Therefore, the freeman must answer and first swear. If land law applies here, four nobles, four freeholders and four unfree men shall swear. In this way, a case involving the king shall be dealt with in court.

GLOSS 78. *Huisman* (*freeman*). This can be understood as concerning hereditary tenure, see *Cod.* 4.66.2, or monopoly, see *Cod.* 4.59, as is stated in *Cod.* 2.15(16).2. Everyone is held to honour his master and not to anger him according to the counsel of Salomon, so that one will not anger the soul of the mighty.

GLOSS 79. *Sikarade mit xii* (*confirm with twelve*). For, rustics and simpletons should be spared. See *Cod.* 6.23.21. And this provision can be nullified for the many causes, mentioned in the *landriucht*.

9. The ninth statute is that a Frisian is obligated to pay the king the tax for keeping the peace and the *huslaga*, amounting to two pennies minted by Reynald. And the pennies should be so heavy that if they are dropped in a bowl, they can be heard over a distance of nine compartments of a house. If someone does not comply, he has to pay a fine of 21 shillings to the *frana* for infringing on the authority of the emperor. Because of this lawful tithe, all Frisians have the right of use of seven free routes to the south: four by water and three by land.

GLOSS 80. *Ferd peuningen* (*tax for keeping the peace*). Note that in view of a peaceful pas …

GLOSS 81. *Ferd penninghen* (*tax for keeping the peace*). Note. In view of a peaceful passage through shipping lanes and roads, everyone is held to pay money to the king and not to another, unless to do so would preserve the peace, as in C.23 q.8 c.22.

The first route by water is the river Elbe, the second is the Weser, the third is the Ems, the fourth is the Rhine. The first route by land is landward to Oldenburg and seaward to Jever. The second: landward to Münster and seaward to Emden. The third: landward to Coevorden and seaward to Stavoren.

If someone obstructs us on any of these routes, he will be fined with 10 marks and he will have to pay the highest penalty for infringing on the authority of the *frana*, that is, 21 shillings. If the Frisians or their merchants are robbed on any of these routes and this can be blamed on the king, then the damage is to be subtracted from the *huslaga* and the people's tax and the loss to be repaired with this money.

Tojens da saun pennigen da saun ruma streta, dat is di tegheda deer alle Fresen tienda hetet: fiower da himelkoningh ende tria dae eerdkoningh. Disse penningen aegh di fria Fresa to lasten op dine alter to der capella deer hi heert mit wiitscip sines presters deer him mit boke ende mit stoele bihot jefta to der haudsto deer dio capelle ut maked is. Dae tree penninghen aegh di fria Fresa sine schelta to lasten deer ur him da ban lath. So aegh se di schelta da grewa deer oen Freeslande is to lastane. So aegh se di grewa to lastane in da palense to Roem foer dine fria Fresa deer se fan commen sint. Jef se deereefter immen oenspreckt foer da fiower penningen dat di tegade deer ma haet tienda naet also last ne se als hi mit riuchta schulde, soe is hi nier oen da wiitedem to witane dat him di prester jechta wille. Jef se aeck immen oensprect om dae tree pennin-
59 gen deer ma huuslaga haet, dat hi so | naet last ne se als hi mit riuchte scholde, wil hem di schelta jechta deer ur him da ban lath, so is hi fri. Ende jef hy dis jechta nelle, soe is di fria Fresa nier oen da wiithum to witane dat[1] hi diin huuslaga oen da riuchte also last habbe als hi to riuchte schulde ti schotte ende ti schielde ende hi toe dere jeertael naet fora lasta ne thoer.

Di grewa deer oen Freesland koninges ban leda schil, di schil wessa edeler bertha boren, dat hi dine palenze[2] riucht fynda moge ende dine fria Fresa onthalda moge ende dat hi des koninges andert naet tielda thoer, stock ner stupa, hendene ner heftene ner heerbeinden men dat hine also frilike[3] toe sine lande seinde.

Compt hit fan dis biscops hallem, soe aegh met toe nimane fan dae thins ende tienda ende hiara schaeda deermei toe beten. Ende hwae soe dat deth soe breckt hi deeroen den alrahagista ban sines frana. Ende tien lioedmerka ban dis frana is een ende tweintich schillinghen.

10. Dioe tiende kest is dat Fresen thoren neen heerferd fora fara dan aester toe dae Wesere ende wester toe dae Flee, suudwirth naet fora soe hya oen[4] jonde weer mogen comma oen den owirra om dat se hyara land bihalde toejenst weeter ende tojenst dyn heydenna hera. Dae baed di koningh Kaerl dat hya fore aester to Hiddeseckere ende wester to da Singfalle. Da bihildent dae lyoed wyth dine koningh Kaerl dat se syn fader Pipwyn[5] fora weldighet ne hadde, dat hya nu ne fareth ner fara thoeren neen heerferd, ner synes bannes plighia, dan aester toe dae Wesere ende wester thoe dat Flee. Truch dat schellet alle dae
60 Fresen wessa fry. |

[1] FG: wiithum dat. [2] FG: palemze. [3] FG: frililike. [4] FG: een. [5] FG: pipwyu.

Against the seven pennies stand the seven routes; this is the tithe which all Frisians call 'tenth': four for the heavenly king and three for the worldly king. A free Frisian has to pay these pennies on the altar at the chapel to which he belongs in the presence of his priest, who safeguards him with stole and Scripture, or at the head church to which the chapel belongs. The three pennies are to be paid by a free Frisian to the *skelta* under whose jurisdiction he resides. In turn, the *skelta* has to pay them to the count who rules over Frisia. In turn, the count has to pay these to the palace in Rome on behalf of the free Frisians, from whom these pennies came. If someone then accuses the Frisians that the four pennies of the tithe which they call 'tenth' have not been paid as they legally should have been, then a Frisian is entitled to take an oath on the relics that the priest can confirm that he received them. If someone also accuses them that the three pennies which are called *huslaga* have not been paid as they legally should have been, and if the *skelta* under whose jurisdiction he resides wants to confirm that he received them, then he is free. And if the *skelta* does not want to confirm this, then a free Frisian is entitled to declare under oath that he did pay the *huslaga* as he legally should and that he is no longer liable during that same year.

The count who is to have authority over Frisia shall be of noble birth, so that he is able to hold court in the palace and defend the free Frisians so that they are not obligated to stand in court against the king, will not have to suffer corporal punishment or the pillory, nor any type of captivity or fetter, but can freely return to their country.

And if the damage can be blamed on the bishop, it is to be compensated by extracting it from the tithe that should have been paid to the church. And anyone who does this has to pay the highest penalty for infringing on the authority of the *frana*. And this penalty of ten marks for infringing on the authority of the *frana* now equals twenty-one shillings.

10. The tenth statute is that the Frisians are not obligated to assist the king in a military expedition which would lead them beyond the river Weser to the east or beyond the Vlie to the west, nor in one which would lead them so far south that they could not get back to the Frisian shores by nightfall because they have to defend their land against the water and against the heathen armies. Then King Charles commanded them to travel as far eastward as Hitzacker and as far westward as the river Sincfal. Then the people stood firm against King Charles and reminded him that his father Pippin had decreed that they need not go on a military expedition nor obey his commands beyond the river Weser in the east and the Vlie in the west. Because of this the Frisians shall be free.

11. Dioe alfte kest is: ferd alle widem ende wesem ende alle warlasem, palmerem ende Roemfarem ende riuchta karfestrem[1] ende alle heyliga sindboden ende oenwaexna kynden bi x lioedmerkum ende dam twyfalda bota deer urswerren habbet wych ende wepen truch ferd ende truch need ende XXI schillingen dae frana.

GLOSSA 82. Isti omnes sunt de iudicio ecclesie quo ad tuicionem et defendendi per sacerdotem xi. q. i. Aliud (C.11 q.1 c.34). Nota. Iniurie et rapine, uidue, orphanis et miserabilibus personis[a] illate, per iudicem ecclesiasticum possunt tueri et defendi, extra de fo. conpe. Ex tenore (X 2.2.11), lxxxvi. d. c. iii. (D.86 c.3); psalmista ⟨dicit⟩ "Oculi eius in pauperem respiciunt"[b] et alibi "Orphano tu eris adiutor".[c] In alys causis tamen principaliter spectant ad forum seculare; de hoc optime in glossa per Bernardum in dicto c. Ex tenore (X 2.2.11),[d] et Innocentius, de offi. delegati c. Significanti. (X 1.29.38).[e] De emendatione istarum personarum dicit, ut extra de iniur. et damp. c. Olim (X 5.36.7), C. unde ui Si quando (*Cod.* 8.4.9), ii. q. i. In primis (C.2 q.1 c.7), de his qui ui metus c. fi. (X 1.40.7). Queritur an uidue spectant ad forum ecclesie. Super hoc ponit Henricus Boic[f] istam distinctionem: an ad protectionem et defensionem, tunc dicendum est quod spectat ad forum ecclesiasticum et sic intelligitur c. Amministratores xxiii. q. v. Regum (C.23 q.5 c.26 and c. 23), aut ad cognitionem[g] et defensionem, et tunc aut agitur[h] de iniuria seu uiolentia eis illata, tunc ecclesia potest cognoscere, ut in c. Si quis de potentibus xxiiii q. iii (C.24 q.3 c.21), aut aliis iuribus[i] et hoc dupliciter, aut possessoria, et tunc ecclesia potest cognoscere[j]—ita notant[k] Innocentius[l] et Hostiensis,[m] de fo. conp. in c. Ex tenore (X 2.2.11)—aut petitoria, et tunc cognitio principa-

---

[1] FG: kerckfestrem.

---

a personis *scripsimus*: persone FG.
b Psalmi 9.30.
c Psalmi 9.35.
d Bernardus Parmensis (†1266) is the author of the *Glossa Ordinaria* to the *Liber Extra*. See the gloss *in iustitia* ad X 2.2.11.
e Innocentius IV, Commentaria, X 1.29.38, n. 1.
f Henricus Boich, Commentaria, X 2.2.11, n. 2.
g cognitionem *scripsimus*: distinctionem *male praem.* FG.
h agitur *scripsimus*: queritur *male praem.* FG.
i iuribus *scripsimus*: iniuriis *male praem.* FG.
j cognoscere *scripsimus*: coguoscere FG.
k notant *scripsimus*: notat FG.
l Innocentius IV, Commentaria, X 2.29.38, n. 4.
m Hostiensis (Henricus de Segusio), Lectura, X 2.2.11, n. 2–3 (Cf. Summa, X 2.2, n. 11).

11. The eleventh statute is: peace to all widows and orphans and all defenceless people, pilgrims on their way to the Holy Grave or people travelling to Rome and people who are observing a forty days penance, and all messengers of the church and underage children. Breach of this peace is to be fined with 10 marks and a twofold fine for harming those who have renounced war and weapons in an effort to attain peace and mercy, and 21 shillings are to be paid to the *frana*.

GLOSS 82. All these persons fall under the competence of the Church as regards their protection and they should be defended by a priest, see C.11 q.1 c.34. Note. Injuries and robberies, inflicted upon a widow, orphans and the unfortunate ones (*miserabiles*), can be corrected and redressed by the ecclesiastical judge, see X 2.2.11 and D.86 c.3. The psalmist says "His eyes look for the poor" and elsewhere "you will offer help to the orphan". In other cases they fall essentially under the competence of the secular court. This is dealt with very well by Bernard in a gloss to X 2.2.11, mentioned above, and Innocent in his commentary on X 1.29.38. The indemnification of these persons is discussed in X 5.36.7, *Cod.* 8.4.9, C.2 q.1 c.7 and X 1.40.7. It has been questioned whether widows have to resort to the ecclesiastical court. In this respect Henri Boic drew the following distinction: as regards their protection and defence, it has to be said that they resort to the ecclesiastical court and in this way C.23 q.5 c.26 and c. 23 are understood. As regards litigation and defence, the claim is based either on the injury or violence inflicted upon them, and in this way the Church can take cognizance of it, as in C.24 q.3 c.21, or on other rights and this in two ways: either as a possessory claim; and then the Church can take cognizance of it—as noticed by Innocent and Hostiensis, commenting on X 2.2.11—or as a petitory claim; and then litigation belongs basically

liter spectat ad iudicium seculare. Ita intelligit Petrus Sampsona[a] et ita potest intelligi c. Regum xxiii. q. v. (C.23 q.5 c.23) et in c. Significantibus de of. delegati in glossa.[b] Et ob defectum iudicis secularis ⟨iurisdictio⟩ bene deuoluitur ad ecclesiam.

GLOSSA 83. *Palmerum romerum* Capientes, occidentes, mutilantes istas ro-
61 mipetas sunt excommunicati et per papam absoluendi, | ut in extrauagantibus quas[c] ponit frater Otto in additionibus suis ti. de sententia[d] excommunicationis (X 5.39): "Item excommunicamus et anathemamus omnes illos qui per se uel per alios quoscunque, personas ecclesiasticas uel seculares ad eandem sedem super suis negocys recurrentes etc.",[e] xxiiii. q. iii[f] "Si quis romipetas et peregrinos (C.24 q.3 c.23), sanctorum oratoria uisitantes, capere aut rebus suis spoliare presumpserint.[g] Donec satisfecerit, communione[h] careat cristiana".

12. Dio tolefte kest is: kerckferd, huisferd, tingferd ende heerferd ende aldeer ma sweslika trouwa lowed bi XXXII reylmerkum, dat is achteendahael merck grate merck. Ende XXI lekena[1] da frana jof een ende XX schillinga dae frana.

13. Dio tretteensta kest is: lyoedferd bi X lioedmerkum ende dera merka ellick bi fyower wedum ende dera weda ellic bi XII penningen.

GLOSSA 84. De comuni pace, extra de treu. et pace c. ii. (X 1.34.2), xxiiii[i] q. iii. Romipetas (C.24 q.3 c.23).

14. Dio fyoerteensta kest is: hwa so of heerneed ende of oer need comt ende een hava haet, fynt hy syn ayn land ende hy bikanna moge syn edel ende syn eckeren ende syn faders staten ende syn nesta megen naemna jof syn[2] broder jef syn baelmond jefta syn stiepfader jefta syn athem *id est*[3] zwager deer syn land urseth jef urbrocht[4] habbe so aegh hi to farane oen syn ayn gode ende op syn edel utoer stryd mit aller Fresena riucht.

[1] FG: lesena. [2] FG: syu. [3] FG: .i. [4] FG: wrbrocdt.

a The *lectura* of Petrus de Sampsone on the decretals is only preserved in manuscripts.
b The gloss *pauperem se dixisset* ad X 1.29.38.
c quas *scripsimus*: quem FG.
d sententia *scripsimus cum Decretalibus*: seutentia FG.
e §12 from the papal bull *In Coena Domini*, which was promulgated from the year 1363. Cf. also §11.
f iii *scripsimus*: iiii FG.
g presumpserint *scripsimus*: presumpserit FG.
h communione *scripsimus*: comunione FG.
i xxiiii *scripsimus*: xiiii FG.

to the secular judgment. In this way Petrus de Sampsone has interpreted it and so one can understand C.23 q.5 c.23 and what is said in the Gloss to X 1.29.38. Moreover, when a secular judge is not available, jurisdiction devolves very well to the Church.

GLOSS 83. *Palmerum romerum* (*pilgrims, people traveling to Rome*). Those who capture, kill or mutilate these pilgrims to Rome shall be excommunicated and must be absolved by the pope, as stated in the circulating documents which brother Otto enshrined in his additions to X 5.39: "Similarly, we excommunicate and anathematize all those who, either by themselves or by whatever other persons, have undertaken to capture or despoil from their belongings ecclesiastical or secular persons, seeking refuge to the same See for the sake of their affairs, etc.", and in C.24 q.3 c.23 "and visiting the chapels of the saints. As long as no satisfaction is given, one will lack the Christian communion".

12. The twelfth statute is: breaking the peace inside churches, houses, at court meetings, during military expeditions and in case of a truce between two feuding parties is to be fined with 32 marks, that is seventeen and a half large marks. And 21 pieces of cloth or 21 shillings to the *frana*.

13. The thirteenth statute is: breaking the people's peace is to be fined with 10 marks, and each mark equals four *wedmarks* and each *wedmark* equals 12 pennies.

GLOSS 84. See X 1.34.2 and C.24 q.3 c.23.

14. The fourteenth statute is: if someone who is released from war captivity or from any form of captivity possesses an estate and if upon return he is able to find his own land again and is able to locate his property and lands and his father's house and is able to identify his next of kin, and if in his absence his brother or his guardian or his stepfather or his brother-in-law have sold or divested it, then he has the right to go to his own property and take possession of it without any legal proceedings according to the law of all Frisians.

GLOSSA 85. De captiuis et postliminio reuersis etc. per totum[a] (*Dig.* 49.15), ubi eis reseruantur omnia iura sua et possessiones restituntur,[b] uide infra in tercio *landriucht*,[c] et Insti. quibus mo. ius § Si ab hosti.[d] (*Inst.* 1.12.5), uerbo postliminium eciam ibi in glossa.[e] Postliminium dicitur a limen et
62 post, quia captus ab hostibus et ultra limina nostri imperii deductus, post | intra[f] limina ⟨reducatur, uel reuertatur. Nam limina⟩[g] sicut in domibus finem quendam faciunt, ita eciam imperii limen ueteres esse uoluerunt; dicitur ergo postliminium,[h] quia post eodem limine reuertebatur,[i] quo[j] amissus erat. Hec Azo C. e. ti. (*Cod.* 8.50) in summa.[k] Est autem postliminium ius amisse rei recipiende ab extraneo et in statum pristinum restituende inter nos et liberos populos regesque moribus constitutum, ff. e. l. Postliminium (*Dig.* 49.15.19). Prosit autem ius postliminii in omnibus que michi ante captiuitatem competebant uel mea erant siue sint res mee iura mea amissa prescripcione uel usucapione. Et si amissa sunt subuenitur michi per restitutionem et in integrum data in rem recissoria ff. ex quibus causis ma. l. i. (*Dig.* 4.6.1), C. de capti. et postli. reuersis l. Ab hostibus (*Cod.* 8.50.2). Non solum prodest ius postliminii reuersis, eciam et redemptis precio, quia redemptio non mutat ius postliminy ff. e. l. Si captiuus § fi. (*Dig.* 49.15.20.2), Azo.[l]

GLOSSA 86. *Oen syn ayn gued* Nisi obstat usucapio idest de mobilibus bonis uel prescriptio, C. de usuca. transforman. l. unica (*Cod.* 7.31.1), C. de prescriptionibus et uel xx. annorum l. fi. (*Cod.* 7.33.12), C. de prescriptionibus xxx. uel xl. annorum l. pe. (*Cod.* 7.39.8).

15. Dio XV kest is: hwa so weduen jefta mageden jefta oderis mannes wyf an nede nympt of hyt jecht jef dat ma him mit campschielde urwint, so schil hy mit XII merkum syn haudlesena jelda ende oder XII merck dis wederjeldis dat sint XXIIII mercka ende deerof aegh hy to jeldane XXI schillingen da frana. Jof

---

a per totum *scripsimus cum M60 et UB*; per iotum BL BN FG KB J109 PB RA.
b restituntur *scripsimus*: restitnuntu FG.
c See text VIII,3.
d hosti. *scripsimus cum Institutionibus*: hoste. FG.
e The gloss *postliminii* ad *Inst.* 1.12.5.
f intra *scripsimus*: *infra* FG.
g reducatur—limina *om.* FG (*homoitel.*). Emendavimus ex Azone.
h postliminium *scripsimus*: postliminum FG.
i euertebatur *scripsimus*: reuertebantur FG.
j quo *scripsimus*: quia FG. Cf. *Inst.* 1.12.5.
k Azo, Summa Codicis, *Cod.* 8.50, n. 1.
l Azo, Summa Codicis, *Cod.* 8.50, n. 10–11.

GLOSS 85. See the entire title *Dig.* 49.15, where all their rights are preserved for them and their possessions are restored, see below in the third *landriucht*, *Inst.* 1.12.5 and the gloss *postliminii* to *Inst.* 1.12.5. The term '*postliminium*' (right to return) is derived from '*limen*' (border) and '*post*' (later), because once captured by the enemies and carried away beyond the borders of our empire, one is later brought back or one returns within these borders, because, since thresholds constitute a certain boundary for houses, the ancestors considered also the borderline of the empire to be a threshold. Accordingly, one speaks about '*postliminium*' (reversion right), because one returned later over the same border across which one was lost. Azo dealt with these things in his *Summa* on Codex title *Cod.* 8.50. The 'right to return' is the right, established by customs between us and free nations and Kings, to recover an object lost from an 'extraneous' and have it restored to its original state, see *Dig.* 49.15.19. The 'reversion right' is beneficial for all things I was entitled to or were mine before captivity, whether they are my things or my rights, lost through long-term or short-term prescription. And if they are lost, I will be saved by restitution. And a remedy for restitution to the original state, is granted against anyone, see *Dig.* 4.6.1 and *Cod.* 8.50.2. The 'reversion right' benefits not only those who returned, but also those ransomed, because ransoming does not alter the 'reversion right', see *Dig.* 49.15.20.2; thus, according to Azo.

GLOSS 86. *Oen syn ayn gued* (*to his own property*). Unless short-term prescription stands in the way, that is, the one of moveable things, or long-term prescription, see *Cod.* 7.31.1, *Cod.* 7.33.12 and *Cod.* 7.39.8.

15. The fifteenth statute is: if anyone commits rape against widows or virgins or a married woman and if he concedes this or he fails the ordeal by combat over this case, he then has to pay his own wergild of 12 marks to avert a death penalty and he has to pay a wergild to the woman with another 12 marks, which makes 24 marks in total, and from this sum, he has to pay 21 shillings to the *frana*. If

hyt self naet habbe deer hyt mey jelda moge, soe agen syn fryonden toe stepane,[1] bi aesga dome ende bi lyoda landriucht.[2]

GLOSSA 87. *Ueduen iefta mageden* Nota ad Sabinianum xi.[a] deflorator virginum "infelicissime mortalium, tu speluncam illam, in qua filius dei natus est et ueritas de terra orta est et terra dedit[b] fructum suum de stupro condicturus ingrederis? non times[c] ne de presepe[d] infans uagiat[e] ne puerpera
63 uirgo uideat, ne mater domini contempletur? Angeli clamant, pastores | currunt,[f] stella desuper rutilat, magi adorant, Herodes terretur, Iherosolim turbatur[g] et tu cubiculum uirginis uirginem decepturus irrepis et uiolas?" etc. C. de epis. et cleri. l. Raptores (*Cod.* 1.3.53), l. 1. C. de rapt. uirgi. (*Cod.* 9.13.1), xxxvi. q.i. (C.36 q.1), de raptori. extra c. Cum causam (X 5.17.6).

GLOSSA 88. *Haudlesena ielda* Quia secundum legem deuteronomii xxii,[h] C. de rapto. l. i. (*Cod.* 9.13.1) et xxvii. q. ii. Omnem § Item (C.27 q.2 c.10). In Leuitico mori debet raptor et oppressor; et uitam redimere potest L ciclis argenti, ut ibi.[i]

GLOSSA 89. *Hyara ferd ar.* C. de sepul. uio. l. ult. (*Cod.* 9.19.6), ff. de iurisdicti. omnium iudicum[j] Si quis (*Dig.* 2.1.7).

GLOSSA 90. *So agen syn fryonden* Contrarium uerum est secundum ius commune. Pena enim tenet suos malefactores, nec ulterius progrediatur metus quam reperiatur[k] delictum. Ibi enim est pena, ubi est noxa. Propinquos ac notos siue familiares submouemus a noxa; hec omnia C. de pe. l. Sancimus (*Cod.* 9.47.22).

16. Dio XVI kest is dat alle Fresen aghen hyara ferd mit hiara fia to beten. Om dat schillet alle Fresen[3] wessa an Saxena merkum utoer stock ende utoer stupa, utoer scheran ende utoer filan ende utoer ander pinen. Ende wirth hy aeck urwonnen ende urdeeld ende wirter urdoemd oen lioda tinge om twa daeddeda[4] ney aesga doem, so aegh ma siin fora hand op dae tinghstapale of to slaen

[1] FG: scepena. [2] FG: landriucdt. [3] FG: frese. [4] FG: ded deda.

a Jerome (347–420), Letter to the deacon Sabinianus, n. 4.
b terra dedit *scripsimus cum Hieronymo*: terra que dedit *male praem.* FG.
c times *scripsimus cum Hieronymo*: timens FG.
d presepe *scripsimus cum Hieronymo*: presepi FG.
e uagiat *scripsimus cum Hieronymo*: uagit FG.
f currunt *scripsimus cum Hieronymo*: currant FG.
g turbatur *scripsimus cum Hieronymo*: turbantur FG.
h Deuteronomium 22.22.
i Leviticus 27.3.
j iudicum *scripsimus cum Digesto Veteri*: gentium *male praem.* FG.
k reperiatur *scripsimus*: reperaitur FG.

he does not possess enough to pay these fines with, then his kin has to help him out, in accordance with the judgment of the *asega* and the land law of the people.

GLOSS 87. *Ueduen iefta mageden* (*widows or virgins*). See the letter to Sabinianus, paragraph 11: Corrupter of virgins, "you, most miserable of the mortals, do you enter this cave, in which God's Son was born and the truth emerged from the earth and the earth produced its fruit, to commit fornication? Don't you fear that the babe will wail from his manger, that the virgin who just gave birth will see you and the mother of the Lord will notice you? The angels rejoice, the shepherds rush up, the star from above lightens, the wise men worship, Herod is frightened, Jerusalem is worried and you creep in and violate the bedroom of a virgin to deceive the virgin?" etc. See *Cod.* 1.3.53, *Cod.* 9.13.1, C.36 q.1 and X 5.17.6.

GLOSS 88. *Haudlesena ielda* (*pay his own wergild*). For, this is in conformity with the rule of Deuteronomy 22, *Cod.* 9.13.1 and C.27 q.2 c.10. In the book Leviticus the robber and oppressor have to die and can purchase their life for 50 shekels of silver, as you can find there.

GLOSS 89. *Hyara ferd ar* (*their peace*). See *Cod.* 9.19.6 and *Dig.* 2.1.7.

GLOSS 90. *So agen syn fryonden* (*then his kin has*). The opposite is true according to the *ius commune*. For, punishment binds its wrongdoers, so that fear will not extend further than where the delict is discovered. After all, punishment takes place, where there is fault. Relatives and acquaintances or housemates we safeguard from fault. All these things are found in *Cod.* 9.47.22.

16. The sixteenth statute is that all Frisians have the right to compensate their wrongdoings with valuables. Because of this, all Frisians will not have to be subjected to punishment by stick or pillory, hot scissors, flagellation or any other corporal punishment in the Saxon territory. And if anyone is found guilty in court and sentenced for two capital crimes according to the judgment of the *asega*, then his right hand is to be cut off at the court anvil by order of the *skelta*

nei schelta doem, bi des keisers oerlef. Haeter aeck hauddeda[1] deen, nachtbrand jefta oder moerddeda, bi aesga doem ende bi lioda landriucht jof hi[2] fia nabbe deer hi mei[3] beta moge, soe aegh hyt toe jelden mit sine ayna halse jef hiit onriuchta ne mey. Aeck jelt hy alle lyodem deer hinghet want moerd schil ma mit moerd beta.

17. Dioe saunteende kest is, ende dis koningh Kaerlis jeften ende aller Fresena riucht, dat alle Fresen tingie bi twira tale ende bi aesga dome ende aller manick
64 wyte him self haet hi deen habbe oen da wyteden, | hit ne se dat hi een wed deen habbe aen een worpena were jefta an kedena[4] tinghe jefta an da banda synde,[5] soe ne mey ma dera deda nene wyteed byeda.

GLOSSA 91. *By twira taele* Iudex secundum allegata parcium debet iudicare et non secundum conscienciam, quia secundum hoc esset iudex et testis ut et locis suis.

GLOSSA 92. *Wyte him self* Quia nemini licet facta propria ignorare, arg. C. de rei uend. l. Si quis (*Cod.* 3.32.11). Tres persone debent esse in iudicio, scilicet actor, reus et iudex, extra de uerbo. sig. c. Forus (X 5.40.10), iiii. q. iiii. c. i. (C.4 q.4 c.1), quandoque quarta persona, scilicet testis.

GLOSSA 93. *Uued deen* Hoc est notorium iuris, extra de coha. clerico. et mulierum[a] c. Vestra (X 3.2.7). Quatuor modis conuincitur aliquis, scilicet per euidentiam facti, secundo per testes, de testibus per totum (X 2.20), tercio per instrumenta,[b] de fide instrumentorum per totum (X 2.22), quarto per confessionem in iudicio factam, extra de resti. spoli. Cum ad sede. (X 2.13.15) et de cohabitione c. fi. (X 3.2.10), si quinto potest addi, scilicet uiolenta presumptio xxxii q.i Dicit Dominus (C.32 q.1 c.2).

Dit sint da XVII kesten[6] deer wi Fresen mit use fia fan koningh Kaerl kapaden ende wy mit riuchta bruka schillet, also langh als landen lidse ende lioed se, tojenst heren ende huusman jof wyt habba moten. Deereefter baed di koningh Kaerl dat wy alle aefte tingh ende alle riuchte tingh hilde also langh so wi lywade ende man efter man lywade, also lyaef so us Godes genade were ende syn hulde ende wi bihalda willet land ende lioed. Ende hwa so us dis riuchtes birawet, so wirt hi birawet dis himelrikes ende alre nedena. Ende hwa so dat riucht halt so wirt him epened dat himelryck ende alle dio nede, want een dei is bettera oen himelrick dan op eerdric M jera: dat spreeck di appostola us Herens

[1] FG: haudeda. [2] FG: hia. [3] FG: deer mei. [4] FG: herena. [5] FG: fynde. [6] FG: keste.

a mulierum *scripsimus cum Decretalibus*: mulieris FG.

b instrumenta *scripsimus*: instrumeuta FG.

and with permission of the emperor. If someone has also committed a major crime, nocturnal arson or other forms of murder and has been sentenced for this in accordance with the judgment of the *asega* and the land law of the people, and he does not possess enough money to compensate for this and is not able to deny these accusations before court, he shall have to pay for it with his own neck. And he who hangs on the gallows pays compensation to the entire people because murder is to be compensated with murder.

17. The seventeenth statute is, and this was a privilege given to us by King Charlemagne and it is the law of all Frisians, that all Frisians have the right to bring a claim before court and defend themselves in court according to the judgment of the *asega* and each has a right to testify of his own actions before court with an oath on the holy relics, unless someone has given a statement before a normal court, a special court or a synodical court; in that case he can no longer deny his acts by swearing an oath on the holy relics.

GLOSS 91. *By twira taele* (*bring a claim … and defend*). The judge should pass judgment according to what parties adduced and not according to his conscience, because according to the latter the judge would also be a witness, bringing along own means of proof.

GLOSS 92. *Wyte him self* (*testify of his own actions*). Since nobody may ignore his own acts, see *Cod.* 3.32.11. In litigation there should be three persons, namely the claimant, the defendant and the judge, see X 5.40.10 and C.4 q.4 c.1, and sometimes a fourth person, namely a witness.

GLOSS 93. *Uued deen* (*given a statement*). That is judicial notoriety, see X 3.2.7. In four ways someone can be convinced, namely by the obviousness of the fact, secondly through witnesses, see the entire title X 2.20, in the third place through instruments, see the entire title X 2.22, in the fourth place through confession in court, see X 2.13.15 and X 3.2.10; if a fifth way can be added, that is, 'strong presumption', see C.32 q.1 c.2.

These are the seventeen statutes we Frisians bought from King Charles with our money. As long as the lands lie and people exist, it is our privilege to observe these among lords and freemen as necessity dictates. After that, King Charles ordered us to observe all things lawful and just, for as long as we would live and man after man would live, with the same intensity as we strive for God's mercy and loyalty to him and we want to preserve land and people. And if anyone robs us of these privileges, he will be deprived of entry into Heaven and all its mercies. And whoever upholds this law will be let into Heaven and all its mercy because one day in Heaven is better than 1000 years on Earth: thus said the apostle of our Lord in a verse. If there would be a man who had 1000

in een ferse. Of deer enich man were deer hede M hauda ende al da hauda een stelen tonga ende da tonga al spreken M jera, so ne mochten hia naet fol sprecka da blydschip deer God sine houden jaen wil. | Ende fan da pinen deer in dae helle sint mey ma naet fol tella. Ende ovir gold ende ovir selvir ende ovir yten ende ovir drincken so is deer in der wrald naet so swetis soe dat Godes ryck ende dat haet neen eynd aeck ne schillet nimermeer eynd habba.

"Pacem et ueritatem et iusticiam diligite" ait Dominus Omnipotens. ve illis "qui iustificant impium pro muneribus[1] et iusticiam, iusti auferunt", ad quos dicit propheta: "perdes omnes qui loquuntur mendacium".

[1] FG: mmuneribus.

heads and all these heads had steel tongues and all these tongues would speak for 1000 years, even then they would not be able to tell the full story of the bliss God wants to give his worshippers. And the pains to be encountered in hell are innumerable. And no earthly gold or silver, food or drink can compare to the sweetness of God's kingdom. And it has no end nor will it ever have an end.

'Love peace, truth and justice' said the Almighty Lord.[5] Woe unto them 'who justify the wicked for reward and take away the righteousness from the righteous',[6] to whom the prophet[7] says: 'destroy those who tell lies'.[8]

5 Cf. Zechariah 8.19.
6 Cf. Isaiah 5.23.
7 The text has *propheta* 'prophet', but since this is a quote from the psalms, *psalmista* 'psalmist' would have been more accurate.
8 Cf. Psalm 5.7.

VII. Prologue to the Seventeen Statutes and Twenty-Four Land Laws

Dit is scryoun, dat wi alsoedeen landriucht halde als God self baed. Hy baed dat wy hilde alle aefte tingh ende alle riuchta tingh. Deerefter badent alle eerdsche koningen. Julius ende Octavianus, also heten da eerdscha koningen deer aerst keyser[1] weren to Roem. Ende aeck deer efter hyarem weren badent.

God joe Moysi twae tafela deeroen screven weren sindriucht ende landriucht deer hy selva screef ende alle da riucht deer dae Israhelscha lyoed heden, da hya in da westenia weren, want God al sine lyoed fan Egiptaland latte. Also lath hy alle daejeen to himele deer dat riucht folgiet ende hwa soe se breckt, so faert hi to der helle. Soe bisluut him God in der helle als hy bislaet da Egiptera in dat Rade Mer, da se sine holdem schadia wolden. Alsoe slut him God in der helle deer dat riucht breckt, want hit God self screef ende badet sine lyoed allen to halden, als hit hilden da koningen Aaron ende Samuel, David[2] ende Salomon ende alle da koningen deer eer Cristus berthe weren ende efter Cristus berthe Cristen worden.

Di forma koningh was Pipwyn ende syn soen di minra Kaerl. Hi was minra
66 ende was doch bettera: hi leet scriwa trouwa ende wird—dat sint kesta |
ende landriucht. Aeck hildent dae koningen deer eefter Cristus berthe weren ende Cristen weren. Di aersta was Julius ende Octavianus, Titus ende Vespasianus, Augustus,[3] Nero, Domicianus, Maximianus, Alexander, Decius, Germanus, Traianus, Adrianus, Tiberius, Gaius, Claudius, Dioclesianus, Anthonius,[4] Aurelius, Constantinus, Julianus, Theodosius, Archadius, Honorius, Galecianus, Valerianus, Marcianus, Numerianus, Theodericus, Conradus, Fredericus: disse koningen jowen alle lyoden kesta ende landriucht ende alla landen syn sonderinga riucht.

---

[1] FG: *keyser* is missing. [2] FG: danid. [3] FG: Augustns. [4] FG: anthoniuus.

VII. Prologue to the Seventeen Statutes and Twenty-Four Land Laws

This is written, that we must observe such land law as God himself commanded. He commanded that we should observe all rightful and lawful provisions. Julius and Octavian were the first secular kings in Rome who became emperors. And the ones who came after these also commanded it.

God gave Moses two tablets, on which were written synodical law and land law, which he himself had written and all laws which the people from Israel had when they were in the desert because God led his entire people out of Egypt. In the same way he leads those to heaven who adhere to the law and he leads those to hell who break the law. Then God incarcerates them in hell just as he did the Egyptians in the Red Sea, when they wanted to harm his followers. Thus God incarcerates in hell those who break the law because God himself wrote it and commanded all his people to observe it, just as the kings Aaron and Samuel, David and Salomon observed it, as did all kings who were born before the birth of Christ and became Christian after Christ had been born.

The first (Frankish) king was Pippin and his son Charles the lesser. He was lesser and yet better: he had agreements and resolutions written down—that means statutes and land laws. The kings who came after the birth of Christ and who were Christian also observed it. The first were Julius and Octavian, Titus and Vespasian, August, Nero, Domitian, Maximian, Alexander, Decius, Germanus, Trajan, Tiberius, Gaius, Claudius, Diocletian, Anthony, Aurelius, Constantine, Julian, Theodosius, Arcadius, Honorius, Gallienus, Valerian, Marcian, Numerian, Theoderic, Conrad, Frederick: these kings gave all peoples statutes and land laws and all nations their distinct laws.

VIII. The Twenty-Four Land Laws

Hyr biginnet da XXIIII landriuchta

1. Dit is dat aerste landriucht aller Fresena deer him di koningh Kaerl jo: dat allermanick oen da sinen bisitte, oen havem ende oen werem ende alles deer hi bitiled haet, hit ne se dat met him mit riuchter tele ende mit rede ende mit riuchta tingade ofwinne, jef dat hy tria lyoedtingh ursete, deer him fan des koninges hallem beden se to halden ende to heran. Ende nel hi deer redia ner riuchtes deytinges bieda, so moet hi habba da oenferd fan dam deer hy oenspreckt, hit ne se dat hy biede fan fyower needschyn een, deer di fria Fresa mit riuchta aegh.

GLOSSA 94. *Dat aller mannick an da sinen sitte* Commodum autem possessionis nemini est auferendum, xii q. v Nulli[a] (C.12 q.5 c.1), C. de rei uindica. l. fi. (*Cod.* 3.32.28), ff. de rei uindica. l. Is qui destinauerit (*Dig.* 6.1.24), Institu. de interdic. § Retinende (*Inst.* 4.15.4), iuncto § Commodum autem possess. (*Inst.* 4.15.4), C. de edendo l. Qui accusare (*Cod.* 2.1.4), C. de petici. heredi. l. Cogi (*Cod.* 3.31.11), C. de probat. l. ii (*Cod.* 4.19.2), ff. si usufruc. peta. l. Vti frui (*Dig.* 7.6.5 in pr.). Lex ii C. de probat. (*Cod.* 4.19.2) dicit: "Possessiones quas ad te pertinere dicis,[b] more iudiciorum persequere.[c] Non[d] enim possessori incumbit[e] probandi necessitas eas ad se pertinere cum te cessante in probatione dominium,[f] id est possessio, apud eum remaneat",
67 C. de iudi. | Properan.[g] (*Cod.* 3.1.13), ibi de actore et reo.

1a. Dyoe forme needschyn[1] is dat him di bannere neen tingh keth haet.

GLOSSA 95. Nota quod citatio sit per uiuam uocem quandoque et quandoque per litteras. Per uiuam uocem pluribus modis. Nam quandoque iudex proprio ore citat et artat talis citatio citatum, quandoque per notarium uel tabellionem xxiii q. v Circumcelliones (C.23 q.5 c.1), quandoque per nuncium publicum et personam iuratam et quandoque per partem fit citatio de mandato iudicis uel ubi hoc habet consuetudo[h] et uenire tenetur. Sed

---

[1] FG: needshyn.

---

a Nulli *scripsimus cum Decreto Gratiani*: Nullus FG.
b dicis *scripsimus cum Codice*: dicas FG.
c persequere *scripsimus cum Codice*: persequetur FG.
d Non *scripsimus cum Codice*: Nec FG.
e incumbit *scripsimus cum Codice*: iucumbit FG.
f id est possessio—om. in Codice Justineano.
g Properan. *scripsimus cum Codice*: Proban. FG.
h consuetudo *scripsimus*: consuetndo FG.

VIII. The Twenty-Four Land Laws

Here Begin the Twenty-Four Land Laws

1. This is the first land law of all Frisians, which was given to them by King Charlemagne: that each man shall have possession of that which is his, whether it be goods or lands or anything he has tilled, unless someone obtains it from him by means of a legal claim, a judgment and a legal court procedure, or unless he fails to appear at the three official court meetings at which the king ordered him to be present. And if he does not want to stand suit there or ask for a legal term, he will lose his property to the man who started a case against him, unless he pleads any of the four impediments which a free Frisian can invoke.

GLOSS 94. *Dat aller mannick an da sinen sitte* (*that each man shall have possession of which is his*). No-one should be deprived of the advantage of possession, see C.12 q.5 c.1, *Cod.* 3.32.28, *Dig.* 6.1.24, *Inst.* 4.15.4, *Cod.* 2.1.4, *Cod.* 3.31.11, *Cod.* 4.19.2 and *Dig.* 7.6.5 in pr. *Cod.* 4.19.2 reads "claim the possessions which you say belong to you through the common way of litigation. The possessor does not have to prove that these things belong to him, because ownership", that is, possession, "remains with him, if you do not succeed in the proof". See *Cod.* 3.1.13 on claimant and defendant.

1a. The first impediment is that the *bannere* did not officially announce the court meeting to him.

GLOSS 95. Note that the summons is sometimes issued orally and sometimes by letter. Orally it can be issued in various ways. For, sometimes the judge issues the summons personally and such a summons imposes limitations on the one summoned; sometimes through a clerk or notary, see C.23 q.5 c.1; sometimes through a public messenger and a sworn person; and sometimes the summons is issued through the other party, by order of the judge or where this is customary to do so, and one is obligated to appear. However, one may swear not to have been summoned,

iurare poterit non fuisse se citatum. Nec credere debet de facili aduersario uel inimico, qui facile mentitur. Quandoque per preconem ciuitatis. Hec sanius et lacius uide in Speculo, titulo de citacione § Sequitur uidere qualiter sit citatio facienda.[a]

GLOSSA 96. *Dat him di bannere* Nunquid isti officiali scilicet *bannere* iudex debet credere? Super hoc dicit Accursius, C. de accu. l. fi. (*Cod.* 9.2.17) quod non,[b] sed Innocentius contra quod sic, extra de prescrip. c. Ad audieciam (X 2.26.13),[c] sed Hostiensis[d] quod arbitrio iudicis relinquitur,[e] sed Speculo, titulo de citatione § Sequitur uidere qualiter citatio fiat, uersiculo 'Sed nunquit'[f] soli nuncio officiali uel executori creditur. Vide ibi.

GLOSSA 97. *Bannere* Est nuncius publicus iuratus fideliter exequi officium[g] suum, extra de offi. delega. c. Prudentiam primo responso (X 1.29.21), de appella. Cum parati (X 2.28.19), arg. de prescript. Ad audienciam (X 2.26.13). Et talis uocatur diuersis nominibus, aliquando nuncius, aliquando missus, aliquando notarius,[h] aliquando officialis, aliquando executor, allegato vi. in Speculo titulo quo supra.[i]

GLOSSA 98. *Nen tingh keth* Id est quod non sit citatus, extra de ma. et obe. c. Inter quatuor (X 1.33.8), quia citacio est exordium iudicy quoad perpetuandam iurisdictionem, de offi. dele. c. Gratum § Nos autem (X 1.29.20 i.m.) et c. Licet, ibi Vti ceperit (X 1.29.30 i.f.). Verum hoc probatur per Innocentium,[j] Vincentium,[k] Tancredum,[l] Goffredum,[m] de probat. c. Quoniam contra falsam[n] (X 2.19.11).

---

a Guillaume Durand, Speculum iudiciale, Lib. II, Part. 1, Tit. de citatione, § Sequitur, n. 1–4.
b Cf. the gloss *subiectam innocentiam feriamus* ad *Cod.* 9.2.17.
c Innocentius IV, Commentaria, X 2.26.13, n. 1.
d Hostiensis *scripsimus*: bost. FG.
e Hostiensis (Henricus de Segusio), Lectura, X 2.26.13, n. 3 et 5.
f Guillaume Durand, Speculum iudiciale, Lib. II, Part. 1, Tit. de citatione, § Sequitur, n. 8.
g officium *scripsimus*: officinm FG.
h notarius *scripsimus*: notaries FG.
i Guillaume Durand, Speculum iudiciale, Lib. II, Part. 1, Tit. de citatione.
j Innocentius IV, Commentaria, X 1.29.27, n. 2.
k The apparatus of Vincentius Hispanus to the *Liber Extra* is only preserved in manuscript.
l Tancredus, Ordo iudiciarius, Lib. I, tit. V § 2.
m Goffredus de Trano, Summa in titulos decretalium, X 1.30, n. 8.
n falsam *scripsimus cum Decretalibus*: flasam FG.

but we should not too easily believe the opponent or adversary, who easily tells lies. Sometimes (the summons is issued) through a bellman of the civil authorities. See on these things, more clearly and extensively, the *Speculum iudiciale* in the title on summons, in the paragraph starting with '*Sequitur*'.

GLOSS 96. *Dat him di bannere* (*that the bannere … him*). Should the judge believe this official, i.e. the *bannere*? On this question Accursius, in his Gloss to *Cod.* 9.2.17, says he should not, but Innocent in his commentary on X 2.26.13, says he should, but Hostiensis states that it should be left to the wisdom of the judge. However, according to the *Speculum iudiciale* in the title on summons, in the paragraph starting with '*Sequitur*', in the fragment starting with '*Sed nunquit*', one should only believe the messenger, official or public delegate. See at that place.

GLOSS 97. *Bannere* (*bannere*). is a public messenger who took an oath to fulfil his office faithfully, see X 1.29.21 in the first answer and X 2.28.19, and an argument can be found in X 2.26.13. And such a messenger is designated by various terms, sometimes messenger, sometimes envoy, sometimes clerk, sometimes official, sometimes public delegate and a sixth designation is brought up in the *Speculum iudiciale*, in the title referred to above.

GLOSS 98. *Nen tingh keth* (*did not … announce the court meeting*). That means that he is not summoned, see X 1.33.8, because the summons is the introduction to the court session, so that it perpetuates jurisdiction, see the second part of X 1.29.20 and the end of X 1.29.30. That this is correct, is proven by Innocent, Vincentius, Tancred, Goffredus, and in X 2.19.11.

1b. Dio oder needschiin is dat him siin fiande dine wei urstorde.

GLOSSA 99. Hoc probatur ff. ne quis eum qui in ius uocatur ui exi. in prin. (*Dig.* 2.7.1) et l. Sed eximendi § Eximere[a] (*Dig.* 2.7.4.pr. i.m.) et de his excusatio siue exceptio[b] dicitur, extra ut li. non contest. c. Accedens ii
68 (x 2.6.4), | ff. de arbi. Si cum dies § Si arbiter, in uersiculo 'quod puto'[c] (*Dig.* 4.8.21.10), ff. de iudic. l. Si locus (*Dig.* 5.1.59) et l. ⟨Si⟩[d] longius (*Dig.* 5.1.18 in pr.), concordantibus.[e]

1c. Dat tredde needschyn is dattet him wynd of onweer ofnoem.

GLOSSA 100. Hec probantur ff. si quis cauc. in iudicio sistendi causa l. ii § "Si quis in iudicio sesisti promisit[f] et ualetudine[g] uel tempestate uel ui fluminis prohibitus, sistere non posset, exceptione adiuuatur" (*Dig.* 2.11.2.3) et uide Speculum, titulo de citatione post principium.[h]

1d. Dat fyaerde needschyn is dat hy fan syochte also syeck were dat hy naet toe tinge comma moghe. Efter dam dwe hy als him syn aesga to landriuchte dele.

GLOSSA 101. Infirmus, personaliter citatus, uenire non cogitur, sed tenetur mittere excusatorem, de dol. et contu. Cum dilecti § Exspectantibus (x 2.14.6 i.m.). Nec uenire tenetur occisus,[i] nec cui mors innuebat uel qui graui necessitate uel persecutione uel naufragio urgebatur, de consec. di. iiii Si[j] (De con. D.4 c.16), v q.iii Si egrotans fuerit episcopus (C.5 q.3 c.1), de procura. Querelam (x 1.38.2).

GLOSSA 102. *Al soe syeck* Nec heres defuncti infra nouem dies luctus euocabitur ad iudicium, in auc. ut cum de appellatione cognos. § Me minimus coll. viii. (*Auth.* 8.12.5.1 [*Nov.* 115.5.1]), C. de sepul. uio. auth. Sed neque (post *Cod.* 9.19.6 [ex *Nov.* 115.5]).

1e. Deemt him aeck di aesgha ter hand dattet him need ofnimen habbe, needbrand, needdaedel jefta daedswima,[1] jefta datter syn jet dytsa schulde, deer ne

---

[1] FG: dadet wima.

---

a Eximere *scripsimus cum Digesto Veteri*: Eximerc FG.
b exceptio *scripsimus*: excepti FG.
c puto *scripsimus*: peto *male praem.* FG, poto *male praem.* BN.
d Emendavimus ex Digesto Veteri.
e concordantibus *scripsimus*: concordat FG.
f promisit *scripsimus cum Digesto Veteri*: promiserit FG.
g ualitudine *scripsimus cum Digesto Veteri*: ualitudinem FG.
h Guillaume Durand, Speculum iudiciale, Lib. II, Part. 1, Tit. de citatione, § Contra, n. 10.
i occisus *scripsimus*: obcessus *male praem.* FG.
j Si *scripsimus*: hy *male praem.* FG.

1b. The second impediment is that his enemies prevented him from coming to court.

GLOSS 99. This is proven by *Dig.* 2.7.1 and *Dig.* 2.7.4.pr. and in view of these texts, one speaks about 'exculpation' (*excusatio*) or 'defence' (*exceptio*), see X 2.6.4, *Dig.* 4.8.21.10 at the end, *Dig.* 5.1.59 and *Dig.* 5.1.18 in pr. and concordant provisions.

1c. The third impediment is that wind or storm prevented him from coming to court.

GLOSS 100. These things are demonstrated in *Dig.* 2.11.2.3, stating that if someone promised to appear in court but, prevented by health reasons or storm or an overflowing river, is unable to come, that person will be helped by a procedural defence; and see the *Speculum iudiciale*, in the title on summons, right after the beginning.

1d. The fourth impediment is that he was so ill that he could not come to court. If this was the case, he is to follow the instructions of the *asega* in concordance with the land law.

GLOSS 101. Someone ill, summoned in person, will not be compelled to come, but is held to send someone to excuse him for his non-attendance, see X 2.14.6 in the centre. Nor the one killed is obligated to come, nor the one who faces death or is burdened with great distress or persecution or shipwreck, see De con. D.4 c.16, C.5 q.3 c.1 and X 1.38.2.

GLOSS 102. *Al soe syeck* (*so ill*). Nor will the heir of the deceased be called to the court during the nine days of mourning, see *Auth.* 8.12.5.1 (*Nov.* 115.5.1) and the authentica *Sed neque ante* (post *Cod.* 9.19.6).

1e. If the *asega* concedes that he was hindered by a legal impediment, be it arson, homicide or severe unconsciousness, or if he was compelled to repair

aegh hi foer to fellane penningh ner penninges wirden, hit ne were dat di aesga dat mit riucht oers bitella muchte.

Als dyo moeder her kindes eerfschip forkaped

2. Dat oder landriucht is, hweer so dyo moder her kyndes eerwe foerkapet jefta foerwixled mit her fryonda reed eer dat kind jerich is, als hit jerich se, likie him di kaep, so halde hitten ende likiet[1] him naet so fare hit oen syn ayn eerwe son-
69 der stryd ende sonder schulde. So hwa so dat kynd bifiucht jefta birawe | op syn ayn eerwe so breckt hy tyen lyoedmerck tojens[2] dine frana dat sint XXI schillingen. Ende alle dae lyoed agen him to helpen ende di frana dat hy comme op syn ayn eerwe deer hy eer bi riuchta aechte, hit ne se dat hioet seld habbe jef seth jef wixled truch dera tria haudneda een, deer hio dis kyndes des lives mede hulp.

GLOSSA 103. Casus in quibus predium rusticum uel suburbanum minoris xxv annis distrahi poterit Co. quando decreto opus non est, ut l. "Predium rusticum uel suburbanum a minore xxv annis alienari[a] sine decreto presidis, nisi parentis uoluntas seu testatoris, ex cuius bonis ad minorem peruenit, super alienando eo aliquid mandasset deprehendatur, nulla ratione potest" (*Cod.* 5.72.3). Ibi uide.

GLOSSA 104. *Forkaped iefta foruixled* Hoc non solum matribus est interdictum uerum eciam et tutoribus et curatoribus, ff. de rebus eorum qui sub tutela uel cura sunt sine decreto iudicis non alienandis uel subponendis l. i in prin. (*Dig.* 27.9.1 in pr. et 2), ubi dicitur "Imperatoris Seueri oratione prohibiti sunt tutores et curatores[b] predia rustica uel suburbana distrahere. Que oratio in senatu recitata est[c] a Tertyllo[d] et Clemente consulibus et sunt uerba eius huiusmodi. § Preterea, patres conscripti,[e] interdicam[f] tutoribus et curatoribus, ne predia rustica uel suburbana distrahant, nisi id ut fieret[g] parentis testamento uel codicilo etc.". Ad idem C. de predi. mino. sine decre. non alie. (*Cod.* 5.71.4 in pr.), id est "Non solum per uenditionem rustica predia uel suburbana pupilli uel adolescentis alienari prohibentur, sed neque transactione neque permutatione. Et multo magis

---

[1] FG: liker. [2] FG: lyoedmerck ende tojens.

---

a alienari *scripsimus cum Codice*: alieoare *male praem.* FG.
b tutores et curatores *scripsimus cum Infortiato*: tutoris et curatoris *male praem.* FG.
c recitata *scripsimus cum Infortiato*: recitat a FG.
d Tertyllo *scripsimus cum Infortiato*: Thedphilo FG.
e conscripti *scripsimus cum Infortiato*: prescripti FG.
f interdicam *scripsimus cum Infortiato*: interdicunt FG.
g nisi id ut fieret *scripsimus cum Infortiato*: nisi uidelicet id fieret *male praem.* FG.

his dyke, he is not obligated to pay a fine, be it in pennies or in kind, unless the *asega* chooses to decree otherwise in concordance with the law.

If a Mother Sells Her Child's Inheritance

2. The second land law is that when a mother sells her child's inheritance or exchanges it with the consent of her relatives before the child comes of age, and if the child then comes of age and the transaction pleases him, let it stay firm, but if he does not like it, let him take possession of his own inheritance without having to undergo an ordeal over it or without having to pay any penalty to the people. Whoever then attacks the child or robs him on his own land is fined with ten marks, to be paid to the *frana*, which nowadays makes 21 shillings. And all people are obligated to help the child and the *frana* has to install him on his own land, which is lawfully his, unless the mother sold or mortgaged or exchanged it because of any of the three major emergencies, which forced her to sell his inheritance in order to save her child's life.

GLOSS 103. There are cases, in which the tenement of someone younger than 25 years, located in the countryside or close to the city, can be taken away. *Cod.* 5.72.3: "a tenement, located in the countryside or close to the city, can in no way, be taken away from someone younger than 25 years without a decree from the provincial governor, unless the last will of the father or testator, from whose patrimony the minor acquired the tenement, ruled something in regard to alienating this tenement". See there.

GLOSS 104. *Forkaped iefta foruixled* (*sells or exchanges*). This is not only prohibited for mothers, but also for tutors and curators, see *Dig.* 27.9.1, which states: "In an address of Emperor Severus it was forbidden for tutors and curators to alienate tenements located in the countryside or close to the city, which address was read aloud in the Senate under the consulate of Tertyllus and Clement, and its wording is as follows.'Moreover, gentlemen Senators, I prohibit tutors and curators to alienate tenements located in the countryside or close to the city, unless this takes place, based on the father's last will or codicil'". On the same issue there is the provision of *Cod.* 5.71.4 in pr., namely "It is not only prohibited to alienate tenements of pupils and adolescents, located in the countryside or close to the city, through sale, but neither through agreement, nor exchange. And even less

donatione nec alio quoquo modo ea[a] transferri a suo dominio possunt". Possunt tamen tutores et curatores mobilia ut uestes detritas et animalia superuacua uendere et distrahere sine decreto[b] iudicis, C. quando decreto opus non est l. fi. (*Cod.* 5.72.4).

GLOSSA 105. *Foerkaped* Quod non licet, C. de predi. mino. l. Non solum (*Cod.* 5.71.4pr) et quasi per totum, C. de his qui ue. eta. impe. l. | iii (*Cod.* 2.44.3), C. si aduersus transac. l. ii (*Cod.* 2.31.2), C. de rescin. uendi. l. ii (*Cod.* 4.44.2), ff. e. l. Pupillorum[c] (*Cod.* 5.37.21). Nota quod mater potest esse tutrix pupillorum, quamdiu secundo non nupserit, C. de leg. tu. l. i. (*Cod.* 5.30.1) et in auth. ibi signata (post *Cod.* 5.30.1 [ex *Nov.* 118.5]) et C. quando mulie. tu. offi. (*Cod.* 5.35.2), in autentica ibi posita (post *Cod.* 5.35.2 [ex *Nov.* 118.5]).

GLOSSA 106. *So faere hi an* C. de predi. mi. l. Ob es (*Cod.* 5.71.12) et l. se. (*Cod.* 5.71.13) et l. Si minor. xxv an. (*Cod.* 5.71.15), ff. de re. eo. Qui sub tu. l. i. § Preterea (*Dig.* 27.9.1.2).

GLOSSA 107. *Sonder schulde* C. de predi. mi. l. Non solum (*Cod.* 5.71.4 in pr.).

GLOSSA 108. *Birawed* dic ut extra de resti. spo. Olim (X 2.13.12) et C. unde ui (*Cod.* 8.4) per totum.

GLOSSA 109. *Dat hi up syn ayn eerwe comme* C. de commod. (*Cod.* 4.23). Dicit lex: "Si quis a pupillo sine tutoris auctoritate rem emerit, ex uno latere tenet contractus, quia qui emit obligatur, sed ex alio latere non, quia pupillus non obligatur, si est lesus".[d]

GLOSSA 110. *Hit ne se dat hioet seld habbe* Nota quod educatio pupillorum ad matrem spectat, si secundo non nupserit, C. ubi pupil. educa. l. i. (*Cod.* 5.49.1) et ff. e. l. i. (*Dig.* 27.2pr), extra de conuersi. Infide. c. Ex litteris (X 3.33.2).

GLOSSA 111. *Him dis liwes mede hulp* Nota quod immobilia sine iuramento minoris per ipsum uendi et distrahi non possunt, quantumcumque careat tutore, quia contractus est irritus et nullus ipso iure, nisi fiat ob es alienum, id est pecuniam debitam et tunc causa cognita et interpositione,[e] C. predi. mi. l. Ob es (*Cod.* 5.71.12) et lege sequenti (*Cod.* 5.71.13) et ff. de rebus eorum qui sub tute. l. i § i (*Dig.* 27.9.1.2) et l. Magis puto § Non passim et sequente (*Dig.* 27.9.5.9–10). Item propter alias causas speciales possunt alienari predia minoris, puta propter dotem C. de amminis. tute. l. Lex § i

---

a ea *scripsimus*: ex ea FG.

b decreto *scripsimus*: deercto FG.

c Pupillorum *scripsimus cum Codice*: Pupllorum FG.

d Cf. *Dig.* 19.1.13.29.

e interpositione *scripsimus*: interpellatione *male praem.* FG.

through donation or some other way can these things be transferred from their ownership". And yet, without judicial decree, tutors and curators can sell and alienate moveable things, such as cast-offs and superfluous animals, see *Cod.* 5.72.4.

GLOSS 105. *Foerkaped* (*sells*). Which is not allowed, see *Cod.* 5.71.4.pr and almost that entire title, *Cod.* 2.44.3, *Cod.* 2.31.2, *Cod.* 4.44.2 and *Cod.* 5.37.21. Note that a mother may be the tutor of pupils, if she does not marry for a second time, see *Cod.* 5.30.1 and in the authentica *Sicut hereditas* allocated to that fragment, and *Cod.* 5.35.2, in the authentica *Matri at aviae* incorporated there.

GLOSS 106. *So faere hi an* (*let him take possession*). See *Cod.* 5.71.12–13, *Cod.* 5.71.15 and *Dig.* 27.9.1.2.

GLOSS 107. *Sonder schulde* (*without having to*). See *Cod.* 5.71.4 in pr.

GLOSS 108. *Birawed* (*robbed*). say as X 2.13.12 and the entire title *Cod.* 8.4.

GLOSS 109. *Dat hi up syn ayn eerwe comme* (*install him on his own land*). *Cod.* 4.23. This provision says: "When someone buys from a child under tutelage without assistance of the tutor, the contract is binding from one side, because the buyer is obligated, but not from the other side, because the child under tutelage is not obligated if he breaches the contract".

GLOSS 110. *Hit ne se dat hioet seld habbe* (*unless the mother sold ... it*). Note that the upbringing of the pupils falls to the mother, as long as she does not marry for a second time, see *Cod.* 5.49.1, *Dig.* 27.2.pr. and X 3.33.2.

GLOSS 111. *Him dis liwes mede hulp* (*to save his life*). Note that immovables of a minor cannot be sold and alienated by his own will without an oath, in the absence of a tutor, because the contract is legally null and void, unless it takes place in view of a debt, i.e. money due, and in that case only after investigation of the case and the issue of a decree, see *Cod.* 5.71.12, *Cod.* 5.71.13, *Dig.* 27.9.1.2 and *Dig.* 27.9.5.9–10. Tenements of a minor can also be alienated due to special reasons, for example, as a dowry, see *Cod.* 5.37.22.1

(*Cod.* 5.37.22.1), ff. de iure doc. l. Ticia (*Dig.* 23.3.62). Item ob necessitatem famis, C. de patribus qui filios distra. l. ii (*Cod.* 4.43.2). Anima enim hominis est cuilibet rei preferenda, C. de sac. san. ecc. l. Sancimus in fi. (*Cod.* 1.2.21.2). Vel ob defencionem pupilli, C. de amminist. tu. l. fi. § Omnem autem dubitacionem (*Cod.* 5.37.28.4), et in quibusdam aliis casibus. Nota C. quando de. opus non est per totum (*Cod.* 5.72); de his uide decretalem Constitutus, de resti. in inte. (X 1.41.8), super uerbo 'debita solempnitas',[a] Johannes Andreae ibidem[b] in Nouella,[c] Speculum, titulo de emp. et uendi. § Nunc dicendum, in pri. et ii calumpna.[d]

71 **2a.** Dyo forme need is: hweer so een kynd jongh is finsen ende fitered, noerd ur | hef jefta ur birgh, soe moet dio moder her kindes eerwe setta ende sella ende her kynd lesa ende des lives bihelpa.

2b. Dioe oder need is: jef da jere diore wirdat ende di heta honger ur dat land faert ende dat kynd honger stera wil, so moet dio moder her kindes eerwe setta ende sella ende capia her bern ku ende ey ende coern, deer ma da kinde des lives mede helpe.

GLOSSA 112. Nam causa uictus licet parentibus filios distrahere ut dicitur C. de patribus qui filios distra. l. ii (*Cod.* 4.43.2) et dicta l. Sancimus in fi. (*Cod.* 1.2.21.2) multo magis bona.

2c. Dyo tredde need is: als dat kind is al stocnaken jefta huuslaes ende dan di tiuestera nevil ende calda winter oencomt, so faert allermanick oen syn hof ende oen syn huis ende an warme[1] gaten, ende dat[2] wiilda dier seket diin holla baem ende der birgha hlii aldeer hit siin liif oen bihalda mey. So weinet ende scryt dat onjeriga kind ende wypt[3] dan syn nakena lyae ende siin huuslaes ende syn fader, deer him reda schuld tojenst dyn honger ende winter nevilcald, dat hi so diepe ende dimme mitta fiower neylen is onder eke ende onder da eerda bisloten ende bitacht. So moet dio moder her kindes eerwe setta ende sella om dat hio da bihield habbe ende biwaer also lang so hit onjerich is dat hit oen forste ner oen honger naet forfare.

[1] FG: waranne. [2] FG: da. [3] FG: wyst.

a The gloss *debita* ad X 1.41.8.

b ibidem *scripsimus*: abidem FG.

c Johannes Andreae, Novella Commentaria, X 1.41.8, *passim*.

d Guillaume Durand, Speculum iudiciale, Lib. IV, Part. III, Tit. de uenditione a minoribus et ab ecclesia celebratis, § Nunc dicendum, n. 1 et seqq.

and *Dig.* 23.3.62. Also for reason of famine, see *Cod.* 4.43.2. After all, the human soul takes priority over some object, see *Cod.* 1.2.21.2. Or, in view of the defence of a pupil, see *Cod.* 5.37.28.4 and in some other cases. See also the entire title *Cod.* 5.72; see on this matter the decretal X 1.41.8 and the gloss *debita solempnitas*, and Johannes Andreae in his *Novella Commentaria* to the same text and the *Speculum iudiciale* in the title on purchase and sale in the paragraph starting with *Nunc dicendum* in the first and second column.

2a. The first emergency is: whenever a young child is captured and fettered, and taken away to the north over sea or over the mountains, then the mother is allowed to mortgage and sell her child's inheritance in order to free her child and save his life.

2b. The second emergency is: if life becomes expensive and grave famine hits the land and the child is about to die of starvation, then the mother is allowed to mortgage and sell her child's inheritance in order to buy her child a cow and an egg and grain, and thus save his life.

GLOSS 112. Since, as a means of sustaining life, parents may alienate their children, as is said in *Cod.* 4.43.2 and in *Cod.* 1.2.21.2, mentioned above, then all the more so, may they alienate their goods.

2c. The third emergency is: if the child is stark naked or homeless and if the dark fog and the cold winter are coming, each man goes to his house and courtyard and to his warm chambers, and the wild animals seek shelter in a hollow tree or the lee side of a mountain in order to protect their lives. Then the underage child cries and weeps and laments his naked body and his homelessness and the fact that his father, who should have saved him from hunger and the winter cold, lies buried in the deep and dim earth under an oaken lid closed with four nails. Then, the mother is allowed to mortgage and sell her child's inheritance because she has to protect her child, for as long as it is underage, from dying from cold or starvation.

GLOSSA 113. *Ende syn fader deer* An pater uel mater debeant pueros alere C. diuor. facto apud quem l. unica[a] (*Cod.* 5.24.1) et in auth. ibi posita (post *Cod.* 5.24.1 [ex *Nov.* 117.7]), C. de alen. li. per totum (*Cod.* 5.25), ff. e. l. Si quis (*Dig.* 25.3.5 in pr.), C. ubi pupil. edu. l. i (*Cod.* 5.49.1).

3. Dat tredde landriucht is: jef di noerdman enen man nimpt ende hi uta lande feerd wirt, so hwa so syn eerwe capet da hwilen ende als hi weer comt int land so fee hi weer oen syn ayn eerve buta lioda schield ende frana ban. Fry scil wessa
72 dat siin bi aesga[1] dome ende onbritsen. | So hwa so him deer oen meert, so aegh hyt dae lyoden to urfollen mit tyen lioedmerkum ende tria pond da frana, dat is XXI schillingen dis koninghes[2] ban.

GLOSSA 114. De materia huius iuris ff. de capti. et postliminio reuersis l. Postliminium per totum (*Dig.* 49.15.19) et C. e. ti. per totum (*Cod.* 8.50). Per restitutionem in integrum data in rem rescissoria ff. ex quibus causis ma. l. i (*Dig.* 4.6.1), C. de postli. reuersis l. Ab hostibus[b] (*Cod.* 8.50[51].12).

4. Dat fiaerde landriucht is: aldeer fader ende moder hyara dochter jaet oen flette hiara ayn eerwe ende hyoet laet uta liuedgarda mit cape ende mit wixle oen een oderne liuedgarda ende her broder dat kera wil, so moet hioet halda mit XII manna deededen. Jef hyt dan aeck naet leta wil da oenspreeck so aegh hy[3] dan to fellane wed ende scholinga bi sextich merkem.

GLOSSA 115. De materia huius iuris ff. de iur. dot. l. Iure succursum[c] (*Dig.* 23.3.6). Dicitur quod iure succurrendum est patri ut, si filia eius moriatur, in solacium eius dos, quam ei dederat, sibi restituatur, ne dotem simul cum filia amittat.

GLOSSA 116. *Jowt hiara dochter aen flette* Dos profecticia est substantia quedam filie a patre in dotem tradita ff. de iure doti. l. Profecticia primo responso et § Si quis patri et § Sed et si curator (*Dig.* 23.3.5 in pr. 2 et 3). Idem et si filiusfamilias dederit sorori sue, est dos profecticia, e. l. § Si filiusfa. (*Dig.* 23.3.5.10). Et hec dos permutari potest, si hoc utile sit mulieri, ff. e. ti. l. Ita constante matrimonio[d] (*Dig.* 23.3.26), ff. de pact. dotal. l. Si mulier dotis (*Dig.* 23.4.21) in fi. et l. Cum maritus (*Dig.* 23.4.29)

---

[1] FG: dat bi sii*n* aesga. [2] FG: koninhes. [3] FG: hyt.

---

a unica *scripsimus*: una *male praem.* FG.
b hostibus *scripsimus cum Codice*: hosttibus FG.
c Iure succursum *scripsimus*: Iuris succursis *male praem.* FG.
d matrimonio *scripsimus cum Digesto Veteri*: matrimonium FG.

GLOSS 113. *Ende syn fader deern* (*and his father, who*). About the question whether a father and mother have to feed their children see *Cod.* 5.24.1, the authentica *Si pater causam* (post *Cod.* 5.24.1), the entire title *Cod.* 5.25, *Dig.* 25.3.5 in pr. and *Cod.* 5.49.1.

3. The third land law is: if the northmen capture a man and take him abroad, and if in his absence someone buys his land and if he then returns home, he has the right to take possession of his property again without having to pay a fine to the people or experiencing an interdiction by the *frana*. His property shall be free and undisturbed according to the judgment of the *asega*. If anyone prevents him from taking possession of his property, this person shall pay a fine of ten marks and three pounds to the *frana* by order of the king, that is 21 shillings.

GLOSS 114. See about the substance of this provision the entire text of *Dig.* 49.15.19 and the entire title of *Cod.* 8.50. By restoring to the original state; a remedy to rescind is granted against anyone, see *Dig.* 4.6.1 and *Cod.* 8.50(51).12.

4. The fourth land law is: if a father and a mother give a portion of their property to their daughter as a dowry and if the daughter then extracts this property out of the family estate by means of selling or exchanging it and if her brother wants her to give it back, she is allowed to keep the property with the assertion oaths of 12 men. If the brother then still wants to pursue his claim, he will have to pay a fine of sixty marks for breaking his promise.

GLOSS 115. See about the substance of this provision *Dig.* 23.3.6. It says that the law renders assistance to the father so that, if his daughter dies, the dowry he gave is restored to him for his comfort so that he will not, together with his daughter, lose the dowry.

GLOSS 116. *Jowt hiara dochter aen flette* (*give ... to their daughter as a dowry*). The *dos profecticia* is the asset which the father of a certain daughter has conveyed as dowry, see *Dig.* 23.3.5 in the first answer and paragraphs 2 and 3. Likewise, also when a son under paternal control has given it for his sister, it is a *dos profecticia*, see *Dig.* 23.3.5.10. And (the composition of) this dowry can be altered, if this is advantageous to the woman, see *Dig.* 23.3.26, *Dig.* 23.4.21 at the end and *Dig.* 23.4.29.

5. Dat fyfte landriucht is: toe hwam so ma land aeschet, sa anderie di aldere mit riuchter taele ende queth: "Dit land deer du my ofaeschest buppa riucht ende toe tinge om ladeste dat caped ic fan ene roemfarende ende feerde ayn ur birge, bede fel ende flaesch ende dat fia aldeermei ende nerda mitta fia bede seel ende lyf". So aegh hi eefter to farane ende binna fiiftiga wikem toe bifin-
73 dane[1] | ende da lioed hem deytingh toe jowane ende hy weer to commane mit twaem roemfarem ende an[2] da lioedwerf to bringane dat hi habbe Godes bod forfold ende hi se mit boke ende mit stola to der eerda bifellen. Dat aegh hy to bitiugen mit twam roemfarem ende hi self tredda, jefta mit XII manna deededem. Aldeermey se hy siker bi lioeda bode ende bi frana ban buta stryd ende hy ne thoer lingera an warende sitta.

6. Dat sexta landriucht is: jefter tweer broren sint ende di ora een wif halet to howe ende to huis mit hoern ende mit drechte, soe weddat him syn fader jefta syn moder jefta syn foermond riucht swesdeel efter sine deghem. Jef syn kynd jefta sines kyndes kynd him urlibbe ende dis kindes aldera naet liwet, soe wil dat kynd dela sines aldfaders lawa ende syn aldmoders lawa ende syn fedria nel naet ende spreckt dat hy een kne nyer se, so aegh dat kynd hine to winnen in den lioedgarda tolwasum mit acht fadermegen ende mit fiower modermegen. Ende jef him frionden breckt, soe moet hi lioed capia deer mit him swerre jef him syn fedria dera wil.

GLOSSA 117. *Ende syn fedria nel naet* Et male filii premortuorum fratrum succedunt simul cum patruis suis in stirpes, C. de legitimis[a] heredibus, auc. Cessante (post *Cod.* 6.58.3 [ex *Nov.* 118.3 in pr. et 127.1]) et in auc. de heredibus que ab intesta.: "§ Si[b] autem defuncto fratres fuerint et alterius fratris aut sororis premortuorum fily uocabuntur" (*Auth.* 9.1.3 in pr. [*Nov.* 118.3 in pr.]).

GLOSSA 118. *Dat hy een knee nyer se* De iure antiquo Insti. de heredi. que ab intest. deferuntur § Cum filius (*Inst.* 3.1.6) et § Et quemadmodum (*Inst.* 3.1.15 in fi.), de iure nouo authenticorum, in auct. de success.[c] ab intest. uel de her. que ab intest. in principio rubrice (*Auth.* 9.1.1 [*Nov.* 118.1]), ex quo elicitur[d] auth. posita C. de suis et legit. libe. (post *Cod.* 6.55.12 [ex *Nov.* 118.1]), in qua sic habetur "In successione patrisfamilias[e] mortui seu

---

[1] FG: *bifindane* is missing. [2] FG: aec.

---

a legitimis *scripsimus cum Codice*: legittimis FG.
b Si *scripsimus cum Authentico*: Sui *male praem.* FG.
c success. *scripsimus*: suceess *male praem.* FG.
d elicitur *scripsimus*: eltcitur FG.
e patrisfamilias *scripsimus cum Codice*: patrisfamilas FG.

5. The fifth land law is: if someone lays a claim to a certain piece of land, then the oldest man in the house has to defend himself in court and speak thus: "The land you are claiming from me illegally and for which you have compelled me to appear before court was bought by me from a pilgrim who went to Rome and took all his possessions with him over the mountains, both skin and flesh and also the money I paid him and he nourished with this money both soul and body". Then the defendant has to go and find proof of this within a period of fifty weeks and the people have to grant him adjournment during this period. After that period he has to appear before court with two pilgrims and testify that the pilgrim he bought the land from has obeyed God's commandment and was buried by a priest. The defendant has to testify to this himself, aided by the testimonies of two pilgrims or by means of the assertion oaths of 12 men. With this, he shall be exempt from further legal claims on the order of the people and he shall not be obligated to undergo an ordeal by order of the *frana* and he need not be under the guarantee of a guarantor any longer.

6. The sixth land law is: if there are two brothers and one of them brings home a wife in a bridal procession, accompanied by the sounding of horns, then his father or mother or tutor, officially allot him his rightful inheritance, to be obtained after the death of the former. If his child or his child's child outlive him and the child's parents have died, and if the child wants his share from his grandfather's and grandmother's inheritance and if his paternal uncle denies him this, saying he is more closely related than his cousin, then the child has a right to claim his share of the inheritance by means of twelve oaths, eight by paternal kinsmen, and four by maternal kinsmen. And if he is not able to find sufficient kinsmen to testify for him, he is allowed to engage people to swear for him if his paternal uncle wants to disadvantage him.

GLOSS 117. *Ende syn fedria nel naet* (*and if his paternal uncle denies*). The sons of brothers, who died previously, inherit unfavourably at the same time with their parental relatives 'by roots (stocks)' (*in stirpes*), see the authentica *Cessante successione* (post *Cod.* 6.58.3) and see in *Auth.* 9.1.3 at the beginning (*Nov.* 118.3 in pr.): "However, if the deceased has brothers, and children of another brother or sister who previously died, these will be called to the inheritance".

GLOSS 118. *Dat hy een knee nyer se* (*he is more closely related*). For the old law see *Inst.* 3.1.6 and *Inst.* 3.1.15; for the new law of the *Authenticum* see *Auth.* 9.1.1 (*Nov.* 118.1) at the beginning of the rubric, from which the authentica *In successione mortui* (post *Cod.* 6.55.12) is derived, which rules: "In the hereditary succession of a deceased *paterfamilias* or son under pater-

74 filiifamilias[a] liberi eius, si sint, omnibus | alys latis succedunt, primi quidem gradus equaliter, nepotes et ulteriores in stirpes", idest in eam partem quam parentes eorum[b] habituri erant, si uiuerint. Vnde, si quis ex uno filio unicum nepotem suscepit et ex alio filio x, tantum percipient unicus[c] nepos[d] ex uno filio, quantum illi decem uel eorum parentes, C. de suis et leg. li. l. ii (*Cod.* 6.55.2) et melius C. de le. her., auct. Cessante (post *Cod.* 6.58.3 [ex *Nov.* 118.3 in pr. et 127.1]), sublata deferentia sexus, id est siue sit uir siue mulier, et patrie potestatis, id est siue sit mancipatus siue non. Et sic semper primo succedunt descendentes[e] sed deficientibus descendentibus tunc uocantur ascendentes, ut in auth. Defuncto posita super l. fi. C. ad tertullianum[f] (post *Cod.* 6.56.7 [ex *Nov.* 118.2]), sumpta de § Consequens autem est, in auth. de her. ab intest. uenien. (*Auth.* 9.1.2 [*Nov.* 118.2]).[g] Defuncto filio sine liberis, parentes, si soli sunt, succedunt salua gradus prerogatiua, si pari gradu sunt, pariter uocantur, paternis quidem maternis dimidia delata, licet dispar sit eorum numerus. Sed et si cum parentibus fratres sorores utrimque coniuncti defuncto supersint, uocantur cum ascendentibus in gradu proximis ut uiriles fiant portiones,[h] exclusa prorsus omni differentia sexus et patrie potestatis. Sexus id est ita bene succedit femina sicut et masculus. Et patrie potestatis, id est quia non refert utrum sit suus uel emancipatus, ubi nulla secundarum nupciarum sit mentio.[i] Hic uult dicere quod pater et mater succedunt filiis, siue contrahunt secundas nupcias siue non. Viso enim qualiter linea descendens et ascendens admittitur, uideam de collaterali. Et sciendum est quod primo uocantur fratres in auct. de her. ab intest. § Reliquum et sequenti, et etiam[j] fratrum filii in primo coll. ix (*Auth.* 9.1.2–3 [*Nov.* 118.2–3]), ex quibus elicitur auth. posita de legit. her. C. (post *Cod.* 6.58.3 [ex *Nov.* 118.3 in pr. et 127.1]) in hec uerba: "Cessante successione linee descendentis et ea que sola sit ascendentis, uocantur primo fratres fratrisque premortui filii in[k] stirpem".

---

a filiifamilias *scripsimus cum Codice*: filifamilias FG.
b eorum *scripsimus*: eoque FG.
c unicus *scripsimus*: unos FG.
d nepos *scripsimus*: nedos FG.
e descendentes *scripsimus*: descendeutes FG.
f tertullianum *scripsimus cum Codice*: terculiauum FG.
g 'Consequens autem esse' is the final line of *Auth.* 9.1.1 (*Nov.* 118.1).
h portiones *scripsimus*: porcones FG.
i mentio *scripsimus*: mensio FG.
j etiam *scripsimus*: ut *male praem.* FG.
k in *scripsimus*: iu FG.

nal authority, his descendants, if there are any, succeed him before all others, those in the first degree for equal shares, the grandchildren and further descendants by roots", i.e. in the share their parents would have had, were they still alive. Hence, if someone has one single grandchild from one son and ten from another son, the one and single grandchild will receive as much as the ten or their parents, see *Cod.* 6.55.2 and even better, the authentica *Cessante successione* (post *Cod.* 6.58.3), irrespective of the difference in gender, i.e. whether one is male or female, and the family status, i.e. whether one is emancipated or not. And thus the descendants always succeed in the first place. But if descendants are lacking, then ascendants are called to the inheritance, see the authentica *Defuncto sine liberis* (post *Cod.* 6.56.7), which is derived from *Auth.* 9.1.3 (*Nov.* 118.3). If a son dies childless, the parents, where they are the only ascendants, succeed to the inheritance subject to the priority of their degree. If they are in the same degree, they succeed equally. Half is given to the paternal ascendants and half, indeed, to the maternal ascendants, no matter how unequal their number is. However, if together with the parents there are also remaining brothers and sisters, through one of the parents related to the deceased, they are called together with the closest ascendants in degree, so that separate portions are made, entirely irrespective of gender and family status. Gender i.e. that a woman succeeds as much as a man. Family status, i.e. because it does not matter whether one is under his father's control or emancipated, where no mention is made of second marriages. This means that the father and mother succeed their son, whether or not they have entered into a second marriage. After having seen in which way the descending and ascending line is admitted to the inheritance, let us now look at the collateral line. And one has to know that first the brothers are called (to the inheritance) and also the sons of the brothers, see *Auth.* 9.1.2–3 (*Nov.* 118.2–3), from which the authentica *Cessante successione* (post *Cod.* 6.58.3) is derived, in the following words: "When there is no succession in the descending line and in the line which is only ascending, first the brothers are called and by roots the children of the brothers who have previously deceased".

7. Dat VIIde landriucht is dat ma emes lawa, aldefaders lawa ende aldmoders lawa, edeles lawa ende tredknia laewa halde sonder stryd mit XII manna | dededem. Jef deer enich man onsprect mit onriuchter tale dan riucht ma mit twam dededem ende bisitte syn ayn eerwe mit aller fresena riucht.

8. Dat VIIIde landriucht is dat ellic eerwe mei leda siin tredknia mit twam dededem toe dade ende to dulge om dat hi is mei fan sine blode commen. Hweer so ma een bannethe[1] werpt op een man deer nen dulg ne haet endma queth dat hi se slain mit bamem jefta huinsen so moet hi tolwasum onswara ende nen meer onbringh daia. Jefter een dulgh is endma biseckt dis daeddellis endma dis dulgis jecht, soe moet syn eerfnama syn tredknia oenleda mit XII manna wytedem. So aeg ma him to jeldene. Dat is landriucht aller Fresena.

GLOSSA 119. Secus de iure communi ut supra satis declaratum est *inda xvste kest*,[a] in allegationibus ibi positis.

GLOSSA 120. *Endma queth* Nec hoc idoneis testibus nec apertissimis documentis approbari possit, C. de proba. l. Sciant cuncti (*Cod.* 4.19.25), ff. de pe. Absen. (*Dig.* 48.19.5), extra de homi. Ex litteris (X 5.12.14).

GLOSSA 121. *Endma dis dulgis iecht* Extra arg. de homi. Ad audientiam (X 5.12.12), ff. ad le. acqui. l. Si putator (*Dig.* 9.2.31), C. quorum appellati. non recipiantur[b] l. Obseruare (*Cod.* 7.65.2 in pr.).

9. Dat IXde landriucht is: soe hwer so di man sine friond bleda siucht ende se oen him fiuchten dulgh jefta daed jefta bede buta sine schield ende hi binna sine tredda kne se, so bete hyt di deer hit deen is truch sine willa. Ende jef hyt beta nelle so swerre hit di ora oen da wyteden dat hyt naet haet deen om neen[2] seeck ner om alde nyd ner om nener slachta willa oers dan dat hi hem helpa wolde. So bete hyt deert om syn schield deen is. So hweer so di dada is ende[3]

[1] FG: ban ther*e*. [2] FG: nee. [3] FG: eu*d*e.

a See text VI,15.

b recipiantur *scripsimus cum Codice*: recipitur FG.

7. The 7th land law is that anyone has the right to retain the inheritance of a maternal uncle, a grandfather or a grandmother, a great-grandfather or a relative in the third degree if one is called to court to stand suit over it, without having to undergo an ordeal over it, with the help of the oaths of 12 men. If anyone makes an illegitimate claim against him, the defendant can exonerate himself by means of two assertion oaths and retain possession of his own estate in accordance with the law of all Frisians.

8. The 8th land law is that each estate holder may rightfully call to court his relatives up to the third degree to act as compurgators in a case of homicide or severe injury by means of swearing two assertion oaths because they are related by blood. If a case of homicide is brought before court but the body shows no wound and the claimant states that the victim has been hit by a bludgeon or hanged, the defendant has the right to exonerate himself by swearing an oath on the holy relics, together with eleven compurgators and after that is not compelled to answer to any more claims brought against him. If the body does show a wound and the defendant denies the charge of homicide but does concede to have wounded the victim, the heir is allowed to call in the testimony of his relatives in the third degree with the oaths of 12 men. Then the defendant has to pay the wergild for the deceased. This is the land law of all Frisians.

GLOSS 119. According to the *ius commune* it is different, as sufficiently explained above in *inda xvste kest*, in the texts adduced there.

GLOSS 120. *Endma queth* (*and the claimant states*). And this can neither be proved by appropriate witnesses nor by the clearest documents, see *Cod.* 4.19.25, *Dig.* 48.19.5 and X 5.12.14.

GLOSS 121. *Endma dis dulgis iecht* (*but does concede to have wounded*). Arguments in X 5.12.12, *Dig.* 9.2.31 and *Cod.* 7.65.2.pr.

9. The 9th land law is: if a man sees his relative bleeding from a wound and if they both fight with the attacker and wound him or kill him or do both and if the two are related within the third degree, then he for whose sake this was done has to compensate. And if he does not want to compensate, the other relative must swear that he did not wound the attacker because of any feud the two of them had, nor because of any old scores, nor for any other sake than that he wanted to help his relative. Then the person for the sake of whom the wounding was perpetrated has to pay the compensation. If there is a dead man

nen dulg oen is mit bamem slagen is jefta di man huinsen is, so moet hi tolwasum onswerra ende nen meer oenbringh daia.

GLOSSA 122. Dicit lex, ad le. ac. l. Qui occidit § fi. (*Dig.* 9.2.30.4), "Si seruus, non mortifere uulneratus, negligentia periit, non de homicidio sed de uul-
76 nere iudicatur", extra de homi. c. Significasti ii (X 5.12.18). |

GLOSSA 123. Nota. Quilibet tenetur defendere uicinum suum, maxime amicum suum, et ei auxilium prestare. Alias sibi est particeps[a] culpe, xxiii q. iii Fortitudo et c. Non inferenda (C.23 q.3 c.5 et 7), ubi dicit Ambrosius "qui a socio suo non repellit iniuriam, cum posit, tam ille in uicio est quam qui fecit". Vide latius, extra de senten. exco. c. Quante presumptionis (X 5.39.47) et Iohannes ibidem in Nouella,[b] de homici. in c. Sicut dignum § Illi autem (X 5.12.6.1) et in decretali Innocentii iiii, de sen. excom. Dilecto, libro vi (VI 5.11.6) et Johannes in Summa confessorum, titulo de homicidio q. xxxiii.[c] Vtrum quilibet tenetur proximum liberare a morte et Raymundus, de homi. § In summa,[d] arg. ff. quod me. causa l. Isti § ult. (*Dig.* 4.2.8.3), C. ad leg. iulia. de ui pub. l. Quoniam (*Cod.* 9.12.6). Dic ut ibi et de hac materia notat Innocentius, de sen. exco. Si uero § ult. in glossa inferentem (X 5.39.3).[e]

10. Dat xde[1] landriucht is: hweer so ma een daedbante werpt op enis mannes schalck, soe moet di hera ontswara mit ene wytede, jefta di schalck schil een heet yrser draga fan da fonte ti da hagha alter. Jef di eerfnama dat riucht naet hera wil jefta oensyaen so aeg ma hem to helpen mit sindriucht, mit ketelfangh jefta mit wyder corbita—dat is sindriucht, deer ma mei helpa schil da eerma mey da rika, da onedela als da edela—jefta mit ene kempa op ti halyane.

GLOSSA 124. *Jefta kneppa werpt* Non tenetur dominus de familia sua nisi mandauerit uel ratum habuerit arg. extra de restit. spo. c. Cum ad sedem apostolicam (X 2.13.15), ff. de ui et ui arma. l. i § Deiecisse autem[f] is uidetur qui mandauit uel iussit et § Sed et si eum quis alius deiecerit ratum habuerit (*Dig.* 43.16.1.12 et 14). Noxa est corpus quod nocet, sicut seruus. Noxia est ipsum maleficium, ut furtum, dampnum, rapina, iniuria. Et quod dominus non sit in culpa, oportet quod prohibeat uerbo et facto

[1] FG: xvste.

a particeps *scripsimus*: perticeps FG.
b Johannes Andreae, Novella Commentaria, X 5.39.47, n. 3.
c Johannes de Friburgo, Summa confessorum, Lib. II, tit. 1, q. 32.
d Raymundus de Pennaforte, Summa de poenitentia, Lib. II, tit. 1, § 14.
e Innocentius IV, Commentaria, X 5.39.3, n. 2.
f autem *scripsimus cum Digesto Novo*: aut FG.

but the body shows no wound and if the victim has been hit by a bludgeon or has been hanged, the defendant has the right to exonerate himself with eleven compurgators and after that is not compelled to answer to any more claims brought against him.[9]

GLOSS 122. The provision of *Dig.* 9.2.30.4 says: "If a slave who is not mortally wounded, died out of negligence, the wrongdoer will be sentenced not for homicide, but for wounding", see X 5.12.18.

GLOSS 123. Note that everyone has to protect his fellowman, especially his friend and offer him help. Otherwise he is guilty of carelessness, see C.23 q.3 c.5 and 7, where Ambrose says: "the one who does not preserve his companion from injury, is as much to blame as the one who acted". See about this at length X 5.39.47 and Johannes in his *Novella Commentaria* to this text, X 5.12.6.1, the decretal VI 5.11.6 of Innocent IV and Johannes in his *Summa confessorum*, in the title on homicide, question 33. On the question whether everyone is obligated to save his fellowman from death see also Raymundus in the title on homicide in the paragraph starting with the words '*In summa*' with as arguments *Dig.* 4.2.8.3 and *Cod.* 9.12.6. Say as in that provision and about this matter Innocent makes a comment in the gloss *inferentem* to X 5.39.3.

10. The 10th land law is: if a charge of homicide is brought against someone's servant, then the servant's master has the right to exonerate his servant of the claim by swearing an oath on the holy relics, or the servant must (undergo the ordeal by fire and) carry the hot iron from the baptismal font to the high altar. If the heir of the deceased man does not want to hear the oath or see the ordeal, the servant is to be helped by taking refuge to the synodical law, by undergoing an ordeal by water or an ordeal by ingestion—because synodical law is established to help the poor as well as the rich, commoners as well as noblemen—or by undergoing trial by combat.

GLOSS 124. *Jefta kneppa werpt* (*brought against someone's servant*). A father and master is not liable for his household, unless he has given a mandate or ratification, see X 2.13.15 and *Dig.* 43.16.1,12 and 14. *Noxa* is the physical entity causing the damage, such as a slave. *Noxia* is the delict itself, such as theft, damage to things, robbery and injury. And, in order for the father and master not to be blamed, he should issue a prohibition in word and

9 This last sentence seems to be a variant version of what is said in the 8th land law. It is unclear how it got here. It is not present in the variant redactions of this text and therefore is probably an error of the editors of *Freeska Landriucht*.

et faciat omnem resistentiam quam potest, ut et in textu et glossa et per doctores in allegatum c. Cum ad sedem (X 2.13.15) et ff. si fa. fur. fe. dicatur l. i (*Dig.* 47.6.1).

77 **11.** Dat alfte landriucht is: hweer | so ma een daeddel werpt op een man fan rederis hoern, fan hondes byt, fan hona eetsele ende fan swines tussche, soe moet ma dis tolwasum onzwara on da wytedem. Fora ne aegh hyt to foranderien.

GLOSSA 125. *Uan rederis hoern* Quando autem animal alicuius dampnum dat, si motum sit ad dandum dampnum contra naturam sui generis, tenetur dominus uel dare quod nocuit pro noxa uel restituere dampnum. Sed non est intelligendum[a] de indomitis, ut sunt ursi, leones, pantheres et alia, quia si ursus a domino fugit et sic nocet, non potest dominus conueniri, quia desinit dominus esse, dum euasit, Insti. et ff. si quadru. pau. (*Inst.* 4.9 et *Dig.* 9.1) per totum et potest colligi extra de iniur. et damp. c. Si bos (X 5.36.3).

12. Dat toelfte landriucht is: haet so tusch deth jefta hoef jefta hona eetsel jefta oenjeriga kynd jefta mannes wyf jefta urbeck deth mitter hand jefta oder onwitenda deda jef hyt on da helligem bringha wil dattet hem were onwilla ende onwald, soe schil ma hit al beta mit halver bota ende neen ferd da lioden ner da frana.

GLOSSA 126. *Unieriga kynd* Intellige de puero doli capace, quia pupillo et furioso subuenitur in maleficiis, quia facultatem deliberandi non habent. Quomodo ergo reus constituitur, qui nescit quid facit, extra de delict. pue. c. ii (X 5.23.2) dicitur.[b] Sepe enim solet in pueris relinqui in ultum, quod in aliis prouecte etatis leges dicunt seuerius corrigendum, quia pater pro delicto pueri sui non debet puniri pena pecuniaria, in Speculo titutlo de sen. execu. § Sequitur uidere uersiculo 'Quit si filiusfa.'.[c]

GLOSSA 127. *Uurbeck deth* Leui culpa precedente, alius non tenetur, C. ad le. cor. de sicca. l. iiii (*Cod.* 9.16.4). Dic ut ibi in glossa.

GLOSSA 128. *Haet so hit deth* Insti. si quadru. pau. feciss. dicatur § Pauperies (*Inst.* 4.9 in pr.) "est dampnum datum sine iniuria facientis; nec enim

a intelligendum *scripsimus*: intelligedum FG.
b Cf. C.15 q.1 c.5.
c Guillaume Durand, Speculum iudiciale, Lib. II, Part. III, Tit. de executione sententiae, § Sequitur uidere, n. 11.

deed and offer all the resistance he can, as in accordance with the text, the Gloss as well as the commentaries of the scholars on the adduced text of X 2.13.15 and *Dig.* 47.6.1.

11. The eleventh land law is: if someone is charged with homicide caused by the horn of cattle, the bite of a dog, the spur of a cock or the tusk of a pig, he may exonerate himself by swearing an oath on the holy relics, together with eleven compurgators. If he has done so, no further case can be brought to court on this matter.

GLOSS 125. *Uan rederis hoern* (*by the horn of his cattle*). However, when someone's animal causes damage, if it was induced to cause the damage contrary to the nature of its species, the owner is obligated to surrender noxally what caused the damage, or to compensate the loss. However, this practice is not to be adopted as regards untamed animals such as bears, lions, panthers and other animals. Since when a bear escapes from his owner and in such a way causes damage, the owner cannot be sued because he ceased to be the owner at the time the bear ran away, see the entire titles *Inst.* 4.9 and *Dig.* 9.1 and you can derive this from X 5.36.3.

12. The twelfth land law is: whatever injuries were caused by a tusk or a hoof or a cock's spur or an underage child or a man's wife or by someone's own hand as a consequence of carelessness or any other unintentional deed, these shall be compensated with half the normal compensation and no fine is to be paid to the people or the *frana* if the defendant will swear on the holy relics that the injuries happened against his will and that he was unable to prevent them.

GLOSS 126. *Unieriga kind* (*underage child*). Understand this as concerning a child capable of fraud, because in wrongdoings the immature and insane are safeguarded since they lack the ability to deliberate. Regarding the question whether one may be held liable, who does not know what he does, is stated in X 5.23.2. Since, in the case of children, one ususally leaves the reprehensible act unpunished, which in case of others of a more advanced age should be censured more severly because a father should not be punished with a monetary penalty for the delict of his child, see the *Speculum iudiciale*, in the title on the execution of a sentence, in the paragraph starting with '*Sequitur uidere*', the fragment with the words '*Quit si filiusfamilias*'.

GLOSS 127. *Uurbeck deth* (*unintentional deed*), with an earlier minor negligent act, otherwise he is not liable, see *Cod.* 9.16.4. Say as there in the Gloss.

GLOSS 128. *Haet so hit deth* (*whatever it does*). *Inst.* 4.9 in pr.: "*Pauperies* is loss inflicted without a wrongful act of the one who caused it; for one

animal iniuriam fecisse dici, quod sensu careat", id est intellectum et ratio-
78 onem non habet. |

13. Dat XIIIste landriucht is: hwa so wida bifiucht jefta birawet, so bete hi her mit twifalder bota ende da liodem dine ferd bi X lyoedmerkum ende tria pond da frana, dat is XXI schillingen des koninges ban. Ende alle dagelix also lang so hi mitta onriuchta rawe sit, soe jelde hy da frana XVI schillingen om dat dio wedue is des koninges mondele.

GLOSSA 129. *Dat xiiiste*[a] *landrincht* Hec iniuria ex qualitate persone est per iudicem existimanda, extra de iniu. et damp. da. c. Olim (X 5.36.7), quod metus ca. c. fi. (*Dig.* 4.2.23), Insti. de iniur.[b] et § Atrox (*Inst.* 4.4.9) et posset dici maior iniuria. Nota. Si quis rem propriam uiolenter inuadit, amittit proprietatem. Si uero alienam, punietur in estimatione illius rei et amittit ius quod in ea re habuit, Si quis in tanta C. unde ui (*Cod.* 8.4.7).

GLOSSA 130. *Onriucht birawed* Spoliatus ante omnia debet restitui cum fructibus[c] perceptis c. i. de resti. spo. (X 2.13.1) et ibi in glossa. Nec tenetur respondere ante restitutionem, extra de or. cogni. c. Cum dilectus (X 2.10.2).

14. Dat XIIIIste landriucht is: so hwa so anderem faert to hou ende to huis mit een opriuchta fana ane lioda werd ende buta frana ban enis domliachtes deis, so haet so ma deer inoer hoff ende huis deth dat is twybeet ende alle dat ma deerut[1] deth of deer needwer dat sel wessa al eferd[2] ende ebeet.[3] Des agen him[4] da lioed ende di frana to helpane om dat him di haudlase here[5] tocommen was. Hwer so di man fiucht to oderis mannes huis ende di ora hine binna wert so haet so ma dan utfiucht dat schil wessa sonder boet ende sonder ferd ende haet so ma infiucht dat is al twibeet.

GLOSSA 131. *Dat xiiiiste landriucht En to huis*. Nota. Qui domum alterius intrauit per uim, tenetur sibi actione iniuriarum, l. Lex cor. ff. de iniuriis et l. Is qui domum ff. e. (*Dig.* 47.10.5 et 23) et Inst. de iniuriis § Sed et lex cor. (*Inst.* 4.4.8).

GLOSSA 132. *Tuibeet* De istis iniuriis et alys nota caput supra proximo cum allegatis cum suis concordantibus, quia locus, tempus et persona reddunt

---

[1] FG: deer wr. [2] FG: een ferd. [3] FG: een beet. [4] FG: hi. [5] FG: *here* is missing.

---

a xiiiste *scripsimus*: xxiiiste FG.
b iniur. *scripsimus cum Digesto Veteri*: ininr. FG.
c fructibus *scripsimus*: frnctibus FG.

cannot say that an animal acts wrongfully, because it lacks understanding", i.e. it has no intellect and reason.

13. The 13th land law is: if a man attacks or robs a widow, he shall compensate her twofold and he shall pay a fine of ten marks and three pounds to the *frana* by order of the king for the breach of the peace, that is, 21 shillings. And for every day he remains in possession of the illegally robbed goods, he shall pay 16 shillings to the *frana* because a widow falls under the king's guardianship.

GLOSS 129. *Dat xiiiste landriucht* (*the 13th land law*). This injury, based on the status of a person, has to be assessed by the judge, see X 5.36.7, *Dig.* 4.2.23 and *Inst.* 4.4.9. And it may be called major injury. Note that if someone forcibly takes possession of his own thing, he will lose ownership. If, however, he takes possession of another's thing, he will be punished in the estimated value of the thing and lose the right he held in that thing, see *Cod.* 8.4.7.

GLOSS 130. *Onriucht birawed* (*illegally robbed*). The one robbed should before all other things be restored, also with the fruits picked, see X 2.13.1 and the Gloss on that text. Before restitution has taken place, he is not obligated to answer, see X 2.10.2.

14. The 14th land law is: if someone goes to another man's house and lands with a raised banner without the consent of the people and without the order of the *frana* in broad daylight, whatever is perpetrated consequently at that estate shall be compensated twofold and nothing that is done out of self-defence shall require a fine for the breach of peace nor compensation. And the people and the *frana* should come to the victim's aid because an illegal armed force came to his house. If someone attacks the house of another man and this man defends himself on the inside, whatever is done by the people inside will not require compensation nor a fine for the breach of peace and whatever is done by the attackers shall be compensated twofold.[10]

GLOSS 131. *Dat xiiiiste landriucht En to huis* (*the 14th land law and to another man's house*). Note that the one who forcefully enters another's house, can be sued by means of the remedy for injury, see *Dig.* 47.10.5 and 23, and *Inst.* 4.4.8.

GLOSS 132. *Tuibeet* (*twofold*) See for these and other injuries the immediately preceding chapter with its allegations and similar provisions, be-

10 This last sentence is variant redaction of this same land law so it largely repeats what has been said before.

iniuriam atrocem, Inst. de iniuri § Atrox (*Inst.* 4.4.9), ff. de iniur. l. Pretor
79 § Atrox (*Dig.* 47.10.7.8) et l. ult. (*Dig.* 47.10.45). |

GLOSSA 133. *Need wer* Nota. Omnes leges omniaque iura uim ui repellere permittunt saluo moderamine inculpate tutele c. Significasti ii. extra de homi. (X 5.12.18), ff. de ui et ui ar.[a] l. i. § Vim ui (*Dig.* 43.16.1.27).

15. Dat XVde landriucht is: hwer so ma wapeldepene[1] det ende swerte swingen of een man onschieldich biint jefta onriucht rawet jefta sonendeis bloedresene deth: dera elkerlyc to bote is XV einsa. Wil ma bisecka, so ontswerre hyt mit fyf wyteden ende mit een fiaeed.

16. Dat XVI ste landriucht[2] is: so hwer so lawa lawiget wirdet utoer sex handen ende deer is nen fader ner moder, broder ner suster, bern ner bernsbern, dat hetet onween lawa. Soe hwa so deer dan sibst to is, di nime da lawa. Jef dat aeck ne se, so dele da oder frionden[3] al like deer hia lyc sib se ende di aesga nime deer of deer hi fander deelscip aeg: een penningh fan allerlikes hand.

GLOSSA 134. *Huaso deer sibst* C. de le. her. auth. (post *Cod.* 6.58.3 [ex *Nov.* 118.3.1]): "Post fratres fratrumque filios uocantur quicumque gradu sunt proximiores, ut pares in gradu pariter admittantur, sublata differentia masculorum et feminarum; sola[b] namque cognatio spectatur in talibus".

17. Dat XVII ste landriucht is, dat dio wedue ner her kind ne thoren anderda om land ner om letar ner om meenteel eer dat kind jerich is. Anders schillet hya anderda om alle seckem bi aesga doem ende lioda landriucht.[4]

GLOSSA 135. De priuilegys uiduarum et orphanorum etc., causa uiduarum et pupillorum principaliter spectant ad iudicium seculare, extra de fo. compe. Ex tenore (X 2.2.11), Innocentius, de off. dele. c. Significantibus[c] et Henricus Boic in c. Ex tenore e. ti. (X 2.2.11), uide glossam ii.[d]

GLOSSA 136. *Ner om meenteel* Melius uide infra de homicidii compositione in libro illo.[e]

GLOSSA 137. *Anders schillet hia* Arg. a contrario sensu quod est in iure fortissimum, ut notatur extra de his que fiunt a prela. c. Cum apostolica (X 3.10.7).

[1] FG: wapel tuyheet depene. [2] FG: ladriucht. [3] FG: froiden. [4] FG: landrieht.

a ui ar. *scripsimus cum Digesto Novo*: ar. ar FG.
b sola *scripsimus cum Codice*: solo FG.
c Innocentius IV, Commentaria, X 1.29.38, n. 1.
d Henricus Boich, Commentaria, X 2.2.11, n. 2.
e See text XII,1–3.

cause the location, the time and the person make an injury atrocious, see *Inst.* 4.4.9, *Dig.* 47.10.7.8 and *Dig.* 47.10.45.

GLOSS 133. *Need wer* (*self-defence*). Note that all legal rules and provisions allow to answer force with force, observing the restraint of an irreproachable supervision, see X 5.12.18 and *Dig.* 43.16.1.27.

15. The 15th land law is: if a man throws another man in the water or pours foul liquids over him or fetters him while he is innocent or robs him illegally or wounds him on a Sunday: the compensation for each of these offences is 15 ounces. If the defendant wants to deny the accusation, he must swear innocence with five oaths on the holy relics or with one property oath.

16. The 16th land law is: if an inheritance falls outside the six hands and there is no father nor mother, brother nor sister, children nor grandchildren, then this is called an unhoped-for inheritance. Whoever is closest related to the deceased then, shall take the inheritance. If there is none, then all relatives shall have an equal share according to their degree of relatedness and the *asega* shall take the fee he is entitled to for the partitioning: one penny from each party.

GLOSS 134. *Huaso deer sibst* (*whoever is closest related*). Auth. *Post fratres fratrumque* (post *Cod.* 6.58.3): "After the brothers and the children of the brothers, all the relatives close in degree are called (to the inheritance) so that those with the same degree are called at the same time, irrespective whether they are male or female because in such matters only relationship counts".

17. The 17th land law is, that a widow nor her child are obligated to stand suit over cases concerning land or servants or the kin's share of a wergild before the child comes of age. In all other cases they shall stand suit in accordance with the decree of the *asega* and the land law of the people.

GLOSS 135. Concerning privileges of widows, orphans, etc. A case of widows and pupils is in principle heard by the secular court, see X 2.2.11, Innocent in his commentary on X 1.29.38 and Henricus Boic in his commentary on X 2.2.11, see the second gloss.

GLOSS 136. *Ner om meenteel* (*nor … of the kin's share of a wergild*). Better, see below on composition in case of homicide in that book.

GLOSS 137. *Anders schillet hia* (*In all other cases they shall*). This is an *argumentum a contrario* which is very solid in legal reasoning, as is noticed in X 3.10.7.

18. Dat XVIII ste landriucht is: hwer so di man oderem oen hand jefta an hielde jout syn gued so is dat alle riucht dat hyt him weder anderda schil dis selva deis deer hyt habba wil, | hit ne se dattet hem tria need ofnime: needraef jefta needbrand jefta nachttiefta. Ende dat se buurkuud ende gaekuud dat hem se gued rawed jefta baernd jefta stellen. So ne thoer hyt him naet anderda hwant nimmen anderis gued fora waria mei dan syn ayn gued.

So haet so di man oderem jout op trowa ende werd ende riuchta fiamonde, waxtet of minret, bede al even. Jef hit alsoe comt dat ma syn huis inbreke ende syn gued nime ende dat aldeermede urstolen wirt, jeft ma dine tief mit riuchte biradie, soe jowe hyt weder ende frome dae manne jeld ende di oera helft nime di grewa.

GLOSSA 138. Nota extra de deposi. c. i. (X 3.16.1). Licuit autem deponenti pro uoluntate sua depositum suum reuocare quandocunque,[a] quia de iure naturali est, d. ⟨i⟩ Ius naturale[b] (D.1 c.7) et ff. e. l. i. § Est apud et § pe. (*Dig.* 16.3.1.22 et 46); "item commodate uel deposite rei restitutio". Et res deterior facta, reddita non uidetur, ff. e. l. iiii § iiii (*Dig.* 16.3.1.16) et extra de deposito c. Bona fides. (X 3.16.2).

GLOSSA 139. *Anderda dis selua deis* Ne sit in mora. Alius tenetur de fortuito, ff. e. l. Si in Asia[c] § fi. (*Dig.* 16.3.12.3).

GLOSSA 140. *Need raef nacht brand* Fugatur iusticia, si uiolencia inferatur, ff. locati lege Si merces[d] § Vis maior (*Dig.* 19.2.25.6), nisi sint in dolo, culpa uel mora, uel minor restituendus fuerit uel pactum interuenerit, uel se obtulerit seu precium interuenerit; Hostiensis[e] et Azo in Summa.[f]

19. Dat nyoghenteensta landriucht[1] is: jeft ma een man bityghet dat hy een famna aen nede nymen haet, jeff hy se jecht, soe jelde hy se twede. Jef hy bisecke, soe ontswerre hy se achtasum aen dae wythedem.

GLOSSA 141. Item nota de raptu uirginum (*Cod.* 9.13) de materia huius iuris.

GLOSSA 142. Eciam uide supra de iure pretorio.[g]

---

[1] FG: landrincht.

---

a quandocunque *scripsimus*: bncunque *male praem.* FG.

b naturale *scripsimus cum Decreto Gratiani*: naturala FG.

c Asia *scripsimus cum Digesto Veteri*: aliam *male praem.* FG.

d Si merces] l. Si res merces BL KB J109 M60 RA UB.

e Hostiensis (Henricus de Segusio), Summa aurea, X 3.16, n. 8 (in fine).

f Summa *scripsimus*: Snmma FG; probably Azo's Summa Codicis; we could not identify the specific fragment.

g See text III,9.

18. The 18th land law is: if someone hands over to another man his goods to hold in trust, then it is law that this man shall return it to the former's possession on the same day he demands this, unless this is made impossible as a consequence of three impediments: robbery, arson or theft. And it should be publicly known that the recipient suffered robbery or arson or theft. In this case the custodian is no longer obligated to return the property because no man is expected to take better care of someone else's property than of his own.

Whatever a man gives another man in good faith and with solid promises to be part of a legal joint ownership, whether the property grows or diminishes, they shall both share equally. If it happens that someone breaks into his house and takes his goods and among this was the shared property, and if the thief is tried before court, he shall return the goods and compensate the person and the count shall take the other half of the thief's possessions.

GLOSS 138. See X 3.16.1, since, if he wishes the depositor may at anytime ask back the thing deposited because this is based on natural law, see D.1 c.7 and *Dig*. 16.3.1.22 and 46; "so is the restitution of something borrowed or deposited". And a deteriorated thing is not considered as returned, see *Dig*. 16.3.1.16 and X 3.16.2.

GLOSS 139. *Anderda dis selua deis* (*return ... on the same day*). So that he is not in default. Otherwise (if he falls into default) he is liable in case of fortuity, see *Dig*. 16.3.12.3.

GLOSS 140. *Need raef nacht brand* (*robbery, arson*). When violence is exerted, justice stands aside, see *Dig*. 19.2.25.6, unless one is in fraud, negligence or default, or something has to be restored to a minor, or a pact was made, or one had accepted liability or agreed to a certain amount of damages, see Hostiensis and Azo in his Summa.

19. The nineteenth land law is: if a man is tried before court of having raped a girl and if he confesses, he shall pay her two thirds of her wergild. If he denies, he shall exonerate himself with eight oaths on the holy relics.

GLOSS 141. See also *Cod*. 9.13 on the subject of this provision.

GLOSS 142. See also above the chapter on the *Older Skelta Law*.

GLOSSA 143. *Dit is riucht: hweersoma een wyf an nede nimpt* Et eciam uide
81 de materia eadem *inda fyfteenda kest.*[a] |

20. Dat XXste landriucht is: hweer so di man fiucht oen heerferd, so bete hi di man twybeeth om dine lioedferd ende tria pond dae frana om dis koninghes ban.

GLOSSA 144. *Twybeet* De hoc Insti. de iniur. § Atrox (*Inst.* 4.4.9). Ex persona dicitur enim iniuria atrox ut si magistratui aut senatori iniuria facta fuerit, ff. de iniuriis l. De iniuria (*Dig.* 47.10.45).

21. Dat XXIste landriucht[1] is: jef di noerdman nymt een man ontankes ende hine sines ontankes uta land feert ende hi oen een torp faert ende hueckene schade det, dat hi een torp baernt jefta wyf nedet, jefta man slacht ende haet so hi eweles deth ende als hi dana fliucht jefta dat hy leesd wirth, als hi weer in dat land comme endma him dat toesidse an da lyoda warve ende an bannena tinge, so queth hi dattet also se. Deer ne haet hi oenbritsen hor schelta ban ner aesga doem ner koninges ferd ner lyoeda wirde, hwant hy deda als him syn hera baed da hi syn schalck was. So schil hit syn hera al beta.

GLOSSA 145. *Syn ayn schalck waes* Seruitus est constitutio iuris gentium qua quis alieno iure contra naturam subicitur. Serui autem ex eo appellati sunt, quod imperatores captiuos uendere iubent ac per hoc seruare non occidere solent. Que et mancipia dicta sunt quia ab hostibus manu capiuntur, Instit. de iu. perso. § Seruitus et § Serui (*Inst.* 1.3.2–3), Insti. quibus modis ius pa. po. sol. § Quod "si ab hostibus captus fuerit parens, quamuis seruus hostium fiat, et tales, si reuersi fuerint, omnia iura pristina recipiunt" (*Inst.* 1.12.5).

GLOSSA 146. *Als him syn hera* Dominus uel pater precipiens tenetur, obediens excusatur, ff. de ac. et obli. l. Seruus (*Dig.* 44.7.20), ff. de re. iu. his "is[b] dampnum dat qui iubet dare; ei nulla culpa est cui etc." (*Dig.* 50.17.169).

21a. Elkes wives weetma dat is acht pond acht einsa ende acht peninge.[2]

[1] FG: landrircdt. [2] FG: pen*in*ge.

a See text VI,15.

b is *scripsimus cum Digesto Novo*: his *male praem.* FG.

GLOSS 143. *Dit is riucht: hweersoma een wyf an nede nimpt* (*This is law: whoever rapes a woman*). See for the same subject also the chapter *inda fyfteenda kest*.

20. The 20th land law is: if a man fights with one of his companions during a military expedition, he shall compensate him twofold because of the breach of the peace and pay three pounds to the *frana* for infringing on the authority of the king.

GLOSS 144. *Twybeet* (*twofold*). See for this *Inst.* 4.4.9, since an injury is said to be atrocious in view of a person, as when injury is done to a magistrate or senator, see *Dig.* 47.10.45.

21. The 21st land law is: if the northmen capture a man against his will and take him abroad against his will and if he comes to a village and causes any damage, such as burning the village down, or raping women, or killing men or any evil deed, and if after that he flees or is released, and if he returns to his homeland and is indicted and tried before court over these crimes, he shall declare that he indeed did these things. In performing these acts he did not infringe on the authority of the *skelta* nor the judgment of the *asega*, nor did he break the king's or the people's peace because he did as his master ordered him while he was his servant. And his master is obligated to compensate everything.

GLOSS 145. *Syn ayn schalck waes* (*was his servant*). Slavery is an institution of the law of nations, by which someone contrary to nature is submitted to another's right. Slaves (*servi*) derive their name from the fact that the emperors ordered that captives be sold and by so doing used to save (*seruare*) them and not put them to death. They are also called *mancipia* ('taken by hand'), because they were by hand (*manus*) taken (*capere*) from the enemy, see *Inst.* 1.3.2–3 and *Inst.* 1.12.5: "If a father was taken by the enemy, although he was a slave of the enemy, in case such persons returned, they regained all their previous rights".

GLOSS 146. *Als him syn hera* (*as his master*). A master or father who gave an order, is liable; the obedient one is excused, see *Dig.* 44.7.20, and *Dig.* 50.17.169: "the one who orders that damage be inflicted is the one who inflicts it; the one is not to blame, who etc.".

21a. The wergild of any woman is eight pounds and eight ounces and eight pennies.

21b. Enis edelis wives weetme is C pond.

GLOSSA 147. ff. de religi. et sump. fu. l. At si quis § Hec actio (*Dig.* 11.7.14.6);
82 uero dicitur quod sumptus | defunctorum parantur secundum dignitatem defuncti; sic a simili uesticia[a] datur mulieri secundum eius dignitatem et secundum uiri facultatem, si non nupserit infra annum luctus, quia uxor senatoris amittit nomen dignitatis, si secundo nubat uiro minoris dignitatis et inferioris, C. de digni. l. Mulieres (*Cod.* 12.1.13), C. de nup. l. Cum te (*Cod.* 5.4.10), extra de fo. compe. c. Ex parte B., in fi. glo. ulti.,[b] de sepul. Is qui li. vi (VI 3.12.3), ibi Archidiaconus.[c] Est arg. ff. de reli. et sumpti. fu. l. At[d] si quis § Hec actio (*Dig.* 11.7.14.6), uersiculo 'equum autem accipitur ex dignitate eius qui funeratus est' et sequitur[e] statim pro modo facultatium[f] sumptum fieri oportere.

22. Dat XXII ste landriucht is: to hwam so ma land aeschet soe andera di aldera ende spreckt: "Dit land deer du mi aef aeschest onriucht ende to tinge om ladest dat lauwede mi myn aldera, myn aldfader ende miin aldmoder. Jef ic se nomia schil ic namne se wel. Deelt mi aeck di[1] aesga to ene wiiteed dat dwe ic. Fora ne thoer ic anderda."

23. Dat XXIII ste landriucht is: aldeer een wif se onfuchten ende hio mit eenre berthe se ende hio ne hab dulgh ner daed ner daedlika deda ner daedlika bloedresen ner bloedrinnenda deda ende hio so fiir wreweled se inoer da binnena burch, dat dio berthe daed se, jef hi se jechte so aegh hi se toe jelden mit jeld ende mit urjeld. Dat jeld als wise lioed lowiad ende dat urjeld bi XII merkum ende her liwes bote mit saun jeldum jefta VIII pond VIII eynsa ende VIII penningen.[2] Jef hi aeck bisecka wil, soe sikerie hi hem mit XII wytedem jefta hi gongh niogen scheren. Jef hi disse ordel nenthera dwaen wil, so biwissie hi him enis berschinses kempa. Dat schil ma binna trim etmelum bifiuchta jefta een soen dwaen als wise lioed quaed, deer godlic ende nadelic ende eerlick se ende riuchtelick.

83 Fan trowa ende fan wirde | ward himelriick stift ende af wirde wardet aeck forfold. Also waerd dat aefte oen eerdrike.

---

[1] FG: di di. [2] FG: pe*n*ui*n*gen.

---

a uesticia *scripsimus*: ueticia *praem.* FG.
b The gloss *exceptionibus aliis* ad X 2.2.15 at the very end.
c Archidiaconus (Guido de Baysio), Lectura super VI decretalium, VI 3.12.3.
d At *scripsimus cum Digesto Veteri*: Ac FG.
e sequitur *scripsimus*: sequitnr FG.
f facultatium *scripsimus*: facultatum FG.

21b. The wergild of a noble woman is 100 pounds.

GLOSS 147. See *Dig.* 11.7.14.6; However, it is said that the expenses for the deceased are in accordance with the dignity of the deceased. Similarly, a wife is given housing in accordance with her dignity and the wealth of her husband, if she does not marry within the year of mourning, because the wife of a senator renounces her name of dignity when she marries for a second time with a man of a minor and inferior dignity, see *Cod.* 12.1.13 and *Cod.* 5.4.10 and the end of the final gloss to X 2.2.15, VI 3.12.3 and the commentary of Guido de Baysio on that text. An argument can be found in *Dig.* 11.7.14.6 in the words "Equitable is understood as in accordance with the dignity of the one buried" and immediately it follows that the expenses should be incurred in accordance with his wealth.

22. The 22nd land law is: if a claim is brought before court over a piece of land, the oldest man in the house shall answer and declare: "The land you are claiming from me illegitimately and for which you have compelled me to appear before court was left to me by my grandparents, my grandfather and my grandmother. If I were forced to state their names I will do so correctly. If the *asega* would judge I should take an oath on the holy relics, I will do so. Other than this, I need not defend myself."

23. The 23nd land law is: if a woman is attacked and she is with child and she does not show any wounds or death or deadly injuries or deadly bleeding wounds or less severe bleeding wounds but she is still abused to such a degree in the womb area that the foetus has died, and if the attacker confesses, he shall compensate her with a wergild and an additional wergild. The wergild for the foetus is to be established by wise men and the additional wergild is set at 12 marks and if she dies herself, her own wergild will be sevenfold or seven times 8 pounds, 8 ounces and 8 pennies. If, however, the defendant wants to deny the accusation, he shall exonerate himself with 12 oaths on the holy relics or he shall undergo an ordeal by fire, walking over nine (hot) ploughshares. If he does not want to undergo any of these ordeals, he shall hire himself a barefooted champion. The trial by combat shall then be held within three days or a reconciliation shall be established, advised by wise men, which is Godly and merciful and honest and lawful.

The kingdom of Heaven was built on faith and truth and it was fulfilled with truth. Thus matrimony came to the world.

24. Dat XXIIII ste landriucht is: hweer so ma een man bitiget dat hi nachtes habbe faren mit barnenda brande ende mit gliander coele toe enis sikeris mannes huse ende him al syn gued ofbaernt deer hy haeth to hou ende to huis oen wald[1] jefta oen werre, deer hi dine lichame schulde of feda ende dae siel of reeda, jef hi des jechtan se, soe comme hi itta fiower hernum mit tien merka weda ende domie dae lioden ende itta herdsteed mit synre haudlesen ende jelde dae manne syn gued twifald jeld als hit syn buren mit him oenbringa willed. Jef hyt bisect, soe schil hy to aller herna likera syn landriucht ontfaen ende strida mit ena berschinsa kempa ende dat fyfte om dine[2] herdsteed. Wirt hy mitta riucht urwonnen,[3] so aegh hy syn haud toe lesen mit tolef merkum ende oder toelef merck om dine herdsteed ende da man syn gued toe jeldane twifalda jelda ende mit urjelde deerur toe jeldane; tria merck dae liodem om dine liuedferd; tria merck dae hellighen op dine franaalter om dine bannena ferd; tria merck[4] da schelta ende dae aesgha om hiara ban ende hyara sibbe[5] unslitande se. Jef di oera deer di moerd nachtbrand deen is aeck mit wytem ende mit wirden biradet wirt oen da liuedwarve dat hy een arra moerddeda eefter der ora deen habbe dat hi dat wreke ende dat moerd deen habbe om een andere deda, so schede dat di aesga bi sine wysdome ende dae lyode nei hiara riucht. Soe isset aller herna aeck een merck, dyoe herdsteed dyo fyfte. Aldus aegh ma dae lioden hiara ferd toe beten.

---

[1] FG: wer*rum*. [2] FG: dtne. [3] FG: urwonuen. [4] FG: merek. [5] FG: stwe.

24. The 24th land law is: if someone is accused of having sought out a certain man's house during the night with a burning torch and live coal and of having burnt all this man's goods which he possessed in his house and yard and which were in his possession and care, and with which he had to feed his body and save his soul, and if the defendant confesses, he shall come to the burnt house and pay ten marks as surety at each of the four corners and compensate the people in this way and pay his own wergild to avert a death penalty at the hearth and on top of that compensate the victim for his loss with twice the worth of the burnt goods as appraised by his neighbours. If the defendant denies the charge, he shall exonerate himself at each corner of the burnt house and fight a judicial duel with the help of a barefooted champion and a fifth duel shall be fought at the hearth. If he loses the duel, he shall pay his own wergild in order to avert a death penalty with twelve marks and another twelve marks because of the hearth and he shall compensate the victim for his loss with twice the worth of the burned possessions and pay an additional wergild; three marks to the people for violating the peace; three marks to the church, to be paid on the high alter, for breaking the decreed peace; three marks to the *skelta* and to the *asega* for infringing on their authority and to pay off liability of his kin. If it can be proven in court that the victim of the nocturnal arson had performed a worse murderous deed against the arsonist, and that this homicide in turn was done out of revenge for a previous act of violence, then the *asega* shall decide wisely and the people according to their law. In that case the arsonist shall pay one mark at each corner and a fifth at the hearth. In this way, the people shall receive compensation for breaking the peace.

IX. The Eight Provisions

Hyr bighinnet da Acht Doemen

84 **1.** Di aersta doem is: hweer so een joncfrou een aefte bigaen schil, soe schil hyoe tolef jeer ald wessa, soe mei hyoe en foermond tziesa. Ende jef dat ymmen ursprecka wil, soe aghet di aesga to riucht to wisen dat hyo dat aefte moge bigaen.

GLOSSA 148. Nota. Sponsus et sponsa fieri possunt, qui sunt septem annorum, sed uir et uxor fieri non possunt, nisi sunt xiiii annorum.

GLOSSA 149. *Soe scil hyo xii ieer ald wessa* Etas ad matrimonium contrahendam in femina secundum leges et canones est xii annorum, ff. de ritu nup. l. Minorem (*Dig.* 23.2.4), notatur de desponsatione inpuberum c. i. (X 4.2.1) in glossa ii[a] et c. Continebatur[b] (X 4.2.6), sed in masculo xiiii, eodem titulo etc.[c]

2. Di ora doem is, dattet kynd aegh synre moder lutterslaen toe jaen XII jeer alomme, aller jera lyck fyf schillinghen, alsoe fyr soe hyoet bihot habbe oenweemd fan acht secken deer hyone fan ocht toe hodene: fan fyore ende fan wallende wettere, fan sade, fan slate, fan horses howe ende fan hona etzele, fan swynes tusch, fan schettes hoerne, ende fan hondis bite ende fan scherpa wepen, als hy sine breyd halet, hit ne se dat hi zwara wil dera acht sekena een deer hyone naet fan hot habbe, soe mey hy bihalda da sextich schillingen. Hit ne se dat hi swara wil als hi saun jeer ald is, dat hy syn gued moge bigaen ende bistaen ende bireda. Ende di aesga aegh him dine eed to stowiane. Ende hi jouwe dan synre moder XXXV schillingen ende hi wesse dan mond synre moder. Soe mei hio mitta lutterislaen capia ende sella ende oen jefta jowa sonder des mondes oerlef ende jelkirs haet hyo nates wald oers dan her ayn ledena.

3. Di tredda doem is, dat di landsata aegh toe witane mit een ede hwaneer hi
85 da heer urgulden | habbe da forma twa jeer. Dat tredde jeer is di landhera nier to witane ho lange hiara eentale se. Als hi him dera heer jecht, soe aegh hi dine ker hor hine urdriwe dan hine sitta leeth.

---

a The gloss *canonibus* ad X 4.2.2.

b Continebatur *scripsimus cum Decretalibus*: Contratinebatur FG.

c Cf. X 4.2.10.

IX. The Eight Provisions

Here Begin the Eight Provisions

1. The first provision is: when a girl is to be married, she must be twelve years old: then she is allowed to choose a husband. And if anyone wants to raise any objection against this, then the *asega* has to confirm her legal right to enter into the intended marriage.

GLOSS 148. Note that persons who are seven years old may become betrothed, but cannot marry before they are 14 years old.

GLOSS 149. *Soe scil hyo xii ieer ald wessa* (*she must be twelve years old*). According to the provisions of Roman and Canon law the age for contracting a marriage is twelve years for a woman, see *Dig*. 23.2.4. This is noted in the second gloss to X 4.2.1 and in X 4.2.6, but for a man it is fourteen, see in the same title.

2. The second provision is that a son, when he brings his bride home, has to pay his mother 'swaddling-payment' over a total period of twelve years, five shillings for each year, if she has kept him uninjured by the eight things she was obligated to guard him against: from fire and boiling water, from a well, from a canal, from the hoof of a horse and from the spur of a cock, from the tusk of a swine, from the horn of cattle, and from the bite of a dog, and from sharp weapons, unless he wants to declare under oath that she did not protect him against one of these eight things, in which case he has the right to keep the sixty shillings. It is also possible for a son to declare himself capable of handling his own affairs and taking care of his property when he is seven years old. In that case, the *asega* has to administer the required oath to him. After that, he shall give his mother thirty-five shillings and from then on be the guardian of his mother. With this 'swaddling-payment', the mother may buy and sell, or give away from it, without having to ask the consent of her guardian and apart from that she does not have any competence but over her own body.

3. The third provision is that a tenant has the right to testify under oath whether he has paid the rent during the first two years of the lease. In the third year, the landlord is entitled to further determine the future duration of their agreement. If the landlord acknowledges that the rent has been paid, he may choose to evict the tenant or let him stay (after the third year).

4. Di fiarde doem is, dat alle lawa agen foerd to gaen als hia deden fan Adam ende Abraham ende fan Ysaac ende al hiara jongheren alont dine hioedlika[1] dey.

GLOSSA 150. utque insti. de here. ab intest. § i (*Inst.* 3.1.1), in Auth. in eodem titulo (*Auth.* 9.1 [*Nov.* 118]) in principio.

5. Di fyfta doem is, dat dae weseken nyme hara aldfaders ende aldmoders lawa mit mara riucht dan se aghen urbeck toe ghaen jefta oen dae syda.

6. Di sexta doem is, datter nimmen aegh sines stiepfaders ner sines stiepmoders lawa. Deer om aegh di halfbroder mit eenre hand to ti faen ende di folbroder mit twam handem toe thi faen toe syn folbroders lawa.

GLOSSA 151. C. communia de success. l. "Affinitatis iure nulla successio permittitur" (*Cod.* 6.59.7) et l. Victo (*Cod.* 6.59.3).

GLOSSA 152. *Aegh di halfbroder* Dicit Azo in titulo Codicis communia de success.:[a] "Sciendum est igitur quod si quis decesserit si quidem sint ei[b] aliqui descendentium, illi omnibus prelatis ⟨succedunt, ita⟩[c] scilicet ut si ex uno filio aliquis, etiam[d] in decimo gradu constitutus, supersit, tamen cum filio defuncti admittantur et erit successio in stirpes, in auth. de her. que ab intes. defe. § Si quis igitur (*Auth.* 9.1.1 [*Nov.* 118.1]) et § Si autem (*Auth.* 9.1.2 [*Nov.* 118.2]). Si uero nullum descendentium relinquat, uocantur primo ascendentes, et primo pater et mater cum quibus et fratres defuncti uocantur, qui ex utroque parente coniuncti erant illi. Item uocantur consimiliter fratrum filii. Si uero pater et mater non supersint, sed auus et auia paterni et materni, dicimus quod cum eis admittantur predicti fratres et consimiliter fratrum filii ⟨in stirpes, licet alii dicant contrarium, ut diximus supra de leg. haer. (*Cod.* 6.58)⟩.[e] Si autem sunt fra-
86 tres ex altero[f] parente coniuncti tantum, et non supersint coniuncti ex | utroque, non succedunt cum ascendentibus; immo repelluntur propter eos. Si uero ascendentes non supersunt, uocantur primo fratres utrinque[g] coniuncti et consimiliter fratrum fily ⟨in stirpes⟩. Eis autem deficienti-

[1] FG: lioedlika.

a Azo, Summa Codicis, *Cod.* 6.59, n. 6.
b ei *scripsimus cum Azone*: ibi *male praem.* FG; emendavimus ex Azone.
c Emendavimus ex Azone.
d etiam *scripsimus cum Azone*: esset *male praem.* FG.
e Emendavimus ex Summa Codicis Azonis, ad *Cod.* 6.58, n. 8.
f altero *scripsimus cum Azone*: utroque FG.
g utrinque *scripsimus cum Azone*: ut'ni FG.

4. The fourth provision is that all inheritances should be passed on the way they have done since the times of Adam and Abraham and Isaac and all their descendants up until the present day.

GLOSS 150. and as in *Inst.* 3.1.1 and *Auth.* 9.1 (*Nov.* 118) at the beginning.

5. The fifth provision is that orphans have more rights to the inheritances of their grandfather or grandmother rather than that these inheritances should go to relatives who are further removed.

6. The sixth provision is that no-one is entitled to the inheritance of his stepmother or stepfather. Because of this, a half-brother is entitled to half a share, while a full brother is entitled to a full share of his full brother's inheritance.

GLOSS 151. *Cod.* 6.59.7 "No succession is allowed based on a right of affinity" and *Cod.* 6.59.3.

GLOSS 152. *Aegh di halfbroder* (*a half-brother is entitled*). Azo says, commenting on title *Cod.* 6.59: "Thus, one should know that when someone has passed away, the descendants, at least if he has some, succeed him in all things which turn up, namely, in such a way that if there would be someone alive, who is found to be even in the tenth degree related to a (predeceased) son, they will, together with the son of the deceased, be admitted (to the inheritance) and succession will take place 'by roots' (*in stirpes*), see *Auth.* 9.1.1 (*Nov.* 118.1). See also *Auth.* 9.1.2 (*Nov.* 118.2). If, however, someone leaves not even one descendant behind, first the ascendants are called (to the inheritance) and first the father and mother are called, together with the (full) brothers of the deceased who were related to him through both parents. Simultaneously, the sons of the brothers are called. If, however, the father and mother are no longer alive but the grandfather and grandmother are, we maintain that the brothers aforementioned are admitted (to the inheritance) together with these (grandparents) and similarly the sons of these brothers, and will inherit by roots, although others maintain this is not the case, as we stated above, commenting upon *Cod.* 6.58. However, if there are living half-brothers, related to the deceased by means of one parent, and no full brothers, related to the deceased by means of both parents, these half-brothers will not succeed alongside the ascendants. On the contrary, they are excluded due to the ascendants. However, if the ascendants are no longer alive, first the full brothers, related to the deceased by means of both parents, are called and at the same time the sons of the brothers by roots. However, if these

bus ⟨uocantur fratres ex altero tantum parente coniuncti et consimilium fratrum filii. Quibus deficientibus⟩[a] optinet regula 'qui prior est gradu, prior est in successione',[b] sublata omni[c] differentia sexus, patrie potestatis et cognationis ⟨et succeditur in capita⟩,[d] in Auth. de here. que ab intest. (*Auth.* 9.1 [*Nov.* 118.1]) in principio et Vt[e] fratrum fily § Reliquum (*Auth.* 9.1.2 [*Nov.* 118.2]), C. de he. legi., auth. Cessante (post *Cod.* 6.58.3 [ex *Nov.* 118.3 in pr. et 127.1]) et auth. Post fratres fratrumque filios (post *Cod.* 6.58.3 [ex *Nov.* 118.3.1])". Sic est de iure. Sed Frisones aliter seruant de consuetudine, ymmo uerius ex corruptela, quia fratris filius ex utroque parente non uocatur cum filio ad hereditatem[f] aui et auie, sed solus filius cum filia tamquam proximior in gradu. Hoc repete supra in sexto et septimo landriucht.[g]

7. Di saunda doem is, dat dioe folsuster nyme her broders lawa ende her halfbroder nyme se half, truch dat hiara odera jeldera him al fraemd was.

GLOSSA 153. Contrarium est uerum de iure auctenticorum de here. ab intest. § Reliquum et sequenti (*Auth.* 9.1.2–3 [*Nov.* 118.2–3]), C. de legit. here., auth. Cessante (post *Cod.* 6.58.3 [ex *Nov.* 118.3 in pr. et 127.1]).

8. Di achtenda doem is: hweer so di man geet[1] fan syn aefta wive to enis anderis mannes wive ende hi deer een berthe oen tiled bi des fiandes sponste ende dio berthe dan waxt ende urslain wirt: dae jelda ende da lawa aeg dio frowe deer dio berthe bi des fiandes sponste ondrein ward als of hioet mit herre ledem wonnen heed ende dio nene fiafollinge deer da berthe to der wrald droech. Aldus ist riucht al der wrald ende ewa der Fresena.

Jef een man haet onaefte bern teyn ende hi dan jout gued minra jefta mara, so moten da bern lawigia op hiara bern al to da tredda. Alsoe moten hia lawigia op hiara folbroder ende op syn folsustera, ist dat hia fan ene liwe bern se. So hya
87 dan des biliowet, so moet dat flotjeftige gued weer in aldeer | hit is utcommen.

[1] FG: geec.

a uocantur—deficientibus *om.* FG (*homoiotel.*). Emedavimus ex Azone.
b regula 'qui prior est gradu, prior in successione' *scripsimus cum Azone*: regula prioris prior erit in successione FG. Emendavimus ex Azone.
c omni *scripsimus cum Azone*: oim FG.
d Emendavimus ex Azone.
e ut *scripsimus cum Azone*: nt FG.
f hereditatem *scripsimus*: dereditatem FG.
g See text VIII,6–7.

do not exist, the half-brothers, related to the deceased by means of only one parent, will be called and at the same time the sons of the brothers. If these do not exist, the rule applies that the individual, related to the deceased more closely, is sooner entitled to the succession, while disregarding any difference in gender, paternal control and consanguinity, see *Auth.* 9.1 (*Nov.* 118.1) at the beginning, just as children of the brothers, see *Auth.* 9.1.2 (*Nov.* 118.2), the authentica *Cessante successione* (post *Cod.* 6.58.3) and the authentica *Post fratres fratrumque* (post *Cod.* 6.58.3)". All this is written law. The Frisians, however, observe something else, based on custom, rather, however, on a corruption, because the son of a full brother is not called to the inheritance of his grandfather and grandmother together with the son, but only the son together with the daughter as being the closest related. Remember this above, at the sixth and seventh *landriucht*.

7. The seventh provision is that a sister is entitled to a full share in her brother's inheritance while her stepbrother is entitled to half a share because her other parent is not a relative of him.

GLOSS 153. The opposite is true according to the law of the *Authenticum*, see *Auth.* 9.1.2–3 (*Nov.* 118.2–3) and the next provision, and authentica *Cessante successione* (post *Cod.* 6.58.3).

8. The eighth provision is: if a man leaves his own wife and goes to someone else's wife and—being seduced by the devil—begets a child with her, and if the child reaches maturity and is killed then the wergild and inheritance shall go to the woman who missed a child because of the devil's temptation as if she had brought this child to the world with her own body and no compensation shall be given to the woman who gave birth to the child. This is universal law and the law of the Frisians.

If a man has begotten illegitimate children and he gives them any goods, be it large or small, then these children may leave these goods to their children up until the third degree. They are also allowed to leave these goods to their blood brother or sister if they had the same mother. If none of these relatives are available to accept the inheritance then these goods, which are considered as dowry, must return whence they came.

GLOSSA 154. *Oen aefte bern teyn* Nota. Liberi autem naturales tantum et non legitimi, de quibus hic loquitur, ab intestato succedunt patri in duabus uncys cum matre eorum. Viriliter hoc dico uxore et prole legittima non superstite, in auth. quibus modis naturales efficiuntur sui § Discretis (*Auth.* 7.1.12 [*Nov.* 89.12]) et ibi uide plenius. Et in bonis maternis succedunt in totum, Insti. ad sena. consul. orfici. § Nouissime (*Inst.* 3.4.3), Speculum, titulo de success. ab intest. uerbo 'nunc[a] de naturalium',[b] Azo in Summa, de natura. li..[c] Nota quatuor sunt genera filiorum scilicet legittimi et naturales ut nati de legittimo matrimonio ut xxxii q. iiii Liberti (C.32 q.4 c.15), aly legittimi et non naturales sed ciuiles ut adoptiui, ut extra de cogna. lega. per totum (x 4.12), Instit. de adopti. (*Inst.* 1.11), aly naturales et non legittimi, ut nati ex concubina que in uxorem potest haberi, ff. de concubi. l. i et ii (*Dig.* 25.7.1–2). De his loquitur hic. Aly sunt nec legittimi nec naturales ut spury, manseres et nochi. Hi in nullo succedunt, nec ex testamento paterno aliquid consequuntur, C. de incest. nupc. auth. Ex conplexu (post *Cod.* 5.5.6 [ex *Nov.* 89.15]), C. de natu. libe., auth. Licet (post *Cod.* 5.27.8 [ex *Nov.* 89.12 et 15]). De materia istorum et eorum successionibus et alimentis a parentibus prestandis et e conuerso uide in auct. quibus modis naturales efficiuntur § Discretis (*Auth.* 7.1.12 [*Nov.* 89.12]), et Hostiensis in Summa, titulo de success. ab intestat. et titulo qui fily sunt legitimi,[d] Instit. ad sena. con. orfici. § Nouissime (*Inst.* 3.4.3). Sciendum eciam illos liberos qui wlgo quesiti sunt ad matris hereditatem hoc senatus consulto admitti, wlgo quesiti sunt qui non habent certum patrem uel cuius pater wlgus est, Inst. de nup. § Si aduersus (*Inst.* 1.10.12). Multo magis naturalis admittitur, C. ad se. con. orfi. l. pen. (*Cod.* 6.57.5). Vel wlgo quesiti sunt qui certum patrem ⟨habent⟩ sed illicitum, puta qui ex coitu nati sunt, qui lege dampnatur, scilicet incesti, adulterii, nephary. Et tales non succedunt in auct. quibus mo. natural. effi. sui (*Auth.* 7.1.15 [*Nov.* 89.15]) § finali. Et si wlgo quesiti sunt procreati ex concubina uel ex coitu non dampnato succedunt in totum et patri duabus uncys non exstantibus legittimis ut in § Discretis (*Auth.* 7.1.12 [*Nov.* 89.12]) et sicut succedunt naturales liberi parentibus. Quando et in quantum, ita et in
88 tantum | succedunt[e] parentes liberis naturalibus e contrario et prestan-

a nunc *scripsimus*: uunc FG.

b Guillaume Durand, Speculum iudiciale, Lib. IV, Part. III, Tit. de successionibus ab intestato, n. 15.

c Azo, Summa Codicis, *Cod.* 5.27, n. 4–12.

d Hostiensis (Henricus de Segusio), Summa aurea, x 3.27, n. 6 et x 4.17, n. 6.

e succedunt] succedebent BL BN KB PB UB.

GLOSS 154. *Oen aefte bern teyn* (*begotten illegitimate children*). Note, however, that only the natural children and not those born out of wedlock, discussed here, under the rules of intestacy, inherit from their father for one sixth, together with their mother. Strongly, I maintain this, if the lawful wife and the progeny born in wedlock are no longer alive, as in *Auth.* 7.1.12 (*Nov.* 89.12) and there you will find much more; and they inherit all their mother's assets, see *Inst.* 3.4.3, the *Speculum iudiciale* in the title on succession by rules of intestacy, in the paragraph starting with '*Nunc de naturalium*', and the *Summa Codicis* of Azo, commenting on *Cod.* 5.27. Note that there are four categories of sons, namely (i) legitimate and natural sons, such as those born from a lawful marriage, see C.32 q.4 c.15, (ii) legitimate and non-natural, but civil sons, like adoptive sons, as in X 4.12 and Inst. 1.11, (iii) natural and illegitimate sons, as born from a concubine, with whom one could have married, see *Dig.* 25.7.1–2—that is the category discussed here—and (iv) those who are neither legitimate nor natural, such as those who are born of conventuals and clerics (*spurii*), of prostitutes (*manseres*) or out of adultery (*nothi*). These do not inherit anything, nor may they acquire something on the basis of the last will and testament of the father, see the authentica *Ex complex nefario* (post *Cod.* 5.5.6) and the authentica *Licet patri* (post *Cod.* 5.27.8). See about these persons, their hereditary succession and the maintenance to be provided by their parents and the same conversely, *Auth.* 7.1.12 (*Nov.* 89.12), Hostiensis in his *Summa*, commenting on the titles X 3.27 and X 4.17, and *Inst.* 3.4.3. One should also know that children, who are 'begotten in extramarital affairs' (*vulgo quaesiti*), by the *Senatus Consultum Orfitianum* are admitted to the inheritance of the mother. 'Begotten in extramarital affairs' are those, whose father is unknown or not married to the mother, see *Inst.* 1.10.12. More so, should a natural son be admitted, see *Cod.* 6.57.5. People are also 'begotten in extramarital affairs', when their father is known but the procreation is illicit, for example, those who are born out of sexual intercourse prohibited by law, namely incest, adultery and crime. And such persons will not inherit, see *Auth.* 7.1.15 (*Nov.* 89.15) in the final paragraph. And if those 'begotten in extramarital affairs' are begotten by a concubine or from a manner of sexual intercourse which is not prohibited, they will be entitled to the entire inheritance (of the mother) and to that of the father for one sixth, if there are no surviving legitimate children, as in *Auth.* 7.1.12 (*Nov.* 89.12) and in such way natural children succeed their parents. Reversely, the parents will succeed the natural children and provide maintenance under the same circumstances and to the same extent;

tur alimenta, ut dicto § Discretis (*Auth.* 7.1.12 [*Nov.* 89.12]) et C. de natura. liber. l. ulti. (*Cod.* 5.27.12) et in auth. ibi posita (post *Cod.* 5.27.11 [ex *Nov.* 117.2]), licet et sicut naturales succedunt matri sic et proximioribus linee materne et econtra sic intelligitur, ff. unde cognati l. Hac parte (*Dig.* 38.8.2) et l. Si spurius (*Dig.* 38.8.4) et minister et dicto § Nouissime (*Inst.* 3.4.3) et ibi bona glossa.[a] Spury, autem, manseres[b] et nochi nec patri succedunt, quia iura agnacionis non habent, ut notat Hostiensis in Summa, titulo de consang. et affi. post principium,[c] nec alicui ex linea paterna. Si quid tali relinquatur restituendum est soboli legitime aut fratri sorori aut patri uel matri. Si predicti non exstant aut exstant dissimulant uel tacuerint, id est duos menses inuadit fiscus res tales et torquet amasiam ut ueritatem dicat de rebus sibi uel alys relictis in dicto auct. Licet (post *Cod.* 5.27.8 [ex *Nov.* 89.12 et 15]) § fi., C. de natura. libe. l. i (*Cod.* 5.27.1). Heres inscitus, si talibus legatum tacitum conferat, quartam suam amittit, C. ad le. falci. l. Eciam (*Cod.* 6.50.3), ff. de usu. cum quidem § In tacito (*Dig.* 22.1.17.2).

a The gloss *admitti* ad *Inst.* 3.4.3.
b manseres] manseris BN KB PB UB.
c Hostiensis (Henricus de Segusio), Summa aurea, X 4.14, n. 2.

see the aforementioned *Auth.* 7.1.12 (*Nov.* 89.12) and *Cod.* 5.27.12 and the authentica *Si quis liberos* (post *Cod.* 5.27.11) located there, although in such a way they also inherit as natural children from the mother and from the closest relatives in the maternal line. On the other hand, *Dig.* 38.8.2 and *Dig.* 38.8.4 are understood in this way and there is also support for this view in the aforementioned provision of *Inst.* 3.4.3 and the fine gloss to this text. Those who are born of conventuals and clerics, of prostitutes or out of adultery will not succeed their father because they lack the right of those related through males, as Hostiensis states in his *Summa*, in the title on consanguinity and affinity, after the beginning. And neither will they inherit from anyone from the paternal line. If something is left to such a person, it has to be restored to the legitimate progeny, either brother and sister, or father or mother. If the aforementioned persons are no longer there, or are there but conceal themselves or are silent, namely two months, the fisc will take possession of these things and one will torture the mistress, so that she tells the truth concerning the things left to her or to others, according to the last paragraph of the aforementioned authentica *Licet patri* (post *Cod.* 5.27.8) and *Cod.* 5.27.1. If a foolish heir would pay such persons a secret bequest, he will lose a quarter (of the inheritance), see *Cod.* 6.50.3 and *Dig.* 22.1.17.2.

x. Exceptions to the 17th Statute

Hyr bighinnet da sex[1] wenden

Dae Fresen tinghaden[2] toejeens dyne koningh Kaerl hor se mosten alle secken mitta wythedem fan wisa. Da noem hy em sex weer off deer alle Fresem froem ende fere was.

1. Dat aerste is: hweer so ma bi liachta dei ende bi schinende sonna tweer heerfanen opriucht ende tween heerkedden mit ofledena[3] togara laet: haet so ma deer fiucht oen dulgen jefta oen daden dat dis al jechta se.

2. Dat oder is: jeft ma ane munthere bifucht mit fade ende mit schrede ende mit falscher muntha an sine schrene jefta an sine schate, an sine bigherdele, an sine budele, so ne mei ma dera deda nene wyteed bieda.

GLOSSA 155. ff. ad leg. corne. de falsis l. "Quicumque nummos aureos partim[a]
89 raserint, partim[b] tinxerint uel finxerint, et si quidem liberi | sint, ad bestias dari, si serui, supremo supplitio affici debent" (*Dig.* 48.10.8), le. sequenti (*Dig.* 48.10.9), C. e. l. i (*Cod.* 9.22.1) et C. de fal. mon. l. i et ii (*Cod.* 9.24.1–2).

3. Dat tredde is: ister een wed deen an een worpena waer jefta an bannena tingha jefta an dae helliga sinde, so ne mei ma dera deda nene wyteed byeda.

4. Dat fyarde is: hweer so ma een wyf an nede nimpt endma hia bifynt binna doram ende binna drompel endma hya deer ut wint mit lioda twangh ende mit frana ban ende hyo wopenropende is, soe ne mey ma dera deda nen wyteed byeda.

5. Dat fyfta is: hweer so een man oderis gued stelt oen der neyltyuestera nacht binna dorem ende binna drompel endma oen him dat fynt oen syn handen, an sine boesme jefta an sine becke, so ne mey ma dera dede nene wyteed bieda, hwant di bondena tyaef ne mei nene schieldigra baria ende dis jechtiga ne mey ma naet bisecka.

---

[1] FG: acht. [2] FG: tighaden. BL, J109, KB, M60, RA: ti*n*ghaden. [3] FG: oen ledena.

---

a partim *scripsimus cum Digesto Novo*: partem FG.
b partim *scripsimus cum Digesto Novo*: partem FG.

x. Exceptions to the 17th Statute

Here Begin the Six Exceptions

The Frisians petitioned King Charles to grant them the privilege to exonerate themselves before court against all types of charges by swearing innocent on the holy relics. He then set apart six types of cases in which they could not swear innocence, which all Frisians considered just and good.

1. The first exception is: if two leaders raise their banners and bring together two armies, accepting all responsibility, in broad daylight and while the sun is shining: whatever is perpetrated there, be it wounds or homicides cannot be denied in court.

2. The second exception is: if a moneyer is apprehended with inferior coins, clipped coins or counterfeit coins in his coffin or his apron, his pouch or his purse, then he is not allowed to swear innocence on the holy relics.

GLOSS 155. *Dig.* 48.10.8: "Persons who have partly scraped off golden coins, partly coloured or counterfeited the same, should, if they are free persons, be left to the wild beasts, and if they are slaves, they should receive the severest punishment", *Dig.* 48.10.9, *Cod.* 9.22.1 and *Cod.* 9.24.1 and 2.

3. The third exception is: if a commitment has been pledged at a regular court meeting or at a decreed court meeting or at an ecclesiastical court, then it is not allowed to deny this commitment by swearing innocent on the holy relics.

4. The fourth exception is: if someone assaults a woman and she is found inside his doors and doorstep and rescued from that place with the help of the people's armed forces and by the commandment of the *frana* and if she was crying for help, then one is not allowed to swear innocence on the holy relics for this act.

5. The fifth exception is: if someone steals someone else's goods in the dead of night, passing someone's doors and doorstep whilst doing so and if the stolen goods are found in the thief's hands, tucked in his clothes or strapped on his back, then one is not allowed to swear innocence on the holy relics for this act, because a thief who has been arrested cannot bring forward someone who is more guilty than he, and that which is evident cannot be denied in court.

6. Dat sexte is: hweer so een man fiucht op een oderem liachtes deis mit igge ende mit oerde ende mit sines selvis handen ende alsoe fyr oenfiucht dat ma him een synre sex ledena binimpt, dattet gersfallich wirt, jef syn lyf ende hi fan dana geet mit blodiga wepen, soe ne mei ma dera deda[1] aeck nen wyteed bieda.

[1] FG: keda.

6. The sixth exception is: if someone attacks another man in broad daylight with sword and spear and with his own hands, and wounds him so severely that he loses a hand or a foot or an eye to such a degree that the limb is completely severed or poked out, or if he loses his life, and if the attacker leaves the site with a bloodstained weapon, then one is not allowed to swear innocence on the holy relics for this act.

XI. The Synodical Law of Central Frisia

1. Cum presidere debet decanus in sinodo accersitis ad se assessoribus, primo dicat antiphonam "Veni Sancte Spiritus" vel "Emitte spiritum coelo Deus qui cor". Deinde querat a circumstantibus, si sit tempus sinodalia excercendi. Quibus consensientibus sic inchoat uoce teutonica.

2. Alle da deer to disse godeshuse to sind here, da ladie ic foerd dat se to sinde
90 comme;[1] jef ma se | oenspreckt, dat se sindelic anderde. Ferd ban ick mi selm ende mine mannen ende alle mannem to da sinde ende fan da sinde, fan da huse ende toe da huse. Dat enich man oderen wald jefta onriucht dwe, dat urbiede ick bi da banne. Ferd ban ic disse godeshuse ende alle godeshusen oen alsodena guede als redelick in dine wethem heert ende riuchtelic incommen se. Dat him nimmen deeroen dwe wald jefta onriucht, dat urbiede ick bi dae banne. Sindslitane urbiede ick, unhlest urbiede ick, alle deerwe soen urbanne ick efter dam dat hit toe claghe commen is.

3. Da fogeden to disse haudsto ende to da capellen deer hyr ut maked sint, dae ladie ick foerd ende monia se bi dae eede deer se sworen, da ma se thoe foegheden kaes, joff dit godeshuis ende disse capellen deer al hyr ut maked sint, alsoe tacht ende timmerad se, oen howe ende oen hoffwerum, oen yrsen ende oen eke ende oen tecke, oen doerem ende oen drompelem, oen boeckum ende oen byldem, oen tzyelken ende oen corporalen, oen gharem ande oen alterleckenen, ende alle secken deer dae heren dae presteren thi dae goedestyenst byhoeff sint, dat jemna se onbanplichtich se.

4. Alle daejenne deer to der haudstoe jefta toe dae cappelum, deer aldeer ut tacht ende timmerad se, eniges jeldis schieldich se ina waxschot, ina buterschot, ina deeckma, ina minra schot jefta ina[2] mara schieldum, deer monie ick alle lioden to, dat se disse goedeshusem hiara schielda eer der clage bitellie, also fyr so se onbanplichtich[3] willet bliwa.

5. Deinde prouocet scabinos. Cum uenerint dicat eis: "Ick monie jo bi da ede deer y sworen da ma jo ti da riuchta kaes ende bi juwer selvis sele dat y da wird
91 sidse ende da leyne lete ende wrogie us | haet y witen deer wrogelick is, se hit oen britsen fyra and onbetta[4] manslachten, hoerdom jefta urhoer, wilinga jefta tawerie. Hwa so byiouna lioden jefta wida lyoden rawet jefta onfuchten habbe, dat y se us foerd bringe."

---

[1] FG: conme. [2] FG: iua. [3] FG: onbanplichtih. [4] FG: an betta.

XI. The Synodical Law of Central Frisia

1. When the dean has to preside the synod and has summoned the assessors, he first has to recite the antiphon "Veni sancte Spiritus" or "Emitte spiritum coelo Deus qui cor". After that, he asks those present whether it is time for the synod to take place. And if they consent, he starts as follows in the vernacular:

2. I summon all those to come to the court who fall under the synod which is to be held at this church; if a case is brought to the synod against anyone, he shall defend himself according to the synodical law. Peace I proclaim over myself and my men and all men going to the synod or returning home from it, leaving their homes and returning to them. I prohibit anyone, by the authority given to me, to exercise violence against someone else or doing someone injustice. Peace I proclaim over this church and over all churches, concerning all goods pertaining to them, insofar as they were acquired legitimately and in conformity with the law. I prohibit anyone, by the authority given to me, to use violence or to do anything wrong against those properties. I prohibit disturbing the synodical procedure or the court order, as well as closing deals outside the synod concerning cases which have already been brought before the court.

3. I summon the churchwardens of this main church and of the chapels which have been established from it and demand of them to assure me by the oath they swore when they were appointed as wardens, that this church and the chapels which have been established from of it are in such a shape that you wardens need not be fined for negligence, as far as roofing and construction are concerned, be it churchyard or church fence, iron, wood or roof, doors or doorsteps, books or statues, chalices or corporals, liturgical vestments or altar cloths, or any of the things the reverend priests need for the liturgy.

4. I summon all those who owe any money to the main church or to the chapels which were roofed and constructed from it, be it because of candle tax, butter tax, tithe, the minor tax or the major tax, to pay these churches the money they are due before they are tried over it, if they do not wish to incur a fine.

5. He then has to summon the jurors. When they have arrived, he has to say to them: "I demand from you on the oath you swore when you took up this office and on your soul, that you shall tell the truth and not lie and bring those cases before the court you know to be punishable under synodical law, whether they concern desecration of holy days, homicides, prostitution or adultery, divination or sorcery. And that you bring before this court those who have robbed or attacked monks, nuns, or clerics."

6. "Bi disse selva moninga so monie ic al juwe lioden by da ede deer se da himelkoningh toe hulde sworen ende bi hiara selvis sele, so haet so hia bet witen dan jemna dat set jemna bringe ende jemna us foerd bringe. Alle falsche clage ende alle onriuchte wroginge da urbiede ic bi da banne. Ende spreck deer bihoef se, ende wi willet jern riuchta als wi best connen ende mogen."

7. Item mandamus pacem nobis et sociis nostris siue famulis nobiscum sinodum sacram uisitantibus in exitu et reditu et in omnibus requisitis, sub pena XX mercarum.

8. Item omnibus et singulis[1] sacrum sinodum uisitantibus similiter pacem, sub pena X mercarum aurearum.

9. Item quod nullus proponat actionem ciuilem, sub pena quinque solidorum.

10. Item quod nullus commitat insilentium uel tumultum, sub pena quinque talentum.[2]

11. Item quod nullus uiduas pupillos et orphanos uexet aut molestet in personis aut in rebus in iudicio seculari, sub pena quinque mercarum.

12. Item mandamus omnibus et singulis personis et curatis quibuscumque nobis subditis unicuique eorum in solidum ut prouideant ecclesiis suis de legittimis et iuratis aduocatis infra quindenam in mediate sequentem, sub pena quinque mercarum.

13. Item mandamus curatis et aduocatis omnibus et singulis ut prouideant ecclesiis suis in tectis et edificiis ceteris et ornamentis, in calicibus et corporalibus et palliis altaris, in missalibus et cereis et ceteris que spectant ad ornatum diuini officii et clausuris ecclesiarum in debita custodia sacramentorum sub pena quinque solidorum ante festum[3] omnium sanctorum.

14. Item mandamus curatis et aduocatis ut faciant nobis debitam denunciati-
92 onem in postsinodalibus nisi de licentia | nostra amplior eis fuerit facta prorogatio sub pena quinque mercarum unicuique eorum in solidum.

[1] FG: sigulis. [2] FG: talenti. [3] FG: *festum* is missing.

6. In the same manner I demand from all your people, on the oath of allegiance they swore to the heavenly king and on their souls, that they report to you anything they know which you do not and that you put it forward for us. By my authority, I forbid any false accusation or unlawful indictment. And speak if it is required, and we will gladly administer justice to the best of our abilities.

7. Similarly, we order peace for ourselves and our companions and servants who are joining us in attending the holy synod, as regards the journey to and from the synod and while performing the duties of the court, on penalty of 20 marks.

8. Peace also to each and everyone attending the holy synod, on penalty of 20 gold marks.

9. We also order that no-one brings a secular claim before the synod, on penalty of five shillings.

10. No-one is allowed to break the silence or disturb the order, on penalty of five pounds.

11. No-one is allowed to injure or trouble widows, underage children and orphans as regards their person or assets before a secular court, on penalty of five marks.

12. We command each and every person and the curates who are subject to us, each of them for the whole, to provide their churches with legitimate and sworn advocates within a period of fourteen days from today, on penalty of five marks.

13. We command all curates and advocates to provide their churches with church buildings and other buildings and other ornaments, with chalices and corporals, and altar cloths, missals and candles and other things which are destined for the adornment of the divine office and with locks of the churches for the obligatory custody of the sacraments, on penalty of five marks, to be in order before All Saints Day.

14. We command the curates and advocates that they give us the obligatory declaration during the postsynodical court sessions, unless we granted them further delay, on penalty of five marks, each of them fully liable.

15. Item mandamus omnibus et singulis debitoribus ecclesiarum presbiterorum et ceterorum quorumque ut soluant eis ante festum omnium sanctorum sub pena solidorum nisi prolixores inter se habuerint dies et conuentiones.

16. Item mandamus omnibus et singulis curatis et aduocatis ut soluant nobis cathedraticum secundum modum consuetum in postsinodalibus, sub pena medii talenti.

17. Item mandamus omnibus et singulis ubique per totum sinodum constitutis, ut reficiant uias publicas ad ecclesias, fossas ecclesiarum et tillen et setten teutonice[1] ante postsinodalia, sub pena solidorum.

Hyr bighint dat syndriucht int ghemeen

18. Dit is syndriucht. Als di biscop sine synd keda wil ende hi sine boda an dit land sent, so schil ma sine sind sex wiken eer keda eer mane halde. So schiler self comma jef hi mei. Jef hi naet mei, so schil incomma syn choerbiscop mit breve ende mit insigel ende mit een guldena fingherliin ende sidsa dat syn hera also sieck se jefta suder ur birgh, dat hi to da setta sind naet comma mochte. So sel syn choerbiscop sindia alleraerst op dyn urherigha deer di decken urherich brocht haet tria jeer ende nioghen sinden.

19. Di decken schil wessa fri ende Freesch ende fulre berthe boren ende syn wyed ende syn riucht onforloren ende enis leka soen. Soe[2] aeg syn sind di haudprester to keden ende da lioed to sekane, alle huismanne. Ende als di biscop tree dagen sindet haet, so schil hi setta ene decken ende hem syn ban bifella bi trim schillingen. So schil ma dis deckens sind xx nachta eer keda eer men halde.

[1] FG: teutunice. [2] FG: fol.

15. We command all debtors of churches, priests or whoever to pay their debts before the festival of All Saints Day on penalty of (five) shillings, unless they agreed on larger terms and conditions.

16. We command each and every curate and advocate to pay us the diocesan levy in the customary manner at the postsynodical court sessions, on penalty of half a pound.

17. We command each and everyone, wherever they are, who fall under the synod to repair the public roads leading to the churches, the church canals, and what is called *tillen* "bridges" and *setten* "plank bridges" in the vernacular before the postsynodical court sessions, on penalty of (five) shillings.

Here Begins the General Synodical Law

18. This is synodical law. When the bishop wants to make it known that his synod will be held and he sends his messenger to the Frisian lands, the meeting of the court must be proclaimed six weeks in advance. Then the bishop shall come himself if he is able to. If he is unable to come, his chorbishop shall come, bringing with him a sealed letter and a golden ring, and he shall say that his superior is so ill or has travelled so far to the south over the mountains that he is unable to come to the synod. Then the chorbishop will first hold synod over disobedient persons who have been declared to be disobedient by the dean for a period of three years or nine synods.

19. The dean shall be free and Frisian and born of free stock and his ordination shall not be nullified and neither shall he have lost his legal status as a consequence of having committed crimes, and he must be the son of a layman. Then the archpriest shall proclaim the synod and the people—that is, all freemen—shall attend it. And when the bishop has presided the synod for three days, he will appoint a dean and give him his authority, the infringement of which is to be fined with three shillings. The synod of the dean shall be made known 20 days in advance.

20. Nu agen da lioed eedswaren to setten. Da schillet wessa fry ende Freesch
93 ende fulre berthe boren | ende also hioechdedich dat hi dis biscops ban beta mey jef hit oen him falt, ende syn landriucht onforloren.

GLOSSA 156. *Eed suara* Est testis uel nuncius iudicis et comitatis iuratus et persona publica cui creditur ratione iuramenti, extra de prescrip. Ad audientiam (X 2.26.13), in citacionibus et denunciationibus illorum criminum, que sunt notoria, C. de accu. l. Ea que (*Cod.* 9.2.7) iiii q. iiii § Aliquando (DG post C.4 q.4 c.2–3 § i), ff. ad se. con. turpil. l. Ab accusatione § Nunciatores (*Dig.* 48.16.6.3) et uocatur aliquando officialis deputatus ad crimina denuncianda iudicibus, ut in c. Circumtelliones xiii q. v (C.23 q.5 c.1). Hodie istorum sunt et alii, uidelicet et presbiter et aduocati testes sinodales qui deferunt crimina episcopis siue decanis, xxxv q. v Epis. (C. 35 q.6 c.7), extra de test. cogen. c. Preterea (X 2.21.7), Speculo, titulo de accu. § i.,[a] hic scias.

Soe agen hine[1] da lioed ende di prester to tziesen ende oen dine sind to bringen. Nu aeg him di decken tofara dine sind dine eed to stowien. Als hi dan dine eed swerren haet, so aegh him di decken een ferdban to dwaen bi des biscops banne dat him nimmen dwe wald jefta onriucht jefta aet eweles sprecke jefta dwe om wroginga, hine schil des biscops ban beta ende twibeet da eedswara. Soe schillet da lioed dine ferd sterkia, hit ne se dat hyt habbe forwrocht mit sine handem jefta mit sine monde. So aegh di huisman sine selvis deda to witen ende fyf synre buren to folgien, haet hi da eedswara deen habbe. Als hi naet blicandis ne haet, soe schil di eedswara bi da laden laya ende bi dae boten als een oer leeckman. Soe ne schil di eedswera naet wrogia, hi ne habbet achtet mit syne prester ende mit sine buren.

21. Haet so di decken wroghet buta da eedswara jefta di prester jefta ander lichte lioed, so ne thoer ma da wirden neen andert jowa hodder to jechtwird ner to seckwird, ner to nene weerwird comma. Aldus ist sindriucht aller Fre-
94 sena. |

22. Jef di eedswara enichne man wroghet om sibbe ende hi dat sibbe naet birecknia mei, so is hi banschieldich.

[1] FG: *hine* is missing.

a Guillaume Durand, Speculum iudiciale, Lib. I, Part. II, Tit. de accusatore, n. 1.

20. Now, the people have to appoint a jury. Its members shall be free and Frisian and born of free stock and so wealthy that they are able to pay the penalty for infringing on the authority of the bishop if they would be fined for this, and not have lost their legal status as a consequence of having committed crimes.

> GLOSS 156. *Eed suara* (*a jury*). This is the witness or the complainant for the judge, sworn before the districts and a public official who, because of his oath, see X 2.26.13, is taken at his word in the summons and denouncements of those crimes, which are notorious, see *Cod.* 9.2.7, C.4 q.4 c.2, the paragraph '*Aliquando*' and *Dig.* 48.16.6.3. And sometimes this person is called 'the official concerned with denouncing crimes before the judges', as in C.23 q.5 c.1. Today, there are also other such persons, such as the priest and the church wardens who as synodical witnesses bring crimes before bishops or deans, see C. 35 q.6 c.7, X 2.21.7 and the *Speculum iudiciale* in the title on the accuser, the first paragraph; here you know it.

Then the people and the priest have to choose them and bring them to the synod. Now the dean has to administer the oath to each member in front of the synod. If he has sworn his oath, the dean shall proclaim a peace over him under the authority of the bishop, so that no-one will harm him or do him injustice or speak badly of him or treat him badly because of his denouncements, on penalty of paying the fine for the infringement of the bishop's authority and compensating the member of the jury twofold. The people shall then affirm this peace unless the member of the jury has committed any crimes in word or deed. A freeman may testify of his own actions towards a member of the jury, assisted by five neighbours as witnesses. If there are no signs of violence on his body, a member of the jury shall bring a case to court in the same way as any layman and be entitled to the same compensations. No member of the jury shall make a denouncement before having consulted his priest and his neighbours over it.

21. Whatever denouncement is made by a dean or a priest or by other sensible people without consultation of the jury, need not be answered, confessed or denied by the defendant, and neither does he need to come up with any kind of defence. Thus goes the synodical law of all Frisians.

22. If a member of the jury accuses a man of being too closely related to his wife and he is unable to demonstrate the degree of their affinity, he shall be fined.

23. Jef hi enichne man wroghet om sonendeis fira, so is di fria Fresa nier to witane tolwasum oen da helligem dan hi aegh enich ban to beten jefta enich hermscheed to ontfaen jef hi onschieldich is; sinte Maria also, sinte Micheel ende alle Godes helligen also; Apostolorum fira ende sinte Laurentius fira sexasum.

24. Jef ma een man wroghet om een onbinaemd moerd deer hi deen habbe oen da wive ende hi des bisecka wil, so moet hi tolwasum onriuchta jef hi onschieldich[1] is.

25. Jef di eedswara wroghet om een reesraef, jef hi bisecka wil, soe[2] is hy nyer tolwasum to onriuchten dan hi thore enich haghera ordel oengaen.

26. Jef di prester ende di eedswara wrogiet enich man om een alterraef, jef hi dis bisecka wil truch sine onschield, soe aegh hi dis tolwasum onriuchta.

27. Jef di prester ene leeckman[3] bitighet mit sine fria foeged dat hi him birawed habbe, lessa jefta mara, also als hyt biwirda wil, jef hi se jecht, so schil hyt saunbeet beta jefta sexasum onriuchta.

28. Jef di leka da prester een[4] faxfangh deth so schil hyt saunbeet beta jefta tolwasum onriuchta.

29. Jef di leka dae prester bitighet eenre quader deda, soe aegh hi him mit sine fria foghed mit ene eed toe sikerien jefta eenbeeth beta.

30. Jef di decken enich man aeschet dat hy syn sind naet alsoe socht habbe[5] als hi mit riuchta schulde, soe schil hy sexasum onriuchta[6] jefta syn ban betha. Jeff him dy decken bythighet dat hy hem dis forma deys urherich were, soe schil hy
95 hem sexasum | onriuchta jefta syn ban beta. Dis ora deis alsoe. Jeff hi him dis bitiget dat hi him dis tredda deis urherich se, soe is di decken nyer mit papen ende mit fiower leecmannen hine toe bitiughen dan hy dae lada se to bieden. Soe hwa so tree daghen herich an da sinde stinsen haet so ne thoer hy dis fiarda deis hor bod ner ban tyelda.

[1] FG: schieldith. [2] FG: sde. [3] FG: lecckman. [4] FG: ecn. [5] FG: habhe. [6] FG: onriuhta.

23. If a member of the jury accuses a man of not having observed the Sunday worship, a free Frisian may exonerate himself by swearing an oath on the holy relics together with eleven compurgators, rather than having to pay a fine or do penance, if he is innocent; this also applies for the Feast of Assumption and that of Saint Michael and of All Angels; for the Feast of the Apostles or that of Saint Lawrence: five compurgators.

24. If a man is accused of having caused a woman to suffer a miscarriage and he wants to deny this, he shall exonerate himself with eleven compurgators, if he is innocent.

25. If the jury accuses a man of having stolen a corpse and he wants to deny this, he has the right to exonerate himself with eleven compurgators, rather than having to undergo a higher ordeal.

26. If a priest and a juror accuse a man of altar robbery, and if he wants to deny this because he is innocent, he has to exonerate himself with eleven compurgators.

27. If a priest, through his free guardian, accuses a layman of having robbed him, to a smaller or greater extent, no matter how he assesses the damage, and if the layman confesses, he shall compensate this sevenfold or he shall exonerate himself with five compurgators.

28. If a layman grabs a priest by the hair he shall compensate him sevenfold or exonerate himself with eleven compurgators.

29. If a layman accuses a priest via his free guardian of a crime, he has to exonerate himself by swearing an oath, or he has to compensate with a single compensation.

30. If the dean accuses a man of not having attended the synod as he should have, he shall exonerate himself with five compurgators or pay the penalty for infringing on the dean's authority. The first day the dean accuses him of being disobedient the defendant may exonerate himself with five compurgators or pay the penalty for infringing on the dean's authority. The second day as well. On the third day, when the dean accuses him of being disobedient again, the dean has the right to prosecute his claim, assisted by clerics and four laymen rather than the defendant can offer to swear oaths of innocence. If someone has attended the synod for three consecutive days, he need not be subjected to any commandment or authority on the fourth.

31. Jef di decken een wyf aeschet ende her des bitiget dat hio een man to urhoer habbe onder her aefte manne; jef hio dis bisecka wil, so wil her dio paepheed ende wise lekalioed finda een handordel.[1] So steet her aefte man ende queth hioe se[2] onschieldich, so is hy se nyer mit ene eed to sikeriane dan hya dat ordel oen to gane. Jef hi se naet sikaria nelle, so schil hio self oen da ordel sikeria ende jef se god sikered, so aeg se her aefta man weer to nimen. Jef hio se aeck urbaernt, soe aegh hi dine ker hor hi se hangie, soe hi se haudie, so hy se drinse, so hi se baerne. Soe moet hi se—fiarda kest—jefta toe him nima jef hit him di wisa prester reth.

32. Jef dy decken enich man aeschet ende hy deer naet to andert is ende hi sine boda aldeer seint ende dat needschyn aldeer biut ende queth dat hi so mogende ne se dat hy deer comma moge, jefta dat hi ur een onwad wetter were eer di sind ket ward ende hi dat oppe da helligem wil bringa, so ne thoer hi fora urfaen dan to da nesta sind der hi aldeer halda schil.

33. Jef binna da trim jerim da decken ymmen urherich wirt, soe schil hy dyn
man dis fiarda jeris da biscop bringha ende di decken ne sel neen man toe ban
dwaen. Soe sel dy biscop dis fyarda jeris alleraerst sindia op dyn urherigha man,
96 deer di decken urherich is, alle dae | tree dagen. Jef hi him eer naet bikanna wil,
soe schil him di biscop efter him laya, toe trim tzierkum aldeer hi dine sind halt.
Ende jef hi se urherich wirt, so schil him di biscop efter him laya to da stoel toe
Utrecht; deer schil hine tree dagen laya. Jef hi deer naet comma ne wil, so aegh
hine dis fiarda deis mit riuchte toe ban to dwaen ende jef hi oen da banne sterft,
soe ne aegh him neen prester to bifellanne, ner neen liacht ur to barnene, neen
pater noster ur to syongane, op neen hof to lidsane. Syn gued deer hi haet, dat
schil oen hofwara allegader.

34. Jeff een man een bern thilet an een wive ende hy se naet jechta nelle als hit boren is, soe schil hyoe her wed jaen op dyn deer hyoe op seyt eer hit enich prester aegh toe depen.

---

[1] FG: haud ordel. [2] FG: sese.

31. If the dean summons a woman to appear and accuses her of sleeping with another man while she is officially married and if she wants to deny this, the clergy and wise laymen will let her undergo the ordeal by fire. If her husband appears before court and states that she is innocent, then he has the right to ascertain her innocence by swearing an oath rather than her having to undergo the ordeal. If he does not want to ascertain her innocence, she has to prove her innocence herself by undergoing the ordeal and if she passes the ordeal, her husband has to accept her again as his wife. If she burns herself, however, her husband has a choice whether to hang her, behead her, drown her or burn her. Or, as a fourth choice, he can accept her again as his wife, if a prudent priest advises him so.

32. If the dean summons someone to appear and the latter does not appear to defend his case and if he sends his messenger and thus offers an official notice that he was unable to come, or that he was overseas when the synod was announced, and if he wants to swear so on the holy relics, this man shall not be excused beyond the next synod which will be held there by the dean.

33. If someone is disobedient within the period of three years the dean holds the synod, the dean shall present this case in the fourth year to the bishop and the dean shall not excommunicate any man. When the bishop then holds the synod in the fourth year, he shall first hold court over this disobedient man, which was disobedient to the dean, for all three consecutive days (on which the court is held). If the man does not wish to confess, the bishop will summon him to follow him to the three churches where he will hold synod. And if he is still disobedient the bishop will summon him to come to the sea at Utrecht; the bishop will summon him to come there for three days. And if he refuses to come there, then the bishop will lawfully excommunicate him on the fourth day and if the dies while being excommunicated, no priest is to bury him, no candles shall be lit for him, no *pater noster* shall be sung for him, and he is not allowed to be put to rest on a churchyard. All his possessions shall go to the church.

34. If a man begets a child with a woman and he does not want to acknowledge it when it is born, she shall provide security against the person she maintains to be the father, before any priest baptises the child.

35. Jeff een wyff staet an dae synde ende queth dat hy des bernes fader se; jof hy dan queth dat hy se nae toe wyve wan, soe is hy nier oppe dae XII scheran to onriuchten dan hioet op him se toe bringen. Jef hi him urbaernt soe aegh hyt bern toe ontfaen ende dine menaeed to festiane ende dae ban toe betane.

36. Jef een wyf her aefte man aeschet an da banda synde, soe aegh him di decken mit laynghen toe andert to bringane, jof hi mei. Jof hi[1] biseka wil, soe is hyoe nyer mitta aefta tiugh,[2] jof hyoet habbe, hine toe winnen dan hi se dera aeftenga toe ontghaen. Jef hy dis riuchtes al urherich wirth, soe aegh hyo dine ferd oen dae guede.

37. Dera[3] scheerna ferst is XLII nachta. Ende dan di man toe synre haudsto toe
97 commane mit syne fyore ende mit syne yrsane, mit syne secken | ende mit sine waxe, syn ambucht to herane, wytat to nymane, lycmissa toe capiane, ordelwyenga toe winnane mit twam schillengen ende da schere in da tzierka to gane.

38. Handyrsen aldus urnacht to dragene, sine lycmissa to herane, *corpus domini* to nimane, ordelwyenga to winnane[4] mit een schillingh penningha. Nu schel ma dis tredda deis da hand schoya, di prester ende sex man mei him; tween[5] fan dis mannes[6] halum ende tween fan des wives halum, fan des deckens halum di prester ende tween man mit him. Jef hia aet sanet, soe sint nier dae fiower da hand to helane dan da tree to urbarnene, hit ne se dat al dioe meente anders hlya wil.

Hyr biginnet da syndriuchta

39. Dat syndriucht gaf us di paeus Leo to Roem ende heet dat wyt hilde also fest als wi dine Cristena nama halda wolde ende wi da suderna riucht herich wolde wessa, hwant wi Fresen alle noerd heerden ende heiden weren.

40. Dat is riucht: hweer so een wiiede stoe is ende di prester een wyeden alter haet ende deer lycfellinga ende kyndkerstinga sint, so aegh aller mana lyc syn deeckma toe jowane ti da godeshuse deer hy binna setten is. Deer aegh aller presterna lyc toe syndiane tria jeer alont dis biscops jeer commet mit mara riucht dan ma dis deckens ban hera thoer jefta dis provestes.

---

[1] FG: *hi* is missing. [2] FG: tingh. [3] FG: Hera. [4] FG: ordelwyenga toe ienst een to winnane. [5] FG: fiower. [6] FG: *mannes* is missing.

35. If a woman appears before the synod and accuses a man of having fathered a child with her, and if he then replies he never slept with her he can prove his innocence by walking over 12 (hot) ploughshares rather than she can pursue her claim. If he burns himself he has to acknowledge the child and pay the penalty for perjury by means of fasting and for the infringement on the authority of the bishop.

36. If a woman brings a case against her husband before a properly announced synod, then the dean has to summon the husband to appear and answer the accusation, if he is able to. If the husband wishes to deny the allegation the woman may win the case against him by producing proper evidence, if she has any, rather than the husband may swear he did not enter into the marriage. If he is totally disobedient to the court, his goods will be assigned to the woman.

37. The term for the ordeal of walking over (hot) ploughshares is 42 days. And then the man has to come to the head-church with his fire and his iron, with his socks and his wax, he has to hear mass, receive the sacramental bread, pay for the mass of the dead, pay two shillings for the consecration of the ordeal and walk over the ploughshares inside the church.

38. A hot iron shall thus be carried on the following day, after hearing the mass of the dead, receiving the *Corpus Domini*, and paying one shilling for the consecration of the ordeal. On the third day, the hand will be inspected by the priest and six men; two relatives of the man, two relatives of the wife, and from the side of the dean the priest, assisted by two men. If they do not agree amongst each other, then the four have the right to declare the hand healed rather than the other three to declare it burnt, unless the entire community wishes to testify differently.

Here Begin the Synodical Laws

39. The synodical law was given to us by Pope Leo in Rome and he ordered us to uphold it just as firmly as we wanted to be called Christians and we wanted to be loyal to the southern law because we Frisians all used to be subjects to the northern kingdom and were all pagans.

40. This is the law: wherever there is a consecrated church and a priest has a consecrated altar there and burials and baptisms take place there, then each man has to pay his tithes to the church to which he belongs. Each priest has to hold synod there during a period of three years until the year comes when the bishop has to hold synod (and the people have to be obedient to these synods) rather than one has to obey the dean's or the provost's jurisdiction.

41. Dis fiarda jeris aegh di biscop to sindiane, jef hy comt, ende sine sind schillet alle huisman seka. Jef immen da prester urherich is binna da trim jerem, so aeg di biscop alleraerst deerur toe sindiane ende jef di biscop dis fiarda jeris naet ne comt so sel di prester dis fiarda jeris sindia als hi dede da tria oer jeer eer di
98 biscop coem. |

42. Dat is riucht,[1] dat da capellapapen da biscop tienia schillet mitta haudprester, al bi dio deer hya deer gued to ledet. So schillet hia den tienst dwaen of da deeckma deer hya nimet ende di deer neen deeckma[2] onfucht di ne thoer neen tyenst dwaen.

43. Soe schil ma riuchta alleraerst, dat deer to clage comt. Als deer is urworden di lyckwey ende di tzierckwey, dat hi naet is fiower mollesfoten breed, dat da fiower mogen dine fyfta to kerka drega, dine dada toe der molda bistedigia, dine heidena Cristen dwaen, dat sel ma riuchta al nei dae riuchte jof ney grata Godes neden; deer ne sint allegader nene lada weder scrioun. Deer schillet wessa reed fiower wegen to da godeshuse to dae quika ende to da dada, hit ne se dat hit stande bi een heerwey, so mei di heerwei wessa ende di tzierckwei ende di lyckwey al een wey, jefta hy stande an ene stedis owere dat ma moghe comma mitta schipes[3] boerde toe da wyda howe. Aldus ist synedriucht[4] alre Fresena.

44. Als deer een stryd is opheven, een ontyd an Paescha moern, an Pynxstera moern ende an Cristesmoern in der tzierka ende dat hellighe *corpus domini* britsen is, di tzylick stirt is, dat font britsen, da helligha biriind ende di prester toe dae bloedis utryn slayn is, soe is deer britsen *munitas* ende *sacrilegium*, soe is dy enghel[5] ire. Soe schel ma om dae openbera sonda dae hermscheed ontfaen ende dae ban beta mitta alrahagista ban mit twa ende sauntigha ponda Agripsera penninghen. Doch soe schellet da Fresen nedena nieta deer Wideken[6] di forma aesga deelde ende efter him Herdrick biscreef bi des paeus henghnese,
99 dat deer | ymmer scholde ghaen ur hals ende ur haed di penning deer toe der montha nye were. Aldus is dat sindriucht aller Fresena.

45. Hweer so deer fuchten is in da godeshuus ende deer naet blicande is, jef ma hit bikanna wil, so scil ma hit beta da ban mit tria ende sextich schillengha. Jef hia[7] se aeck naet schieldich sint, hor so hit faxfangen sint, so duustsleken,

---

[1] FG: riuct. [2] FG: deeck. [3] FG: shipes. [4] FG: synediucht. [5] FG: eughel. [6] FG: undeken. [7] FG: hi*n*a.

41. In the fourth year, the bishop has to hold synod, if he comes, and all freemen should attend his synod. If someone has been disobedient to the priest during the preceding three years, the bishop first has to administer justice over this case and if the bishop does not come on the fourth year, the priest has to hold synod in the same manner he did in the preceding three years, before the bishop was supposed to come.

42. This is the law, that the chaplains together with the archpriest shall provide for the bishop proportionally according to the revenues they receive. They shall pay for serving the bishop out of the tithes they receive and the priest who has no income from tithes need not pay for the costs of the bishop's visit.

43. Then the synod shall judge whichever case presents itself first. If the corpse road and the church road have deteriorated, so that they are no longer four feet wide, so that four persons can carry a fifth to the church, to commit the dead to the soil, or to baptise children, then this shall be adjudicated according to the law or according to the mercy of the almighty God; no rules on how to swear innocence in cases like these have been written. There should be four functioning roads leading to a church, for the living and for the dead, unless one of these roads leads to a main road because then the main road may constitute church road and corps road all at once, or unless the church stands on the shore of an open water so that the churchyard can be reached by ship. Thus goes the synodical law of all Frisians.

44. If a fight has occurred in a church on an untimely moment, at Easter Sunday, Whit Sunday or Christmas day and the holy *Corpus Domini* has been violated, the chalice has been run over, the baptismal font has been broken, the relics have been destroyed and the priest has received a bleeding wound, then the immunity has been violated and sacrilege has been performed, and the angel is irate. Then the perpetrators shall do penance for this public sin and pay the highest fine for the infringement on the authority of the church, which is seventy-two pounds in pennies of Cologne. But the Frisians shall profit from the blessings which Widekin the first *asega* decreed and which Herdrick later put down in writing by consent of the pope, that pennies in good currency always surpass neck and head (i.e. capital punishment). Thus goes the synodical law of all Frisians.

45. If there has been a fight in the church but there are no visible signs of it, and the defendant wants to confess it, he shall pay the penalty of infringing on the authority of the church with sixty-three shillings. If he is innocent, be it of

duuststeten, duustwerpen, soe is di huusman nyer hine to sikeriane twa endesauntigasum mit sine fiower fachtum oen da helligum, dan hi doer daia sind jefta enich ordel jefta oentiugh, dan hi dat bete deer hi naet deen habbe.

46. Hweer so ma claget dat deer faren se inoer dine wedeles werp ende dioe wiiede eerde epened se ende een reesraef deen se ende deer oen britsen se *sacrilegium*[1] ende *munitas*, so ne[2] thoer ma dera gretene nen andert jowa, hit ne se dat ma swigie *sacrilegium*[3] ende grete *munitatem*; so schil dat ordel dela een papa ende tweer leken. So is hi nier oen da helligem tolwasum to onswaren, so aeg hi to daien sind jefta ordel jefta enich oentiugh. Brect[4] him dera ladena so is hi dis rawis alle schieldich, so scheler om da sonda da hermscheed ontfaen ende da ban beta mit LXXII schillengen, ende dat reesraef saunbeet.

GLOSSA 157. Hec actio siue accusatio locum habet uiolato sepulchro ciuium nostrorum non hostium, id est quoquo modo facta deteriore eius condicione, quia diruto sepulchro uel lapso uel statua[a] de monumento euulsa siue sit applumbata uel affixa monumento siue non et datur actio in factum et interdictum quod ui aut clam et competit heredi sepulchri. Si autem dominus nemo est, competit[b] agere uolenti, ff. eodem titulo l. i et ii (*Dig.* 47.12.1–2). Et est pena uiolatoris[c] centum aureorum, qui autem inhabitauerit ducentorum aureorum, ff. et C. eodem titulo (*Dig.* 47.12 and *Cod.* 9.19) in pluribus locis. Est et eciam criminalis actio instituta quoad
100 uiolatores sepulchrorum, nam | "si corpora ipsa extraxerint[d] uel ossa eruerint,[e] humilioris[f] quidem fortune supremo supplicio afficiantur, honestiores in insulam[g] deportantur et religantur aut in metallum dampnentur", ff. eodem l. ult. (*Dig.* 47.12.11). Cetera uero plura uide in Summa Azonis eodem titulo.[h]

47. Hweer so di prester claget dat hi bifuchten se op da fria fielda ende oen him britsen se *sacrilegium* ende *munitas*, so ne thoer hy dera haga gretene nen andert jowa, hit ne se dat ma swigie *sacrilegium* ende grete *emunitatem*; so schil

---

[1] FG: facrilegi*um*. [2] FG: e. [3] FG: sacrlegi*um*. [4] FG: drect.

---

a statua *scripsimus*: statuta FG.
b competit *scripsimus*: cumpetit FG.
c uiolatoris *scripsimus*: uiolatris FG.
d extraxerint *scripsimus cum Digesto Novo*: extaxerint FG.
e eruerint *scripsimus cum Digesto Novo*: emerint FG.
f humilioris *scripsimus cum Digesto Novo*: humiliori FG.
g insulam *scripsimus cum Digesto Novo*: insula FG.
h Azo, Summa Codicis, *Cod.* 9.19, n. 1–6.

hair grabbing, hard blows, hard thrusts, or hard pushes, then the freeman may swear innocence on the holy relics, with the assistance of seventy-one compurgators, coming from his four ancestral branches, rather than having to undergo a trial by the synod or a trial by ordeal or a prosecution, which would imply he would compensate something he did not do.

46. If someone is accused of having trespassed the churchyard and of having opened the holy ground and of having stolen a corpse and because of that having performed sacrilege and violation of the immunity, the defendant need not answer this accusation, unless the prosecutor remains silent about the sacrilege and only accuses the defendant of violation of the immunity; in that case a priest and two laymen shall pass judgment. Subsequently, the defendant may swear innocence on the holy relics, with the assistance of eleven compurgators rather than having to undergo a trial by the synod or a trial by ordeal or a prosecution. If he is unable to procure the required compurgators he will be found guilty of the robbery, and shall have to do penance for this sin and pay the penalty of infringing on the authority of the church with 72 shillings, and compensate the corpse robbery sevenfold.

GLOSS 157. This action or charge is lodged, when a tomb of our citizens, not of our enemies, is violated, that is to say in whatever way its condition is deteriorated because when a tomb is destroyed or broken down, or a statue is loosened from the monument, no matter whether or not it was soldered or affixed to the monument, the heir of the tomb is also entitled to an *actio in factum* and the *interdictum quod vi aut clam*. However, when nobody owns it, anyone who wishes to do so, is entitled to sue, see *Dig*. 47.12.1–2. And the punishment for the violator is 100 gold pieces, but for the one who inhabits the tomb 200 gold pieces, see several texts in the titles *Dig*. 47.12 and *Cod*. 9.19. And violators of tombs may even be criminally prosecuted, because "if they excavated corpses or dug up bones, those of the lower classes will receive the severest punishment, those of the upper classes will be deported to an island and lose their civil rights or be sentenced to hard labour in the mines", see *Dig*. 47.12.11. However, for many more things see the *Summa Codicis* of Azo on the same title.

47. If a priest brings as a complaint that he was attacked out in the field and that accordingly sacrilege and violation of his immunity has taken place, the defendant need not answer this grave accusation, unless the priest remains silent about the sacrilege and only accuses the defendant of violation of the immunity; in that case a priest and two laymen shall order the defendant to undergo

dat ordel wisa een papa ende tweer leken. Soe is hi nyer oen da andert tolwasum to ontriuchtane dan hi to dayen aegh synd jefta ordel jefta enich oentiuch. Breckt him dera ladena, so is hy al schieldich, so schil hi da ban beta mit twa ende sauntiga schillingen ende da papa saunbeet.

GLOSSA 158. Patronus non plus usurpare debet in uacante ecclesia, quam sit a iure permissum, sed quod statutum est ad defensionem, non debet extendi ad depressionem, extra de peniten. c. In quibusdam circa medium (X 5.37.12 i.m.). Nam si quis suum prelatum occiderit uel mutilauerit, si patronus priuatur iure patronatus, si uicedominus uicedominio suo, si uasallus feudo, si aduocatus aduocatia sua, si beneficiatus beneficio suo debet priuari. Debet priuari et heres usque ad quartam generationem. Non habeant illa beneficia, nec heres sui possunt ad sacros ordines promoueri in ecclesia seculari nec in religionem habeant prelaturam, nisi dispensatiue. Et sic nocet irregularitas, proueniens ex delicto alieno. Et est speciale in hoc casu. Hec uide in capitulo allegato inmediate supra (X 5.37.12). Percutiens clericum, Romam petit. Excipiuntur etas, officium, scola, ludus, pellere uim ui, ordinis ignarus, soror, uxor, filia, mater.

48. Hweer so di prester claget om syn faders gued jefta om syn onbannena gued,
101 so schil ma him dis aersta | dey anderda jef ma wil. Ende jef ma naet wil, soe
schil dat ordelandert wisa een papa ende tween leken to da nesta synde to jechtwird jefta to seckwird jefta to riuchta werawird.

49. Als di prester claghet op dine huusman om dine saunda dei deer hy schieldich is to delen ur dine daeda, deer hy gued fan nimen haet, soe mey hi fordera neen pronda aeschia. Claghet hi dan om tria offer, een an Cristesmoern, een oder an Paschamoern,[1] dat tredde aen Pinxsteramoern, so schil ma se him jowa also fyr so dat huus rekende se ende hy habbe ku ende ey. Dat is syn paeplica pronda. Soe ne mey hy fora om neen offer clagia. Claget di prester om fyower seelmoninga, een an Hwita Tornsdei, an Guede Monendei, an sinte Micheelsdey ende an Alraselenadey,[2] soe ne mey hi fordera neen seelmoninga aeschia. Als hy claghet om disse saun ting, so schil ma him dis forma deis anderda jef

[1] FG: paesha moern. BL: pascha moern. [2] FG: alra seleua dey.

an ordeal. Subsequently, the defendant may swear innocence on the holy relics, with the assistance of eleven compurgators rather than having to undergo a trial by the synod or a trial by ordeal or a prosecution. If he is unable to provide compurgators he will be found guilty, and shall have to pay the penalty of infringing on the authority of the church with seventy-two shillings, and compensate the priest sevenfold.

GLOSS 158. A patron should not usurp more in a vacant church than what is legally permitted. However, what is introduced as means of defence, should not cause trouble, see in the middle of X 5.37.12. Since, if someone has killed or mutilated his cleric, if he was patron, he is deprived of his patronage, if vidame of his vidamé, if vassal of his fief, if church warden of his wardenship, and if beneficed of his prebend. Also, their heirs should be deprived of these rights to the fourth generation. They will not possess these privileges and neither can their heirs be promoted to holy orders in the church, served by secular clerics, nor be presented in a church, served by regular clerics, unless after dispensation. And in such a way the irregularity resulting from another's crime is detrimental. And that is exceptional in this case. See the *capitulum* cited right above about these matters (X 5.37.12). Whoever assaults a cleric, should petition Rome. Exceptions exist on the grounds of age, office, school, playing, responding to force with force, ignorance of the other's orders, being sister, wife, daughter or mother.

48. If a priest brings a complaint concerning his father's goods or concerning goods which were appointed to him, the defendant shall answer him on the first day if he wants. And if he does not want to answer, then one priest and two laymen shall order him to confess, deny or defend himself on the next session of the synod.

49. If a priest claims that a freeman should pay him for the necessary mass of the dead for a deceased person from whom the freeman has inherited, he is not entitled to bring a claim for his prebend. If the priest then claims three oblations, one on Christmas Day, the second on Easter Sunday, and the third on Whit Sunday, he shall receive them if there is smoke coming from the chimney of the farmhouse and cows and sheep are present. That is his priestly prebend. A priest cannot claim any further oblations. If a priest claims revenues for four masses of the dead, on Maundy Thursday, on Good Monday, on Saint Michael's Day and on All Souls' Day, he cannot claim any further revenues for reading masses of the dead. If he brings a claim to court concerning these seven cases, the defendant shall give him an answer on the first day, if he desires so. If he

ma wil. Jef ma naet wil, so schillet ordelandert wisa een papa ende tweer leken, ayder to jechtwird jefta to seckwird. So is di prester nyer dat binaemde gued in to winnen mit sine custer, om dat hy alle daghen ita ende drincka schil of sine paeplika pronda.

50. Als di leka bitinget da prester dat hi him een deda habbe deen, soe is di prester him nyer toe sikerien mit sine fria foget deer hi kaes dae hi dine alter ontfingh, dan hi aegh dine fieldferd toe beten ende da leeckman enich bota. Breckt him dera ladena, so weet him sine foged alle schieldich. Haet hi him birawed dera fyf sinnena een jefta dera sex ledena een, so ne moet hy efter dam
102 to nene[1] alter neen missa syonga, neen dada | bifella, neen heidena Crysten dwaen, eer hi dine paeus socht haet willen ende berfoet ende hi weer brocht haet breef ende insigel. So is hi sine sondena siker. So schillet him alle lioed deereefter herich wessa.

GLOSSA 159. Clericus per se uel per alium nomine suo perpetrans homicidium uel membrorum mutilacionem, efficitur irregularis, extra de cle. pug. in duello c. i (X 5.14.1), de raptoribus c. In archiepiscopatu in fine (X 5.17.4 i.f.). Et non solum mutilatio siue truncatio, sed si manus uel pes arefiat[a] ex delicto clerici, ipse efficitur irregularis.

51. Als ma wroget eden deer swerren sint om landcaep, om selvir, om goud, om slain penningen, om standena huis, om quick, om wepen, om weed ende om alrahanda gued, so is di huisman nyer him self toe sikerien ende fyf synre buren him toe folgien dan hi aegh toe dayen sind jefta ordel jefta enich oentiugh. Breckt him dera ladena, so is hi dis menaedis al schieldich,[2] soe schil hy om da sonda da hermscheed ontfaen ende da ban beta mit LXIII schillenghen.

52. Hweer so deer fuchten is ur sette soen ende ur swerren eden ende ur kesten mond,[3] so sel ma da ban beta mit LXIII schillengen, so schillet se om da sonda da hermscheed ontfaen nei hiara presters reed ende seka dine paus willen ende berfoet. Om dine swerta sweng in der cristenheed aegh him nemmen jelkirs neen hermscheed[4] to ty scrywane want se habbet forwrocht godes hulde ende synre helgena.

[1] FG: neue. BL: nene. [2] FG: schieldieh. BL: schieldich. [3] FG: mod. BL: mo*n*d. [4] FG: hermrcheed. BL: hermscheed.

a arefiat] arefiant BL.

refuses, then one priest and two laymen shall order him to either confess or deny. The priest then has a stronger case to claim revenue with the support of his sacristan because he is dependent on his priestly prebend in order to eat and drink every day.

50. If a layman brings a complaint against a priest for having attacked him, the priest can swear innocence, represented in court by his free guardian, whom he chose when he took office of his church, rather than having to pay the penalty for breaking the common peace and compensation to the layman. If he is unable to provide compurgators, his guardian has to admit his guilt. If the priest has robbed the layman of one of his five senses or one of his six limbs, he is not allowed to read any mass anymore, to bury any dead, to baptise anyone, before he has visited the pope in a woollen white robe and barefoot and has brought home a sealed letter of absolution. After that, he is acquitted of his sins. And all people shall obey him again.

GLOSS 159. A cleric who, either by himself or through another on his behalf, commits homicide or mutilates limbs, becomes 'irregular', see X 5.14.1 and X 5.17.4 at the end. And not only a mutilation or amputation will cause him to become irregular, but also when a hand or foot becomes paralysed as a result of the cleric's crime.

51. If oaths that were sworn concerning sale of land, silver, gold, coins, estates, cattle, weapons, textile or concerning any kind of goods are challenged, a freeman can exonerate himself with the aid of five of his neighbours, rather than having to undergo a trial by the synod or a trial by ordeal or a prosecution. If he is unable to provide compurgators he will be found guilty of perjury, and shall have to do penance for this sin and pay the penalty of infringing on the authority of the church with 63 shillings.

52. If certain persons fight in violation of a settled truce, of sworn oaths and of a kiss of reconciliation, they shall pay the penalty for infringing on the authority of the church with 63 shillings, they shall do penance on the advice of their priests and visit the pope in a woollen white robe and barefoot. Because of this unmendable crime within Christianity, no-one except the pope can impose a penance because they have lost the grace of God and his saints.

53. Hwer so enis mannes kempa howen wirt ende mit stryd urwonnen, so aegh
hi self dine meneed to bikannen sonder wroginga, ende di decken synre ban
monia jef met bikanna wil. Hwant Dawid ende Golias dyne forma camp fuch-
103 ten om twira koninga wilker. Aldeerom | aegh ellick man syn selvis deda to
witen, om dat di camp is dera fyf ordela Godes een, dera trina heta ende dera
twira caldera.

54. Hweer so een man of een wyf urwonnen wirdet mit wettercampe ende dattet him comt mit riuchte, soe sint se dera deda alle schieldich, wantet him God opwysd haet. Nu schil ma da ban beta mit LXIII schillingen. Umme da tziisordel also.

55. Hweer so een man jefta wyff hya naet[1] baernd habbet an da wallende wege om een onnaemd moerd offta om moerdbrand, so schil ma him ordelsikeringa wisa an der wallende wege. So is hi nier[2] sikeringem dan hi aeg to daien sind ende ordel. Um dat handyrsen also.

GLOSSA 160. Duella et purgaciones wlgares, scilicet ferri candentis uel aque bulientis, sunt hodie prohibite, quia Deus temptatur et innocens frequenter condemnatur, extra de pur. wlga. per totum (X 5.35). Et si clericus duellum susceperit uel optulerit, deponatur, de cle. pug. in du. c. i et ii (X 5.14.1–2).

56. Hwa so him baernt in da ketelfang, so sciller da hermscheed ontfaen om dine[3] menaeed ende da ban beta mit LXIII schillingen.

GLOSSA 161. Nota quod secundum iura solidus et aureus idem sunt, C. de suscep. prepo. et archa. l. Quotiens, libro x (*Cod.* 10.72[70].5) et C. de veteris nummisma. potest. l. Solidorum libro xi (*Cod.* 11.11[10].1). Et libra auri constat ex lxxii solidis,[a] id est aureis, instit. de pena te. li. in fine (*Inst.* 4.16.3), glossa finali.[b]

57. Hweer so een man Godes riucht brect ende Octavianus ende Moyses ewa
ende al der wrald, dat hi schetten ulvat so aegh him di riuchter tre kerren to
jowen als hi liwet habbe en eetmel alom mit twam hieldem spand, dat hi dis da
wird jechte deer hy deen habbe,[4] ende dat hy dine ker habbe hor hi sine machta
104 by dae lywe off snyde ende syne sonda betterie, | so ma een kolck delve deer dat

[1] FG: *naet* is missing. [2] FG: uier. BL: nier. [3] FG: diue. BL: dine. [4] FG: hahbe. BL, J109: habbe.

a lxxii solidis] lxx duobus solidis BL.

b The gloss *solidorum* ad *Inst.* 4.16.3.

53. If someone's champion is cut down and defeated in a trial by combat, he himself shall confess perjury without challenging this, and the dean shall claim the penalty for infringing on his authority, if the defendant confesses. David and Goliath fought the first trial by combat on behalf of two kings. Accordingly, each man has the right to testify about his own acts because the trial by combat is one of the five ordeals instituted by God; the three hot ordeals and the two cold ordeals.

54. If a man or a woman fails an ordeal by water and when this is established in court, then they are to be found guilty of all allegations because God has imposed this judgment upon them. Now they shall pay the penalty of infringing on the authority of the church with 63 shillings. The same rules apply to the ordeal of the cheese.

55. If a man or a woman have not burnt themselves in the boiling water in an ordeal concerning an abortion or arson, then the legal proof gained from successfully performing the ordeal of the boiling water shall be allotted to them. This proof allows him not to be submitted to a trial by the synod and its judgment. The same rules apply to the ordeal of the hot iron.

GLOSS 160. Duels and public purgations, namely (the ordeals) of red-hot iron or boiling water, are nowadays prohibited, because God is put to the test and often an innocent man is sentenced, see the entire title of X 5.35. And if a cleric accepts or offers a duel, he will be removed from office, see X 5.14.1–2.

56. If someone is burnt in the ordeal of the boiling water he must do penance because of the perjury he committed and pay the penalty of infringing on the authority of the church with 63 shillings.

GLOSS 161. Note that according to the Roman provisions a *solidus* and an *aureus*[11] are the same, see *Cod.* 10.72(70).5 and *Cod.* 11.11(10).1. And a pound of gold consists of 72 *solidi*, that is, *aurei*, see the final gloss to *Inst.* 4.16 at the end.

57. If someone breaks God's law and the laws of Octavian and Moses and of the whole world by performing sexual acts with cattle, after he has been fettered in shackles for a day and a night, so that he confesses the truth of what he has done, the judge has to give this man three choices: cutting off his own genitals

11 The *solidus* and *aureus* were Roman coins of gold.

quick in moge ende dat ma him alles nida bringe, jefta dine tredda ker, dat ma alle dat heer gadrie fan da schettena stirten ende makie een band ende bynden aldeermei ende baerne.

GLOSSA 162. Hoc casu armantur iura at gladio feriantur, Inst. de pub. iudici. § Item lex Iulia (*Inst.* 4.18.8), C. ad le. Iuli. de adulte. l. Cum uir nubit in feminam (*Cod.* 9.9.30[31]), ff. ad le. Cor. de siccar.[a] l. iii § Qui hominem libidinis (*Dig.* 48.8.3.4 i.f.) et in auct. ut non luxurientur contra naturam § ultimo, col. vi (*Auth.* 6.5.2 [*Nov.* 77.1.2]).

58. Hweer so sibbe siden sint ende dan hiara sonden riouwen sint, so schillet se gaen toe hyara decken ende biede him riuchta ban tree schillingen, dat hi se scheda wil. Jef hy se scheda nelle ende hy mara gued habba wil, so schillet se gaen to hara prester ende schedet hiara self, elkerlyck orem urswara, ende di prester scil dine eed stowia, ende neen ban schillet hia da decken jouwa.

59. Hweer so sibbe siden sint ende se togara sittende sint ende di eedswara se wroget ende hia di decken scheda schil, so schillet se om da sonda da hermscheed ontfaen ende da ban beta mit tria ende sextich schillingen.

GLOSSA 163. Et mulier pro causa licita a uiro suo diuorciata[b] recipiet dotem suam integre et etiam percipiet commodum omnium bonorum que uir et ipsa communiter acquesierunt et comparauerunt, extra de dona. inter uirum et ux. c. i (X 4.20.1), ubi de hoc et c. ii (X 4.20.2). Et filii eorum, si habent, erunt legitimi. Si alter parentum ignorauit impedimentum et banna fuerint[c] premissa, filii sunt legitimi, c. Cum inter (X 4.17.2).

60. Hweer so ma[1] een man biclaget om een onnaemd moerd, so is hi nier tolwasum to onswarane dan hi aegh toe daiane sind jefta ordel, jefta enigh oentiugh. Brect him dera ladena, soe schil hi beta dae ban mit trim merkem ende dine liuedferd als hit riucht is ende dat moerd also dyore soe een
105 manslachta.[2] |

[1] FG: Hwecrsoma. BL: (H)weersoma. [2] FG: manslahta.

a de sicarr. *scripsimus cum Digesto Novo*: deciccar FG.
b diuorciata] diuorciaio FG M60 KB RA.
c fuerint *scripsimus*: fuerit FG.

and make amends for his sins, or that a pit shall be dug for the cattle and he shall be put underneath all, or, as a third choice, that all hair from the tails of the cattle will be gathered and a rope will be made from it and he is to be tied by it and then burnt.

GLOSS 162. In this case the legal provisions are provided with arms and equipped with the sword, see *Inst.* 4.18.8, *Cod.* 9.9.30(31), *Dig.* 48.8.3.4 and *Auth.* 6.5.2 (*Nov.* 77.1.2).

58. If a man is too closely related to his wife and they repent their sins, they shall go to their dean and offer to pay the penalty for infringing on his authority with three shillings, so that he will want to divorce them. If he does not want to divorce them and demands more money, they shall go to their priest and divorce themselves, each one abjuring the other, and the priest shall administer the oaths, and they shall not have to pay a penalty to the dean.

59. If a man is too closely related to his wife and they stay together and the juror of the synod brings this case before the court and the dean has to divorce them, then they shall have to do penance for this sin and pay the penalty of infringing on the authority of the church with 63 shillings.

GLOSS 163. And a wife, divorced from her husband for a legitimate reason, recovers her full dowry and she also acquires an interest in all the goods which her husband and she herself together have acquired and obtained, see X 4.20.1, where this is also dealt with in X 4.20.2. And the sons, if they have any, are legitimate. If one of the parents was not aware of the impediment and the marriage banns have been proclaimed, the sons are legitimate, see X 4.17.2.

60. If a man is accused of having caused a woman to suffer a miscarriage, he has the right to exonerate himself with eleven compurgators, rather than having to undergo a trial by the synod or a trial by ordeal or a prosecution. If he is unable to provide compurgators, he shall have to pay the penalty for infringing on the authority of the church with three marks and the legal penalty for the breach of the common peace and compensate this loss of life as if it were a homicide.

61. Hweer so ma een frouwe wroget dat hio een urhoer deen habbe, soe aegh se her foermond to sikerien, jef hi se siker weet. Brect her dera ladena, soe weet se her foermond al schieldich, soe aegh di foermond dine ker, hor hi se fille, so hi se haudie mitta swird deer se onder ghing da se dat aefte bighing, so hi se to him nime. Nu hia se sikeria nellet, soe schel ma om dae sonda da hermscheed ontfaen ende da ban beta mit tria ende sextich schillingen.[1]

GLOSSA 164. De pena adulterantis mulieris C. de adul l. Gratus (*Cod.* 9.9.4) dicitur quod si maritus adulterantem cum sua uxore interficeret etc.

GLOSSA 165. *So aegh di foermond dine ker hor hise haudie* id est secundum antiqua iura.

GLOSSA 166. *Mitta suirde* C. de adulte. l. Quamuis (*Cod.* 9.9.29[30]) in fine, et l. Castitati (*Cod.* 9.9.9). Hoc hodie est reuocatum per auth. hodie ibi posita (post *Cod.* 9.9.29[30] [ex *Nov.* 134.10]).

GLOSSA 167. *So hise to him nime.* Quia ei remittere potest adulterium, Extra de iu. iurandi c. Quemadmodum (X 2.24.25), xxxii q.i Quod autem (C.32 q.1 c.7).

62. Hweer so ma claget om een aeft dat hit tobritsen se endma hit riucht greta schil, soe schil ma hit aldus greta, dat dio frie Fresinne coem oen dis fria Fresa wald mit hoernes hluud ende mit bura oenhlest, mit bakena brand ende mit winna sangh, ende hio breydelike sine bedselma[2] urstoep[3] ende op dae bedde herres lives nette mitta manne ende an moerne opstoed, to tzierka ging, kerckstal stoed, alter arade, da prester offarade ende dat aeft also bigingh, alsoe di fria Fresa mitter frie Fresinne schulde. Soe schil ma dat aeft hirda mit saun buren ende mitta prester deer dae missa sangh ende dat offer ontfingh, deer hya in dae kerka latte, ende mitta[4] kuster deer dae clocke hlette. Soe is ma nyer mit disse nyoghen tyogen dat aeft to sterkien dan[5] hit aegh enich Fresa toe brec-
106 ken. |

63. Hweer so een[6] prester in een capelle comt mit hlote ende mit lioda wilkerre, soe aegh him di persona dine alter toe bifellen, dae kerka, dae stola, dae boecka, dine tzilick, dine fana ende alsoedeen gued als deer binna is to bihodane, deer ma godestienst mey dwaen schil, als hy Gode toe jonghista dei anderde wil dat hyt huede also aeftlyck ende naet urhuere. Toe alla haechtidum aegh hy toe biedane da halta ende da blynda, da siecka, da dulgeda, dat hi him jerne bringe wytat ende missa bi des pauses banne.

---

[1] FG: shill*ingen*. [2] FG: besma. [3] FG: op stoed. [4] FG: mitts. [5] FG: dan dan. [6] FG: eeu.

61. If a woman is accused of adultery, her husband has to exonerate her if he knows she is innocent. Is she is unable to provide compurgators, her husband shall find her guilty and have the choice between whipping her, decapitating her with the sword she passed under when she entered the matrimony, or taking her back. If he does not want to exonerate her, she shall have to do penance for her sins and pay the penalty for infringing on the authority of the church with 63 shillings.

GLOSS 164. Concerning the punishment of the one committing adultery with the wife, it is stated in *Cod.* 9.9.4 that, if the husband caught him in the act with his wife etc.

GLOSS 165. *So aegh di foermond dine ker hor hise haudi* (*her husband shall … have the choice … decapitating her*). That is according to the ancient provisions.

GLOSS 166. *Mitta suirde* (*with the sword*). See *Cod.* 9.9.29(30) at the end and *Cod.* 9.9.9. This is nowadays repealed by the authentica *Sed hodie adultera* (post *Cod.* 9.9.29[30]) which is nowadays inserted there.

GLOSS 167. *So hise to him nime* (*or taking her back*). Since he can forgive her for the adultery, see X 2.24.25 and C.32 q.1 c.7.

62. If a case is brought before the court concerning an illegitimate marriage and the case is to be tried, the accusation shall be presented thus, that the free Frisian woman came under the guardianship of the free Frisian accompanied by the sounding of horns and the clamour of the neighbours, by lit torches and the singing of friends, that she stepped into his bed as a bride and enjoyed her body with her husband and got up in the morning, went to church, heard mass, honoured the altar, paid an offering to the priest and thus entered into matrimony as a free Frisian and a free Frisian woman ought to. Then seven neighbours as well as the priest who read mass and received the offering and who lead her into the church and the sacristan who tolled the bell shall testify of the marriage. In this way, the legitimacy of the marriage can be defended in court with these nine witnesses, rather than that any Frisian can claim it to be invalid.

63. If a priest enters into a chapel by allotment and by the choice of the people, then the archpriest has to transfer to his care the altar, the church, the stole, the books, the chalice, the maniple and all other items needed to celebrate mass, if he wants to answer to God on doomsday that he took good care and did not desecrate anything. He has to provide the lame and the blind people, the sick and the wounded with a mass and the host on all festival days, by order of the pope.

Is hit aen wetterlande, een schip toe habben, deer hi eefter syne gae moge mede fara, to fandiane da syecka. Is hit an gastland, een hinxt to habben, deer hi mede ride eefter sine gae, toe fandiane dae syecka.

64. Forma instituendi: "Auctoritate Domini nostri Ihesu Cristi et autoritate apostolorum Petri et Pauli et auctoritate michi in hac parte commissa et confisa, in presenti beneficio te instituo et de iure tibi collato te inuestio et in corporalem possessionem fructuum, reddituum ac oblationum[1] omnium per presentis libri apprehensionem". Suppledando sibi librum ewangeliorum: "te introduco, tibi curam animarum tocius parrochie et custodiam reliquiarum presentis ecclesie committo in nomine Patris et Filii ⟨et⟩ Spiritus Sanctus. Amen", cantando 'Te Deum' et antiphonam 'Veni Sancte Spiritus' cum uersu de Sancto Spiritu. Ista forma habetur de iu. iu. per Innocentium c. Cum quidam (X 2.24.12).[2]

65. Formula iuramenti: "Ego .n. promitto, iuro et spondeo ab isto die et in posterum reuerentiam et obedientiam domino meo domino episcopo Traiectensi eiusque successoribus canonice substituendis; ac fidelis ero in canonibus seruandis, rebus ecclesieque conseruandis, pensionibus debitisque soluendis, antiquis pensionibus non agendis. Sic me Deus adiuuet et hec sancta ewangelia." Et tunc iurans debet ponere manum super ewangelium "Ego sum pastor
107 bonus",[3] quando iurat. |

[1] oblationem FG. [2] This decretal is of Urban III († 1187) and does not contain a formula of an induction or oath. [3] Iohannes 10.11.

If the chapel lies in wetlands, he shall have a ship in order to travel through his parish to visit the sick. If the chapel lies in dry lands, he shall have a horse in order to ride through his parish to visit the sick.

64. Formula of the induction: "On the authority of Our Lord Jesus Christ, and on the authority of the Apostles Peter and Paul, and on the authority granted and entrusted to me in this territory, I invest in you the present benefice and, based on the right granted to you, I invest in you the corporeal possession of all its fruits, profits and gifts through the handing over of the present book". When handing over the Evangeliary: "I induct you and entrust you the care of the souls of the entire parish and the custody of the relics of the present church in the name of the Father and the Son and the Holy Spirit. Amen". At the same time the *Te Deum* and the antiphon *Veni Sancte Spiritus* with the verse on the Holy Spirit is sung. This formula you can find in X 2.24.12 of Innocent.

65. Formula of the oath: "I, ... (name) promise, swear and pledge, from this day and for the future, respect and obedience to my Lord, the Lord Bishop of Utrecht and his successors who will canonically take his place. And I will be loyal in observing the canons, preserving the assets of the Church, paying the revenues owed and not claim expired periods. So help me God and these holy Gospels". And subsequently the one taking the oath should put his hand on the Gospel of the Good Shepherd, when swearing the oath.

XII. The Younger Skelta Law

1. Dat is riucht. Aldeer di frya Fresa ene oderne to dada slacht ende dat hine jelda schil, soe aegh hi him to biedane twa pond toe jaen, dat hy riuchta jelda ontfaen wil. Soe ist riuchte jeld acht pond tien eynsa ende fioerteenste trimene penningh. So is dio riuchte meenteel fyower pond ende fyf einsa ende saunda twede penningh.

Nu schil ma se da megem dela. Nu schil di broder habba een pond jef hi deer is. Ende jef hi deer naet is, so aegh hit to nimen[1] sines broders soen jefta sines susters soen. Jef hya deer nintera sint, so nima hit di eerfnama self.

Nu aegh di fedria niogen einsa. Jef hi deer naet is, soe aegh hit syn bern jefta siinre susterbern. Jef hia deer ne sint, so aegh hit di eerfnama self.

Nu aegh di eem een hael pond jef hy deer is. Jef hy deer naet is, soe nime hit syn bern jefta syn susterbern. Jeff hyae deer ne sint, soe aegh hit di eerfnama selff. Ende deerfoer toe ferdiane ende toe alle fangha likum deer hy oenfucht.

Nu schillet dae eeftersusterbern oen dae fadersyda habba acht penninghen ende tria eynsa jeff hya deer sint.[2] Jeff hya deer naet sint, soe nymet dy eerfnama selff. Ende diin eed di eerfnama selff toe swaren.

Nu aghen dae eeftersusterbern oen der moedersyda fyff penninghen twae eynsa jeff hia deer sint. Jeff hyae deer naet sint, hyara bern toe nimane ende aldeer weder toe ferdiane.

Nu aghen dae deer dyne ferdeed swared dyne fyaerda penningh off toe nimen, hit ne se dat him siin ewenknee kestighia ende qwe: "Tzies du hor du swerre ende lethe wessa al evendeel".

Nu sinter jeta toe swaren acht freededen.

108 Nu aghen oen der fadersiida dae fyouwer fanghen elkerlyck | XXXVIII penningen. Aldeer agen hia to ferdiane foer alangne ferd ende alderlangne ferd.

Nu sinter tredlingan fyower fangen fan synre modersida.

Nu agen da fangen elkerlyck XXXVII penningen. Aldeer tojenst agen hya to ferdien alangne ferd ende alderlangne ferd.

Nu agen him elkerlyck deer him dine freedeed swert mit sine mond kessa ende deermede da fayte urtigia. Jef immen dine fangh nimen haet deer hi mit riuchta naet aegh, soe schil hine twyschet weerjaen ende mit twam pondem beta. Hwa so dine fangh nimen haet ende wer sine evenkne naet dela wil, so sel hy dine fangh twyschet weerjaen ende mit twam pondem beta.

[1] FG: nimeu. [2] FG: siut.

© KONINKLIJKE BRILL NV, LEIDEN, THE NETHERLANDS, 2023 | DOI:10.1163/9789004526419_016

XII. The Younger Skelta Law

1. This is the law. If one free Frisian kills another free Frisian and he has to pay wergild for it, he has to offer to give the heir two pounds, so that he will be willing to accept the legal wergild. The legal wergild amounts to eight pounds and ten ounces and thirteen and one third pennies. The legal kin's share then is four pounds and five ounces and six and two third pennies.

Now these amounts are to be divided between the relatives. Now the brother, if there is one, shall have one pound. And if there is no brother, the brother's or the sister's son shall take it. If there is none of these either, the heir himself shall take this share.

Now the father's brother has a right to nine ounces. If there is none, his children or his sister's children shall have it. If these are not alive either, the heir himself shall take this share.

Now the mother's brother has a right to half a pound, if there is one. If there is none, his children or his sister's children shall have it. If these are not alive either, the heir himself shall take this share. And for this, he will have to swear an oath of peace and likewise for each share he claims for himself.

Now the second cousins on the father's side shall have eight pennies and three ounces, if there are any. If there are none, the heir himself shall take this share. And the heir himself shall swear an oath for this share.

Now the second cousins on the mother's side shall have five pennies and two ounces, if there are any. If there are none, their children shall take the share and swear the oath of peace for it.

Now those who swear the oath of peace may take a quarter part of the share, unless the other relatives in this group appeal over this before court and say: "You can choose whether you swear the oath and let the shares remain equal".

Now there are eight oaths of peace yet to be sworn.

Now the four relatives entitled to payment on the father's side will receive 38 pennies each. Then they have to swear eternal peace and everlasting peace.

Now there remain four relatives entitled to payment belonging to the third line from the mother's side of the victim.

Now these branches are entitled to 37 pennies each. In return for this they have to swear eternal peace and everlasting peace.

Now each person who swears an oath of peace concerning the killer has to kiss him with his mouth and so refrain from a feud. If someone has taken a share to which he was not legally entitled, he shall pay it back twofold and pay a fine of two pounds. If someone has taken a share and refuses to share it with his relatives in the same degree, he shall pay the share back twofold and pay a fine of two pounds.

2. Als ma enich man weddat to jelde so is dat deiting XXI nachta jef hyt lasta mei. Jef hyt naet lasta ne mei, efta XXI nachta. Jef hyt dan jeta naet mei lasta, dae tredda XXI nachta. Nu schil hi itta forma dei jaen fiower pond ende fyf einsa ende saunda twede penningh. Nu eefta binna een ende tweintich nachta fyouwer pond fyf eynsa ende saunda twede penningh. Itta tredda[1] deytingh eft fyower pond ende fyf eynsa ende saunda twede penningh. Nu sel ma entlike freed halda. Soe ist riucht dat hy toe da lesta dey alle laesta schil, jeld ende meenteel. Nu schil hy dae fryonden monia binna tria ende sexstich nachtem deer him dae meentele jaen schillet, elkerlyck toe sine fordele deer dine fangh samnia[2] schillet mit twam orkenem. Warnet hya se him ende hy dat dae frana claghet, jef hyt bysecka wil, soe schillet[3] hit sidsa tweer orkenen dat hy se monede.[4] Jef hit dae tween orkenen sidsat, soe schil hyt twiischet jaen ende mit twam pondem beta.

3. Jef ma om ane daedne man gretha schil, soe spreckt ma aldus: "Joe sprect dy
109 eerfnama toe | ende ick sine wird ende hy an myne greetwird geet, dat y ane guedne man slayn habbet binna dae alrahagista ferd, dat dullich oen hym deen habbet deer hi lyflaes fan waerd ende banschieldich worden alsoe oenriucht buppa riucht,[5] soe y nu mit riuchta dae ban agen toe beten ende dyne ferd toe jelden, brand ende breck toe thyelden, eerwe ende land toe remen, dyne ferd toe jelden mit twya tachtich ponden, tachtich heren ende tachtich lyoedem". Soe aegh dy grewa dyne man to bannen by des koninghes ban, dat hy dae gretene jouwe jechtwird jefta seckwird. Nu queth di man hy ne thoer, aldus gret, hor jechta ner bisecka. Nu aegh di greuwa dine aesga toe bannane toe een riuchta doem. Soe deelt di aesga dat hi om disse daedbante aldus gret jechta jefta bisecka schil. Nu biseckt hy ende biut toe riuchtane. Nu biut di eerfnama dyne oenbringh. Nu[6] queth di man hy se nyer mit sine dedladem oenschieldich toe wirdane, soe hy thore dyne oenbringh ontfaen. Nu aegh dy grewa dyne aesgha toe bannen dat hi riucht deeroen deel. Nu deelt dy aesgha dat hy nyaer se mitta oenbring him schieldich toe winnane dan hy se mitta edem deer hy byoeth oenschieldich toe wirdane. Nu di eerfnama di oenbringh deeld[7] is, nu

[1] FG: treedda. [2] FG: sannia. [3] FG: schil. [4] FG: moned. [5] FG: rincht. [6] FG: Nn. [7] FG: deel.

2. If someone pledges to pay wergild for a man, the proper period within which this should take place is 21 days, if he is able to pay. If he is unable to pay the money then, again 21 days. If he is still unable to pay, a third term of 21 days. Now, he shall give four pounds and five ounces and six and two third pennies on the first day. And again four pounds and five ounces and six and two third pennies within twenty-one days. After the third period again four pounds and five ounces and six and two third pennies. Now the parties shall keep the peace between themselves eternally. Then this is the law, that on the last day he shall pay everything, wergild and the kin's share. Now within a period of sixty-three days and with two witnesses he has to officially enjoin the relatives who shall give him the kin's share at the house of each of the men who must gather a certain share. If they refuse to pay him, and he files a complaint over this before the *frana*, and if a certain relative wants to deny that the killer enjoined him, then the two witnesses will say that he did do so. If the two witnesses declare this, the relative shall pay the required sum twofold and pay a fine of two pounds.

3. If a case of homicide is to be brought before court, one shall speak thus: "The heir of the deceased accuses you and I am speaking on his behalf and he has delegated his denouncement to me, that you have slain a good man under the highest peace, that you have inflicted the wound to him which caused his death and so became liable for breaking the common peace in such an illegal way, that you now lawfully will have to pay the penalty for breaking the common peace and compensate the breach of the peace, will have to witness that your house is burnt down and demolished, will have to leave your estate and land, and will pay for breaking the peace with two times eighty pounds, eighty for the lords and eighty for the people". Then the count has to order the defendant by the king's authority, to either confess or deny the accusation. Now the defendant says that he, being accused in this manner, is not obligated to confess nor deny. Now the count has to order the *asega* to give expert judgment. Then the *asega* declares that the defendant, being accused for this homicide in this manner, is obligated to either confess or deny. Now the defendant denies and offers to exonerate himself under oath. Now the heir claims the right to confirm his accusation under oath. Now the defendant says he has the right to exonerate himself with the help of the oaths of innocence (he and his compurgators are willing to swear) rather than having to listen to the accusation. Now the count has to order the *asega* to come to a lawful judgment concerning this matter. Now the *asega* declares that the claimant is entitled to accuse the defendant under oath and thus get him convicted, rather than that the defendant is allowed to produce oaths of innocence and thus be found innocent. Now that the heir has been granted the right to confirm his accusation under oath, he

schil hy swara op dae helligem ende naema[1] dine man deer deer slayn is; alsoe als hy greth waes, dat aegh hy toe swarane. Nu di oenbringh sweerren is, nu aegh di grewa dine aesgha toe bannene thi een riuchta doem. So deelt di aesga dat hi foerdghaen schel ende weddia twia tachtich pond: herem tachtich ende tachtich dae lyoedem. Nu hi weddet haeth, nu schil hy ane burgha habba deer
110 alsoe ryck se deer | beta moge herem ende liodem twia tachtich ponda. Nu ist riucht dat hi aegh ane ferd nacht ende dei, dat hi moghe land ende lioed rema ende siin liif helpa.

Nu spreckt hi foerd op dae sex ende bigret dine sexta. Nu queth him di grewa toe ende wisa lioed dat hi deermede ne weer an ferthe ner an fulliste ner fiuchtende da ma dine man sloegh binna da alrahagista frede "also onriucht buppa riucht[2] als i nu mitter haudlesene[3] beta schillet ende brand ende breck tielda". Nu aegh di grewa dine aesgha toe bannane toe[4] een riuchta dome. Nu deelt di aesgha dat neidam deer hi an dat seckwird bitinget wirth, dat hi ti[5] da sikeringha habba schil dine schelta deer him dae ban ur lath ende dera tolwa saun. Jef hi se haet, soe schillet se tiuga dat hi deermede ne were an ferste ner an fulliste ner fiuchtane da ma dine man sloegh binna da alrahagista banne also onriucht[6] ur riucht soe hi[7] nu mitter haudlesene naet betha ne thoren.

Dat is alle riucht, jef him dera utha breckt—dat is biwiis—deer him di aesgha wiisd haet, soe schil hi mitter haudlesene beta. Jeff hi mitter haudlesene beth, soe ne thoer hi neen brand thielda. Jeff hi naet beta nel binna dae aefta deitinghe, soe aegh di schelta dine bannere toe biedane dat hine tweer daghen bodie. Soe schel di schelta dis tredda[8] deis hine selwa bodia dat hi toe houwe comme ende laeste als him di aesgha deeld haet. Nu aegh di schelta dis fiaerda deis toe how te commane ende dat keda dat hine bodet habbe als him di aesgha deelde. Nu aegh di greuwa dine aesgha toe bannene toe ene riuchta[9] doeme. Soe deelt di aesgha dat di schelta dat tioegha schel dat hine fol boedet
111 habbe ende him schillet sex fulghia dis koninghes oerkenen | binna dae banne. Nu ist riucht dat di greuwa dine aesgha banna schil thi ene riuchta doeme. Nu deelt di aesgha dat neidam deer hi boedet waes ende urherich thioeged waes, dat hi mit twaem pondem betha schil endma hine eefta tree daghen dat boe-

[1] FG: naemt. [2] FG: rtucht. [3] FG: haulesene. [4] FG: *bannane toe* is missing. [5] FG: *ti* is missing. [6] FG: onrincht. [7] FG: i. [8] FG: fiaerda. [9] FG: *riuchta* is missing.

shall swear on the holy relics and designate the man who was killed there; the heir has to confirm under oath exactly that of which the defendant has been accused previously. Now that the accusation has been sworn, the count has to order the *asega* to give expert judgment. Now the *asega* declares that the defendant has to take a further step and pledge two times eighty pounds: eighty for the lords and eighty for the people. Now that the defendant has pledged, he shall have a surety who is sufficiently wealthy to be able to pay two times eighty pounds to the lords and the people. Now it is the law that the defendant is entitled to go in peace for a night and a day, so that he may leave the land and the people and so bring his life into safety.

Subsequently he calls the six closest relatives to account and denunciates one of them. Now the count and wise people accuse this man of being a member of the feuding force, offering help and fighting at the time when the victim was killed under the highest peace, "in such an illegal way, that you now lawfully will have to pay your own wergild to avert a death penalty and will have to witness that your house is burnt down and demolished". Now the count has to order the *asega* to give expert judgment. Then the *asega* declares that the defendant, since he was allowed to bring a defence, he shall produce the testimonies of the *skelta* under whose authority he falls and seven of the twelve district witnesses. If he is able to produce them, they will testify that the defendant was not a member of the feuding force, nor offering help nor fighting at the time when the victim was killed under the highest peace in such an illegal way, so that he now lawfully will not have to pay his own wergild to avert a death penalty.

This is the law, if he is unable to produce the required evidence—that means proof—which the *asega* ordered him to, he will have to pay his own wergild to avert a death penalty. If he pays his own wergild to avert a death penalty, he will not have to witness his house being burnt down. If he does not want to pay before the fixed term, the *skelta* shall order the *bannere* to summon the defendant on two consecutive days to appear before court. Then the *skelta* himself shall summon the defendant to appear before court on the third day in order to pay as the *asega* decreed. Now the *skelta* shall come to court on the fourth day and declare that he has summoned the defendant as the *asega* decreed. Now the count has to order the *asega* to come to a lawful judgment. The *asega* then decrees that the *skelta* shall testify before court that he has fully summoned the defendant and six of the king's witnesses within the district shall also testify to this. Now it is the law that the count has to order the *asega* to come to a lawful judgment. The *asega* then decrees that since the defendant has been summoned and officially found in contempt of court, he shall have to pay a fine of two pounds and again be summoned for three consecutive days to bring to

dia schel dat hi twae pond bringhe ende dae haudlesene. Soe aegh di schelta dis fiaerda deis eefta toe commane ende toe kedane dat hine fol boedet habbe. Nu aegh di greuwa dine aesgha toe bannane toe ene riuchta doeme. Soe deelt dy aesgha dat dy schelta dat bityogha schil dat hyne[1] fol bodath habbe ende him schillet folghia sex dis koninghes oerkenen[2] binna dae banne. Nu dat thyoegh ghinsen is, nu aegh dy greuwa dyne aesgha toe bannane thy een riuchta doeme. Nu deelt dy aesgha dat ma hyne tree daghen boedye ende dat hy fyouwer pond bringhe ende dae haudlesene. Soe comt dy schelta dis fyaerda deys ende seyt dat hyne[3] fol boedet habbe. Nu dat bytioeged[4] is ende hy nyoghen hwara bodeth is, so aegh di greuwa dyne aesgha toe bannane thy een riuchta doeme. Nu deelt dy aesgha neydam dat hy nyoeghen hwara boedeth is toe howe ende dat een ende tweyntich manna tioegh ghinsen is, nu aegh aller scheltena lyc thi awane binna sine banne dae branden toe baernane ende dae kedingha toe dwaen. An moerne aegh ma hyne toe sekane thi houwe ende toe huse als ma dis koninghes fyand schil. Hyne schima dan toe brand ende toe breck dwaen. Ist dat hi jeta comma wil ende beta als hy urberd haet eer di fana op were, soe
112 mei hi habba dey ende burgha.[5] Jeff hy naet ne comt eer dy fanna op | were, soe ne mey hi habba dey ner burgha mer mitter ena hand weddia ende mitter[6] ander hand laesta. Jef hy naet betha nelle, soe aegh men toe brand ende toe breck toe dwaen, ferdloes toe lidsen hem ende al syn gued ut dae fordel toe lidsen ende toe wysen alont hi beth mit fyoerteen pondem ende mit fyoerteenste trymene penningh.

Nu dae fersta dera saun di oenbringh swerren is, nu aegh di grewa dine aesgha thi bannane toe een riuchta doem. Nu deelt di aesgha dat nu hi toe brand ende toe breck deen is ende ferdloes leyd is, soe hwa soe hine huset ende howet deereefter nacht ende dei, dat hi beta schil mitter haudlesene. So hwa soe siin gued flet jefta flemt, huset ende howat dei ende nacht, soe aegh hi dis koninges ban toe betane mit twam pondem. Nu aegh di schelta dat ferdloes gued to bisittane to heerna hand ende to lioda wilker.

4. Jef ma greta schil om een lamthe, so queth ma aldus: "Jo sprect di man to dat y him habbe deen een dullich, dine middel ende bede da einden ende oen

[1] FG: byne. [2] FG: oerkegen. [3] FG: dat dat hyne. [4] FG: dat hy bytioeged. [5] FG: burghia. [6] FG: mttter.

court the two pounds and also his own wergild to avert a death penalty. Then the *skelta* shall again come to court on the fourth day and declare that he has fully summoned the defendant. Now the count has to order the *asega* to come to a lawful judgment. The *asega* then decrees that the *skelta* shall testify before court that he has fully summoned the defendant and six of the king's witnesses within the district shall also testify to this. When the testimony has been passed before court, the count has to order the *asega* to come to a lawful judgment. The *asega* then decrees that the defendant be summoned for three consecutive days to bring to court four pounds and his own wergild to avert a death penalty. Then the *skelta* appears before court on the fourth day and declares that he has fully summoned the defendant. Now that this has officially been established and the defendant has been summoned nine times, the count has to order the *asega* to come to a lawful judgment. The *asega* then decrees that since the defendant has been summoned nine times to appear before court and this has been testified by twenty-one persons, each *skelta* now has to light the beacon at night and make the official announcement within his own district. On the next morning, a militia shall go to his estate in the same way one would march against an enemy of the king. His house and goods are then to be burnt down and laid to waste. If he then wishes to come to court and pay the penalty he was fined to before the banner has been raised, he is entitled to a fixed term within which to pay and to a surety. If he does not come before the banner has been raised, he is no longer entitled to a fixed term within which to pay and to a surety, but he shall have to pledge with one hand and pay with the other. If he refuses to pay the fine, his house and goods are to be burnt down and laid to waste, he and his possessions are to be outlawed and all his goods to be confiscated until he pays the fine of fourteen pounds and thirteen and one-third pennies.

Now that the first of seven persons has been officially accused and sentenced, the count has to order the *asega* to give expert judgment. The *asega* then declares that, since the defendant's house and goods have been burnt down and laid to waste and he himself has been outlawed, no-one is to offer him lodgings for a night and a day on penalty of paying his own wergild to avert a death penalty. If someone ships or moves the defendant's goods or stores it for him for a night and a day, he shall have to pay the penalty of infringing on the authority of the king with two pounds. Now the *skelta* shall take possession of the goods of the outlaw for the lords' sake and at the disposal of the people.

4. If someone wants to bring a case before court concerning a paralysis, one shall speak thus: "This man accuses you that you have done him an injury; a wound consisting of a middle part and two ends, and that because of this

da dullich een lamthe also onriucht ur riucht, soe y nu mit riuchta aghen toejenst him to beten ende dine ferd deer mit riuchta deerto heert." Jef hi him dera onschield urmeth, soe is hi nier mitta oenbringhe da bota to winnen dan hi se onschieldich to wirdane. Om een dullich schima aldus greta. Dis is hi eeft nier mitta oenbringhe.

5. "Jo spreckt dis man toe dat y hine fri oenfingen oen da fria fielda oen dis frana wald ende y him nomen an juwe wald ende oen sines selvis onwald alsoe
113 onriucht ur riucht so y nu mit riuchta beta schillet[1] mitter haudlesene." | Jef hy dis ferstis jeret, so aegh hi dat ferst. Jef hi biut to riuchtane soe aegh hy da lada, dat sint tolef eden. Jef ma hine wil hagera greta, so schil ma aldus sprecka: "Ic sprec jo to dat y mi laten mit juwer onriuchter wald to juwe hove ende to juwe huse ende y mi deer hilden an heften ende an heerbeynden an juwer wald ende oen miner onwald nacht ende dey ende an cald yrsen spanden also onriucht ovir riucht soe y nu mit riuchta beta schillet mitter haudlesene, willi jechta ende beta. Willi bisecka, dis wil ick yo also jechta als di aesga deelt to landriuchte dat y dera deda alle schieldich sint." Jef hy queth dat hy aldus gret ne thoer hor jechta ner bisecka, soe wil ick dine aesga banna toe ene riuchta dome. Soe deelt di aesga dat hi aldus gret ayder jechta jefta bisecka schil. Nu bisect hy ende biut to riuchtane. Nu hi an dat seckwird bitinghed wirt an disse bannena tinge, nu is hi nier mitta schelta ende mit dera tolva saun hine to jechtane dan di odera se to onswarane.

6. Allerlyck deer huus ende hof habbet di aegh allerjeralikes een penning to jeldane toe riuchter koninghschielda. Aldeer hy ryckera is, aldeer aegh hy tree penningen toe jouwane, alsoe soe hi habbe fyf inheemde schetten ayder tam ende udertam it sinta Walburga missa—da syn clawa oen der eerda foel.

[1] FG: shhillet.

injury you have caused a paralysis, in such an illegal way, that you now lawfully will have to compensate the claimant and pay the corresponding fine for the breach of the peace". If the defendant pleads not guilty, the claimant is entitled to accuse the defendant under oath and thus get him convicted to pay the compensation, rather than that the defendant is allowed to produce oaths of innocence and thus be found innocent. The procedure in case of other types of wounds is the same. Here the same prevalence of the claimant's rights applies.

5. "This man accuses you that you have captured him, a free man, without the consent of the *frana* in the open field and that you brought him under your power and that you deprived him of his liberty of movement, in such an illegal way, that you now lawfully will have to compensate this by paying your own wergild to avert a death penalty". If he asks for a term, this shall be granted. If he offers to exonerate himself, he shall be granted the right to produce the required oaths of innocence, that is, twelve oaths. If one wants to bring a more serious accusation against the defendant before court, one shall speak thus: "I accuse you of having led me to your house and estate by illegally using force and that you kept me there in fetters and shackles under your control, depriving me of my own control for a night and a day and bound me with cold iron shackles in such an illegal way, that you now lawfully will have to compensate this by paying your own wergild to avert a death penalty if you wish to confess and compensate. If you want to deny this, I will force you to confess these acts, by means of the correct procedure which the *asega* will decree". If the defendant says that he, being accused in this manner, is not obligated to confess nor deny, "I will order the *asega* to give expert judgment". Then the *asega* declares that the defendant, being accused in this manner, is obligated to either confess or deny. Now the defendant denies and offers to exonerate himself under oath. Now that the claimant is entitled to accuse the defendant under oath in this court, he is allowed to have the defendant convicted with the help of the *skelta* and seven of the twelve district witnesses, rather than that the defendant is allowed to produce oaths of innocence and thus be found innocent.

6. Anyone who possesses an estate is obligated to pay the legal king's tax of a penny each year. If someone is richer, he is obligated to pay three pennies, which means he has (at least) five pieces of cattle under his roof which are tame and can be milked at the time of the feast of Saint Walpurga[12]—when his hoe fell to the earth.

12 1 May.

7. Dine huuslaga aegh di schelta to ontfaen in sine[1] banne hwant hi dis koninges foged is ende dis grewa. Dis koninges schielda deer ma huuslaga haet di schil urgulden wessa eer sinte Bavo ende Remigius missa. Ende jef hi se urherich ende urjerich[2] halt, soe schil hi ayder dyne huuslaga twischet jelda ende mit
114 twam schillinghen beta jefta sexasum onswara. |

8. Dat is riucht. Hwam so di schelta des bitiged dat hy sine huuslaga habbe bihalden een jeer ende een oder ende dat tredde, da riuchta koninghschielda: jef hi dis riuchta koninghschielda naet kanna ne wil, so aegh hi him XVIII manna eden to stoyen ende to swaren ende deerefter altida oen orkenschip andert toe lastene. Jef se di huusman naet jelda ne wil ner disse eden tiaen endma him optinget[3] een tingh[4] ende een oder dat tredde ende dat fiarde, so aegh hi toe lasten VIII schillingen da schelta om da urheriga ban. Jef hi se naet weddya nel ner efter lasta, so aegh hi[5] dat fyfte tingh toe syne fordele to lidsen. Soe aghen dis koninghes orkenen in to gaen ende deer ut to achtiane da urherigha ban ende da biwysda bota. Soe hwa so dat wert mit wiche ende mit wepen, so schil hy mit twam ponden beta. Jef hit aeck nimmen ne wert endma dat hues[6] bislut, so bant di schelta dyne aesga toe ene riuchta dome. So deelt di aesga dat hit wita schil di schelta deer dae ban deer lath ende[7] di aesga deer hit mede bitinged is ende dera tolva saun, hor hi se herich dan urherich. Jef di schelta dat bitiuget ende[8] da tolef ende di aesga deer hit mede bitinged is dat him dis man alra aeftera bannena ende alra riuchta fyf tingh[9] urherich worden se alse dat aefte tiug tiuged is ende di tinglose sege ginsen is, so aegh di schelta dine aesga to bannane ti een riuchta dome. So deelt di aesga dat di schelta gungha schil to da fordele aldeer dat huis bilitsen is. Alle riucht ist, dat hi dine waegh inbrecka schil ende neen sletten in da huse. So deelt di aesga tien schillinghen da schelta om dae urherigha ban ende dae grewa twae pond. Dat is riucht dis urherigha ban deer hyr bitinghed sint, dat ma se dae schelta[10] aegh
115 to lasten. |

[1] FG: siue. BL: sine. [2] FG: wrherich. [3] FG: op tiuget. [4] FG: tiugh. [5] FG: hine. [6] FG: *hues* is missing. [7] FG: *di schelta deer dae ban deer lath ende* is missing. [8] FG: oen. [9] FG: tiugh. [10] FG: *dae schelta* is missing.

7. The *skelta* has to collect the (tax called) *huslaga* within his district because he is the king's and the count's representative. The king's tax, which is called *huslaga*, must be paid before the feast of Saint Bavo and Saint Remigius.[13] And if someone disobediently and for a period longer than a year retains the money, he will either have to pay the *huslaga* twofold and pay a fine of two shillings, or exonerate himself with five compurgators.

8. This is the law. If the *skelta* accuses someone that he has not paid his *huslaga*—that is the legal king's tax—for one year, a second and a third: if this man does not want to acknowledge that he has to pay the legal king's tax the *skelta* has to demand an oath from him and 17 compurgators, and henceforth he is obligated to always testify under oath. If a freeman does not want to pay the tax nor swear these oaths, and he is summoned to court once, twice, thrice and a fourth time, he has to pay 8 shillings to the *skelta* for infringing on his authority. If the man does not want to solemnly declare that he will pay this penalty nor pay it afterwards, then the fifth court meeting is to be held at his doorstep. Then the king's witnesses have to enter the house and collect the penalty and the fine that is owed. If anyone hinders this using force and weapons, he has to pay a fine of two pounds. If no-one is using violence but the house is closed up, then the *skelta* has to order the *asega* to give expert judgment. Then the *asega* declares that the *skelta* under whose jurisdiction this person falls and the *asega* before whom the matter was brought to court and seven of the king's witnesses must testify whether this person is defiant or not. If the *skelta* and the king's witnesses and the *asega* before whom the matter was brought to court testify that this man has been defiant concerning all legal authority and all five legal court meetings, and if the legal testimony had been given and the person has been officially declared to be in contempt of court, then the *skelta* has to order the *asega* to give expert judgment. Then the *asega* declares that the *skelta* shall proceed to the front part of the house, where the house has been locked up. It is then completely legal that he breaks down the walls of the house and does not break open the locks. Then the *asega* declares that the *skelta* is entitled to a fine of ten shillings for the infringement on his authority and the count is entitled to a fine of two pounds. As regards the fines for defiance which are established here, it is the law that they are to be paid to the *skelta*.

---

13 1 October.

9. Dat is riucht. Hweer so ma een fiowerfoted schet an raef nymt ende di man dis bisecka wil, soe is di man nyer, jef hi dine schelta haet ende dera tolva saun, hine to bitiugen, soe hi oppe da helligem se toe ontgaen ende jef him[1] dis tiuges breckt so aegh hi him sexasum to ontriuchtane. Jef hi bitiuged wirt so is dio bote da schelta tweer schillinghen, da grewa twa pond.

10. Dat is riucht. Elkerlyck deer een kase deth binna da huse jefta een raef, jef hi bitiuged wirt ende jechtich biradet, so ist twybeet ende dae schelta tweer schillenghen ende dae grewa twae pond.

11. "Ick bitigie jo des dat y dissen man een huisraef deen habbet binna da huse alsoe onriucht buppa riucht als y nu mit riuchta tojenst him beta schillet dat raef dat eenschet ende dat oer ende da schelta tweer schillingen ende dae grewa twae pond to ferd."

12. Alle[2] riucht ist dat di heerwei schil wessa XXVI[3] mollesfota breed. Dine aegh di schelta ende da lioed mit banne to halden. Jef di schelta dine bannena heerwey to wanwirke schowet mitta aefta orkenschip ende dat wanwirck aldeer bitiuged wirt, so schil hi beta tojens dine schelta mit twam schillingem ende dus urnacht an wirke staen ende dat wanwirck an folla wirke bringa twisscha dit ende ur achte dagen. Dat aeg di schelta him mit ban to bifellen dat hyt alsoe laste ende jef hyt also naet dwe, so aeg hyt tojens diin schelta mit twam schillingem beta ende foerd an wirke staen. Jef hy syn bannena wey naet wirtsa nelle ende hyne drewa leth wirda jeer ende dey, soe aegh hyt to beten tojeens dine schelta mit twaem schillingem ende dae grewa twae pond.

116 **13.** Jef di schelta monet om wanwirck, soe monet hy aldus: "Ick monie | jo bi dae ede deer y swerren habbet ende bi juwer siele dat y dae wird sidze hwae dat wanwirck wirtsa schel jefta dae wita beta ende dat wanwirck an fulla wircke bringhe."

---

[1] FG: hi. [2] FG: ALe. [3] FG: vxi. BL: xxvi.

9. This is the law. If someone has robbed a piece of four legged cattle and the defendant wants to deny this, then the claimant, if he has the support of the *skelta* and seven of the twelve district witnesses, he can pursue the proceedings, rather than the defendant has the right to exonerate himself by swearing innocent on the holy relics. However, if he lacks this support, then the defendant may swear innocence with the help of five compurgators. If he tastes defeat, the defendant must pay a fine of two shillings to the *skelta* and two pounds to the count.

10. This is the law. If someone fights inside a house or commits a robbery there and if testimony is brought against him and he is found guilty, he must compensate twofold and pay a fine of two shillings to the *skelta* and two pounds to the count.

11. "I accuse you that you have performed a robbery on this man inside his house, so illegally and in breach of the law, that you shall now compensate him once and a second time for what you have robbed and you will pay two shillings to the *skelta* and two pounds to the count for breaking the peace."

12. It is the law that the main road must be 26 standard feet wide. The *skelta* and the community must maintain this road under his authority. If the *skelta* who has authority over the road inspects it and, confirmed by legal witnesses, finds it in bad repair and if testimony has been given before court concerning the bad repair, then the person responsible shall pay a fine of two shillings to the *skelta* and the next day he has to start with the maintenance of the road and bring it in proper order within eight days. The *skelta* has to command him on his authority to do so and if he does not do it, he has to pay the *skelta* a fine of two shillings and immediately after this start to work on the road. If he does not want to maintain his allotted stretch of road and if he lets it stay in an impassable state for a year and a day, he must pay a fine of two shillings to the *skelta* and two pounds to the count.

13. If the *skelta* enjoins someone because he has not kept an allotted piece of road or dyke in good repair, he shall do so in the following manner: "I enjoin you on the oath you took and on your soul that you will declare truthfully whose responsibility it is to repair this allotment or pay the fine and fully repair this allotment."

14. Dat is riucht. Hweer so een lyckwey an wanwirke is deer ti dae godeshuse gheet, dat ma deer mei fyf aefta tingh binna fyf daghem om tingia truch da need. Hwant ma dat godeshuis deer seka schil, di heydena ende di cristena, di sondiga ende di silligha. Jef dat wanwirck deer bitiuged wirt, so aegh hyt tojenst dyn schelta to beten mit twam schillingem ende dae grewa twa pond. Jef hi eer da tiughe naet toe dome comt ende hi urherich wirt, so aegh ma dis tysdeys dat tingh toe keden ende des wernsdeys toe halden. Jef hi des wernsdeys urherich wirt, soe aegh ma dis deis dat tingh toe keden ende des tornsdeis to halden ende jef hi des tornsdeis[1] urherich wirt, so aegh ma hit dis[2] deis to keden ende des fredis to halden. Jef hi dis fredis urherich wirt soe aegh ma dat tingh[3] dis deis to keden ende dis saterdeis to halden. Jef hy dis saterdeis urherich wirt, so aegh hyt to beten tojeens dine schelta mit twam schillingem ende tojenst dine grewa mit twam pondem, jef hi deer bitioget wirt. Soe aegh ma oen to faren ende da urheerghens of to haliane. Comt hi to dome eer di fana op were, so mey hi habba dei ende burgha. Jef hy bidat alont di fana op were, so ne mey hi deerefter habba dei ner burgha. Jef hi dan beta wil als di fana op is, so schil hi mitta ena hand weddia ende mitter[4] ander hand lasta.

15. Dat is alle riucht.[5] Hweer so een torp is deer een hemmerickhaud is, dat deer
117 een wei om schil | gaen XXVI foten breed, diin aeg di schelta ende da lioed mit ban to halden. Alle deer in da torpe sittet ende diin heemsteed habbet, da agen dine wei to wirtzen also fyr so dio himmerik tocomt fan da utera slaet ende di scil VIII foten wyd wessa.

16. Dit is riucht. Aldeer di syl an wanwirke is endma hit di schelta claget, so is dat riucht dat ma hine aegh to scoyane mitta aefta orkenscyp. So aeg di schelta to moniane hor hit se wanwirck so fulwirck, alsoe tiaende ende also temende als hi mit riuchta schel.[6] Ende jef dat wanwirc deer scowet wirt ende seid, so aegh di scelta dine aesghe to bannane dat hi riucht dele.

Alle riucht is hit. Alle deer hyr scotschieldich sint to disse bannena syl, deren halde mit banne ende mit dome, da habbet allerlyc tojenst dyn schelta urberd tweer schillenghen ende da nu to jowane ende ti da nesta tinghe to lastane, hit ne se dat hia beth[7] tinghia moeghe. So aegh dy schelta da IIII tinghe ende to aller tinghlyckum da urheriga ban to moniane ende da biwysda bota. Jef se

[1] FG: tornsdei. [2] FG: di. [3] FG: tiuegh. [4] FG: mitrer. [5] FG: rucht. BL: riucht. [6] FG: scehl. [7] FG: bede.

14. This is the law. If a cemetery road which leads to the church is in bad repair, this matter must be settled in five proper court sessions within a period of five days because of the urgency of the matter. For people must be able go to church, both pagans and Christians, both sinners and devout people. And when a testimony has been given before court over this bad repair, the defendant shall pay a fine of two shillings to the *skelta* and two pounds to the count. If the defendant does not appear in court before the testimony is given and he is found defiant, the court session is to be announced on Tuesday and to be held on Wednesday. If he is found to be disobedient on Wednesday, the court session is to be announced on that same day and to be held on Thursday and if he is found to be defiant on Thursday, the court session is to be announced on that same day and to be held on Friday. If he is found to be defiant on Friday, the court session is to be announced on that same day and to be held on Saturday. If he is proven to be defiant on Saturday, the defendant shall pay a fine of two shillings to the *skelta* and two pounds to the count. Then the *skelta* and his officers shall go to the house of the defendant to collect these fines. If he comes to court before the banner has been raised, he is entitled to a fixed term within which to pay and to providing a surety. If he waits until the banner has been raised, he is no longer entitled to a fixed term within which to pay and to providing a surety. If he wants to pay the fine after the banner has been raised, he must pledge with one hand and pay with the other.

15. This is the law. If a village is the centre of a number of hamlets, a road must run around it which is 26 feet wide, and which the *skelta* and the people must maintain under his authority. All those who live there and who possess a house are obligated to maintain that road as far as the hamlet reaches until the outer canal and this canal must be 8 feet wide.

16. This is the law. If a sluice is poorly maintained and the case is brought before the *skelta*, then it is the law that the sluice must be inspected with legal witnesses. Then the *skelta* has to demand of the witnesses to declare whether it is in bad repair or in good repair, letting in and letting out water as it should according to the law. And if it is assessed to be in bad repair and if this is declared, then the *skelta* has to command the *asega* to give expert judgment.

This is the law. All those who are responsible for the maintenance of this sluice, who used to do so by virtue of a specific order or a judicial decree, have to pay a fine of two shillings to the *skelta* and they have to pledge it now and pay at the next court session, unless they have a stronger position in the proceedings. Then the *skelta* has to hold 4 court sessions and at each session demand observance of his authority in view of their deviance and payment of the fine. If

disse urheriga banne to da nesta tinghe naet laesta ne willet, so aegh di aesga dat fyfte tingh to wisane to der seeburich ti da mena syl. Jef se deer naet laesta nellet, so aegh dy schelta dine aesgha to bannen[1] ti een riuchta dome. Soe deelt di aesga dat di scelta een man tofara greta[2] schil ende al syne landnathen deer aldeer scotschieldich sin to da syle. So aegh di schelta dine aesga to bannene to ene riuchta[3] dome. So deelt di aesga dat dy schelta ende dera toelwa saun[4] ende dy aesgha deer hit mei bitinghet is dat hiaet bitiugha[5] schillet dat hi mit urheriga banne aldus fyr bitinghet is. Nu dit aefte tiug[6] ghinsen is, nu aeg di schelta dyne aesga to bannene to een riuchta[7] dome. Nu deelt di aesga dat hi
118 deer[8] tofarra gret is ende al sine landnaten deer hi | aldeer schotschieldich sint to da sile neidam dat hia mit urheriga banne aldus fyr bitinghed sint, een tingh ende een oer ende dat tredde ende dat fiarde ende nu dat fyfte, dat se jowa schillet da schelta X schillingen ende da grewa twa pond.

17. Jef ma monet om een syl, so bigint ma aldus: "Ick monie joe bi juwe ede ende bi juwer sele dat y wird sidse hor disse bannena syl also wrocht se mit hore ende mit holte, mit eerda en mit eke, dat hi onbanplichtich se ende also tiaende ende temende als hi mit riuchta schil."

18. Dat is riucht, dat to der bannena seburich een wei binna gaen schil, XXVI fota breed ende binna dae wei schil wessa dis dyckes hilde tria ende sexstich fota jef ma him deermei halda mei. Jef ma naet mei, so sel ma deertoe habba oer LXIII fota toe dikes hilde.

19. Dat is riucht, dat da liued deer dine dyck haldet mit banne ende mit dome, jef se willet mitta dyc infara ende dat land utlidsa, dat hia dat mit riuchte naet habba mogen, hit ne se dat se dat op da helligum swerre an ene ede dat se deer dine bannena dyck naet langera ne halda ne moge mit hore ende mit holte, mit eerda ende mit eke. So deelt di aesga dat se naet lengera ingaen ne mogen, nu di eed swerren is, dan da[9] lettera LXIII fotan ende[10] aldeer staen schillet. Jef da lioed eta een eed biedet dat hiane deer naet halda mogen mit hore ende[11] mit holte, mit eerda ende mit eke, nu di eed swerren is, nu[12] deelt di aesga dat hia lingera ingaen ne mogen mitta diicke dan da tredda LXIII foten. Soe sint da lioed nier him to warane dan se him aegh in toe reman[13] jefta enich tioegh toe ontfaen.

[1] FG: ga*n*nen. [2] FG: een oenfer greta. [3] FG: riucta. [4] FG: toeluasu*m*. [5] FG: bitinghia. [6] FG: ti*n*g. [7] FG: riucta. [8] FG: dome dat deer. [9] FG: ba. [10] FG: en. [11] FG: en. [12] FG: uu. [13] FG: rema.

they do not wish to pay the fine up until the fourth court session, the *skelta* has to hold the fifth court session at the sluice in the seawall. If they do not wish to pay there, the *skelta* has to order the *asega* to give expert judgment. Then the *asega* declares that the *skelta* has to accuse one man first and then all his fellow countrymen who are responsible for keeping the sluice in good repair. Then the *skelta* has to order the *asega* to give expert judgment. Then the *asega* declares that the *skelta* together with seven of the district witnesses and the *asega* under whose jurisdiction the court was held will testify that concerning his defiance to keep the sluice in good repair, proceedings have been brought against this first man up to this point. Now that this legal testimony has been given, the *skelta* has to order the *asega* to give expert judgment. Then the *asega* declares that since proceedings have been brought against this man who has been accused first together with his fellow countrymen who are responsible for keeping the sluice in good repair, at one court session and a second and a third and a fourth and now the fifth, that they now have to pay a fine of 10 shillings to the *skelta* and two pounds to the count.

17. A demand concerning a sluice starts as follows: "I enjoin you on your oath and on your soul to tell the truth, whether this sluice is brought in such a good condition with mud and wood, and with earth and oak, that it is in good repair and letting in and letting out water as it should according to the law."

18. This is the law, that the seawall which must be maintained shall include a road which must be 26 feet wide and together with the road, the seawall shall be sixty-three feet wide if this is sufficient to uphold the dyke. If it is not sufficient, then the seawall may be made another sixty-three feet wide.

19. This is the law, if the people who are obligated to maintain the seawall under the authority (of the *skelta*) and under a decree wish to move the dyke further inland so that some land comes to lie on the outside of the seawall, they are not lawfully allowed to do this, unless they swear an oath on the holy relics that they are no longer able to maintain the dyke with mud and wood, and with earth and oak. Then the *asega* declares, now that the oath has been sworn, that they may not move further inland than the second stretch of 63 feet and remain there. If the people want to swear by means of yet another oath that they are unable to maintain the dyke there with mud and wood, and with earth and oak, and if that oath has been sworn, the *asega* declares that they may not move the dyke further inland than the third stretch of 63 feet. Then the people are more strongly obligated to maintain it, rather that to abandon it or hear witnesses bringing complaints.

20. Dat is riucht, datter schillet wessa alle wettergongen schet to da bannena
119 dyck efter sinte Benedictusdei, | bi sinte Walburga missa to folla wirke, dat ma moge deer onder era ende onder schera.

21. Dat is riucht, aldeer dis salta wetter ingong wirt an da bannena dyck twisscha sinte Benedictus ende sinte Urbanusdei, so hwa so dine dyck aegh ende dat salte wetter inlet ende da lioden schada deth, so is dat alle riucht dat hyt beta schil tojenst[1] dine schelta mit twam schillingem ende foerd an wirke staen.

22. Dat is riucht, deer mit riuchte des bitiged wirt dat syn dyck dis salta wetters ingong deda twisscha sumerisnacht ende[2] lettera evennacht, so haet hi urberd tojenst dyn schelta tweer schillingen ende[3] tojenst dyn grewa twa pond ende dus urnacht an wirke staen. Jef hi an wirke aldus naet ne steet, so aegh hi to betene tojenst dine schelta mit twam schillingem ende dae grewa twa pond ende foerd an wirke staen. Soe aegh di schelta dine aesga to bannene[4] thi een riuchta doem. Nu deelt di aesga, jef hi nelle disse urheergnisse beta ner syn dyck wirtsa, nu agen him da lioed oen to farane mit disse schelta orleff ende disse urheergnisse to haliane. Nu agen him da athen to moniane dat hi an sine dyck fe ende dat hi urnacht an wirke stande. Jef hi dis fiarda deis naet an wirke steet, soe aegh ma da branden ur to stecken. So aegh di schelta dine aesga to bannene thi een riuchta dome. Nu deelt di aesga dat ma om dine bannena dyck beta schel mitter haudlesene. Jeff hy beta wil ende oen syn dyck faen, soe mey hy habba dey ende burgha. Ende jeff hy naet beta nelle eer di fana op is, soe ne mey hy eefter dis hoer dey ner burgha habba men mitter ena hand weddia ende mitter ander hand lasta. Nu hy naet lasta wil, nu deelt di aesgha dat men schil toe breeck dwaen ende ferdloes him ende syn gued eefterdam deer hy ferd-
120 loes leyd is. | Hwa so him huset ende howet, soe aegh hyt mit twam pondem to beten. Sit hi jeer ende dei ende hi naet beta nel, soe schel men als dat jeer om comt uta land driwa ende dela: soe aegh di schelta syn eerwe to bisitten[5] to heerna hand ende dera liodena.

[1] FG: to ieust. [2] FG: ede. [3] FG: en. [4] FG: tolbannene. [5] FG: bisisten.

20. This is the law, that all drains in a public dyke must be closed by Saint Benedict's Day,[14] and fully operational by Saint Walpurga's Day,[15] so that people can plough and pasture the land next to the dykes.

21. This is the law, if between Saint Benedict's Day[16] and Saint Urban's Day[17] salt water flows in through the seawall which must be maintained under the authority (of the *skelta*), then the person who is responsible for the dyke and allows salt water to flow in and cause damage to the residents must lawfully pay a fine of two shillings to the *skelta* and immediately see to it that the dyke is repaired.

22. This is the law, that if it is proven before court that someone's stretch of seawall has been letting in salt water between midsummer's night and the autumn equinox, he has to pay a fine of two shillings to the *skelta* and two pounds to the count and repair it on the next day. If he does not repair it on the next day, he has to pay a fine of two shillings to the *skelta* and two pounds to the count and repair it immediately. Then the *skelta* has to order the *asega* to give expert judgment. Then the *asega* declares that if he does not want to pay the fine for his defiance nor repair his stretch of the seawall, the people have to go to his house with permission of the *skelta* and collect the fine for his defiance there. Now the *atthas* have to enjoin him to go to his stretch of the seawall and start working there on the next day. If he is not doing the repairs on the fourth day, the beacons must be lit. Then the *skelta* has to order the *asega* to give expert judgment. Then the *asega* declares that the defendant must pay his own wergild to avert a death penalty to compensate this negligence of the seawall which must be maintained under a special order. If he wants to compensate and repair the seawall, he is entitled to a fixed term within which to pay and to provide a surety. If he does not want to pay before the banner has been raised, then after this he is no longer entitled to a fixed term within which to pay and to provide a surety, but he shall have to pledge with one hand and pay with the other. Now that he does not want to pay, the *asega* declares that his property must be demolished and he is to be outlawed, including his goods. If someone lets him stay under his roof once he has been outlawed, this person has to pay a fine of two pounds. If he remains at his house for a year and a day and still does not want to pay his fines, he must be driven out of the country after this year: then the *skelta* has to take possession of his estate to the benefit of the lords and the people.

14 21 March.
15 1 May.
16 21 March.
17 25 May.

23. Hwa so des dikes helde delt jefta dyckt jefta mit spada greeft jefta mit ploge eerth jefta mit waine urweit,[1] dat schil hi beta mit dis koninges ban mit twam pondem ende da schelta mit twam schillingem.

24. Jef deer een huisman claghet an bannena tinge da schelta an sine banne dat him[2] een urscher deen se oen dera meenscher an syn ainlika eerwe, so is hi nier deer met opsprekt to riuchtane, jef hyt bikanna nelle, hit ne se dat ma him bitiuga moge mit saun atthem. Jef hi bitioged wirt, so aeg hi da ban to beten tojenst dine schelta mit twam schillingen.

25. Jef een huisman een schet oen eenre meenscher nimt ende hi dat naet biwisa ne mei dattet enich urscher se, soe ist een raef. So aegh hy dis sexasum toe ontswarane ende jef hyt bikant so schil hyt twyschet beta.

26. Jef een man om een overdelta claget an syn ainlika[3] eerwe, so aeg ma dat to bischoien mit des koninges orkenem ende mitta landnatem. Jef ma dat bischowet dat hi da urdelta deen habbe, so aeg hyt to beten tojenst dine schelta mit twam schillingen.

27. Jef een huisman to ene tinge op ene odera claget dat siin eerwe dulven se ende mit raef deerof lat ende hyt bitiuge mei, also graet so hyt achtia wil mitta lioden, so aegh hyt bitiogede raef twyschet beta tojenst dine clagere, dae schelta tweer schillingen ende da grewa twa pond.

28. Jef een schelta dat to[4] clage comt datter een gued stellen se ende jef hi dan
121 seent tojenst dine tief deer dat gued nimen is | ende[5] hine da schelta naet ne andert, so wil di schelta greta: "Ic bitigie jo dis dat y tojenst anen tief seend habbet deer jo gued stellen haet ende is mi naet so andert als hi mit riuchta schulde ende habbet mi birawed[6] mines riuchtis, soe gued so fiower einsa ende fiorteenste trimene penning also onriucht ur riucht so y nu mit riuchta tojenst mi beta schillet". So aegh hi aldus gret aider jechta jefta bisecka. Jef hy ontswara wil, so sintet sex eden.

[1] FG: wrwint. [2] FG: dim. [3] FG: ai*n*lka. [4] FG: *to* is missing. [5] FG: en*de* ende. [6] FG: hirawed.

23. If someone excavates the slope of a seawall or uses it to build another dam or digs into it with a spade or ploughs it or drives a cart over it, he shall have to pay the penalty for infringing on the authority of the king with two pounds and with two shillings for infringing on the authority of the *skelta*.

24. If a freeman complains before court to the *skelta* that someone has illegally pastured the common mark or his own lands within the *skelta's* jurisdiction, then the defendant has the right to exonerate himself if he does not want to confess, unless the claimant is able to procure the testimonies of seven *atthas*. If the defendant tastes defeat, he shall have to pay the penalty for infringing on the authority of the *skelta* with two shillings.

25. If a freeman takes a piece of cattle which is grazing on the common mark and he is unable to prove that it had been grazing there illegally, this is considered as robbery. Then he has to exonerate himself with five compurgators and if he confesses he has to compensate the loss twofold.

26. If a man complains before court because his land has been excavated illegally, then this has to be assessed by the king's witnesses and the neighbours. If it is assessed that the defendant has illegally excavated the land, he has to pay a fine of two shillings to the *skelta*.

27. If a freeman accuses another freeman before court that he has illegally excavated his land and illegally carried away the soil and if he is able to prove this, the defendant has to compensate the claimant twofold for robbery in accordance with the assessment of it by the claimant and the people and he has to pay two shillings to the *skelta* and two pounds to the count.

28. If a *skelta* hears that something has been stolen and that the person from whom the thing was taken has reached an agreement with the thief and that he has not handed over the thief to the *skelta*, then the *skelta* shall accuse this person thus: "I accuse you of having come to an agreement with a thief who has stolen from you and that you have not handed him over to me as should legally have been done and that you have robbed me of my right, worth four ounces and thirteen and a third pennies in such an illegal way and in breach of the law that you will now lawfully have to compensate me for this". Then, having been accused in this way, the defendant is obligated to either confess or deny. If he wishes to exonerate himself, he will have to swear an oath together with five compurgators.

29. Dat is riucht, als di tief finsen is endma him da schelta brinckt, jef him di hals urdeeld wirt, soe ne aegh di schelta dine tief hor hingia ner blinda. So aegh di bannere him to bynden ende to der galga leda. So aegh di man dyne ker hor hine selwa hwe, so hyt mit sine guede winne.

30. Jefter een fynd fonden wirt ende deer nimmen efter comt binna jeer ende binna dei, so agen di schelta half ende di man half deren fonden haet.

GLOSSA 168. De rebus inuentis secundum leges uide Insti. de rerum diuisi. § Thesauros (*Inst.* 2.1.39) et est thesaurus pecunia ab ignotis dominis uetustate temporis abscondita, ut ibi in glosa,[a] C. de thesauris l. i (*Cod.* 10.15.1). Et si per artem magicam inuenitur, tunc cedit fisco, ut in dicta l. i, alius nihil habebit scultetus. Iure autem canonico quidquit "inuenisti et non reddidisti rapuisti.[b] Quantum potuisti[c] fecisti, quia plus non inuenisti", xiiii q. v Si quidquit (C.14 q.5 c.6). Sed iure canonico et nouo iure bona incerta uel certa, quando non exstant hii quibus facienda est restitutio, dispensantur in usum pauperum seu ecclesiarum per episcopum uel ab eo missum, extra de iudeis c. Cum sit (X 5.6.16) ibi "donec in usum pauperum Christianorum secundum prouidentiam dioecesani episcopi conuertantur", et de pe. re. c. Si episcopus, libro vi (VI 5.10.2) in glosa.[d]

31. Jefter een schip an dine owir comt endma hit penda wil, soe aegh hy to gaen mitta schelta ende mitta tolwem ende to jariane datter him dine roder jowa
122 wil ende onder pand setta want hi pandis tojenst him schieldich is. | Jeff hi dera schielda biseckt, so is di scipman nyer mit ene ede ur sine scippes boerd to riuchtane, soe hi thoer pand tielda.

32. Aldeer tween maen om een eerwe entwa sprecket ende him ayder dera nestera werrana urmet ende dat hyt an werrem hede jeer ende dei siker[1] ende onsand[2] ende hi to sine hus ende to sine howe binette riuchtelic ende onraeflic ende "dat wil ick also sterkia als di aesga to landriuchte[3] deelt". Nu deelt him di aesga[4] hockera fan hiarem haet[5] dera toelwa saun deer him oppa dae wara setta wil, so schil hi sitte[6] jef hi sitte moet.

---

[1] FG: sike. [2] FG: onfand. [3] FG: ladriuchte. [4] FG: aesgo. [5] FG: *haet* is missing. [6] FG: *sitte* is missing.

---

a The gloss *thesauros* ad *Inst.* 2.1.39.
b rapuisti *scripsimus*: rapoisti FG.
c potuisti *scripsimus*: potaisti FG.
d The gloss *reseruantur* ad VI 5.10.2.

29. This is the law, if a thief has been caught and brought before the *skelta*, and if he is sentenced to death, then the *skelta* is not obligated to either hang the thief or blind him. Then the *bannere* has to bind him and lead him to the gallows. Then the claimant has the choice between hanging him himself and paying someone to do it for him.

30. If a find is discovered and no-one comes to claim it within a year and a day, half of it shall go to the *skelta* and half to the man who found it.

GLOSS 168. For the Roman rules concerning lost and found see *Inst.* 2.1.39 and this concerns a pecuniary treasure, long ago hidden by unknown owners, as stated in the Gloss to this text and *Cod.* 10.15.1. And if it is found through divination, it will be handed over to the fisc as in the latter provision, otherwise the bailiff will have nothing. However, according to Canon law whatever it was "you have found and you have not restored, you have robbed. You took as much as you could, because you did not find more", see C.14 q.5 c.6. But according to Canon law and the new law (of the decretals) things of which the owner is unknown; and things of which the owner is known, but those to whom restitution should take place are no longer there, are allocated to the use of the poor or the churches by the bishop or the one authorized by him, see X 5.6.16 which reads "until they are diverted to the use of poor Christians according to the providence of the diocesan bishop" and see the Gloss to VI 5.10.2.

31. If a ship sets ashore and someone wishes to seize it, he has to go to the ship with the *skelta* and with the district witnesses and demand from the skipper to hand over the rudder and thus allow the ship to be seized because the skipper owes him a pledge. If he denies owing a pledge, then the skipper has a stronger right to swear an oath over the board of this ship than having his ship seized.

32. If two men argue over an estate and each claims a right of ownership and says he has had the estate secure and uncontested in his possession for a year and a day and that he has been using the house and lands as his own property legally and not as an outcome of robbery, and "I will defend that in court in any way the *asega* asks of me according to the land law". Now the *asega* declares that which of the two (parties) has seven of the twelve district witnesses on his side, who want to install him on his estate, that that party shall take possession of it if he can.

Dat is riucht dat di scelta dera sega monia schil ende als dio sege ginsen is ende di ora oppe da wara set is, so aegh di schelta dine aesga to bannene ti ene riuchta dome. So deelt di aesga dat hi deer op da wara set is, dat di schelta aegh him deer een ferd to bannen dat him nimmen deer an rawie ner naet onriuchtis deer an dwe. Nu hi oppe dat eerwe commen is mit sege ende mit banne ende mit dome, nu is dat riucht dat hi also sitta schil. Jeff hi naet sitta moet, so hwa him oensprecka wil dat hi schil hyne kestigia jefta optingia jefta him sitta leta.

Jef di ora quet[1] dat dat eerwe syn ain se ende di ora quet dattet syn se deer eer oppe dat eerwe ende op da wara sit, nu se bede dera ainlikera[2] werrena urmettet, nu aeg di schelta dine aesgha[3] to bannane to een riuchta dome. Nu deelt di aesgha[4] dattet wita schillet saun des koninges orkenen in der himmeric deer dat eerwe leit. Nu se him wysd sint ende aider him des urmet ende utbiot[5] da orkenen, nu is hi nier mit sine orkenen deer eer an da wara seth is dan di andera. Nu schil di forma sidza bi da ede deer hy da koninghe swoer to hulde ende bi siner selwis zele dat hi da wird sidze, dat dy man deer oppe dae wara
123 des eerwis | set is, dat hy dat eerwe mit mara riucht voer ayn aeg ende mit mara riucht deer op sitta schil voer ain so hyt him rema schil. So schil elkerlyc sidza dera sex mit sonderlinga moninghem dat hi riucht seide dat deer hy hyr om dat eerwe seide.

33. Jeff een frowe her des foermeth dat hio oen her manne voercoft habbe half be ende half bodel ende trymene syn ain, lawiged ende onlawiged, jeff di eerfnama des bisecka wil, soe is hio nier hyne to jechten mit saun orkenen—dat schillet wessa fiower an syner sida ende tre an her syda—dan di eerfnama mitta seckwird ty ongane. Nu ist riucht dat dio frowe schil dat her half in bringa jeff hio dat trymene habba wil. Jef ma deerom monnia schil, so spreckt ma aldus: "Ic monie jo bi da ede deer y da koningh to hulde sworen ende bi juwer selwis sele dat i dae wird sidze hor disse frowe an disse manne foercaped habbe half be ende half bodel ende trymene syn ain ende hi se mit cape an da wara latte ende hio nu an da wara sitta schil mit mara riucht[6] dan hioet enigh man

[1] FG: qnet. [2] FG: aiulikera. [3] FG: aesha. [4] FG: aesha. [5] FG: utbi*n*ot. [6] FG: rincht.

This is the law, that the *skelta* shall enjoin the party to make a statement. And if the statement has been made and the party has been installed on the estate, the *skelta* has to order the *asega* to give expert legal judgment. Then the *asega* declares that the *skelta* has to use his authority to order a peace over the party who has been installed on the estate, so that no-one will rob him there or do anything illegal against him there. Now that he has secured his right to the possession of the estate because of his declaration and with the help of the authority of the *skelta* and the declaration (of the *asega*), now it is the law that he shall take possession of the estate. If he is not able to take possession, anyone who wishes to challenge him must either compel him to take more oaths, or summon him to court, or allow him to take possession of the estate.

If the other party says that he owns the estate and if the party who has been installed on the estate also says that he owns it, and thus both parties claim ownership, then the *skelta* has to order the *asega* to give expert legal judgment. Then the *asega* declares that seven of the king's witnesses from the village district in which the estate lies must give testimony. Now that the king's witnesses have been assigned to the parties and each of the parties claims his rights and tries to persuade the king's witnesses, the party who has been installed on the estate has more rights to prove his claim than the other party. Now the first of the king's witnesses shall swear upon the oath he took when he swore allegiance to the king and upon his soul, that he will speak the truth, and that the man who has been installed on the estate, possesses the estate with more right of ownership and must possess it as his own with more right, rather than having to give it up in favour of the other party. Then each of the other six witnesses shall declare, after having been separately enjoined to do so, that what the first witness said about the estate was correct.

33. If a woman declares that she transferred to her deceased husband half of the profit the estate yielded during their matrimony and half of the movables and (she can therefore claim a right to) one third of the entire property, both acquired through inheritance and otherwise, and if the heir wants to deny this, then she has a stronger right to prove her case with the help of seven witnesses—four from his side and three from her side—than that the heir may invalidate her argument by denying. Now it is the law that a woman must bring in her half if she wants to have a third (of the inheritance). If one wants to enjoin over this, one shall speak thus: "I enjoin you on the oath you swore to the king and on your own soul to tell the truth, whether this woman gave this man half of the profit the estate made during their matrimony and half of the movables and that in return for this he has given her a third of the entire inheritance, and that he legally installed her into the inheritance and that she now

rema thoer." Nu schellet da sex folgia ende da schillet elkerlyc sidza mit sonderlinga ede deer hi da koninge to hulde swoer ende by syner selwes sele, dat hi dae wird sidze, dat dis man riucht seide, nu dat deer hi hyr seide om dat eerwe.

34. Dat is riucht, jef ma een hera oenspreckt dat hi habbe een man to met[1] ende to mele ende hy him habbe eesna joun, dat hi deerfoer anderda schil so haet so ma him op sprect: jechta jefta bisecka; beta jeff hyt bicaent; riuchta jef hyt naet bicaent.

35. Dat is riucht, jef een huusnata syn hera offstelt ende hi des jechtich urwon-
124 nen wirt, soe schil hy beta toejenst syn hera dat een schet ende dat oder. | So ist riucht dat di hera foer syne huusnaet da schelta dat weerjeld jouwa schil om syn ayn gued om dat hine taegh mit met ende mit mele.

36. "Ic bitighie jo des dat y mi mine tollen bihalden habbet also onriucht ur riucht so y se nu mit riuchta jelde schillet." Nu ist riucht dat hi aldus gret anderda schil toe jechtwird jefta to seckwird. Jecht hi, soe is dio tollen twischet. Jef hyt biseckt, soe sintet sex[2] eden, hit ne se dat di schelta habbe tweer synre buren deer deer to andert weren da ma him monade. Jef da tweer dat bitiuged dat hi da tolne weigarade, so is di schelta nier mit twam orkenem him toe bitiogen so hi disse lada habba moge. Jef da tweer dat bitioged, so is dio tolne twischet ende da schelta tweer schillingen ende da grewa twa pond.

37. Jeff een man een orem bitighet dat hi habbe siin ros an raefrede riden an sine moede[3] ende an syne willa, so aegh hyt to beten jef hyt bikant mit twam schillingen jefta twirasum onswara.

38. So hwa so dera seecknese wernt dat ma syn gued biseka wil, so schil hi da bannere jowa twa pond.

39. Allerlyck deer faders lawa ende moders lawa ontfinsen habbe, dera aegh allerlyck ane penningh to jowane thi huislaga jefta allegader dine mara, tre penningen uta huse.

---

[1] FG: mec. [2] FG: scx. [3] FG: mede.

legally owns the property and does not have to concede it to anybody." Now the other six will follow and they must each declare under oath—which they swore to the king—and on their own soul tell the truth, that the first man spoke correctly when he spoke about the inheritance.

34. This is the law, if a master is called to account for someone whom he feeds and nourishes and whom he pays wages, he shall be answerable for any complaint which is brought before court against this servant: he must confess or deny; compensate if the servant confesses; continue the proceedings if the servant denies.

35. This is the law, if a servant steals from his master and he is found guilty of this before court, he shall compensate his master twofold. Then it is the law that the master shall pay the *skelta* his servant's wergild in view of the theft of his own property because the master fed and nourished the servant.

36. "I accuse you of withholding toll I am entitled to in such an illegal way and in breach of the law that you will now lawfully have to compensate me for this." Now it is the law that the person who has been accused in such a way must either confess or deny. If he confesses, he must pay the toll twofold. If he denies, he has to swear six oaths, unless the *skelta* can procure two of his neighbours who were present at the time he was enjoined (to pay the toll). If these two testify that he refused to pay the toll, then the *skelta* has a stronger right to state his case before court with the help of these two witnesses than that the defendant may exonerate himself by taking an oath. If the two neighbours bear witness to this, the defendant must pay the toll twofold and two shillings to the *skelta* and two pounds to the count.

37. If someone accuses a person of having ridden his horse without his permission, against his intention and his will, the defendant must pay a fine of two shillings if he confesses or exonerate himself by swearing innocent together with one compurgator.

38. If someone refuses to allow a court expedition on his estate, when they come to his house (to execute a verdict), he must pay a fine of two pounds to the *bannere*.

39. Each person who has received an inheritance from the father's side of the family or from the mother's side has to pay the king's tax called *huslaga* of one penny, or all heirs together can collectively pay the higher tax; three pennies taken from the whole estate of the deceased.

GLOSSA 169. Pedagia noua institui non debent sine consensu principis, de censi. ca. Innouamus (X 3.39.10). Pedagia dicuntur et que dantur a transeuntibus in locis constitutis a principe, de uer. signi. c. Super quibusdam (X 5.40.26).

40. Hweer so een hemmerickmaer is aldeer da hemmerika gaercommet, so aegh hine to slatane deer der mit sine lande tocomt. Di maer schil acht fotem wyd wessa; dyne aegh nimmen toe sellen ner to capien. |

41. Hwer so di bannena dyck bischowat wirt to wanwirck, so haet so ma deer ut[1] wint, so agen da dyckathen dine hale deel ende di schelta dine halendeel. Is di aesga dermede, so heertet oen trim.

42. Hwer so ma een gued bisitta schil mit des koninghes orkenem so hwam so hit di schelta bifelt dat hyt an hodene nime, so aeg hyt to ontfaen. Jef hyt withseit, so is hi banschieldich.

43. Jef ma een manne bitiget dat hi ane huisbreec deen habbe deer di wiind ingonge ende di reek ut, so aegh hi aldus tigades twirasum onriuchta jefta mit twam schillingem beta.

[1] FG: it.

GLOSS 169. New pedages should not be introduced without consent of the ruler, see X 3.39.10. Tollages indebted by passers-by in places, determined by the ruler, are also called pedages, see X 5.40.26.

40. If there is a canal at a point where several communal marks meet, the person whose own land borders on that canal shall dredge it. The canal must be eight feet wide; no-one is allowed to sell or purchase it.

41. If a dyke which must be maintained under the authority (of the *skelta*) is found to be in bad repair, whatever fine is generated because of this shall be divided between the *dikatthas* and the *skelta*. If the *asega* is involved as well, it shall be divided between these three.

42. If property is to be seized with the help of the king's witnesses, then the one ordered by the *skelta* to take the land into his custody should accept. If he refuses, he is infringing on the authority of the *skelta* and has to pay a penalty.

43. If someone is accused of having unlawfully and violently wrecked a person's house, so that the wind entered the house and the smoke went out, he may exonerate himself with one compurgator or pay a fine of two shillings.

XIII. The Statutes of the Five Districts

Hyr biginnet da wilkerren dis landis mitta fyf[1] *delen*

1. Dit is riucht ende wilker der wysesta ende der riuchtera: dat neen abbet een biwesed kind toe claester ne nime buta reed des eerfnamens ende des mondes. Jef di ora claged, so schil di, deer dat kiind nimt, ende di deer dat jout aider in dat land beta mit tachtich pondem, ende dat kynd weer op syn gued, bi bode dis landis.

2. Jefter een frow nimen wirt mit onwilla ende hio dat ket ende claget, so schil di deer se jout ende di deer se nimt ayder beta dine ferd mit tachtich pondem, ende da frowa hia aider jouwa een haudlesene. Claget dio frowe, als hio fri is, dat se to needwyf wonnen se, so schil ma hit beta mit LII pondem, jef hyt bicand.[2] Biseckt hyt, so[3] aegh hio dine ker her hio dat op him bringe mit her ede ende mit saun dera tolva, so hyo him toreme mitta sinem.

3. Hwa soe oderne ur setta sone ende ur swerren eden ende ur kesten mond daed slacht, so is di ferd tolftich pond in dat land; andere[4] daedslachta tachtich pond.

4. Hwa so oderne bi redena reed ende bi leidera lega openbeerlyc daed slacht, so is di ferd tolftich pond.

126 5. Hwa so fiucht to enis anderis mannis huse, jef | deer een man slayn wirth in da huse, so is dy ferd tolftich pond. Hat so ma der ut fiucht: neen ferd.

6. Hweer so ma een man da agen onwirdelic utbrekt, deer siin riucht bihalden haet, so is dy ferd tachtich pond.

7. Gersfallich lya XXXII ponda. Alle disse ferden sel ma in Fraenkere byriuchta ende lasta.

8. Truchslain haud, utschetten agen, lam lyaa: dy ferd XXIIII ponda.

---

[1] FG: syf. BL, BN, KB, M60, UB: fyf. [2] FG: hyt becand steed. [3] FG: se. [4] FG: anderde.

© KONINKLIJKE BRILL NV, LEIDEN, THE NETHERLANDS, 2023 | DOI:10.1163/9789004526419_017

XIII. The Statutes of the Five Districts

Here Begin the Statutes of the Land with the Five Districts

1. This the law and the statute of the wisest men and the judges: that no abbot shall allow an orphan to enter his monastery without the consent of the heirs and of the legal guardian. If one of these brings a complaint on this matter before court, then he who accepts the child and he who gives it away shall each pay the land eighty pounds and return the child to his estate by order of the land.

2. If a woman is forced into a marriage against her will and she makes this known and brings a complaint before court, then he who gave her away and he who took her shall each pay the fine for having breached the peace of the land with eighty pounds, and each shall pay the woman his own wergild to avert a death penalty. If the woman is a free woman and brings a complaint before court that she has been raped, then this must be compensated with 52 pounds if the defendant confesses. If he denies, she may prove it with an oath and with the oaths of seven out of the twelve district witnesses, or she may assent to his denial.

3. If someone kills another man in violation of a truce, of sworn oaths and of a kiss of reconciliation, he has to pay hundred and twenty pounds for breaking the peace of the land; all other homicides require eighty pounds.

4. If someone publicly kills another man with premeditation and while attacking him from an ambush, he has to pay hundred and twenty pounds for breaking the peace of the land.

5. If someone attacks another man's house and if a man is slain inside the house, the perpetrator has to pay hundred and twenty pounds for breaking the peace of the land. Whatever fighting has been done in defence: no fine is required.

6. If someone shamefully pokes out another man's eyes, he has to pay eighty pounds for breaking the peace of the land.

7. Severed limbs: 32 pounds. All these offences are to be taken to court and paid in Franeker.

8. A penetrating injury in the head, eyes that have been poked out and paralysis of limbs: the fine for breaking the peace is 24 pounds.

9. Dulligh truch dine buck, truch dine hals, truch[1] dat haud ende oder dulginga an[2] frasa des[3] lyves: dy ferd is XVI pond.

10. Dullich truch dine eerm, truch da hand, truch diin schonck ende truch diin foet ende alla oenbrins seer: di ferd is acht pond. Disse ferden sel ma byriuchta in da[4] bifang ende lasta.

11. Bloedresen ende[5] faxfangh ende haet so nier is mitta eden to ongaen dan di onbring: di ferd[6] twa pond; ende dat scillet da atten byriuchta.

12. Hweer so da atthen een man schieldigiet, dat hy dyn ferd britsen habbe, so schil hi mit twam pondem beta. Jef hi biseckt, so schillet hia him dat urtiuch weddia des forma deis, jefta syn eden onfaen, jefta fri lete. Dat tiugh schillet tre atten dwaen; jef da tre athen naet en ena sind, so hera hia syn eed ende tween folgren.

13. Hwa so di schelta urherich tiughet fyff tingh, so schil hine ladia to Fraenker ende deer urtiuga, jefta to da bifanges[7] waer deer hi in sitten is ende deer urtiuga mit saun dera tolvem ende mitta aesga ende mit him selm. So is syn ban X schillenghen ende da fellinga deerom dat hy urherich waerd in dine warff mit twam pondem.

14. Hwa so oderne om een hael pondis schada jefta minra[8] bitiget, so tziese hi, deer met oensprect, hor hy mit ene ede onswerre, so hi dae orem dat toreme.

15. Hwa so orem offaeschet enis halvis[9] pondis wirden jefta meer binna da pond, so moet di, deer met oensprect, mit ene ede ontgaen, hit ne se[10] dat di
127 ora him | kestigie op tweer eden.

16. Umme neen schada, ner om nen penninghschielda, moet ma hagra kestigia, dan op sex eden, hi ne habbe riuchte orkenen.

[1] FG: truich. [2] FG: *an* is missing. [3] FG: dus. [4] FG: uta. [5] FG: eude. [6] FG: fedr. [7] FG: bisanges. [8] FG: *minra* is missing. [9] FG: halnis. [10] FG: hit ne fe.

9. A penetrating injury through the stomach, through the throat, through the head, and other life-threatening wounds: the fine for breaking the peace is 16 pounds.

10. A penetrating injury through the arm, through the hand, through the leg and through the foot, and all wounds which may be proven by oaths: the fine for breaking the peace is eight pounds. All these offences are to be taken to court and paid in the district court.

11. Bleeding wounds and hair grabbing and all deeds for which a defendant can exonerate himself by swearing an oath of innocence rather than that the claimant can substantiate his claim by oath: the fine for breaking the peace is two pounds; and the *atthas* will pass sentence in these cases.

12. If the *atthas* accuse a man of breaking the peace, he has to compensate with two pounds. If he denies, they shall present him the evidence of witnesses on the first day, or accept his oaths of innocence, or let him go free. The incriminating evidence must be corroborated by three *atthas*, but if the three *atthas* are not of one mind, then they are obligated to accept the defendant's oath and those of two compurgators.

13. If a *skelta* proclaims someone disobedient at five successive court sessions, he shall summon him to come to the court in Franeker and there the evidence of witnesses is to be presented, or at the court of the district where he lives, and there the evidence of witnesses is to be presented by seven out of the twelve district witnesses and by the *asega* and by the defendant himself. Then the penalty for infringing on the authority of the *skelta* is 10 shilling and the fine for his disobedience at the district court is two pounds.

14. If someone brings a claim to court over a damage of half a pound or less, then the defendant may choose whether he wants to swear innocence with one oath or concede the claim.

15. If someone brings a claim to court worth half a pound or more, but less than one pound, then the defendant, of whom this is claimed, can exonerate himself by swearing an oath, unless the claimant forces him to take two oaths.

16. No-one can be forced to provide more than six oaths over any loss or debt, except when he is able to produce legally valid testimonies.

17. Hweer so di ene papa claget op dine oderne, so schil aider een riuchter tziesa ende da tweer mitta decken da seke einda, eer hi uta lande fare.

18. Hwa so faert tifora layngem ur bod dera riuchtera, so bete hi mit XX ponda ende dio fer om naet.

19. Hwer so di papa jefta di leka ayder op oderne clagiet, soe schil aider een papa nyma ende da riuchteren een setta, deer da seke einde.

20. Hweer so di papa fan nothschada ende fan smella schada uta[1] bifangh claget, aldeer toe nimen lada jefta bota.

21. Deerwe duistsleken, als hia schaed, so schil ma se da riuchterem leta siaen deerefter itta riuchta deitingh, dat is LXIII nachta. Jechtet him dae riuchteren, dat hiaet schowed habbet, so moet hi mit ene eed winna sine bota. Breckt him dis orkenscips, so moet hi bitigia.

22. Hwa so bitiget een orem, dat hi een raef deen habbe oen syn lande, om een raefeerd, jefta sceerd, jefta meta, jefta eth, jefta delta, so moet hy deer met oenspreckt mit een hala pond beta, jefta sexasum ontswara, hi ne wilt swara mit ene ede, dat hit ne se, dat hyt fan wanwytschip dede, jefta fan wanwisinghe deen habbe ende bete dine schada deer hi deeroen deen habbe.

23. Hwa so mit saemnada sidem oderis land een walde deth, soe schil hyt mit twam pondem beta ende in dine bifanges werf mit acht pondem. Hwam so tynse disse bota to litick, so schil di deer met oensprect beta, als di ora swara wil twyschet[2] dat hit fol bet se ende stedigie niogen eden, hit ne se dat hy habbe riuchte sikeringe, nyoghen eden.

24. Hwa so oderem mit wepeneder hand ende mit landbede in syn eerwe walde deth, so schil hy deer dat land aegh habba dine ker, dat hi da bote nime, acht
128 pond, jefta twybeet, | so dy andera wil mit[3] ene ede ontgaen ende niogen eden
folgie him; twintich[4] pond in dine bifangh ende nene sikeringa.

---

[1] FG: schada cla wta. [2] FG: tuysdhet. [3] FG: mi*nt*. [4] FG: tuntich.

17. If a priest accuses another priest, they shall each choose their own judge, and these two will decide over the case together with the dean, before he leaves the land.

18. If one of them leaves against the order of the judges before summons were issued, he will pay a fine of 20 pounds and his journey is useless.

19. If a priest or a layperson brings a case against the other to court, then each shall choose a priest and the judges will appoint a third party, so that the three of them can pass sentence on the case.

20. If a priest brings a complaint to court over loss of crops and minor loss outside the court's district, then they must accept oaths of innocence or compensation over there.

21. If hard blows have been delivered, the results shall be shown to the judges before the legally established time has elapsed, that is, 63 days. If the judges acknowledge that they have observed it, then he can claim his compensation by swearing an oath. If he lacks this testimony, he must bring an accusation before court.

22. If someone accuses another of having committed a robbery against his land, or of unlawful ploughing, or reaping, or mowing, or grazing, or burrowing, then the defendant shall compensate with half a pound, or swear innocence with the help of five compurgators, unless he wants to swear that he did so out of ignorance or mistakenly and compensate for the loss he has caused.

23. If someone performs acts of violence with the help of a group of kinsmen on someone else's land, he will have to compensate with two pounds and with eight pounds to the district court. If the claimant thinks this compensation is insufficient, then the defendant will have to pay twice the amount the claimant assesses the damage to be, so that it will be fully compensated and nine *atthas* will testify of this, unless the defendant is able to produce the testimonies of nine *atthas* in order to exonerate himself.

24. If someone performs acts of violence with armed forces and with violent land seizure on someone else's estate, then the owner of the land has the choice of accepting the fine of eight pounds or twice the actual compensation, if the defendant wants to swear innocence and have nine *atthas* as compurgators; twenty pounds in the district court and no swearing innocent allowed.

25. Hwa so in oderis huis geet an siin willa ende an dis oderis onwilla, so schil hi beta dine ingongh mit ene pond ende dine utgongh mit ene ora pond, jefta sexasum ontswara.

26. Hwa so oderis huus instaet mit haester hand ende mit ira mode, dat di wynd ingeet ende di reeck ut, so schil hyt beta mit een hala pond ende toejenst dae athen mit twam pondem, jefta sexasum ontswara, hit ne se dat hit da athen bitiuga willet.

27. Hwa so oderis huus instaet mit saemnada sidem, so schil hi beta mit twam pondem tojenst dyn, deer hine schada deen haet ende in dine bifangh mit acht pondem. So schil di huushera swara dine oenbring ende mit ene eed wita haet syn schada is ende niogen eden folghia ende dat twibeet beta.

28. Hwa so anderis huis instaet mit landbede ende mit weepnader hand, so schil hyt beta tojens dyn huushera mit acht pondem ende in den bifangh mit XX pondem.

29. Hwa so anderis huus baernt jefta breckt, speerfallich ende balckfallich, di ferd is tachtich pond, dae huushera tribeet als hyt swara wil ende him nioghen eden folgia.

30. Hwa so capet een schet, jefta schepen weed, jefta fyowerherned dueck, jef di claget,[1] deer hit seld haet, om syn wirden, so schil hyt mit twam orkenem winna, aldeer hy sittende is; hit ne se[2] dat di ora dat urjeld aldeer habbe; so is hi mitta urjeld nier. Jef him dis breckt, so schil di ora mit sine orkenem syn jeld winna.

31. Hwa so orem haet joun handjeftich gued op jeld oen orkenschips andert, so schil hyt winna mit sine burem, jef di ora dat urjeld aldeer haet, aldeer di clager sit binna da hemmerick. Is[3] hit een pond jef min: tweer orkenen. Ist meer dan een[4] pond: saun orkenen.

[1] FG: clager. [2] FG: *se* is missing. [3] FG: *ins*. [4] FG: twa.

25. If someone intentionally enters another man's house against the wish of the other, then he must pay one pound for entering it and another pound for leaving it, or swear innocence with the help of five compurgators.

26. If someone damages another man's house out of anger and spite, so that wind enters and smoke exits the house, he will have to compensate this with half a pound and pay the penalty for breaking the peace of the *atthas* with two pounds, or swear innocence with the help of five compurgators, unless the *atthas* want to produce testimony against him.

27. If someone damages another man's house with the help of group of kinsmen, he will have to compensate the one who has suffered the loss with two pounds and with eight pounds in the district court. Then the owner of the house must swear an oath of accusation and testify under oath what kind of damage was caused and nine *atthas* must confirm this by oath, and this amount is to be paid twofold.

28. If someone damages another man's house in the course of a violent confiscation of an estate with armed forces, he will have to compensate the owner of the house with eight pounds, and with 20 pounds at the district court.

29. If someone burns or destroys another man's house, so that rafters and beams are falling down, then the penalty for breaking the peace is eighty pounds, and a threefold compensation for the owner of the house if he is prepared to give testimony under oath and if nine *atthas* confirm this by oath.

30. If someone purchases a piece of cattle, or a piece of clothing, or a four-cornered piece of fabric, and if the one who has sold it complains before court about the agreement, then he must claim the money in the district where he lives; unless the other party has the money ready; then the other with the money has a stronger case. If the other party does not have the money ready, then the claimant should claim his money with the help of witnesses.

31. If someone has given some goods to another man on credit in the presence of witnesses, he must claim his money with the help of his neighbours, if the other party has the money ready in the district where the claimant lives. If the amount is less than one pound: two witnesses. If the amount exceeds one pound: seven witnesses.

129 **32.** Hwa so claget om | een raef in syn ayn eerwe, so schil hi dat land naemna, deer hi dine schada oen deen habbe. Wil di ora dis ain urmetta etta dei deer di ora nimt, so schil hi dis forma deis to da schelta tiaen om dine aindom, jefta in da atthem. Jef hi to da schelta tiucht, so schil hi in dine bifangh twa pond setta ende di ora deer tojenst; jefta da claegh beta.

33. Hwa so een land sella wil, dat hyt ur sine ghaekerka biede alle dam deer nest wessa willet tree dagen. Jef hit nimmen capet om dat bod, soe aegh hy to da waer toe commen ende aldeer to bieden tree dagen, alle dam deer nest wessa wil. Jef hit dis tredda deis nimmen capet deer nest is, soe aghen da riuchteren hine to ferdien, deer hit oen hiara andert caped, dat him nimmen wald jefta onriucht dwe deeroen.[1]

34. Hwa so claghet om nyercaep ende di ora tioeghtet to da aina, soe fyr soe hy dat tiugh habbe, dat hyt jeer ende dei binetten[2] ende bisetten habbe, so moet hi aldeermei fri wessa; breckt him des tiuges, so fyr so di ora dat nier[3] birecknia mei, so moet hi him dine caep rema.

35. Hueck riuchter in sine eedspil mede nimt, se hit greetman, ehera, attha, schelta, tolfta, asegha, abbet, decken, papa, eedswara, bannere, wil dy clagia deer se jout, so schil di ora sine ker habba,[4] hor hi mit sine ede dis ontgonge ende mit him sex synre buren, so hi da orem toereme mit alsodena tiughe, jef hit is buppa twam pondem;[5] ist binia twam pondem, jefta twa pond, mit twam edem. Wirt[6] hy toe riucht urwonnen,[7] so schil hi dis jeris uta ede. Dat is riucht aller Fresena.

36. Saxes steke ende armborst schette: ayder twybeet.

37. Hwa so op oderis hors sit, an syn willa ende an dis oderis onwilla, so schil hi beta dine opsedel mit een ponde ende dyn ofsedel mit een odera, jefta sexasum onswara.

---

[1] FG: deer decn. [2] FG: binetten. [3] FG: nies. [4] FG: babba. [5] FG: poudem. [6] FG: wtrt. [7] FG: wrwonuen.

32. If someone brings a complaint to court about a robbery on his own estate, he must name the land on which the damage was done. If the other party wants to contest the ownership of the land at the day appointed by the other party, then he will have to appeal to the *skelta* on the first day over the ownership, or to the *atthas*. If he appeals to the *skelta*, he will have to pay a deposit of two pounds in the district court and the other party as well; or he will have to pay what was claimed.

33. If someone wants to sell a piece of land, he must offer it for sale for three days to those individuals in his parish who think they are entitled to purchase it. If no-one wants to buy it, he has to come to the district court and offer it for sale there for three days to those who think they are entitled to purchase it. If none of these persons has purchased it on the third day, then the judges have to proclaim a peace over the person who buys it in their presence, so that no-one does him any harm or injustice as a consequence of this purchase.

34. If someone brings a complaint to court about an alienation of a plot of land to a neighbouring buyer and the other maintains to be the owner; if the other can prove he was in possession of the land for a year and a day, he will be acquitted. If he lacks witnesses and the claimant can demonstrate his neighbourship, then he has to vacate the land.

35. If a judge accepts bribes in his district, be it a *gretman*, *ehera*, *attha*, *skelta*, district witness, *asega*, abbot, dean, priest, juror, *bannere*, and if the one who gave the bribe brings a complaint over this to court, then the defendant may choose whether he wants to swear innocence with the help of the oaths of six neighbours, or whether he wants to give the claimant the option to produce the same amount of witnesses to prove his complaint, if the bribe is higher than two pounds. If it is less or if it is two pounds, he may swear innocence with the help of one compurgator. If he loses the case, he will have to step out of office for a year. This is the law of all Frisians.

36. Being stabbed with a knife or shot by a crossbow: a twofold compensation is owed for each.

37. Riding another man's horse against the owner's will is to be compensated with 1 pound for mounting it, and another pound for dismounting it, or the defendant must exonerate himself with five compurgators.

38. Hiir sint lada scrioun. Herdefanges ende duustslekis, duuststowes ende duustswenges, so schil di man an sine nates hand faen ende swara dat him God alsoe helpe ende riuchte hand trowa, so hi dera deda onschieldich se. Om faxfang so schil hi faen oen synre gara ende swara so him siinre schette fia ti frome wirde so hi onschieldich se. Item bloedresene: twirasum onswara. Metedulgh: fiowerasum onswara. Faxfangh, weedscreed, fliueswerp, bloedresene, duiststeet, duistsleeck, dis is di fria Fresa nier op da helligem to witane dan hi aegh enich tiugh to ontfaen.

38. Here the oaths of innocence are written down. In case of grabbing someone by the shoulders, hard blows or pushes or swings, the defendant must grab the hand of his relative and swear that God may help him and judge over this hand-oath, that he is innocent of this act. In case of hair grabbing he must take his own clothes in his hand and swear on the loss of his cattle that he is innocent. Also, for a bleeding wound: two oaths, for a measure wound: four oaths. Hair grabbing, cutting someone's clothes, pushing someone into the water, bleeding wounds, hard push, hard blow; in case of all these offences, a free Frisian may testify of his innocence by swearing an oath on the holy relics rather than having to listen to any testimony to the contrary.

XIV. The Calculated Tariffs

Hyr biginnet dae birecknada botha

1. Duustsleeck, duuststeet, duustschou, duustsuengh ende herdefengh: allereeck fiower penningen jefta mit eenre hand ontswara.

2. Dustsleeck deer is XXI nachta weden ende wanfel: dio bote is XII graet jefta twirasum ontswara. Eenbeet ende oenbrins.

3. Dustsleeck deer is XLII nachta weden ende wanfel: dio bote is IIII schillinghen jefta fiowerasum onswara. Eenbeet ende oenbrins.

4. Dustsleeck deer is LXIII nachta weden ende wanfel: dio bote is sex schillingen jefta sexasum ontswara. Jef da riuchteren jefta da tolven habbet dat bischowet, so is hi nier mit ene ede oen to bringen. Eenbeet ende oenbrins.

5. Tien duustsleken, XX, XXX, ende een duustsleeck in een kase dat is algaer seid een dustsleeck to recnien, alsoe fiir soe hit naet weden ner wanfel is.

6. Dauiddusinga[1] is dat een menscha slain se also seer, dattet him itta ara dawid ende duset: so is dio bote XXXVI[2] graet. Eenbeet.

7. Duustslekis bote op syn fria hals, fyf fingeren breed twisscha[3] weed ende schreed: dio bote is fiower schillingen jefta fiowerasum onswara ende neen onbringh daya, alsoe fyr soe hit mitter blata hand deen se ende bi hela fel se.
131 Eenbeet ende onbrins.[4] |

[1] FG: Dauid dusniga. [2] FG: xvi. [3] FG: tuissha. [4] FG: *on*.

XIV. The Calculated Tariffs

Here Begin the Calculated Tariffs

1. A hard blow, a hard thrust, a hard push, a hard swinging blow and grabbing a man by the shoulders: each of these 4 pennies or the defendant may exonerate himself with one oath.

2. A hard blow which leaves a man black and blue for 21 nights: the compensation is 12 groats or the defendant may exonerate himself with one compurgator. The compensation is single and the claimant may substantiate his claim with an oath.

3. A hard blow which leaves a man black and blue for 42 nights: the compensation is 4 shillings or the defendant may exonerate himself with three compurgators. The compensation is single and the claimant may substantiate his claim with an oath.

4. A hard blow which leaves a man black and blue for 63 nights: the compensation is 6 shillings or the defendant may exonerate himself with five compurgators. If the judges or the jury have ascertained this, the claimant has more right to swear an oath to substantiate his claim than the defendant has to exonerate himself by swearing an oath. The compensation is single and the claimant may substantiate his claim with an oath.

5. Ten, twenty or thirty hard blows as well as a hard blow in a fight are all to be counted as one single hard blow, provided they do not leave the victim black and blue.

6. Deaf-dizziness means that a man is hit so hard that his ears remain deaf and ringing as a consequence: the compensation for this is 36 groats. The compensation is single.

7. A hard blow on a man's free neck, which has a breadth of five fingers and is located between a man's clothes and hair: the compensation is 4 shillings or the defendant may exonerate himself with three compurgators, and if it is done with the bare hand and the skin is left unscathed, the claimant may not substantiate his claim with an oath. The compensation is single and the claimant may substantiate his claim with an oath.

8. Swymslekis bote is fyf einsa, fiower schillinghen ende fiower graet, dat is dio landis wilker. Item: nei da bota fyf schillinghen. So schillet swara tween trowe maen, dat hia dat oensagen dat hi oen swyme lege, jefta fiowerasum onswara.

9. Tree swymsleken, tree eerdfallen ende tria wapelpina habbet al een riucht ende al een bota. Da hagista: fyf schillingen; da middelsta: xxvi graet; da minsta: xiiii graet.

10. Faxfangh: acht graet jefta twirasum onswara.

11. Birdfangh om den mond: XVI graet.

12. Faxfangh binia oen da buke: XXXII graet.

13. Faxfangh op da aeghhlid: VI graet.

14. Faxfangh ondera eerme: IIII graet.

15. Heerscreden: acht graet.

16. Bird offbaernd jefta kaeld jefta offscherren ur syn willa, soe is dio bote fiardahael pond.

17. Hwam so ma syn haud bischert mit wald, dat ma him halt ende bynt, dat is acht pond ende sexteen graet.

18. Jef ma een frowa mit wald her frislen offsnyt, soe schel ma her beta mit acht eynsem.

19. Jef ma een man syn heer ofsinght, so is dio bote fyf pond; jef met alheel offsinght, soe is dio bote tien pond ende da lada sex eden fan dissem.

20. Hweer so ma een frowa faxfangen deth jefta duustsleken jefta bloedresena jefta jelkirs dulginga ende hio naet fiuchtende is, so is her bote da fiarda penningh mara so met een man dwee. Eenbeet ende oenbrins.

8. A knock-out is to be compensated with 5 ounces, 4 shillings, and 4 groats, according to the statutes of the land. Also: according to the composition tariffs 5 shillings. Two reliable men must swear that they saw the victim lying unconscious, or the defendant may exonerate himself with three compurgators.

9. Three knock-outs, three blows which make a man fall on the ground, and three blows which make a man fall into the water are all to be treated the same and require the same compensation. The highest degree: 5 shillings; the middle degree: 26 groats; the lowest degree: 14 groats.

10. Grabbing a man by the hair: 8 groats or the defendant may exonerate himself with one compurgator.

11. Grabbing a man by the beard around the mouth: 16 groats.

12. Grabbing a man by the hair below the belly: 32 groats.

13. Grabbing a man by the hair on the eyelid: 6 groats.

14. Grabbing a man by the hair in the armpit: 4 groats.

15. Cutting off a man's hair: 8 groats.

16. Singeing a man's beard, or making him bald or shaving off his beard against his will is to be compensated with 3½ pounds.

17. Shaving a man's head with violence, that is that he is held fast and bound, this costs 8 pounds and 16 groats.

18. If a woman's braids are cut off with violence, she must be compensated with 8 ounces.

19. If a man's hair is singed off, the compensation is 5 pounds; if it is singed off completely, the compensation is 10 pounds, or the defendant may exonerate himself with five compurgators.

20. If a woman suffers hair grabbing or hard blows or bloody wounds or any kind of injury and she does not struggle against her attacker, she is to be compensated one-third higher than if a man would suffer this. The compensation is single and the claimant may substantiate her claim with an oath.

Flïueswirp

21. Hweer so een man wirt weet ende wasich fan een orem: dio bote is VIII graet jefta sexasum onswara.

22. Flïueswirp in een banda sylroda: dio bote is V schillingen jefta sexasum ontswara.

23. Jefter een man word worpen in een onwad wetter, dat hi[1] mit aghenem mei siaen hor himel ner eerda, ner dine grond reka mitta handen ner mit foten, soe schil ma him beta mit eenre lioedwirden. Trybeet ende oenbrins jefta tolwasum
132 ontswara. |

24. Bloedresene: VIII pennighen jefta twirasum onswarra.

25. Dio bloedresene blicande onder da claen: XXXII pennighen jefta twirasum onswara.

26. Bloedresena onder da frislem: VIII graet.

27. Bloedresen onder da andlete mit wlite: I pond.

28. Bloedresene trugh da tonge: V schillengen.[2]

29. Bloedresene onder dera tonghe jefta dullich onder da tonghe als hit jelkars is oen da felle.

30. Bloedresena truch dyne hals ende[3] truch da sida: etta eind XVI engelsch ende bi da odera eind also fulla.

31. Jeff een man wirth[4] mangera bloedresen deen, mey hy da bispanna,[5] soe schil ma dat beta jef hi dat swarra wil dattet him deen se to ene steck ofta to ene sleek. So mei ma da twa bloedresena garia to ene meteduligh.

32. Ende tria bloedresena to twa metedulgen ende to eenre bloedresena mei ma da garia.

---

[1] FG: *hi* is missing. [2] FG: shill*engen*. [3] FG: eu*de*. [4] FG: wirht. [5] FG: bispana.

Throwing a Man into Water

21. If a man becomes wet and muddy through another man's doing, the compensation is 8 groats or the defendant may exonerate himself with five compurgators.

22. Throwing a man into a public sluice-way: the compensation is 5 shillings or the defendant may exonerate himself with five compurgators.

23. If a man is thrown into deep water, so that he can see neither earth nor sky with his eyes, nor touch the ground with his hands or feet, he is to be compensated with a small wergild. The compensation is threefold and the claimant may substantiate his claim with an oath, or the defendant may exonerate himself with eleven compurgators.

24. A bleeding wound: 8 pennies or the defendant must exonerate himself with one compurgator.

25. A visible bleeding wound underneath the clothes: 32 pennies or the defendant may exonerate himself with one compurgator.

26. A bleeding wound underneath the tresses: 8 groats.

27. A bleeding wound in the face with mutilation: 1 pound.

28. A bleeding wound through the tongue: 5 shillings.

29. A bleeding wound under the tongue or an injury under the tongue is to be compensated just as injuries elsewhere on the skin.

30. A bleeding wound which penetrates the neck or the side: 16 English pennies for the intrusion and the same amount for the extrusion.

31. If a man suffers several bleeding wounds and he is able to span them, he must be compensated for them if he wants to swear that they were inflicted to him with one single stab or one blow. In this case, the two bleeding wounds may be added up and counted as one measure wound.

32. And three bleeding wounds may be added up and counted as two measure wounds and one bleeding wound.

33. Item: fyf bloedresena schil ma een man beta ende naet mangra ner hit se dat da deen se toe een stecke jef to een sleeke ende ma[1] da bispanna mei.

34. Hweer so een man op syn fria hals slain wirth ende hi haet een bloedresena, dio bote is XVI penninghen.[2]

35. Hweer so een man[3] haet een bloedresene also seer, dat hire oen to bed lidse ende burkud is ende gaekud ende him syn prester fandlet, soe is hi nyer da bloedresene to wytan ende riuchte intaingha aldeertoe.

Fan da haude

36. Hwam so ma[4] slacht jefta mit yrsen syuth jefta mit holte jeff mit stupa oen syn haud, dat ma him snya schil, so aegh hi dan des snides twa einsa. So aeg ma him om toe metten bi da lingra igh bi des tumma knockela langh, aller meta lyc XVI penninghen. Ende dat mei een ede oen to bringhen, dat hy den snei naet deen habbe oem nene fyafollinghe mer om sine liwes sonda.[5]

37. Jeff dii man truchgrioud[6] wert, so is dio boet fiiftahael merck; dat schillet
133 bihoda presteren ende riuchteren bi hiara ede ende bi hiara sele, | dat hi des naet ontbara mochte.

38. Inreed int haud: VIII schillingen.

39. Di beenbreeck in der breinpanna: fiower schillingen.

40. Tre beenbrecken schil ma beta in der breinpanna ende naet meer.

41. Dis elkerlyck schil ma beta mei fiower schillingen.

42. Dio screden oen da haud is fyf schillingen to bote, mey hit meer halda so een meta.

43. Dis forma benis utgongh dera breinpanna: XXXII graet.

44. Dis lettera benis utgong: XVI graet.

---

[1] FG: *ma* is missing. [2] FG: peni*n*ghen. [3] FG: *ma.* [4] FG: Huasoma. [5] FG: sines sonda. [6] FG: trnch grioud.

33. Also: five bleeding wounds inflicted on a man must be compensated, and no more, unless they were done to him by one single stab or blow and he is able to span them.

34. If a man is struck on his free neck and this causes a bleeding wound, the compensation is 16 pennies.

35. If a man has a bleeding wound which is so severe that he has to keep to his bed and this is known to his neighbours and in his village, and if his priest comes to visit him, then he has more right to substantiate his claim to this bleeding wound and also to the side-effects of this deed than the defendant has to exonerate himself by swearing an oath.

Concerning the Head

36. If a man is struck on the head—or shot with iron—with a piece of wood or with a club, such that a physician has to make an incision, then the injured man must receive 2 ounces for this incision. Furthermore, the wound must be measured around along the longer side by the length of the upper knuckle-bone of the thumb, each measure to be compensated with 16 pennies. And the physician has to swear that he did not make the incision for the sake of a (higher) compensation but only for the sake of his patient's health.

37. If a man is trepanned (by a physician), the compensation is 4½ marks. The priests and judges have to confirm with their oaths and upon their souls that he could not do without it.

38. A penetrating injury in the head: 8 shillings.

39. Bone fracture in the skull: 4 shillings.

40. Up to three bone fractures in the skull must be compensated, and no more.

41. Each of these must be compensated with 4 shillings.

42. A cut on the head is to be compensated with 5 shillings, if it is longer than one measure.

43. Protrusion of the first bone splinter from the skull: 32 groats.

44. Protrusion of the second bone splinter: 16 groats.

45. Dis tredda benis utgongh: viii graet. Somlike bota willet dat dis forma benis utgongh se fiouwer schillinghen, dis lettera tween schillingen, dis tredda een schillingh. So schil hyt swara mit ene ede, dat met mochte hera clippa in een lewyn, jef hit foel fan sine kne ur ix stapen; jelkirs thoer met naet beta.

46. Breindulg: tolef pond.[1]

47. Benis onstal: vi graet, to halien mei en eed.

48. Beenstallich: vi graet, sonder eed.

Ergens in da haed

49. Jef en man sprect dat hi[2] dam fiarendel ergra se in da haud jef oen syn haud, so schil hi habba een pond. Spreckt hi dat hy da haldeel eergera se in syn haud, so schil hi habba tria pond; dat schil hy winna mit trim edem.

50. Dio eergens ural in da haud: acht pond.

51. Dio dawid in da haud: iiii pond.

52. Hweer so en man dulget wirt in syn haed jef oen syn haud, dawid him syn haud aldeerfan, so is dio bote achteenstehael pond.

Is hi daef

53. Dawid him syn haud binna jeer ende binna dei, so is dio bote alsoe.

54. Ne mei hi an bedde, an wige ner an weinden, an huis ner an godeshuse, ner mit sine wive alsoe wessa, soe hy eer mochte, ner bi sine fiore, ner an nener ferthe, deer hi ferra schil, soe is dis allerekis toe bote xii graet, bikant ma dis dulgis. Eenbeet ende oenbrins.

Van wirsenakerf

55. Dio forme wirsenakerf: xxx penningen; dio lettere also stoer, dio tredde
134 alsoe. Dera | elkerlyck een eed.

[1] FG: xii pond tolef pond. [2] FG: *hi* is missing.

45. Protrusion of the third bone splinter: 8 groats. Some composition tariffs claim that protrusion of the first splinter would be 4 shillings, of the second 2 shillings, and of the third 1 shilling. Then he must swear with an oath that the splinter could be heard sounding from a distance of nine steps if it fell from knee-high into a bowl; otherwise it doesn't require compensation.

46. A brain injury: 12 pounds.

47. When a bone splinter gets stuck (in the wound): 6 groats, and the claimant has to swear an oath to substantiate his claim.

48. If an injury causes flesh to stick to the bone: 6 groats, without an oath.

Paresis in the Head

49. If a man declares that he is suffering from paresis for a quarter part either inside his head or on his head, then he must receive 1 pound. If he declares that he is suffering from paresis for half a part in his head, then he must receive 3 pounds; he must support his claim with three oaths.

50. Paresis everywhere inside the head: 8 pounds.

51. Insensibility in the head: 4 pounds.

52. If a man is wounded inside his head or on his head, and his head becomes insensible, the compensation is 17½ pounds.

If He Is Insensible

53. If he becomes insensible within a year and a day, this is to be compensated likewise.

54. If he cannot be as good in bed, on a horse nor in a cart, at home nor in church, nor with his wife as he used to be, nor at his fireplace, nor at any expedition he has to undertake, then each of these instances is to be compensated with 12 groats, if the defendant confesses. The compensation is single and the claimant may substantiate his claim with an oath.

Cutting the Wrinkles of the Brow

55. Cutting the first wrinkle: 30 pennies; the second just as much, the third likewise. The defendant has to swear an oath for each wrinkle.

56. Hweer so dio wirsen truchslain is oen dat been endma hit naet scuva mei, dat hit glida ne mei, so is dio arste wirsen een pond, dio oder XXX penningen, dio tredde XX penningen.

57. Jef dat dulgh geet alinga der wirsena ende hio naet tokoren se, soe aegh hit naet meer to bote dan hit jelkirs oen da felle se.

Fan da agenen

58. Dat fore aegh mit XIIII pond.

59. Dat winster mit XIII pondem to beten ende bi da sida V merck sonder wald.

60. Ongneilis[1] inscatinga: sex graet.

61. Dat aegh staerbliind,[2] dioe bote een merck.

62. Jef di aeghappel uta haud is, so is dio bote X pond. Selc haet XX pond ende bi dae sida XXXII pond.

63. Hwer so dat age al stalfestich is in da haude ende hit naet biseppen is, so schil hi een metadulgh oenswara. So mei hi alsodeen intaynga wita oen der sioen alser in der here. So is dio bote dera sioen dera trira deel elkerlyc tredda-hael pond fan der bota, so fyr so dat metedulgh oenbrocht se als fan der heer.

Eergens fan der sioen

64. Hwa so dio[3] sioen fan da age da[4] fiaerndeel ara is, soe aegh hi toe bote treddahael pond. Tribeet.

Fan der sioen

65. Spreckt hi dat dae treddele urlerren se, so is dio bote achtahael pond.

66. Aegbreedkerf[5] buppa da age: XXXII penningen.

67. Dis aeghbreedkerf binia da aghe: XXIIII penningen.[6]

[1] FG: Ongneliis. [2] FG: scaerbliind. [3] FG: di. [4] FG: dio. [5] FG: Regbreedkerf. [6] FG: pe*n*nningen.

56. If the wrinkle has been cut to the bone and one can no longer frown because the skin has become immobile: the first wrinkle is 1 pound, the second 30 pennies, and the third 20 pennies.

57. If the cut traces the wrinkle and the wrinkle has not been cut across, then this injury does not exact a higher compensation than if it were elsewhere in the skin.

Concerning the Eyes

58. The loss of the right eye is to be compensated with 14 pounds.

59. The loss of the left eye is to be compensated with 13 pounds, and according to the custom 5 marks, not counting the compensation for the violent deed which caused it.

60. Damage to the corner of the eye: 6 groats.

61. If the eye is partly blinded, the compensation is 1 mark.

62. If the eyeball has come out of the head, then the compensation is 10 pounds. Some composition tariffs have 20 pounds, and it is 32 pounds according to the custom.

63. If the eye is entirely motionless in the head, and if it is not moist, the claimant may claim a measure wound with an oath. He can then claim the same compensations for side-effects for his sight as is the case with hearing. Thus the compensation for the loss of the three quarters of the sight is 2½ pounds each, provided that, as with hearing, a measure wound has been claimed.

Paresis of the Sight

64. If a man's eyesight is paralysed for a quarter part, he is to be compensated with 2½ pounds. The compensation is threefold.

Concerning Sight

65. If he declares that he has lost three quarters (of his sight), the compensation is 7½ pounds.

66. Cutting the eyelid above the eye: 32 pennies.

67. Cutting the eyelid below the eye: 24 pennies.

Van da kinbacke

68. Hwam so syn kinbacka twa worpen wirt, jefta mit een swerde slayn ende hi synre sondena naet nath,[1] wirt hio bicand, so schil ma hem beta mit XX pondem. Bicant ma him naet, so ne moet hy fora oenswara dan hi[2] da tree delen urlerren habbe: so schil hy habba XV pond. Dat pond is hyr saun graet.

69. Twira tzakena breeck, dio bote is IIII schillingen.

70. Di beenbreck oen der tziaka: XXXII penningen.[3]

71. Snawelbreeck: IIII schillingen ende haet beenbreeck deer ma dan schoye
135 ende dat se XXI nachta weden | ende wanfel, so schil ma dat beta aldeerto. Eenbeet ende oenbrins.

72. Inreed in da tziaka: XVI graet ende in den mond also stoer.

73. Werbreeck, also fyr so dio were tild[4] se fan da tosschen, so aegh hi enis inreed in sine mond ende een weerbrekis ende een wlytwimelsa, so is dera elkerlyc XVI graet.

74. Jef dio weer een dam standen haet, soe aegh dis weerbrekis bote naet meer[5] dan jelkirs on der andleten; dat dullich schil ma beta nei synre meta. Dit is algaer oenbrins.

75. Wlitewimelsa is XXXII penningen, dat schil wessa onder dera[6] neersta wirsene; dat dulligh aldeerthi to beten, alsoe graet[7] als hit is. Oenbrins.

Fan da tonga

76. Dat dullich jefta bloed oen der tongha also als jelkirs oen da felle. Trybeet.

77. Bloedresene trugh da tonge: fyf schillingen ende oenbrins.

78. Dis fellis oenflecht: XIIII penningen.

---

[1] FG: bicant. [2] FG: bi. [3] FG: pe*n*nningen. [4] FG: til. [5] FG: mee*n*r. [6] FG: eera. [7] FG: gsaet.

Concerning the Jaw

68. If a man's jaw is cast in two or struck with a sword and as a consequence he is not as healthy as he used to be, he is to be compensated with 20 pounds, if it has been confessed by the defendant. If it is not confessed, the claimant may not declare any more than that he has lost the three quarters (of his former health), and he is to have 15 pounds then. Here a pound is 7 groats.

69. A fracture of both jaws is to be compensated with 4 shillings.

70. A fracture in the jaw: 32 pennies.

71. Tearing the corner of the mouth: 4 shillings, and whatever breaking of a bone is ascertained then, and if the victim is black and blue there for 21 days, these claims must be compensated in addition. The compensation is single and the claimant may substantiate his claim with an oath.

72. Penetration of the jaw: 16 groats, and penetration of the mouth likewise.

73. A tear of the lip, to such an extent that the lip is elevated from the teeth, this is to be compensated with the compensations for penetration of the mouth, for a tear of the lip, and for a mutilation of the face, each amounting to 16 groats.

74. If part of the lip has been left intact, the compensation for the tear of the lip is not higher than if the injury were located anywhere else in the face; the injury is to be compensated according to its length. The claimant may substantiate his claim with an oath.

75. Mutilation of the face is to be compensated with 32 pennies; this means that the injury must be located beneath the lowest wrinkle; to this must be added the compensation for the injury itself, according to its size. The claimant may substantiate his claim with an oath.

Concerning the Tongue

76. An injury on the tongue or a bleeding tongue is to be compensated as if it were anywhere else on the skin. The compensation is threefold.

77. A bleeding wound through the tongue: 5 shillings, and the claimant may substantiate his claim with an oath.

78. Excoriation of the skin: 14 pennies.

79. Dis adema utgongh: XXIIII penningen.

80. Seweris utgongh: XXIIII penningen.

81. Di beenbrec oen der tziaka ende di beenbreck dis onberna benis, dio bote is elkerlyck[1] XXXII penningen.

82. Tussches breck bote is XXXII penninghen.

83. Keesbreeck: XVI penningen.

84. Tusch gersfallich: VIII pond.

85. Kese gersfallich: IIII pond.

Fan der spreeck

86. Hwa so syn spreeck binimen wirt, so is dio bote X pond; so ne mey hy meer oenswara so da tree delen. Eenbeet ende oenbrins.

Eergen thera spreeck ende dera here

87. Hwa so dio spreec binimen is to da fiarndeel, so is dio bota vi einsa; thi da halndeel: XII einsa; sint da tre delen awei, so sintet XVIII eynsa.

88. Van der here ist also; aldeerto so aegh ma dat dullich to beten.

Fan da noes

89. Hwam so dio noes al of is, so sintet VI pond ende bi da sida XXXII pond.

90. Gerstelkerf oen dere noes: VIII scillingen. Di scilling is hyr I grata.

91. Beenbrec oen dera noes: XV graet.

[1] FG: elkeelyck.

79. The outflow of breath: 24 pennies.

80. The outflow of spittle: 24 pennies.

81. Bone fracture of the jaw and a bone fracture of the root of a tooth are each to be compensated with 32 pennies.

82. The compensation for fracture of a tooth is 32 pennies.

83. Fracture of a molar: 16 pennies.

84. Knocking out a tooth: 8 pounds.

85. Knocking out a molar: 4 pounds.

Concerning Speech

86. If a man has been deprived of his speech, the compensation is 10 pounds; the claimant cannot claim more by oath than (the loss of) three quarters. The compensation is single and the claimant may substantiate his claim with an oath.

Paresis of Speech and Hearing

87. If a man has been deprived of a quarter part of his speech, the compensation is 6 ounces; if he has lost half, the compensation is 12 ounces; if three quarters are missing, the compensation is 18 ounces.

88. The same applies to hearing; to this the compensation for the injury itself must be added.

Concerning the Nose

89. If someone's nose has been completely severed, this is to be compensated with 6 pounds, and according to the custom with 32 pounds.

90. A cut on the nose cartilage: 8 shillings. Here a shilling is 1 groat.

91. A bone fracture of the nose: 15 groats.

136 **92.** Jef dis benis aet ofslain is mitter noes, so is dio bote | XVI graet ende triibeet ende dat dulgh om to metten bi da igge ende aller meta lyck triibeet. Tho disse boethem XXXII pond.

93. Inreed in da noes: XVI graet, dat dulligh[1] deerto ty beten.

Fan da arem

94. Wa so trugh siin aer staet wirth, dio boet is VIII graet.

95. Gerstelbreeck oen da are: XVI penningen.

96. Truch dyne aerlippa: fiiff graet.

97. Ayderis aerclevis boete: III pond, dat is sex eynsa.

98. Birdbreeck:[2] XXXII[3] penningen.

99. Jef dat are al of is slain jefta koren, dio bote IIII schillenghen ende bi da sida VIII pond ende XIIII einsa.

Fan da halse

100. Hweer so di hals is truchstaet, so scil ma hine metta bi da cortera igge, aller meta lyc VIII graet ende itta aidera ein XVI penningen. Ende truch dae sida dat selve riucht.

101. Beenbreck[4] oen da halse: XVI graet.

102. Inreed in den hals also fulla; so fyr so hit metadulgh se ende dat oenbrocht se, so mei hi da bota mit en eed winna, dat dulg beta derto also jelkirs wirt bet. Ende dat dulg on da strotbolla ende dat oenbrocht se, so mei hi des bota mit en eed winna.

103. So moet hi foerd swarra mit en[5] eed den gerstelkerf, so is dio boete XVI graet.

---

[1] FG: dnlligh. [2] FG: Birdbreeck fan da aerem. These last three words represent a rubric that became inserted into the text. [3] FG: *xxx*. [4] FG: Been ereck. J109: Been breck. [5] FG: *en* is missing.

92. If some piece of bone has been cut off together with the nose, the compensation is 16 groats—threefold—and the wound is to be measured around the edge and each measure is to be compensated threefold. To these compensations 32 pounds must be added.

93. Penetration of the nose: 16 groats, and to this the compensation for the injury itself must be added.

Concerning the Ears

94. If a man is stabbed through his ear, the compensation is 8 groats.

95. Fracture of the cartilage of the ear: 16 pennies.

96. Piercing the earlobe: 5 groats.

97. The compensation for splitting each ear: 3 pounds, that is, 6 ounces.

98. Damaging the beard: 32 pennies.

99. If a man's ear has been completely struck off or cut off, the compensation is 4 shillings, and 8 pounds and 14 ounces according to the custom.

Concerning the Neck

100. If a man's neck has been pierced, the wound must be measured along the shorter side, each measure to be compensated with 8 groats, and for each end of the wound 16 pennies. If a man's side has been pierced, he must be compensated likewise.

101. Bone fracture in the neck: 16 groats.

102. Penetration of the neck is to be compensated likewise; if it concerns a measure wound and the claimant has substantiated his claim to this, he may obtain the compensation by swearing an oath, and the compensation for the injury itself must be added, amounting to the same as if it were anywhere else on the body. And if the injury on the throat has been substantiated, then he may obtain the compensation for this with an oath.

103. He may furthermore substantiate his claim to cutting the cartilage by swearing one oath, and the compensation is 16 groats.

***Eergens dera sprecke*[1]**

104. Hweer so een man in dine strotbolla dulghet wirt ende wirt him dio spreecke dae fiaerndeel ara, so aegh hi fiower pond; wirt hio da helfte ara: sex pond.

105. Sint da tweer delen awei: tien pond, allerlyc oen to bringhen mit een sonderlinga eed. Fan der here, fan der sione ende fan der tongha[2] dat selve riucht.

Fan da beenbrecken

106. Beenbreck bynia da brein: XVI graet.

107. Di beenbreeck oen der tziaka ende di beenbreck dis onberna benis, dio bote is elkerlyc XXXII penningen.

108. Di beenbreck[3] oen da halse: XXXII penningen.

109. Di beenbreck[4] opper axla: XXXII penninghen.[5]

137 110. Wydebeens breck: XVI penninghen. |

111. Burstbenis brec: IIII schillingen.

112. Beenbreck on da scholderum: XXXII penningen.

113. Ribbesbenis breck: een einsa.

114. Trya reb schil ma bete ende naet meer.

115. Rib mit swirde tokoren: XXXII penningen allerlyck.

116. Quembenis breck: XXXII penningen.

117. Regbenis breek: twa einsa.

118. Beenbreck oen da eermis mergh ende oen dat tieghmerg: fiower schillengen ende dat inreed in dat eermmergh ende tieghmerg: also IIII schillenghen.

[1] FG: spreckr. [2] FG: to*n*hga. [3] FG: beerbreck. [4] FG: bennbreck. [5] FG: penniughen.

Deterioration of Speech

104. If a man is wounded in his throat, and his speech becomes paralysed for a quarter part, then he must receive 4 pounds; if it becomes half paralysed: 6 pounds.

105. If two-thirds are wanting: 10 pounds, and the claims to each of these parts must be substantiated by the claimant by swearing a separate oath. The same rule applies to hearing, sight, and the tongue.

Concerning Fractures

106. Bone fracture below the brain: 16 groats.

107. Bone fracture in the jaw and a bone fracture of the root of a tooth are each to be compensated with 32 pennies.

108. Bone fracture in the neck: 32 pennies.

109. Bone fracture in the shoulder joint: 32 pennies.

110. Bone fracture in the clavicle: 16 pennies.

111. Bone fracture in the sternum: 4 shillings.

112. Bone fracture in the shoulders: 32 pennies.

113. Fracture of a rib: 1 ounce.

114. Up to three ribs must be compensated, and no more.

115. If a rib has been cut with a sword: each 32 pennies.

116. Fracture of the coccyx: 32 pennies.

117. Bone fracture in the back: 2 ounces.

118. Bone fracture in the marrow of the arm and in the marrow of the thigh: 4 shillings, and a penetrating wound into the marrow of the arm and into the marrow of the thigh: also 4 shillings.

119. Hertbleddis beenbreck: IIII schillenghen.

120. Di beenbreck oen da eermschet: XXXII penningen.

121. Di beenbreek oen da handwirst: XII graet.

122. Di beenbreck binya da ursta knoecla ende dat ursta lyd oen da fingher: XVI penningen.

123. Dy beenbreck oen der ander kaet aldernest: VI graet.

124. Dy beenbreck oen der nesta kaet: twa graet.

125. Di beenbrek oen der knesciwa: IIII schillengen. Aldus sint da beenbrecken oen da sconckum als hia on da eermen, oen da tanen als on da fingheren. Disse vorscriounda dulgh deerto ti beten.

Benena utgong

126. Dis forma benis utgongh sonder dera breinpanna, hweer so hit[1] is on da been: XXXII penningen.

127. Des odera benis utgongh: XVI penningen.

128. Des tredda benis utgongh:[2] VIII penningen. Mit ene ede scil hi dine beenbreck[3] wita eer hi dera bena utgong mei habba. Also als hi dat metedulg onbrocht[4] haet oen dine man deer hyt oenkaltet, so scil hi dine beenbrek ende dera bena utgong allereeck mit ene ede oenbringa, ief hi da boeta habba wil; hi wite self dat hi riucht dwe.

129. Dis onberna benis utgong aeg nen bote.

Fan da liidweien

130. Lydwei op da halsknaep: IIII schillingen, dat dulg deerto ti beten,[5] is hit bloedresen, is hit metedulg, also fyr so hit oenbrocht se; is hit aet mara, aldeerto ti beten.

---

[1] FG: hi. [2] FG: wtgo*n*h. [3] FG: beenbrcck. [4] FG: o*n*hrocht. [5] FG: heten.

119. Bone fracture in the shoulder blade: 4 shillings.

120. Bone fracture in the armpit: 32 pennies.

121. Bone fracture in the wrist: 12 groats.

122. Bone fracture in the upper knuckle or the upper joint of the finger: 16 pennies.

123. Bone fracture in the second bone: 6 groats.

124. Bone fracture in the next bone: 2 groats.

125. Bone fracture in the kneecap: 4 shillings. Thus, the compensations for bone fractures in the legs run parallel to bone fractures in the arms, and the compensations for bone fractures in the toes run parallel to those in the fingers. To these must be added the compensations that are mentioned above.

Protrusion of Bone Splinters

126. Protrusion of the first bone splinter from anywhere except the skull: 32 pennies.

127. Protrusion of the second bone splinter: 16 pennies.

128. Protrusion of the third bone splinter: 8 pennies. The claimant must first testify a bone fracture with one oath, before he can claim a protrusion of bone splinters. In the same way as he has substantiated his claim to a measure wound against the man he is holding responsible, likewise he must substantiate his claims to a bone fracture and a protrusion of bone splinters with one oath each, if he wants to be compensated for it; the claimant may testify himself that he is acting according to the law.

129. The protrusion of the root of a tooth or molar is not to be compensated.

Concerning Sprains of the Limbs

130. A sprain of the nape of the neck: 4 shillings, and to this must be added the compensation for the injury itself, whether it is a bleeding wound or a measure wound, insofar as the claims to this have been substantiated; if it is a little more, this must be compensated too.

138 **131.** Lydwei opper axla: XXXII[1] penninghen. |

132. Lydwei itta eermboga: XXXII penninghen.

133. Lydwey itter handwirst:[2] tweer schillinghen.

134. Lydwey itta wrsta knocla: een eynsa.

135. Etta middelsta knocla: sexteen penninghen.

136. Etta ursta knocla bi dae neyl: XII penninghen.

137. Neylkerff:[3] XVI penningan.

138. Lidwey oen da hande:[4] V schillingen, dat dulgh deerto ti beten. Aldus sint da lidwegen oen sconkum als hia oen da eermen sint, oen da tanen als oen da fingeren.

Synkerf

139. Halssynkerf: IIII einsa.

140. Hoxena synkerf: in aydera hoxena twa sina; elk syn fan dam aider twa einsa.

141. Heelsynekerf: IIII einsa. Jelkirs sint da siinkerf[5] bihala disse sex algaer een einse, mit ene eed to winnen, dat dulg deertoe thi beten.

142. Truchgungende dulg truch dyn eerm ende truch diin schonck: di ingungh ende di utgungh ayder een eynsa,[6] so fyr so deer helis fellis een meta twisscha se; is deer neen meta twisscha, so sintet twa bloedresena.

143. Hweer so di ingungh ende di utgungh[7] is oen fingerem jefta tanum: aider een einsa, hoder so deer minra jefta mara helis fellis atwisscha se.

[1] FG: xvxii. [2] FG: haudwirst. [3] FG: Neykerff. [4] FG: haude. [5] FG: sii*n*kcrf. [6] FG: eysa. [7] FG: en*de* di wtgu*n*gh en*de* di wtgu*n*gh.

131. A sprain of the shoulder: 32 pennies.

132. A sprain of the elbow: 32 pennies.

133. A sprain of the wrist: 2 shillings.

134. A sprain of the lower joint (of the finger): 1 ounce.

135. A sprain of the middle joint (of the finger): 16 pennies.

136. A sprain of the upper joint (of the finger) next to the nail: 12 pennies.

137. Cutting the nail: 16 pennies.

138. A sprain of the hand: 5 shillings, and to this must be added the compensation for the injury itself. Thus, the compensations for sprains of the legs run parallel to those of the arms, and the compensations for those of the toes run parallel to those of the fingers.

Cutting Sinews

139. Cutting the sinew of the neck: 4 ounces.

140. Cutting a sinew in the hollow of the knee: there are two sinews in each hollow, and each of these is to be compensated with 2 ounces.

141. Cutting the sinew of the heel: 4 ounces. Apart from these six cases, cutting a sinew is to be compensated with 1 ounce, to be obtained by swearing an oath, and to this must be added the compensation for the injury itself.

142. A perforating wound through the arm or through the leg: 1 ounce for the intrusion of the weapon and 1 ounce for the extrusion, provided there is a measure of unscathed skin between the two; if this is not the case, then the wound is to be compensated as two bleeding wounds.

143. If the intrusion and the extrusion of the weapon are in fingers or toes: each 1 ounce, irrespective of whether there is more or less than a measure of unscathed skin between the two.

Truch da hand

144. Di beenbrec, truchgongende dulg truch da handbird: een pond, dat dulg deerto thi beten.

Van lamthe

145. Jefter immen sprect dat hi oen sine eermen jefta oen sine handen, oen sine sconken jef oen sine foten lam se, so is dio bote XXVII[1] einsa.

146. Jefter immen haet lam fingeren jefta tanen, so is dio bote een merck.

Eergens oen eermen ende sconken, handen ende foten

147. Jefter immen eergens hab buppa dera lamthe, so is dio minste eergens VII einsa, dio middelste XIIII einsa, dio maeste eergens XXI eynsa; dit is fan eermen ende sconken.

148. Jefter fingeren jefta tanen habbet eergens, so is dio minste een einse, dio middelste II einsa, dyo maeste tria einsa.

139 **149.** Item: dio mare eergens oen da fingeren: | dio aerste XXX einsa, dio oder LII, dio tredde LXXIII, bi hwita penningen to recknien.

Lam tuma

150. Is di tuma lam ende dat hine bihalden haet, so is dio bote III pond.

Eergens oen da tuma

151. Jef di tuma haet een eergens, so is dio minste X graet, dio middelste XX graet, dio maeste XXX graet.

152. Alle eergens schil ma del tiaen to da neilen, naet op da live, ende hia sint in da eermen ende in da schoncken allyck.

Tuma of

153. Jef een menscha dat urste lid fan da tuma of is, so is dio bote IIII einsa.

[1] FG: xxvi.

Perforation of the Hand

144. A bone fracture and a perforating wound in the palm of the hand: 1 pound, and to this must be added the compensation for the injury itself.

Concerning Paralysis

145. If someone declares to be paralysed in his arms or in his hands, in his legs or in his feet, the compensation is 27 ounces.

146. If someone's fingers or toes are paralysed, the compensation is 1 mark.

Paresis of Arms and Legs, Hands and Feet

147. If anyone suffers from paresis in addition to paralysis, then the smallest paresis is to be compensated with 7 ounces, the middle one with 14 ounces, and the largest paresis with 21 ounces; this concerns arms and legs.

148. If fingers or toes suffer from paresis, then the smallest paresis is to be compensated with 1 ounce, the middle one with 2 ounces, and the largest one with 3 ounces.

149. Also, concerning the more severe paresis of the fingers: the first one is to be compensated with 30 ounces, the second one with 52 ounces, and the third one with 73 ounces, to be calculated in white pennies.

Paralysed Thumb

150. If the thumb has been paralysed but it is still attached to the hand, the compensation is 3 pounds.

Paresis of the Thumb

151. If the thumb is suffering from paresis, the smallest paresis is to be compensated with 10 groats, the middle one with 20 groats, and the largest one with 30 groats.

152. All pareses are to be ascertained down towards the nails, and not up towards to the body, and in the legs they are to be ascertained in the same way as in the arms.

Thumb Severed

153. If the thumb of a man is severed at the upper joint, the compensation is 4 ounces.

154. Is hi itta nesta knocla off, soe is dio bote VIII einsa.

155. Is di tuma al of, so is dio bote XII einsa.

Vingeren of

156. Jef dat urste lid fan da scotfinger of is, dio bote is II einsa.

157. In da nesta knocla: IIII einsa.

158. Itta nesta[1] knocla: VIII[2] einsa.

159. Is hi alheel of, so is dio bote XI einsa.

160. Is dat fornsta lid of fan da lange finger, dio bote is twa einsa.

161. In da nesta knocla: IIII einsa.

162. Etta nesta knocla: VIII einsa.

163. Is hi alheel of: X eynsa.

164. Is dat fornsta lid of fan da goldfinger, so is dio bote twa einsa.

165. Etta nesta knocla:[3] IIII einsa.

166. In da knocla deerbi: VIII einsa.

167. Is hi alheel of: niogen einsa.

168. Is dat fornste lid of fan da lytka finger, dio bote is twa einsa.

169. In dae nesta knocla: IIII einsa.

170. Etta nesta: VI[4] einsa.

171. Is hi alheel of: VIII einsa.

[1] FG: uesta. [2] FG: viiii. [3] FG: *nesta knocla* is missing. [4] FG: xi.

154. If the thumb is severed at the lower joint, the compensation is 8 ounces.

155. If the thumb is severed completely, the compensation is 12 ounces.

Fingers Severed

156. If the upper joint of the index finger is severed, the compensation is 2 ounces.

157. If the next joint is severed: 4 ounces.

158. If the next joint is severed: 8 ounces.

159. If it is severed completely, the compensation is 11 ounces.

160. If the upper joint of the middle finger is severed, the compensation is 2 ounces.

161. If the next joint is severed: 4 ounces.

162. If the next joint is severed: 8 ounces.

163. If it is severed completely: 10 ounces.

164. If the upper joint of the ring finger is severed, the compensation is 2 ounces.

165. If the next joint is severed: 4 ounces.

166. If the next joint is severed: 8 ounces.

167. If it is severed completely: 9 ounces.

168. If the upper joint of the little finger is severed, the compensation is 2 ounces.

169. If the next joint is severed: 4 ounces.

170. If the next joint is severed: 6 ounces.

171. If it is severed completely: 8 ounces.

Hand of

172. Jef dio fore hand of is itter handwirst: XXVIII einsa, nei dam dat hio da seininga schil dwaen toejenst da quada gast.

173. Is dio winster hand of: XXVII[1] eynsa.

174. Dio hand craulcruum: een merck.

175. Di eerm, is hi griiplam: een merck.[2]

Foet off

176. Jeff di winstera foet off is itta anckele, soe is dioe boete acht ende tweintich eynsa, nei dam dat hi diin instaep dwaen schil.

177. Is di fora foet off: XXVII einsa.

140 **178.** Is di foet strickhalt: een merck, dit winne hi mit sex sine sibbem. |

179. Yelkerf:[3] XXIIII penningen.

180. Jefta leska on da yle tokoren sint: in da hande ende onder da foten allereeck XVI penningen.

Metedulg[4]

181. Dat metedulg tuscha weed ende screed, so is di man nier mitta oenbringhe dan da lada; so is dio bote IIII schillingen.

182. Jelkirs sint da metedulgh XVI penningen ende dat dulgh mit ene ede oen to bringhen.

183. Metedulgh, inre in den buck: acht schillinghen[5] ende IIII graet; is hit lingera, so aech ma hit to beten buta ney der meta. Aldeerto mei hy beenbreck ende benis utgongh swara, alst riucht wyst.

184. Bloedresan, inre in dine buck: VIII scillingen.

---

[1] FG: xxvi. [2] FG: di eerm griip een merck is hi lam. [3] FG: Delkerf. [4] FG: MEte dug. [5] FG: schilhg*en*.

Hand Severed

172. If the right hand is severed at the wrist: 28 ounces because this hand must perform the blessing against the evil spirit.

173. If the left hand is severed: 27 ounces.

174. If the hand is crooked like a hook: 1 mark.

175. If the arm is no longer able to hold anything: 1 mark.

Foot Severed

176. If the left foot is severed at the ankle, the compensation is 28 ounces because this foot is used for mounting a horse.

177. If the right foot is severed: 27 ounces.

178. If a foot is dragging: 1 mark, and the claimant must substantiate his claim with the help of the oaths of six relatives.

179. Cutting the sole of the foot: 24 pennies.

180. If the wrinkles in the sole are cut: in the hand and under the feet each of these 16 pennies.

Measure Wounds

181. A measure wound between garment and hair: the claimant has more right to substantiate his claim than the defendant has to swearing an oath of innocence; the compensation is 4 shillings.

182. Otherwise, measure wounds are to be compensated with 16 pennies and the claim to the compensation for this wound is to be substantiated by swearing one oath.

183. A penetrating wound in the belly which is a measure wound: 8 shillings and 4 groats; if the wound is longer, it is to be compensated according to the size of the wound. On top of this, the claimant may claim a bone fracture and a protrusion of bone splinters, as the law says.

184. A penetrating wound in the belly which is a bleeding wound: 8 shillings.

185. Bloedis inryn: VII schillingen.

186. Fraesheed des lives, dio boete is tree penningen min dan XXIIII scillingen.

Trucht lyf

187. Hweer so ma een man trucht[1] lyf siuth jefta staet, soe aeg ma him to metten dine curtera wei. So aeg ma dera meta allerlyck[2] to beten mit XVI penningen.

188. Ende dat inre mit VIII schillingen ende dat utwardis also wel.

189. Haet hi een eergens, da aldeerto ti beten.

190. Eergens inoer dat lyf: dio minste VII einsa, dio middelste xiiii einsa, dio maeste XXI[3] einsa.

191. Hweer so een man dulget wirt buppe dera sprideka ende hy dan swara wil da fiaerndel ara, so is dio bote V½ merck.

192. Wil hi swara da haeldel ara, so is dio bote XI merck.

193. Wil hi swara da tre delen ara, so is dio bote XVII merck.

194. Item: wil hi swara dat hi alle dera sondena naet een habbe, deer hi mei boren ward ende opwaxen was, da tre delen awei, so is dio boet XVII merk.

Gersfallich lappa

195. Hweer so en man een dulg wirt howen, slain jefta biten ende een gersfallich lappa off is ende hi dat gersfallich swara wil, so mot ma him naet onswara hi habbe allerweikes een meta; so mot met metta om bi da ig ende liowa den
141 fiaerndel; so is dio mete allerlyck | tribeet. Foerd[4] moet hi swara een lamthe ende di schil wessa eenbeet. Jef hi swara wil bena utgong: al eenbeet. So moet hi swara III synkerf ende tre beenbrecken. Bede tribet.

[1] FG: trncht. [2] FG: alleriyck. [3] FG: xvi. [4] FG: ffoerd.

185. An internal bleeding: 7 shillings.

186. Fear of one's life is to be compensated with 3 pennies less than 24 shillings.

Penetrating the Body

187. If a man is shot or stabbed through his body, then the shorter distance between the two ends of the wounds (the intrusion and the extrusion) is to be measured. Then each measure is to be compensated with 16 pennies.

188. And the penetration is to be compensated with 8 shillings and the outward wound equally high.

189. If a man suffers from paresis (because of this), this is to be compensated additionally.

190. Paresis in the trunk of the body: the least paresis is to be compensated with 7 ounces, the middle with 14 ounces, the highest with 21 ounces.

191. If a man is wounded in his body above the diaphragm and he wants to claim a paresis for a quarter part, the compensation is 5½ marks.

192. If he wants to claim paresis for half a part, the compensation is 11 marks.

193. If he wants to claim paresis for three quarter parts, the compensation is 17 marks.

194. Also: if he wants to claim the loss of three quarters of the health with which he was born and has grown up, the compensation is 17 marks.

Hewn off Piece of Flesh

195. If a man is injured by cutting, hitting or biting, and a piece of flesh has fallen off, and he wants to claim that it has fallen off, he is not allowed to do so, unless the wound has the size of a measure all around; then the wound must be measured around along the edge, and a quarter of this length must be subtracted, and each measure is to be compensated threefold. Furthermore, this man must claim a paralysis which must be compensated single. If he wants to claim a protrusion of bone splinters, this is to be compensated single for each splinter. And he must also claim three instances of cut sinews and three instances of bone fractures. Both of these are to be compensated threefold.

196. Nen[1] dulgh mei ma meer oenswara dan tree beenbrecken ende trira bena utgong ende tria synkerff; disse bota aegh hi allerlyc mit ene ede to winnen, hi wite self dat hi riucht dwe.

197. Swert hi benis utgongh, so schil hi dan oen[2] sine eed habba dat met mochte hera clippa jef hit fan sine kne foel ur IX stapen in een lewyn, dat is in en[3] becken, jelkirs toer met naet beta. Scouwet al dio meent an him en beenbrec ende een lam lid, so ist oenbrins.

Navla

198. Hwa so dulget wirt in dine navla binna dine ringe, dio boet is XX graet.

199. Dis navlabrekis boet is sextahael schilling.

200. Dio eergens in da sida: sextahael pond.

201. Longenscreden: VI schillingen.

202. Miltascreden: V schillinghen.[4]

203. Wanspreke: XXVI[5] graet.

204. Hemelinga: X graet.

205. Wyfstreven: XVI penningen.[6]

206. Spedelspring: XXVI graet.[7]

207. Abel[8] ende incepta: X graet.

208. Hette ende kelde: X graet, ayder mit en ede to halien.

209. Mosdulgh: XXXII penningen.

---

[1] FG: Nnen. [2] FG: een. [3] FG: *in* is en. [4] FG: schilili*n*ghen. [5] FG: xvi. [6] FG: graet. [7] FG: penningen.
[8] FG: Apel.

196. For no injury can a claimant claim more than three instances of bone fractures, three instances of a protrusion of bone splinters, and three instances of cut sinews; he has to substantiate his claim by swearing one oath for each instance, and the claimant himself may testify that he is acting according to the law.

197. If he claims a protrusion of bone splinters, the injured man has to swear that the splinter could be heard from a distance of nine steps if it fell from knee-high into a basin—that is a bowl; otherwise it need not be compensated. If all of the community ascertains that he has a broken bone and a paralysed limb, then the claimant may substantiate his claim with an oath.

Navel

198. If a man is injured within the circle of the navel, the compensation is 20 groats.

199. The compensation for a rupture of the navel is 5½ shillings.

200. Paresis of the side: 5½ pounds.

201. Cutting the lungs: 6 shillings.

202. Cutting the spleen: 5 shillings.

203. Deterioration of speech: 26 groats.

204. Partial mutilation: 10 groats.

205. Tearing off a woman's hood: 16 pennies.

206. Drivelling: 26 groats.

207. Scar tissue which is higher or lower than the skin: 10 groats.

208. (Insensibility to either) heat and cold: 10 groats, the compensation for each to be obtained by swearing one oath.

209. A bruise: 32 pennies.

210. Dio fylmenbreeck:[1] IIII schillingen.[2]

211. Thera fyf sinne allerlyc, dio bote is VI schillingen.

Waldwaex

212. Da waldwaxbot is XXVI[3] penningen.

Fan da pint

213. Hwa so oderem syn tillinga binimt, dio bote is[4] V½ merc.

214. Hweer so en man truch syn machta schetten wirt truch[5] dat fel, dio boet is II einsa, hit ne se dat hi fora sprecka wil; so mei hi habba tria siinkerf: dio aerste haet dio staepsyn, dio oer dio wieldsyn ende dio tredde dio fruchtsyn. Deer moet hi fan bitigia tria onbinaemd moerd, da aegh ma allerlyc to beten so diore so en manslachta jefta tolvasum onswara.

215. Hwa so orem bi sine machtum nimpt ende hine qualic handelet, dio bote is XX penningen.

216. Hwam so ma slacht ur sine machtum bi ira moede, dio bote is XXVI penningen.

142 **217.** Scalsleeck: | IIII schillingen.

Fan da kuntha

218. Jef hio also dulged wirt, dat hio dae heren naet to tancke tienia mei, so is dio bote fioerteenstehael merck; dat wite hio self mit hiere eed.

Eerghens dera frouwa

219. Dio eergens in dine buuck, jef ma se oenkaltia wil: dio hagista eergense dioe bote is niogen einsa. Jef se bi da lesse lya wil, dio bote is fyftahael einsa, soe schil ma dis winna mit ene ede.

220. Di blodis inriin: saun schillinghen.

---

[1] FG: fymel breeck. [2] FG: schillgen. [3] FG: vi. [4] FG: ia. [5] FG: trnch.

210. Rupture of the skin: 4 shillings.

211. The compensation for each of the five senses is 6 shillings.

The Spine

212. The compensation for damaging the spine is 26 pennies.

Concerning the Penis

213. If someone amputates a man's generative parts, the compensation is 5½ marks.

214. If a man is shot through his genitals, through the skin, the compensation is 2 ounces, unless the claimant wants to pursue his claims further; in that case he may claim the cutting of three sinews: the first one is called the 'up sinew', the second the 'wielding sinew' and the third the 'fruit sinew'. He must also claim the killing of three unborn children, and each of these is to be compensated as a case of homicide, or the defendant must exonerate himself with eleven compurgators.

215. If someone grabs another man by his genitals and touches him indecently, the compensation is 20 pennies.

216. If anyone hits a man on his genitals in a fit of rage, the compensation is 26 pennies.

217. A blow on the testicles: 4 shillings.

Concerning the Vulva

218. If a woman is injured such that she is unable to serve the lords to a satisfactory degree, the compensation is 13½ marks; she may testify to this herself by swearing an oath.

Paresis of a Woman

219. Paresis in the belly, if she wants to pursue this claim: the highest degree of paresis is to be compensated with 9 ounces. If she wants to be compensated for the lesser degree of paresis, the compensation is 4½ ounces, and this compensation is to be obtained by swearing one oath.

220. An internal bleeding: 7 shillings.

221. Dis nedera swolles bote is IIII schillengen, da lada sex eden.

222. Hwa so siinre sondena mist, deer hi mei boren ward, jeft ma dat bicant, jefter een man queth dat him ur al syn lya da tree delen urlerren haet ende dyn fiaerndeel bihalden, so is dio bote XLIIII pond. Jef ma dat naet bicant, so ne mei hi meer onswara so da tree delen, dera allereeck mit I eed, so is dio boet allerlyc XI pond; dine fiaerndeel ne mei hi habba, want hi naet gersfallich is.

223. Hwa so orem grypt oen syn hals, dat di adema hor ut ner in mey, dio bote is X penninghen.

224. Hwa so orem onder syn agen spyt onwerdelyc, dio bote is XXVI penninghen.

225. Hwer so ma een man onschieldich oenfucht ende halten oen heften ende oen heerbeinden dei ende nacht, so schil ma dat beta mit een liuedwirden, dat is II penninghen min[1] so achteenstahael einsa, jefta tolvasum onswara.

Van brande

226. Hweer so[2] een man oen siin lithem baernd wirt, so schil met bi epena dulg[3] metta alst wydst is, al bi da lingera igge: aller[4] meta lyc VII penningen min so X einsa.

227. Hwa so oderem baernt, so schil met algaer ommetta bi da iggen ende bi da sidem. So is aller meta lyc tribeet jof hyt bicant; jof hyt naet bicant, so is di oder nier mitta oenbring so di oder to ontgongen ende da tre delen allereeck tribeet.

228. Hwer so een man of een wyf baernd wirt on hiara lyf minra jefta mara
143 ende hit compt fan | ira mode, fan haest jefta fan haester hand, so is dio bote twibeet; wint hit een meta, so schil ma hit metta om dina wei deer hit langist is ende naet omme, ende ist een ticka brand so bete hy da maesta; so ist aeck tribeet.

[1] FG: mim. [2] FG: hneerso. [3] FG: *dulg* is missing. [4] FG: allnr.

221. The compensation for wounding the abdomen is 4 shillings, or the defendant has to exonerate himself with five compurgators.

222. If a man lacks the health with which he was born, and if the defendant has confessed, or if the claimant declares that he has lost three quarters of his health from all over his body and has retained the fourth quarter, the compensation is 44 pounds. If the defendant has not confessed, the claimant may claim no more than a compensation for the loss of three quarters, each to be substantiated by swearing one oath, and each to be compensated with 11 pounds; the fourth quarter he shall not have because nothing has been hewn off.

223. If a man is grabbed by the throat, so that his breath can go neither in nor out, the compensation is 10 pennies.

224. If a man is spat in the face ignominiously, the compensation is 26 pennies.

225. If an innocent man is assaulted and held in fetters and shackles for a day and a night, the compensation is a small wergild, that is, 2 pennies less than 17½ ounces, or the defendant must exonerate himself with eleven compurgators.

Concerning Burns

226. If a man's limbs get burnt, the burn is to be measured at its widest while the wound is still open, all along the longer edge: for each measure 7 pennies less than 10 ounces.

227. If someone burns another man, the wound must be measured all around the edges and the sides. Then each measure is to be compensated threefold if the defendant confesses; if he does not confess, then the claimant has more right to substantiate his claim than the defendant has to exonerate himself by swearing an oath, and each of the three quarters is to be compensated threefold.

228. If a man or a woman gets burnt on their bodies to a lesser or greater extent, and if it was brought about in a fit of rage, out of anger or agitation, it is to be compensated twofold; if the wound is longer than a measure, it must be measured along the distance where it is longest, and not around; and if there are several burns, then the largest compensation is to be paid; then it is also to be compensated threefold.

Van biten

229. Hwer so di man dine oderne bit ende manetich wirt, so schil hi dat dulg beta tribeet, hor hit mara so minra se, ende banscieldich wessa. So is di oder nier to ontgongen dis bites ende swaret, dat hyt habbe deen mit wepender hand ende riuchte bota to reken, dan di oder mitta oenbring. Dine byt ende dine brand met ma bi epena dulg[1] by dera meta ende jelkirs nen dulg. Dine byt ende dine brand aeg ma mit gold to betten want hi mei nimmermeer to haegh bet wirda; deerom schil ma hine al mit goud beta. Theer aegh dy frana VIII pond toe ferden. Theer schil hy dae XII eden om tiaen jef hi dine oenbringh quaen nelle. Dat gold toe jaen om dine brand ende om dine byth.

230. Hweer so een man dulgid wirt ende hi dat kalde yrsen binna hem drecht, so is dio bote VIII pond jefta XVI[2] pond. Nimpt hi VIII pond, so schil ma hem deertoe jelda, of hi sterft. Nimpt hy XVI pond so sint da bota fol biwysd: wirt hy lyf jefta[3] daed fan da dulghe, hi schil oen syn frionden ferdeden swara to mannes[4] liif ende to landes leghere.

231. Haet so een man deth mit tusschen, mit saxe, mit scerpa wepen ende mit armburst, dat aeg ma al twibeet to betane.

232. Een[5] jewelyc man aegh siin bota to delen ur siin broderen, so lange so hia meenbodel sint ende hi syn VI lya gans haet, dat sin da twa agen, da tween foten ende da twa handa.

233. Halsraef dera frowa op her bursten, op her axlum jeff op her tziakum, dio bote is IIII penningen min dan xviii-hal[6] einsa ende twibeet; da lada VI eden.

234. Jef her di mantel ofbritsen wirt jefta dat gold, so is dio bote IX einsa ende
144 twybeet. |

235. Wapeldranck, halsraef, needmond, dio boet is elkerlyck XVIII pond ende XXXII penningen, jeff mit ene ede toe onswaren, ende somlica bota haldet achteenstahael einsa.

---

[1] FG: metma mit bi epena dulg. [2] FG: xvl. [3] FG: itfta. [4] FG: manne. [5] FG: Ten. [6] FG: xviii.

Concerning Bites

229. If a man bites another man and in doing so becomes man-eating, then he must compensate the injury threefold, whether it is large or small, and he shall be excommunicated. The defendant has more right to exonerate himself from the claim to a bite by swearing that he has wounded the claimant with a weapon and to compensate him accordingly, than the claimant has to substantiate his claim. Bites and burns are the only injuries that must be measured before they have healed. Bites and burns are to be compensated with gold because the claimant can never recover completely; that is why the defendant must compensate him completely with gold. The *frana* must receive 8 pounds because of a breach of the peace. The defendant must exonerate himself with eleven compurgators if he denies the accusation. Gold is to be paid in cases of burns and bites.

230. If a man is injured, and he still carries in his body the cold iron that wounded him, the compensation is either 8 or 16 pounds. If he takes 8 pounds, an extra compensation is required if he dies afterwards (as a consequence of the wound). If he takes 16 pounds, this is a full compensation: whether he survives the injury or dies because of it, he and his relatives must swear oaths of peace, which will last for as long as men live and the land lies.

231. Whatever a man inflicts on another with teeth, with a knife, with a sharp weapon, and with a bow, this must all be compensated twofold.

232. Each man has the right to call in the financial help of his brothers when he has to pay compensation, as long as they share an estate, and as long as his six limbs are unscathed, that is: two eyes, two feet and two hands.

233. Robbing a woman of the adornments on her breasts, shoulders or cheeks is to be compensated with 4 pennies less than 17½ ounces, and the compensation is twofold; the defendant may exonerate himself with five compurgators.

234. When her mantle is robbed, or her gold, the compensation is 9 ounces, and the compensation is twofold.

235. Throwing someone into the water, robbing someone's adornments or rape are all to be compensated with 18 pounds and 32 pennies each, or the defendant can exonerate himself with an oath, and some tariffs state that the compensation is seventeen and a half ounces.

Fan bierwerpen

236. Hwa so orem mit bier werpt onder syn aegen, dio boet XVI penningen jefta fiourasum onswara.

237. Halt hi dine cop ende swingt mitta bier, dio bote is[1] IIII penningen jefta mit eenre hand onswara.

Claen toreint

238. Hwa soe orem claen toraint oen syn willa ende ur oers oenwilla, dio bote is XVI penningen. Jeff hi[2] wil dat swara dat hyt him naet habbe deen hor to leck ner toe laster ende nim nidla[3] ende treed ende siet weer gaer; ende deermei set ende seend.

239. Jeff enis mannes hors in een tieder off keppel jefta inoer[4] syne stalle deth aen byt, soe thoer met naet beta; jeff hy stande an heerwei, oen tzierckwei of an een amptmannes huise,[5] so schil hiit beta als off hiit selm deen hede.

240. Jeff enis mans hors dulget wirt, deer hi mit leder bileit haet jefta mit tame halt, so schil hiit beta gelyc and ma hit een man self dwe jefta deen were. Fordera ne mot hi nen intainga meer wita, mer hi mot wel kestigia om syn scada.

241. Jef dat hors dulget en man als di hera dat hors mit tame halt ende mit leder bileit haet, so scil hiit beta jof hiit self deen hede, hit ne were dattet buta des hera wiitsciip were schyn ende ur siin willa ronne.

242. Hwa so op oders hinxt sit in syn willa ende in oders onwilla, so bete hi den opsedel mit I pond ende den offsedel mit I ora pond, jefta sexasum onswara.

Fan quada fia

243. Joulikes fiaes dulg schil ma beta deer hit ledich hlaept.

244. Dis oxa ende jeulikis scettis horn ende swyns tusch ende hona eitzel ende katta biit scil ma beta deer hia leech hlapet ende dis hondis, hit ne se dat hiit nachtis dwe jef als ma stapet op him jef dat men slacht in sine danne, deir hi

[1] FG: es. [2] FG: *hi* is missing. [3] FG: nirla. [4] FG: i*n* oen. [5] FG: hise.

Throwing Beer

236. If anyone throws beer in another man's face, the compensation is 16 pennies, or the defendant must exonerate himself with three compurgators.

237. If he holds the mug in his hands and throws the beer, the compensation is 4 pennies, or the defendant must exonerate himself with an oath.

Torn Clothes

238. If a man tears the clothes of another man on purpose and against the will of the offended man, the compensation is 16 pennies. If the defendant wants to declare that he did not do this in order to mock or defame the claimant, he may take needle and thread and then sow the clothes of the claimant together again; then it will be settled and reconciled.

239. If a man's horse, being on a tether or on a rope, or in its stable, inflicts a bite, no compensation is required; if, however, the horse is standing on a public road, a church road or at the house of a public officer, then the owner must compensate the bite as if he had done it himself.

240. If a man's horse which is saddled or harnessed by the owner is wounded, this is to be compensated just as if it is done or has been done to the owner himself. No further claims may be made then, but in order for the damage to be acknowledged, the claimant may force the defendant to hear his complaint.

241. If a horse which is saddled or harnessed by the owner injures another man, then the owner must compensate this as if he had done it himself, unless it had happened without the owner knowing it, and the horse was running free from its master against his will.

242. Riding another man's horse against the owner's will is to be compensated with 1 pound for mounting it, and another pound for dismounting it, or the defendant must exonerate himself with five compurgators.

Concerning Harmful Livestock

243. Injuries inflicted by any kind of straying livestock are to be compensated.

244. Injuries inflicted by the horns of an ox or of any kind of cattle, or by the tusks of a pig, or by the spur of a cock, or by the bite of a cat, if they are running loose, are to be compensated by the owner, and also a dog's bite, unless it does so at night, or if one steps on it, or if one hits it when it is lying in his dog

145 leit, so toer met naet | beta. Fan disse sprecket hya ontwa, soe schillet dat wita saun synre buren.

245. Dis oxa[1] ende jollikes rederschettes bote ende des swines ende des hona ende dera katta dullich mit haelre bote schil ma dat beta. Jef hia dyn onwilla ende dae wanwytschip dera schaedafticheed biswara willet, so schil met naet beta.

246. Hondes byt, of hi eer biscouden is als eens, twia, tria, so schil met beta lyck jeft di man self deen hede ende oers naet. Aldus ist fan da hond, hit ne se dat hyt dwe als tofara is biscrioun, so ist sonder bote. Mer dwaet disse binaemda dier oers aet, soe schil met beta als forscrioun steet.

GLOSSA 170. Supradicta emenda fiunt, si animalia nocuerunt. Si leduntur animalia, sicut inferius est expressum.

247. Haet so des mannes ayn fia deth, dat schil hi beta eenbeet aldus.

248. Ende dulget hi een dier jefta daeth, dyn schada half toe beten ende ferd herem ner lioden also fyr so dio bote mara naet se dan tria pond ende fioerteen graet, dit is strydheftich schet. Jef dat strydwirdich is[2] ende hi forwonnen wirt, soe schil hi beta heren ende lioden.

GLOSSA 171. Intellige de puero doli[a] capace, quia pupillo et furioso subuenitur in malificiis, quia facultatem deliberandi non habent. Quomodo reus constitueretur, qui nescit quid facit?[b]

Urbec deda

249. Hweer so een man een deda urbeck det jefta mannes wyf det onwillens, jef hyt oen da wytedum wara wil, ther him onwillens were, so schil hyt beta mit haelre bote ende[3] neen ferd da lioeden ner da frana.

Husbrand

250. Jef hit comt fan katta, fan famna, fan hond, fan knappa jefta fan onjeriga kindum, dattet huis wirth a baernen ende sines bures huis aldeer fan baerne, so aegh dat di hera to beten mit haelre bote, deer syn knappa deen haet, hia ne

[1] FG: exa. [2] FG: ief strydw*ir*dich schet. [3] FG: eu*de*.

a doli *scripsimus*: dolo FG.
b Cf. C.15 q.1 c.5.

kennel; in such cases no compensation is required. If an argument arises about this, seven of his neighbours must give testimony.

245. Wounds inflicted by an ox or by any kind of cattle, or by a pig, a cock, or a cat, are to be compensated half. If the owners want to swear that the damage was done against their will and without their knowledge, no compensation is required.

246. A dog's bite, inflicted by a dog that has been corrected on this before, once, twice, or thrice, is to be compensated by the owner just as if he had done it himself, and in no other way. These are the regulations concerning a dog, unless it has bitten under the conditions which have been outlined above, in which case no compensation is required. But if these aforementioned animals do anything else, it is to be compensated as prescribed above.

GLOSS 170. The aforementioned redress will be made, if animals have caused a loss. If animals are harmed, what is noted below will apply.

247. Whatever a man's livestock does is to be compensated single like this.

248. And if a man injures or kills another man's animal, the damage is to be compensated half, and no compensation needs to be paid to either the judges or the people because of a breach of the peace, provided the compensation amounts to no more than 3 pounds and 14 groats; this is the 'duel-worthy price'. If the damage is 'duel-worthy' and the defendant is defeated in court, he has to pay compensation to the judges and the people.

GLOSS 171. Understand this as concerning a child, capable of acting with malicious intent, since the pupil and madman are exonerated for their crimes, because they lack the faculty of deliberation. How can someone be sued, who does not know what he is doing?

Unintentional Actions

249. If a man or his wife do anything against their will, and he wants to swear on the holy relics that it was unintentional, he must compensate it with half a compensation, and no compensation needs to be paid to the people and the *frana* because of a breach of the peace.

House on Fire

250. If this is caused by a cat, a maid, a dog, a servant, or by underage children, so that the house is burnt down, and his neighbours' house also catches fire because of this, then the master has to compensate half of what his servant

habbe urlerren da sex liden een, da twa handen, da twa aghen ende dae tween
146 foten; habbet se dera een urlerren, | so ne thoer met fora beta.

Fan huisferd

251. Hwa so oen oderis huis staet, so schil hyt beta mit een hala pond.

252. Geet di reeck ut ende di wind in, so schil hyt beta mit twam pondem.

253. Staet hi oen doer ende oen drompel, so schil hyt beta mit acht pondem.

254. Geet hy int huis, so is di ingongh ende di utgongh aider twa eynsa.

Steten oen da porta

255. Hwa so staet oen oers porte, soe schilre beta mit een hael pond.

256. Geet hi inoer da porta, so schil hi beta mit twam pondem.

257. Staet hi een boerd ut, soe is dio bote II pond.

Van urwalden

258. Dio alre minste: twa pond jefta fiourasum onswara.

259. Dio minre: IIII pond.

260. Dioe urwald aldernest: VIII pond jefta sexasum onswara jefti hit naet bicant.[1] Dio maeste urwald dio is gersfallich; dat sint daeddellen.

---

[1] FG: *naet* is missing.

has brought about, unless one of them has lost one of his six limbs—the two hands, the two eyes and the two feet; if they have lost one of them, no further compensation is required.

Concerning Domestic Peace

251. If someone bangs against another man's house, this is to be compensated with ½ pound.

252. If smoke comes out of the house, and wind enters the house, this is to be compensated with 2 pounds.

253. If he is banging against the door and the doorstep, this is to be compensated with 8 pounds.

254. If he enters the house, both the entrance and the exit are to be compensated with 2 ounces each.

Banging on the Door

255. If someone bangs against another man's door, this is to be compensated with ½ pound.

256. If he enters through the door, this is to be compensated with 2 pounds.

257. If he knocks out a board, the compensation is 2 pounds.

Concerning Violence

258. The lowest degree of violence: 2 pounds, or the defendant must exonerate himself with three compurgators.

259. The lesser: 4 pounds.

260. The degree of violence which comes next: 8 pounds, or the defendant must exonerate himself with five compurgators if he denies. The highest degree means that something is hewn off: these are cases of homicide.

Weyschettinge

261. Hwa so orem det een weischettinge: twa einsa in Woldenseradeel, in Weimbritseradeel twa pond.

Weymeringa

262. Hwa so oderum een weimeringa det: x engelsch in Woldenseradeel, in Weimbritseradeel een hael pond.

Roadblock

261. If anyone blocks someone's road: 2 ounces in Wonseradeel and 2 pounds in Wymbritseradeel.

Road Obstruction

262. If anyone obstructs someone's road: 10 English pennies in Wonseradeel and ½ pound in Wymbritseradeel.

XV. Currency Conversion and Wergilds

1. In nomine domini amen. Willi hera ende wel forstaen ho dat payment alhyr in Westergo ende in Astergo is ghedaen. Int aerste di Freescha schield is XXX graet fan Starem to Groningen ende di grata is fiower scubben jof fyf Liowerdra penningen.

2. Item dat pond is saun graet ur al dat land, bede in Aestergo ende in Westergo land. Dat grate pond is een Colensche pond, dat is fiower schielden ende in da botem bi hwita penningen so is dat Colensche pond XX graet ende in da Birecknada Bota alsoe.

3. Item di schilling in Westergo land ende in Aestergo land is VI graet. Aestergo litika schillingh di is XII Liowerdera penningen, dat sint twa graet ende tweer Liowerdra penningen. Di schilling in da botem bi hwita pennigen is een grata.

147 4. Item dio eynsa in da Birecknada Botem is XX penningen, dat sint X graet. | Dyo eynse in da botem bi hwita peningen dyo is XX hwiite penninghen,[1] XII hwite penningen een graet. So is dio einse bi hwyte penningen oerhael grata ende tween hwyte penningen.[2] Soe sint tria eynsa by hwyta penningen fyf graet.

5. Item in da Fyf Delen, in Woudenseradeel, in Weimbritseradeel ende in da Hemme, ur al disse delen so is dio merck X schillinghen, dat sint tweer schielden.

6. Item ur Liowerderadeel, Dongeradeel, Danthemadeel, Ferwerderadeel, Tietziercksteradeel ende Ydaerderadeel, in disse sex delen so is dio liuedmerck fiower schillingen ende di schillingh is sex graet. Jef bi da litika schillingh, so is dio merck X schillinghen. Ende soe is di schillingh tweer graet ende tweer Liouwerdera penninghen.

7. Dyo schillinghmerck is XII schillinghen, so is di schillingh sex graet.

8. Dio penninghmerck is VIII eynsa ende dio eynse X graet.

---

[1] FG: penghen. [2] FG: peningen.

XV. Currency Conversion and Wergilds

1. In nomine Domini amen. Listen and understand how payment is done here in Westergo and Oostergo. First, the Frisian *skild* is worth 30 groats between Staveren and Groningen and the groat is worth four *skubben* or five pennies of Leeuwarden.

2. Item, the pound is worth seven groats all over the land, both in Oostergo and Westergo. The great pound is worth one pound of Cologne, which equals four *skilden* and in the compensation tariff in white pennies[18] the pound of Cologne is worth 20 groats and in the *Calculated Tariffs*[19] as well.

3. Item, the shilling in Westergo and Oostergo is worth 6 groats. The lesser shilling from Oostergo is worth 12 pennies of Leeuwarden, which equals two groats and two pennies of Leeuwarden. The shilling mentioned in the compensation tariff in white pennies is worth one groat.

4. Item, the ounce in the *Calculated Tariffs* is worth 20 pennies, which equals 10 groats. The ounce in the compensation tariff in white pennies is worth 20 white pennies, where 12 white pennies equal one groat. Thus the ounce in white pennies is worth one and a half groats and two white pennies. Thus three ounces in white pennies are worth five groats.

5. Item, in the Five Districts, in Wonseradeel, in Wymbritseradeel, in De Hemmen, in all these districts a mark is worth 10 shillings, which equals two *skilden*.

6. Item, in these six districts, Leeuwarderadeel, Dongeradeel, Dantumadeel, Ferwerderadeel, Tytsjerksteradeel and Idaarderadeel, the *liudmerk* is worth four shillings and the shilling is at three groats. Calculated in lesser shillings, this mark is worth 10 shillings. And the shilling is worth two groats and two pennies of Leeuwarden.

7. The *skillingmerk* is worth 12 shillings, and one shilling equals six groats.

8. The *penningmerk* is worth 8 ounces and one ounce equals 10 groats.

---

18 With this the *Compensation tariff of Ferwerderadeel and Dongeradeel* is meant. For this identification, see Nijdam, *Lichaam, eer en recht*, 494.

19 See text XIV.

9. Dio grate merck is XVI schillingen. Soe schil ma dyn schillingh recknia bi sex graet, dat is in da landriucht to recknien hweer dio merck in da landriucht steet. Dioe Liowerdera graet merck is XXIX graet een penningh min. Dio grate merck ur al Aestergoland dio is XII schillinghen. Hweer so ma een man jelt bi alda jeldum, so is dio merck tolef schillingen.

10. Dio reilmerck is fiardahael schillingh ende een twede schillingh.

11. Hwer so een man slain wirt in da Fiif Delen, in Woldenseradeel jefta in da Hemme, soe sint da jelden in elka deel XXII merka ende dio merck is tweer schielden, dat is togara XLIIII schielden ende so is di arsta fang fan disse jelden XII merck ende twa einsa ende di lettera fang is II einsa min so X merck. Item di ferd in Woldenseradeel IX merck. Item di ferd in da V Delen LXXX pond ende in da Hemme also.

12. Dit sint riuchte jelda in Weimbritseradeel. Da jelden sint XXX merka ende di
148 arsta fang is XVIII merk ende diin to | bisetten mit tilla kesten an dyn eerfnama wald ende dyn to legien mit reda jeld bi eenre tyd, ende di lettera fangh is XII merck, dyn to lasten als dio seke seend is ende di kos kest is. Item di ferd is in Weymbritseradeel sex merck.

13. Dit sint da jelden in Lyowerderadeel, in Ferwerderadeel, in Dongeradeel, in Danthemadeel, in Tietziercksteradeel ende in Ydaerderadeel: deer sint da jelden XXVII merck. Soe is dio merck XII schillingen ende di schillingh sex graet.

14. Item dae litika jelden in disse forscryouna delen da sint XXVII merck. Ende dyo merck is dan toe recknien bi XXIIII graet.

15. Dit sint dae jelden in Boerndeel: dae sint XV merck ende dioe merck is tween schielden. Soe sint da togara tritich schielden.

Hyr eyndighet dat Landriucht der Fresena ende alhyrnei folged[1] Keiser Rod-
149 ulphus boeck. |

---

[1] FG: fofged. M60, RA: folged.

9. The great mark is worth 16 shillings. In this case, the shilling is to be calculated at six groats, this is to be calculated in the land law if the mark is mentioned in the land law. The great mark of Leeuwarden is worth 29 groats minus one penny. In all Oostergo, the great mark is worth 12 shillings. If someone pays a wergild in old money, the mark is worth twelve shillings.

10. The *hreilmerk* is worth three and a half shillings plus two-thirds of a shilling.

11. If a man is killed in the Five Districts, in Wonseradeel, in Wymbritseradeel, in De Hemmen, then his wergild in each of these districts amounts to 22 marks, each mark at two *skilden*, which makes 44 *skilden* in total, and the first instalment should be 12 marks and two ounces and the second instalment should be 10 marks minus 2 ounces. *Item*: in Wonseradeel, the penalty for breaking the peace is 9 marks. *Item*: in the Five Districts, the penalty for breaking the peace is 80 pounds and in De Hemmen as well.

12. This is the lawful wergild in Wymbritseradeel. The wergild is 30 marks and the first instalment should be 18 marks, and surety should be given for this to the heirs of the deceased by means of good valuables and this surety is to be exchanged for cash at a set time. And the second instalment should be 12 marks, to be paid when the matter had been reconciled and the kiss of peace has been given. Item, in Wymbritseradeel, the penalty for breaking the peace is six marks.

13. This is the wergild in Leeuwarderadeel, in Ferwerderadeel, in Dongeradeel, in Dantumadeel, in Tytsjerksteradeel and in Idaarderadeel: there the wergild is 27 marks. There, the mark is worth 12 shillings and one shilling equals six groats.

14. Item, the lesser wergild in these districts is 27 marks. And the mark should be calculated at 23 groats.

15. This is the wergild in Bornego: it is 15 marks and one mark is at two *skilden*. This makes a total of thirty *skilden*.

Here ends the land law of the Frisians and after this begins the book of Emperor Rudolf.

XVI. The Book of Emperor Rudolf

1. Dit sint dae riucht ende di oenbighin des Keysers boeck Rodulphus, deer hy dede binna Bordeus[1] da hy da Fresen toefarra him layde ende spreeck aldus, dat se scolden[2] mit him heerferd fara om tria tingh:[3]

alleraerst om dat heilighe land,
jef hit stoe an heiden hand.
Een oer om dat Roemsche land
jeft hit wolde van der crystena hand.
Dat tredde om dat hus bi da Rine
deer heert to da guede sinte Martine.
Dat fiarde om hyara ayn fridome.
Nellet hya dan disse heerferd mit him naet bistaen,[4]
soe wil hi se fan hiara fridoem quyt dwaen.
Ende willet se dan disse fiower thing[5] mit him oengaen,
hi wil hiarem tyenia ende staedik riucht dwaen

om da era dis Freescha fridomes deer hia wonnen heden in da hou to Roem by da alda tyden fan des paus ende koninghes[6] jeften. Hwant hiat deer bicronghen dat se wirden des keisers nathan ende aec al mara heren. Want hia moeten self riucht makia by hiara landis wilker ende bi wisera lyodena ende dera prelatena reed. Ende dy setma scil alsoe wessa dat hi naet ne se seth with da ewa ner with dae alda riucht ner tojenst godes hulde. Jefter een lioedwarf jefta tweer willet ene setma makia buta rede dera wisera ende dera prelatena ende dis landes, so schil ma dine sethma witsprecka ende ne schil ma to nene riucht[7] halda.

2. Di keyser Rodulphus spreckt aldus: alle da riucht ende alle da wilkaren ende alle da sethman deer di keyser Justinianus hede set ende Romulus hede maked ende Julius ende Octavianus heden byscrewen ende bybaned ende di keyser Theodosius efter byscreef ende jemna riucht deer Fresen sint, da sint maked ut twam riuchten deer God Moysi ende Aaron gaf up da birge to Synay; Aaron
150 dat gaestelik ende Moysi | dat wraldsche. Ende hy baed himmen dat se al da wrald byriuchta scholden ende al dajene deer an goede festa trouwa wolden. Hwant hi selwa spreeck: hwa so dat riucht hilde dat hi him dat hymelryck geva wilde ende hwa soe hit toebrecke, dat hi hyae in der hel bisluta wolde als hy dae Egipteren dede in da Rada See da se syne lioden scadie wolden.

---

[1] FG: borders. [2] FG: scold. [3] FG: ti*n*hg. [4] FG: bistaeu. [5] FG: tding. [6] FG: koni*n*gdes. [7] FG: riuct.

XVI. The Book of Emperor Rudolf

1. These are the laws and this is the start of the book of Emperor Rudolf, which he decreed in Bordeus, when he ordered the Frisians to appear before him, and spoke thus, that they should follow him on a military expedition for three causes:

First, because of the Holy Land,
if it would fall into pagan hands.
Second, because of the Roman Empire,
if it was in danger of slipping from Christian rule.
Third, because of the house alongside the river Rhine
which belongs to the good Saint Martin.
Fourth, because of their own freedom.
If they would not want to follow him on these military expeditions,
he would nullify their freedom.
But if they would fight with him for these four causes,
he would serve them and constantly do right by them,

in honour of the Frisian freedom, which they had won in the old days in the court in Rome as a privilege from the pope and the king. Because there they managed to become comrades-in-arms to the king and high lords. Because they were allowed to create their own law, in accordance with their statutes and with the advice of wise men and prelates. And the decree shall have such properties, that it does not go against custom law, nor against the old laws, or at the expense of the worship of God. If one court assembly or two wish to create a decree without consultation of the wise men and the prelates and of the court of the entire land, this decree must be rejected and shall not be considered law.

2. Emperor Rudolf speaks thus: all laws and all statutes and all decrees which Emperor Justinian had determined and Romulus had established and Julius and Octavian had written down and commanded and which Emperor Theodosius after that again put in writing and the law of you Frisians, have all been created out of the two laws which God gave to Moses and Aaron on Mount Sinai; divine law to Aaron and secular law to Moses. And he commanded them to pass judgment to all the world and to all who would preserve their faith. Because he himself said that he would give the kingdom of heaven to anyone who upheld the law and that he would lock up in hell those who broke the law, just as he had done to the Egyptians in the Red Sea when they tried to harm his people.

3. Dit wil ic nu leta staen ende[1] wil joe nya setma kud dwaen, deer ic hab in der keysere boecken ende in des paus boecken langhe socht eer ick dine setma toesamen habbe brocht, want hi in manigha dera koningha boken screwen stond.

4. Dit is dat aerste: dat ma dyne haldere aeg foerd to fynden an da lioedwarve jefta an da bannena sinde om redelika[2] thing bihala om fyower thingh.

GLOSSA 172. Nota ex c. Ex litteris de proba. extra (X 2.19.3) et ex glosis eodem capitulo, quando partium iura sunt obscura uel ubi actoris et rei probaciones sunt eque ydonee et equales, pro reo est ferenda sentencia et contra actorem, nisi in his casibus in textu scriptis, quia promptiora[a] sint iura ad absoluendum quam ad condamnandum, ut dicto cap. (X 2.19.3).

5. Dit is dat aerst fan da fiowerem: hweer so een man leyt oen da lesta eynde,[3] haet so hi dan deth bi sines papa rede, so aech ma da oenspreeck foerd toe fyndane.

GLOSSA 173. Testamentum,[b] pro quo[c] habes ff. de testa l. Si pars iudicancium (*Dig.* 5.2.10). Quando agitur de inofficioso testamento, pocius pro testamento est iudicandum, ff. de inoff. test. l. Si pars (*Dig.* 5.2.10).

6. Dit is[4] dat oder: hweer so een man syn fria hals schil biradia mit liode landriucht[5] ende mit des koninghes oerkenen, so schil ma him an da lioedwarve syn fria hals todela al haet hi dae oenspreeck.

GLOSSA 174. De hoc uide ff. de manumis. le. antepenultimam (*Dig.* 40.1.24), ff. de re iu. l. Inter pares (*Dig.* 42.1.38), ff. de re. iu. l. Libertas (*Dig.* 50.17.122), xii q. ii Cum redemptor (C.12 q.2 c.68). Libertas omnibus rebus fauorabilior est. In liberalibus causis inter pares numero, si diuerse sentencie proferuntur, pro libertate optinet.

151 7. Dit is dat tred: hweer so di fria Frese[6] ofte dio fri Fresenna willet sprecka[7] an da bannena sinde om een aeft dattit britzen se ende hia willet bireya mit lioeda landriucht, soe aech ma hiarem foerd toe fynden.

---

[1] FG: eu*de*. [2] FG: rehelika. [3] FG: eyude. [4] FG: HJs. [5] FG: la*n*drincht. [6] FG: frse. [7] FG: spsecka.

---

a promptiora *scripsimus*: promciora FG.
b Testamentum] tameen M60.
c quo *scripsimus*: qno FG.

3. I want to let this rest for now and announce to you a new decree, which I looked for in the books of the emperor and in the books of the pope for a long time, before I compiled this decree because it was written in many of the books of the kings.

4. This is the first provision: that in all reasonable cases, a secular court or an ecclesiastical court has to find in favour of the defendant, with four exceptions.

GLOSS 172. Note that on the basis of X 2.19.3 and the glosses to this text, when the rights of the parties are unclear and when the evidence, adduced by claimant and defendant is just as effective and of the same weight, sentence should be passed for the defendant and against the claimant, unless in the cases described in the text, since legal provisions are more strongly aimed at absolving a party than convicting him, as in X 2.19.3, mentioned above.

5. This is the first exception of these four: when a man is lying on his deathbed, whatever he then does with the approval of his priest, the court shall find in favour of the claimant.

GLOSS 173. A last will and testament, for which there is the provision of *Dig.* 5.2.10. In legal proceedings concerning an 'undutiful last will' (*testamentum inofficiosum*) one should sooner judge in favour of this last will, see *Dig.* 5.2.10.

6. This is the second exception: if a man has to defend his free neck in court according to the land law and with the help of the king's witnesses, the court shall find in favour of his freedom, even though he is the defendant in a case.

GLOSS 174. See for this *Dig.* 40.1.24, *Dig.* 42.1.38, *Dig.* 50.17.122 and C.12 q.2 c.68. Freedom is to be favoured above all other things. If, in proceedings concerning freedom, in case of an equal number of judges, divergent opinions are presented, the opinion in favour of freedom should prevail.

7. This is the third exception: if a free Frisian or a free Frisian woman want to defend themselves before the synod against an accusation of having entered into an illegitimate marriage and if they want to build their defence according to the land law, the court shall find in favour of them.

GLOSSA 175. *Soe schilma dat aeft gaer dela* xxxiii. q.i Si quis acceperit uxorem (C.33 q.1 c.3). Vnde ⟨uersus⟩[a]

"Stat testamentum, libertas, coniugium, dos,
si sunt equales,[b] que producuntur, utrinque".[c]

Hy habentur extra de proba. c. Ex literis (X 2.19.3), de sen. et re iu. c. finali (X 2.27.26), de fi. inst. c. Inter dilectos (X 2.22.6).

8. Dit is dat fiaerde: hweer so een[1] faeder ende een moeder tyaet tria kynden; tween soenen ende een dochter, ende hara jelderen dan stervet ende hio dan een man nimpt buta reda bedera broren, soe quaet[2] dae broren hio habbe her gued urschelt om dat dat hioet deen haet buta hiara reed. Nu[3] queth her mond hio nabbet naet urschelt, om dine frya wilker deer her ende alla frowen di koningh Kaerl ghaf ende di koning Pipwyn efter biscreeff.[4] Want se agen wald liwes ende ledena and ene[5] foermond toe tziesane. Truch dat aegh ma da frowen foerd to fynden ende dae broren urbek jefta een soene deer wise lyoed lowiad ende redet. Jef dae wysa lioed ne connet naet ureen wirda, soe schil doch der frowa riucht foerdghaen.

GLOSSA 176. Equaliter uero succedit filia cum filio in bonis paternis et maternis, in auth. de here. ab intesta. ue. § i (*Auth.* 9.1.1 [*Nov.* 118.1]), Insti. de successo. ab intesta. (*Inst.* 3.1) in principio, Insti. de. here. quali. et diff. § Sui autem et neccessary heredes sunt filius[d] filia (*Inst.* 2.19.2).

GLOSSA 177. *Ende ane foermond to tziesane* Matrimonium contrahitur consensu uiri et mulieris, extra de spon. et ma. c. Tue (X 4.1.25) et c. Cum locum (X 4.1.14). Et ubi non est consensus nec matrimonium, xxx q. v Aliter (C.30 q.5 c.1), de despon. inpuber. c. Vbi non est (X 4.2.2). Attamen solus consensus sufficit ad matrimonium, xxvii q. ii Sufficiat (C.27 q.2 c.2).

152 9. Dit sint dae fiower slettelen deer dy keiser Rodulphus sette binna Bordeus bi des paves hinghnisse. Dae twae fallet aen da gastelika hand ende da twa oen da wraldscha hand. Jetta sinter sex bihalden, dae swerstae riucht, dae sint fonden

[1] FG: *een* is missing. [2] FG: qnaet. [3] FG: uw. [4] FG: biscrreeff. [5] FG: cne.

a Emendavimus ex Glossa Ordinaria.

b equales *scripsimus cum Glossa Ordinaria*: equa es FG. In FG J109 UB and BL there are manual corrections.

c The gloss *in liberali* ad X 2.19.3.

d filius *scripsimus cum Institutionibus*: filus FG.

GLOSS 175. *Soe schilma dat aeft gaer dela* (*So one should render the marriage valid*). See C.33 q.1 c.3. Hence the verse

> "Last will, freedom, marriage and dowry will hold,
> if the arguments adduced from both sides are equal"

And those cases can be found in X 2.19.3, X 2.27.26 and X 2.22.6.

8. This is the fourth exception: if a father and a mother beget three children; two sons and one daughter, and if their parents pass away and if the daughter then marries a man without having consulted either of her brothers, the brothers will claim she has lost her share of the inheritance because she entered into the marriage without their consultation. Now her husband says she did not lose her share of the inheritance because of the free choice which was given to her and all women by King Charles and which King Pippin later wrote down. Because they have dominion over their own bodies and limbs and the right to choose a husband. Because of this, the court shall find in favour of the women and against the brothers or the parties shall come to an agreement after consultation and on the advice of wise men. If these wise men cannot come up with a solution, the woman's rights shall prevail.

GLOSS 176. The daughter indeed succeeds equally with the son to the paternal and maternal goods, see *Auth.* 9.1.1 (*Nov.* 118.1), at the beginning of *Inst.* 3.1 and *Inst.* 2.19.2: "the necessary heirs (*heres necesarii*) are the son, the daughter (…)".

GLOSS 177. *Ende ane foermond to tziesane* (*and to choose a husband*). A marriage is entered into by the consent of man and woman, see X 4.1.25 and X 4.1.14. And where there is no consent, there is no marriage, see C.30 q.5 c.1 and X 4.2.2. Nonetheless, mere consent suffices for a marriage, see C.27 q.2 c.2.

9. These are the four key provisions which Emperor Rudolf established in Bordeus with the approval of the pope. Two of these fall under the authority of the church and the other two under secular authority. Still, there are six more, the

in der koningha boeken jefta in des paves riucht bisocht. Da tria fallet oen da gastlika hand ende da tria oen da wraldscha hand.

10. Dit is dat aerste: hweer so twer syden togarasitte sint ende nen kynden habbet, jeft hit also falt teleyder bi des fyandes sponst dat hiara aydera oerna oen moerd slaeght mit stock jefta mit stompa jefta mit een scherpa wepene ende hia dera deda bisecka willet, soe schillet hia se sikria mit hiara haudpapa ende mit twam frya foegheden ende mit hiara fiower fachtum ende mit twa ende sauntiga orkenen binna hiara kinne. Ende disse maen schillet onbewillet wessa fan sondlika dedem, fan moerdbrande, fan schaeckrawe, fan nachtrawe, fan manslachta,[1] fan hoerdoeme, fan meneden,[2] dat hi karina festa ne schieldich se. Brecht him dan des riuchtes, so sint hia dan des moerdis alle schieldich. Nu schillet hia den ker fan trim oengaen deer him da koninghen set habbet; hoeder him liawera se dat ma hem in een fiore urbarne, dan ma een stock nyme ende sle ma hem a fara itter herta in dat hit tefta itta regghe ut gonghe, jeft ma hiaram hiara syoen binyme ende reme dat land ende lioed ende betterie[3] hiara sonda. Doch schilla se des koninghes[4] ban betha[5] mit twaendesantigha schillinghem ende dii penningh schil alsoedenis jeldis wessa als in da land ghinse is. Ende schil des paves ban beetha mit twaendesantigha pondem Agripsera penning-
153 hen,[6] dat sint Coelenscha penninghen, ende dat moerd al even dioere | ende dine manslachta myt saun jeldem. Ende haet so hya deer fan lyowat, dat schil an koninges wara. Ne mogen hiaet naet jelda, so schillet da sibsta beta. Habbet se kinden teyn, da ne schellet des naet onnyeta, so schellet hyaet mitta halse beta.

GLOSSA 178. *Nu schillet*[a] *hya* Pena istorum et aliorum malefactorum, uide Insti. de pub. iudi. § Alia denique (*Inst.* 4.18.6).

GLOSSA 179. *Ban beta* nota de bannis soluendis in publicis criminibus; per hoc uide supra *inda lettera kest.*[b]

GLOSSA 180. *Inda lande ginse* Vide concordanciam supra[c] de iure synodali tytulo de adulteriis.[d]

11. Dit is dat oder: hweer so ma diin frya Fresa tho how bodet aen dey ende diin odera ende diin tredda ende hy dan naet comma nel, so aegh ma hyne ita

---

[1] FG: manslacdta. [2] FG: mennede*n*. [3] FG: bctterie. [4] FG: koui*n*ghes. [5] FG: bctha. [6] FG: pe*n*ni*n*nghen.

---

a schillet *scripsimus*: schi let FG.; J109 and UB there are manual corrections.
b See text VI,2.
c supra *scripsimus*: snpra FG.
d See text XI,61.

most difficult ones, which were found in the book of the kings or in papal law. Three of these fall under the authority of the church and the other three under secular authority.

10. This is the first key provision: if a husband and a wife live together and have no children, and if it so happens that—being unfortunately seduced by the devil—one of them kills the other with a club, a bludgeon or a sharp weapon and if they wish to defend themselves against a charge over this act before court, they must swear innocence with the assistance of their archpriests and of two free guardians and of their four ancestral branches and of seventy-two witnesses from their kin. And these men shall not have been indicted for any sinful crimes, arson, forceful robberies, nighttime robbery, homicide, adultery, or perjury, which have obligated them to do a forty days penance (*carena*). If he is unable to procure the required witnesses, they shall be found guilty of homicide. Now they shall have a choice of three options which the kings provided; whether they would rather be burnt in a fire, or that an executioner takes a pole and drives it through their hearts at the front side so that it comes out at the back, or that they are blinded and leave the country and the people in order to atone for their sins. They will, however, still have to pay the penalty for infringing on the authority of the king with seventy-two shillings and the penny shall be of a coinage which is current in the land. And they shall also have to pay the penalty for infringing on the authority of the pope with seventy-two pounds made up of Agrippinal pennies, that is, pennies of Cologne, and the same amount for the murder and compensate the homicide with seven wergilds. And if they still have any property left after this, this shall go to the king. If they are unable to pay, the next of kin shall have to compensate. If they produced children, these will not suffer any damage because of this and the parents will have to pay for their own crimes with their necks.

GLOSS 178. *Nu schillet hya* (*They will, however*). The punishment of these and other wrongdoers, see Inst. 4.18.6.

GLOSS 179. *Ban beta* (*pay the penalty*). Note. This concerns the fine to be paid in case of public crimes; see about this above *inda lettera kest*.

GLOSS 180. *Inda lande ginse* (*current in the land*). See the concordance with the section above on synodical law, the title on adulteries.

11. This is the second key provision: if a free Frisian is summoned to court one day, a second day and a third day and he does not want to come, on the fourth

fyaerda dey to sekane to sine how mit brand ende mit breeck. Jeff hy dan ne haet hor huus ner hoff, so aegh him syn greetman siin riucht to dwaen in da lyuedwarve ende hyne utoer ferd to lidsane, siin lyff ende syn gued. Haet so ma hym dan deth, dat is boetloes ende haet so hy dan deth, dat is twibeet. Als jeer ende dey om comt, so aegh hym siin greetman to da lyuedwaer to layen hor hy beta wil als hy urberd haet. Nel hyt dan naet dwaen, so aegh siin gued an koninghes wara. Wil hy dan inoer ferd comma ende beta deer hy britsen haet, so aegh dy greetman hyne inoer ferd to nymen oen da openbera ware aldeer hyne ut leyde[1] ende jelkirs in nene stoed.

GLOSSA 181. *Dat oeder is* Nota hic quomodo quis proscribitur, nisi propter contumaciam et non pro debito pecuniario.

GLOSSA 182. *Etta fiaerda dei to sekane* In personali actione debet fieri executio in rebus condempnati hoc modo ut primo capiantur mobilia si qua possidet, secundo immobilia, tercio peruenitur ad nomina scilicet suorum debitorum et iura et ad ea que ⟨pre⟩scribentur, ff. de re iudi. l. A diuo
154 Pio § In | uendicione (*Dig.* 42.1.15.2), extra ut lite non contesta. c. Quoniam § fi. (x 2.6.5.8). Formam et modum proscribendi iudicii uide supra *inda scheltena riucht*, ibi *Iefma ane man biiclaghet itta how and hiine wtoer ferd to liidsene.*[a] Verum propter crimen capitale. Et quod fuerit capitale, uide ff. de publicis iudic. l. i et secunda (*Dig.* 48.1.1–2). Aduerte quod proscribitur quis pro crimine publicorum iudiciorum capitali, scilicet pro adulterio, homicidio, mordocheo, maleficio et similibus et non pro debito pecuniario,[b] C. de pen. l. "Qui sentenciam laturus est, temperamentum hoc non teneat[c] ut non prius in quempiam capitalem penam promat seueramque sentenciam, quam in adulterii uel homicidii uel maleficii[d] crimen[e] aut sua confessione aut certe omnium, qui tormentis uel interrogacionibus dediti, in unum conspirantes concordantesque rei finem conuictus sit et sic in obiecto crimine seu flagicio deprehensus, ut uix eciam ipse ea que commiserit negare sufficiat" (*Cod.* 9.47.16). Vtrum publice proscriptus quocumque casu occisus secundum consuetudinem patrie fuerit persoluendus. De hoc sunt opiniones doctorum uarie.

---

[1] FG: leyd.

---

a See text III,56–57.

b pecuniario *scripsimus*: pecuianrio FG.

c teneat *scripsimus cum Codice*: teneatur FG.

d maleficii *scripsimus cum Codice*: maleficio FG.

e crimen *scripsimus cum Codice*: crimine FG.

day a militia will go to his estate and it shall be burnt down and laid to waste. If he then has neither house nor yard, his *gretman* will proclaim the sentence in court and declare him an outlaw, including his body and his goods. Whatever people then do to him will not require compensation but he will have to compensate twofold whatever he does. When a year and a day have passed, his *gretman* will summon him to appear before court and ask whether he is willing to pay the compensation he was sentenced to. If he does not want to do so, his goods will become the property of the king. If he then does want his outlawry to be nullified and compensate the damage he has caused, then the *gretman* has to denounce his outlawry in the same public court in which it was pronounced and in no other place.

GLOSS 181. *Dat oeder is* (*the second is*). Notice the way someone is declared an outlaw here: only because of his default in appearance, not because of his monetary debt.

GLOSS 182. *Etta fiaerda dei to sekane* (*on the fourth day ... will go*). In case of a personal action, the execution on the assets of the one condemned should take place as follows. First the movables, if he possesses any, are seized, and secondly the immovables. In the third place one reaches his rights, namely the claims on his debtors, his rights, and the things he will acquire by prescription, see *Dig.* 42.1.15.2 and X 2.6.5.8. See the formula and wording of sentencing of the outlaw above in the section *inda scheltena riucht*, and there in the lines starting with *Iefma ane man biiclaghet itta how and hiine wtoer ferd to liidsene*. This is true in the case of a capital crime and for the question what is a capital crime see *Dig.* 48.1.1–2. See that someone is declared an outlaw due to a capital crime in public criminal judgments, namely for adultery, homicide, murder, witchcraft and similar things and not for monetary debts. As stated in *Cod.* 9.47.16, “the one who is to pronounce sentence, does not observe the correct moderation in such a way, that he does not impose upon anyone a capital punishment and a severe sentence, unless he is convinced of the crime of adultery or homicide or witchcraft either through his confession or at least through the statements of all those who were left to torments and interrogations, resulting in an identical and concordant outcome of the case. In such a way he is caught in the alleged crime or wrongdoing, that even he himself is hardly able to deny the things he committed”. The question whether the one outlawed in any case has to be put to death, has to be answered according to indigenous law. About this question the scholars of Roman law hold divergent opinions.

12. Dit is dat tredde: hwer so di fria Fresa een soen biseent ende deer aen slachte ur slacht jefta wyda an hare kinde birawet jefta moerdbrand[1] deth jefta urbannena raef fan gaestlika lioden jefta schaeckraef jefta bisit mit onriuchta gued ende hi dan wille fan des keisers hallem riucht ontfaen, so schil met witsprecka ende him to nene riucht staen, hwant hyt self tobritsen haet ende urleren. Ende so moten alle dajen deer wirdet efonden in aldusdeenra sonda ende alle da deer naet friboren sint ende alle dajene deer nene fria spreeck ne habbet. Dit riucht sette di koningh Kaerl ende di paus Leo ende Leo baed dit da lioed to halden.

13. Dit is dat fiarde ende dat langste ende hildma toe riuchte aleer Cristus berthe
155 hwant hit in alla landen | riucht was dat alle dat folck fri was deer binna Roem
boren was. Hwant hit hilden da Krekera heren ende da Egiptera ende da heren fan Media ende fan Babilonia deer weren onder da hera koning Nabugodonosor, deer alle heiden was, ende also dedent da Judan. Da noment da Romera heren oen hiara wald. Da noem hit myn hera her Romulus deer da burich makade ende Numa deer dine penning heet muntia[2] in des keisers forma ende deer hildent LI mit grata arbeide alont Justinianus[3] quam deer God da nede gaf. Hwant hi da alda riucht ende da langa riucht ende alle da riucht deer toe sweer ende to manichfald weren biriuchte ende kirte ende jo orlef dat aller landic wilkerren kerre ende cortera ende bischedelikera riucht noeme truch theerwe dis landis ende netticheid dera liodena. Dit riucht biscrewen da koninghen Pipwyn ende di keiser Philippus deer naet in da rime was.

14. Nu wil ick dit riucht in disse rime ende aeck manegera tosamen[4] bringa want se alle screwen waren ende na tosamen brocht. Nu wil ick biscriwa ende sprecka aldus. Hwer so dy fria Fresa dis jondis utgeet efter sonnaschyn ende eer sonnaopgongh ende to enis anderis huses geet ende dat inbreckt ende deer incrupt, wirt hi dan in da hole biginsen, so haet hi mitter insmuge syn fria hals urleren ende naet fora to biseken dan itta lioedware aldeer hi syn riucht ontfaen schil. Jef hi in dae hole slain wirt soe is syn hals urleren. Jef hi an dae flechtiga foet ende mit fatiende bernte biginsen wirt, alsodeen riucht. Wilkeren ende setma deer juwe lande ende juwe lioden nette se, jef dat di onriuchta tobrecka wil mit nachtdedim, jef hi dan biginsen wirt, so is siin fria hals urleren. Jef hyt to swide maket deis, alsodeen riucht, hit ne se dat hyt om honger jefta om open-
156 bere secka dwe, so haet hi syn fria hals naet urleren. | Doch schil hiit itta riucht

[1] FG: moerbra*nd*. [2] FG: mu*n*iia. [3] FG: iustianus. [4] FG: to famen.

12. This is the third key provision: if a free Frisian enters into a truce and then in violation of this commits a homicide or if he robs a widow and her child or commits arson or illegitimately robs clerics or commits a forceful robbery or illegitimately possesses certain goods, and if he then wants to receive justice from the emperor, he shall be denied this and not be allowed to pursue a case in court because he himself has nullified and lost this privilege. And this applies to all those who have committed sins like these and all those who are not freeborn and all those who do not have the right to speak freely in court. This law was established by King Charles and Pope Leo and Leo commanded the people to uphold it.

13. This is the fourth and the longest key provision and this was considered law before the birth of Christ because it was law in all countries that everyone who had been born in Rome held the status of a free person. This rule was obeyed by the Greek rulers and the Egyptians and the rulers of Media and of Babylon, who fell under the authority of the ruler King Nebuchadnezzar, who was a pagan, and also by the Jews. Then it was considered law by the Roman rulers. Then it was considered law by my ruler, lord Romulus, who had the citadel built and Numa, who commanded coins to be struck with the Emperor's bust and after him 51 rulers upheld the law with great effort until Justinian came, whom God gave mercy. Because he corrected and shortened the old laws and the long laws and all laws which were too strict and too extensive and he gave permission to all countries to compose statutes and shorter laws and laws that were better fit to meet the particular needs of those countries and that would benefit their peoples. This law was written down by King Pippin and Emperor Philip, who were not mentioned in the poem.

14. Now I want to compile these laws in this poem and also many others because they have all been written down but never compiled. Now I want to write down and speak as follows. If a free Frisian goes out at night, after sunset and before dawn, and goes to someone else's house and breaks into it and crawls into it, and if he is then apprehended inside the hole he dug, he has lost his free neck because of this burglary and he will not be permitted to plead not guilty at the court at which he will be tried. If he is killed inside the hole, he will have lost his legal status as a freeman. If he is caught red-handed while fleeing from the site, the same rule applies. If a criminal wishes to violate statutes and decrees which are beneficial to your people and your land by criminal acts during night-time and if he is caught doing so, he will have lost his legal status as a freeman. If someone commits a very serious crime by day, the same rule applies, unless he did it out of starvation or because of an emergency, in which case he will

aerst biseka. Wil ma him dan nen riucht dwaen, soe moet hi da manne dine scade dwaen aider deys jefta nachtis. Jelkirs om alle clena deda deer twiiflic sint, da schil ma itta riucht biseka.

15. Jefter een munter in sinre munthe bigripen wirt mit fade ende mit falschede deer hi deen habbe binna sinre munta, so scil ma him op da staepele siin hand aefslaen. Ende jeft hyt feert in een oera land jefta to een haedmerkade ende hi dan bifinsen wirt, is hit dan binna da Coelscha pond, soe schil ma him da fora hand ofslaen. Jef hit is een Coelsche[1] pond jefta derabuppa, soe is di hals urlern. Is hit toe swide[2] ende buppa disse bannem, soe moet hi dine ketel ontfane.

16. Jefter een schreeder bifinsen wirth mitta urbannena weepen aen sine schaete jefta aen sine screne jefta an sine bigerdele, deer hi bicoren haet, is hit binna da Coelscha pond, so scil ma hyne sine fornsta twa lid ofnima. Sind hit twa Coelsca pond jefta meer, soe schil ma him dae sioen binyma, hoe hyt naet meer ne dwe jeff hoe hyt nene man lerre. Want hit alleraerst urbaeden hede di koningh Numa, want hyne munthia heet. Ende aldeerefter urbaeden hit beide Julius ende Octavianus ende Roemscha heran, beida heidena koninghen ende deer Cristen weren. Also dede hyt mit dadelica gome di goede sinte Peter deer ti Rome was di forma paus. Also habbet dit soer deen bede koninghen ende biscoppen want disse twa tingh in aydera riucht urbaden sint.

17. Jeff disse tween maen ayder fan sine aemthe gheet nioegen stapen ende
comt dan weder gaen ende sprect dan hia se dera deda onscieldich, so scillet
hia se sikria mit riuchta landriucht mit VI edem ende mit saun orkenem ende
mit alsodena riucht als ma deerto set, hit ne se dat hia eer se bischolden een
157 ende | oersta ende tredda stond, so ne mei him dat riucht naet helpa ende hiara
goed schil oen koninges wara.

18. Jeff en man bihala een munthere biginsen wirt op een tolnade merked mit fade ende falschede ende hyt dan tiucht to ene munthere jefta jelkirs to ene manne, willet hia jechta jefta dat hi se urwinna moege mit riuchta landriuchte,

[1] FG: Coelsdhe. [2] FG: snide.

not have lost his legal status as a freeman. But he will still have to defend his case before court. If the victim is denied his right to bring a lawsuit to court, he may reciprocate the damage done to him by the perpetrator either by day or by night. All further small criminal acts which are unclear shall be tried at court.

15. If a moneyer is caught in his workshop with inferior coins or counterfeit coins which he produced inside his workshop, then his hand is to be cut off at the court block. And if he takes these coins to another region or to a principal market and he is caught with them, if the value is one pound of pennies of Cologne or less, his right hand is to be cut off. If the value exceeds that of one pound of pennies of Cologne, he will have lost his neck. If the crime is more serious and exceeds these punishments, he must be boiled in a kettle.[20]

16. If someone is caught clipping money with the illegal instruments for it in his coffer or in his purse, and if the value of the coins he has clipped is one pound of pennies of Cologne or less, the first two joints of his fingers shall be cut off. If the value transcends that of two pounds of pennies of Cologne, he shall be blinded so that he will not be able to do it any longer or teach it someone because this was first forbidden by King Numa, because he ordered pennies to be struck. Later, it was forbidden by both Julius and Octavian and Roman rulers, by both pagan and Christian kings. Likewise, the good Saint Peter, who was the first pope in Rome, forbade it on pain of death. In the same way, both kings and bishops have forbidden it since, because these two things are forbidden in both types of law.

17. If each of these two men takes nine steps away from his workshop and then returns and says he is not guilty of these crimes, he shall prove this according to the land law with six oaths and seven witnesses and with such evidence as will be required from them by the court, unless they have been accused of these crimes once, twice and three times before, in which case the law is unable to help them and their goods will become the property of the king.

18. If someone who is not a moneyer is caught with inferior coins or counterfeit coins and he then traces this back to a moneyer or some other man, and if they want to confess or if he is able to win a lawsuit against them in accor-

20 Or: 'undergo the ordeal by water'. The variant versions of the Old Frisian text are unclear and give rise to both interpretations. Buma and Ebel, *Westerlauwerssches Recht II*, 358–359; Meijering and Nijdam, *Wat is recht?*, 468.

soe schillet hia[1] beta. Mei hi se dan naet jechtane bringa[2] mit riuchte ende mit orkenscyp, soe schil hi self scieldich bliwa.

19. Hwer so ma een man efter sonne sedele ende eer sonne opgonge ti enis anderis huse comt mit samnade sydem ende mit weepnader hand, haet so hi deer indeth dat is twibeet ende hat so ma deer utdeth dat is boetloes ende freedloes. Jef hia fan da huse commet mitta guede ende hia dan bigensen wirdet endma hiarem aet deth, so ist boetloes, want hia scaekraweren weren ende habbet urlern dat hoff, want alle scaekraef ende alle nachtraeff di paus urbeden haet.

20. Dit is dat fyfte: hweer so ma dine fria Fresa urwinna schil, dat schil wessa om fyf ting jeff hiaet deertoe tiaed. Dat aerst is om moerd ende om moerdbrand jef hia bighinsen wirdet. Dat oder is om een scaekraef. Dat tredde is om tiefta. Dat fiarde is om faed. Dat fyfte is um screed.[3] Dit ordel mogen bihoda ende dwaen tre riuchteren ende da scillet swerren habba an da hagista lioedware ende lyc haeg. So mey dio dede ane stal habba ende naet heel bliwa hor fan enen noch fan twam, hit ne se dat hiane an der deda bygripen habbe jefta hym tosaynt se. Jelkirs om nen thing mei ma diin frya Fresa urwinna deer gonge oen siin lyf jefta oen syn gued, hit ne se dat hy deer comme myt wilker oen da lyuedware jefta an bannena thinge jefta an da bannena synde, dat moet habba een stal.
158 Wirth hy dan | an da minra riucht tree daghen bitinget, soe schil met hem ith siinre gaetzierka keda eer ma[4] hine itta lioedware urtioget.

21. Dit is dat sexte: hwer so een man nimpt een frowa ende hi deer kinden bitiucht, jef di man dan sterft eer da kinden jerich sint, soe aegh syn broder jefta syn broders soen da bischirmense an da guede ende an da kynden ende an der frouwa, dat him ymmen dwe wald jefta onriucht ont dae kynden jerich sint, hit ne se dat dio frouwe ene oderne man nime. Soe aegh hy dis mondschettes fan dera frouwa een Colensche pond also fyr soe hy riucht mond habbe wessen der frouwa ende der kyndena. Haet hi dan der frouwa ende der kindena een urrader hiara guedis wessen ende dat openbere se, so is hi een baelmond, also fyr so hit biprowat se mit riuchta landriuchte.

[1] FG: hya hia. [2] FG: bri*ngan*. [3] FG: streed. [4] FG: *ma* is missing.

dance with the land law, they will have to compensate. If, however, he is unable to make them confess by means of a lawsuit and a testimony, he will remain guilty himself.

19. If a man goes to someone else's house after sunset and before dawn with a party of followers and all fully armed, whatever he does to the house or its inhabitants will require a twofold compensation and whatever the inhabitants will do to defend themselves will not require a compensation nor a fine for breaking the peace. If the attackers leave the house with goods and if they are then apprehended and if any harm is done to them in the process, this will not require a compensation because they have made themselves violent robbers and thus have lost their right to bring a case to court, because the pope has forbidden all violent robbery and night-time robbery.

20. This is the fifth key provision: if someone wants to win a case against a free Frisian, this can only be achieved for five types of crime, if the claimant wishes to pursue them. The first is arson or homicide, if they are caught in the act. The second is violent robbery. The third is theft. The fourth is producing inferior coins. The fifth is clipping coins. The judgment in these cases can only be passed by three judges who have been sworn in at the highest people's court or an equally high court. Then the case can be considered valid but not if only one or two judges judge the case, unless the defendant was caught in the act or was sent to them. In no other case can a free Frisian be found guilty before court in lawsuits affecting his life or his goods, unless he comes to the people's court or the special court or the synod by his own free will: then it shall be considered valid. If the proceedings against him in the lower court will require more than three days, this shall be announced to him in his own parish church before he is to be found guilty in the lower court.

21. This is the sixth key provision: if a man marries a woman and he begets children with her, and if the man then dies before the children are of age, then his brother or his nephew have to take the guardianship of the goods and the children and the woman upon themselves, so that no-one will do them any harm or injustice until the children are of age, unless the woman marries another man. Then the guardian is entitled to a fee of one pound of pennies of Cologne from the woman if he has been a just guardian to the woman and the children. If, however, he showed no care for the woman's or the children's goods and if this is publicly known, he is a bad guardian, provided that he has been found guilty of this in court according to the land law.

Jef di mond da kinden to bosta jout eer hia to hiara jerem commen sint, buta rede der moder, soe ne mei dio dede naet staen, want hit di keyser urbeden[1] haet alle needmonda. Jef hit dioe moder deth buta reed dis mondis, so aegh dio dede eft naet to staen, want him di keyser dae mondschip toedeeld haet.

Aldeerom aegh neen frow neen deda toe dwaen buta her manne; hioe ne mei her winna ner forliesa. Da frowen aghen da bihode der kinden ende dis guedis, hit ne se dat hiaet urliese mit trim tingem. Dat aerste is als hia ene oderne man nimet, so ist urlerren, hit ne se dat hioet biburgie da kynden also gued[2] weer toe jouwen als hioet ontfucht. So mei hio foerd in der hoda bliuwa alont dae kynden jerich sint. Dat oder is jef hio dera kyndena eerwe urbrinckt buta rede dis mondis, soe haet hio se eefta urloren. Dat tredde is jef hio se in een claes-
159 ter[3] bringha[4] wil, so ne aeg | hia neen abbet to ontfaen eer hia jerich sint. Jef dat eerwe urbrocht is mit clasterferd jefta mit kape, als hia jerich sint, so fee hia oen hiara ain eerwe mit lioda landriuchta deer him di koningh Kaerl joe. Want alle needmonden fan onjeriga kinden buta reed dis mondis ende dera bihield dat haet di paeus ende di keyser urbeden.

GLOSSA 183. *So aegh syn broder iefta syn broders soen* Instit. de legi. ag. tutela § i (*Inst.* 1.15.1), C. eodem titulo (*Cod.* 5.30). Hodie uero nouo iure auctenticorum agnati simul et cognati. Et proximior gradu prefertur in tutela, sicut in successione, in auct. de success. que ab intestat. deferuntur § Ex his (*Auth.* 9.1.5 [*Nov.* 118.5]), ff. legi. tute. l. Si plures et l. Si relinquero (*Dig.* 26.4.9 et 8) et Insti. de capi. diminui. § Vlt. (*Inst.* 1.16.7) in glosa.[a]

Emen ende eeftersusterlinghen fan der modersida sint alsoe nei toe dae mondscip onjerigha kindena soe dae fedrien ende dae susterlingen fan des faders sida.

GLOSSA 184. Iure auctenticorum, ut supra proxima glosa.

GLOSSA 185. *Dit is dat aerste als ane oderne man* C. quando mulier tutele officio fungi potest l. ii (*Cod.* 5.35.2), et in auth. Sacramentum ibi posita (post *Cod.* 5.35.2 [ex *Nov.* 94.2]), et in auth. de nupci. § Si autem tutelam, collatione iiii (*Auth.* 4.1.40 [*Nov.* 22.40]).

GLOSSA 186. *Hit ne se dat hiaet biburgie* Nota antequam mater admittitur ad tutelam puerorum, debet primo coram iudice obligare res suas et renun-

[1] FG: wrbede. [2] FG: gned. [3] FG: claestera. [4] FG: brigha.

a The gloss *gradu* ad *Inst.* 1.16.7.

If the guardian lets the children enter into matrimony before they are of age, without the consent of the mother, this act shall not be considered to be legally binding because the emperor has forbidden all forms of imposed guardianship. If the mother does this without the consent of the guardian, this shall also not be considered to be legally binding because the emperor has given the guardianship to the guardian.

For this reason, a woman is not allowed to perform a legal act without her husband; she can win nor lose a case. Women have the right to take care of the children and their property, unless they lose this right because of three things. The first is when she marries another man, then she has lost it unless she can provide security that she will give the children back their goods in the same condition and value as she had received it. Then she may continue to look after the goods of the children until they are of age. The second is, if she alienates the inheritance of her children without the consent of the guardian. Then she has also lost it. The third is, if she wants to bring them into a monastery, than no abbot must accept them until they are of age. If the inheritance has been alienated because of entry into a monastery or because of selling it, and if the children then come of age, they can take possession of their own inheritance according to the land law which was given to them by King Charles. Because all imposed guardianship against underage children without the consent and monitoring of the guardian have been forbidden by the pope and the emperor.

GLOSS 183. *So aegh syn broder iefta syn broders soen* (*then his brother or his nephew have*). See *Inst.* 1.15.1 and *Cod.* 5.30. Nowadays, however, according to the new law of the *Authenticum*, those related through males together with next of kin in general. And the one most closely related has preference in the tutelage just as in the succession, see *Auth.* 9.1.5 (*Nov.* 118.5), *Dig.* 26.4.9 and 8, and in the Gloss to *Inst.* 1.16.7.

Uncles and cousins from the mother's side have the same right to become guardian of underage children as uncles and cousins from the father's side.

GLOSS 184. According to the law of the *authenticae*, as in de preceding gloss.

GLOSS 185. *Dit is dat aerste als ane oderne man* (*the first is if ... another man*). See *Cod.* 5.35.2 and the authentica *Sacramentum quidem* (post *Cod.* 5.35.2) and *Auth.* 4.1.40 (*Nov.* 22.40]).

GLOSS 186. *Hit ne se dat hiaet biburgie* (*unless she can provide surity*). Note. Before the mother is admitted to the tutelage, she must first provide security with her assets before the judge, renounce her appeal to the

ciare senatusconsulto uelliano et abdicare secundas nupcias, ut in auct. unde sine prohibitione matris § finali collatione vii (*Auth.* 7.4.2 [*Nov.* 94.2]). Et si secundas nupcias contraxerit, antequam pecierit tutorem filiis dari et antequam racionem tutele et totum quidquit inde debet reddiderit, non solum bona matris sed uitrici sunt filiis obligata. Aliis penis abiectis, in auctentico de nupc. § Si autem tutelam (*Auth.* 4.1.40 [*Nov.* 22.40]). Et debet mater compelli, ut rationem tutele reddat et quidquit inuentum fuerit eam debere integre persoluat, ut ibi.

GLOSSA 187. *Soe mei hio foerd inder hode* Sed non in tutela, quia alius dabitur tutor pupillis a iudice, ut in auctentico de nup. § Si autem in fine (*Auth.* 4.1.40 [*Nov.* 22.40]). |

GLOSSA 188. *Dat tredde is ieff hyose dan inden claester bringhe* De iure canonico mater potest offerre filium religioni inpuberem, xx q. i c. ii (C.20 q.1 c.2) et q. ii c. i (C.20 q.2 c.1). Idem in tutoribus, cum equiparantur in parentibus, xx q. ii Puella (C.20 q.2 c.2).

22. Dit sint da riucht, spreckt dy keyser Roliff, deer ic[1] langhe hadde socht myt grata arbeide eer ick se togadera brocht beida fan da Krekena heren ende fan da Dyonistera heran deer se scryoun hadden ende da heran fan Egiptera[2] lande. Da noment da heran fan Media ende makaden se al to manichfald. Deerefter nomen se da heren fan Babylonia,[3] want hit dii koningh al tostoerde alont hit da heren fan Athenra land toegader weder brochten mit grata arbeyde. Aldeerefter noment da heran fan Lacedemera lande hoder hiia se ne[4] getten ner naet se sie kyrten want se da Juden aerst screwen hadden. Efter disse heran nomen se da heren fan Roem: da tween heran Romulus ende Numa, di ena da burich[5] makade ende dy oder da riucht[6] sette. Da da heren weren daed, da worden da riucht wandeled. Da stodt manich schonen dach alont hit Julius ende Octavianus bycrongen myt crefte dat hya diine mena ferd fan Pardland brochten to Roem in dat hoff. Aldeerom schoep ma hine dine nia nama om da teyken deer aldeer schiiden ende hieten hym Augustus, want tween koningen haddent begonnen to scriwen.

Da dii daed quam
ende da heran beyde nam

[1] FG: hi. [2] FG: egpitera. [3] FG: bahylonia. [4] FG: *ne* is missing. [5] FG: bnrich. [6] FG: ruicht.

Senatusconsultum Velleianum, and abdicate a second marriage, see *Auth.* 7.4.2 (*Nov.* 94.2). And if she enters into a second marriage before she has requested that a tutor be given for the children and before she has given account of the tutelage and has restored all she accordingly owes, not only the mother's assets but also those of the stepfather will serve as security for the children. For other humiliating punishments see *Auth.* 4.1.40 (*Nov.* 22.40). And the mother should be compelled to give account of the tutelage and whatever appears that she owes, she will fully pay, as is stated there.

GLOSS 187. *Soe mei hio foerd inder hode* (*then she may continue to look after the goods*). But not remain tutor, since the judge will provide the pupils with a tutor in a different way, as in *Auth.* 4.1.40 (*Nov.* 22.40).

GLOSS 188. *Dat tredde is ieff hyose dan inden claester bringhe* (*The third is, if she wants to bring them into a monastery*). According to Canon law, the mother can make an immature child enter into a monastery, see C.20 q.1 c.2 and C.20 q.2 c.1. The same holds good for tutors, since they are put on a par with parents, see C.20 q.2 c.2.

22. These are the laws, says Emperor Rudolf, which I had sought with great effort before I compiled them, stemming both from the Greek rulers and from the lords of the Areopagus council in Athens,[21] who had written them down, and from the rulers of Egypt. Then the rulers of Media adopted them and made them too copious. After that, the rulers of Babylon adopted them, but the king invalidated them all until the rulers of Athens compiled them again with great effort. After that, the rulers of Lacedaemon adopted them, who neither compared them nor shortened them because the Jews had written them down first. After these rulers, the rulers of Rome adopted them: the two rulers Romulus and Numa, one built the citadel and the other decreed the laws. When the rulers had died, the laws were changed. Then many beautiful days passed until Julius and Octavian succeeded in forcefully bringing the common peace of Parthia to the court of Rome. Because of the omens that occurred there he was given a new name and they called him Augustus because these two kings had started to write down the laws.

When death came
and took both lords

21 See for this interpretation of *Dyonistera heran*: Wumkes, 'De frijheitsmythe fen it Rudolfsboek', 8n28. For an alternative interpretation (Dionysius Exiguus and the *Collectio Dionysiana*): Gosses, 'By it Rudolfsboek', 115–116.

da waes de leyder dat arbeyd ondaen
alont hith dy keyser Theodosius naem
ende dat arbeyd folbrochte[1]
deer neen man eer ne mochte
alont hit to Justianus quam
deer ma grata dueged fan foernam.
Syn riucht hi kirthe
ende mit dueghed getthe.
Aldus hi se bliuwa leet alont se Kaerl noem
161 deer joe di fridoem fan coem. |
Deer eer sonder erem weren[2]
onder alle mannes fotem
want joe dy dywel dyne raed ghaef
dat y mit wilker aldeertoe comen
dat y dine ayndoem nomen
ith dis norsche koninghes[3] hand
al sonder pand.[4]
Want joe di aersta koningh by syne tydem al fry deeld heede
wantet joen alderen mit dumheit urloren heden.
Aldeerum schillet hia sonder twiwel
da helle bowa mitta dywel.
Dit stoed dy leyder manyghen schoenen dach
alont joe God syne gnade ghaf.
Sinte Willibrord hi ju sante, hoe hi joe dat leerde
dat y fan da nordsca diwelen keerde.
Dine raed hy mit jo noem
datti to da Roemscha herem coem
ende jowen tins ende[5] tiende
dat se joe bischyrmden fan des nordscha koninghes[6] handen.
Dis tiende waerd sonderlyke ontfaen
want y waren eer friboren heran
want joe di aerste koningh efter dae floede
fri deeld hadde
ende jemna fri joun hede Asya land
alont y mit rede in Europa comen.
Aldeer y dyne ayndoem nomen
alont joe God sine naede gaf,

[1] FG: ffolbrochte. [2] FG: wereu. [3] FG: koniughes. [4] FG: band. [5] FG: enhe. [6] FG: koningdes.

the work unfortunately remained unfinished
until Emperor Thedosius took it up
and finished the work
which no man was able to do before
until it came to Justinian
in whom great virtue was perceived.
He shortened his laws
and compared them virtuously.
Thus he let them remain until King Charles adopted them
from whom your freedom stems.
Who before were without honour
under the feet of all men
because the devil had given you the advice
to freely come to the choice
of entering into slavery
under the rule of the northern king
without any surety.
Because the first king in his age had declared you free
but your ancestors had lost this privilege out of stupidity.
Therefore they will undoubtedly
live in hell with the devil.
This subsisted for many fair days
until God gave you mercy.
He sent you Saint Willibrord,
so that he could teach you
how to turn away from the northern devils.
He gave you the advice
to turn to the Roman lords
and pay tithes and taxes
so that they would protect you from the rule of the northern king.
This tax was to be paid singly
because once you had been freeborn lords
because the first king after the deluge
had made you free
and had freely given you Asia
until you came to Europe.
There you entered into slavery
until God gave you mercy:

dat y da heerferd foeren in dat Roemsche land
ende dae burich wonnen toe juwer hand
ende dyne heidene daed sloghen deer da burichheran[1] weren to Roem.
Aldeerom coem y mitta oerdele toe dae fridoeme
deer di leider langhe was urloeren.

23. Nu wil ick joe dit laeta staen
ende wil joe nu leta foerstaen
hoe da alda riucht[2] waren daen
want se da Judan ende dae Greken aerst bigonnen.

Dae Joeden screwen se fan her Moyses boecken ende da Greken fan hiara wys-
doeme ende fan Judaesche scrifte ende da heran fan Egiptera land dae Greken,
dat hia se bynoemen ende aec maeckaden toe riuchte hwat soe hiarem nette
tuchthe want se dat byscrewen an da Dyonistra. Jeft se dede enich man oen-
163 riucht, dat seet oen dae Dyoenistra bysoechthe. | Da Dionistra bitwonghen
fyfteen crona hoghe deer ma droeghe efter Egipto mit folla lowe. Want dioe fal-
sche munthe in Egipto urbaeden waerd alleraerst. Alhyrefter nament dae heran
fan Media dit riucht an hiara wald ende makaden se al toe manichfald nei da
Ebrewischa sidem want ze alle nachtdeden urbeden heden ende alle heiden
weren. Doch se dat toe riuchte hilden ende jelkirs litick bifinghen. Dis wald
stoe naet langhe an hiara hand. Alhyrefter soe noment dae heran fan Babilonia
ende riuchten se[3] bi halsum allerlikum aermen ende rikem. Hwa so da folke
wilde onriucht dwaen, dam deed ma dat hoefd offslaen. Want alle schaeck-
raef ende moerddeda[4] urbaeden heeden ende se dat riucht feste hilden alont[5]
di selwe koningh coem deer se alle wei noem. Alhyrefter noemen[6] disse wald
oen hiara hand dae heran fan Athenera land ende maekaden dae riucht wee-
der deer di koningh fan Babilonia hadde toebritsen. Want hia se weinten oen
da Latinscha tongha, hoe se nene heiden tobrecka ne mochten. Want se dae
riucht setten aerst, hwa soe mit tiefte woerde bighinsen dat ma him syn riucht
dede. Disse heran[7] hilden dit riucht mit eeren alont hit dae Lacedomera heran
noemen an[8] hiara handen, want hiaet hilden mit scanden. Want hia se hodder
ne getten ner toe nener dueged setten. Want hia se alsoe leten staen ont se dae
Roemeren noemen aen hyara handen, deer se joe fan commen sint, want se dae
Roemera heran getten ende setten ende kirten ende aeck soe banden se ende
bischirmden se by dae halse dat hia emmen toebreeke, want se aldeer worden
162 ghaederet ende aldeer scillet hia wirda toebritsen eer dae jonghista dei. |

[1] FG: bnrich heran. [2] FG: riuct. [3] FG: riuhtense. [4] FG: moerdeda. [5] FG: al out. [6] FG: noemeu. [7] FG: heranlde. [8] FG: au.

you went on a military expedition to Rome
and you conquered the citadel
and killed the pagans
who were the lords of the citadel in Rome.
Because of that you regained your freedom,
which had been lost for so long.

23. Now I want to let this rest
and want to let you know
how the old laws were made
because the Jews and the Greeks first made them.

The Jews copied them from the books of Lord Moses and the Greeks from their own wisdom and from the Jewish texts and the lords of Egypt adopted them from the Greeks and they also made into law what they deemed profitable because they wrote it down in the Dyonistra. And if any man did them any injustice, they looked it up in the Dyonistra. The Dyonistra subjugated fifteen high crowns which were worn to high esteem in Egypt. Because it was in Egypt that counterfeit coins were prohibited for the first time. After this, the lords of Media adopted the laws and made them too copious, following Jewish customs because they had forbidden all crimes committed during the night and were all pagans. But they upheld these laws and did not do much otherwise. They did not retain this rule for long. After this the lords of Babylon took possession and they passed severe judgment to both wealthy and poor. Whoever meant to do injustice to the people was beheaded. Because they had forbidden all violent robbery and homicide and they obeyed these laws until that same king came who nullified them all. After this, the lords of Athens came to power and reinstalled the laws which the king of Babylon had nullified. They translated them into Latin, so that no pagan would be able to destroy them. They first made it into law, that when someone was caught in the act of stealing, he would be sentenced before court. These lords maintained the laws honourably until the lords of Lacedaemon adopted them, but they maintained them shamefully. Because they neither compared them nor developed them for the better. They just let them be as they were until the Romans adopted them, and they have come to you via them because the Roman lords compared them and developed them and shortened them, and protected them because they commanded on capital punishment that they not be broken, and there they have been compiled and there they will not be nullified until Judgment Day.

24. Nu wil ic joe disse fiower tingh bitioda deer ick joe om bodet hab.
Dat arste om dat heilighe land: to der selwa heerferd schil y helpe dwaen
truch da eera des himelscha faders,
want hyt jo wal lania mei warlike
di koningh fan himelrik
want hi dat selwe land kaes
da hi hyr nedir an disse wrald commen was.
Want hi ons alle leesde sonder twiwel
fan da helscha[1] diwel.
Jef emmen dit land
wold winnen fan da Crystena hand,
so moete wi deerum alle sterwa doed
ende lesa us uter fiandes noet,
want hit is warlik
onsis faders eerwe an himelrik.

Dat oder is om dat Roemsche ryck jef hit wold fan der Crystena hand ende selschipia with da heidena hand bi rede ende bi falsched dera quade Roemra, want hit leider[2] also fallen is aleer. So sel y een heerferd fara mitta paus ende keisere want hia sint waren juwe riuchte heren. Nelli disse heerferd naet mit him dwaen, so mei jo di paus bisluta din ewiga wei deer ti da himelryc leit. Ende y schillet aec alsoe wal fara om da era deer jo dan wirdet deen in da Roemscha land da jo di fridoem joun ward.

Dit is dat III um dat hus bi da Rine. Jef dat enich landis hera wold oenfaen jefta sinte Martine wold onriucht[3] dwaen, so moetti deerfoer staen mit creftliker hand want hi da sloetelen feert toe juwer siele in dat paed ti da lesta ordele.

Dit is dat[4] fiard, deer joe selwe toheert ende y oenghaen schillet.[5] Jef y ith Gode willet habba dat himelsche laen ende da ewigha crona ontfaen soe moetti strida with da nordscha[6] hand ende mitta suderna hand om juwe ain land ende om juwe fridoem. Want y noemen diine fridoeme alleraerst[7] dae Noe utera archa coem. Want i sint fan koninghes slachte ut boeren, fan Sem, deer di aerste koningh waes efter di floede, deer dis wrald enich kaes. Want hy joe allen fri
164 wessa heet. | Nu horet ho haeg hyt jo bifeel bi synre crona ende bi ju hymelryck scone. Dit stode manich sconen dach alont joe di diwel daer to brochte mit synre falscheid ende mit juwer dumheit dat y deer toe kamen dat y dine ayndoem noemen fan des norsche koninghes handen ende dedin al mit scanden. Dat ne stoed meer dan een[8] half jaer dat y joene riuchter sloeghen daed

[1] FG: helscda. [2] FG: heider. [3] FG: *on*riuct. [4] FG: dt. [5] FG: schiliet. [6] FG: nordseha. [7] FG: aller aerss. [8] FG: eeu.

24. Now I want to tell you about these four things because of which I commanded you to come.
The first is because of the Holy Land: you shall assist in a military expedition there in honour of the heavenly father,
for he will truly reward you for it
the king of heaven
because he chose this same land
when he had come to the world.
Because he undoubtedly redeemed us
from the hellish devil.
If anyone wished to conquer this land
from Christian dominion,
we should all die for it
and redeem us from the devil's reign,
because it truly is
our father's legacy in heaven.

The second is because of the Roman empire, if it threatened to go over from Christian into pagan rule, through the advice and treason of the evil Romans because this has unfortunately happened before. Then you shall undertake a military expedition with the pope and the emperor because they truly are your rightful lords. If you choose not to come on this military expedition, then the pope may cut you off from the eternal road which leads to heaven. And you shall also go because of the honour that was bestowed upon you in Rome when you received your freedom.

The third is because of the house alongside the river Rhine. If any lord would attack it or would do injustice to Saint Martin, you should defend it vigorously because he holds the keys to your souls on the road to the Final Judgment.

This is the fourth, which concerns you yourselves and which you shall undertake. If you want to receive the heavenly reward from God and the eternal crown, you shall fight against the northern kingdom and along with the southern kingdom for your own country and freedom. Because you first received your freedom when Noah came out of the ark. Because you were born of royal blood, from Sem, who was the first king who was ever chosen on this world after the deluge. Because he proclaimed that you be free. Now hear this, how highly he commanded it you by his own crown and by your heavenly kingdom. This lasted for many days until the devil treacherously deceived you and you foolishly decided to enter into slavery of the northern king and disgraced yourselves in doing so. This did not last longer than six months and then you killed

ende brochten syner frowe in grater need ende[1] y juwe fridoem weder noemen. Aldeerefter stoet manich scoenen dach ont hit mit dumheet urloren waerd. Want i alle heyden worden ende mit riuchte des diwels[2] knechten want joe di koningh aldeertoe twangh ende aldeerefter toe manich arbeide ende dedin manighen[3] leide. Dit arbeit was to graet, neen man can joe waerlike seggen dat. Dat stoed[4] thi leider manighen sconen dach alont i to Rome quamen ende yt fan Kaerle handen weeder naemen. Want hit joe dy paus byfeel dat y hilde juwe fridoem ful waerlike[5] by da hagha hymelryck.

25. Dit leta wi nu staen ende wil joe mine fyf ferdban kondich dwaen. Dat aerste,[6] dat ic urbanne alle muntha an juwe land bihala da selwirna, want hit dio haegeste is: da ban ic jo to haldene.

Ick urbanne alle indycken ende alle dammen ur een dyep ende ur bannena faran thi da kerchowe[7] jefta to da tolnade merkaden jefta to da syle deer dat wetter utrenne schil. Da indycken, jef se macked sin buta reed wisera liodena ende des landis ende dera papena ende prelatena ende hy dan birawie da seburich dis wirkis, so ne moet hy naet staen[8] bliwa. Ick urbanne dat da burich ymmen[9] dytze jefte dele dattet salte wetter ingonge. Hwa so dat det, di schil beta mit trim Colinsca pondem. Ick urbanne dattet nemmen haetie da heerstreta, deer gaed truch dat land jefte to een tolnade merkade ofta toe enis |
165 godeshuse. Hwa so hyr wald oen[10] det di schilt beta mit een Coelscha pond.

Ic urbanne alle needmonden fan onjeriga kynden buta rede des mundis end der hera.

Ic urbanne dat deer immen aen jemna lande myn riucht nyme mit wald jefta mit falscha rede jefta mit bede jefta mit cape. Mer hit schillet wessa dajene deer wise lioede ende prelaten in settet bi rede des landis ende da schillet wessa buta alsodena deden als ick buppa biscrioun habbe, jef hia mei ma witsprecka.

Ick urbanne kerckferd, hofferd, soeneferd. Hwa so dera trya enich inbrect so schil hi beta dyne ferd mit sex Coelscha pondem ende triin boeta. Hwam so[11] ma[12] in een hus onder een hinem an nachta stolkens daed slacht ende hi syn riucht naet urlerren haet, soe is di ferd sex Colinsche pond ende twibeet.

Ick urbanne alle falscka wilkaren deer dat neste lyf onterwia willet, want di wilker seit with da ewa ende with dat alda riucht ende with Godes hulde. Want dat neste lyf dat eerwe aegh soe fyr so hi friboren see ende hyt naet urlerren haet mit trim thingem, mit mordbrand, mit manslachta, mit falska urreed an lyff jefta an guede ende dat openbeer se, soe haet hi syn riucht urlern.

---

[1] FG: eu*de*. [2] FG: dwels. [3] FG: manigde*n*. [4] FG: *Dat stoed* is missing. [5] FG: waerike. [6] FG: acrste. [7] FG: kerthone. [8] FG: stacn. [9] FG: ymmer. [10] FG: oeu. [11] FG: Hwaso. [12] FG: *ma* is missing.

your *skelta* and brought his wife in great distress and regained your freedom. Now the freedom lasted for a long time until it was lost because of foolishness. Because you all became pagans and true servants of the devil because the king forced you to do this and after this he forced you to suffer terribly. No man can truly tell how great this suffering was. This lasted many days until you came to Rome and received your freedom again from Charles. Then the pope commanded you by the high kingdom of heaven to faithfully uphold it.

25. Now I want to let this rest and proclaim to you my five peace orders. First, I prohibit the use of any coins except silver coins in your lands because silver is the highest: I order you to obey this.

I prohibit all inland dams and all dams which have been laid in a river or in water roads which are under my command leading to a churchyard or to a toll market or to sluices which channel the water outward. Inland dams that have been constructed without the consent of the wise man and the council of the land and the priests and prelates and that prevent the seawalls from functioning properly, cannot be allowed to stay. I forbid anyone to strengthen or weaken the seawall by means of digging if this leads to salt water passing through. If anyone does so, he will pay a fine of three pounds of pennies of Cologne. I forbid anyone to damage the principal roads which run through the land or to a toll market or to a church. If anyone does so, he will pay a fine of one pound of pennies of Cologne.

I prohibit all forms of imposed guardianship upon underage children which are executed without the consent of their guardian or the *skelta*.

I prohibit anyone to usurp my jurisdiction by force or false counsel or on request or by buying it. But the law shall be upheld by those appointed by wise men and prelates with the consent of the land and these men shall not have been sentenced for crimes I described earlier, otherwise the people will not have to obey these men.

I command peace to all churches and courts and to honour truces. If anyone breaks these forms of peace, he will pay a fine of six pounds of pennies of Cologne and compensate threefold. If any member of a household is killed maliciously during the night and the victim has not lost his legal status, the penalty for the breach of the peace is six pounds of pennies of Cologne and the compensation is twofold.

I prohibit all false statutes which aim at disinheriting the next of kin because such statutes go against the old custom and against the ancient laws and against God's grace. The next of kin is entitled to an inheritance as long as they are freeborn and have not lost their legal status by committing three crimes; arson, homicide, false treason concerning life or goods. If this is publicly known, then they have lost their legal status.

26. Nu wil ick dit lata bliwa ende nel jo naet meer scriwa. Doch wil ick jo I[1] tingh bibanna. Hwant alle da riucht ende alle wilkaren deer juwe land nette sint, so fyr so se wit da ewa naet na se seth, ende juwe fridom ende mene rede ende mene frede ende mene heerferd mit juwe saun selandem om juwe fridoem dat byfalle ick joe to haldane bi juwe halse ende bi dae himelrike ende bi jonre siele ende bi da lesta ordele. Hwaneer i ane hera ur jo tziese, juwe himelryck i urliese. Ick urbiede jo dat i eniga landis hera jowe tins ende tienda mer da
166 riuchta[2] | hofschielda ende dajenne deer dat koninges teiken mit him bringe. Alhyreefter urbiede ick[3] alle koningem ende alle landis herem dat ju immen wald jefta onriucht dwe an juwe fridoem. Hwa so hit jo det buta juwe schield so haet hi siin haud urlerren with da Roemscha heren.

27. Nu wil ic jo jouwa een traest ende een helpa so fyr so y deer om bidde to Almania dat koninghryck. Nu wil ic fan jo scheda. Di rika God bihoed ons bedem. Da Fresen nomen orlef ende foren an hiara hof ende di keiser entwara, deer was een friboren hera. Dit was in da tredda hondersta jeer an sinte Johannesdei to middasomera efter Kaerle der Fresen dine fridoem jo, da disse riucht worden maked ende disse handjefta utjoun.

28. Nu wil ic jo tria tingh condich dwaen deer jo di koningh to Salem haet condich daen, deer Melchisedech was naemd. Nu wil ic corta disse dichta ende disse tingh biriuchta. Dit is dat aerste: hweer so di fria Fresa is eens mit falscheed bifaen so moet hyt twischet wederjouwa ende een hallef Colinscha pond to frede banne. Aldus is dat aerste daen. Dat oder: hweer so di man mit falscheed wirt bifaen so moet hi sex grata pond jaen ende hiara fridom weder nima ende IIII Colinscha pond toe fredebanne dwaen. Aldus is dat tredde da orem lyc ende sinta nede, deer joe di koningh fan Cherub haet condich daen. Dit moten alle Fresen ontfaen deer sint friboren jefta fri spreke habbet ontfaen. Dit is om dat koninghlike slachte daen ende om daejenne deer conath da riuchte urstaen. Alle disse ban deer in disse boke sint biscrewen da schillet wessa bi da grata ponde, dat pond schil wessa bi xx schillingem. Dach schillet Fresen nedena nyeta.

29. Aldus spreec di keyser Philippus ende di koninck Theodericus ende di paeus
167 Alexander ende | spreken fan da wirden deer hya fan dae guede sinte Peter heerden ende seiden dat dio wird scholde dat riucht opnima altida bihala om fyf bischedelika ting. Dit is dat aerste: hweer so een man jefta een frowe leit an

[1] FG: *I* is missing. [2] FG: riudhta. [3] FG: *ick* is missing.

26. Now I want to let these matters rest and not write you any more about it. But I want to command you one more thing. I command you to uphold all laws and statutes that are beneficial to your land, in so far as they do not go against the custom and your freedom and your communal council and your communal peace and your communal military expedition amongst your seven sealands to protect your freedom, on pain of your necks and by heaven and by your soul and by the Last Judgment. If you should ever choose a ruler to rule over you, you will lose the kingdom of heaven. I forbid you to pay taxes and tithes to any other ruler except the lawful king's tax to the person carrying the king's symbols. I also forbid all kings and rulers to infringe upon your freedom in any way. Anyone who does so against your will shall lose his neck before the Roman rulers.

27. Now I want to give you aid and assistance if you ever come to the kingdom of Alemannia for it. Now I want to depart from you. May the almighty God protect us both. The Frisians took leave and went home and the emperor also departed: he was a freeborn lord. These laws and this privilege were decreed on Saint John's Day; exactly three hundred years after Charles had given the Frisians their freedom.

28. Now I want to make known to you three things which the king in Salem, who was called Melchizedek, told you. Now I want to shorten this text and tell it to you. This is the first thing: If a free Frisian is caught with counterfeit coins he shall return it twofold and pay the penalty for the breach of the peace with half a pound of pennies of Cologne. This was the first thing. The second: if a man is caught with counterfeit coins he shall give six pounds of groats and then reclaim his freedom and pay the penalty for the breach of the peace with four pounds of pennies of Cologne. The third is similar to the other two and these are the privileges, which the king of Cherub bestowed upon you. This was done because of the royal house and because of those who can understand these laws. All penalties described in this book are to be paid with pounds of groats, twenty shillings in one pound. Still, the Frisians will enjoy privileges.

29. Thus speak Emperor Philip and King Theoderic and Pope Alexander and they spoke of the truth which they had heard from the good Saint Peter and said that the truth should overrule the law at all times except in five instances. This is the first: if a man or a woman are lying on their deathbeds, and if a claim

lesta einde haet so ma hiarem toaeschet ende sprecket hia danne dat hit urgolden se dat wird moet staen ende haet so hia sprecket dat moet habba ane stal. Al is hit naet redelike daen, so moet hit da wird nederslaen want hyr steet scrioun fan: "In da lesta dei schil God riuchta da heemlika tingh dera liodena ende openberia da tochten der herten".

> In ultimi[1] die iudicii[2] iudicabit Deus occulta hominum et manifestabit cogitationes cordium.

Dat oder is: hweer so een man ende een frouwe dwaet een trouwa, nyster neen man over, willet hya dan bisecka, soe ontgongh se mit hyara sexter hand. Dat riucht[3] moet da wird nederslaen. Mer habbet deerur wessen tween man, soe moet hit staen, want deer steet fan scrioun in da ewangelio: "Tweer menscha tiuech of tree is weer".

> In lege mea scriptum est, quod in ore[4] duorum hominum stat omne uerbum.

want fan der falsckheed steet scrioun aldus: "fulla sonderen schillet opstaen in der oprisenisse der daden ende des ordels ende ghaen fan pina to pinen."

> Multi peccatores resurgunt in resurrexione iudicii[5] et ibunt de supplicio ad supplicium.

Dat tredde is: hweer so een man faert in een oer land jefta in een oer kerspel ende hi een tingh nimt ende feertet mit him jefta dattet him joun wirth endma him dan eefter comt ende mitta guede bifucht ende tiucht hyt dan op een orem so mey hyt ontgaen mit siner sexter hand. Al ist naet redelike deen doch soe mey dit riucht da wird nederslaen. Hwant in der koninga bueckem scrioun
168 steet: | "Dy koningh fan Babilonia ende syne forsten ende syn folck comen ende selden da weerheed tofara dat ansicht des urste riuchters ende bijaraden ydele afgoden ende baeden oen da goldena sela deer dy koningh seth heed. Deerom foerderf di koningh ende syn folck fan honger ende god bidekte syn ansicht fan himmen, want se qualike[6] wrochten".

> Rex Babilonie et principes et populus eius uenerunt et uendiderunt ueritatem ante faciem summi iudicis et cupierunt praua iudicia idolorum[7] et

---

[1] FG: ultimo. [2] FG: indicy. [3] FG: riueht. [4] FG: *in ore* is missing. [5] FG: indicy. [6] FG: qualibe. [7] FG: ydolorum.

is made against them and they say this has already been paid, this shall be considered to be true and whatever they say shall be valid. Even when it is not actually true, it will overrule the truth, for it is written: "On the day of the Last Judgment God will sentence the hidden things of men and will make manifest the counsels of the hearts".

> On the day of the Last Judgment God will sentence the hidden things of men and will make manifest the counsels of the hearts.

The second thing is: if a man and a woman exchange wedding vows and no man is present to witness it, and if they want to deny this later, they can do so with the help of five compurgators. Here the law must overrule the truth. But if two men were present, the vows must stand because it is written in the gospel: "The testimony of two or three men is true".

> It is written in my law, that in the mouth of two men every word stands.

Because on the untruth it is written: "Many sinners rise up again at the resurrection of the Judgment and will go from torment to torment".

> Many sinners rise up again at the resurrection of the Judgment and will go from torment to torment.

The third is: if a man goes to another land or another parish and takes something with him or if it was given to him and if people come after him and he is caught with the object and he then blames it on someone else, he is allowed to swear innocence with the help of five compurgators. Even though this is not reasonable, this law may overrule the truth. Because in the Books of Kings it is written: "The King of Babylon and his princes and people gathered and wasted the truth before the face of the highest judge and desired perverse idols and worshipped a golden statue which the king had established. Henceforth the king and his princes starved to death and God concealed his face from them because they did evil".

> The King of Babylon and his princes and people gathered and wasted the truth before the face of the highest Judge and desired the perverse

> adorauerunt statuam auream, quam constituerat rex. Propterea sine racione rex et principes eius perierunt fame et Deus abscondit faciem suam ab oculis eorum, quia male egerunt.

Dat fiarde is: hweer so een man ende een frowe dwaet togara cleppen jefta dio frowe spreckt dat hio see mit ene kinda joff di man biseckt dis manda, so ontgonge hi mit siner selwer sexter hand. Joff hi jecht dis manda, soe wite dio frow da stonda mit herre sexta hand ende di man di nime dat kynd[1] allinna want hiit self alsoe meende.

30. Dit sint da fyf riucht, spreeck di keiser Frederick, deer da wird schillet nederslaen. Elkers om alle ting deer redelic sint moet dio wird foerdgaen. Also moetin alle daejeen deer riucht urstaed ende willet onfaen. Konet hia se naet urstaen, also moten hia thene man faen. Aeck so moter neen man fan da riucht gaen sonder orlef, want deer steet scrioun: "wesset onderdenich jemna ursten."

> Obedite prepositis vestris.

Ende in der koniga bokem steet scrioun dat dat folc gingh to her Samuel ende seiden dat hi himmen I koning jo deer hia mochten redelic onder libba ende di koning scolde wessa alsodeen dat hi kude riucht urstaen aec ne schil hi him an nen arbeid biswera ende nen onriuchtes pligia. Samuel spreec weder ti da folke hi wolde him dat riucht biscriwa ende jaen deer hia redelick onder libba
169 mocht. | Mer fula des folkis en wolden him naet hera ende seiden: "Seth us en koning deer us biriucht". Samuel spreek weder ellick gongh in syn hus.

> Plures autem noluerunt audire uocem eius, sed dixerunt "constitue nobis regem". etc.

Aldus moghen hit alle lioed urstaen deer riucht willet onfaen. Joff him enich thingh comt to, deer ma sielden urnimt ende ne conet hiaet urstaen, so schillet hia nei hiara presters rede gaen, willet hia redelike libba,[2] want dio riuchtfirdicheed[3] ursteert da onriuchtfirdicheed. Want in us hera passia lest ma dat Herodes God ursmaide ende God spreec to Pilatus: "Ic bin di wei, der wird, ende liand". Ende Pylatus ursmaide God mit onriucht ordel. Deerom urderf hi ende alle onriuchta riuchteren mit him in ewelick in lika seckum.

---

[1] FG: kyud. [2] FG: habba. BL, BN, J109, KB, M60, PB, RA: libba. [3] FG: riucht firhicheed. BL, KB, PB, UB: riucht firdicheed.

> judgments of idols and worshipped a golden statue, which the king had established. Henceforth the king and his princes starved to death without explanation and God concealed his sight for the eyes of those who did evil.

The fourth is: if a man and a woman have sexual intercourse, and if the woman says she is with child and if the man denies having had intercourse, he may prove his innocence with the help of five compurgators. If he acknowledges having had intercourse, the woman shall testify to the time of their intercourse with the help of five compurgators and the man must only accept the child because he was of he same opinion.

30. These are the five laws, spoke Emperor Frederick, which overrule the truth. In all other cases which are reasonable the truth must prevail. In this way all should act who understand the law and want to receive justice. If they are unable to understand it, they will still have to do justice to someone. And no man shall leave the court without permission, because it is written: "Obey your prelates".

> Obey your prelates.

And it is written in the Books of Kings that the people came to lord Samuel and asked him to give them a king under which they could live reasonably and this king should be able to understand the law but would not force them into labour or do them injustice. Samuel answered the people that he would write down the law and give it to them so that they could live under it sensibly. But a majority of the people would not listen to him and said: "Give us a king who will do us justice". Samuel answered again and each went home.

> Many, however, would not hear his voice, but said "establish us a king", etc.

In this way all people who want to receive justice should understand it. If they are confronted with a case which is rare and they are unable to understand it, they should listen to the advice of their priest if they want to live sensibly, because justice destroys injustice. Because in the passion of our Lord one can read that Herod scorned God and God said to Pilate: "I Am the Way, the Truth, and the Life". And Pilate scorned God with an unjust sentence. For that reason he, and together with him all unjust judges, perished in eternity and for one and the same reason.

Et legitur in passione Domini: "Spreuit[1] eum Herodes cum exercitu suo". Et eciam Pilatus ad eum ait: "Quid est veritas?". Et Dominus ad eum: "Ego sum uia, ueritas et uita". Et tamen spreuit eum iniusto iudicio. Propterea ipse periit et omnes iniusti iudices cum illo in eternum et cum una racione.

Jefter enich landis hera jof enich riuchter deth een naemlick onriucht ende hit biprowet wirt openbeer, di haet syn riucht urlerren ende syn era. So ne thoer ma hem naet meer toe riucht staen want in der appostela buecken scrioun steet: "Pilatus[2] is utginsen fan sine tinghstoel ende gingh nei ydele ordelen ter hellen ende nimmermeer weer to commen".

Vnde in actibus apostolorum: Egressus est Pilatus de pretorio suo post praua iudicia etc.

Also wel so schil dijen om siaen hwam hyt riucht jou hor hi aet redelic libbe. Nel hi naet redelick libba, so moet hyt riucht en orem jaen, so ne haet hi deer nen schield fan. Want deer steet scrioun: "Di quada redir ende di quaeda dedir schillet mit liker pina piniget wirda."

Consentientes[3] et agentes[4] etc. |

[1] FG: sprenit. [2] FG: Pilatns. [3] FG: consencientes. [4] FG: agentet.

> And in the Lord's Passion one can read: "Herod with his army despised him". And also that Pilate said to him: "What is truth?". And the Lord said to him: "I am the way, the truth and the life". And yet he despised him with a perverse judgment. For that reason he, and together with him all unjust judges, perished in eternity and for one and the same reason.

Any lord or any *skelta* who passes an unjust judgment and if this is proven publicly, he will have lost his legal status and his honour. And no-one needs to undergo a trial by this judge any longer, because it is written in the Acts of the Apostles: "Pilate left the court and after the unjust judgment went to hell and never returned".

> Thus it is written in the Acts of the Apostles that after the perverse judgments Pilate left his courthouse etc.

In the same way, he who gives away justice should see to it that he lives properly. If he does not want to live properly, he should give the appointment to someone else, so that he is not guilty of anything. For it is written: "The one who gives bad counsel and the one who acts unjustly will be punished in the same manner".

> Consenting and acting, etc.

XVII. Market Law

Hyr biginnet da merckedriucht

1. Dit is riucht, dat di schelta moet tingia ende tingh halda to alle merckadum deer ma utfirdich oen is hwanneer so hi wil, dat offnima hor festa ner fira, om huis, om hussteden,[1] om bodel, om lawa, om tiefta, om falscha wichta, om falscha ielna, om onriuchta tolna, om faed, om screed, om falschene brand, om moerdbrand ende om alle tingh deer da mercked toheert, mer om nen eerwe deer in dine mercked heert ende binna der hemmeric leyt: dat scil ma riuchta als hit to landriuchte heert.

2. Hwa so een hus an ene mercket selt ende hi dine steed bihalt ende di caper dine sedel foerd bitinget cortera jefta langera, so sel ma dat bisetta oen da bannena tinge ho lange hiara eental were, jef di seller moet dine caper ofswara hwanneer hi wil mit alle riucht.

3. Jef een merkedman een steed heert ende hi deer also lange op sit dat hi queth dat hine caped habbe ende di ora biseckt, brect di capere dis aefte tiuges,[2] so aeg di ora dat fri ende trira jeer heer sonder eed, also fyr soe hi se aschia wil ende als hit aldus biradet wirt, so aegh di schelta fyf schillingen.

4. Dat is riucht, dat om huissteden wita schillet saun synre buren ende tween schepenen, alsoe fyr so hia ayn steden habbe an der buirschip, hor hit caep se soe heerd were, ende dat schil ma oen da tinge opbringe.

5. Dat is riucht: deer mit falscher meta oen da merked bigripen wirt jefta an onriuchter wichta hweeroen so hit is onriuchtelike deen, so aegh hi om dat onriucht da schelta XXI schillingen to jouwane also fyr soe een scheppena ende tweer trowe buren bitiugha wille ende in dine merked als hit wilkared is, so is
171 di | wilker alsoe graet als hine dae liued mitta schelta enighiet.

6. Om wanmeta saun schillingen da schelta ende ti da merkedriucht als hit wilkared is.

---

[1] FG: hwsted*en*. [2] FG: ti*n*ges.

XVII. Market Law

Here Begins the Market Law

1. This is the law, that at all market towns to which people are travelling from elsewhere, the *skelta* may hold court whenever he wants—and neither fast-days nor feast-days will be excluded from this—over cases concerning houses, house plots, inventories, inheritances, theft, false balance weights, false textile measuring rods, unlawful tolls, counterfeit or clipped coins, malicious fire-raising and arson and concerning all things which pertain to the market town, but not concerning estates which fall under the market and lie within the boundaries of the village: these matters should be brought before court according to the land law.

2. If someone sells a house in a market town but keeps inhabiting the place and the buyer makes a legal agreement over the duration of the occupancy, whether it be a shorter or a longer period, this is to be settled at court for how long a period they can come to an agreement over, or the buyer may lawfully expel the seller by swearing an oath when he wants.

3. If a merchant rents a house and lives there for such a long time that he claims that he has bought it and the other party contests this, and if the "buyer" is unable to produce the lawful proof by testimony, then the other party has full authority over it and can have three year's rent without having to swear an oath over it if he wants to claim this. And if this has been proven in this way, the *skelta* shall have five shillings.

4. This is the law, that in cases concerning houses seven neighbours and two jurors must give testimony, if they own houses in the town, which they either own or rent, and such a case must be brought before court.

5. This is the law: if someone is caught in the market town with a false measure or with false balance weight, with which it is unlawfully done, he has to give the *skelta* 21 shillings because of this illegal act, if one juror and two reliable neighbours are willing to give testimony on this and he has to pay a fine to the market town as has been decreed; the amount of this fine is such as the people have agreed upon with the *skelta*.

6. In case of measuring inaccurately, seven shillings are to be paid to the *skelta* and to the market court as has been decreed.

7. Om bieres wanmeta: hwa so drinckt lessa so mara, so ne thoer hi dat naet jelda also fyr so hit binna da bierhuse eniged se ende mit riuchte bifulged. So aeg di schelta tweer schillingen dis bannes ende di merked syn riucht alset wilkared is. Spreckt hi buta huus om wanmeta, soe is di tapper nier mit ene eed to ontgaen dan ma mit eniga riucht se to urwinnen. Om da ielna is dat selve riucht.

8. Jef een man mit fade ende mit scredane biginsen wirt, deer in dine merked heert, nimpt ma dine fader onder hammer ende onder tanga, jefta dine screder onder dera schera jefta onder sine falscha onderke, soe ne heert deer fordera neen riucht to, dan ma him da fordera hand ofslee. Wirth hit folbrocht mit riucht, so aeg di schelta dat gued to bisittane to heerna hand ende da treftiga weder to delane ende deer aegh di aesga him een ferd oen to delane also fyr so hyt wille swara tween trowa schepenen dat hi riuchtelyc ontfinsen se.

9. Wirter een munter buta der smitte mit fade bigripen, soe moet hi riuchtes bruka toe ene swirdkempa. Om dine scredere also.

10. Om lauwa deer in da merked lauwiget wirdet, soe aegh di eerfnama dine schelta[1] to da huus to haliane dat hi him riuchtes helpe. Det hy dat naet ende di schelta dat uraeschie om dat bodel, so aeg hi sine bannere to da fordel to seynden dat ma him afara utachtie fyff schillinghen, want se hit him an raef haldet. Nu aegh di schelta dis fyarda deys thi dae fordele to commen ende sines
172 riuchtes te monien. Wernet[2] hia se him, | so aegh di aesga to delen dat hi infare ende mit synre fora hand syn riucht utachtia schil. Wert him immen mit wald, di aech to jowane II pond.

11. Nympt dy tolner onriuchte tollen ende him tre schepnen bitinga willet, so aegh di schelta foer alle da deer hi tollen ur laet fan da fordele fyf schillingen. Dat schil di tolner jowa jefta mit riucht wara mit ene swirdkempa, jefta di aesga deelt him XII eden.

12. Dit is riucht om moerdbrand an da merkade. Wirter en man mit moerdbrand bigripen, so aegh di schelta dine ker hor hi dine man hwe, dan men blynde jefta barne jefta an elende seinde ende syn gued heert an koninges wara ende an heerna hand. Seit met een man op endma dat naet urweer weet, so aegh men

[1] FG: schctta. [2] FG: werwet.

7. In case of inaccurately measuring beer: if someone drinks (beer), be it little or much, the innkeeper does not have to pay this if it has been established inside the inn and it has been brought before court. Then, the *skelta* shall have a fine of two shillings for breaking the peace and the market court shall have the fine as has been decreed. If he accuses of measuring inaccurately outside of the inn, the innkeeper is entitled to exonerate himself by swearing an oath rather than that the claimant may offer testimony against him. The same law applies to inaccurately measuring textile.

8. If a man who partakes in the market is apprehended with inferior coins or clipped coins, and if the counterfeiter is apprehended while working with his hammer and pliers, or the money trimmer while working with his scissors or with his criminal tools, then no other law applies than that his right hand is to be cut off. If this is done according to the law, then the *skelta* shall take possession of this property on behalf of the judges and this is to be distributed among the poor. And the *asega* has to proclaim a peace over this action if two reliable jurors are willing to swear that he was caught in a lawful manner.

9. If a moneyer is apprehended with counterfeit coins outside of his smithy, he can appeal to a judicial duel. The same applies to someone who clips coins.

10. If an inheritance is bequeathed in the market town, the heir has to ask the *skelta* to come to the house and assist him according to the law. If the heir does not do so and the *skelta* demands his share of the inheritance, he has to send his *bannere* to the house and the heir shall pay him five shillings there because they unlawfully denied him this. Now the *skelta* must come to the house on the fourth day and claim his rights. If they deny him access, then the *asega* shall decree that he enters the house and takes with his right hand what is legally his. If someone resists him and uses violence, he has to pay 2 pounds.

11. If a tax collector demands unlawful tolls and three jurors want to find him guilty, then the *skelta* is entitled to five shillings for each house the tax collector exacts tolls from. The tax collector shall pay this or claim his innocence by appealing to a judicial duel, or the *asega* may allow him to swear 12 oaths of innocence.

12. This is the law concerning arson in the market town. If someone is apprehended performing arson, then the *skelta* has a choice whether to hang the man, blind him, burn him or send him abroad, and his goods will be transferred to the property of the king and the judges. If someone is accused of this,

oen to tingiane mit aefta tinghe emmer ur acht daegem. Dat ne mei ofnima ner fira ner festa want hit in da mercked schiin is. So ist riucht to da aersta tinge, ist een eerm man, dat di schelta aeg him onder burga to bringen alont hit bitinget is. Ne mei hi neen burga winna, so aeg hi to swarrane. So aeg hi to gaen dana ont ti da nesta tinge. So aeg him di schelta to andert to bringen alont hit bitinget is. Ist een ryck man deer met oenspreckt, so moet hi burgia op syn ryk alont hi mit riucht fri wirt jefta in da schield urwonnen wirth.[1]

[1] FG: wirh.

but there is no absolute certainty, the man is to be prosecuted before court on eight consecutive days. Fast-days or feast-days are not excluded from this term, since it happened in the market town. Then this is the law that on the first day the *skelta* shall let the defendant, if he is a poor man, provide a surety until the end of the proceedings. If he is unable to find a surety, he has to swear an oath. The defendant is then allowed to leave until the next court session. Then the *skelta* has to make sure he appears before court until the proceedings have been brought to an end. If he is a rich man, he may provide security with his wealth for the period until he has been found innocent or guilty.

XVIII. Unmendable Crimes

Hyr bighinnet da swarta swinghen

1. Dit is een riucht swart swengh: hwa so fiucht ur sette soen, ur swerren eden ende ur keste mond, so haet hi britzen dine heilighe ferd deer hi selve wilkared.

2. Dat is en swart swengh: hwa so dat riucht brect om giricheed jefta om jelkirs
quada meninga, so breckt hi dat deer God selve baed to twang dera sondena,
173 want dat riucht helpet dam deer him selm naet helpa | mei, hit scept riuchte
wreeck op da schielde ende hit bischirmt da onschield.

3. Dit is en swart swingh: hwa so syn riuchta syd urreth so liket hi Judas deer God selva urreed, deer dyn freed keste mitta mond ende[1] dyn weer tobreeck.

4. Hwa so deth disse swarta swinghen jefta ander deda dissem lyck deer aldus quaed sint, so mei him neen prester nen hermscheed scriwa, hi ne seke dine paves to Roem jefta syn wieldiga boda ende him di paus ende dy prester sine hermscheed scriwe ende sette nei nedem ende ney riuchte. Alont dat schel hi buta kerka staen ende nen man hyndera comma dan datter atwischa se nioghen feet. Hi ne moet neen paes nima als dat ander folck: hi schil tojens syn stef passia deer hi oen der hand haet ende hi mei nenis orlefs nieta. Hi schil mangra duget missa deer ma in der cristenheed deth want hi haet him selff deerut brocht mitter quaeder deda.

5. Item dit sint da saun swarta swinghen: hwa so deth moerd jefta moerdbrand jefta bondena scaecraef jefta scaeckraef in gastelika logem jefta gastelika lioden dulghet, frase des liwes jefta daeth jefta ane slachta slacht ur sette soen, ur kesten mond ende swerren eden jefta hwa so een gastelick bihodene onfucht mit symonie. Dit sint da saun swarta swingen deer nimmen oenbinda mei bihala di paus.

[1] FG: cn*de*.

XVIII. Unmendable Crimes

Here Begin the Unmendable Crimes

1. This is an unmendable crime according to the law: if someone fights in violation of a truce, of sworn oaths and of a kiss of reconciliation, then he has broken the sacred truce which he himself promised to uphold.

2. This is an unmendable crime: if someone breaks the law out of greed or any other malicious intent, then he breaks that which God himself commanded in order to control sinful behaviour, because the law helps those who are unable to help themselves, it rightfully brings vengeance upon the guilty and protects the innocent.

3. This is an unmendable crime: if someone deceives his legal relatives then he resembles Judas who betrayed God himself, and who confirmed a truce by a kiss with the mouth and then broke it again.

4. No priest is allowed to let a person who commits these unmendable crimes or other crimes that are as evil as these do penance, unless he (this person) travels to Rome to visit the pope or his authorised representative and then the pope and the priest should decide on the way in which he should do penance, taking into consideration both mercy and the law. Until that time he must stand outside the church and not approach any man further than a distance of nine feet. He is not allowed to kiss the peace board (osculatorium) together with the other people: he is to kiss the staff he is carrying in his hand and he is not allowed to enjoy any privileges. He will miss many favours which are conferred in the Christian community because he has placed himself outside that community through his evil deed.

5. *Item* these are the seven unmendable crimes: if someone performs murder or arson or a violent robbery while holding someone in shackles, or a violent robbery in religious places or if someone wounds clerics so seriously that their life is feared for or kills them, or kills someone in violation of a truce, of a kiss of reconciliation and of sworn oaths, or if someone infringes upon an ecclesiastical immunity by means of simony. These are the seven unmendable crimes that no-one can pardon except the pope.

XIX. On Forceful Robberies

Hyr biginnet da scaeckraeff

1. Dit is een schaeckraef: hwa soe faert onbirades mit onriuchter wald to een standen hus ende deer binimpt da liodem hiara gued deer scholden hiara lyf aff feda ende da seel fan reda, soe brincht hi him self in dera schakera riucht mitta raef. Jef hi deerto bitinged wirt dat hi mitta fia beta schil, so schil hyt al
174 twibeet beta ende dine ferd twifald, alst da liued wilkared habbet. |

2. Dit is een schaecraef: hwa so faert to een birewed[1] scip onbiradet mit onriuchter wald aldeer di man leit on riuchter nerringa deer hi of sculde siin lyf feda ende da seel fan reda, so brinct hi him selva in da scakera riucht. Jef hi deer to bitilet wirt dat hi mitta fia beta scil, so ist twibeet deer hi det ende diin alrahagista ferd twifald, alst da liued wilkaren.

3. Dit is een riucht schaeckraef: hwa soe fiucht oen een fieldfarane man ende oen krameren ende hi an riuchta nerringa is ende nimt him siin gued of deer hy scolde dat lyff fan feda ende da seel fan reda, so brinckt hi hem selff in da scakera riucht ende haet so him di ora man det dat uter needwer, dat is sonder boet ende sonder ferd.

4. Dit is riucht, deer siin godeshuus seka schil om betteringa synre sondena, so aegh hi ferd deer ende dana. So hwa so him schadet in da wei an lyf, in ledem ende in gued, so ist twibeet ende di hagista ferd twifald.

5. Dat is riucht, deer syn sind seka schil om lainga jefta om netticheed dis heiliga sindis, so aegh hy ferd deer ende dana. Hwa so him quaed det an lyf ende an gued, so ist twibeet ende twifald ferden.

6. Dat is riucht, deer siin tingh jef siin werf seka schil om lainga jefta om jelkirs treft dis helga riuchtes soe aeg hy ferd[2] deer ende dana. Soe hwam so ma aet

[1] FG: birawed. [2] FG: fard.

XIX. On Forceful Robberies

Here Begins 'On Forceful Robberies'

1. This is a forceful robbery: if someone goes to a house without the consent of the court and by illegally using violence takes goods from the people that they need to support themselves and save their souls with, then through this robbery he commits a forceful robbery. If he is tried before court and is sentenced to compensate with money, then the compensation is twofold and he shall pay a twofold penalty for breaking the peace, as the people have determined.

2. This is a forceful robbery: if someone goes to a ship that has been loaded without the consent from the court and illegally using violence where someone is doing some honest business which he needs to feed himself and save his soul with, then through this robbery he commits a forceful robbery. If he is tried before court and is sentenced to compensate with money, then the compensation for what he did is twofold and he shall pay a twofold penalty for breaking the highest peace, as the people determined.

3. This is a forceful robbery: if someone attacks a travelling merchant or a peddler who is doing some honest business and if he robs him of goods which he needs to feed himself and save his soul with, then through this robbery he commits a forceful robbery and whatever the assaulted man does out of self-defence requires no compensation, nor does he have to pay a penalty for breaking the peace.

4. This is the law, if someone needs to go to his church in order to do penance for his sins, he has a right to be there peacefully and go back home peacefully. If someone harms him on his way, either his body or his limbs or his goods, the compensation is twofold, and the attacker must pay a twofold penalty for breaking the highest peace.

5. This is the law, if someone has to go to the synod because he has been summoned or to perform certain duties at the synodical court, he has a right to peacefully travel there and peacefully return home. If someone harms either his body or his goods, the compensation is twofold, and the attacker must pay a twofold penalty for breaking the peace.

6. This is the law, if someone has to go to his court because he has been summoned or to perform certain duties at that sacred court, he has a right to be there peacefully and go back home peacefully. If someone harms either his

deth oen lyff jefta oen ledem jefta oen gued, so ist twibote ende di alrahagista ferd aider twyfald, als da liued wilkared habbet.

7. Dat is riucht keninghes setma: dat is treft dat met halde da onriuchte to pinen ende da riuchte liodem to helpe want koninges setma dat is riucht also fyr so hit naet ne se seth tojenst da ewa ende tojenst dat riucht.

8. Dit is riucht als di grewa in dat land compt ende hi | urheriga liued schil seka, so schil hi siin fana fera deer di freda in da lande warat. Widekin heet di forma aesga, deer di aersta doem deelde binna dae Freeska merkum.

body or his limbs or his goods, the compensation is twofold, and the attacker must pay a twofold penalty for breaking the highest peace, as the people have determined.

7. This is the lawful statute of the king: it is necessary to uphold it in order to punish the unjust and to aid the righteous people because the king's statute is law when it does not contradict the *ewa* or the law.

8. This is the law, that if the count enters the country and has to enforce against disobedient people, he must carry the banner which guarantees the peace in the land. The first *asega* was called Widekin, who first gave expert judgment in the Frisian lands.

XX. The Statutes of Opstalsbam

Hyr biginnet da wilkerren fan Opstallisbame

1. In dei nomine amen. Dit is di wilker deer ward eniget MCCC ende XXIII des lettera deis efter sinte Lambertusdei ende wi eniget[1] mitta VI zelandum ende dit riucht ti halden.

2. Dio arste seec: jefter enich landis hera wil enich zeland schaya jefta schanda, hit se biscop jef grewa, dat wi se alle mene in rede ende in dede mit liwe ende mit guede usen fridoem to bihalden.

3. Dio oder seeck is, dat ma alle stellen tingh, hoedeen gued hit se, aldeer ma hit fynt dae riuchta hand weder thi jaene sonder leesne ende hwa so dat gued jef di tieff onthalt mit wald, di schil dat gued wederjaen ende dae riuchterem XX merka. Fan rawe ende fan rawede guede schil ma aldusdeen gued riucht halda.

4. Dio tredda seec is, dat ma alle baerne deer nachtes brand dwaet ende di deer deis brand dwe, di jelden saunfald ende da riuchteren[2] XX merka ende hwa so den moerdbrander onthalt dyn schil ma pinnigia also als fan da onthalderem bischien is. Dit schil ma halda fan da nottredderem also wel.

5. Dioe IIII seeck is: hwa so syn hera urreth jefta selff daed slacht om gued jefta syn friond, di schil ma pinighia als di moerdenaer jef als di nachtbrander, also fyr als hi mit riuchte urwonnen wirt. Hwa so moniken jefta joncfrouwen onthalt deer fan hiara prelate monet sint ti klaester ti kommen, di urbert XX merka. Hwa so hinderet dat hi se naet redelic biriuchta moet, di urbert also wel XX merka.

6. Dio fyfta seec is: hwa so een papa fucht mit wield, di schil him to bettringa jaen X merck ende da riuchteren alsoe fulla.

176 7. Dio sexte seec is: hwa so een riuchter daed slacht in dae wei toe | Opstallisbame, aldeer jefta danne, so schil hi him jelda mit IIII hundert merka, den haudel da erwum[3] ende dyn haudel da riuchterem. Elkers liued deer deer gaet, da jelde ma mit achtiga merkum ende da riuchterem also fulla.

---

[1] FG: eli*ng*ze. [2] FG: riuchrere*n*. [3] FG: herum.

XX. The Statutes of Opstalsbam

Here Begin the Statutes of Opstalsbam

1. In dei nomine amen. This is the statute that was agreed upon in the year 1323, on the second day after Saint Lambert's day[22] and we agreed upon it with the (other) 6 sealands to uphold this as law.

2. The first clause: if any ruler intends to damage or bring shame to any sealand, be it bishop or count, we will all jointly give each other council or assistance and we will fight with our lives and goods in order to uphold our freedom.

3. The second clause is, that all stolen things, whatever type of goods they may be, if they are found, are to be returned to the rightful owner without asking a price for it and if someone hides the goods or the thief and uses violence when they have been found, he must return the goods and give 20 marks to the judges. The same clause is to be applied in case of robbery and robbed goods.

4. The third clause is, that the houses of all those who commit arson by night are to be burnt down, and that those who commit arson by day will have to pay a sevenfold compensation and 20 marks to the judges, and if someone hides the arsonist, he shall be punished in the same way as someone who hides a thief or stolen goods. The same clause is to be applied to rapists.

5. The 4th clause is: if someone betrays his lord or kills him himself for a reward or kills his kinsmen, he shall be punished in the same way as a murderer or an arsonist, if he has been sentenced in court. If someone hides monks or nuns who have been summoned by their prelates to come to their monasteries, he has to pay a fine of 20 marks. If anyone obstructs their being sentenced correctly, he also has to pay a fine of 20 marks.

6. The fifth clause is: if someone violently attacks a priest, he shall pay him 10 marks as compensation and the same amount to the judges.

7. The sixth clause is: if someone kills a judge, either on his way to the Opstalsbam, at the Opstalsbam or on his way back, he shall pay 400 marks as compensation, half of it be paid to the heirs and the other half to the judges. Other people attending the Opstalsbam are to be compensated with eighty marks and the same amount be paid to the judges.

---

22 18 September.

8. Dio VII seec is: huc zeland orem een man of slacht, so schil met jelda mit LX merkum ende da riuchteren also fulla.

9. Dio VIII seec: hwa so da riuchterem in siin dele urherich wirt endma da oder zeland ti helpe ladet, also manich so deer kompt dat aeg hondert merka fan da urheriga ti urbrinse.

10. Dio IX seec is: hwa so des bischinen wirt dat hi wepen drege, di urbert fyf merck.

11. Dyo X seec is: hwer so een riuchter onriuchte riucht jef fynde, dy urbert XX merka.

12. Dio XI seec is, dat ma dine ferde jouwelick halde ende aldeer epenbeer stryd jefta san is, dat schillet da riuchteren riucht sena jefta hia sint menedich.

13. Dio XII seec is: hwa so een leka daed slacht, di jeldene mit VII jeldum ende di jowe da riuchterem saun ferden. Ende lamthe ende oder dolgingha da schil ma alsoe wal saunfald beta.

14. Dio XIII seec is: hwa so een papa daed slacht jefta dyaken jefta subdiaken, di jelda se mit tien fulla jeldem ende mit tien fulla ferdum. Elkers hiara dulginga bet ma mit tien fulla botem.

15. Dio XIIII seeck is: hweer so ma een[1] knappa jefta een famna ti bede jeft jefta nimpt buta rede des mondes ende sibsta eerwena, di haet urberd hundert merk ende dat kynd weder op syn gued bi bode dera riuchtera ende da kinde da wald ti betane als di alde wilker seyt.

16. Dio XV seec is fan lande deer ma kapet jefta selt jefta wandelet, dat di nest se ti winnane ist hera jefta frowe deer fan da fedriem jef fan da swirdsida ut kommen se, hit ne se dat dio der niaer in da sib se ende in da legere dis landis. Ende
177 sint hia lika sib dio swirdsida ende dio spindelsida, so is nier dio swirdsida. |

17. Dio sexteensta seeck is, dat alle lawa deer lawiget wirdet fan gode, dat se aldeer lawie deer se di daed brenghe, hit ne se dat hi op syn lesta tiid mit siin

[1] FG: eer.

8. The 7th clause is: in whatever other sealand a man is killed, this is to be compensated with 40 marks and the same amount be paid to the judges.

9. The 8th clause is: if someone becomes disobedient to the judges in his own district and the other sealands are called to help, then the disobedient man has to pay a hundred marks to each of the sealands that comes.

10. The 9th clause is: if someone is found guilty of carrying a weapon, he has to pay a fine of five marks.

11. The 10th clause is: if a judge passes an unlawful sentence or decrees unjustly, he has to pay a fine of 10 marks.

12. The 11th clause is: each must uphold the peace and if there is a public fight or discord, the judges shall impose a just reconciliation or find themselves perjurious.

13. The 12th clause is: if someone kills a layperson, he has to pay seven wergilds and pay a sevenfold penalty for breaking the peace. And paralysis and other types of injuries are also to be compensated sevenfold.

14. The 13th clause is: if someone kills a priest, or a dean, or a subdean, he has to pay ten wergilds and pay a tenfold penalty for breaking the peace. All other injuries done to them are to be compensated tenfold.

15. The 14th clause is: If someone gives away or takes a boy or a girl into matrimony without the consent of their guardian and of their closest relatives, he shall have to pay a fine of a hundred marks and he has to bring the child back to its own estate by order of the judge and he has to compensate the child for the violence done against it, as the old statute states.

16. The 15th clause is about buying, selling or exchanging land. A man or woman descending from the paternal line or 'sword side' is more entitled to take over the land, unless descendants from the maternal line are of closer descent or their estates lie closer to the land. And if they are equally close in descent, the paternal line takes priority over the maternal line.

17. The sixteenth clause is that all inheritances which consist of goods are brought there wherever death brings them, unless a man decides otherwise in

biegtris[1] rede oderis ordinerie. Hwa so dat inbrect mit onriuchter wald di uerbert XX merka.

18. Dio XVII seec is, dat alle ferdban stande fest deer da grietman dwaet sonder wandel, hit ne se dat da efterkommende riuchteren bi rede IIII dera wisera papena ende enis prelatis in da dele dat oendwe[2] om epenbere netreft ende netticheid ende se hit dan weer riuchte dwe.

19. Dio XVIII seec is: hwa so I man daed slacht ur sette sone ende swerren ede ende ur kesten mond, di schil ut wessa jeer ende dei buta lande ende di paus ti sekan jefta syn bode ende aldeer ti absolverien. Hat hy een stheen huus, dat schil ma thiwerpa. Haeth hy een holten huus, dat heert oen hof ende an konin-ges wara.

20. Dio XIX seec is: hwa so orem agen utbrect, foet ofsle jefta hand, ofkere nose jefta tonge jefta were, dat bet ma als een daedslachta.

21. Dio XX seeck is: hwa so ut disse mena netticheed ende ordineringa ende ut dissa settingha selschipet ende reth jefta swert, fiucht jefta hindreth, di urbert wit da riuchterem XX merka. Ende hwa so disse jenselschipinga ende jenswerringa naet of ne leth, di urbert also wel XX merka.

22. Dio XXI seec is om dera brorena[3] bede.

23. Dio XXII seec is om da monta.

24. Dio XXIII seec is: huck zelandre faert in een oer seland om clage mara of minra, soe schillet him da riuchteren binna trim deghum helpa hoder redis jef riuchtis. Dwa se dit naet, so schil di clager wessa op des greetmans kost ende synre siana alont dio claghe eint se, aider mit rede jef mit riuchte. Is dio clag minre so acht merck, so schil ma thi da oenprovinga jef ti da sikringha habba sex buren ende VII sibben ende een opstallingh. Isse mara, so schil hi habba[4]
178 II opstallingen ende | dae schillet wessa fan dae lande dier dioe claghe oen is.

[1] FG: bigetris. [2] FG: een dwe. [3] FG: browena. [4] FG: habha.

his last hours with the approval of his confessor. If someone infringes on this with illegal force, he has to pay a fine of 20 marks.

18. The 17th clause is that all peaces which have been proclaimed by the *gretman* will be upheld without altering them unless subsequent judges invalidate them with the approval of 4 wise priests and one prelate in the district because of public necessity and usefulness and they again do this in a legal manner.

19. The 18th clause is: if someone kills a man in violation of a truce, of sworn oaths and of a kiss of reconciliation, he shall be outlawed for a year and a day and must leave the land to seek the pope or his authorised representative and do penance there. If he owns a stone house, it shall be destroyed. If he owns a wooden house, this will go into the royal domain and into the property of the king.

20. The 19th clause is: if someone pokes out someone else's eyes, cuts off his foot or hand, cuts off his nose or tongue or lip, this is to be compensated as a homicide.

21. The 20th clause is: if someone infringes upon this public interest, this union and this treaty and makes contrary pacts, gives contrary councils, conspires, fights or hinders it in any way, he has to pay a fine of 20 marks to the judges. And if he does not cease these hostile gatherings or hostile unions, he has to pay another fine of 20 marks.

22. The 21st clause concerns the begging of monks.

23. The 22nd clause concerns currency.

24. The 23rd clause is: if someone from one sealand goes to another sealand because he wants to bring a complaint before court, be it more serious or less serious, this complaint shall be dealt with by the judges within three days, either by giving advice or by passing sentence. If they do not, the claimant shall stay there on the expense of the *gretman* and his household until the complaint has been dealt with, either by counselling or in court. If the complaint concerns a sum less than eight marks, the evidence or testimony shall be provided by six neighbours and 7 relatives and one *opstalling*. If it concerns a higher sum, the claimant will need 2 *opstallings* and these shall be residents of the district where the court is held.

25. Dio XXIIII seeck is: ti der nia settinga habba wi alle meenlyc set dat elck riuchtar deer swert thi da riuchte thi Opstallisbame, dat hy to Paeschum deer comme ende festgade ende creftgade alle da secka des heiligha ferda so fyr so hi riuchtedich bliuwa wil.

25. The 24th clause is: for the new statute, we decreed that each judge who swears the oath of office at Opstalsbam shall come there at Easter and confirm and affirm all paragraphs of this sacred statute, if he is to stay in office.

XXI. A Treatise on the Seven Sealands

Hyr bigint een cleen tractaet fan da Saun Zelanden des gansen landis fan Freesland mei syn tobiheer ende eylanden

Dat aerste Zeland, dat is Westfreesland bi dio oder sida des zees alse Hoern, Enchusen, Medemblic etcetera, hwelc di grewa fan Holland him onderdenich[1] maked haet alderaerst.

Dat oder is streckende fan Starem to Liouwerd alse Westergo[2] ende Doyngaweerfstal, Weimbritse mit al hyara toebiheer.

Dat tredde is heten Aestergo, mei al Smellingaland, Boerndeel, foerdmeer Haudmare,[3] Haskerwald, dae Neersta Walden, ende Rauwerde, Achtzespel[4] ende Colmerland.

Disse twa Zeelanden, als dat oder ende dat tredde, sint eta fry ende oers neen hera bicannet bihalva diin keyser des Roemschen rikes. Mer ontellika schada ende manich oenfiuchtinga ende grata bloedstirtingha habbet disse landen lith om dine frydoem to bischyrmen, hwelck hem is joun fan dine grata koninck Kaerl ende deer to manich sweer striden habbet slain jenst dine grewa fan Holland om hiara land to bischyrmen.

Dat IIII is Stellinghwerf, Scoterwerf, Kunersyl, Geethorn, Fullenhoef, Steenwyck ende al Drentland. Dit Zeland haet bitwongen di biscop fan Utrecht als Drent, Steenwyc, Fullenhoef, Geethoern ende Kunersyl. Mer Stelinchwerf,
179 Schoterland: disse twa sint eta fry, ende grata anfiuchtinga mit grata | orlogem deer hia habbet hand tojenst dat Sticht fan Utrecht.

Dat fyfte Zeland is Langwald, Freedwald, Humers, Mydach, Hunsinga,[5] Fywellingha,[6] Groningen, Aeldambecht, Reyderland, Westerwald mey al da waldem deer aldeerbi lidset twisscha da Eemse ende Westfalen. Dat maeste deel fan disse Zelanden is eta fry ende sommich sint onderdenich joncker Kene ende grewa Ulrick ende sommich sint da Groninghera onderdenich.

Dat sexte Zeland is Eemda mit al Eemderland, Brokmereland, Aurikerland, Aesterghaland, Heerlingerland ende Dole Noerderland mei syn toebiheer. Ende dit edel Zeland, deer ryckst was ende fruchtbaer, hwelck joncker Kene fan Broeckmerland, een neifolger syn faders ende broders in boesheed ende mei quaedheed dit land bitwong, ende make se eerm urmits zeeraweren ende hi spared gastelyck ner wraldsch ende was boes in alle tinghum ende ut da tzerkem naem hi al dat jeld ende clenodien deer hi dat stryd mei feerd.

Dat VII Zeland is Rustringaland, Winingaland ende Buthjaingheraland, hwelc land bisith Sibolt Edesoen, joncker Kene swager. Item Owerlengerland,

---

[1] FG: him haet onderdenich. [2] FG: west*er*gn. [3] FG: ha*n*dmare. [4] FG: aetzespel. [5] FG: Husinga. [6] FG: Sywellingha.

XXI. A Treatise on the Seven Sealands

Here Begins a Short Treatise on the Seven Sealands of Which the Whole of Frisia, Including Its Appurtenances and Islands, Consists

The first Sealand is Westfrisia on the other side of the sea, consisting of Hoorn, Enkhuizen, Medemblik etcetera, which was subjugated first, by the count of Holland.

The other stretches from Staveren to Leeuwarden, consisting of Westergo and Doniawerstal and Wymbritseradeel with all their territories.

The third is called Oostergo, which consists of all of Smallingerland, Boornego, and furthermore Haudmare, Haskerland, the Lage Wouden and Rauwerderhem, Achtkarspelen and Kollumerland.

These two Sealands, namely the second and the third, are still free, and acknowledge no other lord than the emperor of the Holy Roman Empire. But these lands suffered incalculable damage and many attacks and great bloodshed to protect the freedom given to them by the great King Charlemagne, and they fought many hard battles against the count of Holland to protect their land.

The fourth consists of Stellingwerf, Schoterwerf, Kuinderzijl, Giethoorn, Vollenhove, Steenwijk and all of Drenthe. The bishop of Utrecht conquered this Sealand, that is, Drenthe, Steenwijk, Vollenhove, Giethoorn and Kuinderzijl. But Stellingwerf and Schoterland, these two are still free and they fought great battles and great wars against Utrecht.

The fifth Sealand consists of Langewold, Vredewold, Humsterland, Middag, Hunsingo, Fivelgo, Groningen, Oldambt, Reiderland and Westerwolde with all lands that surround it between the river Ems and Westphalia. For the most part, this Sealand is still free but some parts are subordinate to lord Keno and count Ulrich and some parts are subordinate to the people of the city of Groningen.

The sixth Sealand consists of Emden with all of Emderland, Brookmerland, Auricherland, Astringen, Harlingerland and Norderland with its appurtenances. And this noble Sealand, which was the richest and fertile, was maliciously subjugated by lord Keno of Brokmerland—a follower in evil of his father and brothers—who impoverished it by piracy, and spared neither clerics nor secular persons, and he was evil in all respects and took from the churches all money and valuables which he used to finance his war.

The seventh Sealand is Riustringen, Wangerland and Butjadingen, the latter possessed by Sibolt son of Edo, brother-in-law to squire Keno. Further-

Moermerland ende Lingen; dat sint delen disser Zelanden hwelc joncker Kene aec bitwongh ende Focke Ukema disse tria landen fan Keno bileende, ende neen landishera ne mochte disse Zelanden bitwinga bihala disse Focke vorscrioun. Item Segelterland is aec een deel fan disse VII Zelanden ende jout tribuet ende schat den biscop fan Munster. Ende Stheedland,[1] Haedelreland, Wymderland ur dio Wesere sint aeck delin fan disse VII Zelanden. Disse haet betwongen di biscop fan Bremen, mer Dithmers is eeta oenbihinderd.

Hyr eyndichgied da Wilkerren fan Opstallisbame.

---

[1] FG: scheedland.

more Overledingerland, Moormerland and Lengen, which are the parts of this Sealand which were subjugated by lord Keno, and Focko Ukena received these three lands in fief from Keno, and no ruler was able to subjugate these Sealands except for the aforementioned Focko. Saterland is also part of this 7th Sealand and it pays tribute and fee to the bishop of Münster. And Stadland, the land of Hadeln and Wigmodia on the other side of the river Weser are also part of this 7th Sealand. The bishop of Bremen has subjugated these, but Dithmarschen is still unoccupied.

Here end the Statutes of Opstalsbam

Glossary of Untranslated Old Frisian Terms

asega law speaker, legal expert, judge
attha a type of juror
bannere a court official who assisted the *skelta* and the *frana*; bailiff
bodthing commanded *thing* / court session (text III)
dikattha a juror (*attha*) concerned with inspecting dykes (text XII)
ehera village judge (text XIII)
ewa primal customary law, constitution
fimelthing second part of the *bodthing* (text III)
frana magistrate, substitute of the count in Frisia in his absence
gretman magistrate, president of the court, judge (this office replaced that of the *skelta*)
hreilmerk a type of currency: 'textile-mark' (text XV)
liudmerk a type of currency: 'peoples mark' (text XV)
opstalling judge acting on behalf of the League of the Opstalsbam (text XX)
penningmerk a type of currency: 'penny-mark' (text XV)
skelta magistrate, president of the lower court by appointment of the count, judge
skild a type of currency: shield sterling (text XV)
skillingmerk a type of currency: 'shilling mark' (text XV)
skubbe a type of currency (text XV)
wedmark a type of currency: 'textile-mark' (text XV)

Index of Allegations in the Glosses

For the meaning of the abbreviations in the allegations see section 4 (Allegations) in the 'Preface to the Edition and Translation of the Gloss'. The following Roman numeral corresponds with the specific part of the Frisian Land Law, the Arabic numeral(s) (between brackets) with the number of the gloss within that part.